VIOLENCE, AGGRESSION, & COERCIVE ACTIONS

VIOLENCE, AGGRESSION, & COERCIVE ACTIONS

JAMES T. TEDESCHI ■ RICHARD B. FELSON

American Psychological Association, Washington, DC

First printing November 1994
Second printing November 1995

Published by
American Psychological Association
750 First Street, NE
Washington, DC 20002

Copies may be ordered from
APA Order Department
P.O. Box 2710
Hyattsville, MD 20784

In the UK and Europe, copies may be ordered from
American Psychological Association
3 Henrietta Street
Covent Garden, London
WCZE 8LU England

Typeset in Goudy by PRO-Image Corporation, Techna-Type Div., York, PA

Printer: Data Reproductions Corp., Rochester Hills, MI
Cover and Jacket Designer: Anne Masters, Washington, DC
Technical/Production Editor: Molly R. Flickinger

Library of Congress Cataloging-in-Publication Data
Tedeschi, James T.
    Violence, aggression, and coercive actions / James T. Tedeschi and
Richard B. Felson.
      p.   cm.
    Includes bibliographical references and index.
    ISBN 1-55798-257-0 (acid free paper)
    1. Violence.   2. Aggressiveness (Psychology)   3. Social
interaction.   4. Rational choice theory.   I. Felson, Richard B.
II. Title.   III. Title: Coercive actions.
HM291.T375   1994
303.6—dc20

British Cataloguing-in-Publication Data
A CIP record is available from the British Library.

Printed in the United States of America

To Val and Sasha, for
sharing and caring.

James T. Tedeschi

To Sharon, for a fateful smile
in the library 23 years ago.

Richard B. Felson

CONTENTS

PREFACE

Aggression has been studied by biologists, philosophers, and scholars from each of the social sciences. The range of phenomena studied is extraordinarily wide, perhaps greater than that for any other scientific topic. Biologists have noted phylogenetic similarities between species as well as genetic contributions to aggressive behavior. Physiologists have probed for underlying physical causes of violent behavior, such as hormones and brain centers. Psychologists have proposed a number of theories and carried out thousands of experiments to find the causes of aggressive behavior. Sociologists have focused on crime and different forms of group violence. Anthropologists have described cross-cultural variations in violence. Political scientists and historians have recounted and offered explanations for revolutions, civil wars, and wars between nations.

The amount of information and the plethora of theories that have been propagated about aggression are overwhelming. Everyone who writes a book on this topic must make choices about what to put in and what to leave out. Thus, various books have focused on such topics as family violence, criminal violence, biological factors, learning and socialization, revolutions, and war. We chose to write a book that focuses on direct, face-to-face confrontations between individuals in which threats are made or in which one of the parties attempts to impose some form of harm on the other. Our emphasis is on the social interactions of actor, target, and third parties. Although we recognize the role of individual differences and the larger social structure, we emphasize the social situation. In other words, we approach the phenomena from a social psychological perspective.

In the first part of the book (chaps. 1–5), we critically evaluate biological, psychological, and sociological approaches that have a bearing on face-to-face confrontations. In the second part of the book, we present a social interactionist theory of coercive behavior. A critical analysis presented in chapter 6 leads us to abandon the concept of aggression and substitute a language of coercive actions. *Aggression* is seldom used as a descriptive term in the remainder of the book. This theory choice was made with some trepidation because it was anticipated that most readers would not agree with it. However, a reader who, for whatever reasons, prefers the traditional concept should have little trouble making mental substitution whenever concepts of coercion are encountered.

A social interactionist theory of coercive actions is a theory of rational choice. In chapter 7, we emphasize the decision-making process. We focus on three goals of coercive actions: to gain compliance, to restore justice, and to assert and defend identities. Actors who use coercion to achieve compliance are motivated to gain the commodities, services, and safety that the target can mediate for them. A justice motive is associated with attributions of blame, anger, and grievances and, under certain conditions, may instigate coercive episodes. Concern for social identities may also motivate actors to use coercion as a self-presentational tactic. Chapters 7 through 9 are devoted to these three processes.

In chapters 10 and 11, we extend the theory to explanations of the use of coercion by parents against their children and to various forms of sexual coercion. Both of these literatures are pervaded by moral, ideological, and legal concerns and are therefore fraught with minefields for those who wish to separate causal analyses from value judgments. Our social psychological perspective leads us to consider the subjective viewpoint of the actor and the causal role of the target. We are not interested in establishing blame or protecting the victim's image. Our attempt to avoid value judgments and to take a scientific stance should not be construed to indicate that we lack compassion for victims of violent crimes.

In the epilogue, we provide a concise summary of our theory, discuss individual differences that contribute both to the frequency and intensity of coercive actions, and focus on some central disputes and similarities between a social interactionist theory and more traditional theories of aggression, violence, and criminal behavior.

We have written several versions of the chapters in this book over its 4-year incubation period. We have been fortunate that many colleagues and students have been willing to read one or more chapters, even in their underdeveloped stages. Their comments and suggestions have sometimes changed our argument or organization, brought our attention to inconsistencies and additional evidence, and sharpened our presentation. It is a pleasure to publicly acknowledge our debt to them, although to be fair, we should indicate that they do not all share our viewpoint. We thank Roy Baumeister, Hans Bierhoff, Manfred Bornewasser, Katherine Croom, Richard DeRidder, James Driscoll, Marcus Felson, Steve Felson, Mark Leary, Suk-jae Lee, Valerie Melburg, Robert Meyers, Gerold Mikula, Amelie Mummendey, Mitchell Nesler, Sabine Otten, Brian Quigley, Deborah Richardson, Sandra Schruijer, Rich Shuntich, Bernd Simon, Dawn Storr, and George Strand.

JAMES T. TEDESCHI
RICHARD B. FELSON

I

TRADITIONAL THEORIES
AND RESEARCH
ON AGGRESSION

INTRODUCTION

TRADITIONAL THEORIES AND RESEARCH ON AGGRESSION

In this part of the book, we describe and critically evaluate traditional approaches to the scientific study of aggression and violence. Aggression, violence, and related behaviors are studied in a variety of disciplines. The term *aggression* has been applied to an extraordinary range of phenomena: physical assaults, homicides, verbal insults, sarcasm, spouse and child abuse, international and civil wars, predatory behavior, and much else. It is not surprising, therefore, that aggression has been studied in many scientific disciplines. Although in the present book we are concerned primarily with social and psychological factors contributing to the phenomena of interest, it should be recognized that anthropologists, biologists, economists, political scientists, communications researchers, historians, and sociologists have also been involved in studying aggression.

Each scientific discipline has its own level of analysis and develops its own set of theories and methods to explain phenomena. Biologists focus on evolutionary principles, genetic codes, biochemical factors, or central nervous system activity as explanations of aggression. Psychologists tend to focus on internal tensions and frustrations, learned associations, emotions, and perceptions in developing their theories. Sociologists are more apt to focus on social, demographic, and cultural factors to explain aggressive behavior. We examine each of these approaches and note their limitations.

Biologists, and some psychologists, have viewed aggression as responses pushed out by inner forces—such as aggressive drive, anger, hormones, and brain centers (cf. Geen, 1990; Moyer, 1987)—or automatically pulled out by external stimuli, such as frustration and aversive stimuli (Berkowitz, 1989). This type of aggression has been labeled *angry aggression.*

In chapter 1, we describe various mechanisms empirically examined by biologists and evaluate them in light of the available evidence. Among these mechanisms are instincts, hormones, genetic abnormalities, heritability of aggression, and brain centers. Much of the available research has been done with lower organisms, and each of these factors has been linked with aggressive behavior. However, as shall be seen, the generalizability of such findings to explain human aggression is questionable and is seldom corroborated when corresponding research is carried out with human subjects.

One might categorize biologically oriented researchers into strong and weak categories. A strong biological approach to aggression claims direct causal effects between physiological structures that themselves (to a large degree) are products of genetic inheritance and aggressive behavior. For example, one might claim that there is a direct relationship between the concentration of plasma testosterone and aggressive behavior. This hypothesis does not specify the causal path through which biochemicals can bring about complex social actions, such as assaults and homicides.

A weak biological approach claims only that biological factors in indirect ways affect the likelihood and magnitude of aggressive behavior. For example, A. H. Buss and Plomin (1984) have argued that temperament types, which may have heritability components, can indirectly affect aggression. A tendency to be impulsive may increase the likelihood of aggressive behavior, whereas a tendency to be fearful may inhibit it. Intelligence may be another factor indirectly and inversely related to aggressive and criminal conduct. In general, the weak biological approach views physiological structures as possible moderators of aggressive behavior, rather than as direct causal factors. From the evaluation made in chapter 1, we reject the strong biological view and accept the weaker position.

Classic frustration–aggression theory is presented in chapter 2. This theory is an important landmark in the study of aggression because it stimulated extensive laboratory research on aggression by psychologists. The theory attempts to combine built-in biological factors with learning mechanisms to explain aggressive behavior. There is an automatic, prewired connection between frustrating events and the buildup of aggressive drive in the organism, and there is a homeostatic mechanism operating so that the organism needs to reduce the drive by performing aggressive behaviors. Learning comes into play because organisms learn to avoid performing responses that lead to punishment. We show in chapter 2 that research does not consistently support frustration–aggression theory and that there is reason to think that the theory refers to too narrow a range of phenomena.

A major revision of frustration–aggression theory has been developed by Berkowitz (1993), who proposed two systems of aggression: angry aggression and instrumental aggression. Basic to all aggression, according to Berkowitz, is a biological structure, which he refers to as a *rudimentary emotional-response system*. Aversive stimuli activate this system and create in the organism a desire to hurt others. Aggressive behavior that does hurt others serves to satisfy this desire. This rudimentary system is modified by learning and affected by cognitive–associative processes. Berkowitz assembled evidence to support these processes, much of it representing a lifetime of his own research and that of his students. Our evaluation in chapter 2 is that the evidence presented is inconsistent, is subject to demand cues, and has sometimes been misinterpreted by Berkowitz.

The focus in chapter 3 is on physiological arousal and its effects on aggressive behavior. Zillmann (1971) has proposed a theory of excitation transfer in which misattribution is an important factor. Under conditions in which arousal has dissipated sufficiently so that the individual is no longer aware that arousal is still above some quiescent level, he or she may misattribute the leftover arousal to a new situation in which new arousal occurs. The result is a greater cumulative amount of arousal than when the individual has no residual arousal available in the new situation.

According to Zillmann (1971), anger causes aggressive behavior. The arousal accompanying anger can be heightened by residual arousal so that the individual retaliates at a higher level of aggression against a provoker. High levels of arousal can also interfere with cognitive processes, so that cognitive controls (i.e., inhibitors) may be bypassed, and habitual and impulsive behavior may occur. An extensive research program to test the hypotheses of the theory has been carried out by Zillmann and his colleagues. This research is carefully reviewed and critically evaluated in chapter 3. We conclude that the evidence does not consistently support excitation transfer theory. Nevertheless, research has indicated that physiological arousal facilitates aggression but does not instigate it.

Public policy concern has stimulated interest in the effects of sexual arousal on aggressive behavior. We examine the research on viewing pornography and its effects on aggressive behavior. Erotic stimuli and pornography apparently do not instigate or facilitate aggressive behavior specifically directed toward women.

In chapter 4, we present theories that assume that aggression is learned like any other behavior and is a means to achieving goals (A. H. Buss, 1961). Biological theories, frustration–aggression theory, Berkowitz's (1993) theory of angry aggression, and Zillmann's (1971) theory of excitation transfer all treat aggression as a behavior system that is, in important respects, different from other behavior systems. Instrumental and social learning theories (Bandura, 1983; A. H. Buss, 1961) focus on the conditions for learning, maintaining, and performing aggressive responses. According to A. H. Buss, learning any behavior, including aggression, is a function of rewards and punishments, association of stimuli and responses, and extinction processes. Personality, social norms, and other factors will affect the learning process and how an individual will react in a given situation.

Bandura (1983) moved away from the behaviorism expounded by A. H. Buss (1961) and proposed that learning is largely a function of cognitive processes. It is not so much the impact of past rewards that shapes behavior, but the expectation of future rewards that guides behavior. Furthermore, an individual does not need to learn by doing, but may learn by observing others. The central idea of social learning theory is that people learn from and imitate models. Children may learn to be aggressive from observing (often as targets) the punitive behavior of their parents or from viewing models on television or in the movies.

In chapter 4, we make important criticisms of modeling experiments. A review of experiments and field studies indicates that the impact of watching violence on television is very small. Little or no evidence exists for the mechanisms that mediate a relationship between viewing violence and subsequent aggressive behavior. There is evidence of intergenerational transmission of violence, but the relationship is not a strong one. We conclude that there can be little doubt that learning is an important, even a critical factor that must be incorporated into any theory of aggressive behavior. The effects of scripts, means–ends relations, and incentives on aggression have been firmly established.

Finally, sociological theories of violence and crime are discussed in chapter 5. These theories have sometimes been used to explain sociodemographic variation in criminal behavior. The subcultural approach focuses on variation across groups in values conducive to violence and delinquency. Blocked-opportunity theorists interpret crime as an alternative form of achievement or as a way of handling grievances when legitimate opportunities are blocked. Control theorists assume that the incentives for crime are constant but that costs and inhibitions vary. Criminal behavior is likely to occur when internal and external controls are weak and when the routine activities of people create opportunities to commit crime with impunity.

These theories provide ideas that are useful for the study of aggression, although the empirical evidence for some of the theories is mixed. A rational choice approach, which focuses on the instrumental character of crime, provides a basis for integrating many of these ideas (Cornish & Clarke, 1986). Such an approach is compatible with the learning theories presented in chapter 4 and with the approach that we develop in part 2 of this book.

1

BIOLOGICAL FACTORS AND AGGRESSION

Thomas Hobbes (1909), a seventeenth-century British philosopher, speculated that before people formed organized societies, they were like other wild animals. He characterized such primitive humans as *Homo homini lupus*—human wolves. In a state of nature, each human was totally selfish and fought for whatever was desired. As a result, the lives of such people were "nasty, brutish, and short." According to Hobbes, in the absence of social constraints the animal nature of humans was directly expressed in social behavior.

The publication of Darwin's theory of evolution in 1859 (Darwin, 1859/1936) had a profound impact in grounding human behavior in evolutionary history. The implication was that much human behavior might be explained in terms of the same mechanisms that cause behavior in other organisms. Among the biological factors that have been posited to cause aggressive behavior are instincts, genes, pain-elicited reflexive fighting, hormones, brain structures, and an inborn aggressive drive. We examine research carried out on these factors to ascertain their impact on human aggression.

INSTINCTS

In one of the first books written on social psychology, McDougall (1908) attempted to explain all social behavior in terms of instincts. McDougall was the first to identify a social behavior and then invent a coincident instinct to explain the behavior: If men fight one another, it is because they have an instinct for pugnacity. Some forms of complex behavior were attributed to blends of two or more instincts. For example, religious behavior is a complex blend of the instincts of curiosity, fear, self-abasement, and love for parents. McDougall's bag of instincts was sufficiently full to explain any behavior.

McDougall's (1908) theory was exposed as circular in nature. Simply renaming behavior as an instinct, referred to by philosophers as a *nominalistic error,* does not uncover its causes. In an adequate theory of instincts there must be a way of identifying an instinct independent of the behavior it is invoked to explain. The misconception that one has explained a behavior by assigning it to an instinctual tendency has the effect of causing scientists to look no further for its causes. This conceptual difficulty and the rise of behaviorism in psychology turned attention away from instinctual theories of human behavior. A classic experiment by Kuo (1930), in which it was shown that cats learn to kill and eat mice or rats by observing the behavior of their mothers, also increased caution in referring to instincts as the causes of behavior. This type of research suggested that the role of instincts among subhuman animals may have been exaggerated.

Definition of Instincts

The study of animal behavior in natural habitats produced a more sophisticated theory of instincts. Famous ethologists, such as Nobel Laureates Nikolaas Tinbergen and Konrad Lorenz, provided evidence that some behaviors of subhuman animals are carried in the genes. They referred to such prewired behavior patterns as *instincts.* It should be noted that ethologists avoided the nominalistic error made by McDougall (1908). In the more current theories behavior is not explained by instincts but, rather, the behavior is the instinct.

The ethologists identified five characteristics of instincts. First, an instinct is a complex behavior, which is distinguished from a reflex by the amount of time it takes to perform the response pattern and by its goal orientation. A reflex is a simple all-or-none response that occurs instantaneously without the intervention of higher brain centers. In contrast, an instinct consists of a sequential pattern of responses that unfolds over time and achieves some instrumental goal for the organism. For example, an eyeblink in response to a puff of air is a reflex, but a beaver building a dam is an instinct.

Second, instincts are automatically elicited by environmental stimuli, referred to as *releasers*. A releasing stimulus that will elicit an attack by a male stickleback fish is any large, red, and oblong object that invades its breeding territory. These are characteristics associated with competing male sticklebacks (Tinbergen, 1953). However, not all automatic behavior is instinctual. Habits are also automatic in the sense that they are performed in the presence of stimuli without much premeditation and sometimes without awareness. When people first learn to drive an automobile, they may have difficulty executing the correct sequence of responses, but as they gain experience, driving becomes semiautomatic. The difference between instincts and habits is that instincts are inherited.

Third, instincts are innate; that is, the behavior patterns that are identified as instincts are not learned. The behavior patterns referred to as *instincts* are genetically prewired and are triggered by releasing stimuli to which the organism is sensitized by genetic coding. The male stickleback fish does not learn to defend territory during breeding but is genetically prewired to engage in the behavior.

Fourth, instincts are behavior patterns performed by all members of some category within a species: All beavers will build dams and all salmon swim upstream to spawn in lakes. The instinct may be specific to a category of sex, age, or other subgroup of a species, but it characterizes all members of the relevant category. Thus, only male stickleback fish that are breeding will defend territory.

Finally, the strength of the instinctual behavior is affected by biochemical factors. Increased concentration of testosterone will intensify the sexual behavior of male rats, but estrogens will weaken their complex, innate, and automatic copulatory behavior pattern.

There are instinctual behavior patterns among some subhuman species. In considering the question of whether humans have an instinct for aggressive behavior patterns, it is useful to distinguish between predatory and agonistic behaviors (J. P. Scott, 1958). *Predatory behaviors* refer to interspecies killing, where one species preys on the other as a food source. All meat-eating animals must prey on other species for survival. *Agonistic behaviors* consist of threats and fighting between members of the same species. Hobbes (1909) failed to make this distinction when he referred to our species as *Homo lupus*. Wolves are relentless and vicious predators, but they are very cooperative and gentle with one another, almost never killing each other.

There is evidence that the human species is not a predatory animal. According to Napier (1970), the digestive system of the human has the characteristics of a vegetarian, not a meat eater. Human teeth are not as well adapted for eating flesh as are the teeth of a dog or a lion. Old World primates maintained primarily a vegetarian diet, and our ancestors, the "bushmen," depended on nuts and berries for their basic nutrition (Ploog

& Melnechuk, 1970). Furthermore, despite their reputation for bloodthirsty behavior, most humans are reluctant to kill anything larger than a fly or mosquito. Special persons are hired to slaughter animals for meat, and although hunting and fishing are popular sports, they are enjoyed by a minority of the human population.

The kind of human behavior that aggression theorists seek to explain is harmdoing within the species *Homo sapiens*. In respect to agonistic behavior, humans are more like rats than wolves, for rats do frequently kill one another. One might wish to refer to the human species as *Homo rattus*, if an animal analogy is deemed useful. The question to be considered here is whether aggressive behavior by humans against other humans can be explained in terms of instincts. Two forms of agonistic behavior—dominance hierarchies and territoriality—have been firmly established as instinctual in some lower organisms.

Lorenz's Theory of Instinctual Behavior

A particularly influential ethological theory of instincts was offered by Lorenz (1966). His view was that many behavior patterns are inherited and that some force or drive is necessary to activate them. According to Lorenz, energy for a particular instinctual behavior accumulates in the brain areas specific to that behavior pattern. When a releaser is encountered and the energy specific to the particular behavior is present, the instinct is then activated (i.e., performed). If a great deal of energy has been accumulated, the instinct might occur in the absence of an appropriate releaser. This vacuum activity does not occur frequently because there are typically many relevant stimuli that will allow the release of the accumulated energy.

Ethological studies of instincts in lower organisms have established that intact complex behavior patterns are transmitted genetically. These behaviors must be prewired in the brain and, in the case of instincts, are automatically elicited by releasing stimuli. Such prewired behavior patterns exist in most infrahuman animals. However, in many species the individual animal learns to apply the response pattern in a variety of circumstances to achieve certain goals. Thus, a prewired behavior pattern is available for use as an instrument to gain reinforcement and to avoid or escape punishment.

Everyone has observed the two prewired aggressive behavior patterns of the ordinary house cat. The predatory behavior consists of stealthy movements, patient waiting at strategic points, and then a pouncing on the prey. Often the cat will injure the prey without killing it and will then play with it before killing it with a bite on the back of the neck. The cat may or may not eat the prey, depending on prior learning experiences (Kuo, 1930). The agonistic behavior pattern of the cat consists of arching the back, standing the hair on end, baring claws, hissing and screeching, and wagging the tail. Although both the predatory and agonistic response patterns are apparently prewired, when the cat will use them appears to be largely determined by life experiences.

For Lorenz (1966), aggressive behavior is not just a reaction to outside stimuli but results from an inner aggressive drive or inner excitation that must find expression regardless of the presence or absence of releasers. Like a steam boiler, further energy builds up pressure and, if it has no outlet, the organism will explode into violent behavior. Lorenz found two important instincts that appear to regulate the agonistic behavior of animals: dominance hierarchies and territoriality.

Dominance Hierarchies

In most species of animals that live in groups, a typical social structure develops in which individuals are ranked in superordinate–subordinate relationships. In a chicken coop containing four hens—A, B, C, and D—a dominance hierarchy will exist in which, for example, B, C, and D all show deference to A; C and D show deference to B, and D shows deference to C. When A moves to feed in a particular place, all of the others will move out of the way. Any aggression typically follows the line of dominance. So, if A pecks B, B probably will not peck A, but B may peck C. Observations of this kind of behavior have led to the notion of a "pecking order."

A dominance hierarchy may only be loosely structured in some species of animals, and there may be different dominance hierarchies for such biologically based needs as sex and hunger. Intricate dominance hierarchies exist in most primate species. The development of a network of dominance hierarchies was observed in a group of rhesus monkeys in a zoo in Calcutta, India (Southwick, 1967). New monkeys were introduced into a group of 17 monkeys at various time intervals. Subgroups in the established colony exhibited agonistic behavior, depending on the characteristics of the newcomer. New juveniles were attacked by resident juveniles, but were not attacked by resident adults. Similarly, female and male adults attacked strangers of the same age and sex.

A major function of a dominance hierarchy is to assure that the best and strongest of a species survives. If strength, courage, and quickness are associated with survival, and these are characteristics that place an individual high in a dominance hierarchy, then the individual will have early access to food and to mating. In times of scarcity, subordinates may die of starvation, but superordinate members of the species may survive on the scarce supply of food that exists. Furthermore, early or exclusive access to females assures that the genes of the dominant animals are passed on to the next generation.

Dominance hierarchies produce stability by minimizing fighting and killing in the group. Within the context of an established dominance hierarchy, most agonistic behavior consists of threat gestures or postures by superiors and complementary submissive behaviors from subordinates. This arrangement assures that most conflict will be resolved without substantial fighting and harm to members of the group. This benign function of dominance hierarchies was demonstrated by Bernstein and Mason (1963), who placed seven unacquainted rhesus monkeys in a 7.3 m × 14.6 m enclosure and observed their behavior. During the first hour, over 50% of all responses consisted of threats and attacks. Agonistic behavior was 20 times more frequent than during any subsequent hour of observation. The dominance hierarchy established during the first hour was maintained throughout the following 75 days of observation.

The ubiquitousness of dominance hierarchies among social species of animals has led some theorists (Ardrey, 1966; Lorenz, 1966) to explain much aggressive behavior among humans in terms of a struggle for superordinate positions in groups. Despite superficial resemblances between human status systems and animal dominance hierarchies, they serve different functions and operate by different mechanisms.

There are important differences between dominance hierarchies in subhuman species and status hierarchies in human groups. In dominance hierarchies, position is based on such biological factors as size, strength, and speed. In status hierarchies, position is based on social factors, such as education, socioeconomic background, social ties, and other nonbiological factors. Although biology may play a role in determining ability to learn, attractiveness, and social skills, the contribution of biological factors is clearly very indirect and greatly modified by culture. Individual animals determine their own position in a hierarchy, whereas human groups often distribute status to individuals. In addition, human status hierarchies are not necessarily transitive. Person A may be dominant over Person B, and Person B may be dominant over Person C, but Person C may be dominant over Person A. For example, in a family a husband may dominate his wife and the wife may dominate their daughter, but the daughter may be quite successful in influencing her father.

There is a difference in the functions served by dominance hierarchies and status hierarchies. Individual animals who occupy high positions in a dominance hierarchy are more likely to survive when food or water is scarce and are also more likely to pass on their genes to progeny because they have first access to resources and mates. Thus, the major function of dominance hierarchies is to ensure that the best and strongest of the species survives, which is consistent with the principle of natural selection in biological evolution. Individuals in human groups are motivated to achieve status for many reasons. Although biological factors, such as native intelligence, may contribute indirectly to success among humans in achieving status, few social psychologists believe that struggles for status serve a biological function of natural selection.

We conclude that there is no evidence to support the belief that humans are genetically programmed to form dominance hierarchies. Dominance and status hierarchies at first glance look similar, but on closer examination, they can be seen to be very different in terms of their functions, the manner in which individuals achieve superordinate positions, and the normative basis for them. Furthermore, established dominance hierarchies are more important for reducing harmdoing within groups than for facilitating aggressive behavior.

Territorial Behavior

Some species of fish, birds, and mammals will defend a fixed geographical region against intruders of the same species. This territorial behavior typically consists of threats by the defender and withdrawal by the intruder. On occasion, a test of strength may occur, as when two bull moose lock horns. Such encounters seldom lead to serious harm to the loser. In some species, distinctive signs of surrender and deference serve to inhibit fighting, such as when a defeated wolf turns its head away from the victor, exposing its jugular (Lorenz, 1966). This indication of surrender ends the fight and saves the life of the loser.

Territorial behavior in the stickleback fish is instinctive. In his Nobel Prize–winning research, Tinbergen (1953) reported that the male stickleback builds a nest, engages in elaborate swimming patterns to seduce a female to lay eggs in the nest, fertilizes the eggs, and guards them until they hatch and the brood swims away. The male changes from a rather dull hue and develops a red belly during the mating period. The red belly attracts females in a fashion analogous to a male peacock's feathers. The male will defend its nesting territories against any competitive male, that is, any other male that has a red belly. Tinbergen demonstrated that the defender will even attack a red cardboard silhouette. Most of the territorial behavior consists of threat displays, not actual fighting. This territorial behavior is apparently genetically prewired, controlled by hormonal changes, and released by an oval-shaped red object.

Territorial behavior has the biological function of enhancing the survival of a species by preventing overpopulation in relation to the food supply. Territoriality frequently occurs during mating seasons and is closely associated with dominance hierarchies. In such cases, the function of territoriality is natural selection of the genes of the strongest members of the group. Territoriality does not refer to any single class of behaviors. As has been shown, defense of territory can be associated with protecting the young, with food and shelter, and with breeding. Gibbons will fight to defend personal space and also as a group against intruders in their home range (Carpenter, 1940). Furthermore, territorial behavior may not be restricted to intermale aggression, as with the Ugandan kob; it may occur as maternal aggression among lactating females defending a nest area, as with certain mice; or it may be confined to superordinate males in the herding of a harem, as in the sex-related aggression of the walrus.

If *territorial behavior* is defined as the defense of a fixed geographical region against invasion by members of the same species, then the evidence indicates that the gibbon is probably the only truly territorial species among the higher primates (Boelkins & Heiser, 1970). Rhodesian baboons do not fight when they encounter other troops (Washburn & DeVore, 1961). Interchanges in membership are not uncommon among chimpanzees, and several troops may use the same home range (Reynolds, 1965). In any case, defense against "foreigners" is hardly the same as territorial behavior. Refusal to grant membership to strangers in a closed group may or may not be a form of genetically determined defensive behavior. It may well be a learned behavior that is culturally transmitted to the young.

Humans defend territory, although most of their aggressive behavior does not involve conflict over territory. The question here is whether there is a biological determination of this behavior. Humans have no breeding season and do not defend nests or breeding territories. Nor do human males commonly keep harems for their exclusive sexual pleasure. Persons who are in their own primary territory (e.g., home or apartment) feel relaxed and secure in the presence of others (Edney, 1975). People do not typically feel threatened by people who enter their primary areas (Altman, 1975). Furthermore, humans frequently time-share their "territories" and sometimes maintain more than one at any given time (Edney, 1974). In short, there is no automatic pattern of territorial behavior among humans.

Conclusions: Instincts

There are many examples of instincts among subhuman animals. However, as one moves up the phylogenetic scale, there are fewer and fewer examples of instinctive behavior. Almost all of the behavior of the termite is genetically preprogrammed, but it is questionable whether there are any instincts (as defined above) among higher primates. Indeed, it is the lack of instincts that allows organisms to modify and change their behaviors. Although instinctive behaviors must occur, given the right stimulus and organismic conditions, an animal without instincts can make any response to any stimulus. The possession of instincts is associated with rigidity of behavior, whereas learning is associated with flexibility and variation of behavior. Humans do not have instincts associated with dominance hierarchies or territoriality, or any other form of aggressive behavior. A conclusion that humans do not possess instinctual behaviors does not extend to questions about whether they have genetic aggressive dispositions or drives. An organism could have urges to hurt others but no prewired behavior pattern that automatically is elicited by environmental stimuli. We turn now to the question of whether humans have innate drives (or urges) to hurt other people.

INNATE DRIVES AND AGGRESSION

In Lorenz's (1966) ethological theory and in Freud's (1950) psychoanalytic theory, a major factor postulated as causing aggressive behavior is aggressive energy, which is assumed to be part of the organism's genetic makeup. This energy appears to be spontaneous and builds up over time, like steam in a pressure cooker. The buildup of aggressive energy continues until it becomes intolerable and some form of aggressive behavior occurs. The behavior has the function of releasing aggressive energy and returning the organism to a more quiescent state. A very similar hydraulic process has been suggested by a number of learning theories of aggression, as we show in chapter 2.

In tandem with the notion of internal energy, the term *drive* was formulated by learning theorists to indicate that physiological conditions in the organism predispose it to behave in particular ways. It was presumed that the physiological condition (i.e., a need) affected thresholds for perceiving relevant stimuli and readied the appropriate muscle systems to carry out the need-fulfilling (or drive-reducing) behavior. If an animal needs food, it will eat, and if it has a buildup of aggressive energy, it will attack. Just as food alleviates the need for food, attacking fulfills the need to aggress. We refer to such drives as *appetitive* in nature. Appetitive drives are presumed to give rise to appropriate behavior with little or no learning when the relevant environmental conditions are present.

We have occasion in chapter 2 to say more about this topic, but what concerns us here is the physiological basis for energy or drive concepts. It can be categorically stated that there is no known physiological mechanism for storing large amounts of energy in the central nervous system. J. P. Scott (1971) has noted that the organism as a whole is a "mechanism by which energy can be accumulated and stored. However, such energy is not specific to any particular kind of behavior and does not represent motivation" (p. 27).

Although Moyer (1987) agreed with this conclusion, he provided evidence to suggest that neurohormonal mechanisms exist for different types of aggression. Activation of these mechanisms lowers or raises thresholds for performing aggressive responses. These changes in thresholds may give the appearance that internal energy levels are changing, but no independent energy is needed to explain the specific physiological changes that occur.

Physiological needs are cyclical in nature. Animals get progressively hungry if they do not eat, and eating satiates the need. It is a go and stop system that has known physiological determinants. Similar mechanisms exist with regard to thirst and sex. Research has indicated that increases in hunger, thirst, and sex deprivation cause the infrahuman organism to behave more vigorously and to learn more quickly (Bolles, 1967). However, there is no evidence of cyclicity of aggressive behavior or for the hypothesis that increases in delays between harming others produces more vigorous aggressive behavior. In other words, where the drive concept has worked best, there are known physiological mechanisms for the underlying needs and substantial evidence relating deprivation and satiation conditions to environmental conditions and subsequent behavior.

In his early theory of aggression, Freud (1950) suggested that aggressive behavior might result from the damming up or obstruction of the expression of sexual energy. Also, suspicion that sexual drive and exposure to pornography are factors contributing to aggressive behavior by men against women has raised questions about the relations between sexual drive and aggression. No physiological basis has been identified for this association, if indeed there is one. The mechanisms underlying sexual behavior are quite different from those associated with fighting (J. P. Scott, 1971).

Current knowledge about physiology indicates that there is no inborn energy that requires release in the form of aggressive behavior. Furthermore, no mechanism of any drive associated with go and stop signals for onset and offset of aggressive behaviors, respectively, has been found. Indeed, the available evidence indicates that there are different systems of aggressive behavior in infrahumans. There is no evidence for an underlying wellspring of energy that pushes or impels the organism to engage in hostile behavior.

GENETIC DETERMINATION OF AGGRESSION

The field of behavioral genetics has been developed to examine the inheritance of traits, temperaments, and behaviors. In humans, this research takes the form of examining commonality of traits and behaviors (concordance) among identical twins in comparison with that of fraternal twins or of other siblings. We next examine some of the issues and findings in this complex area of research, especially as they concern human aggression. In addition, we briefly review research on abnormalities in chromosomes to examine whether gender differences in aggressiveness might be due to genetic factors.

Recent research in behavioral genetics has provided evidence for inheritance of various characteristics in humans. It is reasonable to ask whether differences in aggressiveness in humans can to some extent be attributed to inheritance. This question has been addressed by comparing identical twins with fraternal twins and by comparing identical and fraternal twins who were raised in different environments.

Comparisons of Identical and Fraternal Twins

Studies of inherited cognitive abilities and personality traits have predominately concentrated on the comparison of identical and fraternal twins. Identical twins are monozygotic (Mz), which means that they come from the same fertilized egg. They are duplicates of one another, sharing 100% of their genes. Fraternal twins are dizygotic (Dz), which means that they develop from separate eggs and share 50% of genes, as would any pair of siblings. The rationale of twin studies is that because Mz and Dz twins share the same environments, differences between them must be due to heredity. The equal-environment assumption appears reasonable if one considers that both types of twins share the same womb, the same age, and the same sex (if opposite-sex Dz twins are excluded). Furthermore, they share the same parents and family-rearing practices.

Several studies have reported a higher concordance in aggressiveness between Mz twins than between Dz twins (Horn, Plomin, & Rosenman, 1976; Loehlin & Nichols, 1976; Rushton, Fulker, Neale, Nias, & Eysenck, 1986; Scarr, 1966). Each of these studies used self-report methods of determining level of aggressiveness. For example, Rushton et al. had 573 twin pairs rate themselves on an aggressiveness questionnaire consisting of 23 items. Sample items include "I try not to give people a hard time" and "Some people think I have a violent temper." A correlation of .40 was obtained for Mz twins, whereas a zero correlation was obtained for Dz twins. Just the opposite pattern was obtained by Canter (1973), who reported that 39 pairs of Mz twins were less similar to each other on the Foulds Hostility Scale than were 44 pairs of Dz twins. No significant heritability effect was found among adult male twins on a self-report measure of aggressiveness (Brunn, Markkanen, & Partanen, 1966) or on a measure of hostility (Vandenberg, 1968).

A behavioral criterion of aggressive behavior that has been frequently examined by social psychologists was used in one twin study (Plomin & Rowe, 1979). Children were shown films of a person hitting a plastic clown and were then given an opportunity to hit the clown. Twin correlations were about .45 for the aggressiveness of both Mz and Dz twins; thus, no genetic influence was found. Laboratory measures of personality traits typically have failed to demonstrate any genetic basis (Plomin, 1981), perhaps because such observations are too specific to identify traits that unfold across time and situations.

Other researchers have examined the heritability of criminal behavior. An examination of six twin studies of juvenile delinquency found little evidence for genetic influence (Gottesman, Carey, & Hanson, 1983). In eight studies of adult criminality, there was more concordance between Mz twins than between Dz twins (Cloninger & Gottesman, 1987). However, heritability existed only for crimes against property and not for violent crimes. Christiansen (1974), in a sample of Mz and Dz twins who had been convicted of crimes in Denmark, reported somewhat higher concordance rates for crimes against the person among Mz twins than among Dz twins. Whether this difference was significant cannot be determined, because Christiansen did not carry out any statistical tests. A meta-analysis of 38 family, twin, and adoption studies found only a weak gene–crime correlation, and the relationship was weaker in higher quality adoption studies and for research conducted after 1975 (G. D. Walters, 1992). In summary, the findings across studies are inconsistent, but it seems likely that there is some small relationship between genetic factors and criminal conduct. It is not known at this time what these genetic factors are.

Equal-Environment Assumption in Twin Studies

If the environment shared by Mz twins is more similar than that experienced by Dz twins, then differences found in research on behavioral genetics could be interpreted either to result from shared genes or to result from environmental differences. Research has indicated that identical twins are more often confused for one another than are fraternal twins (Cederlöf, Friberg, Jonsson, & Kaij, 1961; Cohen, Dibble, Grawe, & Pollin, 1973; Nichols & Bilbro, 1966) and that parents have more similar expectations for Mz than for Dz twins (Scarr, 1968). Mz twins report sharing more friends, spending more time together, and making more similar choices in lifestyles than do Dz twins (Scarr, 1968; R. T. Smith, 1965). The fact that Mz twins look more alike than Dz twins is due to heredity, but the greater similarity of reactions by others to Mz twins is a factor that creates greater similarity of social environment for Mz twins than Dz twins. If Mz twins look alike, share a social identity, and strive for similarity, and these factors produce common responses from significant others, then the fact that Mz twins are more similar in personality characteristics than Dz twins may be attributable to environmental and not genetic factors.

Loehlin and Nichols (1976) attempted to evaluate the criticisms cited above of the equal-environment assumption. They found that environmental factors—such as whether Mz twins shared a room, played together, or had the same teacher—did not affect the similarity of their personalities as measured by the California Personality Inventory. Furthermore, Plomin, Willerman, and Loehlin (1976) found that parental perceptions of the physical similarity of Mz twins were not significantly related to parental evaluations of the personalities of the twins. These two studies did not exhaustively examine all aspects of the social surroundings of the Mz twins, such as number of same friends or shared activities, nor did they directly examine aggressive behavior. Thus, it may be concluded that some of the factors that might negate the equal-environment assumption have been shown to be unimportant. It is an open question whether other factors make the environments of Mz twins more similar than would be the case for Dz twins.

In an ingenious study, a sample of twins was obtained in which twins were asked to identify whether they were Mz or Dz, and then blood tests were carried out to establish zygosity (Scarr & Carter-Saltzman, 1979). Only 60% of twins were correct about their zygosity. Thus, four groups of twins were created: true Mz and Dz twins and misidentified Mz and Dz twins. The intelligence scores of Mz twins were found to be more highly correlated than scores between Dz twins, regardless of twins' perceptions. On the other hand, similarity of personality was greatest between true Mz twins and between Dz twins who believed they were Mz twins. The lack of a difference between these two groups implies that there must be an environmental basis for the similarity.[1] Measures of physical appearance, such as height, skin reflectance, and muscle development, indicated that Dz twins who were physically more alike and had similar personalities were also more apt to mistakenly believe that they were Mz twins. It is plausible to argue that the physical similarities produced a more similar environment for the Dz twins who believed they were Mz twins. The results of this study do not resolve the issue of whether similarities in personalities of Mz twins can be attributable to genetic or environmental factors (or both).

Adoption Studies and the Heritability of Aggressive Behavior

A powerful technique for studying behavioral genetics is the adoption design. Children who live with foster parents can be compared on any characteristic with their biological parents and their foster parents. If there is more commonality with the foster parents, environment must be the cause, but if there is more commonality with the biological parents, then genetic factors must be the cause. If Mz and Dz twins are reared in separate adopted homes and Mz twins are more alike than are Dz twins, then the difference must be due to genetic factors.

In a study involving a small sample of adolescent twins raised apart, high correlations were found for Mz twins on almost all personality measures, including neuroticism, risk taking, self-control, social potency, achievement motivation, alienation, aggression, and conformity to rules (Tellegen et al., 1988). Mz twins raised apart and raised together were more alike than were Dz twins raised by adoptive parents. The fact that almost all of

---

[1]Genetic determinants are not ruled out, because they might play a more remote causal role. For example, Dz twins who believed they were Mz twins look alike because they share more genes related to physical appearance, and because they look alike, other people treat them as if they were identical twins. The belief that they are Mz twins might, in turn, have effects on how others react to them and how they relate to one another, causing them to be more similar in personality than Dz twins who do not look alike. Thus, the lack of a difference in personality traits between Mz twins and Dz twins who thought they were Mz twins might be due to rather direct genetic effects among the former and more remote genetic effects among the latter.

the personality traits assessed by self-report questionnaires showed such a strong heritable influence may indicate that there are more general factors associated with the self-report measures that account for such findings. For example, general intelligence and temperament types have been found to have strong heritability components (Plomin, DeFries, & McClearn, 1990). Perhaps intelligence and temperament are correlated with self-report measures of personality. If so, then Tellegen et al.'s results may be indirectly reflecting the heritability of intelligence and temperament.

Comparisons of Mz and Dz twins reared together or reared in separate households indicated a substantial heritability of a self-reported tendency to act impulsively when angered (Coccaro, Bergeman, & McClearn, 1993). A longitudinal study has shown that self-reports of impulsivity in adolescents are predictive of antisocial behavior (Luengo, Carrillo-de-la-Peña, Otero, & Romero, 1994). Impulsive behavior has also been associated with chemical actions in the brain. An increase in serotonin has been shown to produce response inhibition in humans (Karli, 1991). A depletion of serotonin, on the other hand, produces hyperactivity in associated brain structures, which, in turn, increases the speed of responses to stimuli. Thus, converging evidence suggests the possibility that biochemical actions in the brain, which are to some degree heritable, may facilitate or inhibit impulsive behavior, which in turn may be linked to antisocial and, perhaps, aggressive behavior.

Adoption studies have confirmed results of the twin studies showing a heritable component of criminality. Mednick, Gabrielli, and Hutchings (1984) found that 15% of adopted boys in Denmark were criminals when their adoptive parents were criminals, 20% were criminals if their biological parents were criminals, and 25% were criminals if both biological and adoptive parents were criminals. Parent–offspring data suggested somewhat less genetic influence than did the twin data. Again, as in the nonadoptive-twin studies, the genetic influence was on criminal behavior generally, not specifically on violent criminal behavior. Any genetic determination of aggressive behavior would presumably more directly affect violent behavior than nonviolent behavior (criminal or otherwise).

Although the correspondence between fathers' criminal behavior and their sons' criminal behavior may not be large in adoption studies, the impact of genes on behavior could still be substantial. Figure 1.1 shows the relationships between the criminal behavior of fathers and sons as well as the genetic contributions to the behavior and from father to son. Assume a correlation of .10 between the criminal behavior of fathers and sons. Because a father's genetic makeup accounts for 50% of his son's genetic makeup, the effect of his genes on his sons must be $x = .50$. Whatever the genetic contribution to aggressive behavior, it would be the same for fathers and sons; thus, the effect of genetic makeup (path y) is the same for fathers and sons. Given that the values of x and r are known, one can

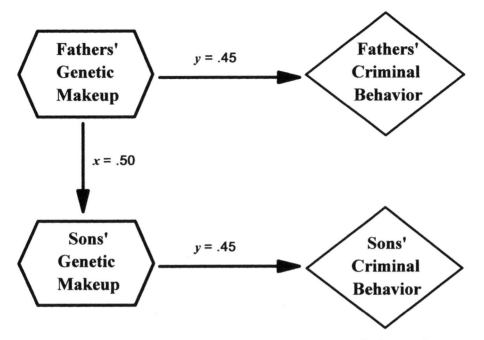

Figure 1.1. A model of path coefficients reflecting genetic contributions to the correlation between the criminal behaviors of fathers and sons.

solve for the value of y (i.e., the genetic contribution to criminal behavior). According to the basic path theorem, the correlation between any two variables is a multiplicative function of the paths connecting them. The paths contributing to the correlation between fathers' and sons' criminal behavior are the genetic contribution to aggressive behavior of both and the genetic contribution of fathers to sons. Thus, if $r = x \times y \times y = .10 = .50 \times y^2$, then $y = .45$. A trivial correlation of .10, therefore, implies a substantial genetic effect on behavior.

Gottfredson and Hirschi (1990) used a similar example to claim that genetic effects are weak. However, contrary to their conclusion, we have shown that nonsignificant correlations may disguise a substantial genetic effect between the behavior of biological fathers and their children. On the other hand, the small but significant correlations between the behavior of biological fathers and sons that have been observed in adoption studies are consistent with substantial genetic effects.

The method of making simple comparisons between Mz and Dz twins in adoption studies has been subjected to criticism (L. W. Hoffman, 1985). Prospective parents must be screened by adoption agencies. Adoptive parents are typically higher in IQ and socioeconomic status than biological parents who give their children up for adoption. Adoptive parents may be selected for personal qualities; similarity to the children in terms of height, race, and religion; and marital stability. Adoptive parents are also likely to be older than biological parents. In general, adoptive parents represent a narrower range on most characteristics than do biological parents, a factor that would alter the estimates of genetic influence in adoptive families (Lewontin, Rose, & Kamin, 1984). The correlations among adoptive family members probably underestimate the effects of socialization.

Abnormal Chromosomes

Males of most species are more aggressive than females. This generalization must be tempered by the recognition that female gibbons, rhesus monkeys, and lions are as aggressive as their male counterparts (Moyer, 1987) and that lactating females of many species are quite aggressive in defending their young against intrusions by male members of the same species. If males are generally more aggressive than females, then the implication is that aggressive behavior is carried somehow in the genes and that the Y chromosome, which determines that a fetus will be male, may be the carrier.

In one study of a prison population (Jacobs, Brunton, Melville, & Brittain, 1965), an abnormal combination of chromosomes that includes an extra Y was implicated as the cause of aggressive behavior. The XYY combination occurs in 1 out of 1,000 males. But in the prison studied, more than 1 out of 100 males were XYY. The extra Y chromosome could be interpreted as giving the individual with an XYY pattern an extra dosage of male aggressiveness.

A study carried out in Denmark found that the percentage of normal men who had criminal records was 9.3% but that 40% of XYY men had committed criminal offenses (Witkin et al., 1976). Most of the crimes committed by the XYY individuals were minor property offenses; such individuals were not overrepresented in the commission of violent crimes. This same study found that XYY men scored lower on intelligence tests and achieved a lower educational level than did XY men. There is evidence that intelligence and educational level are associated with criminal behavior (see chap. 5). In addition, it may be that lower intelligence affects the likelihood of being apprehended for criminal behavior. It is interesting to note that XXY men, who have an extra female-linked chromosome, are also overrepresented in prison populations (Witkin et al., 1976).

Conclusions: Genetic Determination of Aggression

What conclusions should be drawn that are relevant for understanding human aggression from these studies of behavioral genetics? The most reliable findings across various kinds of research designs are that genetic factors are important in determining general intelligence, alcoholism, and schizophrenia. Aspects of temperament, such as activity level and emotionality, may also be genetically transmitted. Any of these factors may contribute indirectly to aggressive behavior.

The evidence shows a heritable component for aggressive behavior when self-report methods are used either by subjects themselves or by their parents, but not when aggressive behavior is directly observed in laboratory situations. The problems associated with the equal-environment assumption of twin and adoption studies raise a question about whether reliable estimates of genetic and environmental effects are obtained in these studies. Last but not least are questions about the validity of the criterion measures used.

Caution about drawing firm conclusions regarding genetic determination is also warranted, because no specific mechanism has been proposed for how genes produce the phenotypes studied. Genes are chemicals programmed to control and change proteins. Genes do not cause behavior, so how could genes affect aggression? In lower organisms, androgens and neural regions can control aggressive behavior, and hereditary processes operate to control androgens and neural development. However, in humans these physiological mechanisms have not been shown to operate in controlling aggressive behavior. The lack of a specific physiological process that directly mediates aggressive behavior, which is known to be affected by the action of genes, weakens the case for a heritable component of aggression.

A favorite statement among behavioral geneticists is "genes are not destiny." Behavior is not preestablished in some Lamarckian fashion by genetic codes, and there is no genetically required behavior. Genes never operate apart from environments. It can also be said that organisms never behave in environments apart from their genetic makeup. It is our view that genetic factors do not directly cause aggressive behavior but, rather, that they have either indirect or moderating effects on aggressive behavior. It can be accepted that there are innate structures, some of which will be considered below, that may allow or facilitate classes of behavior but that would not be considered direct causes.

REFLEX FIGHTING

Pain inflicted on an animal by outside forces, as distinguished from somatic or deep-body pain (like a bellyache) is a reliable cause of attack behavior in subhuman animals. When an animal experiences intense pain, it attacks whatever is perceived as the source. In studies of reflexive fighting, two animals are typically placed in a closed area and then one is given an electric shock. When the space is small, the shocked animal attacks the innocent bystander as if the latter had bitten it. Attacks may even be directed at inanimate objects. For example, harnessed monkeys who had painful shocks administered to their tails responded by biting tennis balls (Azrin, Hutchinson, & Hake, 1967).

Reflexive fighting will not occur under mild shock conditions or when the space occupied by the animals is not small. The intensity and duration of fighting among monkeys was a direct function of the amount of shock delivered to them (Azrin, Hutchinson, & Hake, 1963). These findings have been interpreted as indicating that aggression is a reflexive reaction to pain and that the behavior pattern is a stereotyped one.

Johnson (1972) has suggested that pain-elicited responses are neither reflexive nor aggressive. Intermale fighting among rats is a highly stereotyped ritual. The pattern consists of chattering of teeth, piloerection, arching of the back, and fluffing of the fur, a presentation of the flank to the other rat, jostling, and then hyperactivity, including leaping, kicking, biting, and wrestling on the ground. Rats attempt to bite each other on the back and avoid the underside of their opponent. During pauses in the fighting, each rat will take a defensive "boxing" posture, standing on hind legs and facing the foe with forelegs extended and belly exposed. However, it is typically only this defensive boxing posture that is elicited by shocks. The extension of the body upward may have the function of reducing contact with the electrified grid floor rather than of aggressing against the other animal.

Some evidence is inconsistent with the interpretation of shock-induced behavior as reflexive fighting. When a rat is shocked and a second rat is introduced a few seconds after the shock is terminated, little fighting is observed (Roediger & Stevens, 1970). When only one member of a pair of rats is shocked, the animal experiencing pain will display escape or avoidance responses rather than attack behavior (Knutson, 1971). Furthermore, predatory behavior is not induced by painful shocks. Rats who do not normally kill mice do not kill them when given painful shocks (Karli, 1956; Myer & Baenninger, 1966).

It is not only questionable whether responses to shocks are "aggression," but they are probably also not reflexive. Most reflexes, such as eyeblinks, are easily conditioned to various stimuli (e.g., lights and tones). Shock-elicited boxing responses by rodents are not easily conditioned; in one study, thousands of pairings of a tone with painful shocks brought about only weak and inconsistent boxing responses to the tone (Vernon & Ulrich, 1966). Also, what a shocked animal does depends on the available target. Wild rats who are shocked do not attack familiar objects (Galef, 1970), and mice-killing rats who are shocked will not attack baby rats (Myer & Baenninger, 1966).

Reflexive attack responses to pain have not been demonstrated in humans. Although a woman who hits her thumb with a hammer may yell "damn!" it is not reflexive that she will throw the hammer at whoever happens to be around. We have occasion in chapter 2 to discuss human responses to aversive stimulation. For now, we may conclude that there is no incontestable evidence for reflexive fighting elicited by painful stimulation in either infrahuman animals or humans.

HORMONES AND AGGRESSIVE BEHAVIOR

Among most animal species, including humans, it has been commonly observed that males are larger, stronger, more active, and more aggressive than females. Research has indicated that sex differences in aggression are moderate in size and are stronger among preschoolers than among college-age samples (Hyde, 1986). Although there are important exceptions to this general rule, the sex differences in aggressiveness are sufficiently prevalent to implicate androgens, which are biochemical factors associated with sex, as causes of the relevant characteristics. Sex-related hormones have been identified as important determinants of gender identity, sexuality, mood and the menstrual cycle, activity level, and aggression. The most important androgen associated with being a male is testosterone, which is manufactured in the gonads.

Infrahuman Research on Testosterone Effects

Most of the research on the effects of hormones has been conducted with rodents. Research techniques have included injecting the animal with testosterone, castrating it, or measuring natural levels before, during, or after behavioral episodes. According to F. A. Beach (1974), there are three ways that hormones act to influence the individual: (a) They can momentarily affect the musculature and either facilitate or impair performance of specific behaviors; (b) they may affect the sensory system and thus modify the perception of stimuli; and (c) they can modify the physiological structure of the organism and its long-term capacity or readiness to respond in particular ways. The question here is whether any of these effects, specifically identified with testosterone, affect aggressive behavior.

High levels of testosterone have been associated with both sexual and aggressive behaviors in seasonally breeding animals (Bernstein, Gordon, & Rose, 1983). Exposure to testosterone in adults produces temporary changes in behavior. Hormonal stimulation during adulthood is necessary for the production of aggressive behavior in mammals (Svare & Kinsley, 1987). Conversely, castration reduces the intensity of aggressive behavior (Beeman, 1947). Breeders have long known that castration of horses, cats, and dogs decreases agonistic behavior.

The decline in aggressiveness in castrated rodents is affected by previous fighting experience. Postcastrate animals will maintain their positions in dominance hierarchies (Maruniak, Desjardins, & Bronson, 1977). Male mice who had considerable experience and success in fighting persisted in fighting after castration for a much longer period than did inexperienced animals (Schecter & Gandelman, 1981). An injection of testosterone reinstates the aggressive behavior of castrates (Tollman & King, 1956), but only if they have previous fighting experience (Connor & Levine, 1969). The failure to establish a clear relationship between levels of testosterone and intensity of aggressive behavior (Leshner, 1978) suggests a "permissiveness effect." That is, the presence of testosterone permits aggressive behavior to occur, whereas its absence disallows such behavior. This permissiveness effect is importantly modified by the previous learning experience of the organism.

In early stages of development, a fetus is dimorphous with respect to gender. An XX genetic background is usually associated with the absence of testosterone, and therefore, the individual develops feminine characteristics with respect to internal and external structures of the reproductive system. Female mice who are carried in an intrauterine position between two males are exposed to the testosterone produced by their siblings. Such females exhibit behavior more characteristic of intermale aggression than do females positioned between two other females in the intrauterine environment (Gandelman, vom Saal, & Reinish, 1977). They are more aggressive toward intruders and more vigorous in defending territory. Male fetuses that are exposed to low levels of testosterone tend to act more like females as adults. Male mice positioned between two females in the intrauterine environment are less aggressive when exposed to testosterone as adults than are adult males that had been positioned between two males in utero (vom Saal, 1979).

A female mouse exposed to testosterone during a critical period of fetal development undergoes masculinization. The female shows malelike physical characteristics and engages in behaviors typical of a male (Svare & Kinsley, 1987). It is important to note that the affected behavior is not identical to that displayed by males. Females will not attack males; attacks tend to be restricted to unfamiliar juvenile males, although lactating females tend to attack all intruders. Svare and Gandelman (1975) found that the presence of testosterone early in life was related to aggression toward a conspecific when testosterone is also present in adulthood. That is, the impact of testosterone in the adult organism is dependent not only on past learning but also on perinatal experience with androgens. Structural changes, such as size and secondary sex characteristics, that occur because of exposure to testosterone in utero have been associated with subsequent sexual and aggressive behavior of the affected animals.

Human Research on Androgen Effects

Research has yielded ambiguous results about the impact (if any) of androgens on human aggressive behavior. Although much of the research has focused on the effects of testosterone on male aggression, recent interest has been manifested in the effect of premenstrual hormone changes in women and on female aggression. We turn now to an examination of these two areas of research.

Testosterone and Male Aggression

Many of the results obtained in testosterone research in humans are difficult to interpret. For example, Kreuz and Rose (1972) found no significant correlation between the amount of testosterone in the blood of incarcerated men and the number of times they had been placed in solitary confinement for breaking prison rules. No relationship was established between levels of testosterone, frequency of fighting, verbal aggression, or scores on the Buss–Durkee Hostility Inventory. However, further statistical analysis revealed that the 10 men who had most frequently committed violent offenses during adolescence had higher testosterone levels than did prisoners with a less violent adolescent history.

There is also a problem in establishing causation from cross-sectional correlational data. It is just as plausible to suggest that aggressive behavior raises levels of plasma testosterone as it is to hypothesize that increases in testosterone cause aggressive behavior. It has been reliably established that in infrahuman fighting between males, there is an increase in plasma testosterone in the winner, whereas a decline in testosterone occurs in the loser (Rose, Bernstein, & Gordon, 1975). Analogous findings have been reported among humans. Winners of college wrestling matches exhibited greater increases in circulating testosterone than did losers (Elias, 1981), and winners in a doubles tennis match exhibited elevations in testosterone, whereas losers showed a decline (Mazur & Lamb, 1980). If testosterone was the cause of these differences, it is not clear that the competitive behavior involved was aggression.

Testosterone levels can be greatly increased through the use of steroids. Research has shown that steroids, like natural levels of testosterone, increase the aggressiveness of infrahuman animals (e.g., Haug, Brain, & Kamis, 1985). There are legal and ethical problems associated with doing similar research using humans. However, some athletes take large doses of this synthetic derivative of testosterone because, when combined with vigorous workouts, it helps develop muscles and strength. Most of the available human research focuses on comparing the self-reports of hostility and aggression by athletes who have used steroids with the self-reports of those who have not. For example, Yates, Perry, and Murray (1992) compared weight lifters who did use steroids with those who did not use steroids. The steroid users had higher scores on the Buss–Durkee Hostility Inventory than did nonusers. A problem of interpretation is the possibility that the steroid users might have been more aggressive than nonusers even before they started taking steroids. Furthermore, expectations that the use of steroids will increase hostility and aggression might be responsible for behavioral changes in steroid users. Prospective studies of steroid effects on aggression, if any, have yet to be carefully carried out.

Testosterone levels can be reduced by surgical removal of the gonads or by chemical means. It is reasonable to ask if such methods reduce aggressive behavior. In some countries, criminals convicted of violent sex acts have been subjected to castration and, more recently, to chemical treatments that counteract and nullify the presumed effects of testosterone. Research findings of the effects of castration obtained from six European countries indicated only a 2.2% recidivism rate for 3,186 cases (Sturup, 1968).

Chemical means have also been used to treat sexual offenders by lowering their sex drive. Testosterone antagonists, such as cyproterone acetate and medroxyprogesterone acetate, have been reported to successfully reduce deviate sexual behavior in criminal offenders (Laschet, 1972; Money, 1980). Caution is required in interpreting such results because the men were simultaneously undergoing psychotherapy or counseling. Furthermore, the focus of these studies was the sexual conduct of the men, including homosexuality, and not the violence or aggressiveness of their behavior.

It would not be surprising if the research on surgical and chemical castration indicated some relationship to sex drive and sexual misconduct. The general question here, however, is whether reduction of testosterone reduces aggressive behavior in general, not only in relation to sexual gratification. There is no evidence that castration will affect aggressive behavior that does not involve sexual misconduct.

Premenstrual Tension and Aggression

The belief that males in all species of animals are more aggressive than females has important exceptions. Among bees, only the females possess stingers and defend against predators. Male wasps and praying mantis are generally dominated by the female (Johnson, 1972). Females of many species show a maternal aggression pattern of behavior in which they attack intruders—even the paternal animal—who approach their offspring. Female aggression has been hypothesized to be associated with estrogens.

In humans, women do not invariably display maternal aggression; indeed, there is no behavior pattern in humans analogous to that displayed by lower animals, such as female mice. However, clinical reports indicate that some women experience irritability and tension for seven days before and a couple of days after menstruation (Dalton, 1964; Hamburg, 1966). This cycling of negative mood states and associated behavior patterns has been referred to as the *premenstrual tension syndrome* (PMTS).

A number of behavior patterns have been associated with PMTS. Women make more suicide attempts and are more likely to succeed in committing suicide during the premenstrual period (Mandell & Mandell, 1967). Women imprisoned for violent crimes were more likely to be confined to their rooms for disciplinary reasons during the week before menstruation (Hands, Herbert, & Tennent, 1974). In another study of female prison inmates, a correlation was found between the infliction of physical and verbal abuse on others and PMTS (D. Ellis & Austin, 1971). Women are more likely to commit violent crimes just before and immediately after menstruation than at other times in the menstrual cycle (Dalton, 1964; Moyer, 1971).

The findings discussed above have been subjected to a number of methodological criticisms. These have been summarized by Svare and Kinsley (1987):

> First. . . [there is] no general agreement by individuals working in this area as to what constitutes negative affect and mood; therefore, there is tremendous variation from study to study in what behaviors are actually measured. Second, because most of the work in this area has focused on unusual populations, including prisoners and patients in psychiatric wards, the extent to which the findings can be generalized to the average, cycling female is limited. Third, much of the older and even some of the more recent work in this area fails to measure plasma hormone levels, thus preventing any reasonable conclusions concerning estrogen and progesterone involvement. Finally, the social expectations of many developing females during menstruation is [sic] rarely considered as a major source of variation and a causal factor by itself. (pp. 42–43)

A hint that estrogens may be implicated in the association of premenstrual cycle and moods and behaviors was obtained in a report that women taking birth control pills did not experience PMTS (Hamburg, Moos, & Yalom, 1968). It is known that there is a drop in the level of progesterone in the blood during the week prior to menstruation and that birth control pills contain progesteragenic agents.

The hypothesis that maintenance of progesterone levels by pharmaceutical means will eliminate PMTS has received no supporting evidence. A review of the relevant research found no relationship between levels of ovarian hormones and PMTS (e.g., Dalton, 1982). Furthermore, the well-known postpartum blues were found to be unrelated to estrogen or progesterone levels before, during, or after giving birth.

The psychological effects associated with the menstrual cycle have not been traced to any physiological causes. Moyer (1987) came to the following conclusion:

> It must be recognized that the menstrual cycle is a phenomenon loaded with psychological meaning in most cultures. It therefore seems unlikely that the psychological changes associated with the period just prior to

the onset of the menses are exclusively or even primarily of physiological origin. (p. 52)

The impact of cultural factors on PMTS is suggested by the fact that reports of symptoms vary widely as a function of religious affiliation (Brain, 1984). Although many women in some religions experience PMTS, women in other religions seldom or never do so. Attitudes and expectations associated with the menstrual cycle may be self-fulfilling. Women who knew they were in a study of menstruation-related symptoms reported more symptoms than women who did not know (AuBuchon & Calhoun, 1985; Rogers & Harding, 1981). Klebanov and Jemmott (1992) reported two experiments in which women were given either true or false information about the timing of their premenstrual period. The authors found effects of both expectations and actual premenstrual period on the number of symptoms manifested by women. However, aggressive behavior was not specifically examined in any of these studies.

Conclusions: Hormones and Aggression

The impact of biochemical factors on human emotions and behavior is not precisely known at the present time. After reviewing the relevant research, Svare and Kinsley (1987) concluded that they were "not aware of a single study indicating that hormones directly alter behavior in humans by acting on the central nervous system" (p. 45). Nevertheless, it is not unreasonable to tentatively believe (in the absence of conclusive evidence) that hormones play some indirect role on the aggressive behavior of individuals. An interaction of hormonal factors and external events may affect thresholds of anger or perhaps augment or intensify aggressive behavior. Such speculation about the possible complex and indirect role of hormones on human behavior is not inconsistent with the existing evidence.

NEUROMECHANISMS AND AGGRESSION

The examination of neural mechanisms, particularly in terms of brain centers controlling aggressive behavior, has primarily been focused on infrahuman animals. There are good reasons, as we shall show, for reviewing the evidence separately for infrahumans and humans.

Infrahuman Research

Exploration of the neural mechanisms underlying aggressive behavior patterns has produced some interesting findings. One important method of research has been the use of electrical stimulation in different specifiable locations in the brain. A wire is inserted in a site in the brain and attached to an electrode positioned on the skull. By telemetry (i.e, radio waves) the wire can introduce an electrical stimulus to the brain site. Then the scientist can determine if there is any reliable behavior pattern that accompanies a particular level of shock in a specific site. We may characterize this research as a search for go and stop centers for aggression in the brain.

The area of the brain most intimately involved with emotions and motivation consists of a set of structures referred to as the *limbic system*. A key structure in the limbic system is the hypothalamus, which is associated with the control of eating, drinking, sexual behavior, and the regulation of hormones. The amygdala, another small structure in the limbic system, has also received a great deal of attention in research as a site for control over aggressive behavior.

In a representative study, cats accustomed to coexisting peacefully with rats had electrodes implanted in the lateral hypothalamus (Wasman & Flynn, 1962). Low levels of electrical stimulation caused the cat to pace back and forth in the cage. Slightly higher levels caused the cats to attack a rat that it had previously ignored and to kill it with a surgical bite on the back of the neck. Such electrically induced attacks were quite specific and were so unemotional that they have been called "quiet biting attacks" (Flynn, 1967). The electrical stimulation did not cause indiscriminate attacks against irrelevant objects, horse meat, or the experimenter (Flynn, Vanegas, Foote, & Edwards, 1970).

Electrical stimulation of the medial hypothalamus caused cats to indiscriminately attack almost anything, including the experimenter (Egger & Flynn, 1963; Roberts & Kiess, 1964). Although the latter behavior was accompanied by strong emotion or arousal, it did not appear to be directed toward the satisfaction of any goal. Quiet biting and emotional attacks can also be elicited by stimulation of different regions of the hypothalamus in rats (Panksepp, 1971).

The aggressive responses performed by electrically stimulated animals do not occur irrespective of environmental factors. Electrical stimulation of the anterior hypothalamus of a rhesus monkey did not elicit attacks against inanimate objects or humans, but when the monkey was placed in a cage with a female and a larger and dominant male, stimulation produced attack specifically directed against the dominant male (Robinson, Alexander, & Bowne, 1969). The result was a violent fight. When this sequence was repeated a number of times, the pattern of dominance and submission was reversed between the two male monkeys.

Remember that the aggressive behavior patterns of infrahumans tend to be stereotyped (prewired) and specific to the species or family of animals. Animal research has indicated that there is no unitary aggressive pattern of behavior. Instead, different response systems can exist within a particular species of animal, each with specific and different functions. After reviewing studies of electrical stimulation, lesions, and recordings of the brains of cats and rats, D. B. Adams (1979) proposed that there are three response systems—offense, defense, and submission—and two activating systems—motivating stimuli and releasing–directing stimuli. He speculated that these same systems exist in primates. Moyer (1987) has proposed that there are seven different aggressive behavior patterns that can be identified by their neural and hormonal bases and the stimuli that elicit them. Included in this typology are intermale fighting and predatory, fear-induced, territorial, maternal, irritable, and instrumental aggression.

The most important lesson to be learned from the research on brain stimulation and lesioning with infrahuman species is that there is no unified aggression center in the brain. Fighting, predatory behavior, defense, flight, and other specific forms of behavior that are ritualistic within the species can be elicited from various sites in the mammalian brain. Although a great deal of research has been done with the hypothalamus and its role in controlling aggressive behavior, caution is needed in interpreting the findings. In one study, even when the hypothalamus was neurally isolated from the rest of the brain and, therefore, could not influence behavior, cats continued to engage in normal aggressive behavior (G. D. Ellison & Flynn, 1968).

Human Research on Neurosystems and Aggression

Clinical observations of patients who have suffered from brain tumors, accidents, or diseases that damage the brain provide many case studies of claimed association between lesions in the brain and aggressive behavior. Almost all of the sites in the limbic system have been linked to aggressive behavior in clinical case studies.

Some of the case studies report dramatic changes in behavior. For example, an electrode was implanted in the amygdala of a woman described as kind, friendly, and submissive (H. E. King, 1961). When the woman was exposed to electrical stimulation, she became hostile. Once during stimulation she shouted in an angry voice, "Quit holding me. I'm getting up. You'd better get somebody if you want to hold me! I'm going to hit you." Although she raised her arm, she didn't strike the experimenter, perhaps because he turned off the stimulation. Apparently, this woman's anger could be elicited or turned off by the onset or offset of electrical stimulation.

Another dramatic case study was reported by Moyer (1987). A young man, Charles Whitman, went on a spree of violence, killing his wife and mother. In a letter started before the double murder, Whitman reported experiencing overwhelming violent impulses. He also requested that after his death an autopsy should be performed to see if he had a physical disorder. He said he had tremendous headaches and was the victim of irrational thoughts. The desire to die was connected with murdering his wife and mother, because he did not want them to be embarrassed by his actions and to be left alone in a cruel world.

During the single counseling session with a psychiatrist 2 months before the violent spree, Whitman had indicated an impulse to climb a tower on the campus of the University of Texas and to shoot passersby. After killing his wife and mother, he carried out this impulse. He took a high-powered rifle, climbed the tower, shot and killed the receptionist, and for the next 90 minutes shot at anyone he could get within his telescopic sight. By the time Whitman was killed by police sharpshooters, he had shot 24 people walking across the Austin campus, killing 14 of them. An autopsy established that he had a brain tumor. The precise location of the tumor could not be established because of extensive damage from gunshot wounds.

One might conjecture that Whitman's sudden outburst of violence had been building as pressure on his brain increased. However, there is no direct evidence for such a causal hypothesis. It is just as plausible that the headaches and depression were conditions that he had learned to respond to with anger and, finally, with suicidal attack against others. Whitman's own writings indicated that his actions were not impulsive, but were planned in advance (Valenstein, 1973). A number of studies have reported changes in the behavior of patients who suffer brain tumors in the frontal lobes and various parts of the hypothalamus (cf. Moyer, 1987). Behavior change in the direction of more irritability and aggressive behavior is not invariable. Brain tumors are associated with a multitude of other changes occurring in the lives of patients.

Methodological problems abound in case studies of natural lesions and with electrical stimulation studies of humans. The studies involve small numbers of subjects and many variables, typically under conditions in which there is little control over factors that could account for the findings (Hinton, 1981). For example, Heath (1981) reported that rage and violence were consistently produced when sites in the amygdala and hippocampus were stimulated in 12 violent patients. One must remember that these patients were violent before entering the hospital. Also, these patients might have resented being subjected to surgery to implant electrodes. A learned disposition to react violently when provoked combined with perceptions of unjust treatment could be important factors accounting for why these patients reacted violently to electrical stimulation.

Another approach to studying brain sites is to locate areas that suppress aggressive behavior. Psychosurgery has been reported to ameliorate or eliminate aggression. For example, Sanjo (1975) reported that posteromedial hypothalamotomy caused calming in 94% of cases. Most authorities believe that such surgery produces a general sedative effect and is not specific to any neural circuits controlling aggression. Brain surgery is a radical treatment and is carried out only with patients who are extremely violent and uncontrollable. The available evidence regarding the effects of psychosurgery has indicated that cutting away part of the brain (i.e., ablation) within some sites, particularly the temporary lobes and the amygdala, may produce some ameliorative effects among patients (Brain, 1984; Moyer, 1987). However, critics have noted that less than 40% of patients show marked improvement and that the criteria of improvement applied in these studies have not been very precise (D. Carroll & O'Callaghan, 1981).

Conclusions: Neurosystems and Aggressive Behavior

Research on sites for eliciting and suppressing aggressive behavior must be evaluated in terms of incredibly difficult problems of control and interpretation. Consider some of the difficulties associated with studies in which researchers attempted to localize centers of aggression in the brain:[2]

1. Electrical stimulation is not the same kind of event as a patterned volley of physiological signals. Consequently, generalizations from research using electrical stimulation to the brain to the natural functioning of the brain may not be warranted.
2. Stimulation activates many neurons other than those at the specific site chosen. Any action in the brain is like throwing pebbles in a pond—some ripples occur at the edge and not at the place where the stone hits. Similarly, biochemical changes are produced by electrical stimulation, which may in turn produce remote effects.
3. All the other cerebral content at the time of the electrical stimulation is unknown and uncontrolled. Any electrical stimulation would at best be only a component part of a pattern of brain activity.
4. It is extremely difficult to generalize from animal research to humans for two important reasons: (a) The human brain is more complex, and (b) the behavior of infrahumans is more simple and ritualistic. Thus, the brain sites studied may not have the same connections or functions in animals and humans, and it is difficult to generalize from such specific and ritualized aggressive behaviors as intermale fighting in rodents or predatory behavior of cats, because there are no comparable genetically prewired and stereotyped behavior patterns in humans.

---

[2]We have distilled these criticisms of research on locating sites in the brain for aggressive behavior from Ervin, Mark, and Stevens (1969); Moyer (1987); and Brain (1984).

The human brain is an extremely complex organization of over 10 billion cells. The mysteries of this tangled knot will probably not be unraveled in our lifetime. Thus, it is unlikely that we will find neurological answers to the causes of human aggression. Yet, the physiological evidence with regard to sites in the brain should not be ignored. Abnormalities, such as tumors, may affect mood states or, in some other indirect way, may affect the aggressive behaviors of individuals.

SUMMARY AND CONCLUSIONS

Anthropomorphism is a generalization of unique human characteristics to infrahumans. An owner may refer to the loyalty or love of a house pet, inappropriately attributing unique human characteristics to the pet. Scientists are more prone to make inferences in the opposite direction. Generalizations of infrahuman characteristics to humans are sometimes justified, but often this reasoning by analogy is either too simple or completely unjustified. Although lower organisms may inherit instinctual behavior, humans do not. Furthermore, the development of language and culture by humans has transformed, redirected, and obscured whatever biological tendencies that may be coded in the genes. Attempts to understand the complex behavior of humans by using analogies to the simpler, agonistic behavior of infrahumans are like trying to explain why a jet plane flies by describing the principles of simpler vehicles, such as wheelbarrows (Boulding, 1968).

The complexity of human behavior must be recognized when comparisons are made with lower organisms. We have shown that aggressive behavior patterns in lower organisms are ritualistic and easily recognized. For example, the intermale, maternal, and intruder–defender patterns of aggressive behavior in rats appear to be separate response systems under the control of distinct physiological mechanisms and associated environmental conditions. There are no such easily recognizable and typical behavior patterns in humans. People use tools—such as knives, guns, and bombs—to settle disputes that often focus on symbolic goals like self-enhancement, freedom, religion, and nationalism. Although individual humans may seek retribution, there is no evidence that infrahumans are motivated by a concern for justice. Virtually any response performed by a human can be used to hurt others. Pushing a finger against a button may cause a bomb to explode or may launch a missile carrying a nuclear warhead. Pulling a finger may depress a trigger on a rifle, handgun, or automatic weapon. Speaking a few sentences in a calm voice may conclude a contract with a hit man to kill another person. These considerations lead us to agree with J. P. Scott (1970), who has concluded that "[because of] man's unique genetic composition, no direct analogies (of agonistic behavior) from any other species to man are justified" (p. 570).

All organisms, including humans, are limited by their genetic endowments. However, biological capacities do not provide an adequate explanation for complex human actions. The capacity to speak neither means that all humans will speak nor explains or predicts what people will say if they do speak. The stance taken in this book is that genetic factors may affect mood states, emotions, and other internal conditions that may indirectly affect the likelihood of aggression under certain conditions. In general, we view biological factors as playing a remote causal role, often moderating aggressive behavior in humans.

2

FRUSTRATION, AVERSIVENESS, AND AGGRESSION

Four decades ago, five psychologists at Yale University published a classic book entitled *Frustration and Aggression,* in which they proposed a theory that continues to be influential in the social sciences (Dollard, Doob, Miller, Mowrer, & Sears, 1939). These psychologists borrowed some core ideas from psychoanalysis. Their primary purpose was to transpose the insights of Sigmund Freud into a more scientific language. Freud's ideas, although often ingenious, lacked the precision of definition and testability of rigorous scientific theories.

Dollard et al.'s (1939) frustration–aggression theory brought the study of aggression into the psychological laboratory. Subsequently, the limitations of frustration–aggression theory led Leonard Berkowitz (1982) to revise it. In his theory of reactive aggression, Berkowitz assumed that aversive experiences activate the desire to hurt others. A number of factors may facilitate or inhibit aggressive behavior when a person is exposed to aversive stimulation. The organism also learns instrumental aggression, where the goal is not to hurt, but to achieve some other goal; but reactive aggression is almost always associated with instrumental aggression.

In this chapter, we review the seminal ideas of Sigmund Freud. We then describe frustration–aggression theory and some of the research it has generated. After evaluating frustration–aggression theory, we describe and critically evaluate Berkowitz's revision of it.

FREUD'S THEORY OF AGGRESSION

Freud borrowed ideas from many sources in literature, philosophy, and the natural sciences and combined them with keen observation and insight into psychoanalytic theory. From physics he borrowed the law of conservation of energy, which indicated that energy might be transformed or diffused but could not be lost. In psychoanalytic theory, psychic energy is the basis of all human activity. A person gains psychic energy from his or her biological system; this energy does not dissipate but must be used or spent.

In the most recent version of psychoanalytic theory, Freud (1933) proposed two basic drives, or sources, of psychic energy: *Eros* and *Thanatos*. Eros is the productive, creative, and positive form of psychic energy, whereas Thanatos is the destructive, death-seeking force within each individual. These forces were considered to be of biological origin and to accumulate over time. Of course, individual differences in amounts of Eros and Thanatos occur, just as they do for biological characteristics.

Both Eros and Thanatos require expression and produce various forms of behavior, ranging from masticating food to making love. If psychic energy is denied expression because of inhibition or fear, it will further accumulate, building up pressure like steam in a boiler. Failure to release psychic energy in small amounts may allow sufficient accumulation for a psychological explosion to occur: A person who has been passive and withdrawn from others may suddenly erupt and commit a violent act.

Before he developed the concept of Thanatos, Freud (1950) had developed a frustration–aggression theory to explain destructive behavior. Blockage of the expression of positive energy (Eros) was frustrating to the individual and led to attacks against the source of frustration. However, there are occasions when the individual cannot attack the source of frustration; for example, the source may be too powerful or dangerous, or the source may be unavailable. According to Freud, the negative energy created by the frustrating event had to find an outlet. A safer, substitute target may become the victim of the pent-up, destructive energy that the individual must release. In this way, a frustrated person who, for whatever reason, is inhibited from attacking the source of frustration displaces the negative energy from the original target to a substitute target. This theory of displaced aggression has powerful intuitive appeal because it provides an explanation of irrational behavior, such as when a person attacks a total stranger for no apparent reason.

Freud believed that the negative energy created by frustration had to find behavioral expression. He referred to this energy expenditure as *catharsis*. The notion that energy must be expended explains why inhibition of aggression against a source of frustration causes displacement. It is a case of energy seeking an outlet, when it has been prevented from expression in its primary path. Displacement of aggression is an expression of the need for a catharsis of dammed-up energy. This mechanism led Freud to believe that socially acceptable activities might drain off destructive energy and provide substitutes for aggressive behavior. For example, a football player may expend whatever destructive energy has built up and, as a consequence, be less likely to harm others after playing than before the game.

The basic concepts of Freud's theories are metaphorical and do not yield testable hypotheses. It is not clear what psychic energy is or how it could be measured. If Freud's concept of psychic energy is a metaphor, then it cannot be measured: There is no way to determine if psychic energy builds up following frustration or if it dissipates following the expression of aggressive behavior. It is this type of ambiguity that led the Yale psychologists to undertake a translation of Freud's insights into a more scientific (i.e., testable) theory.

FRUSTRATION–AGGRESSION THEORY

The most rigorous theory in psychology in 1939 was the evolving behavior theory of Clark Hull, who was a much admired psychologist at Yale University. All of the authors of *Frustration and Aggression* (Dollard et al., 1939) had worked with Hull as graduate students. Each represented a different specialty area within psychology: Dollard in clinical psychology, Doob in social psychology, Miller in physiological psychology, Mowrer in learning theory, and Sears in developmental psychology. Historically, it was a rare convergence of psychologists from different research areas around an integrative theory.

Basic Processes

The basic processes postulated in frustration–aggression theory can be stated very simply. Frustration produces aggressive energy, which activates aggressive behavior. *Frustration* is defined as any event or act of others that prevents an organism from obtaining a goal that is actively being pursued. More formally, frustration is "an interference with the occurrence of an instigated goal-response at its proper time in the behavior sequence" (Dollard et al., 1939, p. 7). Physical barriers, lack of relevant resources, legal and social rules, active interference from others, and many other events may prevent an organism from obtaining goals or may delay goal attainment.

In their 1939 book, Dollard et al. postulated that the connection between frustration and the buildup of aggressive energy (or drive) was innate.[1] Aggressive drive served to energize available aggressive responses. Sometimes this process is referred to as an "instigation to aggression." In the naive and inexperienced organism, there is a hierarchy of innate aggressive responses. The responses in this set vary in strength. The strongest, or most dominant, response is activated (i.e., energized or instigated) by aggressive drive. Thus, frustration creates aggressive energy, which in turn activates dominant aggressive responses.

Amount of Frustration and Aggression

The strength of the instigation to aggression (i.e., the amount of aggressive energy generated) varies directly with three factors. First, the amount of frustration (or accumulation of aggressive energy) is directly affected by the strength of the response that is frustrated. One variable that affects the strength of the response is intensity of drive. For example, taking food from a hungry dog should produce more aggressive behavior than taking food from a satiated dog. Another variable affecting the strength of the aggressive response is the value of the goal: Taking away a child's favorite toy should produce a more negative response than taking a rarely used toy.

Second, the degree of interference with a response is directly related to instigation to aggression. For example, a comment by another person while you are trying to solve an intellectual problem may be a little annoying, but having someone talk to you continually throughout the attempt to solve the problem will be very frustrating. Time delays may also be frustrating: A companion who keeps you waiting for 30 minutes causes more frustration than one who is only 5 minutes late.

A third factor contributing to the strength of frustration is the number of frustrated responses experienced by the individual. According to an interpretation by Berkowitz (1962), repeated interferences indicate that a range of nonaggressive responses have been ineffective in removing obstacles to reaching a goal. The ineffectiveness of nonaggressive responses may increase the likelihood that aggressive responses will occur.

Aggressive Behavior Is Reinforcing

Figure 2.1 shows the hydraulic model adopted by frustration–aggression theorists. As can be seen, a set of events, identified as frustration,

---

[1]N. E. Miller (1941) soon modified the view that the connection between frustration and aggression is innate. He took the position that frustration might increase the likelihood of many kinds of responses, including regression, renewed attempts at problem solving, and withdrawal. Aggressive responses are the strongest responses aroused by frustration and will occur until they are weakened and competing responses are strengthened. When modification of the strength of all the responses occurs, frustration may elicit nonaggressive responses. Despite this change in the theory by Miller, most scholars have continued to interpret frustration–aggression theory as it was originally formulated.

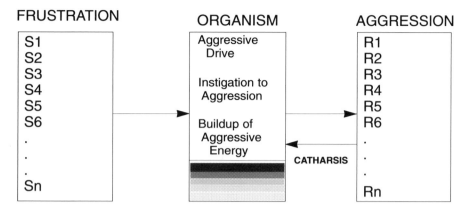

Figure 2.1. A schematic of frustration–aggression theory.

causes a buildup of energy in the organism. The greater the amount of aggressive energy, the more probable it is that the organism will perform one of the responses in the set identifiable as aggressive. Performance of an aggressive response reduces the amount of aggressive energy, a process that is equivalent to Freud's concept of catharsis.

Aggressive responses are considered self-reinforcing because they reduce the negative "drive state" produced by frustration. A negative drive state is assumed to be uncomfortable or painful, and responses that reduce or eliminate this condition will be experienced as reinforcing. The self-reinforcing nature of aggressive behavior guarantees that particular responses will gain strength because the more they are performed, the more they are reinforced. This self-reinforcement increases the likelihood of aggressive behavior when the organism is frustrated. The reduction of aggressive drive makes it unlikely that the organism will immediately perform another aggressive response when no further frustration has been encountered. Thus, the association between frustration and a particular aggressive response is strengthened by reinforcement associated with drive reduction, but the performance of the same behavior again requires a new buildup of drive for activation.

Learned Inhibitions

Dominant aggressive responses can be weakened through punishments. If the organism performs an aggressive response that is followed by punishment, it learns to inhibit that response. Learned inhibition is, in effect, a weakening of a dominant response so that it takes a lower position in the hierarchy of aggressive responses. One possible consequence of learned inhibition is that the organism will subsequently perform a different aggressive response, one that has taken the dominant position over the weakened response. This response substitution is one form of displacement, where the energy that formerly activated one response toward the frustrator now activates a different response against the same target.

If any aggression directed toward a frustrating agent elicits the expectation of punishment, then all such behavior may be inhibited. In such a case, the aggressive energy produced by the frustration accumulates and may lead the organism to make more intense aggressive responses on subsequent occasions. N. E. Miller (1948) proposed how the fear of punishments (as one drive) and aggressive energy (as a competing drive) intersect one another so that a sufficient quantity of aggressive energy may override fear of the target and lead to intense aggressive behavior. This process is represented by a person who appears to be able to tolerate a great deal of frustration over time and then suddenly blows up and engages in uncharacteristic and intense aggressive behavior.

Anticipation of punishment for performing aggressive behavior is also a source of frustration. This additional frustration should cause the individual to aggress more strongly against the agent responsible for the inhibition. This sequence can take the form of a vicious circle of frustration, buildup of aggressive energy, inhibition of aggressive behavior, more frustration, and so on. Either the individual will eventually build up sufficient aggressive energy to overcome the inhibition or, if the inhibition is strong enough, some form of displaced aggression will occur. If the inhibition is specific to one type of aggressive response, then response substitution may occur. For example, if a mother punishes a child for kicking her in the shins, but not for shouting names at her, then the child should inhibit the kicking response and perform the shouting behavior.

Displacement of Aggression

The accumulation of aggressive energy over frustrating experiences, along with the need of the organism to expend this energy, leads to a second form of displaced aggression. Instrumental learning theory has shown that animals that have learned a specific response to particular stimulus conditions will also perform the learned response to novel stimuli. The more similar the novel stimulus is to the original training stimulus, the more likely it is that the organism will perform the learned response to the novel stimulus. This principle of stimulus generalization leads to the prediction that the more similar a second person is to a frustrator toward whom all aggressive behavior is inhibited, the more likely it is that the organism will direct aggressive behavior to the second, substitute individual. In this way, an innocent third party may become the target of aggressive responses.

The mechanisms proposed by Dollard et al. (1939) are consistent with the generalization that aggression is always caused by frustration. However, they did not propose that frustration always leads immediately or directly to aggression. Learned inhibitions may prevent the individual from engaging in aggressive behavior, damming up the generated aggressive energy and delaying its expression until some later frustrating event occurs. Thus, frustration only sometimes leads to aggression.

Research Generated by Frustration–Aggression Theory

In more than 5 decades since Dollard et al. (1939) proposed the frustration–aggression theory, a great deal of research, criticism, and theoretical revisions have occurred. We first provide a summary overview of the evidence and then examine some of the criticisms that have been offered. Finally, we describe major revisions of the theory that have arisen from attempts to cope with the conceptual and empirical problems associated with the original version of frustration–aggression theory.

Laboratory experiments have been focused on the three major aspects of the Yale theory: the direct effects of frustration on aggression, catharsis, and displacement toward substitute targets. A summary examination of this research provides a basis for evaluating the theory.

Direct Effects of Frustration on Aggressive Behavior

In the most direct tests of frustration–aggression theory, researchers present subjects with some task to complete and then introduce some event that interferes with task completion. Task interference was manipulated by Haner and Brown (1955), who promised children a prize if they were successful in pushing marbles through holes in a board within a stated time period. In this experimental game, children who did not succeed could try again by pushing a plunger, like the levers used to send a ball into play on a pinball machine. The number of marbles that were successfully pushed through the holes was manipulated by the experimenter. It was assumed that more frustration would be experienced the closer the children got to the goal before failing. The measure of aggressiveness was the strength with which a child pushed the plunger. The results showed that children exerted more force in pushing the plunger when they had more marbles in the holes before the time period expired (and they failed). Thus, the more frustration experienced by the children, the harder they pushed the plunger.

Unfortunately, it is difficult to evaluate these and similar results (e.g., Olds, 1953) as supportive of frustration–aggression theory. The problem is with the measure of aggressiveness. Dollard et al. (1939) defined aggression as "an act whose goal-response is injury to an organism" (p. 11). Pushing a plunger or energetic behavior of other kinds does not appear to have the goal of harming anyone and, hence, is problematic as a measure of aggression.

Research has indicated that some kinds of frustration do not increase aggressive behavior. Failure at an experimental task (Epstein, 1965; Yarrow,

1948), failure to achieve a better scholastic grade (A. H. Buss, 1966b), or time-out from positive or token reinforcements (Jegard & Walters, 1960; R. H. Walters & Brown, 1963) did not cause subjects to be more aggressive. However, researchers conducting studies in which frustration is operationalized as personal insult, subjects are given high levels of shock by another person, or subjects experience some form of injustice have found that increased aggression does occur (Berkowitz, 1965a; A. H. Buss, 1961; Geen, 1968; Gentry, 1970; Hartmann, 1969).

Frustration is comparable to a condition of nonreward; that is, an organism who seeks a goal fails to achieve it. In his theory of frustrative nonreward, Amsel (1958) proposed that the removal of anticipated rewards—an essential feature of frustration—energizes behavior but does not affect the class of behaviors that occur. In other words, whatever behaviors are subsequently performed after the experience of nonreward will be more vigorous than they otherwise would have been, but there is no specific selection of aggressive responses. Wagner (1966) compared studies of nonreward with those using electric shocks as punishments and concluded that both lead to arousal and energizing of subsequent response. Invigorated responses of some types might be labeled *aggressive* by observers even though there was no intent to cause harm (G. C. Walters & Grusec, 1977).

A. H. Buss (1961) argued that attack, and not frustration, is a reliable cause of aggressive behavior. He distinguished between frustration and attack on the grounds that attack does not necessarily involve any thwarting or blocking operation. For example, a verbal attack or insult may not block an ongoing goal activity by the target person. In one experiment, Gentry (1970) compared goal blockage with attack and found that attack produced more anger and aggression than did frustration.

One approach to understanding the contradictory pattern of results on the relation of frustration and aggression was to make a distinction between kinds of frustration. Pastore (1952) and A. R. Cohen (1955) both showed that unjustified (or arbitrary) frustration was associated with anger but that justified (or nonarbitrary) frustration was not.

Simple distinctions between different kinds of frustration (see also Amsel, 1958; J. S. Brown & Farber, 1951; Feshbach, 1970; Rosenzweig, 1944) have not provided a consistent integration of the experimental literature. Tedeschi, Smith, and Brown (1974) argued that the concept of frustration is too broadly defined. Operational definitions have included all of the following: (a) nonreinforcement after consistent experience of reinforcement, (b) interference to prevent completion of a response sequence that previously had been reinforced, (c) delay of reinforcement, (d) change in incentive conditions so that a subsequent reward is of less value than a previous one, (e) task failure, (f) lowering of self-esteem, and (g) insult or physical attack.

In an exhaustive examination of the concept, Lawson (1965) found no characteristic reactions to these alternative operationalizations of frustration that would allow them to be treated as functionally equivalent. Lawson concluded that the concept of frustration is a commonsense term that was useful as a starting point for scientific investigation but has outlived its heuristic value and should be excised from the scientific vocabulary. More precise terms, such as *delay of reinforcement, withdrawal of reinforcements,* and *attack,* have evolved over the years of studying frustration. Considerable evidence has indicated that these more precisely defined conditions do not produce the same behavioral outcomes (Bandura, 1973).

Catharsis

The linear model proposed in frustration–aggression theory is that frustration creates "aggressive energy," that this energy motivates aggressive behavior, and that aggressive behavior reduces the amount of aggressive energy. The clear implication of this model is that the performance of aggressive behavior should reduce both aggressive drive and the probability of aggressing again immediately.

Most current interpretations of aggressive energy are in terms of anger arousal, physiological tension, or autonomic nervous system (ANS) arousal. The most extensive investigations of the catharsis hypothesis using measures of physiological arousal were carried out by Hokanson (1970). Male college students were exposed to insults from another person while attempting to work on an intellectual task. Measures of blood pressure indicated elevation following provocation. Half of the students were then given an opportunity to give shocks to the provocateur, and half were given a neutral activity for a comparable period of time. In apparent support of the process of catharsis, subjects who gave shocks showed a dramatic decrease in systolic blood levels. Hokanson and his colleagues, like most other experimental psychologists who have studied aggression, used procedures requiring subjects to administer electric shocks. They were curious about what would happen if subjects could choose between performing an aggressive response and a more positive behavior. Procedures were devised to provide subjects with such a choice, and these new procedures produced results that contradicted the catharsis hypothesis.

A confederate, identified as a "fellow student," was allegedly given an option to shock the subject, to provide a token reward, or to signal a "pass" on a given trial. In fact, the confederate was instructed only to deliver shocks. When given the opportunity, male subjects retaliated with shocks, and the rapid catharticlike reductions in physiological arousal were observed. On those occasions when men did not reciprocate shocks, their systolic blood pressure was slow to recover to normal levels. Female subjects displayed opposite patterns of behavior and arousal reduction. Women tended to respond to shocks with a conciliatory (i.e., reward) counterresponse and showed catharticlike arousal reduction afterward.

These results indicate that reduction in arousal was not an automatic, biologically based process of catharsis, as is postulated in frustration–aggression theory. The completion of any sequence of responses, aggressive or nonaggressive, in which the goal is achieved leads to a reduction of arousal. The actor may maintain high levels of arousal even after performing an aggressive response if retaliation from the victim is anticipated or the actor experiences chronic anxiety (Geen & Quanty, 1977).

The second part of the hypothesis of catharsis is the question of whether performance of an aggressive response decreases the amount of aggression when the actor is given another, immediate opportunity to attack a victim. According to several reviews of the literature, the answer is no (Bramel, 1969; Geen & Quanty, 1977; W. Weiss, 1969). In a representative study (Mallick & McCandless, 1966), children were blocked from obtaining a goal by another child. Subsequently, half of the frustrated children were engaged in target shooting with a toy gun, whereas the others simply talked to the experimenter. Then all of the children were given the opportunity to harm the frustrator by interfering with his attainment of a desirable goal. Contrary to the catharsis hypothesis, subjects who had engaged in aggressive play with a toy gun were just as punitive against the frustrator as were those who had simply talked to the experimenter. Furthermore, aggressing against the frustrator did not lower expressed hostility toward him.

A typical procedure in studies testing the catharsis hypothesis is to have a confederate attack or verbally insult subjects and, after subjects have had an opportunity to act aggressively against the confederate, to give them yet another opportunity to harm the confederate. According to the hypothesis, subjects should be less likely to harm the confederate on the second opportunity because they had already had an opportunity to discharge aggressive energy.

A classic version of these procedures was implemented by Thibaut and Coules (1952), who gave half of their subjects an opportunity to verbally attack someone who had insulted them and did not give the other subjects an opportunity to retaliate. Subjects who had been given an opportunity to retaliate were less negative toward the confederate later on than were subjects who had not had an opportunity to strike back. These results, at first glance, appear to support the catharsis hypothesis. However, additional data showed that subjects who had been given an opportunity to retaliate seldom did so. If no aggression was expressed, then catharsis should not have occurred. The unexplained results indicated that a fair opportunity to get even reduced negative evaluation of the insulting confederate, even though there was no overt aggressive behavior.

The most frequent finding in laboratory experiments has been that performing an aggressive response increases aggressiveness (cf. Geen & Quanty, 1977). For example, Green, Stonner, and Shope (1975) gave some subjects the opportunity to retaliate against a confederate who had shocked them, had other subjects simply watch the experimenter shock the attacker, and had another third of subjects simply wait for a short interval before entering the last phase of the procedures. Then, all subjects were given an opportunity to shock the attacker in connection with another task. Subjects who had retaliated against the attacker were more punitive when given still another opportunity to shock him than were the other two groups of subjects. This leaves evidence directly contradictory to the catharsis hypothesis and a question (to be addressed later) about why aggressive behavior sometimes facilitates still more aggression.

Displacement

Most of the research on displacement focuses on substitution of targets. The general principle is that the more similar a second target is to the frustrator, the more likely it is that inhibition of aggression toward the frustrator will lead to harmdoing against the secondary target. However, the greater the anticipated harm that produces inhibition toward the frustrator, the more the inhibition will generalize to secondary targets (N. E. Miller, 1948). In this latter instance, the individual may be inhibited from harming a secondary target who is too similar to the frustrator. How one measures degree of similarity between targets has not been systematically addressed, and hence, in most of the available research displaced aggression toward substitute targets has been examined without concern for degree of similarity.

Tedeschi and Norman (1985a) have reviewed more than 4 decades of research on displacement. They concluded that although there is a preponderance of research to support a displacementlike process, there is a subset of studies that produced negative findings. One explanation for inconsistent findings is that the procedures used to produce frustration are usually quite complex in terms of how they are interpreted by subjects. The experimenters' intentions to introduce frustration into the situation may instead allow other social psychological factors to operate, and it may be these uncontrolled processes that cause displacementlike behavior.

An example of this type of experiment is the classic study carried out by N. E. Miller and Bugelski (1948). Young men at a Civilian Conservation Corps camp were asked to fill out an adjective checklist assessing their attitudes toward Mexican and Japanese people. The men were promised that after dinner they could go to Bank Night at the local movie house. Instead, the men were subjected to a series of difficult and arduous tests (and hence, to failure), which resulted in canceling their night out. Among the tests given to the men following frustration was another assessment of their attitudes toward Mexicans and Japanese. The attitudes toward these groups were less favorable after dinner than they had been before dinner. These results were interpreted as supporting the displacement hypothesis.

The men had been frustrated by an experimenter, who could not be directly attacked, and they displaced their aggression onto a minority group.

A closer examination of the data suggests another interpretation of the findings. The measure of attitudes consisted of 20 adjectives, 10 positive and 10 negative. The men were asked to check the adjectives that were descriptive of the target group (i.e., Mexicans or Japanese). There was no change in the number of negative adjectives checked following frustration; however, the number of positive adjectives checked was fewer on the second assessment. N. E. Miller and Bugelski (1948) reported that the men made spontaneous comments expressing their anger at camp officials and experimenters, and, in a footnote, the authors provided an alternative interpretation of their findings:

> The results were probably produced by the joint operation of two factors: (1) a tendency to be less cooperative with the experimenter and hence to check less items and (2) a tendency to give the foreigners a slightly less favorable rating. (1948, p. 440)

In other words, withdrawal of cooperation from the experiment as indicated by fewer responses on the tests might account for the change in responses to minority groups after the frustration. Withdrawal of cooperation can be interpreted as aggression directed against the experimenters, who had frustrated the men. Support for a displacement hypothesis would seem to require that the subjects should have shown increased hostility to the relevant ethnic groups, and clearly they did not.

Another explanation for what appears to be suppression of aggressive behavior in one situation and its appearance in another was offered by Bandura and Walters (1959). They found that aggressive boys had suffered severe punishment by their parents but had been encouraged to be aggressive outside the home. These aggressive children may have simply learned to discriminate when to be aggressive, because they were punished for it at home but rewarded for it elsewhere.

Despite the possibility of alternative interpretations and a small group of negative findings, there is still a set of impressive studies showing reliable displacement effects. Reliable effects were found in a series of studies in which essentially the same procedures were used (Doob & Wood, 1972; Konecni & Doob, 1972). Subjects were annoyed by a confederate while they failed at a task and were then given an opportunity to shock a third party. It was found that subjects shocked a third party just as much as they did the annoying confederate.

What is puzzling about this body of research is that frustration–aggression theory assumes that aggressive energy, which is dammed up by learned inhibitions but pushes for expression, is released through attacks on substitute targets. Yet, as we have shown, the evidence is overwhelming that there is no process of catharsis. Thus, the theoretical process that is supposed to cause displaced aggression does not occur, yet displacement does appear to occur. The upshot is that although frustration–aggression theory is wrong about the reason for displacement, the theory was useful in generating a phenomenon that now needs another theoretical explanation. We provide alternative explanations in chapters 8, 9, and 12.

Conclusions: Classic Frustration–Aggression Theory

Overall, the evidence is not supportive of the model shown in Figure 2.1. The concept of frustration is apparently too broad and encapsulates events that are not associated with aggressive behavior. Research has revealed a variety of frustrating conditions that do not instigate aggression. One cannot help but note that there are many people who appear to find frustration an interesting and desirable state: A mountain climber would not be challenged by a mountain that offered no frustrations, nor would a golf course without obstacles be much fun. Some forms of frustration may motivate positive or creative behavior and thus may give more excitement and worth to goals that are pursued by people. Consistent and repeated frustration may cause learned helplessness and depression rather than aggression.

The assumption that an organism is biologically prewired so that frustration always creates an instigation to aggress (i.e., aggressive energy) that remains until it is discharged by aggressive behavior is also contradicted by the evidence we reviewed in chapter 1. Recall that biologists have found that an organism is not capable of storing energy or of cumulating energy over time.

It is not surprising that the first systematic and scientific theory of aggression has greatly influenced the way that harmdoing behavior is interpreted in all of the social sciences. The theory was sufficiently precise as to allow experimental disconfirmations as well as support for the theory. Thus, as is the case with all good scientific theories, frustration–aggression theory produced evidence of its own limitations. The attempt at theory building that allowed disconfirmations of the theory has provided a foundation on which newer theories can build. Some social scientists have concluded that frustration–aggression theory is sufficiently flawed that a completely new approach should be tried. Leonard Berkowitz, however, has attempted to dress up the classic theory in new clothes. His view involves two systems of aggressive behavior, one of which is intended to revitalize classic frustration–aggression theory.

BERKOWITZ'S TWO SYSTEMS OF AGGRESSIVE BEHAVIOR

A major new theory has been constructed by Leonard Berkowitz in an attempt to account for both the failures and successes of frustration–

aggression theory. As we shall show, Berkowitz assumed that organisms react aggressively when they experience aversive stimulation. Not all frustration is aversive, and thus frustration does not always lead to aggression. Berkowitz's view allows for both reactive and instrumental aggression. Reactive aggression refers to the innate–biological propensity of the organism to impulsively attack the source of aversive stimulation. The goal of reactive aggression is to hurt the target individual. Instrumental aggression is the use of harmdoing to obtain other goals. In instrumental aggression, harming another is not reinforcing in itself but is simply one way of gaining what the harmdoer desires. Berkowitz proposed that every act of harmdoing probably involves both systems of aggression. But he further proposed that the impulsive reactive system is more important in understanding the violent behavior of human actors.

Reactive Aggression

An unpleasant experience creates an urge to hurt that gains reinforcement and satisfaction from harming the source of the aversive stimulation. Aversive stimuli are associated with a readiness to flee or to fight in all organisms. According to Berkowitz (1981a), "all aversive events, whether frustration, deprivations, noxious stimuli or environmental stresses, produce an instigation to aggression as well as a desire to escape or avoid the unpleasant situation" (p. 174). Which tendency will dominate will depend on the individual's learning history. In the inexperienced organism, the dominant tendency is to fight.

Berkowitz (1981a) stated that

> the aggressive tendencies may be oriented partly toward the termination or reduction of the aversive stimulus, but at the human level, they are also directed toward doing injury. That is, those who are in physical or mental pain are inclined to hurt someone even though their aggression cannot lessen their own suffering, and even if the victim is not the source of their suffering. (pp. 174–175)

Berkowitz (1988) redefined *frustration* as "the nonfulfillment of an expected gratification" (p. 3). Frustration may be associated with positive or negative responses by the individual, depending on how the frustration is experienced. Interruption of ongoing goal activity may be experienced as challenging, may be accompanied by a change of goals, or may be aversive. The inconsistent results obtained in studying the effects of frustration can be understood if we differentiate between those occasions when frustration is aversive and those when it is not. If the frustration is experienced as aversive and the stimulus conditions are such that fight responses are stronger than flight responses, the individual will engage in reactive aggression.

In reviewing the contradictory findings regarding the effects of arbitrary and nonarbitrary frustration on aggressive behavior, Berkowitz (1988) argued that arbitrary frustration is more unexpected than nonarbitrary frustration. Because unfulfilled expectations are aversive, arbitrary frustration is more aversive than nonarbitrary frustration. Furthermore, the justifications accompanying nonarbitrary frustration inhibit aggressive behavior. Thus, the greater aggression following arbitrary frustration is attributable both to the inhibitions accompanying legitimate frustration and to the added aversiveness associated with arbitrary frustration. Berkowitz (1988) claimed that legitimate frustration may also be experienced as aversive and may cause aggressive behavior.

People avoid frustrations because frustrations are usually unpleasant. The factors associated with strength of frustration noted in frustration–aggression theory, such as the value of the goal and the degree of interference, have this capacity because they affect the degree of aversiveness experienced by the organism. Generally, it is aversive stimulation that causes reactive aggression, and certain kinds of frustrating experiences may be aversive.

Although Berkowitz's (1993) primary focus was on reactive aggression, he acknowledged that many acts of aggression can be understood as learned instrumental behavior. Aversive stimulation and its associated negative affect are not necessary, although they are sufficient to create an instigation to aggressive behavior. People may learn that aggressive behaviors can help them attain interpersonal objectives, and so they may come to rely on such techniques. Nevertheless, Berkowitz (1989) proposed that reactive aggression almost always accompanies instrumental aggression. Although a person may aggress to attain other rewards, the aggressor also gains some pleasure by hurting the victim.

As the organism gains experience, its responses increasingly are guided by cues in the environment. This instrumental learning of aggressive responses is grafted onto the innate system of reactive aggression. Aversive stimulation builds up aggressive drive or instigation to aggression.[2] However, without an appropriate cue, the desire to hurt will not automatically be given expression in aggressive behavior by a mature individual.

Neither catharsis nor displacement processes are assumed in cue-arousal theory. Berkowitz (1964) offered a very creative solution to the inconsistent findings regarding catharsis. He proposed that an individual will express less aggression immediately following an aggressive response when the aggressive behavior (a) achieves its goal and, hence, no further behavior is required; (b) elicits feelings of guilt or remorse, which inhibit

---

[2]Although Berkowitz (1993) denied postulating an aggressive drive underlying the system of reactive aggression, he continually referred to the "desire to hurt," which is activated by aversive experience. Furthermore, hurting another person appears to appease this desire. We cannot distinguish this terminology from the language of drive theory.

subsequent aggressive behavior; or (c) is followed by changes in the environment that increase the expectation of costs for further behavior of the same kind. These processes do not depend on the buildup or release of aggressive energy.

Berkowitz sometimes referred to the desire to hurt as *aggressive arousal.* This arousal will simply be maintained by the organism until an appropriate aggressive stimulus is present, and then an aggressive response will occur. Under strong aversive conditions, impulsive aggression may occur in the absence of relevant cues. Some cues may be inhibitory and may restrain the individual from performing aggressive responses despite exposure to aversive stimulation and an accompanying increase in aggressive drive or arousal. In agreement with frustration–aggression theory, Berkowitz (1989) assumed that inhibition of aggression leads to an accumulation of aggressive drive, so that later aggressive behavior may be more intense than the circumstances would seem to warrant.

Role of Cognitions and Emotions

Berkowitz (1983b) has argued that the emotion of anger only indirectly affects aggressive behavior. Anger is a parallel process to aggressive drive, but it is only the latter that directly affects behavior. Anger may facilitate aggression by increasing the probability that the individual will interpret stimuli as aggressive cues, thus increasing the range of stimuli that will evoke aggressive behavior. A particular emotional experience may elicit memories of past episodes, and these activated memories—if they are associated with aggression—may serve as internal aggressive stimuli that will evoke aggressive behavior, given that the individual has experienced some form of aversive stimulation.

Attributions and cognitions of the individual can affect emotions and the degree of aversiveness experienced by the individual. For example, the belief that someone intentionally interfered with goal-oriented behavior may be aversive because it is frustrating and also because the other person engaged in an unfriendly or aggressive act toward the individual (Dyck & Rule, 1978).

Cognitive associations can also affect the degree of hostility expressed toward innocent third parties. If senior citizens are frequently associated with aversive events, the individual may perceive all older people as aversive and, as a consequence, may direct hostility toward them when aggressive drive is aroused. This displacementlike process does not depend on the need for catharsis but is based on both an underlying aggressive drive that is aroused by aversive experiences and the way that the individual forms cognitive associations.

A person experiencing negative affect has an instigation to aggression but will not attack a substitute target unless there is some symbolic connection between the target and the source of aversive stimulation. The cognitive elements in such symbolic connections involve aversiveness for both the substitute target and the frustrating agent, and the two persons must be categorized as belonging to a common social category. It is through such associations that frustrations can lead to prejudice and acts of violence against people because of their ethnic, racial, or religious identity.

A summary of Berkowitz's theory of reactive aggression is shown in Figure 2.2. Aversive stimuli arouse negative affect, which in turn causes an instigation to aggression in the form of an "urge to hurt." Negative affect may prime associated cognitions that may lead directly to instigation to aggression. Associated cognitions also produce negative affect, further increasing the instigation to aggression. Unless inhibitions intervene, the instigation to aggression causes aggressive behavior.

Research Generated by Berkowitz's Theory

Berkowitz and his students have produced an enormous amount of research on aggression over the past 30 years. They have examined the effects of aversive stimulation; the question of whether aggression is itself reinforcing; the cue properties of targets that elicit aggressive behavior; the instigating effects of aggressive stimuli; and the impact of arousal, emotions,

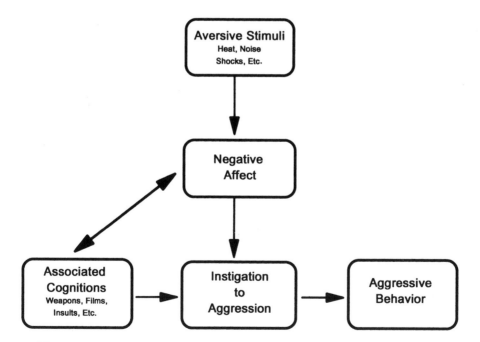

Figure 2.2. A schematic of Berkowitz's (1993) theory of reactive aggression.

and cognitive associations on aggressive behavior. We turn now to a critical analysis of this research program.

Aversive Stimulation and Aggression

Berkowitz (1982, 1993) has relied heavily on the research carried out on subhumans to justify his postulate relating aversive stimulation directly to reactive aggression. He uncritically cited the literature on reflex fighting that we reviewed in chapter 1. For example, he interpreted the studies by Azrin et al. (1967)—showing the direct relationship between degree of aversive electric shock and fighting in monkeys and between exposure to extreme heat and fighting—as supportive of a reflexive aggressive response to aversive stimulation. However, as was noted in chapter 1, closer examination of this research indicates that animals typically engage in only a portion of ritualistic aggression in response to aversive stimulation, and furthermore, the responses did not appear to be simple reflexes. Recall that it is extremely difficult to condition reflex fighting to neutral stimuli. This fact is apparently directly contrary to the assumption made by Berkowitz (1986) that instrumental aggression is appended to or built on the innate reactive aggressive system of the organism.

The tendency of learning theorists to view aggression as following similar processes in both humans and other animals has seldom been questioned. Although cue-arousal theory appears to plug more cognitions and emotional labeling into the theory when humans are responding, the basic principles of reactive and instrumental aggression are applied to other organisms as well. Despite Berkowitz's (1983a) attempt to show the similarities between the processes that produce aggressive behavior in animals and humans, a careful examination of the research on aversive stimuli and aggression indicates that different results have been obtained with animals than with humans.

A common experimental procedure in the study of human aggression was invented by A. H. Buss (1961). Subjects are given the role of teachers, and a confederate is given the role of learner. The learner is given a list of pairs of words and is given a short time to learn them. Then the teacher reads the first of the pair, and the learner is asked to provide the second word. Typically, the teacher and learner are in different rooms, and communications are carried out over an intercom system. Placed in front of the teacher is an aggression machine that is described by the experimenter as capable of delivering shocks through a finger electrode attached to the learner. In fact, the learner–confederate never receives any shocks. There are 10 buttons on the machine, indicating intensities from low to high, and by keeping the finger on the button the teacher can deliver a shock of longer duration. The subjects may be given a shock represented as an intermediate intensity to establish that it is unpleasant or painful.

When the learner's response is correct, the teacher says "good" or "correct" over the intercom, and when the learner's response is incorrect, the teacher delivers an electric shock to the finger of the learner. The intensity and duration of the shock are left to the discretion of the teacher. The context for all of this is an explanation by the experimenter that the research is concerned with the effects of punishment on learning.

Researchers of the effects of noxious stimuli on aggression have typically used the teacher–learner procedures. Human subjects have been exposed to uncomfortable temperatures, noise, air pollution, territorial invasion, high population density, and personal space violations. The most extensive research on the effects of heat was carried out by R. A. Baron and Bell (1975, 1976; P. A. Bell & Baron, 1976, 1977). The general procedures, which had been developed by A. H. Buss (1961), have a confederate either insult or flatter subjects. Then the subjects watch a model (a second confederate) deliver high-intensity shocks as punishments for mistakes made by a learner on a word association task. Subjects then served as teacher for the performance of the first confederate and could select shocks of intensities from 1 to 10 for wrong responses. Subjects participated throughout the experiment either in comfortable temperatures (72 °F– 75 °F) or under hot conditions (92 °F–95 °F).

The results were contrary to expectations. First, the observation of a model had no effect on shock intensities administered by subjects. Second, the tendency was for insulted subjects to reduce their aggressiveness in hot conditions and for flattered subjects to increase shock intensities under hot conditions. Although insulted subjects delivered more shock in the cool condition than did flattered subjects, there was no difference between subjects in the hot condition. These results were replicated in a second study (R. A. Baron & Bell, 1976).

To accommodate these findings with their theory, R. A. Baron and Bell (1976) suggested a curvilinear relationship between negative affect and aggression. In comfortable conditions there are little or no negative feelings, and at extremely high levels of negative affect the predominant response may be to escape.[3] The most aggressive behavior should therefore occur when the person experiences moderate levels of stress.

R. A. Bell and Baron (1976) tested the curvilinear hypothesis by placing subjects in comfortable or hot conditions while exposing them to an insulting or flattering confederate, who was similar or dissimilar to them in attitude. Attitude dissimilarity has been associated with less liking for a stranger (cf. Byrne, 1971). Pretesting was carried out to ascertain the degree of negative feelings that this combination of conditions created in subjects.

---

[3]It should be noted that participants in experiments seldom exercise their right to discontinue and, hence, do not show a strong desire to escape even when they are quite uncomfortable from exposure to high temperatures.

An analysis indicated that the greatest amount of shock was administered by subjects in the most negative condition (i.e., hot, insult, and dissimilar person) and the least amount of shock was used in the most positive condition (i.e., comfortable temperature, flattery, and similar person). In general, the results were consistent with a curvilinear hypothesis.

One must be cautious in interpreting these results. When qualitatively different aversive stimuli are combined into a total amount of experienced aversiveness, there is no control for possible variations in cognitive meanings. Each of these aversive stimuli has different meanings to the individual. This confounding makes it difficult to ascertain whether it was the negative affect experienced by the subjects or some cue that was introduced into the situation by the complex set of stimuli presented to them that was responsible for the variations in aggressive behavior. A more satisfactory test of Berkowitz's (1982) hypothesis regarding aversive stimuli would be to manipulate a single continuum of a particular aversive stimulus, such as a larger range of temperatures, and show that there is a curvilinear relationship between aversiveness of temperature and aggression.

Berkowitz and Thome (1987) have examined the impact of exposure to cold temperatures on the use of rewards and shocks by female subjects. They had female subjects place one hand in very cold (7 °C) or warm (23 °C) water. All of the women in the warm condition were told to expect pain. Some of the women in the cold conditions were led to expect pain, and some were not given this expectation. The women were told that the study was concerned with how supervisors evaluated superordinates under stressful conditions. Subjects then evaluated a partner's ideas concerning a series of problems by delivering shocks or providing rewards. Finally, measures were obtained of how aversive, unpleasant, and painful the subjects found the experience to be. An abridged summary of the results is shown in Table 2.1.

Analyses comparing the cold–expect pain condition with a combination of the other two conditions indicated that subjects who were exposed to the most aversive condition reported the most aversive experience and were most punitive toward a confederate who in no way had annoyed or attacked them. A closer look at the data indicates some inconsistency for an interpretation in terms of an aversiveness–aggression relationship. Ratings indicated that the subjects in the two cold conditions reported similar degrees of aversiveness in the situation. However, the subjects who did not expect pain displayed a lack of aggressiveness similar to that of subjects in the warm condition. If the subjects in the two cold conditions experienced similar degrees of aversiveness, one must ask why they did not display similar levels of aggression. In addition, the reliability of the finding is in some question because Berkowitz, Cochran, and Embree (1981) found in two experiments that aversive experience with cold water did not affect the number of punishments given to a confederate, but that it was related

TABLE 2.1
Aversiveness and Effects on Punitive Reactions

Condition	Rating of Experience				Response by Subject	
	Unpleasant	Painful	Aversive	Annoying	Rewards Given	Punishments
Very Cold Water, Pain Expected	8.13	7.27	6.73	8.07	17.3	3.1
Very Cold Water, Pain Not Expected	7.13	4.93	5.67	6.40	21.7	1.3
Warm Water, Pain Expected	2.53	1.13	2.07	2.60	20.9	1.6

Note. Ratings were on 9-point scales ranging from 1 (*not at all*) to 9 (*very much*). From "Pain Expectation, Negative Affect, and Angry Aggression" by L. Berkowitz and P. R. Thome, 1987, *Motivation and Emotion, 11*, pp. 190–191. Copyright 1987 by Plenum Press. Adapted by permission.

instead to withholding rewards when subjects had been told that punishments would probably hurt the target person.

Another type of aversive stimulus is noise. Research has shown that exposure to excess noise may be associated with high blood pressure (S. Cohen, Evans, Krantz, & Stokols, 1980), increase in symptoms of stress (Pennebaker, Burnam, Schaeffer, & Harper, 1977), and annoyance (Goodman & Clary, 1976; Hitchcock & Waterhouse, 1979). Noise above 60 dB is physiologically arousing (Kryter, 1970; Poulton, 1978) and, according to Berkowitz's (1982) theory, should be associated with aggressive behavior.

To test the impact of aversive noise, Donnerstein and Wilson (1976) first exposed subjects to a confederate who evaluated their essays quite harshly or favorably. Then, while wearing earphones and being exposed to noise levels of 65 dB or 95 dB, subjects served as teachers in the teacher–learner procedure described above. Subjects exposed to the higher intensity noise were more punitive than were subjects exposed to lower intensity noise, but only when they had first been exposed to a punitive confederate.

It appears that high-intensity noise at least sometimes facilitates aggressive behavior (see reviews by R. A. Baron, 1977; Mueller, 1983; Rule & Nesdale, 1976a, 1976b). One should remember, however, that although so-called environmental stressors, such as noise, may initially produce arousal as an alarm reaction, adaptation is a typical longer-term phenomenon (Glass & Singer, 1972). Furthermore, arousal to stressors is greater when they are unpredictable than when they can be foreseen (Lazarus, 1968; Mueller, 1983). Adaptation to and predictability of noxious stimuli reduce or eliminate their aversiveness. Thus, generalization of laboratory findings of the relationship of noxious stimuli and aggression to environments where stressors exist may be limited to situations where the aversive stimuli have been recently introduced or where they are unpredictable.

These conditions can be incorporated into Berkowitz's (1989) theory by shifting the locus of aversiveness from the physical effects of environmental stimuli to cognitive appraisals of stimuli. Berkowitz (1983b) vacillated between viewing the aversiveness as in the stimulus and as due to interpretations of the stimulus by the person. He stated, "It is not the stimulus' objective nature in itself that determines its aversiveness but its meaning (i.e., the associations it has for the person)," and then, several lines later, said,

> what the individual experiences depends to a considerable extent on how the sensory input is psychologically processed. He receives the aversive stimulation and interprets it in some way, thus determining the magnitude of the negative affect that he experiences. And it is this negative affect that evokes the instigation to aggression. (1983b, p. 119)

In the first quote, Berkowitz (1983b) said that aversiveness is not in the stimulus but, rather, is a product of a person's processing of the information through cognitive filters. In the second quote, Berkowitz indicated that a person receives aversive stimulation and that the degree is moderated by cognitive processes. In the latter statement, the aversiveness of the stimulus appears to be in the stimulus and not just in the appraisals of the individual. This apparent contradiction can be resolved by assuming that young organisms react to the physical attributes of stimuli but that mature organisms have learned to ignore or have become habituated to some stimuli and have learned that other stimuli are associated with negative outcomes. The problem with this theoretical move is that it appears to contradict the assumption that aversive stimulation instigates reactive aggression without cognitive mediation. Because cognitive meanings would always intervene in mature organisms to interpret experiences as aversive, one could not argue, as Berkowitz (1983b) did, that reactive aggression occurs without cognitive mediation.

Researchers have examined the impact of aversive stimuli other than temperature and noise on aggressive behavior. However, the evidence with respect to crowding, invasion of personal space, air pollution, and territorial invasion is much too sparse to allow for any conclusions relevant to the effects of these aversive stimuli (see review by Mueller, 1983).

In summary, we must conclude that the evidence does not strongly support the view that aversiveness instigates impulsive aggression. Where the evidence is supportive, there are typically flaws in the designs, procedures, or measures of the experiments that have been performed. On the other hand, aversiveness may augment or raise the level of aggressive behavior that is instigated by other factors. Exposure to aversive noise or excessive heat after a person has been insulted may amplify the intensity or duration of shocks delivered to the rude person.

Aggressive Cues and Aggressive Behavior

The function of cues and arousal in reactive aggression has been demonstrated in a study in which subjects were paired with a confederate, who was introduced either as a speech major or as a physical education major interested in boxing (Berkowitz, 1965b). The confederate either behaved in a neutral fashion or insulted the subjects. Subsequently, some of the subjects viewed the fight scene from the motion picture *The Champion*, in which Kirk Douglas receives a terrible beating, while other subjects saw a neutral film about canal boats. The subjects who saw *The Champion* were given a preliminary legitimating statement indicating that Douglas deserved the beating he was about to receive. Finally, all of the subjects were given an opportunity to evaluate the confederate's design of a floor plan for a house by shocking him through a finger electrode. The subjects had to provide a minimum of 1 shock (*excellent design*), but could deliver as many as 10 shocks (*poor design*).

The results of this study were complex, but generally indicated that the confederate identified as a boxer received more shocks than did the confederate identified as a speech major, even when no insult had occurred. Viewing the fight scene, which was assumed to create more arousal in subjects than viewing the film about boats, did not automatically trigger aggressive behavior unless an appropriate external cue was present. When subjects had not been insulted, there was no difference in the number of shocks administered to the confederate, regardless of which film they had seen. The most shocks were given by subjects who had been insulted, had seen the violent film scene, and had been paired with the confederate identified as a boxer. These results have been widely interpreted as providing strong support for Berkowitz's (1965a) cue-arousal theory.

The tendency of aggression theorists, such as Berkowitz, has been to use notions of drive and arousal interchangeably. In the series of studies using the fight scene from *The Champion*, the rationale was that viewing the fight scene would increase arousal in subjects, causing those who had been insulted or attacked to be more aggressive when an appropriate target was available. Results tended to support this hypothesis.

It is instructive to take a closer look at the procedures used in one of these studies (Berkowitz & Geen, 1966). In a 2 × 2 × 2 design, subjects were shocked either frequently or infrequently by a confederate, witnessed the fight scene or viewed a neutral film, and then had an opportunity to shock the confederate, whose name was either Bob Anderson or Kirk Anderson. Subjects who were shocked frequently, saw the violent film, and were able to shock Kirk gave the confederate more shocks than did subjects in any of the other groups. A review of the procedures used and later failures to replicate these results suggests that they may have been attributable to demand awareness and not to high levels of arousal (Tedeschi & Norman, 1985a).

Consider the sequence of events experienced by subjects in the following critical conditions. (a) A subject was frequently shocked by a stranger (an alleged peer) or insulted by him. A subject probably considered this a most unexpected occurrence in the context of a scientific project. An analogy would be to a situation in which a person shared a waiting room in a physician's office with another patient, who then initiates an interaction for the purpose of attacking him or her. (b) The confederate identified himself as *Bob* or *Kirk*. (c) Each subject was asked to fill out a mood questionnaire or had his or her blood pressure taken, as an assessment of anger level. (d) The subject was shown a fight sequence from *The Champion*. (e) A synopsis of the story was given to subjects following the film, for the purpose of justifying (according to a norm of reciprocity) the beating that Kirk Douglas received. (f) The experimenter remarked about the coincidence that the confederate's first name was *Kirk*, just like Kirk Douglas. (g) Subjects were given an opportunity to evaluate the confederate's essay by giving him shocks. (h) Subjects were asked how friendly or hostile they felt toward the confederate. Some subjects might have interpreted this sequence of events as indicating that the experimenter expected them to retaliate against their attacker (i.e., the confederate). Because the mean differences between experimental conditions in this type of study are always very small, just a few hypothesis-aware and compliant subjects could account for the findings.

Geen and Berkowitz (1967) failed to replicate their original finding when they omitted the justification segment from their procedures. A series of studies have shown that justified aggression synopses were required before subjects in violent film conditions demonstrated an enhanced aggression effect (Berkowitz, 1965b; Berkowitz, Corwin, & Heironimus, 1962; Berkowitz & Rawlings, 1963; Meyer, 1972b). Berkowitz and Geen (1967) also failed to replicate the original name-mediated aggression finding. The name-mediated aggression was found only when five of the most anxious men in each experimental group were dropped and the data were reanalyzed. The most anxious men should have been experiencing the most negative affect and, hence, should have been the most aggressive men in each group. In addition, it is intellectually puzzling that the name *Kirk* was associated with the violent film and hence became an appropriate aggressive stimulus when the confederate had attacked the subject, but was not an appropriate cue when arousal was produced only by watching the violent film.

Aggressive Stimuli and the Weapons Effect

Berkowitz (1983a) proposed that aggressive cues as conditioned stimuli can evoke aggressive responses. Another effect that can be produced by aggressive stimuli is to prime cognitions associated with unpleasant emotions, thereby strengthening the aversiveness of an existing negative emotion. These two proposed effects of aggressive stimuli have been applied to weapons. Guns are aggressive stimuli, and Berkowitz (1981b) has argued that they may not only elicit aggressive behavior, but may also create aggression that otherwise would not occur: "Guns carry with them meanings that increase aggression: They create aggression that in the absence of guns would not exist. It is in this sense that the trigger can pull the finger" (p. 12).

Berkowitz and LePage (1967) used the essay-writing paradigm to examine the hypothesized weapons effect on aggressive behavior. Subjects and a confederate wrote essays and were asked to evaluate each other's essays by delivering electric shocks. The best evaluation was 1 shock and the worst was 10 shocks. The confederate first evaluated the subjects' essays and gave them either 1 or 7 shocks. When subjects entered the room with the shock apparatus to evaluate the confederate's essay, they found a shotgun and revolver on the table near the shock key. In an associated-weapons condition, subjects were told that the weapons belonged to the confederate who was conducting an experiment using them. In an unassociated-weapons condition, subjects were told only that weapons belonged to someone else who must have been doing an experiment in the room. A control condition was also used in which no weapons were present. The results showed that the presence of guns had no effect when subjects received only 1 shock but that when subjects received 7 shocks, they gave more shocks in the associated-weapons conditions than in the control condition. Subjects in the unassociated-weapons condition did not give more shocks than subjects in the control condition.

Berkowitz's (Berkowitz & LePage, 1967) claim that he had found support for a weapons effect was sharply challenged by Page and Scheidt (1971), who noted that suspicion was reported by a large number of subjects in the associated-weapons condition. According to Berkowitz and LePage, many subjects in the associated-weapons condition were suspicious about the confederate. Page and Scheidt claimed that the weapons effect obtained in the associated-weapons condition was due to demand cues. When subjects who had been strongly attacked were given an opportunity to give shocks to a confederate who was said to be doing an experiment using the weapons, they could decide to give fewer or more shocks. The presence of weapons near the shock key might be interpreted by subjects as indicating they should give more shocks, especially when the reason given to them for their presence did not eliminate this demand hypothesis. If the weapons effect was a reliable phenomenon that occurs in the absence of subject suspicion and demand cues, it should have been manifested in the unassociated-weapons condition. Yet, there was no difference between the number of shocks given by subjects in the unassociated-weapons condition and the control condition.

The controversy about the validity of the weapons effect has motivated a number of subsequent studies. A. H. Buss, Booker, and Buss (1972) replicated the exact procedures of the Berkowitz and LePage (1967) study, changing only the cover story in the associated-weapons condition: Subjects were told that the guns were left there by the confederate, who was going to give them to a friend. No weapons effect was found. Other attempts to replicate the weapons effect either have failed (D. P. Ellis, Weiner, & Miller, 1971; Page & Scheidt, 1971) or have found the opposite effect of the presence of weapons reducing the amount of aggression by subjects (Fischer, Kelm, & Rose, 1969).

Berkowitz (1993) has cited Frodi's (1975) study with Swedish high school students as a solid demonstration of the weapons effect. Frodi used the essay-writing paradigm. A confederate delivered one or seven shocks to the students. Subjects were then exposed to weapons, baby objects, or no objects when they evaluated the confederate's essay. Both the level of confederate attack and the stimulus conditions affected aggressive behavior. Subjects gave more shocks when they received more shocks, and they gave more shocks in the presence of weapons than in the other two conditions. Unlike prior studies that have shown a weapons effect only in high-attack (or high-anger) conditions, Frodi found it for both the low- and high-attack conditions. This result could indicate that the demand value of the weapons was so strong for Swedish children that it affected their behavior whenever the weapons were present. A demand-cue interpretation is supported by Frodi's report that 23% of subjects were suspicious about the confederate and 9% correctly answered a question about the purpose of the objects next to the shock key.

A meta-analysis of 31 weapons effect studies (M. Carlson, Marcus-Newhall, & Miller, 1990) indicated a nonsignificant effect of weapons on aggressive behavior. The procedures of these 31 studies were examined so that the studies could be assigned to one of two categories: a high hypothesis awareness–high evaluation apprehension category or a low hypothesis awareness–low evaluation apprehension category. An analysis showed that conditions in past experiments coded as high evaluation apprehension or high hypothesis awareness were associated with inhibition of aggression, whereas conditions coded as low in these two factors were associated with increased aggression. This result, we believe, is not clearly interpretable because it was based on an inappropriate coding of the data. Lumping evaluation apprehension and demand cues reveals a misunderstanding by M. Carlson et al. about how these factors function in psychological experiments.

According to Rosenberg (1969), *evaluation apprehension* is anxiety experienced by subjects who want to avoid being perceived as psychologically maladjusted by an experimenter. The implication is that subjects will avoid acting in ways that may lead others to perceive them as maladjusted. Demand cues, on the other hand, are unobtrusive instructions or other stimuli that indicate to subjects how the experimenter would like them to behave. In its strongest form, demand cues give away the experimenter's hypothesis to subjects, who then compliantly act to confirm the hypothesis. In its weaker form, demand cues simply guide behavior without hypothesis awareness. Typically, the responses that subjects are allowed to perform in experiments are extremely limited: They can evaluate someone more or less positively, give more or less shock, and so on. Any cue that indicates which direction the experimenter expects would be a demand cue.

Evaluation apprehension is primarily concerned with avoiding responses that might convey psychiatric symptoms, and demand compliance is associated with choosing responses believed to be desired by the experimenter. These two motivations may produce opposite responses in experiments on weapons-eliciting effects on aggression. If subjects believe that giving shocks to another person would lead the experimenter to perceive them as psychologically maladjusted, they should give less shocks. If, on the other hand, subjects believe the experimenter expects them to use more shocks, then they should give more shocks.

Berkowitz and his students acknowledged that the presence of weapons may have both inhibitory and facilitory effects on aggressive behavior. They stated that

> weapons do not always stimulate aggression. In fact, many individuals frequently seem to "bend over backward" to avoid aggressive reactions in the presence of weapons. . . . Based on people's previous experience with firearms, they may have very different associations to firearms which may determine whether inhibitory reactions or stimulating effects will predominate. (Turner, Simons, Berkowitz, & Frodi, 1977, pp. 375–376)

The problem with this individual-differences explanation is that it does not help explain the opposite effects produced in laboratory settings in which subjects are randomly distributed to experimental conditions.

The weapons effect depends on the meaning that the presence of weapons conveys to subjects. Weapons give some clue as to what is a socially desirable response in the experiment—what will achieve a favorable identity. If the experimenter is studying aggression or maladaptive behavior and will monitor the subjects' behavior, aggressive behavior may be inhibited. This explains why high awareness–high evaluation apprehension subjects inhibited their aggression. On the other hand, if the weapons indicate that the experimenter is favorable to or tolerant of aggression, then they should facilitate an aggressive response. The lack of reliability of findings across studies of the weapons effect may be due to procedural differences that induce evaluation apprehension or provide demand cues.

According to the meta-analysis (M. Carlson et al., 1990), the only study that has produced a reliable weapons effect was carried out by Turner and Simons (1974). It is important, therefore, to carefully examine their study. They created high evaluation apprehension by telling subjects that the experiment was concerned with psychological adjustment. If subjects believed that hurting another person frequently with electric shocks is a symptom of maladjustment and they also wanted to appear normal, they might give fewer shocks. In fact, high evaluation subjects displayed inhibition of aggression in the weapons condition. The claim by Turner and Simons (and by Berkowitz, 1993) that these results showed that *demand awareness* has inhibitory rather than facilitory effects on the weapons effect, indicates a failure to distinguish between evaluation apprehension and demand compliance.

A key study showing an inhibiting effect of evaluation apprehension on aggression was done by Simons and Turner (1976). In high evaluation apprehension conditions, subjects were told that the experimenter was concerned with how well adjusted they were. This instruction was omitted from the low evaluation apprehension condition. All subjects were strongly attacked by the confederate and were then given an opportunity to retaliate in the presence or the absence of weapons near the shock key. At the conclusion of the experiment, subjects were given a questionnaire probing for hypothesis awareness. Subjects were then identified as high or low in hypothesis awareness. The conditions of the experiment and the results are shown in Table 2.2.

An overall analysis indicated that the data should be collapsed into four cells—High and Low Evaluation Apprehension × Presence and Absence of Weapons—for further analysis. Hypothesis awareness had no effect in the experiment. However, the researchers made comparisons between all eight conditions, a procedure that was statistically unjustified, and by doing so claimed to demonstrate a weapons effect. As can be seen from Table 2.2, the number of shocks given by subjects in the low evaluation apprehension, low hypothesis awareness, and weapons condition was not

TABLE 2.2
Mean Number of Shocks Delivered in the Experimental Conditions

Weapons Condition	Low Evaluation Apprehension		High Evaluation Apprehension	
	Low Hypothesis Awareness	High Hypothesis Awareness	Low Hypothesis Awareness	High Hypothesis Awareness
Weapons	5.286_a	4.375_{ab}	4.875_{ab}	4.143_{ab}
No Weapons	3.333_b	4.500_{ab}	5.143_{ab}	5.250_a

Note. Means having common subscripts do not differ from one another. From "Evaluation Apprehension, Hypothesis Awareness, and the Weapons Effect" by L. S. Simons and C. W. Turner, 1976, *Aggressive Behavior, 2*, p. 82. Copyright 1976 by Wiley. Adapted by permission.

greater than any of the other conditions except for the low evaluation apprehension, low hypothesis awareness, and no weapons condition. It is not clear why high demand cue and high evaluation apprehension had no effect on the aggressive behavior of subjects. Instead of showing a weapons effect, these results may indicate that demand cues are associated with the presence of weapons.

Is Reactive Aggression Reinforcing?

Berkowitz (1993) has proposed that aversive stimulus conditions produce negative affect—sometimes referred to as *negative arousal* or as an *appetitive aggression drive state*—which in turn increases the readiness of the individual to engage in aggressive behavior. Harmdoing satisfies or reinforces the organism by reducing the aggressive drive state, much like eating food reduces the hunger drive. It is fair to ask, then, whether there is evidence to support the postulation of an appetitive aggressive drive in humans.

Whether aggression is intrinsically rewarding is a difficult question to answer, because it is necessary to discount any possible instrumental purpose for the behavior. After reviewing the animal literature, R. N. Johnson (1972) concluded that the natural aggressive behavior of animals is confined to instrumental aggression. Animals fight to survive, to get rid of the presence or interference of other animals, to protect their young, to gain or defend position in a dominance hierarchy, to gain access to food, and for other reasons (J. P. Scott, 1958).

Berkowitz (1993) postulated that pain cues should be directly reinforcing to the individual because harming a victim is a goal of appetitive aggressive drive. Support has been obtained from several studies in which pain cues increased the aggressiveness of subjects (Feshbach, Stiles, & Bitter, 1967; Hartmann, 1969; Swart & Berkowitz, 1976). In a study by Sebastian (1978), subjects either were or were not angered by a confederate and subsequently served as the teacher in a teacher–learner paradigm. Subjects received high-, low-, or no-pain feedback from the confederate conveyed by meter readings. Angered subjects rated the experiment as more enjoyable the greater the pain indicated by the victim. Furthermore, the enjoyment ratings of the angered subjects were related to their level of aggression toward a third party on the following day.

In a series of studies, researchers have also found that pain cues inhibit aggressive behavior (R. A. Baron, 1971; Geen, 1970; Rule & Leger, 1976). R. A. Baron (1979) has suggested that level of provocation was low in the studies in which pain cues inhibited aggression and was high in those studies in which pain cues increased aggression. He proposed that under low provocation, pain cues elicit empathy, an emotional state that may include identification with the victim and a concomitant reduction in aggressive behavior. Alternately, high provocation produces anger, which is aversive, and high aversiveness interferes with the experience of empathy. When empathy is low and the person has an aversive experience, pain cues reinforce aggressive behavior and should be associated with increased aggression. R. A. Baron (1979), Eliasz (1981), and Ohbuchi, Ohno, and Mukai (1993) reported experimental results that appeared to support these hypotheses.

At this time, there is no widely accepted explanation for all of the contradictory results obtained for the effects of pain cues on aggressive behavior. The role of pain cues in aggressive behavior is complex and not fully understood, but it seems apparent that empathy and gender are factors implicated in how an individual reacts to them (Eagly & Steffen, 1986). We may conclude that the research on the effects of pain cues on aggressive behavior does not provide strong support for Berkowitz's theory of reactive aggression.

Appetitive Drive

An important feature of Berkowitz's system of reactive aggression is that it describes aggression as reactive, impulsive, and not mediated by the prior plans or goals of the organism. In this sense, reactive aggression is unintentional (we have more to say about this in chap. 6). The behavior is analogous to burning one's hand on a stove: The hand is pulled quickly away as a reflex action, and no prior conscious plan to carry out the action is required. Berkowitz (1981c) has pointed out the involuntary aspects of reactive aggression and indicated that, given the right circumstances, the individual may display impulsive outbursts of violence. The right circumstances include experience of aversive stimulation and the presence of releasing aggressive cues in the environment.

Basic biological drives, such as thirst and hunger, display a cyclicity related to deprivation. The more hungry the organism gets (until some point of habituation), the more intense the drive becomes and the more vigorously the organism will seek or consume foods. Eating food reduces the drive, and the organism stops food-related activity. There is no evidence of a cyclicity of intensity in aggressive behaviors that might be associated with a drive state. Nor is there any empirical basis for assuming a biological mechanism that generates aggressive energy and that compels people to hurt one another.

Zillmann (1983) noted that the concept of drive was used to explain the energizing of behavior—the motor that runs the machine. Research on the brain has revealed activation patterns (i.e., excitatory reactions) that some theorists have assumed are consistent with the notion of drive. However, Zillmann pointed out that physiological arousal tends to activate any ongoing behavior pattern and is not specific to any particular response system, such as aggression.

"Drive" was a popular concept in the influential theory of Clark Hull in the 1940s and 1950s, and it played a central role in frustration–aggression theory. It was believed that organisms were born with a few biological drives that, through laws of association, could generate any number of secondary drives, such as hope or fear. Berkowitz (1989) appeared to take the view that reactive aggression is a basic drive and instrumental aggression is an acquired drive.

The recent history of learning theory has shown a major shift away from the concept of drive. Bolles (1967) provided an exhaustive examination of the drive construct that was important in the general abandonment of the concept. The evidence he reviewed was not strongly supportive of the hypothesis that drives energize behavior or that they summate into a generalized drive level (such as seemed to be inferred by Berkowitz, 1986, when he combined appetitive and instrumental drives). The arguments and evidence weighed by Bolles marked a historical shift away from drive theory by specialists in learning. Instead of looking inside the organism for what pushes out behavior, learning theorists have shifted their focus outward and have found better theories that rely on stimulus conditions, past associations, and incentive conditions. It is the future-oriented organism that now runs through mazes in psychology laboratories. In other words, all behavior is assumed to be instrumental in nature.

Conclusion: Berkowitz's Theory of Reactive Aggression

Berkowitz has focused primarily on establishing a system of reactive aggression and has attempted to show how it serves as the basis for the learning of instrumental aggression. He hypothesized that the system of reactive aggression follows different laws than do other systems of behavior. Convincing evidence would, however, need to be provided to establish that there is such a separate system of behavior. Berkowitz has referred to reflex fighting, the causal relationship between aversive stimulation and aggression, the impact of aggressive stimuli in augmenting aggressive behavior, the weapons-eliciting effect, and the aggression-enhancing effect of pain cues as support for postulating a system of reactive aggression. Our close examination of the evidence raises questions about each of these relationships and justifies a healthy skepticism about the existence of a system of reactive aggression.

SUMMARY AND CONCLUSIONS

In an early view that he later abandoned, Freud (1950) believed that frustration caused aggressive behavior. He postulated that frustration creates negative energy, which must be expended by the frustrated person. Catharsis occurs because the negative energy is discharged by aggressive behavior. Displacement occurs because the frustrated person may be inhibited from attacking a powerful frustrator and may redirect the negative energy toward a substitute target. Freud's insights were presented in a metaphorical language, and ambiguities in the concepts made the theory impossible to test.

A group of Yale psychologists (Dollard et al., 1939) developed a more formal theory of the relation between frustration and aggression. They proposed that frustration generated an aggressive drive, which in turn activated a class of aggressive responses. Unless inhibited, the strongest of the responses in the class would be performed. Performance of an aggressive response reduced drive (catharsis), which was reinforcing and strengthened the response. Punishment creates inhibition of aggression, and when aggression is inhibited, the drive produced by frustration may lead to displacement. Research has shown that displacement is a reliable phenomenon, but because a process of catharsis has not been established, the frustration–aggression explanation for displacement is clearly inadequate. In chapter 12, we offer alternative explanations for target substitution effects.

According to frustration–aggression theory, aggression is always caused by frustration, although sometimes inhibitions delay the activation of the behavior. Contrary to the theory, research has shown that frustration does not always lead to aggression. Rather than abandon frustration–aggression theory, Berkowitz (1989) set out to fix it. He proposed that when frustration is aversive it does lead to aggression and postulated two systems of aggressive behavior. Reactive aggression occurs as an impulsive reaction to a desire to hurt another person when the actor has an aversive experience. Instrumental aggression is grafted onto the system of reactive aggression but represents learned behavior that has the purpose of achieving incentives and avoiding punishments.

Evidence has been gathered to establish the existence of a special system of reactive aggression. Berkowitz and his students have worked tirelessly over 30 years to examine the effects of aversive and aggressive stimuli as well as pain cues on aggressive behavior. Unfortunately, close examination of this research indicates inconsistencies and contradictions, in addition to the likelihood that demand cues are pervasive in some studies, such as those focusing on the weapons effect. Nevertheless, it is reasonable to conclude that aversive stimuli do facilitate, but probably do not instigate, aggressive behavior. In the social interactionist theory presented in chapters 6 through 9, we suggest mechanisms by which aversive stimuli facilitate aggressive episodes and the conditions under which such facilitative effects are likely to occur.

Another important contribution of frustration–aggression theory and Berkowitz's revision of it is the conceptual classification of causes of aggressive behavior. A distinction has been made between instigation, facilitation, inhibition, and disinhibition. An *instigator* is a direct cause of aggressive behavior. A *facilitator* increases the likelihood or intensity of aggressive behavior but has no effect in the absence of an instigation. *Inhibition* consists of factors that decrease the likelihood or intensity of aggression when an instigator is present. Finally, *disinhibitors* make it more likely that aggressive behavior will occur, or they may intensify aggressive behavior when both instigators and inhibitors are present. These distinctions have been and will likely continue to be very important in the development of theories and research on aggressive behavior. We use these distinctions in the social interactionist theory that we present in the second half of this book.

3

PHYSIOLOGICAL AROUSAL
AND AGGRESSION

Physiological processes have been assumed by traditional theorists as fundamental in the instigation of aggressive behaviors. For both Lorenz (1966) and Freud (1950), instinctual energies drawn from physiological processes and embedded in genetic features of the organism impel the individual to engage in aggressive behavior. The frustration–aggression theory proposed by the Yale psychologists (Dollard et al., 1939) postulates an inherently biological connection between frustrations and the generation of aggressive energy that, in the absence of inhibitory forces, eventuated in aggressive behavior. Berkowitz's (1989) theory of reactive aggression also assumes a biologically based relationship between the experience of aversive stimulation and an increase in aggressive drive.

In all of these theories, the instinct, drive, or aggressive energy was believed to be specific to activating aggressive behavior. We have argued, however, that such concepts are inadequately defined and are unsupported by the available physiological evidence. Current specialists in ethology and learning theory have largely abandoned or radically changed concepts of instinct and drive. However, theorists have not abandoned energy-related concepts altogether. Physiological arousal has been proposed as an important component of aggressive behavior. Schachter's (1964) revolutionary two-factor theory of emotion and research on misattribution processes has influenced the subsequent conceptualizations of how arousal is interpreted by the individual.

Arousal is quite different from a drive state. Drive states directly cause behavior, whereas arousal states only indirectly do so. Once a drive is activated, it is maintained until a response is performed that is specific to reducing the drive. Although a drive inevitably produces an associated behavior, arousal can dissipate without affecting behavior. According to Schachter (1964), arousal is diffuse and undifferentiated, and interpretation of arousal in terms of specific emotional states is arbitrary and easily manipulated. Arousal may be interpreted in alternative ways, depending on situational cues. It is the interpretation and not the arousal per se that mediates subsequent behavior.

Zillmann (1983) has proposed that arousal from two different sources may combine and be attributable to the same source. He referred to this process as *excitation transfer*. When the combined arousal is attributed to anger, the individual is likely to be more aggressive than would have been the case if only the anger-producing cue had been present. Zillmann's theory has generated a number of interesting experiments, and it has been modified to explain findings about how viewing pornography affects aggressive behavior.

In this chapter, we critically examine Schachter's theory of emotions, the misattribution process, Zillmann's excitation transfer theory, and research on pornography and aggressive behavior.

SCHACHTER'S THEORY OF EMOTIONS AND MISATTRIBUTION OF AROUSAL

For many decades, physiologists and psychologists have searched without success for the biochemical and neurological cues that people use to discriminate between the various emotions they experience. According to Mandler (1979, p. 298), the available evidence indicates that emotions involve only general, global, and diffuse arousal. He concluded that the only reliable distinguishing feature of emotional states that can be tied to physiological factors is general ANS arousal. ANS arousal is manifested in increased heart and respiration rates, sweating of the palms, constriction of the blood vessels, dilation of the pupils, and other reactions. Distinct and separate emotions are apparently not linked to specific neuronal or hormonal factors. If Mandler is correct, then a significant question is, How do individuals know what emotions they are experiencing? That is, how is one emotion distinguished from another? There are apparently no discriminative cues that arise from internal physiological processes that can be used as a basis for inferring one's own emotional states. Schachter (1964) has proposed that cognitive interpretations help people label their arousal and that it is plausible that arousal produced by one stimulus could be misattributed to some other source.

Schachter's Two-Factor Theory of Emotions

In his two-factor theory of emotions, Schachter (1964) shifted the emphasis away from physiological states to the individual's cognitive interpretations of stimulus situations. Whenever individuals experience physiological arousal, they do a cognitive search for information to help interpret what emotion is being experienced. This information-processing view of how people attribute emotions to themselves postulates that two factors are necessary for the labeling of an emotion: physiological arousal and social cues.

A prototypical emotional experience includes a perception of a situation and physiological arousal. These two processes occur simultaneously (Reisenzein, 1983). For example, if you were walking in the woods and encountered a large black bear, your perception of the bear and physiological arousal would take place simultaneously. Which emotion you attribute to yourself would depend on your interpretation of the situation. Past learning about the destructive capabilities and behavior of bears would be associated with expectations of possible harm and, hence, would cause you to label your arousal state as *fear*. The basic assumption of Schachter's two-factor theory of emotions is that people must first experience physiological arousal and link it to cues in the situation before cognitive appraisals can provide the basis for attributing a particular emotion to themselves.

There are occasions when people experience arousal prior to any perception of stimuli that could have created it. When individuals have such unexplained arousal, they are motivated to search for an explanation and use social cues to define the specific emotion that is being experienced. Such a situation was produced in an experiment performed by Schachter and Singer (1962), in which they gave pills containing epinephrine, a stimulant, to subjects. Some subjects were told that they would experience side effects of itching, headache, and numbness of the feet. Other subjects were correctly informed that they would experience symptoms of arousal, such as increased heart rate, trembling of the hands, and flushing of the face. The latter subjects had a ready explanation for the arousal produced by epinephrine, but the misinformed subjects did not. All subjects were then exposed to either an euphoric or an angry person and subsequently were asked to indicate their own emotional feelings. Misinformed subjects reported feeling more of the same emotion as the other person in the experiment than did correctly informed subjects.

This result was interpreted as showing that subjects who had no ex-planation for their arousal used social cues as a basis for inferring and labeling their emotional state. Such a labeling process implies that emotions are not inborn but are learned through the socialization process. Like language, the types and forms of human emotions are culturally determined. Just as a camel rancher in North Africa may have 50 different names for stages of pregnancy in a camel and most of the rest of us think of it as a question of "either or," so there may be wide variations in emotional vocabularies between cultures. However, according to Schachter (1964), emotional ex-periences are inextricably connected to physiological arousal.

Despite intense criticism of the methods and findings of the Schachter and Singer (1962) and other studies as well as of Schachter's theory generally (cf. Neiss, 1988; Reisenzein, 1983), the idea that emotions involve inter-pretations of undifferentiated arousal has had an important impact on the study of aggression.

Misattribution of Arousal

It is plausible that if individuals label arousal in accordance with situational cues, then it might be possible to get them to relabel their arousal by manipulating cues. In an experiment designed to test this idea, Nisbett and Schachter (1966) asked subjects to submit to a series of in-creasingly intensive electric shocks and to tell the experimenter when the shocks became too painful to tolerate. Before the onset of the shocks, each subject had been given a placebo pill. Half of the subjects were told that they would experience arousal symptoms, whereas the remainder were told to expect other types of physical side effects. The hypothesis of the study was that those subjects who were led to misattribute some of their discomfort to the pill rather than to fear or pain associated with the shocks would be able to tolerate higher shock intensities. On the other hand, subjects who expected no arousal or discomfort from taking the pill would attribute all the arousal they experienced to the shocks and, therefore, would tolerate less intense shocks. The results supported these hypotheses. Arousal-in-structed subjects tolerated 4 times the amperage accepted by subjects who had not been led to expect arousal symptoms from ingesting the pill. In other words, subjects who had expected arousal symptoms from ingesting the placebo misattributed some of their arousal state—which, in fact, had been caused by the anticipation and delivery of electric shocks—to the effects of the pill. The interpretation of emotional states in terms of available cues (a cognitive process) lessened the negativity of their experience.

If situational cues heighten or reduce negative emotional states, then they may affect the probability and the intensity of aggressive behavior. Suppose a person who is already in an aroused state is the target of an insult. The insult should produce additional arousal. If the person attributes all of the arousal to the insult, he or she will experience more anger than would have been experienced if no residual arousal had been present when the insult occurred. On the other hand, if the arousal from the insult is attributed to whatever happened before the insult, then the person is likely to feel less angry.

Theories and research have been developed to explain the conditions under which added sources of arousal can enhance or reduce aggressive behavior. A general theory of transfer of arousal to enhance aggressive behavior was proposed by Zillmann (1979) and is referred to as *excitation transfer theory.*

ZILLMANN'S THEORY OF EXCITATION TRANSFER

Excitation transfer is a process proposed by Zillmann (1979) in the framework of a more general theory of aggression. We describe his theory and the role played by excitation transfer in facilitating aggressive behavior. Then we critically examine the program of research that has been carried out to evaluate the theory.

Theory

Zillmann (1979, 1983) proposed that three factors are important for explaining aggressive behavior: (a) the evocation of excitation or arousal associated with emotional states, (b) the dispositions or learned behavior patterns of the individual, and (c) the monitoring function of higher cognitive processes that appraise the appropriateness of both emotional states and courses of behavior. Endangerment of the person's well-being produces a temporary increase in sympathetic arousal. Endangerment is defined in terms of pain, discomfort, and debasement—all of which produce an emergency reaction in the form of physiological arousal and learned behaviors. Arousal states energize and intensify behavior, but which behavior occurs is a function of learning and not an automatic reaction to the arousal state itself. Learned reactions allow the individual to respond to emergency situations without having to rely on time-consuming higher cognitive activity for guidance.

According to Zillmann (1988), cognitive regulation of aggressive behavior is greatly impaired under high levels of arousal. At very high levels of excitation, well-learned aggressive habits may be activated without cognitive guidance. This kind of reactive aggression—similar to the impulsive aggression proposed by Berkowitz (1989)—is restricted, however, to situations in which the individual is provoked or attacked by another person.

However, a person who is attacked and experiences a high level of arousal will not retaliate unless predisposed to do so by past learning.[1]

Provocation in the form of annoyances, frustration, insult, and attack has been shown to increase physiological arousal in the ANS (e.g., Hokanson & Burgess, 1962; Hokanson & Shetler, 1961). Zillmann (1983) suggested that such a sequence does not imply a simple causal relationship between arousal and aggression. Provocation elicits plans for retaliation that correspond to the level of attack: The stronger the provocation, the greater the excitation, or arousal, and the more intense the aggressive behavior. The arousal does not instigate aggressive behavior but amplifies whatever aggressive behavior is chosen by the individual.

Any source of residual arousal that adds to arousal associated with anger will further intensify any subsequent aggressive behavior. Excitation transfer occurs when the individual experiences two successive sources of arousal but attributes the combined arousals to only one of the sources. The transfer of residual arousal only occurs during a specific phase of dissipation. The course of dissipation of arousal has three stages. At the first stage of arousal, the person can identify the source of excitation. At the second stage, the level of arousal dissipates to a level that is above a steady state, but the individual can no longer report experiencing it. In the last stage, the arousal completely dissipates. It is only when a secondary source of arousal is in the second stage and can be misattributed to provocation-produced anger that it can produce excitation transfer and heightened aggressive behavior.

Two questions have been addressed in research on the effects of residual arousal on aggressive behavior. The first question concerns whether separate sources of arousal combine to increase the intensity of aggressive behavior in the absence of provocation. The second question focuses on the effects of excitation transfer on enhancing anger and aggression that is instigated by some provocation by the target person.

Combined Arousal and Unprovoked Aggressive Behavior

The earliest study examining the effect of combined sources of arousal on unprovoked aggressive behavior was carried out by Geen and O'Neal (1969). Some subjects viewed a segment of a prizefight scene from the motion picture *The Champion*, whereas the remainder watched a control film showing excerpts from sports activities. All subjects then evaluated a confederate's essay by delivering shocks to him. During the evaluations, some of the subjects were exposed to noxious white noise through head-

---

[1]Zillmann (1983) and Berkowitz (1989) appear to disagree on this point. According to Berkowitz's theory, the aversiveness of being attacked should elicit reactive aggression unless it is specifically inhibited.

phones, and others were not exposed to the noise. Arousal was not produced by any action of the confederate, who did not insult or attack the subjects. The subjects who had viewed the fight scene and had been exposed to the noxious noise during the evaluation delivered more shocks to the confederate than did subjects who had neither viewed the fight film nor been exposed to noxious noise. The results were interpreted as showing that two sources of arousal, viewing a fight film and being exposed to noxious noise, combined to enhance the intensity of an appropriate response in the situation (the delivery of electric shocks).

Other results reported by Geen and O'Neal (1969) were not entirely consistent with the combined-arousal hypothesis. Subjects who had viewed the presumably arousing fight scene but had not experienced the noxious noise gave no more shocks than did subjects who had merely viewed the control film. Furthermore, subjects who experienced noise gave the same number of shocks as those who did not when both had seen the control film. In other words, subjects were more aggressive when they experienced two sources of arousal than when they experienced none, but two sources of arousal did not produce more aggression than only one, and one did not produce more aggression than none. Although it is possible that it required two sources of arousal to achieve instigation of aggression, no attempt was made to measure arousal in the experiment, so there is no assurance that subjects were actually aroused or that the experimental manipulations had their intended effect. This criticism of Geen and O'Neal's study is important because it is the only study purporting to show that arousal has an impact on aggressive behavior by unprovoked subjects.

Combined Arousal and Provoked Aggression

Konečni (1975) studied the impact of secondary sources of arousal on the aggressive behavior of subjects who had been provoked. In his experiment, some subjects were insulted by a confederate, whereas others were not provoked. Various subgroups of subjects from the provoked and non-provoked conditions were then exposed to combinations of complex–simple and loud–soft sounds while they were delivering electric shocks to the confederate. Although no measure of arousal was obtained, it was assumed that loud and complex sounds caused more arousal than soft and simple sounds. Consistent with these assumptions, exposure to loud sounds and complex–soft sounds led subjects to deliver more shocks than did exposure to simple–soft sounds. However, these effects of sound were only observed in subjects who had previously been provoked by the confederate. Similar findings were reported by Donnerstein and Wilson (1976).

Zillmann's (1983) theory of excitation transfer was used to explain these findings. The combined arousals from the provocation and the secondary source of arousal (noise) enhanced excitation levels over that which provocation alone would have produced. The noise produced a secondary source of arousal that combined with the arousal produced by the provocation. Subjects interpreted the combined arousal as stronger anger, and the guiding cognition was that the level of retaliation should be proportionate to the level of provocation. Subjects who were not provoked might have experienced high levels of arousal from other sources, but they did not label their arousal as *anger* and did not have a guiding cognition for retaliation that would be enhanced by any secondary sources of arousal.

In a carefully done study, Zillmann (1971) had subjects express a number of attitudes to a confederate. The confederate signaled agreement with the subjects' attitudes by turning on a light and signaled disagreement by shocking the subjects. To establish a high level of provocation, the confederate shocked all subjects on 9 out of 12 opportunities. Subsequently, subjects viewed one of three feature-length films: *Marco Polo's Travels* (an educational film), *Body and Soul* (a violent film about a pugilist), or *The Couch* (an erotic film including nudity and precoital behavior). In pilot research, heart rates, blood pressures, and skin temperatures associated with viewing these films were measured, and it was established that the erotic film produced the most arousal and the educational film induced the least arousal.

Finally, in a teacher–learner procedure, subjects decided what level of shock intensity to use in punishing errors made by the confederate on a word-association task. Subjects who viewed the erotic film delivered the most intense shocks, those who watched the violent film gave intermediate shocks, and those who were exposed to the educational film delivered the least intensive shocks. Thus, when a secondary source of arousal was interpolated between provocation and retaliation, subjects were more aggressive toward another person than when a secondary source of arousal was not present. However, the reliability of such findings may have been specific to the films that were shown. Zillmann and Johnson (1973) found that viewing a violent film did not enhance the aggressiveness of provoked subjects but that viewing a neutral film reduced the intensity of aggressive behavior.

The next logical step was to show that any source of secondary arousal could produce excitation transfer. A diffuse source of arousal that is not typically interpreted in terms of emotional states is physical exercise. Zillmann, Katcher, and Milavsky (1972) manipulated both the level of provocation and the amount of exercise-produced arousal in subjects. A confederate directed low or high attack against subjects in the form of electric shocks. Half of the subjects in each attack condition were required to engage in strenuous bicycle pedaling; the remaining subjects were comfortably seated and performed a simple, sedentary task. Physiological measures established that pedaling produced more arousal than did the sedentary task. In the final teacher–learner phase of the procedures, subjects in high-attack conditions gave higher shocks than did those in low-shock conditions. A finding interpreted as supporting excitation transfer theory showed that subjects who had been exposed to high attack and had engaged in subsequent physical exercise gave the most intense shocks to the confederate. However, close examination of the data indicated that, overall, there was only a small (and not statistically significant) difference between the exercise–high-attack and the no-exercise–high-attack conditions. Thus, the only justifiable conclusion from these results is that the level of provocation was directly related to intensity of retaliation but that there was only a slight impact, if any, of exercise. In other words, the researchers' claim that the results supported excitation transfer theory does not appear to be justified.

Zillmann, Johnson, and Day (1974) identified subjects in terms of how quickly they showed physiological recovery after vigorously riding a bicycle. One or two weeks later, subjects were given either a few or many shocks by a confederate and then rode a stationary bicycle. Some subjects were immediately placed in the teacher role and given the opportunity to shock the confederate, whereas other subjects waited until the exercise-produced excitation could dissipate somewhat before they were provided with opportunities to shock the confederate. Subjects who did not recover rapidly from exercised-produced arousal gave more intense shocks, but only when they had experienced a high level of provocation from the confederate. Subjects who had been identified as most proficient in recovery from the excitation produced by exercise and subjects who had not been vigorously attacked were unaffected by the secondary source of arousal.

Zillmann has argued (1983) that the impact of excitation transfer is restricted to retaliatory behavior. This stipulation differentiates his theory from drive theory: A drive would energize any ongoing behavior, whereas arousal is mediated through emotional labeling and cognitive appraisals. In an effort to differentiate between these two types of energy-related theories, Zillmann and Bryant (1974) gave subjects both immediate and delayed opportunities to aggress against another person. Subjects who had either been aroused by physical exercise or engaged in a sedentary task played a game of Battleship with a confederate. The subject was to hide his or her ship on a 6 × 6 squared board, and the confederate's task was to find it. The subject could interfere with the confederate's ability to play by delivering noxious noise of varying intensities to him. Play commenced 2 minutes after the initial period of exercise or sedentary activity. After the first game, some subjects overheard the confederate call them "the dumb ass" in a conversation with the experimenter, and some heard only a neutral comment. Six minutes later—a delay designed to allow the excitation of provoked subjects to dissipate—subjects played two more games of Battleship.

No difference in frequency or amount of noise given to the confederate prior to provocation was found. In other words, arousal produced by physical exercise in and of itself had no impact on aggressive behavior. However, differences between conditions did occur after subjects were provoked. Subjects in the provoked and physical exercise condition delivered more intense noises to the confederate than did subjects in any of the other conditions. A puzzling result in this study, which has apparently gone unnoticed, is that among subjects who engaged in the sedentary activity, there was no difference in either the frequency or the intensity of noise delivered in a comparison between provoked and unprovoked subjects. The provocation alone was not sufficiently strong to produce anger and retaliation. Theoretically, residual arousal can only intensify aggressive behavior that has been instigated by some other factor, but provocation alone did not instigate aggression. According to an arousal interpretation of the manipulations in the experiment, provocation should have produced arousal, arousal should have been labeled as *anger,* and more aggressive behavior should have been displayed by provoked subjects. Thus, although some of the findings reported by Zillmann and Bryant (1974) may be interpreted to support Zillmann's theory, the entire pattern raises questions about the specific mechanism by which provocation and exercise together intensified aggressive behavior.

Combined Arousal Effects and Anger

A corollary of Zillmann's (1983) theory of excitation transfer is that memory of anger is affected by unidentified secondary sources of arousal. If a person is angered at a time when arousal produced by a secondary source is in Stage 2 of dissipation, but for some reason the target person is not available for retaliation, all arousal—including that produced by provocation—will dissipate. A subsequent encounter with the target reminds the person of the provocation and reinstates the total amount of anger experienced on the previous occasion. If this corollary is valid, it should be expected that excitation transfer can occur even when aggressive behavior is postponed for a lengthy period of time.

Bryant and Zillmann (1979) carried out a field study to test the corollary about the carryover of excitation transfer despite considerable delay between provocation and opportunity for aggressive behavior. Students in a large course were broken up into smaller discussion groups. Students saw one of three films that a pretest showed produced different levels of arousal. Subsequently, some of the students were treated rudely by a guest instructor, whereas the remainder were treated in a neutral fashion. Eight days later, subjects were asked to evaluate the guest instructor. Which film subjects had seen did not affect ratings made of the guest instructor if they had not been rudely treated. However, among provoked subjects, those who had seen the most arousing film also gave the guest instructor the worst ratings. This result indicated that the hostility of subjects who had been provoked 8 days earlier was affected by an excitation transfer from viewing an arousing film.

According to Zillmann (1983), high levels of arousal reduce cognitive control. For this reason, a person who experiences a high level of anger may not be receptive to explanations offered for the provoking behavior of another person. Excitation transfer could contribute to this lack of receptivity because it increases the level of anger experienced by the person. Zillmann, Bryant, Cantor, and Day (1975) carried out an experiment designed to show that excuses or justifications for the behavior of a provoking person mitigate aggressive reactions when subjects experience intermediate levels of arousal, but not when subjects are highly aroused. Subjects were treated rudely by an experimenter and then either engaged in a sedentary task or exercised strenuously on a bicycle. All subjects then witnessed the experimenter treating an assistant rudely. The assistant provided an excuse for the experimenter's conduct to only half of the subjects. The subjects then provided evaluations of the experimenter that, purportedly, would affect future job decisions about him.

Subjects who did not engage in strenuous exercise were less angered and provided less negative evaluations of the experimenter, replicating a similar finding by Zillmann and Cantor (1976). The excuse did not affect the evaluations by subjects who rode a bicycle and, presumably, were at high levels of excitation at the time the excuse had been offered. These results appeared to support Zillmann's (1983) view that there is less cognitive control of aggressive behavior at high levels of arousal. However, as in many of the studies carried out in this program of research, there was also a contradictory finding. In a comparison of the subjects who had not been offered an excuse for the experimenter's rude behavior, there was no difference between subjects who did and did not ride the bicycle. This constituted a failure to replicate prior findings by the same researchers of a transfer effect of physical activity on the aggressive behavior of provoked subjects.

Bornerwasser and Mummendey (1982) failed to replicate excitation transfer effects associated with riding bicycles in two experiments. Subjects were exposed to high or low provocation from a confederate and subsequently either did or did not ride a bike. Although measures established that autonomic excitation was strong under high provocation and was affected by strenuous exercise, there was no excitation transfer effect on the intensity of aggression directed by subjects against the confederate.

Conclusions: Zillmann's Excitation Transfer Theory

Zillmann's theory is based on the assumption that anger mediates aggressive behavior along with cognitive controls and that the experience of anger includes both physiological arousal and a cognitive labeling process. Diffuse arousal brought about by secondary sources, such as noise and physical exercise, may be integrated with and added to arousal produced by provocation or endangerment and, thus, may enhance the experience of anger and intensify subsequent aggressive behavior. This misattribution process occurs only after the secondary arousal has dissipated somewhat and is no longer attributed to its original source. Excitation transfer occurs only when an individual is provoked and does not affect the intensity of aggressive behavior of unprovoked persons. Excuses and justifications may mitigate the degree of anger experienced and the intensity of subsequent aggressive behavior, but not when the provoked individual is under high levels of excitation and his or her cognitive control is weakened.

We were puzzled by an apparent discrepancy between the theoretical description of excitation transfer and the procedures typically used to investigate it. The theory proposes that partially dissipated arousal transfers forward to a subsequent experience of arousal. If a person is aroused by noise, violent films, or exercise and (after arousal dissipates somewhat) is then attacked or provoked by another person, the residual arousal from the first experience should transfer to and heighten the anger resulting from the second experience. The most frequently used research procedures, however, first provoke the subjects and then expose them to secondary sources of arousal. If excitation transfer occurs forward in time, then the dissipation of anger should add to the arousal attributed to noise, perceived violence, or the vigorousness of exercise. If our observation is correct, then it could be concluded that the hypothesis of excitation transfer has not yet been adequately tested.

One could argue that the opportunity to retaliate against the provoker reinstates the anger experienced earlier or that the degree of anger experienced when provoked is maintained throughout the experiment and the secondary source of arousal adds to the anger that subjects experience, causing heightened arousal and more intense aggressive behavior. This has not been the mechanism proposed by Zillmann (1983) in reporting his research. Rather than appealing to a post hoc explanation of prior results, one could test the theory in a more straightforward way by exposing subjects to secondary sources of arousal first, provoking them, and then giving them an opportunity to retaliate against the provoker. Reversing the order of presentation of events to subjects in laboratory experiments may change the way that subjects interpret stimuli. The meaning of watching a violent film may be quite different to a subject who has been attacked than to someone who has not been attacked. The lack of control for the interpretations that subjects have of why they are riding bikes or viewing violent or pornographic films may be responsible for some of the inconsistencies in the results of this program of research. As Neiss (1988) has pointed out, it is difficult, if not impossible, to separate or unconfound the cognitive and arousal effects of experimental manipulations of stimuli.

Whatever conclusion is drawn about the merits of Zillmann's theory and the process of excitation transfer, the theory has given impetus to research investigating the facilitating effects of arousal on aggressive behavior. We next examine the evidence and new theoretical suggestions relevant to how exposure to sexual stimuli and arousal states affect aggressive behavior.

SEXUAL STIMULI AND AGGRESSIVE BEHAVIOR

Sigmund Freud (1933) suggested an association between sex and aggression. He observed that intimate sexual relations frequently include sadistic and masochistic behaviors. According to Freud, these behaviors occur in normal relationships and can be considered pathological only when they become the focus of the sexual interaction rather than simply a component of it. Berne (1964) has proposed that anger may increase sexual arousal and pleasure in both men and women. The research on the effects of testosterone, reviewed in chapter 1, also has suggested a link between sexual and aggressive behaviors. High concentrations of testosterone in male animals have been associated with both intense sexual and aggressive behaviors. However, we have indicated that there is no compelling evidence that such a mechanism occurs in humans.

Schachter's (1964) two-factor theory of emotion, Zillmann's (1983) notion of excitation transfer, and the concept of misattribution have revived interest in linking sex and aggression. Over the past 15 years, a series of experiments have been carried out in which subjects are exposed to sexual stimuli and then allowed to aggress against another person, who may or may not have provoked them. These experiments have produced apparently contradictory findings. The researchers have developed hypotheses to explain the conditions under which opposite effects have been obtained. A small group of social psychologists has carried out most of this research, and all of them believe that under specified conditions, arousal produced by sexual stimuli can intensify aggressive behavior. We review this area of research in some detail and subject it to critical evaluation, which until now has not been carefully done.

Early Research

Zillmann (1971) found that viewing an erotic film increased the aggressiveness of subjects who had been provoked by the victim. He also established that an erotic film created more arousal in subjects than did aggressive and control films. Similar findings were reported by Meyer (1972a) and by Zillmann, Hoyt, and Day (1974).

Bandura (1971) argued that emotions do not cause aggressive behavior but that emotional arousal facilitates and intensifies aggressive behavior. According to Bandura, the facilitating effect of emotional arousal occurs only when the individual is already prone to act aggressively. This implies that if the organism is predisposed to behave nonaggressively, then emotional arousal will facilitate nonaggressive behavior. In other words, arousal energizes any behavior that is dominant in the situation.

In an experiment testing Bandura's social learning theory, subjects read either erotic passages or a short science fiction story (Jaffe, Malamuth, Feingold, & Feshbach, 1974). They then had an opportunity to deliver shocks to a confederate, who had not provoked them in any way. Comparisons indicated that male subjects gave more intense shocks than did female subjects, and both male and female subjects gave more intense shocks if they had been exposed to erotic materials rather than to science fiction materials. Jaffe et al. proposed that some link between sexual arousal and aggressive behavior would account for their findings.

In the same year and journal the exact opposite finding was reported. R. A. Baron (1974a) had a confederate either attack the subjects with electric shocks and give each a negative written evaluation or provide the subjects with positive evaluations. Subjects were then each given a notebook containing picture cutouts. In a nonaroused condition the pictures were of inanimate objects, whereas in an aroused condition the pictures were of nude women taken from *Playboy* magazine. In a teacher–learner situation, subjects were then given opportunities to deliver electric shocks to the confederate. The most intense levels of shock were delivered by subjects in the nonaroused and attacked condition. When subjects were not provoked or when they had been exposed to nude pictures, they displayed lower levels of aggression. The effect of observing nude women eliminated the effect of attack and lowered aggression to the level shown by unprovoked subjects. This result is similar to those obtained by R. A. Baron and Bell (1973, 1977); R. A. Baron (1974b); and Donnerstein, Donnerstein, and Evans (1975) and appears to disconfirm both Bandura's and Zillmann's theories.

Hedonic Tone Hypothesis

One hypothesis that might explain the pattern of results obtained in the experiments described above is that some forms of erotica are experienced as pleasant (i.e., having positive hedonic tone) and, thus, detract from the negative emotional experience of anger (R. A. Baron, 1974a, 1974b). In such cases, exposure to erotica following provocation should reduce aggression. However, some forms of erotica may be experienced as unpleasant (i.e., having negative hedonic tone), and the negative arousal may combine with the arousal produced by provocation, enhancing anger and subsequent aggression. Hedonic tone theory proposes an algebra of positive and negative arousal states that, when summed, contribute to increasing or decreasing the intensity of aggressive behavior following provocation.

L. A. White (1979) tested the hedonic tone hypothesis. In a preliminary study, color slides of a large variety of heterosexual and homosexual acts were rated by subjects. Sets of slides were selected to produce high or low sexual arousal and to produce positive or negative hedonic tone. It would be expected that high negative hedonic tone of the sexual stimuli would add to anger and aggression, but only when the sexual stimuli produce high arousal and the subjects are angered. When sexual stimuli produce high arousal but are positive in hedonic tone, there should be a decrease in the aggression of angered subjects. If subjects are not angered, none of the sexual stimuli should have an effect on aggression. Only partial support was found for the hedonic tone hypothesis. Sexual stimuli that produced high arousal with a positive hedonic tone did reduce the intensity of shocks that angered subjects delivered to another person. However, sexual stimuli that produced high arousal and negative hedonic tone did not enhance aggressiveness.

Arousal–Affect Hypothesis

Zillmann, Bryant, Comisky, and Medoff (1981) modified R. A. Baron's (1974a, 1974b) hedonic tone hypothesis slightly and explicitly tied it to a mechanism of excitation transfer. An arousal–affect hypothesis proposes both an excitation component and an affective component for arousal. Each component from residual arousal adds separately to arousal produced by anger, and incompatible positive affect subtracts from anger-produced arousal. High excitation and negative affect from residual arousal would both add to anger-produced arousal, whereas positive affect would reduce anger-produced arousal. Thus, the net contribution of residual arousal in increasing or decreasing anger and aggression depends on the separate additive (or subtractive) components of excitation and affect.

According to the arousal–affect hypothesis, the specific content of the stimuli should not be relevant to excitation transfer. It is not the erotic or nonerotic nature of the stimulus that should modify aggressiveness, but only the excitatory and affective components of residual arousal produced by any type of stimulation that should transfer to anger and aggression.

Preliminary testing of stimuli while using both physiological and psychological measurements allowed Zillmann et al. (1981) to identify erotic and nonerotic stimuli that had high or low excitatory potential and negative or positive affect. Subjects overheard a confederate call them "stupid" for opinions that they had expressed toward women's liberation, viewed one of six possible kinds of stimuli, and then used noxious noise against the confederate as part of the defensive strategy in playing a game. Subjects in the high-excitation–negative-affect condition were more aggressive than subjects in the high-excitation–positive-affect condition. These results supported the arousal–affect model and showed that the erotic or nonerotic content of the stimuli (i.e., amount of arousal produced) was not an important factor in the excitation transfer process.

It is important to note that some other neglected findings in Zillmann et al.'s (1981) study were inconsistent with the arousal–affect hypothesis. There should have been more excitation transfer in the high-excitation–negative-affect condition than in the low-excitation–negative-affect condition; however, there was no difference. Similarly, there should have been a difference within the positive-affect conditions between subjects in the high- and low-excitation conditions, but again there was not. The reliability of the results is also in question because Zillmann and Sapolsky (1977), using similar procedures, failed to find any effects of erotica on the use of noxious noise, despite the fact that independent measures established that the erotica were experienced as more exciting than the nonerotic stimuli. The authors suggested that the nonerotica might have been boring and that subjects may have experienced it negatively. Thus, the pleasant arousal produced by the erotica and the negative arousal associated with the boredom of watching the nonerotic film contributed equal amounts of arousal to excitation transfer. Such a post hoc explanation does little but point out the lack of appropriate controls in the experiment. There should have been one condition in which subjects were not exposed to any stimuli, that is, a group with no excitation transfer.

Sapolski (1984) presented a table listing the results of 10 studies in which predictions from the arousal–affect model were tested and showed that in 9 out of 29 tests, the theory was not supported. We would have to conclude, therefore, that the evidence does not strongly support either the arousal–affect hypothesis or the revised excitation transfer theory.

Feshbach and Malamuth (1978) offered an interesting hypothesis as a nonarousal explanation for the effects of sexual stimuli on aggressive behavior. They suggested that exposure to erotica or X-rated sexual stimuli disinhibits taboo sexual behavior and will generalize to other forms of antinormative behavior. Although their hypothesis did not organize the contradictory findings generated by researchers, it provided a possible mechanism through which demand cues may operate in these studies. Implicit in the presentation of sexual stimuli to male subjects may be that the experimenter condones or at least is more tolerant of taboo behavior, especially when the stimuli involve particularly serious antinormative behavior, as in films depicting rape and other forms of sexual violence. The permissive atmosphere may disinhibit aggressive behavior because subjects may be less concerned about negative evaluations by the experimenter. Sexual stimuli may also be demand cues, as were the weapons in the experiment by Berkowitz and LePage (1967), described in chapter 2. No one has directly tested this demand-cue hypothesis to date; thus, it must remain conjectural for now.[2]

Sex Differences and Effects of Arousal

A number of studies have shown that in laboratory experiments men are more aggressive than women (Bandura, Ross, & Ross, 1963; A. H. Buss, 1963; Jaffe et al., 1974; S. P. Taylor & Epstein, 1967).[3] However, both men and women have consistently been shown to be more aggressive against men than against women (R. A. Baron & Bell, 1973; A. H. Buss, 1966a; Dengerink, 1976; Frodi, Macaulay, & Thome, 1977; Kaleta & Buss, 1973; S. P. Taylor & Epstein, 1967).

Donnerstein (1980) has argued that the tendency to be more aggressive against male victims may occur because of a social norm against harming women, and there may be conditions when disinhibited men harm women more than they do other men. Exposure to erotica that portrays violent scenes of rape and sadomasochism may disinhibit aggressive behavior by men against women who have provoked them. Disinhibition may be especially likely when men have been exposed to violent pornography in which the female victim emits expressions of pleasure during or after being raped, suggesting that women enjoy such treatment. Men who view such films may be induced to believe that forceful sexual acts are desired by women, and they may be encouraged to be more aggressive against women.

According to Donnerstein (1980), the arousal produced by exposure to erotica generally intensifies aggressive behavior against both male and female targets. Thus, the arousal produced by erotica explains why angered men were more aggressive against both men and women. Norms against men hurting women may cause inhibition of aggression and may produce results indicating that men are more aggressive against other men than against women. Donnerstein argued that a perception that women are willing victims, fostered by nonviolent pornography, is a disinhibiting cue and should increase aggressiveness by men against women. Thus, arousal produced by erotica should intensify aggression against women when subjects are disinhibited.

Donnerstein and Barrett (1978) reported that exposure to erotica increased the aggressiveness of angered male subjects but that these subjects

---

[2]It is not necessary for subjects to be aware of the experimenter's hypothesis for demand compliance to occur. Generally, subjects have little choice of alternative modes of behaving in experiments. In aggression studies they can typically give more or they can give less aversive stimulation to a person who has attacked them. Any cue that suggests one rather than the other alternative may have a significant impact on what the subjects do.

[3]R. A. Baron (1977) has argued that a sex difference occurs only when subjects are not provoked. When provoked, men and women display similar degrees of arousal, anger, and aggression toward a same-sex person (R. A. Baron & Bell, 1973, 1977; Frodi, 1977; Gentry, 1970).

gave more shocks to other men than to women. These researchers were convinced that inhibitions toward hurting women in laboratory conditions were interfering with the powerful impact that pornography can have on aggression toward women. Furthermore, nonviolent forms of erotica may not provide the cues necessary to elicit aggression. If it is necessary to expose male subjects to violent pornography to elicit more aggression toward women, then it may be the violence and not the sexual aspects of the pornography that contributes to increased aggressive behavior.

An experiment was devised to disinhibit subjects so that they would believe that aggressive behavior would be approved of by the experimenter and to examine the effects of violent pornography (Donnerstein & Hallam, 1978). In the first phase, a male or female confederate gave nine shocks to subjects, indicating a negative evaluation of essays that subjects had written. Subjects were then exposed to either an aggressive or erotic film containing homosexual acts between two women or they were not exposed to a film. Finally, in a teacher–learner situation subjects were given an opportunity to shock the confederate with the Buss aggression machine. "Disinhibition" consisted of instructions by the experimenter encouraging subjects to shock the confederate. After 10 minutes of quiet rest, subjects were given a second opportunity to deliver shocks to the confederate.

The results showed that on the first set of teacher–learner trials, subjects who viewed the aggressive or erotic films delivered more intense shocks to the confederate than did subjects who saw no film and that there were no differences as a function of sex of target. On the second set of teacher–learner trials, however, a separate statistical analysis indicated that men who had been exposed to erotica were more aggressive against female learners than against male learners. Thus, when subjects were told to shock a confederate who earlier had frequently shocked them and they had viewed a film depicting sexual behavior between two lesbians, subjects gave more shocks to the female confederate than to the male confederate.

In a subsequent study, Donnerstein (1980) backed away from these complex procedures. In an essay-writing procedure, a male or female confederate either gave male subjects many shocks or gave only one shock. After the male subjects were angered, they were exposed to one of three films: (a) a talk show interview, (b) a young couple engaged in consensual sexual actions, or (c) a man with a gun forcing a woman to have sexual intercourse. The talk show film produced less physiological arousal in pretesting than did the other two films.

Results showed that the least aggression occurred in the neutral film condition and that the most aggression occurred in the aggressive and erotic film condition. The subjects were more aggressive against female than male victims only in the aggressive and erotic film conditions. A puzzling aspect of this finding is that it occurred whether the subjects had been provoked or not. Although a manipulation check indicated that provocation produced more anger than did the control condition, all subjects rated themselves on the nonangry side of a 5-point scale, anchored by *angry* (5) and *nonangry* (1).

The strong effect of the aggressive and erotic film on subjects who expressed little anger may be explained by the strong impact of the film as a demand cue. Some subjects were attacked by a woman, were exposed to a film in which a man attacked a woman, and then were given a socially sanctioned opportunity to attack the provoking woman. In this condition, subjects were more aggressive than in the other conditions, in which one or more of these elements were omitted. For example, when subjects were attacked by a woman, viewed a talk show, and were given an opportunity to attack the provoking woman, the subjects were not very aggressive.

Still another set of procedures was invented to demonstrate that violent pornography can increase aggressiveness against women (Donnerstein & Berkowitz, 1981). After male subjects had been angered by either a male or female confederate, they viewed one of four films with varying subject matter: (a) a talk show, (b) sexual behavior of consenting adults, (c) aggressive–erotic behavior with a positive outcome, and (d) aggressive–erotic behavior with a negative outcome. The last two films were the same except for the endings. A young woman arrives to study with two young men, who have been drinking. They tie her up, strip her, slap her, and sexually attack her. In the positive-outcome condition, the woman is shown smiling and on friendly terms with the men. Prior to exposure to this version of the film, subjects were told that the woman would become a willing participant in the sexual activities. In the negative-outcome condition, the woman is shown suffering during the last 30 seconds of the film, and the introduction had indicated that she would find the experience humiliating and disgusting.

The pattern of results indicated that it is possible to create conditions in which men will aggress against women more than against men after being exposed to a pornographic film, but that these conditions are very restrictive. If a man is attacked by a woman, views violent pornography with a positive ending, and is given a legitimated opportunity by an authority in the situation to retaliate against the provoker, then the viewing of violent pornography may increase the intensity of aggressive behavior. The presence of erotica in the film appeared to be irrelevant. The same effect might be obtainable after viewing any film showing violence against women. In a subsequent experiment, Donnerstein and Berkowitz (1981) used the same procedures and the same four films. A female confederate either frequently shocked subjects (indicating a negative evaluation) or gave them only one shock (indicating a positive evaluation). Subjects each viewed one of the four films and then were given an opportunity to shock the confederate. The researchers reported that "for angered subjects both the positive and negative aggressive erotic films increased aggression above that displayed in the neutral and purely erotic film conditions" (Donnerstein & Berkowitz, 1981, p. 720). It was also reported that nonangered subjects in the positive-ending aggressive–erotic film condition delivered higher levels of shock than did nonangered subjects in the neutral or erotic film conditions. This latter finding was attributable to the power of the violent content of the film to arouse an aggressive drive in the viewers and the reduced inhibitions produced by the positive outcome of the film. The idea is that if women want to be hurt and they like it, then men should be motivated to hurt them. According to Donnerstein and Berkowitz, male subjects can be induced to have this idea, at least for a short time in the laboratory. Apparently, the effects of even violent pornography tend to be short lived. Malamuth and Ceniti (1986) found no effects of long-term exposure to either violent or nonviolent pornography on male subjects' use of aversive stimulation against women.

Research on Pornography and Aggression

In reviewing the effects of pornography on aggressive behavior, Donnerstein and Linz (1986) concluded that "there is no evidence for any 'harm'-related effects from sexually explicit materials" (p. 615).[4] Inconsistency of findings and interpretative problems have been endemic to this area of research. Across studies there has been a lack of standardization of erotic stimuli, even by the same experimenters. Among the sexual stimuli used have been cutouts of pictures from magazines, drawings copied from pornographic literature, and clips from X-rated feature films. Verbal labels have been given to these stimuli, such as *beefcake, cheesecake,* and *aggressive pornography,* and they are treated as if they vary only on the single dimension of arousal. The meaning of the sexual stimuli in the context of the cover story given by the experimenter and the sequence of events experienced by the subject cannot effectively be held constant while only the intensity of arousal produced by all of these events is manipulated. Simply put, it is not possible to manipulate arousal in the laboratory without also affecting the meanings that subjects give to the manipulations.

The extremely narrow set of conditions under which viewing violent pornography disinhibits aggression by men against women may be explained in terms of demand cues. When an experimenter legitimates attacking a woman after she has attacked a male subject and the man has been shown a rape scene that has a positive outcome, men are more aggressive against women. The results from other experiments on the effects of viewing sexual stimuli on aggressive behavior have not provided systematic evidence favoring any known theory and have not provided a basis for any practical

---

[4]Research on the effects of pornography on attitudes toward women has been equally inconsistent. See our discussion of this topic in chapter 11.

generalizations for public policy. This is a dismal conclusion after so much work has been done.

SUMMARY AND CONCLUSIONS

The research by Zillmann (1983) and his associates has not provided consistent and reliable support for the notion of excitation transfer or for Schachter's (1964) two-factor theory of emotions. The transfer process posed by excitation transfer theory carries some dissipated arousal forward from a secondary source to a provocation situation and adds to the arousal associated with anger. The typical research procedures, on the other hand, first induce provocation and subsequently provide a secondary source of arousal, and only then are subjects given an opportunity to aggress against the person who angered them. Thus, the sequence of procedures in most research and the process posed by Zillmann's theory have not been the same. If this analysis is correct, then the research would not be a good basis for evaluating the theory; thus, it remains for excitation transfer theory to be thoroughly tested.

In an important analysis of the concept of physiological arousal, Neiss (1988) argued that it is not possible to manipulate intensity of arousal states without also affecting psychological processes.[5] We have shown that experimenters have manipulated exercise, exposure to violent and pornographic films, and exposure to threats and aversive stimuli from others. It should be expected that what individuals think about their experience will vary across these different stimulus conditions, even if the degree of arousal is at the same level in all conditions. These manipulations induce arousal states, but they also carry psychological meaning for the individual. Thus, clear interpretations of studies on excitation transfer in terms of arousal affects cannot confidently be made.

We noted at the end of chapter 2 that the concept of drive, which is at the base of frustration–aggression theory, has been abandoned by learning theorists, who invented the construct. Psychophysiologists have also abandoned the notion of undifferentiated arousal (Neiss, 1988; Venables, 1984). In a classic paper, Lacey (1967) dealt a death blow to the notion of general arousal. He showed that electroencephalographic, autonomic, motor, psychological, and other behavior systems are imperfectly correlated and complex interacting systems. Within the ANS, which most psychologists refer to when they speak of arousal, the relationships between independent measurements are very weak. For example, one study (Eliot, 1964) found few significant correlations between measures of heart rate,

---

[5]We would soften Neiss's (1988) point. It may be very difficult to separate arousal from cognitive meanings, but it may not be impossible.

skin potential, skin-conductance level, and skin-conductance response. The problem of measuring autonomic arousal is compounded by the fact that the relationships among factors appear to vary both within individuals over time and across individuals. Cattell (1972) cautioned that a minimum of six physiological measures are necessary to provide a reliable index of autonomic arousal. Few studies relating arousal to aggressive behavior have used as many as three measures, most have used no more than two, and some have only inferred arousal from scales administered to subjects asking them about their experiential states. The last approach is suspect because research has typically indicated low and even negative correlations between reports of emotional experiences and autonomic responses (Buck, 1985).

Excitation transfer theory assumes a process of misattribution; however, the evidence for a misattribution process is less than overwhelming (Cotton, 1981; Reisenzein, 1983). Schachter and Singer's (1962) original experiment, which spawned the idea of misattribution, has been subjected to a great deal of criticism (cf. Leventhal, 1980), and other researchers have failed to replicate the original findings (G. Marshall & Zimbardo, 1979; Maslach, 1979).

Research has tended to support Zillmann's (1983) view that high arousal interferes with cognitive control and, consequently, disinhibits aggressive behavior. Such a mechanism would account for impulsive aggression. Furthermore, arousal may interfere with the impact of excuses and justifications in the inhibition of aggressive behavior. We incorporate these effects of emotional arousal into the social interactionist perspective presented in the second half of this book.

In conclusion, research on generalized notions of arousal has produced a babel of contradictory data. What we have learned from what may otherwise be considered a cul-de-sac of research is that intensity and valence of emotional state do appear to intensify aggressive behavior, but only under specific sets of conditions. These conditions are that the individual is provoked and chooses a harmdoing response in the situation. Research has also established that viewing nonviolent pornography does not affect aggressive behavior.

4

LEARNING THEORY AND AGGRESSION

The approach to psychology for the first half of the twentieth century was based on learning theory. Although psychoanalysis was emergent, it was never accepted as a legitimate scientific theory. The most prominent psychologists of the time included Ivan Pavlov, Edward Thorndike, Edward Chase Tolman, Clark Hull, B. F. Skinner, Hobart Mowrer, and Kenneth Spence—each of whom had proffered a major theory of behavior. The application and development of these theories to aggressive behavior has been led by Arnold Buss and Albert Bandura. As we show, Buss's theory was a transitional one that focused attention on social factors and personality as variables affecting aggressive behavior. Bandura's social learning theory has been very influential in the study of how people learn aggressive behavior by observing others and has stimulated research on the effects of observing violence in the mass media and the impact of physical punishments by parents on the child's aggressive behavior. In this chapter, we briefly review some basic ideas from learning theory, describe and evaluate the theories of Buss and Bandura, and examine research on the effects of mass media and the intergenerational transmission of violence.

93

CLASSIC LEARNING THEORIES AND AGGRESSION

Learning theories attempt to explain changes in behavior over time by relating environmental factors, such as stimulus associations and reinforcement contingencies, to processes that occur within the individual organism, such as drives and expectations. Controversies between learning theories have focused on the mechanisms that are presumed to mediate observed changes in the behavior of animals and humans.

Three major classes of learning theories of aggression have been proposed: (a) classical conditioning, (b) instrumental learning theory, and (c) cognitive learning theory. Most contemporary psychological theories of aggression include processes proposed by all of these theories. In this chapter, we describe these theories and some of the current controversies that motivate research in human aggression.

Classical Conditioning

Laws of classical conditioning were established by Ivan Pavlov at the turn of the twentieth century. These laws stipulated how reflexes and well-learned behaviors occurring in specific situations could be associated with new stimuli. For example, in his studies with dogs, Pavlov (1927) succeeded in conditioning dogs who already salivated in the presence of meat powder to also salivate in the presence of the sound of a tuning fork, which at the beginning of training did not elicit salivation. Pavlov's theory of classical conditioning is essentially a theory of stimulus substitution in the initiation of already-occurring responses.

Classical conditioning principles are important for Berkowitz's cue-arousal theory of aggression. Recall the experiment reported in chapter 2 in which weapons were placed on a shock apparatus. Subjects in a weapons condition gave a victim more shock than did those in a no-weapons condition (Berkowitz & LePage, 1967). According to Berkowitz, the sight of the weapons elicited associated ideas, images, and emotional reactions learned by subjects in the past. These internal reactions then served to enhance the aggressive responses of provoked subjects. This kind of analysis has led Berkowitz (1981b) to conclude that the trigger can pull the finger.[1]

Instrumental Learning Theory

Theories of instrumental learning are more concerned with changes in behavior. Thorndike (1913), an early instrumental theorist, focused on

---

[1]Many current researchers in the area of cognition and emotion have moved away from classical conditioning principles when discussing the development and learning of meanings and rules that regulate behavior.

how the organism learns to perform new responses to environmental stimuli. For Thorndike, reinforcements strengthened stimulus-response associations, and punishments weakened associations. This law of effect was the primary principle underlying the learning process. If aggression reduces an unpleasant internal state, removes obstacles to the attainment of reinforcements, or protects the organism from external dangers, then it is more likely to occur in a subsequent and similar situation. The law of effect also proposes that punishment of aggressive behavior will reduce the likelihood of reoccurrence of similar behavior. Research has found that reinforcements appear to strengthen aggressive behavior but that the effects of punishments are very complex.

Reinforcement of Aggressive Behavior

Reinforcements can be used to train animals to fight. Mice paired with a restricted mouse gained a history of success in fighting and soon began to attack all mice (J. P. Scott, 1958). The removal of a negative state, referred to as *negative reinforcement,* has a similar effect. N. E. Miller (1948) shocked rats but turned off the electric current when they began to fight. Removal of the shock was associated with fighting, and rats exposed to the training procedures displayed an increase in fighting behavior. Research with children has indicated that aggressive behavior increases when it is successful in eliminating attack by other children (Hartup, 1974) and in reducing or avoiding aversive treatment by others (Patterson, 1982). Aggressive children learn that they can reduce unwanted behaviors of others by using aggression.

An undesirable response can be eliminated, according to learning theory, by rewarding a competing response. As the rewarded response increases in strength (i.e., frequency), it will replace the undesirable response, which is not rewarded and hence is weakened. This response substitution principle was demonstrated to be applicable to aggressive behavior by P. Brown and Elliot (1965). They observed 3- and 4-year-old children during free-play periods at a nursery school and counted the number of physical aggressive responses (e.g., hits, teases, interferences, and strikes) and verbal aggressive responses (e.g., threats and disparagements) performed by each child. After establishing the base rates of aggressive behavior for 2 weeks, teachers selectively praised cooperative and peaceful behavior and ignored aggressive behavior. Another 1-week observation period followed; then, after another 3-week delay, the reinforcements of nonaggressive behavior by teachers were reinstated for another 2-week period. A final week of rating the aggressiveness of the children completed the study.

Results indicated that the reinforcement of cooperative and peaceful behavior produced a dramatic, immediate decrease in both physical and verbal forms of aggressive behavior. Although verbal aggression remained low through the following 3-week delay period, physical aggression returned to its pretreatment level. A further decrease in both physical and verbal forms of aggression occurred during the second treatment period. These results are consistent with the belief that aggressive behavior follows the general law of learning substitutive responses.

Cowan and Walters (1963) used a ratio schedule of reinforcements with young boys. They gave some boys marbles every time they punched a toy clown and gave other boys marbles after every third or every sixth punch. When the reinforcing marbles were no longer provided, the continuation of the aggressive behavior was stronger, the lower the ratio of reinforcements the children had received. This result is consistent with a partial reinforcement effect, which has been demonstrated to occur for a wide range of responses across many species of animals (cf. Hilgard & Bower, 1975). The *partial reinforcement effect* refers to the fact that the lower the ratio of reinforcements received by organisms, the more slowly they will learn, but the more resistant the learned behavior will be to extinction (i.e., elimination).

Consistent with the principles of classical conditioning, it has been found that neutral stimuli can take on secondary reinforcing properties by repeated associations with primary reinforcers. According to Keller and Shoenfeld (1950), "a stimulus that is not originally a reinforcing one . . . can become reinforcing through repeated association with one that is" (p. 232).

The acquisition of a secondary reinforcer can be illustrated by procedures frequently used in a Skinner box. An animal is trained to press a bar to obtain a food pellet. A light is turned on after the bar press and just before the pellet appears, and the light remains on for a couple of seconds after the pellet is received. After a number of trials, the light becomes a secondary reinforcer; that is, the light can now be used to condition the animal to perform a new response.

If a stimulus is frequently associated with a large number of primary reinforcers, it may gain strong reinforcing powers. Powerful secondary reinforcers paired with many reinforcements are referred to as *generalized reinforcers*. Verbal statements of approval, disapproval, approbation, credit, and blame can be interpreted as generalized reinforcers. Parents frequently accompany tangible rewards with statements of approval and indicate disapproval while delivering corporal or other forms of punishment. Aggressive conduct may also earn approval from the peer group and bring whatever privileges that accompany being a dominant member of a peer group (Buehler, Patterson, & Furniss, 1966).

Punishment and Aggression

Instrumental learning theorists view punishment as a stimulus. One viewpoint is that punishment is an aversive stimulus, that is, a stimulus that the organism experiences as unpleasant. Primary punishing stimuli are believed to be inherently aversive; they include electric shocks, loud noises, pinching, air blasts, intracranial brain stimulation, biting, bright lights, and stimuli aversive only to particular species (e.g., snakes for chimpanzees). Thorndike's (1913) law of effect provided a test of a stimulus as aversive: If an organism attempts to escape from or avoid a stimulus, then the stimulus may be considered a punisher (i.e., it is aversive).

Research has established that punishment of previously reinforced responses suppresses them. Chasdi and Lawrence (1955) divided nursery school children into two groups and allowed them to play with dolls. One of the groups was verbally criticized for displaying aggression during play. The children who were punished displayed less hostility and aggression in subsequent doll play than did children in the control condition. Unfortunately, it is difficult to interpret these results, because the aggressive behavior involved was with inanimate objects and probably involved fantasy.

Response suppression effects have been more clearly shown in infrahumans. Fighting between pairs of rats can be suppressed by randomly presenting electric shocks (Azrin, 1970), by pinching the rats' tails (Baenninger & Grossman, 1969), and by electrically stimulating a hypothalamic center in the brain (Stockman & Glusman, 1969). Aggression, if one follows A. H. Buss's (1961) definition, requires delivery of noxious stimuli to another, presumably live, organism. The strength of the suppression of aggression is directly related to the intensity of the aversive stimulation (Appel, 1963; Azrin, 1960; Camp, Raymond, & Church, 1967). Thus, the effects of punishment on aggressive behavior appear to be the same as the effects of punishment on any other form of behavior.

G. C. Walters and Grusec (1977) noted that punishing stimuli, such as shock, sometimes facilitate or invigorate rather than suppress behavior. They attributed this energizing effect of shocks to the ability of any stimulus, including aversive stimuli, to acquire the ability to serve as a signal for positive reinforcement. That is, an aversive stimulus may be associated with rewards and, hence, may act as a cue in the same way that bells and lights do in instrumental learning. For example, a child may learn that attention and hugs follow a spanking, and to gain these nurturant responses from parents, the child may engage in negative attention seeking.

The energizing effects of punishment have been attributed to a change from reinforcing to nonreinforcing conditions, sometimes referred to as *frustrative nonreward* (Amsel, 1958; J. S. Brown & Farber, 1951). The increase in motivation adds to the amount of drive in the organism, thereby intensifying subsequent behavior. The more vigorous behavior following frustrative nonreward or punishment is more likely to be interpreted as aggression than are less intense responses, even though in the former there is no intent to cause harm.

Punishment may suppress behavior because it causes the organism to engage in responses that are incompatible with the previously learned (and now suppressed) behavior (Guthrie, 1939). For example, if punishment causes the organism to freeze, it will not continue to fight with another animal, despite past successes in fights. Punishment may also undermine the organism's motivation to perform certain behaviors (Estes, 1969): If a child disrupts a classroom to seek approval from peers, punishment might have the effect of reducing his or her motivation for approval rather than reducing the specific behaviors involved in classroom disruption.

A. H. BUSS'S THEORY OF AGGRESSION

Arnold Buss (1961, 1971) applied the instrumental learning theories of Thorndike and Skinner to aggressive behavior. The organism has no innate mechanism that requires expression or that ensures that specific stimuli will activate harmdoing behavior. According to Buss, aggressive behavior is learned, like any other instrumental behavior, through rewards and punishments. *Aggression* simply refers to a subclass of all behaviors and is to be explained in the same fashion as rats pressing bars in a Skinner box. Buss (1971) considered a behavior to be aggression whenever "one individual delivers noxious stimuli to another" (p. 9).

A. H. Buss distinguished between angry aggression, which is reinforced by pain cues, and instrumental aggression, which is directed toward achieving other goals. Although this distinction is consistent with Berkowitz's (1989) two systems of reactive and instrumental aggression, Buss considered instrumental aggression to be more important. Instrumental aggression was further described as including physical and verbal, active and passive, and direct and indirect aggression.

Physical aggression consists of inflicting pain on another organism. *Verbal aggression* is a vocal response that delivers noxious stimuli in the form of rejection and threat. Direct aggression occurs in the presence of and is aimed at the victim, whereas indirect aggression may consist of harming the victim from a distance. Forms of indirect aggression include spreading vicious gossip and slashing the tires of a victim's automobile. Active aggression requires an instrumental response that delivers the noxious stimulation to the victim, whereas passive aggression involves an action or inaction that blocks the target person from obtaining a desired goal. The harm experienced by the victim of passive aggression often occurs in the absence of the aggressor. Active and direct aggression allow the victim to clearly identify and retaliate against an aggressor, whereas passive and indirect aggression may allow the aggressor to escape identification, responsibility, and punishment.

A. H. Buss specified that the strength of a particular aggressive response is a function of four factors. First, a history of reinforcements for aggressive behavior will increase its strength. An animal with extensive experience of fighting and a history of winning (i.e., reinforcement) will be more aggressive than one with little antecedent experience or a history of losing (i.e., punishments). Second, antecedent experiences may affect the individual in a way that intensifies aggressive responses to subsequent events. Third, social facilitation of aggressive behavior will occur if social norms support the expression of hostility in a given group. Finally, temperament or personality may directly affect and strengthen aggressive behavior. Characteristics such as the impulsiveness of the individual and an ability to tolerate frustration are aspects of personality that affect the probability and intensity of aggressive behavior.

Reinforcements and Instrumental Aggression

The frequency and magnitudes of rewards and punishments are proposed to strengthen or weaken aggressive behaviors, thereby affecting both the probability of their occurrence and their intensity. Support was provided for this generalization by Geen and Pigg (1970). Half of their subjects were given verbal approval by the experimenter for delivering shocks, whereas the other subjects were not praised. Verbally reinforced subjects gave more shocks that were of higher intensities than did nonreinforced subjects. Furthermore, reinforced subjects subsequently provided more aggressive responses in a word association test. Similar findings were reported by Loew (1967), who rewarded hostile verbal responses made by college students. In comparison with students who had been rewarded for affectively neutral words, students in the hostile-reward condition subsequently delivered more punishments to another person. Geen and Stonner (1971) found that subjects who were praised for increasing intensities of shocks in the teacher–learner situation were more punitive toward the learner than were nonreinforced subjects.

These verbal reinforcement studies are not without interpretative problems. A very serious source of contamination in social psychological experiments is in the form of demand characteristics. Sometimes experimenters inadvertently include procedures in their research that provide cues to subjects about the behavior that the experimenter wants to confirm a hypothesis. When an experimenter praises subjects for performing a particular response, it would be a fairly significant cue for informing them about what the experimenter desires. There has been strong evidence that subjects will comply to almost any demand or suggestion made by an experimenter (Orne, 1962). Thus, a demonstration that subjects will do what the experimenter clearly wants them to do is hardly a generalizable principle about the enhancing effects of secondary reinforcers.

An information interpretation of social reinforcers is consistent with a demand-characteristics explanation of the enhancing effects of verbal praise on the use of electric shocks by experimental subjects. Social reinforcers may be effective because of their information value, not because they reward the individual. When an adult says "good" to a child, it informs the child about what behaviors the adult wants the child to perform. To the degree that the child wishes to please the adult or foresees that complying will achieve instrumental objectives, the more effective the social reinforcer will be.

Clearly reinforcing aggressive behavior does increase its frequency, and, given the appropriate contingency conditions, reinforcement may also directly affect escalation of intensity. Furthermore, partial reinforcement effects and response substitution also apparently apply to aggressive behavior. These findings are supportive of A. H. Buss's view of aggression as instrumental behavior.

Antecedent Experiences

The state of the organism prior to an event that instigates aggression is important in determining the strength of aggressive responses. An individual who has previously experienced attack, frustration, or annoyance may be more aggressive than someone who has not had these experiences. Annoyers are aversive stimuli not specifically directed at the individual, may at times be experienced as frustrating or irritating, and may contribute to causing aggressive behavior. A. H. Buss accepted that arbitrary frustration may sometimes lead to aggression, but he also recognized that the individual may learn almost any other response to frustration. However, the exact conditions under which annoyers lead to aggression are unknown at the present time.

The physiological arousal and tension associated with the emotion of anger intensifies aggression. Anger has drive properties and can lower the threshold for aggressive behavior. However, anger does not always lead to aggression, and many forms of instrumental aggression occur without anger as an antecedent condition. The emotion of anger is a temporary state of the organism and is to be distinguished from hostility. The latter is an attitude that endures over time and involves negative evaluations of people and events. Hostility develops out of rejection, past attacks, and deprivations and may be inferred when aggressive attacks appear as acts of vengeance.

Social Facilitation

The probability and form of aggression will to some extent depend on social factors, such as victim characteristics and social norms. Victim characteristics may be viewed within the context of stereotypes held by the actor. People tend to have stereotypes about members of various social categories. Members of stereotyped groups may be disliked, and it may be easier to aggress against a disliked person than against an attractive person. Donnerstein, Donnerstein, Simon, and Ditrichs (1972) found that White students delivered more intense shocks to Black victims than to White victims when the victims could not retaliate but were less aggressive toward Black victims when the victims could retaliate. However, laboratory research has not always provided support for this hypothesis. It has been found that highly prejudiced White subjects were more aggressive against Black victims but that they were also more aggressive against White victims than were less prejudiced subjects (Genthner, Shuntich, & Bunting, 1975). Similar results were found in a comparison of prejudiced and relatively unprejudiced Black subjects (L. Wilson & Rogers, 1975).

Gender is a victim characteristic that affects the likelihood of aggression. The norm that men should not harm women is reflected in the finding that college men gave less intense shocks to women in a teacher–learner paradigm than to other men (A. H. Buss, 1966a; S. P. Taylor & Epstein, 1967). However, women do not hesitate to give intense shocks to men. This norm is learned at an early age: Shortell and Miller (1970) found that sixth-grade boys and girls gave higher intensities of noxious noise to boys than to girls.

A. H. Buss suggested that group tendencies and attitudes toward aggression will affect the level of aggressiveness of individuals in the group. Children imitate those around them; if models display aggressive behavior, then children will follow in their footsteps. Furthermore, if there is considerable aggression in a group, the likelihood of being attacked is high, and anger stimuli are probably frequent and intense. Countering aggression with aggression may also be praised and valued in certain groups, thus encouraging individuals to be aggressive and reinforcing such behavior.

Personality and Temperament

Temperament refers to characteristics associated with behavior that remain relatively unchanged over the course of an individual's life. The aspects of temperament that A. H. Buss associated with aggressiveness are impulsiveness, intensity of reaction, activity level, and independence.

Individuals differ in their ability to delay gratification and to tolerate frustration. Some people tend to react to any frustrating circumstance with immediate reactive aggression. Such an impulsive person will quickly respond to anger-provoking situations. Although a disposition to be aggressive will depend on the consequences of aggressive behavior (rewards and punishments), an impulsive person is more likely to be aggressive than is a more deliberative and tolerant person.

In two studies using the Buss aggression machine, Caprara et al. (1986) investigated temperaments of irritability and emotional susceptibility. *Irritability* was defined as a readiness to take up an offensive attitude, and *emotional susceptibility* was assumed to reflect a tendency to be defensive. Subjects identified through responses on paper-and-pencil tests as high in irritability or high in emotional susceptibility were more aggressive than those identified as low in irritability or emotional susceptibility. These differences in aggressiveness between temperament types must be interpreted cautiously because they only occurred in conditions where the subjects had been given feedback that they had performed poorly on a task and when they had been aroused by intense physical exercise. It is possible that emotionally susceptible and irritable people interpret their experiences differently from people who have opposite personalities and that the interpretations, not the temperament types, mediate the aggressive behavior. In other words, temperament may be indirectly rather than directly related to aggressive behavior.

Evaluation of A. H. Buss's Theory

The theory proposed by A. H. Buss enriches basic instrumental learning theory as applied to the study of aggression. Buss pointed to antecedent experiences specifically related to frustration, exposure to aversive conditions, success in aggressive encounters, social facilitation by others, and the personality of the individual as factors contributing to aggressive behavior. In other words, Buss attempted to bring together aspects of learning theory, social psychology, and the study of personality to explain aggressive behavior.

The strong emphasis on principles of learning at the core of his theory required that A. H. Buss emphasize the past experiences of the individual as the primary cause of current behavior. The view of the person is of someone who is pushed by historical forces to engage in any current behavior, depending on environmental circumstances that trip off the learned associations. In fairness to Buss, it should be noted that his theory evolved in a historical era when behavioristic learning theory was at its height. Current learning theories emphasize the pull of anticipated consequences (i.e., incentives) and not the push of past rewards and punishments. The organism is now viewed as a kind of decision maker who assesses choice alternatives in terms of the probabilities and values of outcomes and then responds on the basis of an evaluation of those alternatives (Hilgard & Bower, 1975). Bandura's (1973, 1983) social learning theory is an example of such an approach to explaining aggression.

BANDURA'S SOCIAL LEARNING THEORY

Bandura (1973, 1983) has developed a cognitively oriented social learning theory of aggression that does not depend on internal drives. The major cause of aggression, according to Bandura, is the pull of anticipated positive consequences (i.e., incentives). People weigh the potential gains of engaging in aggressive behavior against the potential costs of doing so. Aggression occurs when the anticipated net gains outweigh the anticipated outcomes for alternative possible behaviors. It is these anticipated outcomes, and not the automatic reactions determined by frustration or aversive stimulation, that produce aggressive behavior. Robbers and rapists are motivated by the gains or pleasures anticipated by their actions and not by antecedent experiences of pain. Of course, humans may miscalculate or have distorted or unrealistic notions about means–ends relations.

Aversive conditions will facilitate rather than cause aggressive behavior, but only when the individual has previously learned to respond that way to aversive stimuli. Bandura did not subscribe to Berkowitz's (1982) view that aversive stimuli are innately associated with an appetitive drive to hurt others. Instead, Bandura believed that reactions to negative events depend on the cognitive evaluations of the individual. Frustration, negative affect, or anger can lead to any kind of response, depending on the learning history and current circumstances of the individual. For example, Davitz (1952) found that aggressively trained children were more aggressive following frustration, whereas cooperatively trained children were more cooperative following frustration.

Bandura (1983) stated that "most aggressive activities—whether they be dueling with switchblade knives, or vengeful ridicule—entail intricate skills that require extensive learning" (p. 4). This learning process is not to be confused with the performance of the behavior. Social learning theory clearly distinguishes between learning a behavior pattern, the factors that instigate the behavior, and the conditions that maintain the skill that has been learned.

Acquisition of Aggressive Behavior

Although people sometimes learn aggressive behavior through trial-and-error processes, most complex skills are learned vicariously. People learn by observing others (i.e., models), who use various skills to obtain goals in a variety of situations. Family members, acquaintances in the community, and symbolic models in the mass media all contribute to the learning of the individual.

Learning by observation involves four interrelated processes (Bandura, 1977). First, the individual must notice or pay attention to the cues, behavior, and outcomes of the modeled event. Second, the observations must be encoded into some form of representation in memory. Third, these cognitive processes are transformed into imitative response patterns that are new for the individual. Finally, given the appropriate inducements or incentives, the learned behavior pattern will be performed.

A large number of studies have been carried out to demonstrate these processes of observational learning. In the procedures typically used, young children have been given the opportunity to observe an adult who has access to a number of props in a room. The props include crayons and coloring books; a ball; a rubber mallet; a toy gun and associated arrows with rubber tips; and, most prominently, a large inflated plastic clown (referred to as *Bobo*). The adult model approaches Bobo, makes hostile comments, and then hits Bobo on the head with the mallet, picks Bobo up and throws it to the floor, repeatedly punches it on the nose, kicks it, and so on. In some instances, another person enters the room and rewards the model for good behavior with a candy bar. The children are then either asked to recall as much as they can of what they observed or are placed in a room with props, where their behavior is observed.

The above procedures have produced a rich set of findings. Children have imitated a model's aggressive conduct if the model is reinforced for the behavior. In a study by Hicks (1968a), children saw a model receive praise, condemnation, or no evaluation from another adult for aggressive behavior directed toward Bobo. The children exhibited the most imitative aggression when the model had been praised and showed the least imitation when the model had been condemned. When the adult who had sanctioned the model was not present, the type of sanction had no impact on imitative aggression. Thus, when the incentive was removed from the situation, children no longer imitated the aggressive behavior of the model who had been rewarded. Although children may not immediately imitate the behavior of models, the effect of observing aggressive behavior may occur after long delays. It has been found that children can recall or repeat aggressive behavior months after they have watched a model perform it (Hicks, 1968b).

According to Bandura (1983), characteristics of the model are important in the learning of imitative aggression:

> Models differ in the extent to which their behavior is likely to be successful in producing valued outcomes. People are most frequently rewarded for following the behavior of models who are intelligent, who possess certain social and technical competencies, command social power, and who, by their adroitness, occupy high positions in various status hierarchies. (p. 128)

Research has indicated that model characteristics do affect imitation of aggressive behavior by children. Grusec and Mischel (1966) found that high-status regular teachers were imitated more than low-status substitute teachers. Nurturant models were also more imitated by children. However, liking for a model did not affect the punitive behavior of college students toward another person who had insulted them (R. A. Baron & Kepner, 1970).

Instigating Conditions for Aggressive Behavior

Once a behavior pattern is learned, it can be used as a way of manipulating the environment to achieve desired outcomes. Social learning theorists have specified a number of instigators for vicariously learned aggressive behavior, including incentives, modeling, instructions, and delusions (Bandura, 1983, pp. 18–20).

Observational learning conveys information to the individual about what types of actions are likely to be rewarded (or punished) and the stimulus conditions under which it would be appropriate to engage in them. When an individual is in a situation similar to one in which a model had been observed, relevant cognitive associations learned vicariously are likely to occur, an anticipation of the desired outcome attained by the observed model is elicited, and aggressive behavior is performed as a means to attain the anticipated and desired goal. It should be noted that no drive or energy is postulated as pushing the person into behaving; rather, the cognitive associations that allow the person to anticipate the future pull the behavior.

The individual can also learn by observing models to anticipate that aggressive behavior would incur costs. Bandura (1983) suggested that the effectiveness of punishment will be affected by the probability and value of the punishment, its timing and duration, the benefits to be gained from aggressive action, and the perceived availability of alternative means to achieving the goal. Punishment may be an ineffective method for inhibiting aggressive behavior because it carries risks of escalation and counterattack. By using punishment, an agent serves as a model, and if the agent controls the observer–target, then the model's behavior is reinforced. This modeled action can then teach the observer–target to use punishing means to attain desired goals in interaction with others. Thus, children who experience corporal punishment at the hands of their parents engage in more fighting (Bandura & Walters, 1963; S. Glueck & Glueck, 1950; M. L. Hoffman, 1970). The evidence can also be construed to indicate that children who engage in fighting are more unruly and, as a consequence, are more often punished by their parents (see chap. 10). Bandura (1986) suggested that often a form of reciprocal determinism occurs: Misbehaving children are punished by parents, and the children imitate the aggressive behavior, bringing about further punishment, and so on.

In an aggressive encounter, Bandura (1973) proposed, expressions of pain by the victim serve as strong inhibitory cues and tend to reduce or stop the relevant behavior. All societies establish strong norms prohibiting violent and destructive actions, although there is a narrow range of justifying conditions for such actions. Pain cues therefore elicit fear of sanctions and self-censure, both of which contribute to a lessening of injurious behavior. Of course, strong incentives may override the inhibitory effects of pain cues, but the latter are not directly reinforcing to the individual. Bandura's position on the effects of pain cues was contrary to that of Berkowitz (1982), who postulated that pain cues reinforce and facilitate appetitive aggression. Recall from chapter 2 that research has produced contradictory findings, supporting and disconfirming both positions.

Observation of models may both teach observers to behave aggressively and instigate performance of aggressive behavior. We have shown that observing a model's success may arouse an expectation that imitative behavior will gain similar rewards. This learning process may not eventuate in an aggressive behavior until the appropriate incentive condition occurs.

According to Bandura (1983), there are four processes by which modeling can instigate aggressive behavior: (a) A *directive function* of modeling serves to inform the observer about the causal means–ends relations in the situation. Careful observation of another person's behavior provides information about the stimulus-response-outcome contingencies in particular situations. By extracting a general principle from observing the model's experience, observers can develop the expectation that under the same conditions, if they imitate the model, they will receive the same outcome obtained by the model. (b) A *disinhibitory function* of a model teaches observers that they can avoid punitive outcomes associated with aggressive conduct. For example, observation of an aggressive model who does not experience any retaliation or punishment may reduce the observers' inhibitions toward engaging in aggressive behavior. (c) Observation of others who engage in aggressive behavior causes *emotional arousal* in the observers, which may increase the likelihood of imitative aggression or may heighten the intensity of aggressive responses. Research has shown that watching fighting increases emotional arousal in children (Cline, Croft, & Courrier, 1973) and in adults (Zillmann, 1971). This increase in emotional tension can contribute to the intensity of subsequent aggressive behavior. (d) Observation of a model may have stimulus-enhancing effects by directing the observers' attention to the kinds of implements or tools being used. When models in experiments use, for example, a rubber mallet or a dart gun against the Bobo doll, the children observing the model's behavior have their attention directed to the use of these tools and their application against targets.

Instructions also serve as instigators of aggressive behavior. In all societies people are taught to obey rules or orders from high-status others. In a series of classic studies of obedience to authority, Milgram (1974) has shown that subjects will deliver increasingly intense shocks to victims who shout for them to stop. Observation of others who obey similar orders increases the tendency to conform and do what one is told (Powers & Geen, 1972).

Maintaining Conditions

So far, we have examined how aggressive behavior is learned and the conditions that activate it. Social learning theory also proposes mechanisms for maintaining the behavior over time. The outcomes of behavior tend to control the likelihood of its future performance. Positive expectations may activate aggressive behavior, but negative consequences and unfulfilled expectations will decrease the tendency to repeat it. On the other hand, the successful achievement of goals through aggressive behavior will encourage the individual to engage in such behavior on future occasions.

An incredible range of conditions may be experienced as reinforcing by an individual. Among them is the reduction of aversive treatment by others. Children who are targets of attack but successfully terminate the aversive treatment by counteraggression learn to be very aggressive in their own conduct (Patterson, Littman, & Bricker, 1967). The individual may fight back even when the immediate consequences are painful if it is believed that such episodes will deter future abuse.

Self-Regulatory Mechanisms

An important feature of social learning theory is the operation of self-regulatory mechanisms. The individual develops referential standards against which to judge his or her own conduct. These standards are acquired both by direct experience and by observing others. When a person's own conduct fails to meet internal standards, the person makes a negative self-evaluation and may then administer self-punishment in the form of self-censure or self-contempt. When conduct meets or exceeds internal standards, the individual makes a positive self-evaluation and may administer self-reward in the form of pride or self-satisfaction.

The individual's internal standards are made in the context of social norms, social comparison processes, and direct experience. The anticipation of self-censure or self-satisfaction can serve to regulate behavior. Anticipatory self-reproach for aggressive conduct inhibits such behavior. On the other hand, there are people who take pride in engaging in aggressive actions. Self-congratulation is a form of self-reinforcement for effectiveness in achieving goals and gaining the respect of other people.

The evidence for self-regulation as applied to aggressive behavior is meager and indirect. Heightened self-efficacy for aggressive behavior was found among more aggressive children in one correlational study (Perry, Perry, & Rasmussen, 1986). Children rated as aggressive by their peers were more confident than were nonaggressive children of their ability to aggress, that their aggression would produce rewards, and that their aggression would reduce annoyances and attacks by other children. The researchers acknowledged that the belief that "aggression pays" (i.e., is an effective way to control others) may serve as a rationalization by aggressive children for their antinormative behavior rather than as a cause of it.

The development of self-regulatory processes does not place all aggressive behavior under self-control. Bandura (1983) stated that

> people do not ordinarily engage in reprehensible conduct until they have justified to themselves the morality of their actions . . . . reprehensible conduct is made personally and socially acceptable by portraying it in the service of moral ends. (p. 31)

Cognitive reinterpretations can take the form of justifying the aggressive behavior, by minimizing, ignoring, or misconstruing the consequences, or by dehumanizing or blaming the victim. Such justifications disinhibit behavior that otherwise would be considered reprehensible and would be inhibited by anticipations of self-punishment.

Evaluation of Social Learning Theory

Research has shown that social learning is an important factor in learning new behaviors. The role of modeling in instigating aggressive behavior and the mechanism of self-control postulated by Bandura (1983) have received less support. Questions have been raised about the interpretation of children's behavior in the Bobo experiments. In addition, some general conceptual and philosophical questions have been raised about social learning theory. We now examine some of these criticisms.

Interpretations of Bobo Studies

A major tenet of social learning theory is that children often learn behavior vicariously and that behavior is also instigated and maintained by models. There can be little question that children do learn what responses to perform by watching a model who is reinforced for punching, kicking, and battering Bobo. Furthermore, children who are given the opportunity will perform many of the same responses. Characteristics of the model, such as nurturance and status, have been shown to increase the likelihood of imitation. All of these findings provide strong support for the theory.

Despite the reliability of the findings discussed above, a question remains about the description of a child's imitative behavior as aggression. Tedeschi, Smith, and Brown (1974) argued that most research on harm-doing is guided by conceptual definitions that an aggressive response is either a behavior that does harm or a behavior where harm was intended. There are no reports in the literature of any damage done to Bobo either by models or by children. Indeed, Bobo is specially constructed to absorb rough treatment.

Is it likely that preschool children intend to harm Bobo after they observe a model fail to do so? The children may simply interpret the situation as rough-and-tumble play or a game of follow the leader. There is no intent to harm in rough-and-tumble play. Unlike aggressive responses, rough-and-tumble play is typically accompanied by smiles and laughter, and the participants remain together afterward (Aldis, 1975). There is no evidence that young children intend to harm Bobo in modeling experiments. Thus, it is questionable whether the behavior studied in Bobo modeling experiments is aggression. Furthermore, preschool children who engage frequently in rough-and-tumble play are less aggressive than other children (Rubin, 1982).

In a study describing the modeling procedure to college students, the observers were asked to evaluate a model and a child in a modeling procedure (Joseph, Kane, Nacci, & Tedeschi, 1977). The model was either destructive or constructive in play toward Bobo (and was reinforced for the behavior), and the child's behavior was described as either *destructive* or *constructive*. Observers attributed imitative behavior of the child to the conduct of the model. The child was perceived as nonaggressive either when behavior was constructive or when hitting and pummeling Bobo imitated the behavior of the model. A child was perceived as aggressive only if his or her behavior was destructive and the model's behavior was constructive. These results suggest that the model is perceived as a permission giver in the modeling situation (Siegel & Kohn, 1959).

Social learning theory ignores the social context within which behavior is learned or performed. One might ask if the behavior learned in the modeling procedures causes children to become more aggressive in playground situations. There is no evidence that such generalization occurs. Few studies have demonstrated the imitation of aggression when live targets are used. Hanratty, Liebert, Morris, and Fernandez (1969) found that children engaged in more assaultive behavior toward a person dressed as a clown after watching a film in which a model assaulted an adult dressed as a clown. These actions included verbal insults, aiming a toy gun at the clown and shooting it, and hitting the clown with a plastic mallet. Interpretation of this behavior as aggression is rendered problematic because clowns are associated with slapstick antics and the children may have believed that it was appropriate to direct assaultive behavior toward the clown.

Results of modeling studies carried out with college students (e.g., R. A. Baron & Bell, 1975) have supported the precepts of social learning theory. However, the laboratory situation is a relatively normless situation in the sense that the standards for behavior are unclear (Nemeth, 1970). Under these conditions, the behavior of subjects is clearly influenced by the observation of other subjects (Asch, 1951). Outside the laboratory many models are available. It is not always clear why an observer chooses to imitate one model rather than another when the models engage in opposite or incompatible behaviors and both are rewarded.

Some Conceptual Issues

Social learning theory does not distinguish between aggressive behaviors and other kinds of behavior. People learn how to manipulate their environment to achieve goals. Behaviors tend to be viewed as skills the person learns, and these skills can be applied to any number of situations. A child may learn to hit, kick, and pummel in the laboratory and then may apply these skills in some other situation if he or she perceived that using them can achieve interpersonal objectives. Unfortunately, even if one accepts this analysis, there is no clear picture of what instigating conditions (i.e., social situations) will evoke which skills. In a similar criticism, Pepitone (1974) charged that social learning theory "does not specify in advance what stimuli control aggression nor what constitute reinforcing events" (p. 770). In the absence of these details, it is impossible to carry out an experiment that could disconfirm the theory.

It is not at all clear in social learning theory how aggressive skills can be differentiated from nonaggressive skills in the absence of social contexts. Suppose aggression is defined as any behavior that could potentially harm someone. In the Bobo studies, hitting and kicking does no harm, but the skills that are learned can potentially do harm. That is why Bandura calls such behavior *aggression*. However, almost any human behavior has the potential to do harm. Consider such skills as pushing buttons, talking, and throwing objects. Any of them could be applied in a specific situation to harm someone. Should these skills be considered aggressive because, in some context after learning them, a person could use them to launch a nuclear missile, contract with an assassin to kill someone, or throw bricks through someone's window? The problem with using potential harm as a criterion for an aggressive response is that almost any human skill can be used to harm others. The consequence would be that all human behavior would have to be considered as aggressive. Nevertheless, the learning-performance distinction in social learning theory is a useful one. We are interested in both how people learn skills and the social conditions in which they will use the skills. The order of events is not only in the direction of learning skills and then applying them, but also the other way around. Given sufficient incentive, people will find ways to achieve their goals. People do not just apply skills to situations, but also form desires that require learning new skills: A person who is frightened may purchase a gun and learn to fire it as a form of self-defense. In general, social learning does not consider the role of social motivation in human behavior. In the social interactionist theory presented in chapters 6–9, we identify the circumstances that elicit harmdoing behavior and the social motives underlying such behavior.

Whatever its shortcomings, Bandura's theory is the most sophisticated theory of aggression from a learning perspective. Few psychologists question the importance of modeling in the study of human behavior or the view that anticipations of future consequences guide human behavior. Yet, social learning theory does not account for emotional outbursts and self-destructive behavior. Also, despite its name, the focus of social learning theory is on the individual, and the theory tends to ignore the reciprocal actions of people engaged in social interactions.

MASS MEDIA VIOLENCE AND VIEWER AGGRESSION

One place where violent behavior is frequently observed is on television and in films. There has been great concern among the public that some viewers, particularly children, will imitate some of this violence. Bandura (1973, 1983) proposed a variety of processes that he believed would lead to media effects on violence. We discuss these processes and suggest some additional ones that may have implications for media effects. Then we review the empirical evidence regarding the general link between media violence and the aggressive behavior of viewers.

Theoretical Mechanisms

The most prominent view of the effect of viewing violence in the mass media is that audiences may imitate violent actors (National Institute of Mental Health, 1982). Extrapolation from laboratory research on modeling would suggest that vicarious reinforcements and legitimation of violent actions would increase the tendency to imitate them. Berkowitz (1993) proposed that exposure to aggressive stimuli may prime emotions and thoughts in the viewer, which then leads to performance of aggressive actions by the viewer. It is also possible that viewing many violent actions would desensitize the individual, so that harm done to other people would be perceived as less negative than it was before exposure. People may also get a false idea of reality from observing a great deal of violence on television and may develop unrealistic fears. These fears and time spent watching television may keep an individual away from routine activities that would increase the risk that he or she would be involved in aggressive encounters. We examine each of these processes more closely.

Imitation of Media Models

Bandura (1973) has argued that television can shape the forms that aggressive behaviors take. Television can teach skills that may be useful for committing acts of violence, and it can direct the viewer's attention to behaviors that they may not have considered. For example, young people may mimic karate and judo moves, or they may learn effective tactics for committing violent crime. Young children may imitate cartoon characters who engage in extreme and fantastic levels of violence from which the target quickly recovers. This information may give direction to those who are already motivated to engage in aggression. Such a modeling process could increase the frequency of violence if people who are motivated to harm someone choose a violent method that they have observed on television as opposed to some nonviolent form of aggression.

There is anecdotal evidence that bizarre violent events have followed soon after their depiction on television, suggesting a form of copycat behavior. In one widely reported case in Boston, Massachusetts, six young men set fire to a woman after forcing her to douse herself with fuel. The scene had been depicted on television 2 nights before. In another instance, four teenagers raped a 9-year-old girl with a beer bottle, enacting a scene similar to one in the made-for-TV movie *Born Innocent*. Such incidents may be coincidental, but they suggest the possibility that unusual and dramatic behaviors on television are imitated by viewers who would never have imagined engaging in such behaviors otherwise.

Modeling can also be used to explain contagion effects observed for highly publicized violence, such as airline hijackings, civil disorders, bombings, and political kidnapping. The tendency for such events to occur in waves suggests that at least some viewers imitate real events that are reported on television. However, the central argument about the relationship between viewing violence on television and viewers' aggressive behavior focuses on fictional events.

Vicarious Reinforcement and Legitimations

Bandura (1973) suggested that television may inform viewers of the positive and negative consequences of violent behavior. Audiences can be expected to imitate violent behavior that is successful in gaining the model's objectives in fictional or nonfictional programs. In addition, when violence is justified or left unpunished on television, the viewer's guilt or fear about engaging in violent behavior is reduced.

It is not at all clear what message is learned from viewing violence on television. In most plots, the protagonist uses violence for legitimate ends, whereas the villain engages in illegitimate violence. The protagonist acts in a measured way against the villain, usually using violence as a last resort. Violence may be used in self-defense or to mete out an appropriate level of punishment to a dangerous or threatening criminal. Although an occasional television program or movie will legitimate vigilantism or the illegal use of force by police, such programming is rare. Television conveys the message that although some forms of violence are necessary and legitimate, criminal violence is evil.

The lessons learned from the media about violence may be similar or redundant to the lessons learned about the use of violence conveyed by other sources. In fact, we suspect that, with the exception of pacifists, most viewers approve of the violent behavior of most protagonists. The influence of television on viewers who already agree with its message would be weak at best. Unlike in real life, the illegitimate use of violence is almost always punished on television. Thus, one could argue that television violence might reduce the incidence of criminal violence, because crime never pays for TV criminals.

Two other factors may limit the effects of any message about the legitimacy or the rewards and costs of violence. First, because the audience is usually aware that the violence is fictional, they may not take any message seriously. Modeling is more likely to occur after viewing nonfiction than after viewing fiction (Berkowitz & Alioto, 1973; Feshbach, 1972). Second, the violent contexts and provocations observed on television are likely to be very different from the contexts and provocations people experience in their own lives. Viewers take context and intentions into account before they model aggressive behavior. Geen (1978) found that, when provoked, college students were more aggressive after viewing vengeful aggression but not after viewing a boxing match (see also Hoyt, 1970). For most subjects, a boxing match is a special context that does not provide information on how to behave in other contexts.

Some viewers may miss the more subtle aspects of television messages. This is particularly likely to be true for young children, who may focus on overt acts rather than on the intentions or contexts in which such acts occur. Collins, Berndt, and Hess (1984) found that kindergarten and second-grade children were relatively unaffected by an aggressor's motives in their understanding of a violent program. They focused more on the aggressiveness of the behavior and its ultimate consequences. However, even if young children imitate the violence of models, it is not at all clear that they will continue to exhibit violence as they get older. When they are older and they pay attention to the intentions and context in violent television, their behavior is more likely to reflect the messages they learn. It is at these later ages that their violent behavior can be dangerous.

Cultural Spillover

Straus (1991) argued that some viewers ignore the distinction between legitimate and illegitimate aggression. According to cultural spillover theory, violence in one sphere of life leads to violence in other spheres (Straus, 1991). This carryover process transcends the bounds between legitimate and illegitimate aggression. In an analysis of the distribution of violence in the United States, L. Baron and Straus (1987) found that the higher a state's score was on a Legitimate Violence Index, the higher its rate of criminal violence was. The index measures the extent to which violence has been used for socially legitimate purposes, such as the frequency of capital punishment and corporal punishment of children. However, even if state statistics are accepted as a meaningful unit of analysis, there are alternative explanations for these correlations. For example, it is likely that high levels of crime lead to more punitive responses from both citizens and governments.

Cognitive Priming

A classical conditioning or cognitive priming approach suggests that modeling does not depend on how viewers interpret the content of media violence. Berkowitz (1984) suggested that the aggressive ideas in violent films can activate other aggressive thoughts in viewers through their association in memory pathways. When one thought is activated, other thoughts that are strongly connected are also activated. Immediately after a violent film, the viewer is primed to respond aggressively because a network of memories involving aggression is retrieved. Any environmental cue can initiate the retrieval of aggressive material from memory. Similarly, Huesmann (1982) suggested that children learn problem-solving scripts in part from their observations of others' behavior. These scripts are cognitive expectations about a sequence of behaviors that may be performed in particular situations. Frequent exposure to scenes of violence may lead children to store scripts for aggressive behavior in their memories that may be recalled in a later situation if any aspect of the original situation—even a superficial one—is present.

Josephson (1987) examined the combined effects of exposure to violent television and retrieval cues in a field experiment with second- and third-grade boys. The boys were exposed to either a violent film—in which a walkie-talkie was used—or a nonviolent film.[2] Later they were interviewed by someone holding either a walkie-talkie or a microphone. After the interview, the boys played a game of field hockey, and their aggressive behavior was recorded. It was predicted that boys who were exposed to both violent television and a walkie-talkie would be most aggressive in the game, because the walkie-talkie would lead them to retrieve scripts associated with the violent film. The hypothesis was confirmed for boys who were, according to teacher ratings, aggressive. Boys who were identified as nonaggressive inhibited their aggression when exposed to the walkie-talkie and the film. Josephson suggested that for these nonaggressive boys, aggression may be strongly associated with negative emotions such as guilt and

---

[2]The boys were also frustrated either before or after the film.

fear, that, when primed, may inhibit aggression. If we accept this post hoc interpretation, it suggests that media violence may increase or inhibit the violent behavior of viewers depending on a viewer's initial predisposition. Such effects are likely to be short-term, and they may have no effect on the overall rate of violence.

Desensitization

Frequent viewing of television violence may desensitize audiences to violence and lead to indifference. Experimental subjects who viewed violent films were less aroused by violence later on (Thomas, Horton, Lippincott, & Drabman, 1977; for a review see Rule & Ferguson, 1986). Heavy viewers of television violence tended to respond less emotionally to violence than did light viewers. However, there is no evidence that desensitization affects violent behavior.[3] Nor is it clear what effect should occur. If viewers become desensitized to violent behavior on television they may become indifferent to its message. In other words, desensitization may reduce the effects of any lessons learned from television violence. As Geen (1983) suggested, if violence is punished on television, indifferent viewers are less likely to learn inhibitions. Indifference would not increase violence by viewers but would instead offset any tendency for television violence to decrease violence among viewers.

Desensitization causes viewers to be less anxious and sensitive about violence. If anxiety about violence inhibits the use of violence, then a lessening of this anxiety might cause a viewer to be more tolerant of violence. This hypothesis has not been directly tested. Evidence cited above has shown that heavy viewing of violence decreases arousal to violence, not anxiety about violence. Although the relationship is complex, the evidence generally shows that arousal can have a direct short-term effect on violence (Zillmann, 1983). If viewers are exposed to a heavy diet of television violence, one might argue that they will be less aroused by violence and, therefore, less likely to engage in violence.

Creating Unrealistic Fear

Bandura (1973) claimed that television distorts knowledge about the dangers and threats present in the real world. The notion that television viewing fosters a distrust of others and a misconception of the world as dangerous has been referred to as the "cultivation effect" (Gerbner & Gross, 1976). There is evidence that heavy television viewers are more distrustful of others and overestimate their chances of being criminally victimized (for a review see Ogles, 1987). The assumption is that these fears will lead

---

[3]It is well known that medical students, who frequently work with cadavers, become desensitized to the gore associated with surgery, but there is no evidence that physicians are more violent than other groups of people.

viewers to perceive threats that do not exist and, therefore, to respond aggressively. It is just as plausible that such fears would lead viewers to avoid aggressive behavior against others if they feel it is dangerous and might lead to victimization. People who fear crime may also be less likely to go out at night or to go places where they may be victimized. If viewing television violence increases fear, it might decrease the level of violence.

Routine Activities

The routine activities approach to crime, which we discuss in chapter 5, suggests that watching television can decrease the incidence of violence in society (Messner, 1986; Messner & Blau, 1987). According to this approach, crime should be less frequent when the routine activities of potential offenders and victims reduce their likelihood of contact. Because people watch television at home, the opportunities for violence, at least with people outside the family, are probably reduced. When people watch television, they may also interact less often with other family members, so the opportunities for domestic violence may be reduced. Messner (1986) and Messner and Blau (1987) found that cities with high levels of television viewing have lower rates of both violent and nonviolent crime. However, in an aggregate analysis of this type, one cannot determine the specific viewing habits of offenders or victims of criminal violence.[4]

Criminal violence is most common among young men, so any activity that keeps young men apart is likely to decrease the incidence of violence. One can imagine many leisure activities that young men might choose on a Saturday night that would increase their risk of engaging in violence. (Perhaps everyone would be safer if young men stayed home and watched violence on television.)

Empirical Evidence of Media Effects on Aggression

The hypothetical mechanisms discussed above do not lead to clear predictions about the effects of exposure to media violence on the aggressive behavior of viewers. In this section, we discuss the empirical evidence regarding media effects. The general relationship between exposure to media violence and aggression has been examined in laboratory experiments, in field experiments, and in longitudinal analyses based on correlational data.

Laboratory Experiments

There is abundant evidence that subjects in laboratory experiments who observe media violence tend to behave more aggressively than subjects

---

[4]Viewing violent television and viewing television are so highly correlated across studies that it does not matter which measure is used in analysis. The notion of catharsis provides an alternative explanation, but it cannot explain the negative relationship between exposure to television violence and the incidence of nonviolent crime.

in control groups. Meta-analyses of these studies have revealed that these effects are consistent and substantial (see Andison, 1977; Hearold, 1986). Experimental studies have also shown that exposure to violent pornography leads to higher levels of aggression against women under certain conditions (e.g., Donnerstein, 1980). Nonviolent pornography, on the other hand, does not appear to encourage aggression against women in the laboratory (see chap. 3).

There are a number of reasons to question the generalizability of laboratory experiments in this area (Cook, Kendzierski, & Thomas, 1983; Freedman, 1984). First, it is not clear whether the measures of aggression in these studies reflect violence outside the laboratory. In experiments, aggression is legitimated and even encouraged by a high-status experimenter, and there is no possibility of retaliation or punishment.

Second, Freedman (1984) questioned the external validity of laboratory studies. He noted that only a small selection of violent shows are viewed by subjects. These shows are probably chosen for the purpose of maximizing effects rather than for their representativeness. Outside the laboratory, violent programs are mixed with other types of programs, which might dilute their effects.

Third, demand cues are particularly strong in these studies. Showing violent films is likely to communicate a message about the experimenter's values and expectations. In particular, these films may communicate a permissive attitude on the part of the sponsors that may disinhibit a subject's aggressive behavior (Reiss, 1986). Subjects who are more aggressive after viewing violence in these experiments have not necessarily internalized the values presented in the media.[5] Such an interpretation is consistent with Hearold's (1986) meta-analysis, which also included studies of effects of exposure to media violence on antisocial behavior generally. The effects of media violence on antisocial behavior were just as strong, if not stronger, than the effects on violence. This suggests that subjects assume a more permissive atmosphere when they are shown a violent film and that their inhibitions about misbehavior generally are reduced. Also, Leyens, Parke, Camino, and Berkowitz (1975) found that subjects delivered more shock to another person when they anticipated that the experimenter would show them violent films; they did not have to actually see the films. Although the investigators attributed this effect to priming, demand cues may have been involved. An experimenter who is willing to show a violent film is perceived as more permissive or more tolerant of aggression.

The argument that laboratory experiments overestimate media effects was disputed by Friedrich-Cofer and Huston (1986). They noted that the

---

[5]Wood, Wong, and Chachere (1991) suggested that demand cues are a type of "sponsor effect" that occurs outside the lab as well. The key issue is whether the values presented in the media have been internalized.

stimuli used in experimental research are brief and often less violent than the television programs typically available at home. In addition, subjects are less likely to be aggressive in laboratory settings because they are inhibited by the presence of experimenters. They concluded that experimental research may underestimate media effects rather than exaggerate them.

Whatever the effects obtained in experiments, external validity is a significant issue. Extralaboratory settings are complex, and many factors coexist that would be controlled in experiments. As a result, any extrapolation of experimental results to real-world settings is problematic. The external validity of experimental results on viewing violence needs to be established in natural settings (Freedman, 1984).

Hennigan et al. (1982) carried out a natural experiment on the difference in crime rates between American cities that had television and those that did not. No effect of the presence or absence of television was found on violent crime rates in a comparison of the two kinds of cities. Furthermore, when cities without television obtained it, there was no increase in violent crimes. Thus, there was no evidence of a relationship between viewing television and aggressive behavior.

The effects of highly publicized events on fluctuations in the homicide and suicide rate over time were examined by Phillips (1983). He found an increase in the number of homicides after a heavyweight championship fight, but only if the fight occurred outside the United States and was highly publicized. Modeling effects were only observed when the losing fighter and the crime victims were similar in race and sex, and the days on which increased homicides occurred were different for Black and White victims: The loss of a prizefight by a White fighter was followed by increases in deaths through homicide of White men on Days 2 and 8. Similarly, the loss of a prizefight by a Black fighter was followed by an increase in homicide deaths for Black men on Days 4 and 5.[6]

This research has not gone without criticism (J. N. Baron & Reiss, 1985; Freedman, 1984; see replies by Phillips, 1986; Phillips & Bollen 1985). An unresolved question raised by Freedman was why effects tended to occur on different days for different races. No causal mechanism is provided to explain the appearance of the modeling effect, its disappearance, and its reappearance at a later time. In addition, the evidence is contradicted by Geen's (1978) finding that subjects in a laboratory experiment were more vengeful after viewing vengeful aggression than after viewing a boxing match.

Field Experiments

The evidence from field experiments is much more inconsistent than that from the laboratory studies. Freedman (1984) reviewed a number of

---

[6]The rise in the homicide rate was not canceled out by a subsequent drop, suggesting that the prizefights affected the incidence and not just the timing of homicides.

such studies that have been carried out in residential homes (Feshbach & Singer, 1971; Leyens, Parke, Camino, & Berkowitz, 1975; Parke, Berkowitz, Leyens, West, & Sebastian, 1977).[7] In these studies, boys were exposed to violent or nonviolent programming, and their aggressive behavior was observed in the following days or weeks. Each of the studies had some important methodological limitations. For example, although the boys in each treatment lived together, the studies used statistical procedures that assumed that each boy's behavior was independent. Even if one overlooks the limitations, the results from these studies are inconsistent. In fact, one of the studies found that the boys who watched violent television programs were less aggressive than the boys who viewed nonviolent shows (Feshbach & Singer, 1971). Similarly, emotionally disturbed children were generally more aggressive during lunch and recess after viewing nonaggressive cartoons than they were after viewing aggressive cartoons (Kadow & Sprafkin, 1993).[8]

Wood, Wong, and Chachere (1991) provided a meta-analytic review of field studies of short-term effects of media violence on unconstrained social interaction. In all of these studies, children or adolescents were observed unobtrusively after being exposed to either an aggressive or nonaggressive film. In 16 studies, subjects engaged in more aggression following exposure to violent films, whereas in 7 studies, subjects in the control group engaged in more aggression. In 5 of the studies, there was no difference between control and experimental groups.

Recall that laboratory experiments found that exposure to media violence generally leads to antisocial behavior. Similar general effects on antisocial behavior have been found in field studies. L. K. Friedrich and Stein (1973) exposed nursery school children to violent cartoons, neutral films, or prosocial television for 12 days over a 4-week period. They found some evidence that children who were exposed to violence displayed more aggression during free play. However, they also found that children who watched violent television had lower tolerance for minor delays and lower task persistence and displayed less spontaneous obedience to school rules. Perhaps viewers imitate the low self-control behaviors of the characters they observe in television and films, rather than violence specifically.

Longitudinal Analyses

Longitudinal studies have been performed to examine whether viewing television violence has a causal effect on subsequent aggressive behavior.

---

[7]We are not aware of any field experiments that have examined the effects of exposure to violent pornography on aggression toward women. Malamuth and Check (1981) did find that college students who viewed films depicting women as victims of violence expressed more rape-supportive attitudes several days later.

[8]Subsequently, Friedrich-Cofer and Huston (1986) suggested that the boys who watched the nonviolent shows disliked them and that their frustration led them to be aggressive.

These studies have estimated the effect that exposure to television at an initial time period has on aggressive behavior measured at a later time period. The main longitudinal evidence for a causal link between viewing violence and aggressive behavior has been provided by Eron, Huesmann, and their associates (Eron et al., 1972; Huesmann & Eron, 1986). The earlier reports examined the effect of exposure to television violence at age 8 on aggressive behavior at age 18. A measure of viewing television violence at Time 1 was obtained by asking parents the names of their children's four favorite television shows. These shows were coded for the level of violence depicted. Aggressive behavior at Time 2 was measured by ratings of aggressiveness by peers, self-reports, and the aggression subscale on the MMPI.[9]

There are some serious methodological shortcomings to Eron et al.'s (1972) studies (see Freedman, 1984; Surgeon General's Scientific Advisory Committee on Television and Social Behavior, 1972). First, the measure of television exposure was based on parents' beliefs about the favorite programs of their children. Parents may not be aware of what their children's favorite shows are, and these shows may be weakly related to the child's total exposure to violence on television. In fact, later research found that parental reports of their children's favorite programs was not strongly correlated with the self-reports of their children (Milavsky, Kessler, Stipp, & Ruben, 1982). Second, effects of television violence were only found for boys and only on the peer nomination measure. Finally, the peer ratings included items referring to antisocial behavior that does not involve aggression.[10]

Three-year longitudinal studies of primary school children were carried out in five countries: Australia, Israel, Poland, Finland, and the United States (Huesmann & Eron, 1986). Aggression was measured by the same peer nomination measure as the one used in the earlier research. The children were asked to name one or two of their favorite programs and to indicate how often they watched them. Complex and inconsistent results were obtained. In the United States, there was no significant effect of television violence on the later aggressiveness of male subjects, but there was a relationship for female subjects (Huesmann & Eron, 1986). An effect of the violence of favorite programs on later aggression was found only for boys who rated themselves as similar to violent and nonviolent television characters (not specifically related to their favorite programs). A similar conditional effect was found for male subjects in Finland, but there was no

---

[9]An important requirement of such studies is that they control for the aggressiveness of the viewer at the earlier time period when looking at the effect of earlier exposure on later aggression. Huesmann, Lagerspetz, and Eron (1984) did so in later reanalyses of their data.

[10]There are other methodological problems with this study. The Time 2 peer nomination measure was obtained after graduation from high school and was based on what the person remembered about the behavior of schoolmates. Furthermore, only 50% of the original sample was interviewed at Time 2, and this latter group contained significantly fewer of the more aggressive children than did the original sample.

effect of viewing television violence on later aggressiveness of female subjects (Lagerspetz & Viemero, 1986). In Poland, a direct effect of violence in favorite programs was found on later aggressiveness for both male and female subjects (Fraczek, 1986). However, this study carried out the regression analyses somewhat differently from the studies in the other four countries. Fraczek combined the 1st- and 2nd-year measures of television violence, controlled for the 1st-year aggressiveness score, and predicted the degree of aggression by viewers in the 3rd year. It is not clear why Fraczek did not report an analysis predicting 2nd- or 3rd-year aggressiveness from the 1st-year measure of exposure to television violence. No effect of early viewing of television violence was found on subsequent aggressiveness for either male or female subjects in Australia (Sheehan, 1986) or among children living in a kibbutz in Israel (Bachrach, 1986). It was reported that a television effect was found for city children in Israel when the measure of aggression was a single item asking "who never fights." But the effect did not occur on the same peer nomination measure that had been used in the other cross-national studies.

Milavsky et al. (1982) obtained negative evidence in a large-scale, methodologically sophisticated longitudinal study based on data collected from 3,200 students in elementary and junior high schools in Fort Worth, Texas, and Minneapolis, Minnesota. The measure of exposure to television violence consisted of a checklist of prime-time and weekend programs. Students simply circled the programs they had watched in the past 4 weeks and a number to indicate how many times they had watched particular programs in that time period.[11] The authors refined the peer nomination measure of aggression used by Eron et al. (1972) to include only intentional acts of harmdoing; items measuring general misbehavior were excluded. There was no evidence that any of the measures of exposure to television violence affected changes in aggressive behavior over time. The authors looked for effects by using corrections for measurement error, a variety of time lags, different subsamples, and alternative measures of exposure to television violence and aggressive behavior. In spite of a thorough exploration of the data, they found no evidence that exposure to violence on television affected the aggressive behavior of children. Although the coefficients in most of the analyses were positive, they were all close to zero and statistically insignificant.[12]

What conclusion should be reached from results of these longitudinal studies about the effects of viewing television violence on subsequent aggressive behavior? The study that used the most accurate measurements

---

[11]Also included were parental reports of a child's favorite programs and self-reports by children of their favorite programs. These measures of exposure to television violence were poor indicators of overall exposure.

[12]The pattern of positive correlations led some critics to reject Milavsky et al.'s (1982) conclusion of no effect (T. D. Cook et al., 1983; Friedrich-Cofer & Huston, 1986).

failed to find an effect. In the studies in which an effect was found, the relationship was between favorite show violence and subsequent aggression, rather than between the amount of exposure to television violence and subsequent aggression, and Milavsky et al. (1982) did not replicate that effect. The findings reported in the cross-national studies were inconsistent and had as many negative findings as positive ones. Therefore we conclude that longitudinal studies have not conclusively demonstrated a relationship between the amount of violence viewed on television and subsequent aggressive behavior.

Conclusions: Viewing Violence and Its Effects on Aggressive Behavior

It is difficult to draw firm conclusions about the effect of exposure to media violence, given the inconsistent findings. On the basis of his review of the evidence, Freedman (1984) concluded that the causal effects of exposure to television have not been demonstrated. After reviewing the same evidence, Friedrich-Cofer and Huston (1986) were convinced that there is an effect. Although the evidence is not conclusive, we agree with those scholars who think that exposure to television violence probably does have a small effect on violent behavior (e.g., T. D. Cook et al., 1983).

We base this tentative conclusion on the following evidence: the consistent results from the laboratory experiments; the supporting evidence from some field experiments; Phillips's (1986) research into the effects of highly publicized violence on homicide and suicide rates; the tendency for hijackings and political violence to occur in waves; and the anecdotal evidence that bizarre events on television are sometimes followed by similar events in the real world. We suspect that media effects are not consistently observed because they are weak and affect only a small percentage of viewers. Exposure to violence in books and magazines, radio, movies, music, and video games may also affect some members of audiences. These media are transmitters of culture that include norms (e.g., self-defense), standards of justice, retributive behavior, and other values related to justifying violence. It would be surprising if exposure to these media had no impact on the values, decisions, and behaviors of some members of an audience.

If exposure to media violence does affect the violent behavior of viewers, the mechanism is unclear. It seems reasonable to believe that the media directs viewers' attention to novel forms of violent behavior they would not otherwise consider. This effect should not be especially tied to television viewing, but should also be associated with reading books, going to the movies, and listening to the radio. However, it is not clear what lesson the media teaches about the legitimacy of violence or to what extent that message repeats lessons learned from other sources of influence. We think that the message is ambiguous and is likely to have different effects on different viewers. Out of the millions of viewers, there may be some with highly idiosyncratic interpretations of television content who may intertwine the fantasy with the problems of their everyday lives, and, as a result, they may have an increased probability of engaging in a violent action.

INTERGENERATIONAL TRANSMISSION OF VIOLENCE

Social learning theory is the basis for the hypothesis that children who are physically punished by their parents tend to use violence themselves when they become adults. The idea that violence is transmitted across generations is widely accepted by researchers who study family violence (e.g., Widom, 1989b) and has had a great impact on public discourse. It is sometimes interpreted to mean that children learn to engage in violence when they observe any form of physical punishment (Straus, 1991). At other times, only severe forms of physical punishment—that is, child abuse—are posited as having a causal effect.[13]

The evidence regarding the intergenerational transmission of violence has been based on correlational data (for a review see Widom, 1989b). In a national survey of almost 10,000 cases of child abuse, 14% of the mothers and 7% of the fathers reported that they had been abused in their own childhoods (D. Gil, 1973). Note that this study was based on retrospective self-reports and, like many of the studies in this area, included no control group. There have also been large-scale surveys of the adult population examining the relationship between family violence and violence in the next generation (e.g., Owens & Straus, 1975). Kalmuss (1984) found that marital aggression was associated with having been the target of physical violence as a teenager as well as with witnessing violence between parents when growing up. These studies have also been based on retrospective self-reports. In addition, there have been prospective studies in which children who have been identified as physically abused are studied again when they become adults. These studies (two of which are described in greater detail below) have also shown a relationship between child abuse and violent behavior later in life (McCord, 1983; Widom, 1989a).

The basic problem with these correlational studies is that a variety of causal interpretations are possible. First, evidence has shown that children who misbehave are more likely to be physically punished by their parents (see chap. 10). Because there is substantial stability in aggressive behavior over time (Olweus, 1979), punishment may correlate with aggression in

---

[13]The use of corporal punishment by parents is discussed in chapter 10.

adulthood. Second, parents and children are exposed to a similar environment, which may produce a spurious relationship between the aggressive behavior of parents and children.[14] Third, the genetic similarities between parents and children may also produce similarities in their behavior (DiLalla & Gottesman, 1991). Fourth, respondents who engage in violence as adults may exaggerate their own mistreatment as children to excuse their antinormative behavior. Criminal offenders or adults with emotional or behavioral problems can blame their predicament on their "unhappy childhoods." Therapists and other mental health professionals (who were the sources of information in some studies) may also find that child abuse is a convenient explanation for behaviors that are otherwise difficult to understand.

Even if a causal effect of parental violence on the violence of their offspring could be established, there is some evidence that it may not be the result of modeling. A number of studies have shown that many forms of child mistreatment are associated with antinormative behavior (see McCord, 1991). For example, in a prospective study, counselors described the interaction between 232 boys and their parents as either loving, rejecting, neglectful, or punitive (McCord, 1983). The criminal records of these boys were then compared in adulthood. The evidence suggested that children who had been mistreated in any of these ways were more likely to have criminal records as adults. Punitiveness was not more strongly associated with violent crime than were other forms of maltreatment.

Widom (1989a) used court records to compare children who were either neglected, physically abused, or sexually abused. Later arrests for juvenile delinquency, adult offenses, and violent adult offenses were compared with arrests for a matched control group. Both physical abuse and neglect were associated with arrests for violent offenses later on. Although the effect of physical abuse was slightly stronger, adults who had been both physically abused and neglected were no different from controls. Independent effects of physical abuse and neglect on nonviolent delinquency or crime were not examined. Matt (1992) used clinicians' reports to examine relationships of physical abuse and psychological neglect by parents with assaultiveness and delinquency for a sample of emotionally disturbed children. She did not find that the relationship between physical abuse and assaultiveness was stronger than the relationship between other combinations of parental maltreatment and children's misbehavior.

These studies suggest that any form of parental maltreatment results in a greater likelihood of misbehavior by offspring. They are consistent with the conclusions from a meta-analysis of longitudinal studies of the effects of family variables on conduct disorders and delinquency (Loeber & Stouthamer-Loeber, 1986). These studies show that lack of parental supervision,

---

[14]Controlling for social class does not sufficiently rule out spuriousness.

lack of parent–child involvement, and parental rejection are the strongest family factors in the prediction of misbehavior. Marital conflict and parental criminality were medium-strength predictors, whereas harsh discipline, parental health, and parental absence were weak predictors.

It may be that children model the self-control behavior of their parents. It is also possible that maltreatment interferes with the relationship between parents and children or that parents who mistreat their children are less likely to use constructive methods of conflict resolution. Such processes are likely to reduce parental influence and thereby increase the likelihood of misbehavior.

In summary, the intergenerational transmission of violence has not been adequately demonstrated. The process is very difficult to study because of measurement problems and because longitudinal data over a generation are required. Studies are needed in which the offspring's behavior is measured early in childhood as well as later. Then, the effect of physical punishment or abuse on changes in the frequency of violent behavior over time can be examined. It appears that the intergenerational transmission of violence—if it exists—is not specifically tied to modeling but is part of a more general process: Poor parenting and maltreatment lead offspring to have behavioral problems.[15] These behavioral problems lead to further maltreatment. We examine this interaction process between parents and children more closely in chapter 10.

SUMMARY AND CONCLUSIONS

Learning theorists assume that aggressive behavior is not fundamentally different from any other kind of behavior. The classical conditioning of aggressive behavior indicates how it can be redirected from one target to another—a case of stimulus generalization. Aggression is an instrumental behavior that is acquired through processes of trial and error, instructions, and observation of models. Behavior that is reinforced is strengthened, and behavior that is punished is either suppressed for a while or extinguished.

A. R. Buss proposed that aggressive behavior is affected by reinforcements, the past experiences of the person, the social environment, and the personality of the person. Reinforcements will increase both the frequency and intensity of aggressive behavior. An individual who has experienced more frustrations and negative behavior from other people will respond more aggressively when new frustrations arise than will a person who has had fewer such experiences. The social milieu will affect aggressive behavior for several reasons. Exposure to many aggressive people may involve any individual in aggressive episodes, and the presence of aggressive models

---

[15]Biological factors may also play a role in the genesis of these behavioral problems (see chap. 10).

increases the likelihood of imitation. Social norms may inhibit or increase the frequency of aggressive behavior. Aspects of personality—such as impulsiveness, hostility, and fearfulness—may act as moderators of aggressive behavior.

Bandura's social learning theory views the individual as future oriented and aggression as instrumental behavior directed toward achieving anticipated rewards or avoiding punishments. Modeling plays a central role in social learning theory. Observation of models who are rewarded for aggressive behavior instigates imitation by observers. It is important to distinguish between learning and performance. A person may learn how to do things without doing them. Most skills must be practiced and maintained to be effective. When a person possesses skills, they may be used when opportunities arise to achieve desired interpersonal outcomes. People also learn self-control through mechanisms of self-reinforcement and self-punishment. Internal controls can act as inhibitors of aggressive behavior.

Social learning theory has had a major impact on the study of television violence and intergenerational transmission of violence. The link between viewing violent films and aggressive behavior has been established in laboratory experiments. Various theoretical mechanisms—such as the development of unrealistic fear, priming, and desensitization—have been associated with viewing violence. However, these mechanisms have not been reliably associated with subsequent aggressive behavior of viewers. Field research and longitudinal studies of viewing television violence have provided inconsistent findings. Some studies show a small effect of viewing violence on the aggressive behavior of viewers, and other studies indicate no effect. We concluded that viewing violence may affect a few people but that it probably has little or no impact on the aggressiveness of most people. The research on the intergenerational transmission of violence indicates a general association between poor parenting and maladaptive behavior of children, but the evidence has not established that modeling is a factor.

5

CRIMINOLOGICAL THEORIES

Sociologists and criminologists typically study interpersonal aggression under the rubric of crime.[1] Because some acts of interpersonal aggression, particularly those that involve physical violence, violate the law, this strategy seems reasonable.[2] Many crimes result in some sort of harm to others. Unfortunately, the criminological literature has largely been ignored by social psychologists who study aggression. This neglect is surprising given that much of the interest in the study of interpersonal aggression is stimulated by concern over the frequency of criminal violence. In addition, as we show, most of the people who engage in violent crime also engage in other forms of crime and deviance. Clearly, criminological theories are relevant to the study of interpersonal aggression.

Sociological theories of crime are designed in part to explain sociodemographic variations in crime. The traditional theories of aggression discussed in the first four chapters ignore the dramatic variation in levels

---

[1]There is a separate literature on domestic violence, some of which is discussed in chapter 10.

[2]Crime and aggression include overlapping sets of behaviors that could be described with a Venn diagram. Some acts of aggression, particularly those involving physical violence, are crimes. Some criminal acts involve aggression, whereas others do not.

of violence in different segments of the population. In every society where it has been studied, violence is committed overwhelmingly by young men (Gottfredson & Hirschi, 1990). In the United States, 87% of those arrested for murder and aggravated assault and 93% of those arrested for robbery were male (Bureau of Justice Statistics [BJS], 1983). In addition, 72% of violent crime offenders were under 30 years of age. More violence was committed by 18-year-old men than by people of any other age category.

Neither frustration–aggression theory nor social learning theories can explain the demographic topography of violence. It seems unlikely that young men commit more violence because they experience higher levels of frustration than do young women or people of other ages. A social learning theorist might argue that young men are more likely to observe successful aggressive models (their peers) and to receive rewards for imitation. Yet, although modeling is a factor in the transmission of violence, it cannot explain the origins of the models' behavior. What is needed is an explanation of why the models imitated by youth are more aggressive and why young men are more likely to be rewarded for violence.

Poor people more often commit violent crimes than do people from the middle and upper classes: 40% of men in jail or prison in 1982 had been unemployed at the time of their arrests, in comparison with 8.4% in the overall male population, ages 18–54 years (BJS, 1983). About 40% of all jail and prison inmates had completed high school in comparison with 85% of 20–29-year-old men in the U.S. population. There are also substantial race differences in the commission of violent crimes. According to the 1983 statistics, Blacks, who make up 12% of the U.S. population, committed 49% of the homicides.

Explanations of class and race differences in criminal violence in the United States could posit particularly high levels of frustration among the poor or among Blacks. However, class and race differences in the incidence of nonviolent crimes cannot be explained by the frustration–aggression hypothesis because most of these crimes do not involve aggression.

Traditional theories of aggression do not explain the substantial cross-cultural variation in the level of violence. The homicide rate for young men in the United States is over 7 times the rate in Canada, about 18 times the rate in England, and about 44 times the rate in Japan (Fingerhut & Kleinman, 1990). Southerners are more likely to engage in homicide than are persons born in other regions of the United States (Nisbett, 1993). There is no evidence that Americans are more frustrated than Europeans or Japanese or that Southerners are more frustrated than Northerners. It could be argued that there are more aggressive models available and greater rewards for violence in the United States, but then it would be necessary to explain why this is so.

In this chapter, we review and critique three types of sociological theories. *Subcultural theories* emphasize socialization of certain values, such as toughness and excitement. These values produce violence and delinquency, particularly among youth. *Blocked opportunity theories* propose that violence is used to attain goals when legitimate means are limited. Higher rates of crime among the poor and among minorities are attributed to a lack of educational and economic opportunities. A theory of self-help proposes that people use violence to settle their grievances when the opportunity for institutional recourse is blocked. *Control theories* assume that most people have inclinations to use violence and to commit crimes but that inhibitions prevent them from acting on them. These theories focus on internal and external controls and the routine activities that create opportunities for crime. We discuss each of these approaches, emphasizing their application to the explanation of criminal violence.

VIOLENT AND DELINQUENT SUBCULTURES

Subcultural theories attribute violence and delinquency to socialization by deviant groups. Groups are assumed to vary in values, attitudes, and beliefs that promote these behaviors. Violence is valued by some groups in certain situations, and it enhances the status of those who use it. The origin of these group differences is rarely addressed. Cultural theories may be better at explaining the amplification of group differences than they are at explaining the origin of these differences.

Subcultural theories place particular emphasis on peer effects among young people. There is considerable evidence that youth who have delinquent friends are more likely to engage in delinquency. This association is due to both peer influence and self-selection: Delinquents tend to choose other delinquents as friends. Research attempting to statistically disentangle these two causal processes has indicated that both peer influence and self-selection are operating (for a review, see Matsueda, 1988).

We first review theories that posit subcultures of delinquency among youth. We then focus on the subculture-of-violence thesis, because that theory has received the most attention in the literature.

Subcultures of Delinquency

Subcultural theories attempt to explain sociodemographic variation in violence and crime. Some theorists have suggested that special subcultures of delinquency develop among young lower-class men. W. B. Miller (1958) suggested that lower-class culture is a distinctive tradition with a long history. He listed six "focal concerns" in lower-class culture, four of which are directly related to violence. First, there is an emphasis on toughness, or on being fearless and skilled in combat. Second, there is a "search for excitement" that, he argues, results from the nature of work in the lower class; that is, lower-class men seek "cheap thrills" because their work is dull and repetitive. A third theme is a belief in fate or a tendency to see outcomes as predetermined and unalterable. People who think that they cannot prevent negative outcomes are more willing to use violence in spite of its risks than are people who view their outcomes as under their control. Finally, there is a concern with autonomy or freedom of action. A person with this concern might be expected to assert, "No one is going to push me around."[3] These themes symbolize adulthood for lower-class males.

A. Cohen (1955) argued that members of the middle class value ambition, individual responsibility, cultivation and possession of skills, the ability to postpone gratification, rationality, personableness, and control of aggression, whereas members of the working class value dependence on primary groups, spontaneity, and a freer use of aggression. Conflict is therefore likely when working-class children enter schools dominated by middle-class values. Working-class children find it difficult to win the favor of the adults in charge.[4] It is not that working-class children reject middle-class values but, rather, that they feel degradation in the classroom because they are judged by adults with different values. As a result, working-class children orient themselves to friends who appreciate them and offer an alternative source of status. By redefining the status criteria, working-class children turn a disadvantage into an advantage.[5] They come to value the opposite of middle-class standards, and they develop a separate culture. Cohen described this counterculture as *nonutilitarian, malicious,* and *negativistic.*

G. Sykes and Matza (1961) suggested that the values held by delinquents are similar to the values of the general society but that certain ones are given more emphasis: "The delinquent has picked up and emphasized one part of the dominant value system, namely the subterranean values that coexist with other, publicly proclaimed values possessing a more respectable air" (p. 717). These subterranean values include a search for adventure, excitement, thrills, and big money. Violence and other forms of delinquency are means to pursue these values.

Subculture-of-Violence Thesis

Most of the theories presented in this chapter attempt to explain all forms of criminal behavior. An exception is Wolfgang and Ferracuti's (1967)

---

[3]The other two concerns are with getting in and out of trouble and with the ability to outsmart or con others. W. B. Miller (1958) and others who posit special values for lower-class people do not consider the possibility that middle-class people with these values are more likely to fall into the lower class.

[4]Because the child's educational opportunities are blocked, A. Cohen's (1955) theory could also be classified as a blocked opportunity theory.

[5]Similarly, Kobrin (1951) suggested that adolescent delinquency is a form of defensive adaptation to the inability to meet certain middle-class goals.

thesis of the subculture of violence. This subcultural theory posits a distinctive set of values to explain the high rates of violence among some minorities and among poor people. These values are particularly likely to be held by young men and are associated with the concept of machismo. Members of these subcultures are more likely to value a "quick resort to physical combat as a measure of daring, courage, or defense of status" (Wolfgang & Ferracuti, 1967, p. 153). Members place great value on toughness and excitement and a low value on the importance of human life. A wide range of circumstances are considered by members of the subculture as justifying violence. For example, a slightly derogatory remark that might be viewed as trivial in the general population is likely to be seen as an occasion for violent retaliation. The failure to respond to provocation is likely to meet with derision from the group.

The subculture-of-violence thesis has been used to explain higher rates of violence in the southern United States. Gastil (1971) identified pre–Civil War traditions in the South that have tended to legitimize violence: a strong sense of honor, an interest in military affairs, the persistence of dueling long after it disappeared in the North, and a tendency to carry weapons. Hackney (1969) argued that historically Southerners, particularly White Southerners, have viewed themselves as victims of a larger, hostile environment. He attributed this "southern identity" to the defeat and devastation experienced by the South in the Civil War. As a result of these grievances and feelings of persecution, Southerners were more likely to resort to violence than people from other regions. J. S. Reed (1971) suggested that there is a southern tradition in which disputes are handled privately, without the involvement of formal authorities. Sometimes the private handling of grievances involves violence. Finally, Nisbett (1993) attributed the southern subculture of violence to the settlement in the South by immigrants from herding communities in Scotland and Ireland and the continuation of herding in some parts of the South and West. Herders tend to be extremely vigilant and are quick to retaliate because they are economically vulnerable to theft. Nisbett found that the dispute-related homicide rates of small cities were higher in those states with high numbers of southern-born residents.[6] He also found higher homicide rates in areas where herding is more likely to occur.

A schematic of the processes proposed by the subculture-of-violence theory (and other subcultural approaches) is presented in Figure 5.1. As can be seen, values mediate the relationship between sex, age, class, race,

---

[6]There is some debate over whether the South is the most violent region when poverty, age structure, and percentage of the population that is Black are controlled (e.g., O'Carroll & Mercy, 1989). Nisbett's (1993) study is more convincing than other studies because he examines the pattern for different size cities and restricts the analysis to cities with mostly White populations. He found a strong relationship between the number of Southerners living in a state and the homicide rate of cities under 200,000, controlling for poverty and other variables.

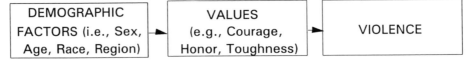

| DEMOGRAPHIC FACTORS (i.e., Sex, Age, Race, Region) | → | VALUES (e.g., Courage, Honor, Toughness) | → | VIOLENCE |

Figure 5.1. A schematic of the subculture-of-violence thesis.

and region on the one hand, and violence on the other. The basic idea is that certain segments of the population are socialized to have stronger values associated with violence than are other members of society. These values are particularly likely to lead to retaliation when a person has been pro-voked. Tests of subcultural theories must show that sociodemographic vari-ables predict values (e.g., toughness) and that values predict violence.[7]

Values and Violence

In a few studies, researchers have examined the relationship between values and violent behavior. In the most well known study, Ball-Rokeach (1973) examined attitudes and values in relationship to self-reported vio-lence among a national sample of the general population.[8] A small rela-tionship was found between the respondents' approval of violence and the frequency of violence, but there was no relationship between violence and values regarding courage and having an exciting life. Although these results appear to disconfirm the subculture-of-violence thesis, the study does have methodological problems (see Erlanger, 1974). The most significant limi-tation was that values were measured by single items, when better reliability could have been obtained by constructing scales and including multiple items for each value.

The effect of values on violence was examined in a longitudinal study of high school boys (Liska, Felson, Chamlin, & Baccaglini, 1984). The researchers attempted to sort out statistically the causal relationship of feelings of resentment and revenge with self-reports of violent behavior. It is important to determine whether values affect behavior, whether behavior affects values, or whether both are a function of some third variable. The study found a reciprocal relationship, with the effect of values on behavior stronger than the reverse effect. The effect of values on behavior was stronger when the values were strongly held. This effect suggests that if many people are ambivalent about the use of violence, as we suspect they

---

[7]Even if these relationships were found, one must then show that values mediate the relationship between sociodemographic factors and violence. Evidence for mediation would be indicated if the relationship between sociodemographic factors and violence disappears when values are statistically controlled.

[8]Ball-Rokeach (1973) distinguished between attitudes and values. She defined *attitudes* as the organization of beliefs toward an object or situation (e.g., approval of violence) and *values* as beliefs about desired end states or modes of conduct (e.g., being courageous). We do not make this distinction in our discussion.

are, then values will be weak predictors of violence overall.[9] We would conclude from this study that values do affect violent behavior, although their effects are weak.

The values associated with violence may be part of a more general set of delinquent values. R. B. Felson, Liska, South, and McNulty (in press) found that measures of approval of retaliation were highly correlated in a negative direction with students' academic values, across individuals and across schools. Approval of retaliation predicted nonviolent forms of delinquency (rule breaking in school and theft or vandalism) as well as it predicted interpersonal violence. This evidence suggests that it may be more accurate to speak of *subcultures of delinquency* than of subcultures of violence.

Class, Race, and Regional Differences in Values

Researchers have examined the relationships of race and class to values associated with violence. Ball-Rokeach (1973) found that education and income had a slight negative effect on approval of violence but no relationship to the other values measured. Erlanger (1974) found little or no race or class differences in approval of interpersonal violence in response to various provocations. Rossi, Waite, Bose, and Berk (1974) found few class or race differences in the ranking of the seriousness of various crimes. In general, these studies show that minorities and the poor disapprove of violent criminal acts just as much as the rest of the population.

Another way to test subcultural theories is to examine the effects of violence on status among Blacks, the lower class, or any other group with higher levels of violence. Group members who are particularly violent should be accorded higher status in groups that value violence. The evidence does not support this hypothesis. Erlanger (1974) found that lower-class men who engaged in more fistfights tended to have lower status than lower-class men who did not have many fights. Erlanger and Winsborough (1976) obtained similar findings with a sample of Black men.[10] The validity of the conclusions reached in these studies is questionable, however, because each relied on self-reports of status (i.e., "perceived respect") rather than on the perceptions of other group members. People tend to be self-serving in their attributions and may perceive positive responses from others even in situations where others have negative evaluations of them. In addition, the

---

[9]The relative strengths of these reciprocal effects depend on the value and behavior in question. Matsueda (1989) found that the effect of delinquency on attitudes toward honesty and cheating was stronger than the reverse effect.

[10]Erlanger and Winsborough (1976) relied on simultaneous equation models to control for the possibility that status and violence have a reciprocal relationship.

studies did not examine the context of the reported fights or whether the violence engaged in by the men was perceived as a legitimate reaction to provocations. Someone who bullies others or starts fights with group members is likely to lose status, but someone who fights only when provoked or who only bullies outsiders may gain status.

There is evidence for regional difference in some values related to violence. Southerners are more likely to have favorable attitudes toward war, are more likely to approve of corporal punishment, are more opposed to gun control, and are more likely to favor violence for self-protection and in response to insults (Nisbett, 1993). For example, southern men are more likely to approve of the right to kill someone in defense of home or family or as a violent response to insults to girlfriends or sexual assaults on one's daughter.

Socialization Versus Social Control

As indicated above, subcultural theories of violence and delinquency emphasize socialization. Groups socialize individuals to certain values (e.g., courage or toughness); individuals internalize those values and then act accordingly. An alternative explanation has been suggested by the study of the relationship between values and violence among high school boys, described above (R. B. Felson et al., in press). Felson et al. found that the values of schoolmates affected violent and other delinquent behavior, when they controlled for the boy's own values. If a boy went to a school where retaliation was valued, he was more likely to engage in violent behavior, regardless of his own values. This finding suggests that certain schools have subcultures of violence–delinquency and that the subcultural effect is due to social control rather than to socialization. In other words, the violence reflects impression management and compliance rather than internalization.

The causal model tested by R. B. Felson et al. (in press) is represented in Figure 5.2. Social control is implied by the fact that the values of schoolmates had a direct effect on the violent behavior of the boys (Path A).[11] A socialization explanation is represented by indirect effects of schoolmates on behavior. Schoolmates' values affected a boy's own values (Path B), which in turn affected his behavior (Path C).[12]

The role of impression management in response to social control by the peer group is suggested by evidence that lower-class delinquents endorse middle-class values in private but not in front of their peers (Short &

---

[11]Left out of Figure 5.2 are the unmeasured mediators of school effects on violence, such as instigating actions by third parties and individual perceptions of how the audience will react.

[12]Values regarding retaliation predicted other nonviolent forms of delinquency at the school. This finding suggests that the values related to violent and nonviolent delinquency are similar and supports our earlier statement that it may be more appropriate to speak of a subculture of delinquency than of a subculture of violence.

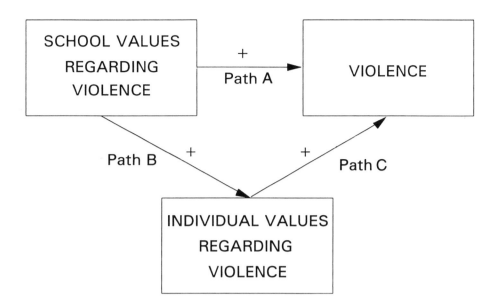

Figure 5.2. A schematic of the effects of peer values on boys' values regarding violence and on their violent behavior.

Strodtbeck, 1965). This audience effect implies that the delinquency of lower-class youth at least partially reflects their misconceptions of the values of their peers. The pluralistic ignorance of these young men leads them to engage in delinquent behaviors to present themselves favorably to their peers.

Subcultures may be more likely to develop among smaller social units, such as schools and gangs, in which individuals engage in frequent social interaction and in which social control processes are likely to operate. The subculture-of-violence thesis may be more useful as an explanation of small-group differences in violence than as an explanation of race, socioeconomic status, or regional differences. This limitation is an important one, because the original purpose of the subculture-of-violence thesis was to explain sociodemographic variation.

Even if class, race, or regional variation in values were related to violence, it seems inappropriate to use the term *subculture*. This term is generally used when there is variation across social groups in members' values. Although the value placed on violence may be high in one group relative to other groups, it is not necessarily high in an absolute sense. Furthermore, the term implies a consensus, in this case a consensus in beliefs about the desirability of violence within some social units. It seems inaccurate to assign poor people, Blacks, or Southerners to a subculture of violence when the overwhelming majority of these group members disapprove of violence. It may make more sense to restrict the use of the term *subculture* to small groups, such as gangs, in which there is more likely to be a consensus.

Social Contexts and the Legitimation of Violence

The discussion above implies that the subculture-of-violence thesis has not been adequately tested. The available research does not capture the complexities in the legitimation of violence. As we show in later chapters, attitudes toward the legitimacy of violence depend on the context in which that violence is used. Whether a violent act is viewed as legitimate or not is likely to depend on who the target is and what he or she did to provoke the response. Violence may be approved of when it is a response to an attack but not when it involves unprovoked bullying. In some gangs, unprovoked violence may be viewed positively if it is directed against members of other gangs. As indicated by Wolfgang and Ferracuti (1967), there may be variation across groups in the tendency for individuals to perceive themselves as under attack and to take offense. Because group variation in these norms and legitimating beliefs have not been examined, the subculture-of-violence hypothesis has not been given an adequate test. We are not ready to reject the hypothesis that groups vary in what they consider to be legitimate uses of violence.

Luckenbill and Doyle (1989) offered a model for examining the subculture of violence that takes into account some of these subtleties. They described an interpersonal dispute as a consequence of three successive events: (a) a person must perceive a negative outcome as an injury for which someone is to blame, (b) the victim must express the grievance to the offender and demand some form of reparation or apology, and (c) the offender must reject the victim's claim. When the claim is rejected, the interaction becomes a dispute. The aggrieved party may respond to these disputes by capitulating, by eliciting the help of third parties, or by using force. Luckenbill and Doyle stated that there are subcultural differences in the way grievances are handled in certain situations. They also hypothesized that young adults, men, Blacks, lower income persons, and urban and southern residents (in the United States) are more likely to retaliate when they have been publicly attacked by persons of equal status. This theory does not explain the origin of subcultural differences in the handling of grievances in disputes.

A test of these hypotheses requires measurement of values that takes into account the situational context of the dispute, including the identity of the person who engages in the initial act that another finds offensive. Luckenbill and Doyle (1989) recommended that scenarios of different situations be presented to respondents, who would then be asked to role-play and indicate how they would respond. In this way, it might be determined when respondents would take offense, whether they would protest to the harmdoer, and whether they would use force if they could not get redress for their grievance. Research using scenarios of this type has not yet been performed.

BLOCKED OPPORTUNITY THEORIES

Subcultural theories propose that those who commit crime have a special set of values.[13] In contrast, most theories that stress blocked opportunities assume that offenders have the same values as other people, but they lack the opportunity to attain those values through legitimate means. Crime is an alternative means to gain status, money, and the redress of grievances when legitimate means are unavailable. Particular emphasis is placed on the barriers to opportunity produced by social class and race. It is argued that poor people and minorities engage in more violent and nonviolent crime because they lack the opportunity to achieve what they value by using conventional means.

Opportunities for Conventional Success

According to the most well known version of blocked opportunity theory, violence and other forms of crime are the result of a disjunction between goals and means (Merton, 1957). The theory emphasizes culturally defined goals in society, such as money and status, and acceptable means for achieving those goals, such as educational attainment. When individuals lack the opportunity to achieve conventional goals with conventional means, they are more likely to turn to crime. For Merton, then, crime is an "innovation" that is attractive to those people who lack legitimate opportunities. Thus, lower-class boys value financial success and status like everyone else, but they lack the opportunities to attain these values by legitimate means. As a result they use violence and other illegal acts to obtain money and to gain status among their peers.[14]

---

[13]Or at least they place greater emphasis on certain values (G. Sykes & Matza, 1961).

[14]The approach implies that violence is used as a last resort. Legitimate means of attaining status are considered first, and violence is used only if these activities do not look promising. There is a preference for legitimate means—because of socialization or because they entail less costs than illegitimate means—and if legitimate opportunities are available they will be used. Cloward and Ohlin (1960) suggested that violence is used as a last resort when delinquents fail at other types of crime. They agreed that when legitimate opportunities are blocked people turn to illegitimate means, but they argued that Merton's theory is unclear about the type of criminal activity that will be chosen. Cloward and Ohlin attempted to explain why some young men choose a violent criminal career. They argued that young men turn to violence when both legitimate and nonviolent criminal opportunities are not available. There is apparently a preference for nonviolent crimes for financial gain. Success in such crimes requires the development of connections with mature criminals, fences, and law enforcement officials. The failure to establish connections makes a "stable criminal career" impossible, and young men then turn to violence. These choices are made quite consciously. Evidence (cited above) that offenders do not usually specialize in violent versus nonviolent crimes contradicts this theoretical approach.

Blocked opportunity theory predicts that youth with high aspirations and low expectations for achieving those aspirations should engage in more delinquency. The evidence concerning whether a disjunction between aspirations and expectations produces delinquent behavior is mixed at best (for a review, see Elliot, Huizinga, & Ageton, 1985). Two studies have indicated that youth who aspire to go to college are less likely to engage in delinquency (Hirschi, 1969; Liska, 1971). Expectations about whether they were actually going to college had no effect. These results indicate that ambitious young people are less likely to engage in delinquency than youth with lower aspirations, no matter how pessimistic they are about achieving their goals.[15]

If crime is an alternative method of obtaining money when legitimate means are blocked, then one would expect an effect of unemployment on pecuniary crimes, both violent and nonviolent. The evidence is mixed on whether unemployment leads people to commit more such crimes. Although those who commit crime are more likely to be unemployed, the causal interpretation is unclear (for a review, see J. Q. Wilson & Herrnstein, 1985). Those who commit crimes may have trouble getting jobs, or they may have individual characteristics that affect both unemployment and crime.

The hypothesis that crime is a method of obtaining status or approval when conventional means are blocked is more complex. A young man who wants the approval of his parents and other adults but does poorly in school cannot switch to crime to get their approval—his behavior will have the opposite effect. Instead, he must switch his significant others to deviant peers who will give him the status or approval that he desires. To the extent that status is a commodity (like money), unconnected to specific people, it can be achieved by substituting criminal behavior for conventional behavior.

Opportunities for achievement in conventional society are affected by many factors besides class and race. Lack of opportunity to achieve desired goals may also be a consequence of a person's own limitations, which could be environmentally or genetically based. Young people with limited intellectual ability or preparation may find it more difficult to achieve in school and may turn to violence and other forms of delinquency to achieve status (Gottfredson & Hirschi, 1990; J. Q. Wilson & Herrnstein, 1985). Research has consistently shown a negative correlation between delinquency and intelligence test scores (for a review, see J. Q. Wilson & Herrnstein, 1985). In general, any individual characteristic that has a detrimental effect on conventional forms of achievement may increase the attractiveness of vio-

---

[15]Farnsworth and Leiber (1989) found that high school boys who had both high economic aspirations and low educational expectations were most likely to be delinquent. However, they failed to control for the additive or main effect of educational expectations.

lence or other forms of delinquency as an alternative source of status and other benefits.

Gottfredson and Hirschi (1990) rejected the idea that crime is an adaptation to blocked opportunities, claiming that criminal offenders are not farsighted enough to consider that future success in conventional activities is unlikely. However, it does not require farsightedness for a young man to notice that he is doing poorly in school. He may be responding to his present situation rather than to his future prospects. Therefore, it is at least plausible that those who do poorly in conventional activities (for whatever reason) might turn to alternative means of attaining status or money. The available evidence regarding blocked opportunity theory, however, is generally not supportive.

Violence as Self-Help

The theories above focus on barriers to educational and economic achievement. Another form of blocked opportunity theory focuses on barriers to the use of legal resources in handling one's grievances. According to Black (1983), when people with high status have grievances, they have the opportunity to get legal recourse in the criminal justice system. They have confidence that if they call the police, the offender will be apprehended and punished. Black argues that legal recourse is not as readily available to persons with lower status, particularly when their status is lower than the status of the person with whom they have a grievance.

For a variety of reasons, people with low status avoid the criminal justice system. They may expect that their charges will not be believed or that the police cannot be trusted. At any rate, their assumption that the legal system is unavailable leads them to engage in self-help. They attempt to settle grievances by punishing the victim themselves, meting out their own brand of justice. Thus, Black (1983) argued, many crimes are attempts at informal social control. Crimes of social control are moralistic acts that are similar to gossip, ridicule, vengeance, punishment, and law. They reflect the fact that the state does not have a monopoly on the use of force and that when the formal control apparatus of the state is ineffective, informal violence is used as a substitute.

Self-help crimes usually involve people who know each other, because grievances are unlikely between strangers. Black (1983) interpreted most instances of nonfelony homicide and assault as self-help. Self-help is the motive in many burglaries and robberies that involve offenders and victims who know each other. Some of these crimes involve a form of debt collection. Some forms of vandalism can be interpreted as an attempt by youth to punish adults generally. In this case, punishment is directed at targets with whom the offender has no personal grievance. Targets are punished because they share some social category with someone with whom the offender does have a grievance. Here there is some notion of collective liability, where an aggrieved party blames the entire group for the misbehavior of one member.

Dollard (1957) used a self-help argument to explain the high level of violence among Blacks in the South. He identified a double standard, under which crimes between Blacks were ignored by authorities whereas Black crime against Whites, which was rare, was punished severely:

> The formal machinery of the law takes care of the Negroes' grievances much less adequately than that of the whites, and to a much higher degree the Negro is compelled to make and enforce his own law with other Negroes. . . . The result is that the individual Negro is, to a considerable degree, outside the protection of the white law, and must shift for himself. This leads to the frontier psychology. (pp. 274, 279)

There are other factors besides status that affect the tendency to use self-help. Black (1983) suggested that an absence of formal authority produces high levels of violence. Where legal systems are absent, undeveloped, or ineffective, or when third-party mediators are unavailable, self-help should be common. Self-help is also more likely when the grievance is against a family member, because legal authorities are less likely to intervene in such cases. Thus the theory of self-help provides one explanation for the high frequency of domestic violence. Finally, persons involved in other forms of criminal activity, such as drug sales, are more likely to use self-help because the law is not available to them when grievances develop over business matters. Obviously, a drug customer who is shortchanged cannot protest to the police or the Better Business Bureau.

Self-help theory implies an inverse relationship between informal social control and the effectiveness of legal forms of social control because the former is a substitute for the latter. Massey and Myers (1989) attempted to examine this relationship by researching trends in lynching, execution, and incarceration in Georgia between 1882 and 1935. Lynching could be interpreted as a form of self-help among Whites who developed grievances against Blacks. There was no relationship between lynching and legal forms of control. These results do not support the idea that lynching was a response to perceptions by Whites that legal forms of social control were inadequate for controlling Blacks.

Massey and Myers (1989) did not control for the rate of crime, which may be related to formal and informal control (see Figure 5.3). The rate of crime positively affects both informal (Path A) and formal social control (Path B). A result of these relationships is that when crime rates go up, a positive relationship will occur between the two forms of control. This positive relationship is not due to one form of control affecting the other but is caused by variation in crime rates. When crime increases, so do both

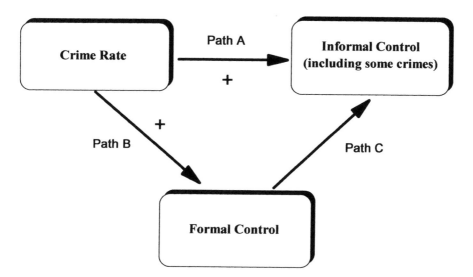

Figure 5.3. The relationships among crime, informal control, and formal control.

formal and informal control. Any real negative effect of formal and informal control (Path C) would be disguised unless the effects of the crime rate are statistically controlled. If some crime is itself a form of informal control, it would also result in a positive relationship between informal control and formal control. The greater the number of crimes committed, the greater the number of people who are sanctioned by the criminal justice system. The situation is complicated because self-help crimes are a social control response to crimes motivated by other reasons. These complexities make it difficult to evaluate self-help theory on the basis of statistical analyses of aggregate data.

Self-help theory predicts that victims of lower status are less likely to report crimes to the police than are victims of higher status. Evidence from victimization studies is generally not supportive of self-help theory. Minorities who are victims of household burglary and motor vehicle theft are just as likely to report the crime to the police as other victims (BJS, 1983). Black crime victims are more likely than White crime victims to demand that police make an arrest (Black & Reiss, 1970). On the other hand, the higher the income of victims of household burglary and motor vehicle theft, the more likely they are to report the crime to the police (BJS, 1983).

Black's (1983) theory is important because it draws the connection between formal and informal control. We suspect that decisions about how to handle grievances have an impact on violent behavior. Decisions about whether to punish a transgressor through violence are probably affected by the perceived opportunity to use the legal system or some third party to redress one's grievance. Self-help theory is interesting because it shows how nonviolent crime (such as the drug trade) can produce violent crime if grievances occur in the course of business that cannot be handled in the criminal justice system. It may also help explain class and race differences in criminal violence as well as why family violence is so frequent. However, the evidence regarding race effects on the reporting of crime suggests that the theory exaggerates the importance of status in the availability of law, at least in the United States today. Furthermore, relatively few crimes involve the grievances of lower status offenders against higher status victims; in most crimes, the offender and victim are of similar status (e.g., Wolfgang, 1958). We know of no research in which the effect of the relative status of the offender and victim (or grievant) has been examined.

CONTROL THEORIES

Whereas subcultural and blocked opportunity theories focus on the incentives for crime, control theories focus on the costs. Control theories assume that there are plenty of incentives for criminal behavior and that there is not much variation in the degree to which people appreciate the benefits of crime. In spite of strong incentives, most people do not engage in serious crime. Most people want money or have grievances against others, but few people commit robbery and assault. The question raised by control theories is not Why do people break the law? but, rather, Why does anyone obey the law? It is assumed that violence and other forms of criminal behavior would be more frequent if it were not for factors that inhibit these behaviors.

Inhibitory factors include both external controls and internal controls. External control involves the threat of punishment. *External control* can refer to both informal social control, such as disapproval, and formal control, such as criminal prosecution. *Internal control* includes internalized moral beliefs, respect for law, self-control, and favorable self-esteem (Reckless, 1961).

External Controls

Three theories focus on external controls. One emphasizes the role of criminal sanctions as a deterrent to crime. Another emphasizes social ties that inhibit crime because they make it more costly. A third stresses the routine activities that create opportunities for crime because they leave targets unguarded and offenders unsupervised.

Formal Control

Deterrence theory emphasizes formal control and the deterrent effect of legal sanctions. Criminologists distinguish three aspects of punishment in their discussion of punishment by legal authorities: severity, certainty, and celerity. Most research suggests that certainty of punishment is a more important deterrent of crime than severity (Tittle & Logan, 1973).[16] However, certainty and severity of punishment probably do not affect behavior independently. No matter how severe the sentence, individuals might not be deterred if they think that apprehension and conviction are unlikely (cf. Gibbs, 1975).

Many criminologists do not have much faith in the ability of the police and legal system to reduce crime through more extensive patrolling or through more effective sanctions. The inability of the police to monitor behavior and apprehend suspects and the difficulties of criminal prosecution in a democratic society limit the effectiveness of criminal sanctions. For these reasons, formal control may be less important than informal control. Informal and formal controls may also be, to some extent, redundant in their effects (Hirschi & Gottfredson, 1990). Those people who are deterred from criminal violence by formal controls may already be deterred by informal controls, whereas those who commit criminal violence are not deterred by either form of control. Finally, incarceration may interfere with successful employment after release, which may in turn lead to continued involvement in crime over the life course (Sampson & Laub, 1993).

Bonds to Conventional Others

Hirschi (1969) has developed the most influential theory of informal social control. He proposed that people violate norms when informal social control is ineffective. Informal social control will be ineffective when the individual's bond to conventional society is weak. The conventional bond consists of four elements. First, there are the attachments that the individual has with conventional others, such as parents, that make him or her more susceptible to their influence. When people are concerned about their status with others, they are more likely to conform. Second, the social bond is a function of commitments. Commitments are investments of time and energy that people have made toward achieving conventional goals. Once people acquire goods, reputations, and prospects, the costs of getting caught for misbehavior increase. They do not want to risk losing these accumulations. In other words, the uncommitted have little or nothing to lose, whereas the committed have developed a stake in conformity (Toby, 1957). Third, involvement in conventional activities decreases the level of criminal activity. A person busy with conventional activities has less time for criminal activity. This is consistent with the commonsense idea that idle hands do the Devil's work. Finally, Hirschi includes one form of internal control in

---

[16]In contrast, labeling theory suggests that punishment leads to more crime, because the labeling of a person as a criminal creates a self-fulfilling prophecy.

his list of controls: Conventional beliefs, such as respect for law and for the police, inhibit delinquent behavior.

Research generally has shown a negative relationship between the strength of social bonds and delinquency. Wiatrowski, Griswold, and Roberts (1981) found that high school boys who were close to their parents and had positive attitudes toward school reported lower levels of delinquent behavior. An alternative causal interpretation of these relationships is that delinquency affects social bonds or that some individual characteristic affects both social bonds and delinquency, producing a spurious relationship between social bonds and delinquency.

Some researchers have attempted to use longitudinal data to isolate the effects of social bonds on changes in delinquency. Sampson and Laub (1993) found that boys with strong attachment to their parents were less likely to be involved in delinquency at age 14, according to both official reports and reports from teachers, parents, and the boys themselves. The study controlled for retrospective accounts from parents of how difficult the boy was at a younger age as well as for other variables. They also found strong effects of school attachment on delinquency. Liska and Reed (1985) found that attachment to family, but not attachment to school, reduced levels of delinquency. The evidence indicated that for these high school boys, low attachment to school was a consequence rather than a cause of delinquency: Participation in delinquent behavior reduced interest in school.[17] In another longitudinal study, Sampson and Laub (1990) examined the effect of social bonds on subsequent criminal behavior among young adult men (ages 17–25 years). Job stability and strong marital attachment decreased the likelihood of future criminal behavior, when delinquency at earlier ages was controlled. Family and work obligations also help explain why people engage in less crime when they get older. However, much of the age–crime relationship remains when these factors are controlled (Rowe & Tittle, 1977), which suggests that other factors are involved as well.

There is some dispute in the literature over the causal mechanism involved in the effects of social bonds. Some studies indicate that the effects of conventional ties are largely mediated by attitudes toward crime (e.g., Matsueda & Heimer, 1987). When attitudes about breaking the law are controlled, the relationship between delinquency and attachment to parents and peers, broken homes, and other measures of social ties disappears. This finding appears to contradict expectations derived from control theory. Hirschi's (1969) control theory implies that the effects of social ties are mediated by the costs of delinquency, and not by attitudes (Matsueda, 1988). Attitude effects imply a socialization process and not social control. We interpret this research as indicating that social control and socialization

---

[17]It may be that school attachments have an impact at earlier ages than was examined in this study.

processes are intertwined. Low social control permits youth to develop attitudes that lead to delinquency. In our view, differences between control theories and socialization theories (such as differential association and subcultural theories) are blurred.

Opportunities for Crime

The routine activity approach emphasizes the situations that provide an opportunity for crime rather than personal characteristics of individuals that might lead them to commit crimes (M. Felson, 1993). L. E. Cohen and Felson (1979) stated that a situation that provides an opportunity for a predatory crime requires three elements: a likely offender, a suitable target, and the absence of capable guardians. For a crime to occur, there must be contact between offenders and victims and the absence of third parties who might act to prevent such behavior. Crime is more likely to occur when routine activities, such as those associated with leisure and work, bring together offenders and victims in the absence of effective guardians. "Changes in the daily life of the community alter the amount of criminal opportunity in society, hence altering crime rates" (M. Felson, 1986, p. 121).

The routine activity approach is particularly useful for explaining changes in crime rates over time and variations in crime rates in different locations. L. E. Cohen and Felson (1979) provided evidence that the increase in crime since the 1960s was due to increases in rates of travel outside the home, single-person households, college attendance and labor force participation among women, and the percentage of households left unattended during the day. They show that the dispersion of activity away from households over time is positively related to official rates of homicide, assault, rape, robbery, and burglary.

Supervision is critical in explaining crime according to the routine activity approach, particularly the supervision of young people, because they are "likely offenders." Thus, Sampson and Laub (1993) found that boys are much more likely to engage in juvenile delinquency if they have been inadequately supervised by their mothers. Low parental supervision helps explain why delinquency is more frequent in broken homes (Matseuda & Heimer, 1987). Lack of supervision also helps explain the consistent finding that the greater the number of children in a family, the greater the likelihood that each child will be delinquent (e.g., West, 1982). Crime is likely to be more prevalent when the ratio of guardians to potential transgressors is low.

In a community where people know other people, there is less opportunity for crime, because offenders can be readily identified and punished. When a child's parents can identify the boy who has been bullying their son, they can seek intervention by the bully's parents, particularly if they know them. Crime may occur more frequently in urban areas because of increased contact and greater anonymity. The "dispersion of kinship and friendship over a wider metropolitan space and the auto-mobilization of the population" (M. Felson, 1986, p. 123) make informal control more difficult. The ability of offenders to travel to areas where they are unknown and the availability of the automobile gives them opportunities for crime that they would not otherwise have. The physical environment may be important because it can affect the visibility of criminal acts to third parties (see Brantingham & Brantingham, 1990).

Any activity that causes young men to congregate in one location will also increase the likelihood of violence, because young men are the segment of the population most likely to engage in violence. Schools create more opportunities for contact between young men and thereby create many criminal opportunities. Thus, evidence suggests that young men of low status engage in less delinquency after they drop out of high school (Elliot & Voss, 1974). Large schools have higher crime rates because there is less supervision, a greater concentration of delinquent-prone youth, and a lower rate of involvement in conventional school activities (M. Felson, 1993).

In an attempt to evaluate routine activities theory, L. E. Cohen, Kluegel, and Land (1981) examined the effect of variables representing lifestyle and proximity on an individual's risk of victimization for assault and other crimes, controlling for income, race, and age. The study was based on the National Crime Survey, a collection of interview data from hundreds of thousands of respondents nationwide. Victimization was found to be most likely when people were unemployed and unmarried and when they lived near the central city and low-income neighborhoods. Kennedy and Forde (1990) examined determinants of victimization of a variety of crimes, using the Canadian Urban Victim Survey. They found that residents who patronized bars, who worked or went to class, or who went out for a walk or drive at night were more likely to be victims of assault than those who do not engage in these activities (see also Miethe, Stafford, & Long, 1987).

Routine activity theory (M. Felson, 1993) may be relevant to dispute-related violence as well as to predatory violence. Routine activities that bring together potential adversaries are likely to lead to higher rates of violence. Thus, the frequency of violence in some bars may result from young intoxicated men being together in a single location. The key predictor of the frequency of violence in bars (as reported by bartenders) is the age of the clientele (R. B. Felson, Baccaglini, & Gmelch, 1986).

Third parties are less likely to serve as guardians in dispute-related violence than in predatory violence. Domestic violence occurs more frequently if the nuclear family is isolated from the extended family (Parke & Collmer, 1975). Extended family may serve as guardians in preventing violence directed against spouses and children. Legal authorities are less likely to intervene in dispute-related violence. Antagonists are less likely to be vulnerable to legal charges because it is often difficult to establish who is the victim and who is the offender. In some circumstances, third parties may encourage the antagonists or take sides.[18]

In general, the evidence indicates that routine activities affect the likelihood that individuals will be involved in violent events. At the aggregate level, routine activity variables predict variation in the rate of violent crime. Explanations for variations in the frequency of violence across social units and over time must take into account variations in illegitimate opportunities that tempt individuals to commit violent acts. Rates of violence are likely to be high when people engage in activities that increase the likelihood of physical contact between potential offenders and victims (or between antagonists) and that decrease the level of supervision.

Internal Controls

Theories focusing on internal controls emphasize stable individual differences in the tendency to engage in violence or commit crime. The stability of individual differences in aggressive behavior over time has been demonstrated in a variety of countries (see Farrington, 1989). Olweus (1979) reviewed results from 16 studies of the stability of aggressive behavior. The age at which aggressive behavior was initially measured varied from 2 years to 18 years, and the follow-up ranged from 6 months to 21 years later. The average correlation coefficient between earlier and later measures of aggression was .68. Farrington found that nearly half of a sample of young men who had been convicted of assault or robbery had been rated as aggressive by their teachers at 8–10 years of age. In comparison, only 20% of a control group of men who were never convicted had been rated as aggressive.

The approach of control theories to internal controls is different from the approach of subcultural theories in two respects. First, when control theories discuss values, they focus on inhibiting values, such as moral beliefs. Subcultural theories, however, emphasize values (e.g., toughness) that act as behavioral incentives. Second, the theories emphasize different sources for values. Control theories assert that inhibiting values fail to develop because of inadequate socialization by the family and other conventional institutions. Subcultural theories emphasize successful socialization of values favoring crime by deviant groups.

We discuss three theories of internal control: Freud's (1938) theory

---

[18]Routine activities are likely to affect domestic violence differently than they affect violence outside the home. Activities that draw people away from their homes are not likely to increase violence in the home; if anything, these activities would have the opposite effect.

of the superego, G. Sykes and Matza's (1957, 1961) theory of neutralization techniques, and Gottfredson and Hirschi's (1990) theory of self-control.

The Superego

Psychoanalytic theory provides the most well known explanation of deviant behavior that emphasizes internal controls. In Freud's (1938) personality system, the superego was used to explain the inhibition of a person's primitive antisocial desires. The superego is the internalized agent of social control that operates through the effects of the ego-ideal and guilt. The ego-ideal sets a standard for desirable behavior, and guilt is a form of self-punishment for undesirable behavior. The superego develops early in a normal childhood, if a child identifies with the same-sexed parent. A person who has an underdeveloped superego lacks standards or values that allow for self-regulation or control. As a consequence, a person with a weak superego lacks inhibitions about performing antinormative actions. In more current scientific jargon, a person who frequently ignores rules, norms, and laws is labeled a *psychopath* or a *sociopath*.

A highly developed superego should be associated with consistent moral behavior across situations and throughout the life of the person. Yet, evidence of considerable situational variation in antisocial behavior (Hartshorne & May, 1929) and the decline in criminal behavior as people get older is not consistent with psychoanalytic theory.[19] Modern criminologists are more likely to speak of internalized moral beliefs that inhibit crime under some circumstances rather than a superego that rigidly controls all antinormative behavior.

Techniques of Neutralization

G. Sykes and Matza (1957) characterized a delinquent as an "apologetic failure [who] drifts into a deviant lifestyle through a subtle process of justification" (p. 667). Like many of the theorists described above, they emphasized the similarity between the values of violent criminals and the general population. The key difference between those who commit crime and those who do not is in the tendency to use techniques of neutralization. These excuses and justifications permit criminals to maintain their self-esteem when they break the law. The role of neutralization techniques, then, is to disinhibit delinquent behavior.

G. Sykes and Matza (1957) identified five techniques of neutralization: (a) the denial of responsibility, in which offenders explain their behavior in terms of social forces beyond their control (e.g., poverty or abuse); (b) the denial of injury, in which offenders deny that there has been any great

---

[19]Although individual differences over time are somewhat stable, there is also a general decline in aggressive behavior as people age.

harm; (c) denial of the victim, in which the victim is perceived as having been deserving of harm; (d) condemnation of the condemners, in which offenders focus on their own mistreatment at the hands of authorities; and (e) appeals to higher loyalties, in which they explain their behavior in terms of loyalty to family or friends.

G. Sykes and Matza (1957) reported three observations to support their theory: (a) delinquents usually exhibited guilt or shame when they violated the law; (b) delinquents approved of people who conform, which indicates that they have similar values; and (c) delinquents usually distinguished between appropriate and inappropriate targets, which shows that they have moral concerns.

Hagan (1985) argued that if the incentives to commit crime are large enough, neutralizations are unnecessary. Furthermore, he argued that G. Sykes and Matza's (1957) approach exaggerates the importance of guilt and shame and that neutralization techniques may simply be rationalizations given after the fact. People who engage in violence are likely to give accounts to justify or excuse their antinormative behavior. Expressions of remorse can be a form of unauthentic impression management, publicly expressed but not privately believed. Even if these expressions of remorse are not sincere, it would not rule out the possibility that they might have a causal impact. People may be more likely to engage in behaviors when they believe they can effectively excuse or justify them to others at a later time. It may be that individual differences in the propensity to rationalize behavior—to act in spite of one's moral values—are important in explaining individual differences in violent behavior.

The hypothesized causal effects of techniques of neutralization on delinquency have not been empirically studied. Longitudinal studies are necessary, because it must be demonstrated that the prior learning of techniques of neutralization subsequently affects behavior. Techniques of neutralization may be only one factor that by itself does not increase violence and delinquency but that when combined with other factors does play a causal role. A deeper analysis would require an understanding of the conditions under which techniques of neutralization are learned and used by individuals.

Self-Control

Gottfredson and Hirschi (1990) assumed that everyone is tempted to commit crimes when opportunities exist but that internal controls inhibit most people from performing criminal acts. The possibility of quick payoffs with little effort appeals to those who lack self-control. People with low self-control tend to be "impulsive, insensitive, physical (as opposed to mental), risk-taking, short-sighted and nonverbal" (1990, p. 90). Because they consider short-term benefits but not the long-term consequences of their actions, they are more likely to become criminal offenders. Gottfredson and Hirschi attributed the lack of self-control to the failure of family socialization when children are young. Evidence presented above that individual differences in violence and delinquency appear in childhood and then become stable is consistent with this claim.

A lack of internal controls in an individual should be manifested in numerous impulsive and rule-violating behaviors. In terms of criminal acts, a lack of internal controls should be indicated by a wide range of crimes rather than by specialization in any one type of crime. Lack of internal controls combined with opportunities that tempt the individual are the factors that cause deviant behavior in general. For the individual who lacks self-control, "the use of force or fraud is often easier, simpler, faster, more exciting, and more certain than other means of securing one's ends" (Gottfredson & Hirschi, 1990, p. 12).

There is considerable evidence that those who commit violent crime tend to commit nonviolent crime and other deviant acts as well. Studies of arrest histories based on both official records and self-reports have shown a low level of specialization in violent crime. West and Farrington (1977) found that 80% of adults convicted of violence also had convictions for crimes involving dishonesty. Violent acts were related to noncriminal forms of deviant behavior, such as sexual promiscuity, smoking, heavy drinking, heavy gambling, and having an unstable job history.

A. Blumstein and Cohen (1979) examined the arrest histories of individuals who had been arrested for aggravated assault. They found that the probability of arrest in a given year was .19 for aggravated assault, .14 for robbery, .11 for theft, .10 for drugs, and .08 for burglary. These results show that the probability that violent offenders will be arrested for additional violent crimes (assault and robbery) is only slightly higher than the probability that they will be arrested for nonviolent crimes. Knowing the type of crime that violent offenders have committed is not very helpful in predicting the type of crime they will commit next.[20] Also, factor analyses have indicated that individual differences in criminal violence reflect a general tendency toward crime rather than a specific tendency toward violence (D. W. Osgood, Johnston, O'Malley, & Bachman, 1988).

Evidence that most offenders are versatile makes it plausible that many of the individual differences associated with all forms of crime are the same. Traditional theories of aggression assuming that aggression consists of a special system of behaviors are challenged by this evidence of versatility (see Gottfredson & Hirschi, 1993). The evidence suggests that individual differences in the propensity to engage in criminal violence reflect individual

---

[20]A study in Denmark (Brennan, Mednick, & John, 1989) revealed evidence of some specialization for violent offenses among offenders with a high number of arrests. However, when two offenses were committed simultaneously, the worst offense was coded. Because violent offenses were more likely to be coded, the study exaggerated the level of specialization.

differences in deviance, but not individual differences in the tendency to do harm. It is important to consider versatility in the search for personal characteristics that predict violence. Most individual-differences factors involved in violent behavior develop early in life, are fairly stable (at least until adulthood), and account for nonviolent criminal behavior as well.

Gottfredson and Hirschi (1993) emphasized self-control because it can account for why the same people who engage in violent crime also tend to smoke, engage in heavy drinking and gambling, and become involved in accidents. However, the notion of self-control is never clearly defined, though it appears to be associated with the failure to adequately consider costs prior to acting. In addition, although criminals may also engage in risky and deviant noncriminal acts, most people who smoke, drink, and gamble do not commit serious crimes. In other words, criminals may be impulsive, but many impulsive people are not criminals. Therefore, it seems unlikely that the traits associated with self-control are the only individual-differences factors related to violence (or crime). Another individual-differences factor may be the person's moral beliefs, which Hirschi (1969) discussed in his earlier work. Also, individuals' differences in sensation seeking may help explain versatile criminal behavior. Thrill seekers are likely to engage in a variety of risky activities, not because they fail to consider the costs but because they enjoy the risk.

SUMMARY AND CONCLUSIONS

All of the theories discussed in this chapter treat crime and violence as goal-oriented behavior. Criminal behaviors are means of achieving values, including money and status. Blocked opportunity theories explain crime as an alternative means of obtaining money and status when legitimate means are perceived as unavailable or ineffective. In addition, violence is a way of settling grievances when access to the legal system is perceived as unavailable. Subcultural theories focus on the values of group members. In delinquent groups, toughness, fighting skills, and honor are valued, and violence is a way of obtaining and protecting status. Young men in such groups may engage in violence even if they have not internalized values conducive to violence. Control theories explain crime in terms of opportunities and inhibitions. It is assumed that there are incentives to engage in prohibited conduct for everyone but that most people are inhibited by external and internal controls. People are more likely to give in to their temptations when their routine activities create opportunities to engage in criminal behavior unobserved by disapproving third parties, when their ties to conventional others are weak, and when they lack moral inhibitions or self-control.

Rational choice theories of crime, which focus on the instrumental character of crime, provide a basis for integrating the various theories (Cornish & Clarke, 1986; J. Q. Wilson & Herrnstein, 1985). This approach assumes that individuals choose to commit crimes to obtain rewards, avoid punishments, or both. Criminals examine the probabilities of success and failure as well as the potential rewards and costs that are associated with criminal conduct. The decision process is rational only from the perspective of the actor, who may have inadequate information, idiosyncratic values, and optimistic views about probabilities and costs. Given the way the actor views decision alternatives, the choice represents the best outcome among those that are considered. Rational choice theories attempt to explain the decision to initially become involved in crime as well as the decision to commit a particular crime. In chapter 7, we present a decision-making model that is very similar to the rational choice approach to crime.

A rational choice model could be applied to each of the theories of crime reviewed in this chapter. A blocked opportunity refers to an alternative that has a low probability of success. When an illegitimate opportunity with a perceived high level of success is compared with a legitimate opportunity to achieve values that has a low probability of success, the actor is more likely to choose the illegitimate means. A delinquent subculture places a high value on fighting skills, physical courage, risk taking, and a willingness to defend honor. These values serve as incentives for group members to engage in physical violence and other forms of delinquency. When there are weak external controls, the decision maker will believe that the costs for criminal behavior are low and, hence, will be apt to choose it as a means to attain valued outcomes. Routine activities produce opportunities where crime has a good chance of success and a low probability of punishment. A rational choice interpretation of internal controls might focus on the negative moral value assigned to criminal acts or the neutralization of these values through rationalization. It would also emphasize the failure to consider long-run costs by people with low self-control.

II

A THEORY OF
COERCIVE ACTIONS

INTRODUCTION

A THEORY OF COERCIVE ACTIONS

Our main goal in this book is the exposition of a new theory of harmdoing that will revitalize research and build bridges between research traditions that have maintained separate concepts and minitheories. It is curious how well segregated the literatures on aggression, social conflict, and criminal violence are. Aggression theorists seldom discuss conflicts, threats, and punishment; conflict theorists only infrequently use the term aggression; and criminologists do not usually refer to theories of aggression to explain criminal violence. For many reasons, these separate literatures do not overlap. Perhaps most significant is that the various social sciences have different levels of analysis and different methodological orientations. Psychologists prefer laboratory experiments, whereas sociologists and criminologists prefer surveys, observational studies, and statistical analyses of crime rates.

In the chapters in this part, we present what we call a *social interactionist approach.* The theory assumes that harmdoing is goal-oriented behavior that develops out of social interactionist processes. We use this theory to organize a wide array of studies, some of which have not heretofore been interpreted as part of the aggression literature. Of course, this organization has been carried out on a post hoc basis. Its value consists of showing how different research traditions can be explained by a single theory and by novel hypotheses that are generated for future tests.

The first task of theory construction is to develop a clear set of concepts. In every book on the topic of aggression, the authors examine the problem of defining the term. Some authors offer a different definition in hopes of circumventing the problems acknowledged earlier, but their subsequent discussion of the topic is not at all affected by their revision. We critically examine definitions of aggression in chapter 6, concluding that current concepts of aggression are inadequate and that it is possible to capture most of the phenomena referred to by aggression theorists with concepts associated with coercion. We recognize that many scholars will resist replacing the concept of aggression with coercive actions. This is not a requirement for understanding our theory. The reader can simply mentally search and replace the terms and chalk up the terminology of our theory to our own idiosyncrasies. Nevertheless, we hope to demonstrate that our social interactionist theory can explain the phenomena of interest to aggression scholars and has a wider scope than theories of aggression.

We present a summary of social interactionist theory at the end of chapter 6, in which we suggest that there are three primary social motives for using coercion: (a) to influence others to obtain some benefit, (b) to express grievances and establish justice, and (c) to assert or defend social identities. Although one of these motives may be salient in any given coercive episode, it is not unusual for all three to be implicated in a single coercive interaction.

A decision-making model is presented in chapter 7. Actors are viewed as making "rational choices" based on their perceptions of the value of outcomes, the probability of success in achieving those outcomes, the negative value of the costs, and the probability of costs for engaging in the contemplated act. A limited form of rationality is involved in many coercive decisions. Decisions to use coercion are often made quickly, under the influence of emotion or alcohol, resulting in a failure to consider costs or alternative choices.

In chapter 7 we also discuss the use of coercion to achieve compliance. Coercion is viewed as one of a number of methods that people use to change the behavior of others. Sometimes coercion is used as a last resort after noncoercive methods fail. Any factor that decreases the decision maker's estimate that a noncoercive form of influence will be successful will increase the probability that coercion will be used.

The use of coercion to establish justice is discussed in chapter 8. The justice process begins with a negative event, which is perceived as antinormative. If the perpetrator is blamed for violations of norms, an offended party will become angry, will form a grievance, and may carry out retributive action against the perpetrator. Such retributive actions may also involve social control, in that they are intended to deter the offender from repeating the offense.

Finally, we discuss the use of coercion to establish or protect desired identities in chapter 9. Some coercive actions involve assertive self-presentation, where the actor attempts to intimidate the target or establish a reputation as a tough, strong, or courageous person. Coercion used to protect identities is probably much more frequent than coercion used to assert or enhance identities. The typical sequence is that a person interprets an action of another as an attack on a desired identity, experiences humiliation and lowered status, and acts in a manner calculated to save face or restore status. One rather direct way to save face is to lower the status of the provoking person by insult or counterattack and place oneself in a superior position.

6

COERCIVE ACTIONS AND AGGRESSION

A theory of coercive actions focuses on the social functions of harm-doing actions.[1] The social context and interpersonal objectives of the actors are emphasized as of prime importance in explaining actions, although the impact of biological, developmental, and personality factors are recognized. The focus of traditional theories on intrapersonal factors—such as hormones, brain centers, frustration, arousal, stress, instincts, and learning—as proximal causes of aggression is viewed as at best misleading and at worst simply wrong. In the theory that we present in this and the following chapters, the central concern is with social interaction and situational factors.

We argue that the theoretical language used by traditional theorists, especially the concept of aggression, is flawed and that it would be helpful

---

[1] The term *social interactionist* should not be confused with the term *symbolic interactionism*, although there are some similarities. Both viewpoints stress the importance of the cognitive constructions of the individual actors and of social interaction. However, the social interactionist view emphasizes decision making, incentive and costs, and the motives for social actions, whereas symbolic interactionism does not.

in changing the direction of theory and research to develop an alternative way of conceptualizing the basic phenomena of interest. The concept of aggression is examined, an alternative language in terms of coercive actions is offered, and an outline of a social interactionist theory explaining why people perform such actions is provided. A social interactionist perspective emphasizes social conflicts, power and influence, social identities, and retributive justice. Although this social psychological approach emphasizes situational factors, it includes cognitions, preferences, and emotions as important features of social actions.

THE CONCEPT OF AGGRESSION

The function of observational concepts in science, according to Kaplan (1964), is to classify events in a manner that allows theoretical explanation in terms of causes.[2] The classification of organisms was an important step in the development of a theory of biological evolution. Any particular observational concept may be considered a good one if it facilitates the theoretical goals of understanding and explaining the classified events. There are instances in the history of science where observational concepts have impeded the development of knowledge. An example is the concept of phlogiston, which delayed the formulation of a theory of gases (Mason, 1962).

The way one organizes phenomena into descriptive units clearly has important theoretical implications. Kaplan (1964) pointed to a paradox of conceptualization: "The proper concepts are needed to formulate good theory, but we need a good theory to arrive at proper concepts" (p. 53). In Part 1 of this book, we presented conceptual and empirical problems with traditional theories of aggression. It is time to ask whether the term *aggression* and its qualifying adjectives are useful as descriptions of phenomena. The two most frequently used definitions of aggression may be referred to as *behavioristic* and *attributional*. We turn now to a critical examination of these two definitions.

Definitions of Aggression

Behavioristic

A. H. Buss (1961) defined *aggression* as any behavior that produces harm or injury to another or, more technically, any "response that delivers noxious stimuli to another organism" (p. 1). Biting, hitting, shooting, and

---

[2]This statement does not deny that observations and methods are affected by theories and does not assert that fact can be separated from theory (Kuhn, 1962). Observations are made under conditions that produce reliable perceptions in independent observers (Meyers, 1988).

stabbing another person are obviously responses that deliver noxious (i.e., unpleasant) stimuli to the victim and, hence, are considered aggressive responses. The behavioristic definition was offered in an attempt to avoid questions about the internal or cognitive states of the organism and to refer to tangible responses. The task of the behaviorist, then, is to develop a theory to explain why actors engage in such aggressive behavior.

The behaviorist agenda seems at first glance to be a plausible and clear approach to a scientific study of aggression. However, it is reasonable to ask some questions about the behavioristic definition. The behaviorist concept of aggression includes all responses ($R1$, $R2$, $R3$ . . . Rn) that produce noxious stimuli to another. A number of critics (e.g., Bandura, 1973; Kaufmann, 1970; Tedeschi, Melburg, & Rosenfeld, 1981) have asked whether the behavioristic definition includes behaviors that are not aggression and, hence, is too broad or whether it excludes relevant responses and, therefore, is too narrow.

Consider a shooting accident. A person at a rifle range aims a rifle at a target, misses it, and the shot wounds a person who is taking a walk nearby. The person clearly inflicts harm to the victim and, according to the behavioristic definition, the harmdoing behavior should be labeled *aggression*. However, accidental outcomes and intentional outcomes are not explainable by the same set of causes. Accidental outcomes are not foreseen and are not under the control of the actor. Intentional outcomes are foreseen and serve to motivate the actor. The two sorts of episodes represent different processes and require separate explanations. No theorist includes accidents, mistakes, and involuntary behaviors in a definition of aggression.

The behavioristic definition also excludes responses that most social scientists believe should be included as aggression (Bandura, 1973; Berkowitz, 1962; Kaufmann, 1970). For example, suppose that a sniper along a Los Angeles freeway fires his rifle at passing motorists and, because he is nervous or a poor marksman, fails to hit anything. Note that no target has been physically harmed. Therefore, the behavior would not be aggressive according to a behavioristic definition of aggression. Yet, all the muscle movements of the sniper in terms of lifting, aiming, and firing the rifle are the same as those that might be performed by a successful murderer. The difference between the unsuccessful sniper and a successful one is not in the behavior but in the outcome. Therefore, it appears inconsistent to include only successful harmdoing as a criterion for including a behavior in the class referred to as *aggression*. Moreover, the causal factors involved in the sniper's decision to shoot are likely to be the same whether he hits or misses the target.

A. H. Buss (1971) recognized these difficulties with the behavioristic definition of aggression and offered a revised definition: "the attempt to deliver noxious stimuli regardless of whether it is successful" (p. 10). It is fair to ask a behaviorist, What does "attempting" look like? A determination that an actor is attempting to do harm requires an inference by observers (or by the actor) about the goals of the actor and is not amenable to a strictly behavioristic description. To ascribe attempting to the actor, an observer must take the role of the actor: "the actor is in a situation in which I would say I am attempting to hurt someone; therefore, the actor is attempting to hurt someone." Thus, Buss's attempt to rescue the behavioristic definition required that he give up a strict behavioristic orientation. A further difficulty for a behavioristic definition is the observation that there are occasions when a person may intend to harm someone by not doing something. A failure to provide aid when someone is drowning may be an act of murder, as was the case in Theodore Dreiser's (1929) famous novel, *An American Tragedy.* Not doing something can hardly be regarded as a response without twisting words.

Attributional

In 1939, Dollard et al. expressed an attributional definition of aggression in the technical jargon of the learning theory prominent at that time: "behavior whose goal-response is the inflicting of injury on some object or person" (1939, p. 3). In contemporary language, the statement may be revised as defining aggression as any behavior whose intent is to harm (Berkowitz, 1962). The attributional definition appears to correct the problems associated with a behavioristic definition because accidents are excluded and intentional responses that do no harm are included within the class of behaviors identified as aggression.

A description of different kinds of acts would not be sufficient to identify aggressive responses from an attributional perspective. It must also be established that the actor intended to injure or kill the victim. A mistake during target practice that results in a person being shot would not count as aggressive behavior because the harm is unintended. On the other hand, a sniper who intends to do harm but fails to do so would be considered to be acting aggressively. It is the attribution about the actor's intentions that is crucial for identifying aggression, typically accompanied by some response believed to be activated by the intention. The actual infliction of harm is not a necessary feature of the attributional definition.

The attributional definition does not include unintentional responses; can be accommodated to inaction that results in harm; and includes responses that were intended to do harm, but failed to do so. The problems associated with the behavioristic definition of aggression thus appear to be resolved. The attributional definition also provides the basis for making further distinctions among types of aggression, including instrumental and angry aggression (see our discussion of Berkowitz in chap. 2). These distinctions depend on what the actor's intention is in performing the relevant response. In instrumental aggression, the intention is to harm in order to attain some outcome, whereas in angry aggression the intent is only to cause harm to the victim, and no other outcome is sought by the actor.

An important conceptual problem is raised by the attributional definition of aggression. Whereas aggressive behavior can be identified only when intent to do harm is present, there has been a failure to provide an adequate definition of *intent* or a set of rules for establishing when a person has harmful intentions. In laboratory research on aggression conducted with human participants, no tests or measurements of intentions are reported. It is simply assumed that if the behavior is nonaccidental, it is intentional.[3] A clear explication of the concept of intent might contribute to theoretical progress in the study of harmdoing actions.

The Concept of Intention

Heider (1958) proposed that an intention is a plan that guides action. Although this definition appears plausible, a precise definition of *plan* has not been explicated (see G. A. Miller, Galanter, & Pribram, 1960). Kaufmann (1970) has proposed that an intent to perform an aggressive behavior is an expectancy greater than zero that an attack will harm a target. If a person believes there is any probability that a behavior will harm another person and then engages in that behavior, then it can be said that the harm was intentional and the behavior can be referred to as aggression.

The concept of expectancy is rooted in cognitive learning theory (e.g., Tolman, 1966) and in current theories of decision making (Simon, 1979). It refers to a mental representation of experienced contingencies that is triggered by some environmental or mental cue. By developing expectancies of means–ends relationships, the individual gains control over the environment to obtain desired outcomes.

The notion of intent as an expectancy is an advance because it is specific and rooted in psychological theories of learning and economic decision theories. However, it is inadequate by itself for characterizing the set of behaviors referred to as aggression. Dentists expect that some of their procedures will cause pain for their patients, but no one labels dentists *aggressors*. This is because dentists do not want to deliver pain—they do not value harm to the target. The acts performed by the dentist produce multiple outcomes: pain, better dental health, and financial remuneration. The dentist values better dental health and, presumably, the money that is earned. If dentists could carry out their procedures without causing pain, they would surely do so. Furthermore, the pain inflicted on patients by dentists is not causally related to any goals pursued by the dentist. Pain is

---

[3]Although intention could be defined as *nonaccidental behavior*, no theorist has explicitly offered such a definition. Any such definition would require a definition of what an accident is, and presumably such a task would require an examination of intentions—a circular reasoning problem.

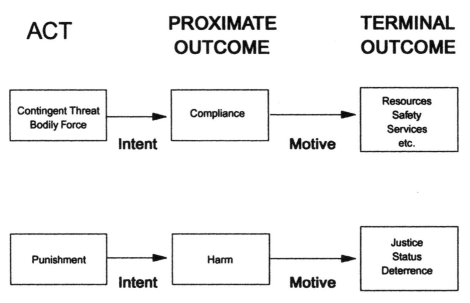

Figure 6.1. The components of coercive actions.

a by-product of dental work, not a means to an end; it is incidental to the dentist's goals. In contrast, the Nazi dentist in *The Marathon Man* inflicted pain in an attempt to extract information from the character played by Dustin Hoffman. In this case, the dentist valued pain because it was a means to an end that he valued.

Given these considerations, we define an *intentional action* as an act performed with the expectation that it will produce a proximate outcome of value to the actor. The proximate outcome is valued because of its causal relationship to some terminal outcome. In social interactions, it is typical that a chain of events transpires before a valued terminal outcome is attained (see Figure 6.1). For example, a boy threatens his sibling in order to get the television control, so he can watch a particular program. The source issues a threat to the target, and, if the target complies (a proximate out-come), the source achieves the valued terminal outcome (in this case, watching the valued TV program). Because compliance is an outcome that is instrumental to achieving the value that motivates the actor, it has derivative value for the source. The expectation that the proximate outcome of compliance will achieve a valued terminal outcome bestows value on compliance.[4] In an attempt to test the above conception of intent, Quigley, Croom, and Tedeschi (1993) presented subjects with scenarios in which information was provided about an actor's perceived probability of harming

---

[4]The representation of intent as the probability of attaining a proximate outcome and the value of the terminal outcome may sometimes be too simple. The decision maker may also contemplate the probability that the proximate outcome will lead to the valued terminal outcome.

another person and the value of harming the person. Subjects were asked to infer the strength of the actor's intention to harm the victim. The strength of the attributed intention to do harm was affected by both probability and value.

One way to conceptualize this complicated chain of events is to accept Schutz's (1967) distinction between intent and motive. He proposed that an *intent* refers to the outcome desired by an actor and a *motive* refers to the reason for valuing the outcome. Schutz stated that intent refers to the "in order to" reason, whereas motive refers to the "because" reason. In our example, the child uses a threat in order to get the other child to hand over the channel changer (the intentional component of the action) because he values watching the television program (the motive of the action).

Intent and motive are associated with every human action. This assumption is important because it distinguishes a social interactionist approach from most traditional theories of aggression, which propose a distinction between angry or reactive aggression and instrumental aggression. For example, in Berkowitz's (1993) theory (see chap. 2), the goal of angry aggression is harm to a victim. Angry aggression is performed automatically—that is, without cognitive mediation—when elicited by aversive stimuli. However, our theory assumes that all harmdoing is instrumental to achieving valued terminal outcomes, such as tangible goods, personal safety, retributive justice, and the restoration of favorable social identities. From a social interactionist perspective, all harmdoing behavior is cognitively mediated.

The intentions of the actor play no formal role in Berkowitz's theory. Our view explicitly incorporates decision making by the actor as causal in determining what he or she does. If an act is expected to do harm and the harm is valued, then, by our definition, the act is intentional. Thus, probabilities and values of proximate and terminal outcomes associated with a chosen act (i.e., its intent and motive) are explanatory in the theory of coercive actions.

RESPONSES AND ACTIONS

Traditional psychological theories, influenced greatly by positivism and its derivative, behaviorism, attempt to describe and explain responses. Psychologists have predominantly taken an individualistic, intrapsychic, and mechanistic perspective in developing theories of human behavior. The traditional stimulus–response associationism characteristic of the first part of the twentieth century has been supplemented by a variety of organismic factors, including cognitions, affect, motives, and personality traits. Nevertheless, the overall perspective still emphasizes a causal sequence that ends with the organism's skeletomuscular response. The notion of response is taken as unproblematic and as simply a datum presented more or less directly to the senses.

Philosophers, and a few social psychologists (e.g., Harré & Secord, 1973), have raised questions about the adequacy of the concept of response as a way of describing what a person does. The term *response* refers to physical movements made by an organism. These movements typically require the use of striate muscle groups. Unfortunately, one cannot describe what a person is doing by pointing to the muscles being used. If one is to understand what a person is doing, one must refer to goals that are being pursued. When a person considers a possible action, he or she does not usually contemplate which striate muscle groups to use. Rather, the focus is typically on how to manipulate aspects of the environment to achieve specific goals. In other words, actions by definition involve means–ends relations (Tolman, 1966).

Consider John Wilkes Booth's assassination of Abraham Lincoln.[5] A mechanistic description of the event might be as follows: Certain cells firing in the motor cortex of Booth's brain caused his hand to grasp a gun, his arm to raise his hand and hold it still in a particular direction, and his finger to exert force against a metal trigger, causing the hammer to trip, igniting a small explosion, ejecting a shell through the barrel into a trajectory that eventually entered Lincoln's body in the area of his head, and initiating physiological processes that terminated Lincoln's life the next day.

It would be tempting under this mechanistic description to say that Booth's assassination of Lincoln was caused by neural firings in the motor cortex. However, the same movements could have been used in firing at a fixed target or a rabbit, or even in playing with a toy gun. The explanation of the movements is not sufficient for understanding why Booth assassinated Lincoln. A complete physiological description of brain states and muscle movements would not provide an explanation of the relevant action. It is not the firing of the gun that is of interest in a description of what Booth did, but his intent and motive in firing it. Indeed, it was not known that Booth had killed Lincoln at the time of the shooting.[6]

The available descriptions of what Booth did are listed below from the most molecular (M1) to the most molar (M5) levels:

M1 → Booth moved his finger.
M2 → Booth fired the gun.
M3 → Booth shot Lincoln.

---

[5]For the following discussion, a great deal is owed to Dretske (1988), including the example of Booth and Lincoln.

[6]Although Booth killed Lincoln when he shot Lincoln, the president did not actually die until the next morning. Although this may be a strange way to talk, it is clear that when Booth shot Lincoln a set of physiological reactions were set into motion that could not be reversed, and, because they ended Lincoln's life, it is not unreasonable to describe Booth as killing Lincoln when he fired the fatal shot. If Booth had died before Lincoln died, Booth would still have killed Lincoln (Dretske, 1988).

M4 → Booth killed Lincoln.
M5 → Booth assassinated Lincoln.

A molar level cannot be explained by more molecular levels. Thus, M5 cannot be explained by M1, M2, M3, or M4, because they are all in M5. Which description is chosen (M1 or M2 or ?) is important because how one describes and defines behavior is integrally related to the way one explains it.

To focus on elementary movements is to see only the trees but not the forest. A more holistic, or molar, description of what someone is doing is incorporated in the concept of action. The most important features of actions are their goal-oriented character and their association with social rules. One is not likely to gain a satisfactory answer to the question of why Booth assassinated Lincoln by looking for physical causes, such as activity in brain centers or endocrine secretions. A sociopsychological question most likely has a sociopsychological answer, not a physiological one.

Peters (1958) suggested two reasons why "we can never specify an action exhaustively in terms of movements" (pp. 5–6). First, an action is identified with a particular goal. Booth is described as assassinating Lincoln because of the belief that his goal was to kill the president. The means used are less important for explaining the event than is the goal of the actor. Booth happened to kill Lincoln by firing a gun, but the same result could have been achieved in numerous other ways. Second, actions can fail of their purpose, but movements just occur. Unless there is reference to a goal, behavior cannot be said to succeed or fail, to be intelligent or stupid, or to be efficient or clumsy (Peters, 1958). Booth's action succeeded because his goal was to kill Lincoln; had Lincoln survived, the action would have been unsuccessful. Booth did not shoot Lincoln to cause Lincoln to suffer pain; his ultimate or terminal goal was to administer retributive justice and remove Lincoln from a position of power. Shooting and killing were instrumental in achieving these goals.

Reflexes are not classified as actions because they are not under the control of motives or decision making by the person. Movements caused by physical force applied by another person also are not actions. If you grab a friend's hand, place a pistol in it, point it at someone, and force the friend's finger against the trigger, and despite his or her resistance, a victim is killed, you would have performed the action, not your friend. Under these conditions, the friend did not have control over his or her muscle movements (you did), and the friend had no orientation toward the goal of killing anyone (although you may have).

The frustration–aggression theory of aggression is an example of a mechanistic view of human behavior. It takes as the datum to be explained a response that is "pushed out" by internal forces in the organism. The theory can be applied to all organisms because they all make movements.

All aggressive responses are conceived as reactive to inner organismic pressures, although they can be modified or inhibited by expectations and environmental factors. In contrast, actions are always "pulled" by the expected value of terminal goals. Actions are guided by future expectations, which are shaped by past experience, observation, creativity, and situational factors. Social learning theory and instrumental theories of aggression tie responses to goals expected by the organism, and, in this sense, they move closer to an action-oriented approach.

Some biological approaches also take a mechanistic view of human behavior. Biological factors can cause responses, but they have only an indirect role in explaining harmdoing actions. Because responses are physical movements, they can be genetically coded. Actions, on the other hand, involve expectations and values—symbolic phenomena—and are unlikely to be genetically coded. It is also unlikely that there is a genetic code for the value an individual places on harmdoing. Alternatively, it is plausible that activity levels, conditionability, and arousal levels are genetically coded, because they have physical elements. In some circumstances, these aspects of temperament may indirectly affect the probability that a person will engage in actions involving harmdoing, the intensity of such actions, or both.

COERCIVE ACTIONS

A *coercive action* is an action taken with the intention of imposing harm on another person or forcing compliance. Actors engaged in coercive actions expect that their behavior will either harm the target or lead to compliance, and they value one of these proximate outcomes. The value they attach to compliance or harm to the target arises from their belief about the causal relationship between compliance or harm and terminal values. There are many values that might be pursued through coercive means. For example, actors might value harm to the target because they believe it will result in justice, or they might value the target's compliance because they believe it will lead to tangible benefits.

There are three types of coercive actions: threats, punishments, and bodily force. A *threat* is a communication of an intention to harm the target person. *Punishment* refers to an act performed with the intention of imposing harm on another person. Threats can be used either to compel compliance by the target or to impose harm on the target. In the latter case, a threat may be intended to cause fear in the target, which may be considered a form of harm.

Bodily force is the use of physical contact to compel or constrain behaviors of another person. The basis for success in achieving compliance through bodily force may be superior bodily strength, the use of implements or weapons, or the unexpectedness of the attack. A purse snatcher may shove a victim or a parent may carry a protesting child to her bedroom at bedtime. Such actions are not intended to punish but to force compliance. The target may perceive the action as harmful, but from the actor's point of view, harm is an incidental outcome or by-product of the bodily contact.

There is at least one instance in which harmdoing actions are not classified as *coercive actions*. Some instances of deception (including lying, entrapment, and fraud) may involve an intention to harm, but they constitute persuasion rather than coercion. No information about harm is communicated to the target (as in a threat), and thus, harm is not a consideration in "forcing" a particular decision on the target. In other words, a negative side-payoff for making the wrong decision is not a factor in whether or not the target will do what the source wants. The decision to believe a lie is left to the target, as is the case with any other form of persuasive communications. It might be said that actors who use deception give targets information that leads them to choose to act in ways that harm themselves.[7]

Threats

There are basically two types of threats: contingent and noncontingent (Tedeschi, 1970). A *contingent threat* is a communication demanding some form of compliance and indicates that the source will impose harm on a target for noncompliance.[8] In a contingent threat, a source states, "If you don't do what I want, then I will do X," where X is something the source believes the target does not want done.

Contingent threats may take a compellent or a deterrent form. Compellent threats demand that the target perform a specific action or else be punished, whereas deterrent threats demand that the target not perform a specific action or else be punished. A compellent threat demands that the target engage in a particular behavior; the target has no choice except to do as demanded or be punished. On the other hand, a deterrent threat demands that the target not engage in a particular behavior.

Threats may also be noncontingent. A source may simply communicate "I will do X," where X is a harm. A *noncontingent threat* is a coercive action that is usually intended to frighten or humiliate the target person. Fear and humiliation are harms imposed on the target by the threatener; hence, noncontingent threats may be conceived as a form of punishment.

---

[7]Although some threats give targets a choice about whether to comply, it is a lesser-of-evils choice; the target will be harmed for compliance or for noncompliance.

[8]This definition of *threat* is consistent with the view that some forms of utterances are actions or performatives (Austin, 1961). Other examples of speech acts are promises, excuses, and apologies.

Threats are often tacit or implied rather than explicit. A facial expression, a bodily posture, the phrasing of a sentence, and a multitude of other subtle means can communicate threats. An expression of anger may be used to communicate a threat. Such threats are likely to be nonspecific with respect to the punishment the actor has in mind, as if the actor were saying "If you don't do X, I will harm you in some way." Threats may also be nonspecific with respect to the demand the actor has in mind, as when a bully behaves in a threatening manner but makes no specific demands.

There are occasions when tacit threats are perceived when none are intended. Miscommunication is likely due to the ambiguous nature of tacit threats. Tacit threats are difficult to decode and are likely to be less successful in achieving compliance than explicit threats (Fisher & Ury, 1981). To the extent that tacit threats are reliably transmitted and decoded by targets, they should function in the same way as more explicit threats. Actors may prefer to make the threat ambiguous so that, if challenged, they can deny that a threat was intended.

Punishment

Psychologists tend to use Thorndike's (1913) empirical law of effect as a basis for defining *punishment:* It is a stimulus that the organism avoids or from which it escapes, and the organism will do nothing to obtain it. Punishment, according to this view, is an aversive stimulus condition that could be nonsocial in origin, such as a bolt of lightning or the prick of a thorn.

A second view identifies punishment as any event that reduces the probability of an antecedent response (G. C. Walters & Grusec, 1977). Such events include the production, removal, or delay of a stimulus. For example, the removal of a reward may reduce the probability of a response, or an increase in the time between the response and the reinforcement may weaken a learned response performed by an animal. If so, the event is considered a punishment whether or not it was brought about by another organism or by some other means.

It is not clear in these definitions whether the criterion for identifying a punishment is the goal of the actor or the consequences on the responses of the target. What should be said about a person who administers a noxious stimulus, expecting it to weaken a response, but it fails? Furthermore, the focus on the goal of weakening responses appears rather narrow in the context of the various motives an actor can have for imposing costs on another person.

A third view identifies punishment as a penalty applied in response to wrongdoing. This commonsense view refers to a legitimate form of harm-doing and thus has a positive connotation. However, such a definition of punishment compounds the act of penalizing and the legitimacy of such an action. In social interactionist theory, punishment is confined to acts that intend to do harm, and the question of legitimacy is treated as a separate factor.

We define *punishment* as an action performed with the intention of imposing harm on another person. Kleinig (1973) suggested that the basic point about a punishment, when effective, is that it imposes outcomes on another person. It may take away a desired resource, force the person to accept an undesired outcome, or prevent the choice of a desired outcome. Recall the distinction between harmdoing acts and punishments. It is possible to harm another person without intending to do so. In addition, punishments may fail of their purpose and would have to be qualified by such terms as *inadequate, ineffective,* or *misguided* (Kleinig, 1973). A person may aim a rifle at another person and pull the trigger but miss the target. If the actor intended to harm the target person, it is considered to be a punishing action, whether or not the action succeeds in doing harm.

Tedeschi (1970) suggested that there are qualitatively different types of harms. He distinguished between physical harm, deprivation of resources, and social harm. *Physical harm* refers to physical events that cause pain, biological harm, or physically unpleasant experiences. Punching, stabbing, or shooting a person are impositions that do biological harm to the person and may also produce discomfort or pain.

Deprivation of resources refers to the restriction of opportunities, removal or destruction of material possessions, or interference with social relationships that the target values. An obvious example is a robbery: Victims are threatened with physical injury unless they hand over their valuables. Sabotage, arson, the use of time-outs by parents, and fines levied by magistrates in small-claims courts are some other examples of this class of harms.

Social harm involves damage to the social identity of target persons and a lowering of their power or status. Social harm may be imposed by insults, reproaches, sarcasm, and various types of impolite behavior. However, there are many occasions when attacks on identity are perceived when none are intended. Impoliteness, negative evaluations, mild reproaches, and disagreements may be perceived as identity attacks when they are not. Although these are not coercive actions, the target may perceive them as aggressive and may retaliate (see chap. 9). One action may impose more than one type of harm. For example, incarceration probably involves all of these types of harm. The inmate experiences the physical harm associated with the violent subculture of prison, does not have access to the resources he or she may have had outside of prison, and acquires the stigma associated with being a convicted felon. Assaults and child abuse result in physical harm, but they almost always also involve social harm. Rape results in social harm but often results in physical pain as well. These examples refer to harmful outcomes caused by physical means.

Coercive Actions and Aggression

Tedeschi (1970) and Tedeschi et al. (1974) proposed that a theory of coercive actions would explain those events referred to under the generic concept of aggression. The concept of aggression is discarded as a technical term in the theory, although we would follow convention by using aggression as a general orienting concept to refer to this area of study (Tedeschi et al., 1981). If we did not, there would be little communication between those with our perspective and those whom we believe are interested in the same basic phenomena.

It is fair to ask why we chose a language of coercive actions rather than the traditional language of aggression. To answer such a question requires a comparison between the new and traditional languages. Perhaps the most important feature of a language of coercion is that it clearly points to social explanations for harmdoing. Instead of searching inside the person for drives, brain centers, hormones, arousal patterns, or other internal sources of behavior, one looks to the social context. The language of coercive actions implies that these behaviors involve social influence: The actor is motivated to effect a change in the target.

The definition of coercive actions and the attributional definition of aggression each emphasize the role of intent. However, those who use the attributional definition never define what they mean by *intent,* and, in the case of the frustration–aggression hypothesis, the causal process implies that there is no intent. A theory of coercive actions provides a definition of intention and incorporates it into the causal process resulting in harmdoing. Coercive actions are guided by expectations about the immediate outcomes they will produce, such as compliance or signs of suffering by the target person. These proximate goals are valued because they are expected to bring about the terminal outcomes that motivate the actor to use coercion. As we show in the next chapter, this definition of intent can be tied into decision theory. The actor's expectations and values are causal factors in the decision-making process.

A theory of coercive actions expands the range of phenomena to be explained to include contingent threats. An actor's intent in communicating contingent threats is to gain compliance and not to harm the target. Thus, the term *aggression,* which is defined in terms of an intent to harm, does not appear to include contingent threats. Although it could be argued that contingent threats are a form of instrumental aggression, some alteration in the definition of aggression would be necessary.

An important heuristic reason for using the concept of coercion is that it points to and clearly includes a range of phenomena that has heretofore not been perceived as within the scope of aggression theories. Threats and punishments play an important role in the literatures on deterrence, social control, grievances, coercive power, social conflicts, bargaining, and retributive justice. However, these literatures have remained segregated from the literature on aggression throughout their parallel histories over the past 30 years. Aggression theorists rarely talk about social conflict or social control, topics that should be central concerns. On the other hand, conflict and control theorists ignore the aggression literature, rarely even using the term *aggression*. Often, they talk about threats and punishment, thus using the language of coercive actions.

The concept of coercion carries less of a value connotation than does the concept of aggression. Values are introduced through a distinction made by many aggression theorists between legitimate and illegitimate aggression. A parent disciplining a child and a police officer subduing a resisting offender are dispute-related actions that are considered legitimate, whereas rape and robbery are unprovoked and illegitimate actions. Such a distinction implies that the two groupings of behavior have different explanations. This implication is reinforced by examining the range of research discussed by aggression theorists (cf. R. A. Baron & Richardson, 1993; Berkowitz, 1993; Geen, 1990). There is no discussion of why parents punish children (unless it is abusive) or why criminals are punished for their offenses. Instead, aggression theorists focus on behaviors that they believe are antinormative or morally wrong. The view taken here is that legitimacy is in the eye of the beholder and is not a descriptive feature of an action. What the scientist considers morally wrong or justified should not be imposed on a description of the action to be explained, because other scientists are likely to have different moral values. The result is a value-laden concept of aggression.

Actors often believe that their actions are justified, no matter how heinous or grotesque the outcome. Hence, a distinction between legitimate and illegitimate actions is neither appropriate nor useful unless placed within the perspective of the person making the value judgment. The reasons why criminals use coercion are not different in kind from the motives of siblings or parents to resolve household disputes. Of course, aggression theorists could simply drop the distinction between legitimate and illegitimate actions, and eliminate the value problem. This conceptual step would expand the scope of research on aggression to include all actions that have the intent to harm, including parents punishing children and judicial authorities punishing criminal offenders.

The conceptual distinctions between contingent and noncontingent threats and various kinds of punishment allow for new and interesting theoretical questions. In the well-established literature on the modeling of aggression, it is possible to suggest new hypotheses. If children imitate parental models, do they imitate the specific form of coercive action used by parents? If parents use punishments that involve deprivation of resources, but not physical punishment, will children tend to imitate the specific form of punishment? Many other questions of this sort can be generated from the new language.

A theory of coercive actions may not explain all behaviors involving intentional harmdoing. An actor may use deception or some other persuasive technique to harm other people. Perhaps these noncoercive ways to do harm can be explained in the same way as coercive actions, but because of the difficulties associated with defining these noncoercive actions we chose not to include them in the present theory. Nevertheless, the scope of a theory of coercive actions is rather large and captures most of the phenomena discussed by aggression theorists as well as much that is not. Violent and nonviolent criminal acts and most laboratory experiments on aggression that require subjects to administer noxious stimulation to another person are clearly included. In addition, the scope of the theory includes fights between family members, workers, friends, and acquaintances; parental discipline of children; deterrence of unwanted behaviors; escalation of conflicts; and much else.

SOCIAL INTERACTIONIST THEORY OF COERCIVE ACTIONS

The term *social interactionist* was given to the present theory of coercive actions for two reasons. First, the theory interprets coercive actions as social influence behavior; that is, coercive actions are intended to produce some change in the target person. An insult is an attempt to cast the target into a negative social identity, a contingent threat is used to achieve compliance, and a noncontingent threat is intended to inspire fear in the target person. Second, the theory emphasizes the social interaction between antagonists in coercive interchanges. The relationship between the parties and the dynamics of the interchange between them are central for explaining coercive actions.

The social interactionist approach could be described as a *decision theory*. The person is viewed as a decision maker, whose choices are directed by the values, the costs, and the probabilities of obtaining different outcomes. The alternatives considered by actors in coercive encounters can sometimes be extremely limited. Actors may not consider alternatives when they enact previously learned scripts, when their emotional level is high, or when they are intoxicated.

Harm experienced by the victim and compliance attain their value because of the outcome values that they mediate. These terminal values are the motivation for coercive actions. Anything that people value can motivate a person to use coercion. Coercion can be used to attain information, money, goods, services, and safety. Because coercion usually involves risk, it can be a source of excitement and entertainment. Coercion can also be used to exact retributive justice and to bring about desired social identities. Because we view justice and identities as key values in the decision to engage in coercion, we devote a chapter to each.

A social interactionist approach emphasizes the perspective of actors, whose values and expectations are important in the evaluations of decision alternatives. Actors often view their own coercive actions as legitimate and even moralistic. Their definitions of the situation—including their beliefs about blame, justice, and social identities—are important in how they respond in these interactions. Coercion often occurs without premeditation and is a spontaneous reaction to the actor's perceptions of opportunities, normative requirements, and provocations. In many situations, there is a dynamic interplay between actors who may have divergent perspectives about the instigation of hostilities and the locus of blame.

Coercive actions can be either proactive or reactive. Proactive actions are directed against parties that, even from the actor's point of view, have done nothing provocative. They usually involve acts of exploitation in which an individual uses the target for some selfish purposes. Actors may be attempting to demonstrate their power or to force compliance. Reactive coercion develops when a person uses coercion in response to a perceived attack or norm violation by another person. Whereas homicides and assaults are more likely to be reactive, robbery, rape, and bullying are typically proactive.

The theory we propose in the next three chapters borrows heavily from other theories in a variety of research areas. The discussion of anger is drawn from Averill's (1982, 1983) work on perceived wrong as the source of anger. Specific processes involved in perceived injustice and the assignment of blame are incorporated from the literature on attribution processes (e.g., Ferguson & Rule, 1981). Bandura's (1983) social learning theory is the source of much that is said about incentives and learned inhibitions. Processes associated with retributive and redistributive justice are borrowed from theories of justice behavior and equity (e.g., Donnerstein & Hatfield, 1982; Mikula, 1993). Finally, the concepts of social identities and accounts are adopted from theories of self-presentation and symbolic interactionism (e.g., Goffman, 1959; M. R. Scott & Lyman, 1968; Tedeschi, 1981).

Many ideas are also borrowed from criminology and sociology (see chap. 5). Violence is interpreted as redressing grievances and as a form of social control (Baumgartner, 1988; Black, 1983; Goode, 1971). Furthermore, interpretations of the social interaction preceding criminal violence (e.g., R. B. Felson, 1978, 1982, 1984; Luckenbill, 1977) are borrowed. For example, we have incorporated the finding that coercion tends to occur when informal social controls are weak and when routine activities create opportunities (L. E. Cohen & Felson, 1979; Hirschi, 1969). Some of the functions of punishment and the conditions of its effectiveness are elucidated by deterrence theorists. Finally, theory and research from scholars who have taken what is known as the social interactionist approach to child abuse (e.g., R. L. Burgess, 1979) provide insight into why coercion is used against children.

These theories are consistent in their underlying assumption that coercion is goal oriented and that the processes underlying coercion are social psychological. Unlike the frustration–aggression hypothesis, the study of coercion is integrated with the study of human behavior generally. The application of a theory that explains a wide scope of behavior is preferable to a unique theory of aggressive behavior on grounds of parsimony. Simple and well-established processes in the social sciences—grievance expression, justice and reciprocity, attribution processes, conflict and social influence—are applied to explanations of coercive actions.

SUMMARY AND CONCLUSIONS

The focus of a theory of coercive actions is to explain why actors use coercion in social interactions with other people. One conceptual task that was considered essential in developing such a theory was to explicate concepts of intention and motive. An intentional act was defined as a behavior performed with the expectation that it will produce a proximate outcome that is valued by the actor. The value of the proximate outcome can be derived from the terminal value that the proximate goal is instrumental in attaining. The value of the terminal outcome is considered the motive for performing an action. For example, contingent threats are intended to achieve compliance (i.e., a proximate outcome) from target persons, and compliance is associated with other valued (terminal) outcomes. Punishments are intended to impose harms on target persons (the proximate outcome), and the harm that is done is perceived as instrumental to achieving other (terminal) values, such as retributive justice.

A coercive action has been defined as an action taken with the intent to impose harm on another person or to force compliance. The scope of coercive actions is broader than has typically been associated with the topic of aggression. Theories of aggression have been constructed to explain harm-doing behavior, but a theory of coercive actions also explains the use of contingent threats to achieve compliance. The association of threats and punishments in everyday life indicates that they should be explained by a single inclusive theory. Furthermore, in contrast with aggression theories, the processes that explain legitimate and illegitimate coercive actions are essentially the same. Thus, the intentions and motives of parents who use coercive actions to control or change the behavior of their children are not fundamentally different from the actions of a robber who seeks compliance and booty from a victim.

A social interactionist theory interprets coercive actions as a form of social influence. The actor is viewed as a decision maker who imposes harms or forces compliance to achieve valued outcomes. The factors that are important in making decisions to use coercion are presented in the next chapter.

7

DECISION MAKING AND COERCION

Coercion is goal-oriented behavior, and the use of coercion should be viewed as the result of a decision-making process. In some situations, actors must decide whether or not to use coercion. In other situations, the choice may be between coercion and persuasion or some other social influence technique. If a decision is made to use coercion, actors must decide what form of coercion to use: whether to threaten or punish, what to threaten, and if punishment is chosen, whether it should take the form of physical harm or social harm. If physical harm is preferred, should the goal be to inflict some pain, to incapacitate, or perhaps even to kill the target person? If social harm is preferred, should it be a subtle put-down disguised by humor or a direct insult? If an insult is chosen, what should the content of that insult be? Tactical decisions must be made about how to defend oneself, what strategies to use during a conflict, and when and how to terminate a coercive interaction. Coercive encounters usually involve a series of such decisions as actors respond to the changing behavior of the antagonist.

In this chapter, we examine the decision-making process in coercive interactions. A decision-making model has been applied to instances in which an actor uses coercion to achieve compliance (e.g., Tedeschi,

Schlenker, & Bonoma, 1973; Tedeschi, Schlenker, & Lindskold, 1972). In this model, threats, bodily force, and punishments are considered as alternatives to noncoercive methods of influence as ways to affect desired changes in the target person. Influence is exerted to achieve desired outcomes. Compliance by the target can mediate many kinds of benefits for the source of influence. Harming the target may also contribute to values associated with retributive justice and social identities, which we discuss in chapters 8 and 9, respectively.

A short review of basic decision-making processes indicates the factors involved in the choice of coercive behavior. There are a variety of decision models that have been developed, and we avoid the technical issues that are involved in choosing between them. Instead, we provide a generic model that outlines general factors that affect the way actors make decisions. The basic assumption of any decision theory is that an evaluation of alternatives is carried out by a person prior to acting. A decision maker's actions may appear impulsive because prelearned scripts and other factors may limit the alternatives that the individual considers, thereby reducing decision time and the latency of response.

The actor's values provide incentives for coercion, and they affect whether coercion is preferred over other action alternatives. A value is a preference and has been referred to by Rokeach (1979) as a prescriptive belief.[1] In the language of reinforcement theory, a value is the degree of reward associated with an outcome (Homans, 1961). Coercion is likely when there is value conflict with other people, particularly when that conflict is intense. Costs, such as those imposed by targets and third parties, serve to inhibit coercive actions. Risk taking is an important feature of the decision to engage in coercive actions. The situational factors and individual differences that affect risk taking are described and linked to the decision-making process. Consumption of alcoholic beverages may facilitate or disinhibit the use of coercion. We examine the complex set of physiological, psychological, and situational factors that link consumption of alcohol and the use of coercion.

The relative power of interacting parties affects the choice of coercive actions. In general, the greater the coercive power and the less the noncoercive power possessed by an actor relative to another person, the more likely the actor is to engage in coercion. Finally, coercion is typically an alternative to more benign forms of influence, such as persuasion and prom-

---

[1]Formal theories distinguish between values and utilities. Values have some objective standard, such as dollars, whereas utilities are subjective and refer to the worth to the particular individual. A similar distinction is made between probabilities and subjective probabilities. To simplify the exposition here (at the risk of confusing the more sophisticated reader), we use the terms *value* and *probability* to refer to subjective value and subjective probability, respectively.

ises. Factors that lower confidence in noncoercive forms of influence will be shown to increase the likelihood that coercion will be used.

DECISION MAKING AND COERCIVE ACTIONS

There are two basic processes involved in decision making: the generation of alternatives and the evaluation of them. The first process involves the development of specific expectations or beliefs about what consequences will likely follow particular actions. Individuals learn by imitation or trial and error the potential ways they may respond in particular situations and the consequences that are likely to follow. These learning principles are well described by social learning theory (see chap. 4).

The evaluation of alternatives has been the main focus of decision theories and, to some extent, cognitive-learning theories. There will be no attempt here to provide the details of competing decision and learning theories or to provide a technical exposition of utility models. Instead, we apply a generic theory of decision making to the choice to use threats, bodily force, or punishments against another person.

A central tenet of a decision theory is that individuals examine decision alternatives prior to acting. Decision theories developed by economists and game theorists have primarily been prescriptive or normative in nature and assume the complete rationality of the decision maker. However, real people are clearly not rational in this sense. Simon (1979) proposed that individuals have a bounded rationality. He meant that within the context of limited capacity to process information, biases in information processing, and other constraints, individuals make what they think is the best decision among the alternatives that are considered. In other words, the individual chooses to engage in an act because it appears to him or her to be the best alternative available in the situation. *Rationality* in this context means that if the observer considered the same alternatives, had the same values, and estimated the same probabilities and costs as the decision maker, the observer would decide in the same way.

The individual is viewed as exercising some foresight before acting. However, the decision making may occur so quickly that the behavior appears impulsive or spontaneous. In other instances, the actor may construct a general or specific plan in advance. The extent of long-term planning has been examined in studies of criminal behavior. Feeney (1986) found that most robbers have a highly casual approach to their crime. Over half said they did no prior planning, and few did any detailed planning. Few perpetrators of homicide and assault—"crimes of passion"—plan their crime (Luckenbill, 1977; Wolfgang, 1958). Most crime, including violent crime, does not involve much planning before the crime event. Nevertheless, we assume that criminals decide to engage in their illegal behavior. Crimes of opportunity may only require a go–no go type of decision by an actor who considers taking advantage of the situation to achieve values.

Elements of Decision Making

The basic elements involved in a decision include the value of the outcome, the probability of success in achieving that outcome, the negative value of the costs, and the probability of costs for engaging in the contemplated act. The expected value associated with a choice alternative is a form of net gain of expected values minus expected costs. The greater the anticipated value of an outcome that can be achieved by performing a coercive act, the more likely it is that a coercive act will be performed. Alternatively, the greater the anticipated costs for performing a coercive act, the less likely it is that a coercive act will be performed.

The outcomes of choices are never completely certain. A person can only estimate the probability that an outcome will occur if a particular act is chosen. When a decision maker's estimation of probable success in attaining a valued outcome by performing a coercive act increases, the likelihood that a coercive act will be performed increases. Thus, aggressive children report that it was easier for them to perform coercive actions and that they were more confident of positive outcomes than nonaggressive children (Perry et al., 1986). Alternatively, when a decision maker's estimated probability of incurring costs by performing a coercive act increases, the likelihood that a coercive act will be performed decreases. Note that subjective probabilities may or may not be consistent with objective criteria (when they exist) or considered realistic by other people. Actors can also manipulate their risks. Robbers select weapons, victims, and settings that increase their probability of success (Letkemann, 1973; Luckenbill, 1980).

Decision theories propose some criterion or rule that a person uses in choosing between decision alternatives. One criterion of choice that is frequently proposed is the minimax principle. The individual chooses to maximize expected gains or to minimize expected losses. Another decision criterion is the *satisficing principle*, which is the implementation of any decision alternative that appears satisfactory or good enough without evaluating all the possibilities to find the best one. Satisficing may be more applicable to coercive encounters because these encounters usually involve strong emotions and a limited time frame requiring split-second decisions. Most rational choice theories of crime view decision making similarly (e.g., Cornish & Clarke, 1986). In some situations, the minimax criterion may be adopted because the person may perceive the choice is between the least of evils and may act to minimize expected negative outcomes. There are also strong individual differences in the tendency to focus on probabilities, rewards, or costs in decision making (J. S. Carroll, 1978).

Decision-making theory can be applied to the development of a coercive or aggressive personality as well as to the decision to use coercion in a particular situation. Individuals are likely to have coercive or aggressive personalities if they have a history of positive outcomes when using coercive behavior. A similar distinction is made in criminology between involvement in criminal careers (or criminality) and the decision to commit a specific crime (Gottfredson & Hirschi, 1986).

Scripts and the Generation of Alternatives

Frequently, only one choice alternative is initially considered in a given circumstance. One way to cognitively represent these behavioral inclinations is in terms of scripts (Abelson, 1976). *Scripts* have been described as programs for behavior stored in memory that, when elicited, may serve as guides to behavior. According to Huesmann (1988), "a script suggests what events are to happen in the environment, how the person should behave in response to these events, and what the likely outcome of those behaviors would be" (p. 15).

A script is acquired through a social-learning process involving modeling and reinforcement. When the behavior associated with a script has been used repeatedly and successfully in the past, it will be activated more readily. If strong enough, an activated script will be followed by the scripted action, unless there are strong inhibitory factors present. Strong scripts of this sort are associated with habitual behavior.

Schank and Abelson (1977) proposed an influence theory based on a general script-based "persuade package." It is assumed that individuals are motivated to pursue a limited set of goals—including acquisition of physical objects, power, and authority—to gain compliance and acquire knowledge. The *persuade package* is defined as a small, standard set of influence tactics that induce a target to do something. The individual encodes, stores, and retrieves information that can be used in influence settings. The scripts in a persuade package are ordered in a hierarchy based on their strength and are considered one at a time. The means are ordered in terms of asking, invoking a role obligation, giving reasons, bargaining, and coercing. If the script considered meets a satisficing criterion, a behavior consistent with it will be enacted. If the script is rejected, the next script in the hierarchy will be considered, and so on. Coercion is assumed to be a means of last resort, to be used only when the other modes of persuasion fail.

Rule, Bisanz, and Kohn (1985) also advanced the idea that a package of scripts may be associated with a sequence of alternative actions. They proposed that the number of goals achievable by each type of influence is a small, finite set. Goals are linked to a small, standard set of methods, and when a particular method fails, additional methods will be tried. Bisanz and Rule (1989), in an exploratory study, found that subjects had distinct preferences for types of influence, with most of the subjects placing negative tactics at the bottom of the list. J. W. White and Roufail (1989) and Aguinis, Nesler, Hosoda, and Tedeschi (in press) obtained similar findings.

Environmental cues may activate a particular script, a process that has been referred to as *priming* (Berkowitz, 1984). Such cues only influence which alternatives are generated and do not automatically lead to a decision. In other words, people are more likely to engage in coercion if some cue brings to mind a coercive script, but a decision must still be made about whether to engage in the behavior.

That people behave in habitual ways is not contradictory to the view that they make decisions and act intentionally. Decision makers may use nonanalytic or analytic strategies (L. R. Beach & Mitchell, 1978). A nonanalytic strategy involves a predictable and rapid response. The apparent lack of cognitive processing and the speed of reaction may lead others to perceive it as impulsive and mindless. When a particular situation occurs, a person may apply a preformulated rule or heuristic to guide actions that have been already evaluated. Even when the actors do not consider alternative actions, but simply implement scripts, they retain the capacity to veto the scripted action, depending on on-the-spot evaluations of probability and magnitude of costs. Parents with scripts involving physical punishment may appear impulsive when they strike their children. For these parents the use of violence is a nonanalytic strategy and a first rather than a last resort. They do not initially consider alternative responses.

An analytic strategy involves an examination of alternatives and an application of rules to choose between them. Minimaxing and satisficing are rules for choosing between alternatives. Huesmann (1988) has argued that a person will evaluate the appropriateness of an elicited script in terms of social norms and the likely consequences that would follow its performance. If a child's misbehavior occurs in a public setting where the use of physical punishment might be embarrassing, parents who might otherwise "mindlessly" use coercion may reject their initial choice and consider noncoercive alternatives. Publicity affects the choice of cognitive strategies and moves the decision maker into an analytic strategy. According to L. R. Beach and Mitchell (1978), nonanalytic strategies are more likely to be used when the task is a familiar and easy one or the task is complex and difficult to solve.

Dodge and Crick (1990) have suggested that scripts including coercive acts will be more easily accessed if a person has a limited response repertoire, as would be the case for a skill-deficient person. The person with a limited repertoire has fewer choices to consider, and so each choice is more accessible. The finding that aggressive boys proposed fewer solutions in hypothetical conflict situations than did nonaggressive boys (Gouze, 1987) supported the script availability hypothesis. Furthermore, Slaby and Guerra

(1988) and Keltikangas-Järvinen and Kangas (1988) found that nonaggressive adolescents generated more alternative and constructive methods for dealing with social conflicts than did aggressive adolescents. Together these studies show that scripts involving coercion are more accessible to aggressive people and that such accessibility is due to lack of knowledge about how to resolve social conflicts in noncoercive ways. The generation and implementation of scripts is consistent with a decision model of human actions.

Values and Coercion

Values have an impact on the decision-making process in two ways. They provide the incentive for behavior and affect the means people choose to get what they want. Rokeach (1979) made a similar distinction between terminal values and instrumental values. *Terminal values* refer to goals that serve as incentives for behavior. Coercion can be instrumental in obtaining a wide range of terminal values. Coercion can be used to attain the terminal values identified by Foa (1971): love, status, information, money, goods, and services. It is also used to protect one's physical well-being and security. As suggested in the previous chapter, retributive justice and favorable social identities are particularly important incentives for the use of coercion.

The term *procedural values* is frequently used in the literature on social justice (see Mikula, 1993) and appears to be equivalent to Rokeach's notion of instrumental values. Procedural values refer to preferences for modes of conduct. It is assumed that procedural value combines with terminal value, producing some net value associated with the outcome expected by choosing a particular action. There are individual differences in procedural values that may affect the decision to engage in coercive actions. Although one person may view the use of physical violence as undesirable and wrong, another person may view such coercive behavior as justified or required to attain terminal values.

Conflicts Over Terminal Values

Boulding (1965, p. 172) facetiously defined *conflict* by referring to the Duchess's Law borrowed from *Alice in Wonderland* stating "the more there is of ours, the less there is of mine." The reference here is to the fact that the values (or goals) of two persons in interaction are frequently incompatible. Two children may want to watch different television programs or want the last piece of cake, and two adults may vie for the same romantic partner. Conflict may also occur over procedural values—over the means rather than the ends. Parents may agree that a child's behavior should be changed but disagree about how to correct it. Conflicts that are based on incompatible terminal values are usually more difficult to resolve than those based on incompatible procedural values (Deutsch, 1969).

The potential for conflict and coercion is greater when there is a scarcity of available resources. Scarcity involves a relationship between the supply of a resource and the demand for that resource. The greater the demand relative to supply, the greater the value of the resource. The greater the value of the scarce resource, the more intense the conflict between the contending parties.

Conflict over scarce resources is an important factor in producing coercive episodes. Mbuti men fight over hunting territories (Turnbull, 1965). The scarcity of women is a key feature of fighting and killing among the Yanomamo men of Brazil (Chagnon, 1977). In an experiment, C. S. Fischer (1969) operationalized conflict intensity as the scarcity of resources available to subjects in a bargaining situation. The greater the quantity of resources that could be divided by the subjects, the less intense the conflict was assumed to be. A direct linear function was found between scarcity and the number of threats used by the bargainers.

There are three possible outcomes in conflict situations: withdraw and give up the desired resource, bargain with the other contenders to divide up the resource and accept something less than desired, or attempt to take the lion's share of the resource. Each person can choose from among a variety of influence tactics in an attempt to obtain more favorable outcomes in conflict. Noncoercive forms of influence are not likely to be effective when conflict is intense. Bribes and promises would have to exceed the value of the contended resource to be effective. Adversaries typically are skeptical of arguments made by each other because of the belief that the other is attempting to gain an exploitative advantage. Hence, persuasion tends to be ineffective as a means of influence in intense conflict situations. As the intensity of conflict increases, the probabilities estimated by the two parties that noncoercive modes of influence will be successful will decrease, thereby increasing the likelihood that coercive acts will be performed. In other words, coercion is more likely when the stakes are high.

Conflicts over tangible goods and the division of labor were found to be the most important basis for fights between siblings (R. B. Felson, 1983). Examples of such conflicts include the use of the family television set and the assignment of a particular chore. The potential for conflict is high within a family because of competition for resources and privileges and the distribution of responsibilities. When the rules governing allocation are unclear, the potential for conflict is even greater. These structural features of family relations explain why fights between siblings are more frequent than fights that children have with all other children combined (R. B. Felson, 1983).

Sunk Costs That Add Value

Coercive actions are frequently costly to an actor, partly because they are likely to be reciprocated by the target person. When people suffer some material loss or physical injury after an initial act of coercion, they may attempt to recoup the loss. Alternatively, they may have invested resources in a long-running conflict and feel the need to justify their investment. In other words, the costs already incurred in a coercive interaction—the "sunk costs"—provide an added value for additional use of coercion. There is hope that the next round of actions will turn the tide in one's favor and allow one to recoup or justify prior losses.

People who have incurred costs may engage in greater risk taking; that is, they may engage in acts that have a low probability of succeeding. The lower probability assigned to the success of a coercive act may be compensated by the added value of recouping or justifying the sunk costs. Paradoxically, the expected value of success for a second coercive act may increase with the failure of an immediately preceding coercive act. People may then become entrapped in an escalating coercive cycle in which they experience increasing costs. This process was illustrated in an experiment in which expected costs and gains had early effects on limiting entrapment by subjects, but had little effect after they had already absorbed substantial costs (Brockner et al., 1982).

The process of increasing commitment to conflict with increases in sunk costs was demonstrated in a dollar auction game (Teger, 1980). The rule of the auction was that the first and second highest bidders would have to pay the auctioneer but that only the highest bidder would receive the dollar. The typical sequence in the auction was that one person would bid, say, 25 cents and another would bid 30 cents. The lower bidder might consider withdrawing, but if no further bids were offered, the quarter would be lost without gaining anything. It therefore appears better to bid higher— say, 35 cents—with the hope of gaining the dollar and a profit of 65 cents. The other bidder thinks in exactly the same way and bids higher to recover the possible loss with the hope of a profit. It is not unusual in this situation to have bids of two or three dollars to obtain the one dollar that is at auction. Teger (1980) found that subjects were influenced first by the incentive of winning the dollar, then by the hope of recouping sunk costs, and last by the motive to defeat the other bidder.

Procedural Values

Procedural values affect decisions about whether to use coercion and, if coercion is used, its form and severity. Procedural values may inhibit or facilitate the use of coercion. A negative procedural value for coercion detracts from the net value of an associated outcome, whereas a positive value for using coercion adds value to an outcome. For example, parents who value physical coercion as a means of influence will spank their children more than parents who disvalue physical punishment.

When coercion is used to gain compliance, it is often as a last resort. Research on sexual coercion among people who know each other has shown that coercion tends to be used after noncoercive means of influence have failed (see chap. 11). Most heroin users avoid violent means to get money for the drug if nonviolent means are available (P. J. Goldstein, 1981). A study of conflict resolution tactics showed that most respondents considered coercive action as the method of last resort in their disputes with other adults (Peirce, Pruitt, & Czaja, 1991). Furthermore, perceived normativeness was a better predictor of the rank ordering of procedures than was rated self-interest. However, 62% of subjects who took the role of a tenant in a dispute with a landlord indicated that, although they did not like using coercion, they would use it if the other means for resolving the conflict failed.

In some situations and for some individuals, coercive means of social influence are considered first. Subjects who possessed both reward and coercive power in a prisoner's dilemma game used threats and punishments against an opponent more often than promises and rewards (Lindskold & Tedeschi, 1970; MacLean & Tedeschi, 1970). Subjects may have perceived coercion as more effective than noncoercion for at least three reasons: (a) Coercion was viewed as more controlling, and therefore more effective, than noncoercion; (b) promises were less likely to be effective because trust was minimal; and (c) the opponent could not retaliate in these studies and so the costs of using coercion were low.

Decision models have alternative ways of interpreting situations in which an actor avoids coercion because of moral values. Actors may assign a negative procedural value to coercion or assign more positive procedural values to other methods of influence and conflict resolution. Alternatively, actors may be inhibited by the moral costs and the guilt they would experience if they engaged in coercion. Finally, individuals may avoid certain coercive choices because they imply unfavorable moral identities. Procedural values can affect the decision to use coercion in all three of these ways.

Actors may not even consider certain forms of coercion because of their procedural values. Most people do not consider robbery as a means to obtain money. Conversely, it is likely that at least some forms of coercion are considered by most people. Even relatively noncoercive parents use some forms of punishment. Although Eskimos do not contemplate physical attack when they are angry, they do shun people as a form of punishment (Briggs, 1970).

Men and women differ in the types of coercion they use when they have a grievance. Although men are clearly more likely to use physical coercion, women are just as likely to use verbal means of attack (Eagly & Steffen, 1986). Research on schoolchildren in Denmark indicated that girls are more likely than boys to use indirect means to harm a target when they are angry (Bjorkqvist, Lagerspetz, & Kaukiainen, 1992). For example, peer nominations in a classroom of 15-year-olds showed that girls were more likely to try to spread vicious rumors as revenge and to irritate others to cause a loss of temper.

There are also strong cultural differences in procedural values related to coercion. Cultural variation in how individuals handle grievances and attacks on their identities are discussed in chapters 8 and 9. There may also be subcultural variation in procedural values. According to the sub-culture-of-violence thesis, procedural values related to the use of coercion and physical violence vary across social groups and sociodemographic categories within cultures (see chap. 5). In some subcultures, coercion may be the preferred method for handling disputes, and violence may be the preferred method of coercion (Luckenbill & Doyle, 1989; Wolfgang & Ferracuti, 1967).

Costs and Coercion

In general, the expectation of costs should deter an individual from performing a contemplated action. The higher the estimated probability of costs and the greater the negative value of those costs, the less likely it is that the individual will choose to perform a coercive action. The concept of costs in decision theory is analogous to the concept of learned inhibitions in traditional theories of aggression. Anticipation of costs (i.e., negative outcomes) inhibits the person from choosing a particular act.

An actor must consider different types of costs before deciding to use coercion. Opportunity costs are those voluntarily incurred by the actor for having the chance to exercise influence. Target-imposed costs are those inflicted by the target, usually in response to something the actor has done, but sometimes in a preemptive fashion. Third parties may also impose costs on a source for engaging in coercive actions.

Opportunity Costs

Opportunity costs are associated with time, effort, foregone outcomes, and the expenditure of resources. The effects of resource expenditure on the use of contingent threats were examined by Tedeschi, Horai, Lindskold, and Faley (1970). Subjects were provided with the ability to send threats to a target in a competitive game. When the target failed to comply with the subjects' demands, they were given an option to administer punishment by taking 10 points away from the target. Three opportunity-cost conditions were created: (a) It cost the subjects nothing to administer punishment for noncompliance with their threats; (b) 5 points were automatically subtracted from the subjects' scores each time they punished the target; or (c) the cost for each punishing action was 10 points. Tedeschi et al. found that subjects maintained high credibility for their threats no matter what the level of costs; if they made a threat, they carried it out if the target failed to comply. However, subjects sent fewer threats as the costs increased. These results show that subjects took into account the cost of coercive acts before deciding to send threats but that once threats were transmitted, they were committed to backing them up.

Opportunity costs play a role in the commission of violent crime. The purchase of a gun requires a resource expenditure, and a mugger's search for a suitable victim and setting involves costs of time and effort. Some criminal offenders prefer robbery to burglary because they find it to be an easier crime to commit. Breaking into a dwelling requires more effort than a personal confrontation (Feeney, 1986; Petersilia, Greenwood, & Lavin, 1977).

Opportunity costs may play a role in the inhibition of physical violence during robberies and rapes. Offenders may avoid injuring victims because the injury might render victims incapable of compliance. In robbery, offenders who require compliant actions by a victim—to open a safe, for example—limit their use of force (Luckenbill, 1980). Experienced bank robbers may limit the level of threat to avoid panicking the victims and making them too fearful to comply (Letkemann, 1973). Rapists may avoid extremely violent behavior because that might result in their victims being unable to comply with their sexual demands (cf. M. Felson, 1993).

Threats may be less costly than other forms of social influence in some situations. Promises can be more expensive because they require the provision of a reward. It may be easier to threaten than to construct a persuasive verbal argument. Threats also take less time to communicate than persuasion. Thus, parents who want a child to comply quickly may choose to threaten rather than persuade.

A successful threat requires no further action by the source. When contingent threats are successful in gaining compliance, there is no need to punish the target. The only opportunity costs are those associated with maintaining surveillance; the source of influence must expend time and effort to ascertain whether the target has complied. When the target does not comply, the threatener must either impose the threatened punishment, which may be costly, or lose credibility. Thus, actors are more likely to make contingent threats when they expect compliance. When actors believe compliance is unlikely, they will avoid threatening outcomes that will be costly for them to enforce. Because it is difficult for actors to predict compliance, they are often mistaken about the probable effectiveness of their threats. Some homicides and assaults apparently occur because actors make threats and fail to obtain the expected compliance. They are then committed to carrying out the threat (Luckenbill, 1977).

An actor will typically need to have direct access to exert influence on another person. A connection must exist between the two persons (Dahl, 1957). Access to great resources or high status may allow an actor's influence "from a distance," but the opportunity costs of influence increase with distance from the target (Homans, 1961; Thibaut & Kelley, 1959). The source is likely to have difficulty communicating with a target who is not nearby, and surveillance to ascertain compliance or behavioral change is more costly and difficult. Furthermore, it is not easy to modify demands or manage a timely delivery of rewards and punishments from a distance. People view connections as opportunities for face-to-face influence.

Target-Imposed Costs

Target-imposed costs are those that can be inflicted on the initiator of a coercive interaction by the target. The use of threats often elicits resistance and counterthreats, and the imposition of punishment often invites retaliation. In general, actors are less likely to engage in coercion if they expect retaliation. Thus, a history of resistance by a target should reduce the likelihood of coercion by a source, whereas a history of appeasement should increase the likelihood of future coercion.

A number of studies have shown that fear of retaliation acts as a deterrent. Evidence shows that there is less use of physical punishments by male college students when they believe the other person has the capability of retaliating (cf. Donnerstein & Donnerstein, 1973; Shortell, Epstein, & Taylor, 1970; L. Wilson & Rogers, 1975). In interviews of 1,874 prisoners in 10 states in the United States, 43% said they had decided at least once not to undertake a crime because they believed the potential victim was carrying a gun (Wright & Rossi, 1986). People who believe they can control, limit, or overcome any resistance by a target will not be deterred by the prospect of retaliation.[2]

Fear of retaliation may play a role in interracial violence, according to a study of college men based on the teacher–learner paradigm (Donnerstein et al., 1972). White men delivered more shocks to Blacks than to Whites when they could attack with impunity. They delivered more shocks to Whites than to Blacks when they believed that retaliation was probable. Fear of Blacks evidently acts a deterrent to White violence against Blacks in the United States.

Confidence that one can achieve compliance through coercion is associated with the perceived probability of target-imposed costs. An actor who expects compliance from a target will not be deterred by the possibility of target-imposed costs.[3] A compliant target is one who gives in and does not retaliate. Thus, the greater the confidence that a target will comply to a threat, the less the perceived likelihood that the target will retaliate.

---

[2]In the context of Bandura's (1986) social learning theory, confidence of success in gaining compliance and controlling the reactions of the target person are factors involved in self-efficacy.

[3]This statement is made in the context of a single coercive episode. The actor may be deterred if the target is expected to seek revenge at some later time.

Findings consistent with this generalization were obtained from children identified as aggressive by their peers. Expected outcomes for engaging in aggressive behavior were shown to be different in children who had been rated as aggressive or nonaggressive by their peers (Boldizar, Perry, & Perry, 1989). Aggressive children were less concerned about retaliation by the victim, minimized the importance of peer rejection for engaging in the behavior, and were much less concerned about negative self-evaluations than were nonaggressive children. Boys were also less concerned about retaliation than girls, which may help explain why they were more likely to use coercion. Overconfidence may be a factor in the failure of formal deterrence to curtail criminal behavior. Men who are habitual criminals frequently overestimate the chances of success for their antisocial actions (Claster, 1967). They expect to avoid punishment for their criminal conduct.

The inhibitory force of expected costs of retaliation may be overridden by other values. In general, when the expected values to be attained are greater than the expected costs, the individual will use coercion. R. A. Baron (1973) found that threatened retaliation only reduced the level of coercion when subjects had not been previously angered by the subject (see also Knott & Drost, 1972). Presumably, when subjects had been provoked, they were concerned with retributive justice and their social identities, and they retaliated despite the costs. When important values are at stake and exceed the magnitude of costs, anticipation of costs will not inhibit the use of coercion. The importance of these social values may also explain why expectations of retaliation did not deter subjects representing competing trucking companies from using a gate to block the path of their opponents (Deutsch & Krauss, 1960, 1962).

The expectation of resistance and retaliation may cause the actor to increase the level of coercion (i.e., to increase the magnitude of threats and punishments). There is evidence that robbery offenders are more likely to physically attack a victim when they anticipate resistance (Luckenbill, 1982). If the goal pursued is sufficiently valued and it is believed that an increase in the level of coercion will attain the goal, the anticipation of resistance may escalate the magnitudes of the threats and punishments used by the source.

Costs of Noncoercion

Sometimes the expected costs of a noncoercive choice are greater than the expected costs of a coercive choice. In this case, the actor must make a least-of-evils choice. Even the most conservative and timid people may take great risks when they see coercion as their only reasonable choice. Thus, people may anticipate costs if they do not retaliate when they have been attacked. By retaliating they may be able to deter their antagonist and third parties from future attack. When the actor expects that the attack will be life threatening or involve some other unacceptable cost, he or she may attempt to incapacitate or restrain the antagonist.

Luckenbill (1982) examined resistance by victims in 201 cases of armed robbery in which the robber's opening move was to make an explicit or implicit threat of death or serious injury for noncompliance. Active resistance to a robber who possessed a lethal weapon occurred under two circumstances. First, when robbers issued a noncontingent threat communicating an intent to harm victims no matter what they did, the best alternative was to take some preventive action. Active resistance provided the best or only alternative to escape serious injury or death. The victim opposed the robber in all 22 cases in which it was believed that force would be used indiscriminately. The second circumstance in which victims resisted a robber possessing a lethal weapon was when they did not believe it was possible to comply with demands. When a victim was unable to obey and believed that noncompliance would cause the robber to inflict injury or death, opposition was the only possible way to avoid the punishment. In all 17 cases in which victims believed that compliance was not possible, they actively opposed the robber.

Bank robbers sometimes face a similar least-of-evils choice. Bank robbers reported that if cornered by the police they would rather have a shoot-out than surrender (Letkemann, 1973). They believed that the police would claim that they resisted arrest and would shoot at them no matter what they did. R. B. Felson and Steadman (1983) found that victims were more likely to be killed during a violent encounter when they had a weapon. When the victim has a weapon, the offender may believe it is a kill-or-be-killed situation. The fact that women are more likely than men to kill their spouses in self-defense may be at least partially explained by the fear inspired by the greater physical prowess of men (for a review, see Dobash, Dobash, Wilson, & Daly, 1992). The offenders in all of these incidents may believe it is either kill or be killed, and so they use coercion in self-defense.

In general, when the expected costs of compliance are greater than the expected costs of noncompliance, the target person will resist the threats of a source. When a target believes a source intends to carry out a noncontingent threat, it is likely that some action to prevent or avoid the expected punitive act will be taken. One form that preventive action can take is the seeking out of third parties to mediate, protect, or form alliances against the threatener. Of course, the ultimate protection against a noncontingent threat is to incapacitate or to kill the source.

Impaired social relationships that result from the use of coercion are a cost that a target can impose on the actor. Coercive actions may decrease the target's liking for the source. Such social costs tend to inhibit the use of coercion. There is considerable evidence that actors who use coercion are evaluated more negatively by the target (cf. Tedeschi et al., 1973). Changes in attraction in response to punitive acts are also affected by initial levels of liking between the two parties. Low-attraction subjects—who expected a disliked person to deliver shocks to them—did not change level of attraction when they were shocked frequently, but they indicated increased liking for the other person when that person delivered the shocks infrequently (Stapleton, Nelson, Franconere, & Tedeschi, 1975). The opposite effect occurred between subjects who had been induced to like one another. There was no change in liking when subjects were shocked infrequently, but there was a substantial decrease in liking when subjects were shocked frequently. Apparently, initial levels of liking affected expectations about the other person's probable use of shocks, and changes in attraction occurred only when expectations were disconfirmed. One generalization from these findings is that the use of coercion against a friend is damaging to the relationship, whereas use of coercion against an enemy merely maintains the status quo.

Costs Imposed by Third Parties

A person might consider the impact that the intervention of third parties would have on the probable costs of performing coercive acts. A brother or father may intervene on the side of an abused wife, a mother may intervene when a father punishes a child, or a police officer may arrest men engaged in a fight. The fear of punishment from these third parties may deter the use of coercion.

Control theories of crime, discussed in chapter 5, emphasize the role of costs imposed by third parties. (Refer to that chapter for a more extensive discussion and a review of the relevant evidence.) The evidence shows that both formal control and informal control affect the likelihood of coercive behavior. Formal control involves legal punishments, whereas informal control involves disapproval and sanctions from parents, teachers, and others outside the criminal justice system. Because the ability of the police to monitor behavior is so limited, formal control may be less important than informal control. Informal and formal controls may also be to some extent redundant in their effects (Gottfredson & Hirschi, 1986). Those people who are deterred from criminal violence by formal controls may already be deterred by informal controls, whereas those who commit criminal violence are not deterred by either form of control.

Informal control depends in part on relationships with conventional others. When social bonds to conventional others are strong, the costs of engaging in criminal forms of coercion are high, and the individual is likely to be deterred (Hirschi, 1969). Informal control also depends on the visibility of coercive behavior to third parties. Routine activity theory suggests that violent crime is more likely when activities bring together violent-prone people in the absence of third parties who might serve as guardians (L. E. Cohen & Felson, 1979). More than 75% of all arrests for crimes of rape and robbery occur as a result of reports from bystanders or victims

(Black, 1970; D. Smith & Visher, 1981), and arrests occur more frequently when bystanders are present at the scene of the crime. Would-be criminals are apparently aware of the greater risks of deviant conduct in the presence of third parties and more often victimize another person when they are alone (Flanagan, Van Alstyne, & Gottfredson, 1982). These studies indicate that the mere presence of third parties serves to deter criminal conduct (cf. R. L. Shotland & Goodstein, 1984).

The role of parents as agents of control has been demonstrated in intervention studies carried out by Patterson (1982). Parents of preadolescents with behavioral problems were taught behavior modification techniques. The parents of these children differed from parents of normal children in not knowing how to punish. Their punishment tended to be erratic and inconsistent, and as a result, children could not predict what the outcome would be when they misbehaved. The parents were taught how to set clear rules, monitor their children's behavior, and establish contingencies for rewards and punishments. The program was quite successful, particularly in reducing the coercive behavior of children.

Baumgartner (1993) emphasized the role of third parties in her cross-cultural study of physical violence between husbands and wives. In many cases, husbands can assault their wives with impunity because of their superior physical strength, unless wives have the support of third parties. Kinship alliance structures, therefore, affect the incidence of the use of physical coercion by husbands. The nearer their families of origin, the less apt women are to suffer physical beatings from their husbands. The brothers and father of an abused woman may seek revenge against the husband. Conversely, when the kin live far away, the husband is less deterred by any threat of retaliation.

Individuals may be deterred from using coercion because they have observed others being punished for coercion. Modeling or vicarious learning can affect calculations of the level and probability of costs (see chap. 4). Criminologists refer to the effect of formal sanctions on observers as *general deterrence* and distinguish it from *specific deterrence*, or the effect of punishment on its target (see chap. 5). Most research has suggested that certainty of punishment is a more important deterrent of crime than severity (Meier & Johnson, 1977; Paternoster, 1989). These factors probably interact in their effects. No matter how severe the sentence, individuals might not be deterred if they think that apprehension and conviction are unlikely.

Age differences in estimations of the probability of costs may help account for the strong negative correlation of age with verbal and physical aggression (Steadman & Felson, 1984) and of age with violent (as well as nonviolent) crime (Wilson & Herrnstein, 1985). The few empirical studies in which this basic relationship has been examined have not been very successful in explaining why young people engage in more crime. It might be argued that stronger bonds to conventional others through marriage and children explain why most criminals retire by age 30, but evidence indicates that social bonds explain only a small part of the relationship (Rowe & Tittle, 1977).

Evidence supports the hypothesis that as people get older their perceptions of the probability of costs associated with criminal activity increase. In interviews, ex-offenders reported that as they grew older they began to realize that the law of averages was against them (Cusson & Pinsonneault, 1986). The more crimes they committed, the more chance there was of being apprehended and ending up behind bars. Many ex-offenders reported fear associated with seeing a partner killed by police or being wounded during a crime. One reported that his accomplice tried to kill him to get all of the loot. In some cases, the decision to stop performing criminal acts was made as a result of a traumatic incident and, in other cases, because of accumulated learning experiences.

The deterrent effects of police arrest on husbands' violence against wives have been examined in field experiments. An initial study (Sherman & Berk, 1984) showed a deterrent effect of arrest on later assaults by husbands. This research has had a major impact on police arrest policies, and at the time of this writing, the policy of police in many localities is to make an arrest in these situations. However, the most recent study suggests that the effects of arresting husbands in these disputes are complex and that, in the long run, they may lead to an increase in violence by husbands (Sherman & Smith, 1992). An arrest may also lead to further deterioration in marital relationships or to later retaliation by husbands.

The celerity of punishment may have an impact on the effectiveness of deterrent threats (Gibbs, 1986). Celerity refers to the timing or delay of punishment following the objectionable behavior. It is well known in the psychology of learning that the greater the delay of reinforcement, the less impact it has on behavior. More immediate negative consequences should deter impulsive people who normally discount such consequences when they are expected to occur in the distant future. Celerity has generally been ignored in the criminal sanctions literature, possibly because punishment immediately after an offense does not occur in most legal systems. The issue of celerity is probably more relevant for informal sanctions, because they often occur immediately.

How celerity is cognitively processed is not known, but one possibility is that remote consequences are perceived as less likely to occur. When an event is predicted for the future, individuals may believe that intervening events will occur to change circumstances so that the predicted event will not occur. If these conjectures are sound, people should be more optimistic about remote, in comparison with proximate, negative outcomes. Remote punishments would therefore have less impact in reducing coercive behavior than would proximate punishments.

Attitudes Toward Risk

Because the use of coercion is often costly, the decision to use coercion usually entails risk. People who are willing to take risks are more likely to use coercion. Individuals differ in their tendencies to be risk aversive or risk seeking. Lopes (1984) found that risk-aversive subjects focus on avoiding negative outcomes, whereas risk seekers focus on achieving positive outcomes. Thus, risk avoiders weight their worst outcomes (i.e., large losses or small gains) more than their best outcomes (i.e., large gains or small losses), whereas risk seekers weight the best outcomes more than the worst outcomes. In other words, risk-aversive subjects ask "what can I lose?" whereas risk-seeking subjects ask "what can I gain?" Risk-seeking subjects have higher levels of aspiration than do risk-aversive subjects. Lopes (1984) found that risk aversion is by far the most common orientation of subjects (see also Schneider & Lopes, 1986).

In studies by Lopes and others, experimenters instructed subjects on the risks of different choices rather than allowing the subjects to estimate the risks themselves. Survey research has indicated that people tend to underestimate risks. People underestimate the likelihood that they will be victims of accidents, robberies, unemployment, infertility, serious illness, or divorce (Harris & Guten, 1979; Kirscht, Haefner, Kegeles, & Rosenstock, 1966; Robertson, 1977; Weinstein, 1984). According to this research, adolescents engage in risky behaviors because of a perception of invulnerability and the belief that they have control over events. A tendency to underestimate risks or the belief that one has sufficient control over events to avoid costs should increase the probability that one will use coercion.

People are more likely to be risk takers when they are faced with the possibility of losses than when they have opportunities for gains. When choosing between alternative gains that have the same expected values, subjects predominantly choose the alternative with the highest probability of success. For example, given a choice between A—a 100% probability of winning $1,000—or B—a 50% chance of winning $2,000—(both A and B have an expected value of $1,000), subjects overwhelmingly chose A. However, when the choice was between alternative losses, subjects tended to be risk seeking (Kahneman & Tversky, 1979; Laughhunn, Payne, & Crum, 1980; C. A. Williams, 1966). Thus, if the choice is between a certainty of losing $1,000 or a 50% probability of losing $2,000, subjects choose the greater risk (Kahneman & Tversky, 1979). Subjects were willing to risk losing more to have a chance of losing less. This may help explain why people sometimes resist coercion (e.g., during a robbery) even when it is risky. Targets experience a certain loss if they fail to resist. Although resistance is risky—it may bring greater losses—it provides an opportunity to avoid any further losses.

Emotions and Risk Perception

The cognitive component of fear is the anticipation of a specific harm. The response to fear is to avoid, escape, or somehow remove or control the source of anticipated harm. A schoolboy who is afraid of attack from other boys may arm himself with a knife or gun to "protect" himself. Resort to threats and preemptive attacks may be motivated by fear of the target person. Toch (1969) found that prison inmates reliably displayed violence in reaction to specific kinds of facial expressions, verbal statements, and skeletal movements of other men. Violent men tended to perceive such social cues as dangerous, and they interpreted their own preemptive violence as self-protective. Toch's observations indicate that actions that appear innocent to one person may be interpreted as threatening by another.

Strong emotions (e.g., anger and fear), which are involved in many coercive encounters, may increase risk taking. Strong emotions tend to focus the person's attention on ongoing events, with the result that future consequences may be ignored. Strong emotions reduce information processing and shorten time perspective. The prototypical example is the outraged husband killing his wife or her lover in a fit of passion. One reason for people to count to 10 when they are angry is to give them time to think about the potential costs of alternative courses of action. It can be expected, therefore, that people experiencing strong negative emotions will be more likely than other people to engage in coercive actions that have long-term costs.

Risk as Value

Decision theories generally view risk taking in terms of the probability components. Actors tend to avoid risk by choosing actions that have a high probability of success and a low probability of producing costs. However, some individuals in some circumstances view risk taking itself as a value (R. Brown, 1965). They may value the excitement of coercive activities. Young men, in particular, may be attracted to the risks of a violent encounter. They may enjoy a certain degree of personal danger or the risk of getting caught by the police. Alternatively, when decisions are made in public, the individual may be concerned about how audiences will evaluate risk taking. Studies show that under certain conditions groups make riskier decisions than individuals (e.g., Isenberg, 1986). People who are willing to take only small risks may be perceived as timid and fearful, whereas those who take greater risks may be perceived as more courageous. Actors who value the identities associated with engaging in risky behavior are more likely to engage in coercive behavior (Weigold & Schlenker, 1991).

Evidence that risk taking affects social identities was provided in a study by Dahlbäck (1978). Subjects were given a risk-taking questionnaire that had allegedly been filled out by another person. In one condition, the other person had chosen predominantly conservative alternatives, whereas in a second condition, the decision maker had chosen predominantly risky alternatives. The risk taker was perceived as more fearless, less anxious, tougher, and less easily scared than was the conservative decision maker.

An identity as a tough and courageous person is more valued in men than in women and is usually associated with a masculine identity. The preponderance of research indicates that men take more risks than do women (Block, 1983; Ginsburg & Miller, 1982; Kogan & Dorros, 1978). The tendency of men to take risks and of women to be risk aversive has been shown to be associated with juvenile delinquency (Keane, Gillis, & Hagan, 1989).

Alcohol and Coercive Actions

Correlational studies have consistently shown a strong relationship between intoxication and criminal behavior. Wolfgang and Strohm (1956) found that in 64% of criminal homicides one of the parties was drinking alcohol. Shupe (1954) found blood alcohol levels exceeding the standard for legal intoxication in over 75% of offenders who committed acts of criminal violence. Similar findings were obtained by researchers in Finland (Virkunen, 1974). In the United States, there is a tendency to associate drinking with machismo. Men drink and get drunk twice as often as women (Cahalan, 1978; Harford & Gerstel, 1981), and they are 3 to 4 times more often problem drinkers and alcoholics than are women (Malin, Wilson, Williams, & Aitken, 1986). Moreover, men drink more often in public places with same-sex friends than do women (Harford, 1978; Leland, 1982). These sex differences exist for all ages, ethnic groups, geographic regions, educational levels, and incomes (W. B. Clark & Midanik, 1982; Leland, 1982). The fact that men drink more than women and that alcohol facilitates and disinhibits coercive actions may help explain why men are more violent than women.

It is reasonable, given the association of alcohol with violence, to look for a mechanism by which ingestion of alcohol leads to aggressive behavior. Alcohol has physiological effects on perception and arousal, is associated with cognitive deficits, and is consumed by people who have strong expectations of how it will affect them.

Physiological Effects of Alcohol

Alcohol consumption is associated with physiological arousal. Small amounts of alcohol may produce increased heart rate (Levenson, Sher, Grossman, Newman, & Newlin, 1980). However, larger doses of alcohol produce sedative effects (Wallgren & Barry, 1970) and reduce the individual's responsiveness to stressful stimuli (Levenson et al., 1980).

It might be postulated that arousal produced by low levels of consumption of alcohol would add to a general aggressive drive and that this additional energy would intensify or facilitate aggressive behavior. Such a view would be consistent with both Berkowitz's (1993) theory of reactive aggression and Zillmann's (1983) theory of excitation transfer. Both theories predict that people who ingest low levels of alcohol and experience heightened arousal should be more aggressive than people who ingest high amounts of alcohol, which should decrease arousal. The correlational studies, reported above, appear to contradict such a prediction. Furthermore, S. P. Taylor and Gammon (1975) reported that subjects who ingested larger doses of bourbon or vodka were more aggressive than subjects who drank smaller doses. These findings indicate no clear relationship between the arousal effects of alcohol and aggressive behavior.

It has been suggested that alcohol impairs higher cognitive processes (Hull, 1981; Zeichner & Pihl, 1979). Alcohol has been shown to impair motor learning, reaction time, word recall, and perceptual-sensory tasks (J. M. Levine, Kramer, & Levine, 1975; M. E. Miller, Adesso, Fleming, Gino, & Lauerman, 1978; Vuchinich & Sobell, 1978). However, the inebriated individual may sometimes compensate and perform normally on difficult cognitive tasks (R. M. Williams, Goldman, & Williams, 1981).

An inebriated individual may be less sensitive to the contingencies of interpersonal behavior and to the outcomes of his or her own behavior. Indirect support for this hypothesis was found in a study that manipulated the behaviors of a confederate either to be contingent on those of the subjects or to be random (Zeichner & Pihl, 1979). Subjects were provided with an aversive noise from an experimental partner (actually a confederate) to signal the beginning of a trial, and to terminate the noise the subject had to push one of five shock-intensity buttons on a modified Buss aggression machine. In one set of conditions, the aversiveness of the noise subjects received was manipulated to be contingent on the intensity of shock they delivered to the confederate. In a second set of conditions, the degree of aversiveness of the noise was randomly determined. Subjects who drank alcohol were more aggressive than those who did not. Furthermore, subjects who imbibed were equally aggressive in the contingency and noncontingency conditions, whereas subjects who did not drink were more aggressive in the random-order than in the contingency condition. Thus, although sober subjects are attentive to the contingencies that regulate social behavior, those who drank alcohol were not attentive to them.

There is some evidence that intoxicated persons are less attentive to inhibitory cues, especially when the instigation to aggressive behavior is strong. C. M. Steele and Southwick (1985) referred to situations involving strong instigation to aggression and salient inhibitory cues as "inhibitory conflict." They had coders rate conditions in 34 experiments as high or low in inhibitory conflict. They then carried out a meta-analysis of the studies. The results showed that drinking alcohol had a disinhibitory effect on the extremity of social behavior (including aggression) when there was high inhibitory conflict. Furthermore, the greater the intoxication, the greater the disinhibitory effect of alcohol under high inhibitory conflict. The results of the meta-analysis supported the view that alcohol impairs cognitive functioning so that the individual no longer pays attention to inhibitory factors. However, it would be desirable to carry out an experiment to directly test the inhibitory cues hypothesis.

Research has shown that drinking alcohol may be associated with the perception of threat in competitive situations. In the competitive reaction-time game, subjects do not know how much shock the other person has preset for them to receive should they lose on a particular trial. In threatening situations, subjects who drink alcohol may attribute more hostile intentions to other people and therefore use higher shocks themselves either to deter or to punish the threatening person. This hypothesis was tested in a simple two-group study in which subjects were either given alcohol to drink or given a placebo (Schmutte, Leonard, & Taylor, 1979). Subjects were then asked what intensity of shock they thought their opponent would set for the first trial of the reaction-time game. The effect of alcohol consumption was to increase the estimate of expected shock from the opponent. However, there was no effect of alcohol consumption on the levels of shock intensity set by subjects. Thus, the study failed to show a clear mediation effect of alcohol-induced expectations of increased threat on punitive behavior.

In another experiment, the threat was removed from the reaction-time game by having the confederate indicate opposition to using shocks and vow to use only the lowest intensity setting. Subjects who had ingested alcohol and subjects who drank a placebo set very low shock settings in the no-threat condition (S. P. Taylor, Gammon, & Capasso, 1976). Subjects who had imbibed were most aggressive when the confederate was not committed to low-shock intensity settings. These results indicate that drinking may increase threat perception and may sometimes lead to coercive behavior.

Alcohol Expectancy Effects

Stereotypes and expectancies are associated with drinking alcohol. In a survey of over 400 respondents in the United States (S. A. Brown, Goldman, Inn, & Anderson, 1980), the expectations of moderate drinkers was that imbibing alcohol increases social assertiveness, increases a feeling of power and aggressive behavior, and reduces tension and anxiety. If these expectations reveal themselves in self-fulfilling prophesies, people who drink may become more aggressive. However, there may be cultural differences in expectancies associated with imbibing alcohol. In Western European countries, alcohol is associated with congenial social relations rather than considered a means of transforming one's personality.

A clear alcohol expectancy effect was obtained in the teacher–learner situation (Lang, Goeckner, Adesso, & Marlatt, 1975). Subjects were either told they would drink alcohol or told they would not be drinking alcohol. Half of the subjects in each condition were given alcohol, and half were given a nonalcoholic drink. Some of the subjects in each condition were provoked by the confederate–learner, and others were not provoked. Subjects who thought they had consumed alcohol gave more intense shocks to the confederate than those who thought they had consumed only tonic, irrespective of the actual content of their drinks. This expectancy effect occurred in both the provocation and the no-provocation conditions.

The expectations associated with drinking alcohol are apparently related to quantity consumed (Pihl, Zeichner, Niaura, Nagy, & Zacchia, 1981). Half of the subjects in alcohol and placebo conditions were told that they would consume a small dose of alcohol, and the remainder were told that they would consume a large dose. In fact, the amount of alcohol given to subjects in the alcohol condition was the same for every subject. Subjects then participated in a modified Buss paradigm. Subjects who were told they had received a large dose of alcohol gave more intense shocks to the confederate than did subjects who had been told they had received a small dose, irrespective of whether subjects were in the alcohol or placebo conditions.

Drinking may be a self-handicapping strategy that mitigates responsibility for whatever the inebriated individual does (Jones & Berglas, 1978). If the person believes that drinking will provide an acceptable excuse for engaging in antinormative or inappropriate behaviors (Sobell & Sobell, 1973), then consumption of alcohol may disinhibit the individual to perform such behaviors (Marlatt & Rohsenow, 1980). According to this analysis, expectancies associated with drinking alcohol disinhibit deviant behaviors (see also Crowe & George, 1989), such as inappropriate sexual advances and aggressive conduct, but should have little or no effect on socially appropriate behaviors. In an examination of 36 experiments, Hull and Bond (1986) found that antisocial behaviors were more strongly affected by alcohol expectancy.

People are more likely to engage in risky actions when inebriated. Mongrain and Standing (1989) found that subjects were more likely to engage in risky driving in a computer simulation after drinking alcohol than before drinking. It is not clear what the process is that mediates an effect of alcohol on risk taking. However, the idea that having a drink gives one courage is consistent with the alcohol–risk relationship.

Conclusions: Alcohol and Coercion

Imbibing alcohol can facilitate coercive actions. A person who has been drinking may become less attentive to social cues and may make more hostile attributions of intention. Drinking may also cause a narrowing of perception to immediate cues with disattention to remote events or abstract principles (C. M. Steele & Southwick, 1985). These cognitive deficits make it more likely that a drunk person will become involved in coercive episodes. A drunk person may also be more impolite and abusive and more apt to take offense and provoke coercive incidents than when he or she is sober.

Drinking alcohol can also disinhibit coercive actions. People expect that drinking bolsters courage, and the sedating effect of alcohol contributes to a reduction of fear and anxiety. A drunk person is less attentive to social norms and the evaluations of others. These effects reduce the perception of costs and, hence, increase the likelihood that coercive actions that are antinormative or viewed negatively by an audience will be performed. In addition, the belief that drunkenness serves as an excuse for antisocial behavior may disinhibit someone from performing coercive actions.

EFFECTS OF POWER ON DECISION MAKING

Interpersonal power refers to the capacity to cause someone to do something they would not otherwise do (Dahl, 1957). Note that it implies a relation between at least two parties and is not an attribute of an individual. *Coercive power* refers to the capacity to force change with threats or punishment, whereas *noncoercive power* refers to the capacity to influence others with noncoercive means, such as persuasion and promises.

The power relations between parties affect the likelihood that one or both of them will use coercion against the other, and the effectiveness of a person in using noncoercive means of influence is inversely related to the frequency with which coercion will be used.

Coercive Power

Kipnis (1976) proposed an "iron law of power" that holds that the greater the advantage of an influencer relative to a target, the more likely "directive" strategies will be used to gain compliance. Derivative from this law is the generalization that actors are more likely to engage in coercion when they have more coercive power than a target and the target resists requests or commands (Kipnis & Schmidt, 1983). Those with a power advantage are likely to perceive higher probabilities of success in using coercion and—because retaliation is perceived as less likely—lower probabilities of incurring costs. Also, any expected costs are likely to be of a lower magnitude.

Relative coercive power is affected by the relative skills and resources of the antagonists and their allies. When physical coercion is an option, physical size and strength may be important. The possession of weapons alters the power equation in violent encounters. That is why a gun is sometimes referred to as a *great equalizer*. Physically weak or fearful people can gain an advantage over stronger, intimidating adversaries when they possess a gun.

A number of experimental studies have shown that a subject's coercive power relative to an antagonist is positively related to the use of coercion. Several studies have found that as the magnitude of an available punitive resource increases, the frequency of its use increases (C. S. Fischer, 1969; Hornstein, 1965). W. P. Smith and Leginski (1970) gave subjects the ability to send threats of a fine and to impose fines on their adversary in a bargaining situation. The magnitude of the fine was varied among groups and could be 20, 50, 90, or 140 points. The greater the magnitude of power they possessed, the more frequently subjects used threats. It must be remembered, however, that the magnitude of punishment that can be used in laboratory experiments is quite low and that the temptation to use unilateral power to coerce compliance from a target is encouraged by the competitive nature of the games in which the power is distributed.

When subjects in a reaction-time game were frequently defeated by their opponent, they delivered less intense shocks than when wins and losses were equally distributed (Epstein & Taylor, 1967). Dengerink and Levendusky (1972) found that subjects delivered less intense shocks to an opponent who could retaliate with even more intense shocks than when shock intensities were equal. These results indicate that a power advantage encourages the use of coercion in competitive situations and that a disadvantage in coercive power discourages its use.

Relative coercive power is affected by the perception that the antagonist is willing to use that power. Perception that a person is hostile and dangerous induces in others a belief that failure to comply with threats will be followed by punishment. Thus, armed robbers use an intimidating voice and threatening language to communicate that they mean business (Letkemann, 1973). In addition, research has shown that dislike for a powerful threatener, in comparison with a more attractive threatener, increased the probability of compliance by a weak target person (Tedeschi, Schlenker, & Bonoma, 1975). There are payoffs, then, for having the reputation of a "badass."

Relative coercive power is dependent on the role of third parties. Actors may have less power than antagonists when standing alone, but they may be advantaged if they have an ally. Research on coalition formation has shown that weaker parties are better able to attract allies (Gamson, 1964). The anticipation of third-party intervention may encourage weaker actors to use coercion because they expect to be protected. It has been found that younger siblings were more likely to initiate an attack against an older (and presumably stronger) sibling when they could reliably expect a parent to intervene and punish the older sibling (R. B. Felson, 1983; R. B. Felson & Russo, 1988). The tendency of parents to protect and side with younger siblings encourages them to engage in coercive actions against older siblings. Alternatively, when parents did not intervene or when they gave supervisory authority to the older sibling, the number of fights between siblings was lower.

Common sense indicates that the superior size and strength of men should play a role in physical violence among heterosexual couples. However, evidence indicates that women are just as likely as men to engage in physical violence against their spouses and that they are just as likely to be the first to use violence (e.g., Straus, Gelles, & Steinmetz, 1980). In addition, violence is apparently just as frequent in committed lesbian relationships as in committed heterosexual relationships (Brand & Kidd, 1986).[4] These patterns suggest that spousal violence is related to the conflicts created when people live together rather than to sexism (cf. B. Carlson, 1992).[5] When conflicts occur in intense relationships, women are willing to use violence even against men with superior coercive power.

Differences between men and women in coercive power do affect violence in marital relationships, however. First, women sometimes use objects and other weapons to counter the physical advantage of men (McNeely & Mann, 1990). Second, the level of coercion that women use is often much lower than that of men (Dobash et al., 1992). In the escalation of conflict, women are much more likely to be injured or killed. When they kill their husbands, it is more likely to involve self-defense than when husbands kill their wives (Dobash et al., 1992). In the United States, 57% of spousal homicides involve a husband killing his wife. The ratio of husband victimization to wife victimization is much more asymmetrical in other countries (M. I. Wilson & Daly, 1992).[6] In summary, we suspect that in the modal case of wife abuse, there is an escalation of conflict in which both husbands and wives use violence. As a result of the greater coercive power of men, as well as gender differences in the tendency to use extreme forms of violence, women are more likely to be injured or killed.

Credible Threats and Preemptive Attacks

The effect of relative coercive power on the use of coercion is even more complex than implied by the discussion above. This complexity is apparent in the causal diagram depicted in Figure 7.1. The diagram shows

---

[4]However, one must be concerned with the representativeness of the sample of lesbians in this study.

[5]In fact, traditional beliefs about women may inhibit violence against them if they emphasize chivalry.

[6]The U.S. rate is apparently affected by race: Black women are more likely than Black men to kill their spouses.

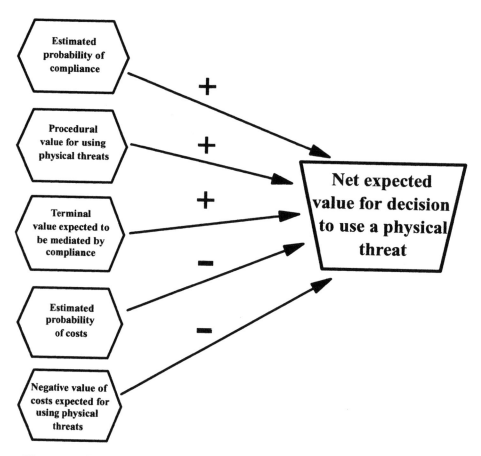

Figure 7.1. Factors considered in the decision to issue a threat of physical harm.

that powerful actors are more likely to engage in coercion because of higher probabilities of success and lower probabilities and costs associated with its use. The result is a direct effect of relative coercive power on the use of threats and punishments. However, the diagram also suggests two reasons why actors with low coercive power might be more likely to engage in a preemptive attack.

First, weaker actors may engage in preemptive strikes in anticipation of attack. An actor at a power disadvantage may expect an attack by the more powerful party. The weaker person may use coercion as a means of deterrence and as a means of communicating an unwillingness to submit passively to coercion by the more powerful adversary. An experiment in which the relative punitive power of two bargaining opponents was manipulated provided evidence that weakness may encourage the use of coercion (Lawler, Ford, & Blegen, 1988). Each pair of subjects was assigned to one of three power capability conditions: equal power, low inequality, or high inequality. The two bargainers could issue threats and impose fines on each other during the 15 bargaining rounds. Power capability was manipulated in terms of the amount of fines that each person could impose. It was found that the greater the inequality in punitive capabilities, the more frequently both bargainers used fines. Furthermore, the weaker party in the high-inequality condition threatened most frequently. This last result suggests that the weaker bargainer anticipated that the more powerful adversary would try to use the superior fine capability to gain a bargaining advantage.

Second, when weaker actors make threats, they may engage in preemptive strikes to demonstrate the credibility of their threats. They may find it necessary to actually attack the antagonist to make their threats believable. The threats of powerful actors, conversely, are likely to be believed because they assume that their antagonists are aware of their power. Their antagonists are likely to be fearful because they anticipate a greater likelihood of harm, and so they are more likely to be compliant and docile. Knowing that their threats are believable, more powerful actors may not find it necessary to engage in demonstrations of their willingness to use coercion.

These two relationships have been demonstrated in research on robbery. In the typical robbery, the offender threatens physical punishment unless the victim hands over some material good. The threat is a contingent one, and if the victim complies, the offender is unlikely to engage in physical punishment (Luckenbill, 1982) because he has achieved his goal. Robbers are less likely to physically attack and injure victims when they are armed with a lethal weapon (Conklin, 1972; P. J. Cook & Nagin, 1979; Hindelang, 1976; Kleck & McElrath, 1991; Luckenbill, 1980). Possession of a gun apparently provides these criminals with a credible threat. Alternatively, an unarmed offender is more likely to physically attack the victim, usually as an opening move. This preemptive attack may be used to increase the believability of the threat or to force the victim to comply. In addition, armed robbers are less likely to meet resistance and therefore are less likely to find it necessary to punish victims for failing to comply (Luckenbill, 1980).

An implied threat may be enough to deter any misbehavior and avert the necessity of punishment. If an actor is known as a "tough guy" or as someone with a bad temper or a history of coercion, others may avoid anything that might offend him. In families where children fear their parents, there may be relatively few overt acts of coercion (Goode, 1971). Thus, the appearance of tranquility may reflect compliance to a standing threat and not necessarily a lack of coercion. On the receipt of an order, the frightened target might engage in a form of "preemptive compliance."

The effects of unequal power capabilities on the performance of coercive actions have been summarized in bilateral deterrence theory (Lawler, 1986). In general, when parties have equal power, each is apt to be deterred by the threat of retaliation from the other. An individual who has superior power is tempted to believe that threats will be successful in gaining compliance from weaker opponents. Weaker parties, however, are apt to expect powerful opponents to use coercion and to tend to use coercion themselves to preempt attack and communicate an unwillingness to give in to the intimidation of others. When a high power source is confident of gaining compliance and has little expectation of retaliation, a high level of coercion occurs (Michener & Cohen, 1973; Michener, Vaske, Schleifer, Plazewski, & Chapman, 1975). The opposite also occurs. When a high power source does not expect compliance to an offensive use of coercion and has a high expectation of retaliation, a low level of coercive actions occurs (Lawler & Bacharach, 1987; Lawler et al., 1988).

Target Selection

The discussion above implies that actors are likely to select targets who have less power than themselves. Particular individuals who are relatively weak may be chronic victims of attacks by more powerful people. Research on victims of peer aggression has found that a small subset of available children are consistently victimized (Patterson, Littman, & Bricker, 1967). The victims tended to reward the coercive behavior of their attackers by giving in to their demands. Olweus (1979, 1984) also found that bullies tended to pair up with particular "whipping boys." In comparison with both bullies and their other classmates, whipping boys were found to be socially isolated, anxious, passive, and afraid to defend themselves. Boys who had been identified as victims when they were 13 years old tended to be classified that way again 3 years later, despite significant changes in teachers, classmates, or even, schools.

Olweus (1979, 1984) also found a smaller group of "provocative victims," who engaged in behavior that irritated others, such as teasing, and were characterized as hot tempered. This subgroup can be classified as both high in aggressiveness and high in victimization. The tendency of provocative victims to bring about retaliation has also been found in laboratory experiments (Kimmel, Pruitt, Magenau, Konar-Goldband, & Carnevale, 1980; Michener et al., 1975). Perry, Kusel, and Perry (1988) found two groups that were identified by their classmates as victims, which they referred to as *high-* and *low-aggressive victims*. These studies indicated that weakness encourages the use of coercion and that provocations by weak parties invite strong retaliation, dislike, and subsequent victimization.

Noncoercive Power

Factors that directly affect the perceived efficacy of noncoercive influence attempts inversely affect the use of coercion. The hypothesis is that actors with greater noncoercive power will engage in less coercion because they are likely to anticipate success using noncoercive means. When the intent of the actor is to gain compliance, coercion is considered as a last resort because of the costs usually incurred in using it. In some instances, there is a transition from noncoercive to coercive forms of influence, as when a child does not comply with a polite request and the parent issues a threat in an attempt to gain compliance.

Noncoercive power includes the capacity to influence others through persuasion and the provision of rewards. Actors who have reward power (i.e., control of material resources), social skills, good reputations, and self-confidence about their ability to use noncoercive forms of influence are likely to be more successful in getting their way. People who have low confidence in noncoercive means of achieving interpersonal goals are likely to use coercive means.

Reward Power

An actor who lacks reward power should be more likely to engage in coercive actions (Molm, 1988). Support for this hypothesis has been provided in field studies of organizations (Kanter, 1977) and the family (Patterson, 1984). These studies indicated that the structure of relative power may be rather complex. The parties may be equal or different with respect to either reward or coercive power bases. When both parties have reward power, they can work out an exchange, but when one person has more reward power and the other person possesses more coercive power, it is likely the person with a coercive power advantage will engage in threatening and punishing acts to obtain desired outcomes. Molm (1988) proposed that imbalanced coercive power should lead to more coercive acts when it favors an actor who is disadvantaged in reward power.

Social Skills

To get along with others and to influence them requires a variety of social skills. Actors who lack these skills are more likely to use coercion. Bandura (1973) argued that people may engage in coercion because they lack abilities that would allow them to effectively cope with interpersonal problems. A person who fails to solve social problems by noncoercive methods may turn to verbal aggression that may lead to physical aggression. In support of these observations are studies indicating that people involved in violent incidents lack skills in managing conflict and do not possess good problem-solving skills (Cantoni, 1981; Claerhout, Elder, & Janes, 1982). Recall also the evidence from the literature on scripts and aggression showing that nonaggressive adolescents propose more alternative and constructive methods for dealing with social conflicts than do aggressive adolescents (Gouze, 1987; Keltikangas-Järvinen, & Kangas, 1988; Slaby & Guerra

1988). There is also evidence that parents with poor child-management skills are more likely to engage in child abuse (see chap. 10).

A number of researchers in the area of human aggression have proposed that deficiency in verbal skills is related to the probability that physical punishments will be used in social interactions. Toch (1969) found that violent men in prisons reported that insults and verbal attacks challenging their masculinity provoked them to physically attack their victims. These men used violence to resolve social conflicts because they often did not possess the verbal skills that would allow them to win verbal battles.

An anecdote from a Dick Cavitt television interview of Jake LaMotta illustrates the relationship between lack of verbal skills and the use of coercion. Jake LaMotta was a prizefighter during the 1950s whose life was portrayed in the movie *Raging Bull*. Cavitt asked LaMotta whether he had fought frequently as a kid on the streets in New York City. When LaMotta responded affirmatively, Cavitt asked why, and LaMotta said that other kids could "argue good" and he could not, so when he got into an argument, he would win by punching the other kid out. This anecdote can be used to understand the fact that violent criminals have lower intelligence than nonviolent criminals (J. Q. Wilson & Herrnstein, 1985). Poor social skills make it difficult to effectively engage in persuasion and, therefore, increase the likelihood that the individual will use coercion. A person without information cannot make effective arguments, and a person who is inarticulate cannot create persuasive communications. A failure to understand nonverbal cues, ignorance of social norms governing interaction, and other indicators of lack of social skills also impede individuals in their quest for interpersonal goals by noncoercive means. People who lack relevant skills and cannot effectively use persuasion and who frequently do not possess resources to offer as rewards or as exchange either must refrain from exercising influence and give up the hope of attaining many values or must use physical forms of coercion as a means of attaining them.[7]

An argumentative deficiency interpretation of spouse abuse has focused on the lack of verbal skills by victims as well as offenders (Infante, Chandler, & Rudd, 1989). Argumentation skills require that a person can effectively present and defend a position on an issue and verbally attack other positions. If a person cannot effectively engage in argumentation, he or she may resort instead to blaming, insults, and threats, all of which make it more likely that the target person will retaliate and an escalation of coercive actions will occur. There is evidence for this process in incidents of domestic violence where it is found that abused women tend to be deficient in communication skills (Jansen & Meyers-Abel, 1981). According to Coleman (1980), 55% of male offenders reported that they were

---

[7]This generalization is consistent with the blocked opportunity theory of criminal violence (see chap. 5).

provoked by swearing and attacks on their character by their female victims. In a study that compared abusive with nonabusive men, it was found that abusive husbands reported their wives as more verbally aggressive in attacking their identities (D. Goldstein & Rosenbaum, 1985). There is also evidence that people who are intoxicated—which presumably interferes with their communication and conflict-management skills—are more likely to be killed during a violent encounter (Felson & Steadman, 1983).

Reputation

An individual's reputation may facilitate or hamper the effectiveness of various forms of influence. Individuals who are attributed expertise, attractiveness, status, trustworthiness, and credibility should find it easier to use persuasion and other noncoercive forms of influence (cf. Tedeschi et al., 1973). The impact of these factors—often referred to as *bases of power* (French & Raven, 1959)—is demonstrated in studies that typically manipulate characteristics of a source of influence, who is either fictitious or a confederate assisting the experimenter, and present some form of social influence to subjects. Research shows that sources who are more expert, attractive, trustworthy, and credible and who are higher in status are more effective in using persuasive communications than are sources who are low on these characteristics (cf. Tedeschi & Lindskold, 1976). In general, it can be said that any factor increasing the effectiveness of noncoercive forms of influence (or confidence that noncoercive influence will succeed) reduces the likelihood of a coercive action.

There is abundant evidence that liking increases the effectiveness of noncoercive forms of influence (cf. Tedeschi, Lindskold, & Rosenfeld, 1985). It should be expected, therefore, that liking should decrease the use of coercion between people. Krauss (1966) found that subjects who liked one another used gates less frequently to block each other in the trucking game than did subjects who disliked one another. Dislike for another person is associated with an increase in coercion. Peer rejection is related to the aggressiveness of children (Coie & Dodge, 1983; Olweus, 1977). Aggressive children are not without friends, however. Small cliques of aggressive adolescents (and bullies) form coercive clusters and provide mutual support for each other (Cairns, Cairns, Neckderman, Gest, & Gariepy, 1988; Olweus, 1979).

People learn through experience and observation how their reputations have an impact on the influence process. Such learning is represented by expectations, including estimates of the probabilities of success in using various influence modes. People with impeccable reputations for honesty and trustworthiness will develop confidence in their ability to influence others through persuasion, and people who are perceived as dangerous may be confident in their ability to get their way with others by using coercion.

Self-Confidence

When a decision maker lacks confidence in other types of influence as a means of gaining interpersonal objectives, he or she is more likely to use coercion. Confidence can be translated into estimated probability of success (or failure) in achieving goals and is related to Bandura's concept of self-efficacy. According to Bandura (1986), "outcome expectations and personal aspirations depend on perceived self-efficacy. . . . People are disinclined to strive for rewards requiring performances they judge themselves incapable of attaining" (pp. 430–431). Self-efficacy may also be conceived as a generalized expectancy of success that is derived from an individual's past history of achievements and social comparisons made with relevant other persons (Gecas, 1982). A person may experience self-efficacy with respect to some situations but not others (W. James, 1950). Individuals who have a history of successful social influence through coercive means may develop self-confidence in coercive means to solve interpersonal problems, particularly when alternative noncoercive means have not been effective in the past.

People with low self-confidence are typically ineffective in using noncoercive influence. Indirect support for this proposition was obtained by Ransford (1968), who found that people who felt powerless and isolated were perceived by acquaintances as more aggressive than were more self-confident people. In simulations of supervisor–subordinate relations, low self-confidence of a supervisor was associated with more use of coercive actions to gain compliance from subordinates (Goodstadt & Kipnis, 1970; Instone, Major, & Bunker, 1983). Lindskold and Tedeschi (1971) found that children who had lower scores on a paper-and-pencil measure of self-esteem used more threats and punishments than did high-self-esteem children.

Success at Conventional Activities

The discussion above focuses on the decision to use coercion in a particular situation when noncoercive techniques are expected to fail. Success in using coercion may be relevant to the development of a coercive influence style or aggressive personality. According to the blocked-opportunity theory of crime, violence may be used when opportunities to attain goals or values with legitimate means are limited (Merton, 1957; see chap. 5). Coercion is an alternative means to gain status and money when legitimate means are unavailable. Thus, the higher rates of crime among the poor and minorities may be attributable to a lack of educational and economic opportunities. More generally, it can be expected that any individual characteristic that has a detrimental effect on conventional forms of achievement—whether it is caused by discrimination or some other factor—may increase the attractiveness of coercion (or crime) as an alternative source of status and other benefits. A young man with below-average intelligence or a short attention span is likely to find school more difficult (and thus more costly) and not a source of status. Such a person might turn to nonconventional activities to achieve status. He might be able to get approval and respect from his peers for his skills in fighting or his courage in risk-taking situations.

SUMMARY AND CONCLUSIONS

Decision theory is useful in understanding coercive encounters, even those that are emotionally charged. Although coercive actions may sometimes appear impulsive, it is proposed that they result from quick and sometimes careless decisions rather than involuntary behavior. The level of information processing may be limited, and actors may follow a satisficing principle by implementing decisions that appear satisfactory or good enough without considering all possibilities. Some coercive actions are habitual (or "mindless") and are elicited by specific conditions associated with social interactions. Actors with prelearned scripts may be predisposed not to consider alternatives; however, they remain capable of inhibiting their initial choice if the expected costs seem high. Because of a limited time frame, actors may make decisions that they would not have made if they had more time to consider other alternatives or the consequences of engaging in coercive actions.

People engage in coercive actions to achieve what they value. These values include retributive justice, favorable social identities, or any benefit that might result from another person's compliance. When there is interpersonal conflict, coercion is sometimes perceived as an effective means of influencing the other party. When the incentives are high—for example, under conditions of scarcity—and when the actor anticipates a high probability of success, coercive actions are more likely. Decisions are affected by procedural values as well as terminal values. Many people view physical coercion as morally questionable, and they either avoid it or use it as a last resort.

Coercive actions are inhibited by the expected costs that are associated with them. Coercion involves opportunity costs associated with effort, time, and expended resources, and it involves costs imposed by targets and third parties. Actors are inhibited from using coercion when they believe that their actions have a probability of producing costs and when those costs exceed expected gains. However, when the expected costs of noncoercion or doing nothing are great, actors may feel they have little choice but to use coercion. In addition, some people are risk takers, and they focus on the values they can achieve with coercion and discount the costs.

Drinking alcohol has been found to be highly correlated with many forms of violence, including homicides, physical assaults, and suicides.

Research has found that alcohol produces cognitive deficits and a tendency to make hostile attributions. The individual's time perspective contracts, he or she feels more powerful and courageous and there is less concern about the evaluations of others. These effects make it more likely that a person will become involved in a coercive episode. The more a person underestimates costs, disregards costs, or has an exaggerated sense of control over the situation, the more likely she or he will use coercion. All of these effects of drinking alcohol disinhibit the use of coercion.

Actors who possess superior coercive power are more likely to use coercion because they anticipate that they will be successful and that their costs will be low. When targets comply with their threats, it is unnecessary to engage in overt acts of punishment. Weaker actors are usually less likely to use coercion, but they may engage in preemptive attacks, because they wish either to deter an attack or to give their threats credibility. Actors with greater noncoercive power, conversely, are more likely to use persuasion and other noncoercive means to encourage others to comply.

8

PERCEIVED INJUSTICE AND THE EXPRESSION OF GRIEVANCES

Many coercive actions are motivated by the value of justice. The key form of justice relevant to coercive actions involves retribution. *Retributive justice* refers to the belief that blameworthy behavior ought to be punished. The issue of retributive justice is invoked when actors are blamed for harmful or antinormative actions. When people blame someone, it is likely that they will become angry and form a grievance against the offender. We propose that the formation of a grievance motivates the individual to restore justice. Attempts to restore justice may take the form of punishment of the offender or other actions that may be preliminary to subsequent coercive interactions.[1] According to Lerner (1981), justice refers to "an appropriate correspondence between a person's fate and that to which he or she is entitled—what is deserved" (p. 12). People believe that virtuous behavior should be rewarded and blameworthy behavior should be punished. Rules of justice arise and are enforced in social groups as a means of avoiding,

---

[1]The word *punishment* in its vernacular usage typically includes this moral connotation. In our framework, punishment is an action that may be motivated by many factors. One motivation for using punishment is to administer retributive justice.

213

regulating, and adjudicating conflicts between social units (Kelsen, 1957). Thus, the punishment of blameworthy norm violations, which is necessary for social control, comes to be morally valued. Although social institutions have been created for punishing norm violators, retributive justice also occurs in informal face-to-face interactions.

The way in which justice is administered varies considerably across cultures. In societies that do not have legal systems or other institutionalized grievance procedures, people are more likely to take justice into their own hands. Norms are established for when it is justifiable to punish another person, what the appropriate form of punishment should be, and what the magnitude of it should be (Pepitone, 1984). For example, studies of the Dafla hill tribes of northeast India (Furer-Haimendorf, 1967) and of pre-colonial New Guinea society (DuBois, 1961) have shown that people will immediately attack those who offend them. If a person does not seek redress for injuries or slights suffered, he or she acquires a reputation as weak and indecisive and is more likely to suffer subsequent transgressions by others.

In societies that have extensive formal institutions of social control, informal control is still an important mechanism for restoring justice. Black (1983) proposed that the legal system and private retribution are alternative methods of handling grievances. Some people use the police and the courts to satisfy their grievances, whereas others engage in self-help and punish the violator themselves. Many acts of criminal violence reflect decisions of offenders to settle grievances themselves when they perceive that police are unavailable or ineffective. The factors that affect the availability and efficacy of the legal system were discussed in chapter 5 and are not repeated here.

Some theorists (Lerner, Miller, & Holmes, 1976; Walster, Berscheid, & Walster, 1973) view justice behavior solely in terms of self-interest. Inequity for self is presumed to cause a negative arousal state, which motivates the individual to engage in equity-restoring actions. Restoration of equity eliminates the negative arousal state. A different and less hedonistic view was offered by Hogan and Emler (1981), who suggested that group members learn to comply with authority and respond to social expectations. Furthermore, people learn to invoke legitimations for their own behavior in the context of the social norms of their society. According to Hogan and Emler, "perceptions of injustice . . . are followed by aggressive reactions that may serve one's selfish best interests but are not prompted by considerations of self-interest" (1981, p. 136).

We view equity-restoring behaviors as actions oriented toward a valued outcome (equity) rather than as responses instigated by a negative drive state. Justice is not confined to the narrow self-interests of the individual. Although justice and deterrence usually go hand in hand, justice is independently valued. People want to see misdeeds punished even when they are not the victims. In this chapter, we focus on attempts to restore justice by people who believe that they have been victimized, because these are the people most likely to want retribution.

A central feature of the justice restoration process is the formation of a grievance. The term *grievance* has been defined as a judgment by people that another person, a group, or an institution has unjustly harmed them (see Felstiner, Abel, & Sarat, 1980–1981; Stafford & Gibbs, 1993). This definition may be inadequate because people respond to perceived intentions as well as to the outcomes of actions (Heider, 1958). Sanctions for intended harms that are unsuccessful are stipulated in the criminal law. A number of experiments have found that an actor's intention to harm was punished whether or not the antagonist was successful in meting out the harm (Epstein & Taylor, 1967; Geen, 1968; Gentry, 1970; Nickel, 1974; Pisano & Taylor, 1971). On the basis of this research, we think the definition of grievance should be expanded to include actions perceived as wrongful whether or not harm is actually done (see also DeRidder, Schruijer, & Tripathi, 1992).[2] Most, but not all, proscribed behaviors are viewed as harmful.[3] The formation of a grievance requires an attribution of blame as well as a negative evaluation of the behavior. The grievant is then likely to experience anger at the target and to be motivated to restore justice.

The first part of this chapter focuses on the formation of grievances. Factors that lead people to believe a norm violation has occurred and the processes that contribute to the attribution of blame to a transgressor will be examined. It is also important to evaluate the role of anger in the development of coercive interactions. What the person does after forming a grievance depends on many factors. Expressions of grievances sometimes lead to coercive actions, but they may lead to settlement of disputes. When retributive justice is the goal of a grievant, it is necessary to examine factors that affect the level of punishment that is meted out.

PERCEIVED NORM VIOLATIONS

The first step in the formation of a grievance is the perception that a norm has been violated and that an injustice has been done. People perceive injustice when they do not get what they believe they are entitled to get by virtue of what they have done or who they are (Mikula, 1984). This judgment depends on the perceiver's point of view as well as the behavior of the alleged offender. We first focus on perceivers and their expectations about behavior. Then we consider the offender's behavior,

---

[2]Fine (1979, 1983) proposed that people do not form grievances unless they believe something can be done to restore justice. We are not convinced that her research strongly demonstrated this condition but leave it open to future research to settle the issue.

[3]Sometimes harm is attributed to actions to justify their prohibition.

including the types of violations they engage in and the factors that affect the likelihood that they will violate norms.

Expectations and Negative Judgments

One theme of this book is that human behavior can be understood only in a social context of interdependent goals and actions. Social context is an integral part of the way people make judgments. Social expectations about appropriate behavior (in the form of norms) are the foundations of perceptions of injustice. It can be assumed that an individual has a storehouse of normative expectations about how people (or types of people) should comport themselves in a variety of situations. Individuals are likely to be censorious when these expectations are not fulfilled. If actors also attribute blame to the perpetrator, they have a grievance.

Thibaut and Kelley (1959) discussed the experience of outcomes in terms of the individual's expectations (see also Homans, 1961). They proposed that individuals form an expectation of what is the least acceptable outcome for any interaction, which is technically referred to as a *comparison level*. The simplest description of comparison level is that people with high expectations will be disappointed with outcomes that people with lower expectations experience as satisfying. For example, Best and Andreasen (1977) found that middle-class consumers reported greater dissatisfaction with goods and services than did lower-class consumers. If we assume that middle-class consumers have higher expectations than lower-class consumers, then the difference in dissatisfaction can be explained in terms of comparison level. The use of coercion in response to violation of expectations was demonstrated in Homans's (1950) study of a bank-wiring observation room. Men would ridicule or punch in the arm ("bing") coworkers who were "ratebusters."

A person may be evaluated negatively for failing to perform an action when that action is expected. A police officer may be blamed for not intervening in an incident in which an intervention is expected. In a study of police response to criminal acts, Bober (1991) found that acts of omission and acts of commission were judged as equally intentional and blameworthy when they resulted in harmful consequences. Omissions do not directly cause harmful consequences, they simply allow them to occur. Not only do observers attribute intent to the passive perpetrator, but they must also have some normative beliefs about what the perpetrator should have done and blame him or her for not acting according to the norm.

Many harmdoing actions are not perceived as illegitimate or antinormative by either actor or recipient. In all societies people are socialized to believe that under specified conditions particular individuals have the right to inflict pain or deprivations on others. For example, parents are expected to punish children, and judges are expected to punish convicted felons.

However, even for punishments given by parents and judges a standard of fairness is applied. The punishment that is administered should be similar to that given to relevant comparison others. Karniol and Miller (1981) stated the rule as "all cases of A are given treatment X" (p. 76). Those who believe they have been punished too harshly are likely to feel aggrieved. This fairness doctrine is illustrated in a comment by a former student who played for the Green Bay Packers under Vince Lombardi: "Was he fair? Yes, he treated us all like dogs." When the dictum "treat like cases alike" is violated, then even legitimate authorities may be perceived as acting unfairly. The reverse process of treating unlike cases alike will also be perceived as unfair. A 15-year-old adolescent may believe he no longer legitimately qualifies to be spanked but that a 7-year-old sibling does qualify.

Expectations are based on both temporal and social comparison. In the case of temporal comparison, people compare a present outcome with outcomes they have experienced in the past. Students with high standardized test scores are more likely to be dissatisfied with an average grade than are students with low test scores (R. B. Felson, 1984). Teachers can anticipate more grievances from the former than the latter. Social changes that improve the opportunities of people bring about rising expectations with the potential for increasing dissatisfaction. Political scientists (e.g., Gurr, 1970) have long recognized this process as the basis for violent revolutions.

In the case of social comparison, reference groups provide standards or levels for expectations. When the outcomes people receive are less than those of other members of their reference group, they experience relative deprivation (Runciman, 1966). The classic study of relative deprivation found that U.S. Air Force personnel in the U.S. Army were more dissatisfied than military police with the promotion system even though promotions were more frequent for air force personnel (Stouffer, Suchman, DeVinney, Star, & Williams, 1949). The feeling of greater relative deprivation among air force personnel was attributed to the fact that the higher rate of promotions created higher expectations for promotion and paradoxically increased the level of dissatisfaction. A more recent study (J. P. Adams & Dressler, 1988) found that elderly people perceived less injustice than young people in an African American community in the U.S. South. The explanation offered for this finding was that older African American people had been socialized to have lower expectations with regard to rights and opportunities than younger people raised after revolutionary civil rights legislation had been enacted. Young people in general tend to be less tied to traditions and more idealistic and rebellious than their elders.

Relative deprivation theory does not provide a basis for predicting whom a person will choose as a comparison other (Schruijer, 1990). In addition, none of the theories that focus on expectations is adequate for explaining the formation of grievances because they do not consider the process of attributing blame for unsatisfactory outcomes. Nevertheless, the relative nature of judgments about issues of fairness and legitimacy must be recognized in any theory of grievances.

Folger (1986) proposed a referent cognitions version of relative deprivation theory that does take blame into account, at least indirectly. He focused on the development of resentment, which he defined as "hostile feelings toward someone responsible for one's own unfavorable outcomes" (1986, p. 34). Two factors contribute to resentment: the is–ought discrepancy in terms of outcomes (the *should* component) and the belief that outcomes would have been more favorable if the other person had acted otherwise (the *would* component). A prediction from this perspective is that subjects with a high referent comparison, who believe that another has acted in an unjust way to block a favorable outcome, will be resentful. In an experiment to test this prediction, subjects were induced to develop high or low referents for outcomes, and the experimenter justified or did not justify a blocking action (Folger, Rosenfield, & Robinson, 1983). Subjects were most resentful in the high referent–no-justification condition (the *should* condition). In a second experiment, it was found that when subjects did not believe that improper behavior by another would affect outcomes (an absence of the *would* condition) they did not indicate resentment (Folger & Martin, 1986).

Types of Norm Violations

Recent research indicates that norm violations can be classified into a rather small set.[4] Mikula, Petri, and Tanzer (1989) asked subjects drawn from samples in Austria, Bulgaria, Finland, and Germany to recall circumstances when they were unjustly treated. Analyses showed that their responses were organized into three basic types of injustice (or norm violations): distributive, procedural, and interactional.

Distributive justice refers to a fair allocation of benefits, a fair distribution of responsibilities, and recognition of performance or effort. Violations of rules related to distributive justice may form the basis of a grievance and lead to coercive interactions. For example, people may feel aggrieved about thefts, defective products, vandalism, unfair grades, and family members who do not do their share around the house. Siblings fight most often over the division and use of property and the division of labor (chores) in the household (R. B. Felson, 1983); their most frequent source of conflict was over what television show to watch.

The social structure of a society affects the types of distributive conflicts that arise. In polygynous societies, cowives tend to quarrel over sexual

---

[4]We adopt the definition of *norms* as opinions or beliefs of members of a group about how they should or ought to behave in a specific situation (see DeRidder, Schruijer, & Tripathi, 1992, for other characteristics or dimensions of norms).

access to husbands, wealth distribution, and disciplining of children (Levinson, 1989). In tribal societies that are egalitarian, conflicts seldom occur about political control (Knauft, 1987). In societies where property is shared, conflicts seldom develop over property.

Procedural justice refers to the means used by individuals to resolve conflicts of interest—the meta-rules that legitimize distributive norms. Among the means used to resolve conflicts are face-to-face bargaining, mediation, and arbitration. Meta-rules include those procedures and values that legitimize authorities and the means for determining credit and blame, including the legitimation of punishments. Violations of rights; interference with opportunities; constraints on freedoms; and arbitrary procedures, authority, or punishments will be perceived as forms of injustice.

Interaction justice involves conformity to norms about demeanor, respect, and politeness toward other people. Interaction justice was by far the most important category of unjust events reported by respondents in the data collected by Mikula et al. (1989). The most frequent unjust experiences referred to lack of loyalty, lack of regard for the feelings of others, selfishness, accusations or censure, hostility, and failure to keep agreements. By far the greater number of unjust incidents clustered around concern for social identities, which indicates that defensive self-presentation (see chap. 9) may also be a factor in many instances of perceived injustice. Similar types of injustices were reported in a study by Messick, Bloom, Boldizar, and Samuelson (1985). Subjects listed vicious gossip, rudeness, and lack of punctuality as unfair things that other people did.[5] Bies (1986), Bies and Moag (1986), and Tyler (1988) have all emphasized the role of politeness and respect in judgments of injustice.

Men and women attribute different types of injustices to each other. Among couples, men were more likely to be upset about women being moody, whereas women were more likely to complain about men being condescending, neglective, and inconsiderate (D. M. Buss, 1989a). Among dating couples, women were more likely than men to be angry about demands for sexual intimacy and the touching of their bodies without permission. In general, physical contact and touching are the most intimate and personal form of interaction, and anyone initiating physical contact must normally gain the assent of the other person (E. T. Hall, 1959; Mehrabian, 1972).

Levinson (1989) examined sources of grievances in spousal violence in small-scale and peasant societies. Data were collected from ethnographic reports in the Human Relations Area File for 90 societies. Allegations of adultery were a common source of grievances leading to wife beating in these societies (see also Daly & Wilson, 1988). A husband was also likely

---

[5]Subjects also listed exploitation and selfishness as unfair things people do, which indicates problems with distributive justice.

to beat his wife when she failed to perform her duties or when she failed to treat him with the degree of respect that he expected. In many societies, wife beating is seen as a legitimate method for men to maintain their authority in the household and can occur in response to any offense, however minor.

Any single action by another person may violate more than one type of justice. Tyler (1988) found that people who had contact with police or courts perceived the procedures as more fair if they had been treated with respect. In other words, interaction justice contributed to the perception of procedural justice. A particularly important example of actions that violate more than one type of justice are physical punishments perceived as arbitrary by the victim. Physical violence may be judged to violate norms of procedural and interaction justice. Arbitrary physical punishments violate the rights of people and convey a negative evaluation of the victim's social identity.

Factors That Produce Norm Violations

From our point of view, targets often play an important causal role in the development of dispute-related coercive interactions. People who engage in antinormative behavior are more likely to be targets of grievances and are more likely to become involved in coercive interactions. When people express their grievances, the alleged norm violators are likely to express countergrievances, and a retaliatory cycle may develop. Thus, people who engage in antinormative behavior are likely to be involved in coercive interactions—sometimes as targets, sometimes as perpetrators, often as both. Evidence that individuals who engage in frequent transgressions are more likely to be targeted for violence comes from the literature on child abuse. That literature suggests that children with behavior problems are more likely to be the targets of abuse (see chap. 10).

Any factor that increases the likelihood that norm violations will be committed should lead to grievances and coercive interactions. Alcohol is a factor that sometimes leads people to engage in behaviors that others find offensive. If reproached for their behavior, intoxicated people may feel aggrieved and, because of lowered inhibitions, may retaliate. Thus, alcohol can play a role in both the initial norm violation that leads to conflict and the escalation of the conflict. This scenario is consistent with evidence that alcohol use is common in homicide victims as well as offenders (Wolfgang, 1958).

Stress may be another factor that leads a person to be the target of grievances. There are many studies that show a positive correlation between physical violence and stress (cf. Mueller, 1983; Straus, 1980). The effects of stress, like the effects of aversive stimuli in the laboratory, are generally assumed to be due to some sort of frustration–aggression mechanism. Our view is that stress has negative effects on performance and increases violations of politeness norms and that these effects on behavior often contribute to the development of coercive episodes.

There is considerable evidence that stress negatively affects performance in school and work (e.g., S. Cohen, 1980; T. H. Holmes & Masuda, 1974; Motowidlo, Packard, & Manning, 1986). In addition, people who are stressed may be more likely to violate interaction norms (R. B. Felson, 1978). Because of their negative mood states, stressed individuals are less likely to be polite and friendly, to feign positive emotions, or to show ritualized support for others. This process is depicted in Figure 8.1. If distressed people are likely to perform less competently, violate expectations, or annoy others, then they are likely to become the focus of grievances and participants in coercive encounters. Evidence for this process comes from research showing that experience of stressful life events is more strongly related to being a target of violence than to the perpetration of violence (R. B. Felson, 1991). The correlation between stressful life events and violence disappears when the incidence of the stressed person being the target of aggression is controlled. Apparently, distressed people engage in more aggression because they are targeted by others. It may be assumed that the reason that distressed people are victimized by others is that they

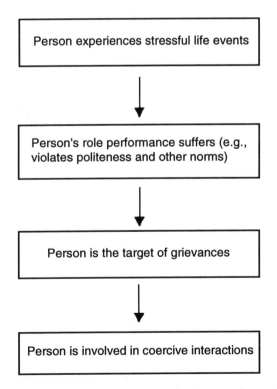

Figure 8.1. The effect of stress in producing coercive episodes.

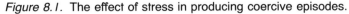

engage in behaviors when stressed that irritate or provoke other people. This complex social process, instigated by stressful circumstances, is consistent with a social interactionist rather than a frustration–aggression explanation.

The tendency for transgressions to lead to violence may be a factor in the explanation of the versatility of people who commit crime. As suggested in chapter 5, evidence suggests that those who commit violent offenses are likely to commit a variety of offenses. People who commit transgressions are more likely to become involved in conflicts with others. Others may be offended by their stealing, drinking, and drug use, or their drinking or drug use may lead them to engage in other offensive behavior. Such behavior is likely to lead to attempts by others to control them and sometimes to violent encounters.

Coercion will occur more frequently in social contexts in which rules are frequently violated. In general, the greater the level of conflict and the less clear the rules for resolving conflict, the more likely grievances will develop. R. B. Felson (1983) suggested that one reason siblings fight so frequently is that siblings share material goods and participate in a household division of labor, and the rules for the use of goods and the division of labor are unclear. Sibling fights typically reflect realistic conflict and not rivalry over status or parental attention.

ATTRIBUTIONS OF BLAME

Whenever people observe unexpected or unwanted behavior by others, they search for an explanation for such conduct (Wong & Weiner, 1981). This search may lead them to attribute blame (or responsibility) to the actor. Sometimes people think no one is to blame, and sometimes they blame themselves and believe they deserve what happens to them. In this section, we examine the tendency to attribute blame to someone for performing an antinormative action.

An attribution of blame may represent the end product of a number of discrete steps of information processing, involving a series of inferences about the impact of the situation and of internal factors within the actor. The attribution process may be described as a decision tree (Rule & Nesdale, 1976c). A depiction of the series of inductive steps in assigning blame is presented in Figure 8.2. The observer first makes a judgment about whether the actor or some external factor caused the negative outcome. There is some evidence that causal attributions are independent of evaluations of behavior and that respondents are able to differentiate judgments of causation and blame (Fincham & Jaspars, 1983; Harvey & Rule, 1978). If a decision is made that the actor caused the outcome, the observer considers whether the outcome was intended or unintended. A judgment that the

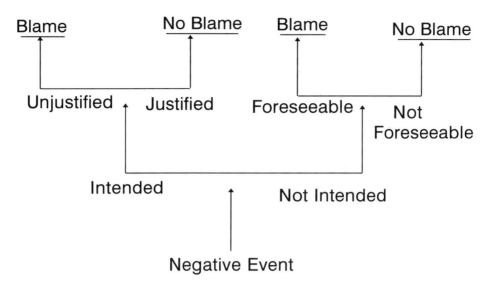

Figure 8.2. The series of inferences that lead to the attribution of blame.

actor could not control the outcome will lead to an inference that the outcome was unintended. If the wrong is intended, the observer makes a judgment about whether the actor's intention was justified or unjustified.[6] The actor will receive a high level of blame for an antinormative act. The actor may also receive some blame for engaging in behavior whose negative consequences were unintended but forseeable.

When examining attributions of blame, it is important to consider the divergent perspectives of perpetrators and targets. Both motivational and cognitive processes contribute to divergent perspectives. Prior expectations of observers also affect their attributions of blame. Finally, it will be suggested that people with a tendency to assume hostility in others overattribute blame to others.

Attributions of Intentions

Among the conditions that contribute to the inference that an actor intended the misdeed are judgments that the actor had the ability to do so, knew before the act that harmful consequences would occur, and was free to engage in some alternative behavior (Heider, 1958; Jones & Davis, 1965). Attribution of intent may also be affected by the degree of effort expended by the actor (Joseph, Kane, Gaes, & Tedeschi, 1976), facial expressions of the actor (Forgas, O'Connor, & Morris, 1983), and the costs incurred by the actor (Epstein & Taylor, 1967).

---

[6]We adopt the polar opposites *justified* and *unjustified*, but Rule and Nesdale (1976c) referred to *justified* and *malevolent*.

Substantial evidence has cumulated to show that the level of sanctions recommended or delivered to would-be harmdoers is proportional to the amount of harm intended by an actor. An example of this reaction to intentions is a study carried out by Epstein & Taylor (1967) in which the reaction-time game was used. You will recall that a confederate and a subject preset shock levels to be delivered should the other person lose on the next trial of the game. They then played a trial of the game. At the end of the trial, the loser received the level of shock preset by the winner and both players saw the level of shock preset by the other. This procedure allowed a programming of the confederate's behavior so that the intensity of intended harm could be manipulated independently of inflicted harm. Thus, holding inflicted harm constant across conditions of the experiment, the magnitude of intended harm was manipulated on trials when the subject won and, hence, did not receive the shocks. It was found that the shock intensities set by subjects were directly affected by the level of intended harm by the confederate.

Retribution is scaled both to degree of intended harm and to the amount of harm actually done. Nickel (1974) suggested that when intended harm and inflicted harm differ, subjects respond to intent. Ohbuchi and Kambara (1985) found that the degree of intent to do harm serves as the basis for the level of retribution when chance intervenes to blunt the force of an attack. They created experimental conditions in which the intensity of shocks received by subjects actually decreased over time, whereas the perceived intent of the harmdoer increased over time. The failure to implement the intended amount of harm occurred because of an electrical problem with the shock apparatus. In this situation, subjects retaliated in proportion to the actor's intent and not the actual harm done.

Unjustified Norm Violations

The justifiability of norm violations has been examined in research on the differential effects of arbitrary and nonarbitrary frustrations. *Arbitrary frustration* refers to unjustified deprivation or blocking of a goal, whereas *nonarbitrary frustration* refers to a deprivation that can be rationalized to the frustrated party as legitimate or equitable. People are likely to become aggrieved when they believe that they have been unjustly or arbitrarily frustrated. In other words, perception that another person is violating a norm leads to an attribution of blame. Note the contrast between a justice explanation for arbitrary frustration and Berkowitz's (1988) explanation in terms of a frustration–aggression mechanism. He suggested (p. 4) that arbitrary frustrations disrupt expected goal attainments and that it is the unexpectedness of the interruption rather than its injustice that produces the negative reaction by the frustrated individual.

Pastore (1952) found different reactions to arbitrary and nonarbitrary frustrations. Some subjects were provided with descriptions of arbitrary frustrations, such as "You're waiting on the right corner for a bus, and the driver intentionally passes you by." Other subjects were presented with examples of nonarbitrary frustrations, such as "You're waiting on the right corner for a bus. You notice that it is a special on its way to the garage." The subjects indicated more anger in the arbitrary than in the nonarbitrary condition. A. R. Cohen (1955), using similar role-playing procedures, obtained similar findings. Recall from chapter 3 that Zillmann and Cantor (1976) found that prior justification muted the degree of anger experienced by subjects who were attacked by an assistant of the experimenter. Furthermore, it has been reliably found that arbitrary frustration causes subjects to give more negative evaluations of the frustrating person (Rule, Dyck, & Nesdale, 1978; Worchel, 1974).

Blame and Perceived Aggression

The conditions that lead people to label an action as *aggression* are similar (or identical) to those that bring about an attribution of blame. This relationship was noted by Cahn (1949), who stated: "Nature has thus equipped all men to regard injustice to another as personal aggression" (p. 24). An actor's behavior is perceived as aggressive when three necessary conditions are met: (a) The actor is perceived as attempting to punish or to constrain the behavioral alternatives and outcomes for a target person, (b) an observer attributes intent to do harm to the actor (irrespective of the actor's real intentions), and (c) the action is considered by the observer to be antinormative (Tedeschi et al., 1974). DeRidder and Syroit (1992) explicitly tested reactions of observers to a number of scenarios and found that perceptions of aggression were entirely consistent with judgments of injustice. They concluded that perceived aggression is a subset of events judged to be unjust. There are unjust events that are not perceived as aggressive, but all episodes perceived as aggressive are considered unjust by the observer.[7] The strong relationship between attributions of blame and perceived aggressiveness was indicated by a correlation of .83 between the two measures (Lysak, Rule, & Dobbs, 1989).

R. C. Brown and Tedeschi (1976) have shown that the offensive use of coercion was labeled by observers as aggressive, whereas the defensive use of coercion was not. Subjects viewed a live dramatization of a barroom scene. Each of four groups witnessed a different scene and was asked to rate the actors. One man instigated an argument over a seat that was being

---

[7]Earlier, we referred to an unpublished dissertation study by Bober (1991), who found that there was no difference in the amount of blame between committing a harmful act and omitting an act that allowed harm to occur. However, committing an act that caused the harm was perceived as more aggressive than the omission of an act that allowed the harmful consequence to occur. There is a hint in these results that there is more to perceived aggression than the attribution of blame.

saved by the other man for his female companion. The instigator either threatened the other man by asking "Are you looking for a shot in the mouth or something?" or made the threat and attempted to use force by taking a swing (which missed). In two other conditions, the defensive man either made a counterthreat or used counterforce by striking the instigator hard in the stomach.

The results showed that the instigator was rated as very aggressive in all conditions. However, the defensive use of force, where the only real damage occurred, was not perceived as aggressive. In fact, the harmdoing actor in the latter condition was not perceived as any more aggressive than in a control condition where he was not involved in any altercation. The fact that the most damaging action was perceived as least aggressive across all of the scenarios is a striking demonstration that the normative context of the action, rather than the behavior itself, determines how it is labeled and whether blame will be attributed to the actor.

Typically, in teacher–learner, essay evaluation, and competitive re-action-time game experiments on aggression, subjects who give more shocks to the confederate have been viewed as more aggressive, irrespective of the amount of shocks they initially receive from the confederate. However, the R. C. Brown and Tedeschi (1976) study indicated that the defensive use of force is not perceived as aggressive by nonpsychologists.

Favorable responses to the defensive use of force were also shown in a series of experiments carried out by Kane, Joseph, and Tedeschi (1976). They provided students with written descriptions of various conditions typically used in the essay evaluation procedures in laboratory studies of aggression. Targets who in the scenario were shocked first and then retal-iated with the same or fewer shocks than did their adversary were rated as defensive, nonaggressive, and good, even when they gave a high number of shocks. These results can be attributed to the perceived legitimacy of proportional retaliation for arbitrary attacks by the naive observers. Almost identical results were obtained by Stapleton, Joseph, and Tedeschi (1978) when they provided observers with information about various conditions typically used in the reaction-time game. Tit-for-tat responses by subjects were not perceived as aggressive and bad, but escalation of shock intensities (usually performed by confederates) was perceived as offensive, aggressive, and bad.

The results of a scenario study indicated that the effect of the mag-nitude of harm on perceived aggression depends on its antinormativeness (Löschper, Mummendey, Linneweber, & Bornewasser, 1984). Intent, norm deviation, and degree of injury were manipulated in eight different sce-narios. The perception of aggressiveness was higher when the magnitude of harm was greater, but only when the harm was intended and the act was antinormative. A high level of harm that was not intended, or if intended was not antinormative, was not labeled as aggression. The implication is that the attribution process leading to blame does not occur when an action is viewed as justified (see also DeRidder, 1985).

Political sympathies were shown to affect perceptions of violence in a study carried out during the Vietnam War era. Respondents who supported the war tended to view the behavior of antiwar demonstrators as violent, whereas respondents who were opposed to the war viewed police use of force against the demonstrators as violent (Blumenthal, Kahn, Andrews, & Head, 1972). The researchers concluded that violence, like truth and beauty, is in the eye of the beholder and not in the action itself.

Foreseeability and Controllability

Actors may be blamed for unintended negative consequences, although not usually as much as they are for intended harmdoing. If an observer makes a judgment that the negative outcomes caused by an agent's behavior are unintentional, an analysis will be made to ascertain whether the consequences of the act were foreseeable or unforeseeable (see Figure 8.2). Research results indicate that if the consequences are viewed as foreseeable, then they should have been avoided, and the actor will be blamed for not avoiding the harmful consequences (Fincham & Shultz, 1981; Rule & Nesdale, 1976c). Weiner (1985) has found that responsibility will be attributed to an actor only when observers believe the negative events are controllable. If negative consequences are perceived as beyond the actor's control, the actor will not be held responsible for them. Mikula (1993) has also found that controllability is an important factor in judgments of injustice.

When harmful consequences are severe, it is more likely that perceivers will attribute blame to the actor (Affleck, Allen, Tennen, McGrade, & Ratzan, 1985; Affleck, Pfeiffer, Tennen, & Fifield, 1987; Rosen & Jerdee, 1974; Shaver, 1970; Vidmar & Crinklaw, 1974; Walster, 1966). People apparently believe that more severe consequences should be more foreseeable and avoidable than less harmful outcomes. In a review of the research on self and other blame, Tennen and Affleck (1991) concluded that there is a distinct tendency to blame others for traumatic events. For example, a high percentage of women blamed a particular man for unwanted pregnancies (Major, Mueller, & Hildebrandt, 1985).

When a harmful outcome is seen as having been forseeable, negligence or recklessness may be attributed to the actor. Negligence is attributed when an actor does not take sufficient care for the interests of others when performing an act. If a person is perceived as negligent in causing harm, blame will be attributed (Walster, 1966). What constitutes "sufficient care" depends on expectations about appropriate behavior—what a "reasonable person" would do, in the language of legal theory. According to Hart (1968), blaming individuals for negligent acts is reasonable because it provides an incentive for negligent harmdoers to act with greater care in the future. Thus, blaming negligence serves as a deterrent. However, instead of individuals being punished for engaging in an action, they are punished for not performing an action.

A person who acts recklessly may also be blamed for any negative consequences that may occur. Hart (1968) has defined a reckless action as "wittingly flying in the face of a substantial, unjustified risk, or the conscious creation of such a risk" (p. 137). If the risk is viewed as justifiable, conversely, it will not be perceived as reckless. The effect of justifiability was demonstrated in an experiment performed by Melburg and Tedeschi (1981). Subjects read a scenario describing an ambulance driver who was driving at high speed and hit a child who darted across in front of the ambulance. When a critically ill patient was in the ambulance, the driver was not perceived as responsible for the accident, but when the person in the ambulance had only a slight injury, the driver was judged as reckless, responsible, and blameworthy for hitting the child.

Divergent Perspectives Between Actors and Targets

Most of the above generalizations about perceived blame and aggression are based on research examining reactions by third-party observers to hypothetical situations represented in stories. There is some evidence that the perspective of the observer—as actor, victim, or third party—affects the attributions made about an actor's antinormative behavior.

Divergent perspectives were first demonstrated in aggressive encounters in a role-playing study of aggressive interactions by Mummendey, Linneweber, and Löschper (1984). They found that subjects who took the actor's role tended to view their own behavior as provoked by others, whereas those who took the victim's role tended to perceive attacks as unprovoked.

Mikula and Heimgartner (1992) showed divergent perspectives in a different context. They asked each of two marital partners to report instances of unfair behavior by the other partner. Each was also asked to respond to a series of questions about the events the other partner thought were unfair. Perpetrators rated the events as less serious and unjust, thought their causal contribution to the events was smaller, and considered their actions as more justified than did victims.

Divergences in perspectives are partially due to motivational biases. On one hand, actors are motivated to avert or mitigate blame and to avoid or limit retribution and, therefore, are apt to minimize injustices that they perpetrate. Targets, on the other hand, have a vested interest in exaggerating the degree of harm done and the responsibility of actors because such attributions justify their own reactions, increase the amount of reparations (if any), maximize sympathy from others, and so on.

Mikula and Heimgartner (1992) found that the victims' perceptions of injustice were based on causality, intention, and lack of justification for the perpetrator's actions. These same factors, however, did not predict the degree of injustice perceived by the perpetrator. Similar findings were obtained by Baumeister, Stillwell, and Wotman (1990). Respondents were asked to provide a story of an incident in which they perpetrated an anger-provoking incident and a story in which they were the victims. In their accounts, perpetrators frequently denied the significance of negative consequences and referred to happy endings for the incidents described. Victim accounts referred to the lasting negative consequences associated with the incidents and the lingering resentment they felt. The vested interests of perpetrators to close the issue (happy endings) and of the victims to keep it open (lingering resentment) may be reflected in these reports.

Blaming others may involve self-justification. Warner (1986) stated this idea succinctly: "Our exoneration is their culpability" (p. 145). Likewise, as Novaco (1976) expressed it: "There is nothing wrong with me; there is something wrong with you" (p. 1125). It is important to justify the use of coercion, particularly when harm is done to a victim.[8] Blaming another person for one's actions justifies them and may avoid condemnation or other forms of punitive reactions. Alternatively, when people blame themselves, they exonerate the perpetrator. They are the guilty party and thus feel guilt. The question raised by the direction of blame and anger (in or out) is one of innocence and guilt.

Divergences in perspectives are also due to cognitive biases. Observers tend to make a "fundamental attribution error," overattributing events to personal factors and discounting situational factors (Ross, 1977). Observers, on one hand, tend to attribute the actor's behavior to personal factors because they often lack historical information about the actor and because the observer's attention is focused on the actor. Actors, on the other hand, are more aware of their own history, and their attention is focused on the situation. The tendency of observers to make internal attributions leads them to blame actors for their behavior, and it leads actors to perceive themselves as responding to situations. Whatever their bases, divergent attributions about unjust acts contribute to a widening of differences and the intensification of conflict between individuals (Horai, 1977; Orvis, Kelley, & Butler, 1976).

The tendency for observers to weigh negative information about an actor more heavily than positive information is likely to lead to attributions of blame (Kanouse & Hanson, 1971). The negativity bias is probably due to the tendency to assume that positive behaviors are attributable to social norms and other external factors. Negative information is more difficult to

---

[8]Blaming others may also be a form of self-justification. When defective products are produced by a group, blaming others can be a way of avoiding responsibility.

explain in terms of external factors and is therefore likely to be perceived as internally caused. It may be related to the general tendency to attribute unexpected behavior to internal causes (Jones & McGillis, 1976). The negativity bias helps explain why people hold grudges. They never forget the misdeed because they believe that it showed the actor's "true colors."

Prior Expectations About the Target

A heuristic that is apparently involved in attributions of blame consists of expectations related to prior impressions of individuals. Good people are expected to engage in good actions, and bad people are expected to engage in bad actions. Fauconet (quoted in Heider, 1944) noted the effect of prior impressions on moral evaluations of a person:

> Persons dreaded for their brutality are the first ones to be suspected of a violent crime; despised persons of a mean act; and those who arouse disgust of an unclean act. People with bad reputations are accused and convicted on the basis of evidence which one would consider insufficient if an unfavorable prejudice did not relate them to the crime in advance. On the contrary, if the accused had won our favor we demand irrefutable proof before we impute to him the crime. (p. 363)

The tendency to mitigate blame for likeable others and to make harsher judgments against less likeable others has been found in several experiments. In some of these studies, differences in interpersonal attraction were created by establishing attitude similarity or dissimilarity (Byrne, 1971). Observers perceived harmdoers with similar attitudes as more justified than harmdoers with dissimilar attitudes (Nesdale, Rule, & Hill, 1978; Turkat & Dawson, 1976; Veitch & Piccione, 1978). Observers also recommended lower punishments for offenders who were similar to themselves than for offenders who were different (Mitchell & Byrne, 1973).

Physical attractiveness may also mitigate blame. College students were given a description of a child who attacked a dog or attacked another child and caused mild or severe harm (Dion, 1972). The story was accompanied by a picture of an attractive or unattractive child, who was identified as the harmdoer. The unattractive child in the severe harm condition was perceived as acting in a more antisocial way, as more apt to engage in similar actions in the future, and as more unpleasant than the attractive child.

Jury decisions reflect the mitigating effect of the attractiveness of defendants. In a retrospective study, criminal court judges were asked to review trials over which they had presided (Kalven & Zeisel, 1966). Each judge described the verdicts reached by juries, the decisions he or she would have made in the absence of a jury, and the reasons for disagreements between the two verdicts. The judges disagreed with the juries in 962 cases.

They attributed 11% of these disagreements to the positive or negative impressions of the defendant formed by the juries.

In our scheme, the decision to impose retributive justice on an offender is based on a prior attribution of blame. It is possible that liking the offender both mitigates blame and, holding blame constant, reduces the amount of retributive punishment administered. However, the meager evidence now available suggests that attraction mitigates the amount of blame and subsequent retribution only when the intentions of the attacker are ambiguous (Hendrick & Taylor, 1971; Ohbuchi & Izutsu, 1984; Stapleton et al., 1975).

Expectations about how others are likely to behave and standards of conduct may be based on an actor's group membership (Tajfel, 1978). There is a general tendency to attribute a higher level of blame to members of out-groups than to members of the in-group. An ethnocentric bias was displayed by Hindu subjects, who attributed undesirable behavior by in-group members to external factors but made internal attributions for identical behavior by Muslims (D. M. Taylor & Jaggi, 1974).

In a similar study, Schruijer et al. (1994) gave members of the Italian Communist Party a scenario in which two men had an altercation at a cafe, which culminated in one punching the other in the nose. One of the men was a Communist and the other was a Fascist; the role of harmdoer and victim varied. Communist subjects were asked to judge the scenario and to explain an in-group or out-group actor's harmdoing toward an in-group or an out-group victim. Results supported the notion of an in-group bias: Out-group actors were seen as more aggressive and intentional in their actions than in-group actors. Attribution bias was also found in a study of jail inmates and correctional officers (Kagehiro & Werner, 1981). Both groups read scenarios depicting four altercations in which inmate misbehavior and retribution by officers were manipulated to be moderate or severe. Inmates were more apt to find mitigating circumstances for the misbehavior of an inmate than were officers.

The stereotypes held by observers may affect attributions and judgments made about the behavior of other people. Duncan (1976) found that race of the actor affected how violent he was perceived to be. White subjects viewed a videotape of an interaction between two men. One of the men shoved the other during a heated discussion. If the protagonist was Black, more than 66% of the subjects perceived his action as violent, independent of whether the other person was White or Black. If the protagonist was White, less than 17% of the subjects perceived his behavior as violent, independent of whether the other person was White or Black.

A negative stereotype may have the opposite effect on the level of blame when guilt for an action has already been established. Individuals may be attributed less responsibility for their antinormative behavior if they are members of lower status groups or social categories that are expected to engage in antinormative behavior. Unexpected behavior carries more information value (Jones & McGillis, 1976) and is more likely to lead to an internal attribution (Thibaut & Riecken, 1955).

Low expectations for lower status groups may explain the inconsistent evidence on the effect of race on sentencing. In some jurisdictions, Blacks receive more severe sentences than Whites, but in others they receive similar sentences or even more lenient sentences (Chiricos & Waldo, 1975). Although prejudiced judges may assign a more severe sentence to Black offenders than to White offenders, they may also treat Black offenders more leniently because they expect such behavior from Blacks and they view their behavior as reflecting low internal causality.[9] Conversely, the behavior of a White offender, particularly one who is middle class, may be viewed as unexpected and therefore more informative about the person. A prosecutor once told one of us that he recommended severe sentences for lawyers who had committed a crime because "they ought to know better." Thus, negative stereotypes can lead to either more severe or less severe treatment, depending on the expectations of the observer.

Hostility Bias in Attributions

When individuals interpret another person's behavior as hostile, they are likely to feel aggrieved and to retaliate. A number of studies have shown that particularly coercive individuals are likely to interpret others' behavior as hostile, even when it is not. Toch (1969) observed that violent men who had been incarcerated had a paranoid style of attributions, which often caused them to engage in what they conceived as preemptive attacks. Parents who interpret children's crying and misbehavior as intentional and defiant are more likely to engage in child abuse (e.g., Frodi & Lamb, 1980; Larrance & Twentyman, 1983).

Additional evidence comes from studies of aggressive boys. Nasby, Hayden, and DePaulo (1979) found that institutionalized, aggressive boys displayed a tendency to attribute hostility to other boys, even when stories were constructed to imply prosocial motives. In an experiment with elementary school children, Dodge and Newman (1981) found that aggressive boys sought less information about another person, made more hostile attributions toward fictitious others, and remembered hostile pieces of information better than did nonaggressive boys. The researchers proposed that aggressive boys have developed an expectancy that others will respond to them in hostile ways. They make quick attributions of hostility where none exists, and these biased attributions lead to coercive actions against

---

[9]In a personal communication (February 1994), Roy Baumeister suggested that judges may sometimes be more lenient toward Blacks because they are sympathetic with the special problems that many Blacks face in a racially biased society.

their peers. Dodge and Somberg (1987) found that when boys perceived a peer as hostile, they were more likely to direct coercive actions against him. The circle is closed when their coercive actions bring about retaliation by the victims and confirm their original expectation of hostile actions.

The hostility bias is likely to be manifested when the target has engaged in behavior that might be perceived as a provocation. To test this proposition, Dodge and Coie (1987) developed a scale to measure reactive aggressiveness—such as striking back when provoked and overreacting to annoyances—and proactive aggressiveness—such as using force to dominate others and bullying behavior. They found that boys who scored high in reactive aggressiveness had a strong hostility bias in making attributions but that proactive aggressiveness was not related to attributional bias. It may be concluded that some of the coercive behavior of young boys is related to the belief that they are frequently victimized by others, and their use of coercive actions is perceived by them as defensive and justifiable.

ANGER AND COERCION

Anger is an emotion associated with the cognitive process of attributing blame to other people. Thus, anger is an emotion that accompanies most grievances. In other words, a grievance or perceived injustice is the cognitive element of anger. This point of view is supported by a study in which college students were asked to recall incidents that made them feel angry (Averill, 1983). They mostly recalled events that were described as intentional and unjustified or as harmful and avoidable. Averill concluded that the most important fact about anger is that it is a reaction to some perceived misdeed.

The relationship between perceived injustice and anger was demonstrated by Klein and Bierhoff (1992). In three scenario studies, distributive justice (pay) and procedural justice (selfish interest of supervisor) were manipulated in the context of a relationship between a supervisor and a subordinate. Subjects were asked to assume the role of the subordinate and to evaluate the fairness of the situation, the degree of anger they would experience, the value of the relevant activity, and the motivation required for success in the future. The main finding was that when perceived fairness was controlled, the effects of distributive and procedural justice on anger, devaluation of the activity, and achievement motivation were no longer significant. In other words, anger was not experienced, and negative reactions did not occur unless a prior judgment had been made that injustice had occurred.

The person's internal experience of anger must be distinguished from displays of anger. People may display anger whether they feel it or not, and they may behave calmly—and even smile—when they feel angry. Shouting or angry facial expressions may appear to be automatic reactions to the experience of anger, but they can be controlled by the individual. Among the Utku Eskimos, expressions of anger are seldom displayed (Briggs, 1970). Children are taught to isolate themselves when they feel angry. Conversely, The Yanomamo of Central America encourage male children to make fierce displays of anger (Chagnon, 1977).

Experience of Anger and Coercion

The emotional aspects of anger can have indirect effects on coercion. Figure 8.3 depicts the effects of anger on attention, retrieval of scripts, and intensification of the behavior of the individual. An angry person is apt to reflect on the unjust episode and to focus on the perpetrator. Attention is focused on the present to the disregard of the future, and as a result, the angry person may react without regard to future costs. From the perspective of decision theory, the angry person does not act in spite of the costs but would be inhibited by them if they were taken into consideration at the time the act was initiated. In other words, an angry actor often does not consider the costs associated with engaging in coercive behavior.

Anger arousal disrupts and disorganizes cognitive processes. A tendency of angry people is to simplify information processing and to make judgments that are more black and white than in calmer circumstances (R. K. White, 1968). Arousal affects the speed of information processing and reduces attentional capacity (Masters, Felleman, & Barden, 1981; Meichenbaum & Gilmore, 1984). Complex behaviors are disrupted. The verbal behavior of an angry person may become disorganized, and it may become more difficult for them to clearly express a grievance. It is cognitively easier to verbally abuse the other person than it is to present a well-

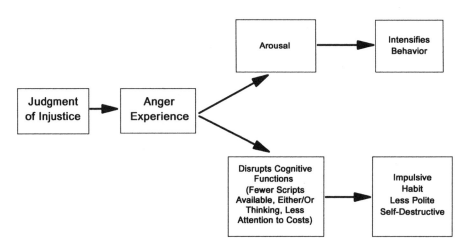

Figure 8.3. The effects of anger experiences on subsequent actions.

234   A THEORY OF COERCIVE ACTIONS

organized and persuasive communication about the legitimacy of one's complaint. Deleterious effects of anger arousal on cognitive processes may cause reactions to become more crude and impulsive. Thus the admonition to count to 10 when angry (cf. Tavris, 1982).

The energizing function of anger has long been recognized and has been explained by the activation of the sympathetic nervous system. Anger arousal is sometimes indicated by an increase in the volume of the individual's voice, the slamming of doors (or telephones), and other vigorous muscular responses. Another result may be more intense coercive behavior.

In summary, anger disrupts cognitive functioning and increases the amplitude of motor responses. The individual tends to focus on the anger-inducing incident and his or her victim status to the disregard of other information that might contribute to a resolution of the interpersonal conflict. The result is that the person is less attentive to politeness norms, is less articulate in expressing grievances, and is less inhibited by potential future costs of various action alternatives. These anger-induced reductions in social skills and concern for long-term consequences are likely to exacerbate relationships with the other person and to disinhibit the actor's use of coercion.

Social Functions of Anger Displays

A display of anger can be used to convey the degree of injustice experienced by the angered person. An expression of anger focuses the accused person's attention on issues that concern the grievant. An expression of anger communicates commitment to resolving the grievance and may be used as an implicit threat, because anger is frequently associated with coercion. In addition, anger expressions are claims that the actor has socially valued attributes and is deserving of respectful behavior by the blameworthy individual. Finally, anger displays may be perceived as accusatory, insulting, or disruptive by others, who perceive the actor as violating politeness norms. These verbal and nonverbal behaviors may therefore be the first step in an escalating cycle of conflict between individuals. When both disputants communicate strong anger, an escalation of hostilities is the most likely outcome.

The display of anger is neither automatic nor reactive, nor does it have a single goal, such as inflicting injury on others. The multiple functions of anger in social interactions have been obscured by the tendency of some theorists to confuse expressions of anger with reactive aggression. As we have seen, anger has energizing, disruptive, expressive, self-presentational, and defensive functions (Novaco, 1976).

EXPRESSION OF GRIEVANCES

Once a grievance is formed, what the individual will do depends on a number of conditions. Among these conditions are the type and magnitude of harm experienced, the importance and salience of the rule that has been violated, the relationship to the other party, the remediability of the harmful consequences, the account provided by the perpetrator, the costs of various actions, and the expected reactions of the harmdoer and third parties. These factors will determine whether the grievant decides to do nothing, reconsiders and decides that the norm violator is not blameworthy, forgives the norm violator, makes a claim for some form of reparation, or attempts to punish the miscreant. These possible reactions by a grievant are displayed in Figure 8.4.

The communication of grievances and anger frequently has the constructive function of instigating solutions to interpersonal problems. Failure to communicate perceptions of unfairness and attributions of blame often interferes with the smooth interactions of people. When one or both parties communicate their cumulated resentments, the result is often restoration of better relationships between them. Tavris (1982) has argued that the chief function of the expression of anger is to mend troubled human relationships. Averill (1983) found that 76% of college students who had been targets of an angry person said they better understood their own faults following the other person's expression of anger. These students reported that the relationship with the other person was frequently strengthened following an angry episode. Alternatively, Baumeister et al. (1990) found that grievance expression had a negative impact on the relationship between people. They interpreted the inconsistency of results as due to the fact that the disputes involved in their study were more severe than those in the Averill study.

We first discuss costs and other factors that inhibit the expression of grievance. We then describe the social interaction process that occurs after

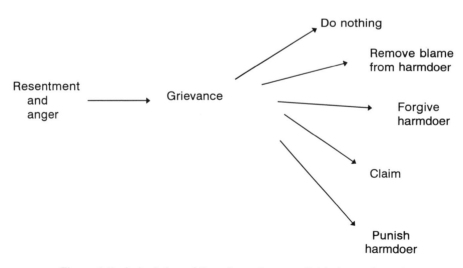

Figure 8.4. A depiction of the alternatives available to a grievant.

a grievance is expressed. That process usually begins with a claim, often in the form of a reproach. Sometimes the target attempts to avoid blame by engaging in some type of remedial action. In other instances, the target rejects the claim, and an escalatory process develops in which both actors engage in retributive justice.

Inhibition of Grievance Expression

In his research on anger episodes, Averill (1983) found that anger seldom led to aggression or to intensified conflict between individuals. Indeed, in most instances people who were angered did not communicate their grievances to the offender. When minor offenses are perceived, the amount of conflict stirred up by attempts to restore justice may simply not be worth it to the grievant. Thus, suburban residents frequently avoid conflicts by doing nothing when they blame their neighbors for norm violations, such as walking on the grass, dogs barking, noisy parties, and so on (Baumgartner, 1988). R. B. Felson (1984) also found that many respondents indicated that they were angry at someone but did nothing. The likelihood of doing nothing when aggrieved was higher when the offender was someone with whom grievants worked or a relative outside the immediate family. Conversely, grievances were readily expressed in the immediate family.[10]

Grievants may do nothing primarily because of the costs anticipated for engaging in actions to redress grievances. Grievants may keep silent because they fear retaliation or because they do not want to destroy their relationship with the offender. In a survey, respondents reported that they frequently did not express their grievances because they did not want to induce conflict or damage the relationship with the offender (Deshields, Jenkins, & Tait, 1989). Grievants may also wish to avoid an embarrassing scene. The rules of conversation require politeness and deference (Goffman, 1971). People usually go to considerable effort to hide any critical opinions they may have; they bend over backwards to avoid any slights. As a result of these rules, many grievances go unexpressed, and many coercive encounters are nipped in the bud.

The grievant must also consider the probable reactions of the offender to demands for explanations or apology, claims of reparation, or attempts to administer punishment. The perpetrator of injustice may control significant future reinforcements that would be withdrawn by any unilateral justice-restoring action undertaken by the grievant. In many instances, the unjust person has superior status to the grievant and cannot be challenged without incurring unacceptable costs. In a study of U.S. Air Force reservists,

---

[10]Unpublished data obtained by Felson (University at Albany, State University of New York, 1994).

Thibaut and Riecken (1955) found that high status protected an individual from open criticism and disapproval by inferiors.

The style of handling grievances is strongly affected by cultural context. In Japanese society, people are very concerned about maintaining good relationships with others and avoiding disrespect (Ohbuchi, 1991). Japanese generally wish to avoid open conflict with others and will often do nothing when they have grievances. Americans are more confrontational than Japanese when they have grievances and may feel the need for assertiveness training if they do nothing. There are numerous books exhorting Americans not to hold it in but to express their grievances.

The choice to do nothing lets the injustice stand unrectified, unless third parties intervene to restore justice. The grievant may ruminate about the unjust incident, interpret subsequent events in that context, and experience increasing resentment toward the offender. The perpetuation of perceived injustice is also associated with depression and learned helplessness, which interfere with adaptive behavior (cf. Tennen & Affleck, 1991). These subjective reactions to the original incident may last for years afterward (Silver, Boon, & Stones, 1983).

The "straw that broke the camel's back" phenomenon may occur. The last small injustice experienced by the grievant in a chain of injustices may suddenly evoke a strong punitive response. There are two processes that may cause such an overreaction: (a) grievances against a single individual cumulate over time, and (b) general resentment develops as a result of injustices perpetrated by a number of other people. Thus, a person who is treated unjustly by one person (and justice has not been restored) may react more strongly to an injustice perpetrated by a second person. Both of these processes have been interpreted as built-up frustrations that lead to aggressive behavior (Dollard et al., 1939). They have also been identified with overcontrolled personalities, who fail to react to injustices but suddenly lash out against an offender. Such reactions sometimes result in homicides (Megargee, 1970).

Reproaches, Claims, and Negotiation

The initial expression of grievances takes a variety of forms. The grievant may demand an explanation for the wrongdoing. In this case, the grievant suspends judgment and allows the offender (or "suspect") to account for the negative behavior. Alternatively, the grievant may assume the offender is to blame and may make a claim against the offender for some remedial action. The claim may be a demand for an apology or a demand for restitution when harm has been done. The grievant may also reproach the offender. In this case, the grievant openly blames and criticizes the offender. The reproach may involve an implicit claim for some remedial action or it may be a form of social punishment.

A coercive interaction is more likely to result when reproaches are severe than when they are diplomatic (Fincham, 1992). Severe reproaches are likely to elicit equally negative defensive reactions (cf. Cody & McLaughlin, 1988; R. L. Weiss & Heyman, 1990). The line between reproach and insult is ambiguous. In fact, many severe reproaches involve an insult in which the grievant attacks the offender's character rather than the offender's actions (Cody & Braaten, 1992). Targets may perceive reproaches as attacks even when the reproacher attempts to be diplomatic. Another reason for the aggravating effect of severe reproaches is that grievants who use them have prejudged the offender's guilt and are predisposed to rejecting any account (Cody & Braaten, 1992). Because a public commitment to the offender's guilt has been made, the grievant will feel constrained to defend the original accusation. A grievant who later honors the account has spoiled the identity of the accused person and implicitly acknowledges doing so. The accused person may form a countergrievance. To avoid this cost, the grievant is likely to reject the account.

In general, the more harm experienced by the individual, the greater the restitution demanded in claims. The specific content of claims depends on the type of harm that was experienced. Destruction or removal of commodities may lead to a demand for replacement or repair, imposition of constraints may be associated with demands for their removal, and aspersions on social identities may lead to demands for retraction or public apology.

The course of interaction subsequent to the issuance of a claim depends on the reaction of the perceived offender. The offender may comply to the demand, may make a counteroffer, or may reject the claim as illegitimate or outrageous. Compliance resolves the grievance and ends the interaction sequence that had begun with the negative event and attribution of blame. Although some permanent damage may have been done to the relationship between the two parties, justice will have been restored and the resentment felt by the grievant will be lessened. This catharsislike effect is related to the removal of anger and resentment and not to processes hypothesized by frustration–aggression theory, such as reduction of general arousal or aggressive energy.

A second reaction by the offender to a claim is to make a counteroffer. In this case, the offender neither complies to the demand nor completely rejects it. They can try to negotiate a solution to the dispute, although either or both may be tempted to use coercive means to gain a solution closer to their own initial position than is desired by the other party. Coercion is more likely to be used when conflict intensity is high and there are no clear rules or norms to govern the negotiation process.

Negotiation processes have been carefully examined by scholars who study social conflict (cf. Pruitt & Rubin, 1986; Walton & McKersie, 1965). Aggression has been interpreted as struggle tactics in negotiation and social conflict (Pruitt, Mikolic, Peirce, & Keating, 1993). A thorough review of this complex and vast literature is beyond the scope of this book (but see discussions in chapters 7 and 9). However, it is clear that perceived injustice, grievances, and coercive behavior are central in many social conflicts.

Some negotiation takes place in the presence of third parties who may help mediate and resolve the dispute to the satisfaction of both people. A grievant may seek the aid of third parties to mediate a dispute or to punish the offender and help restore justice. A person may go to the police, hire an attorney, or seek the help of mediators from dispute settlement programs—a recent innovation in many communities. The use of coercion is less likely in a dispute when third-party mediators are involved.[11]

A third reaction that can occur in response to a claim is a total rejection of the claim and denial of responsibility. The grievant may then perceive the offender as lying or as attempting to minimize the degree of harm done. The grievant may see the refusal as a challenge to his or her judgment, to standards of justice, or to his or her worth as an individual. A refusal may expand the scope or intensity of a grievance when the grievant perceives it as a further norm violation. The target of the claim may believe the grievant is exaggerating the degree of harm, is misinterpreting what happened, or is seeking some advantage by pressing the claim. The alleged offender may feel victimized, attribute blame to the original grievant, and develop a countergrievance. This dynamic typically is involved in an escalation of hostilities between two parties.

Remedial Actions and De-escalation

Remedial actions are often taken by an accused person to remove or mitigate blame or to gain the forgiveness of the grievant. A grievant, like a higher court, may review a judgment of blame against another person. Such a reevaluation may lead to removal of blame and withdrawal of the associated grievance. The most usual basis for removal of blame is an account offered by the offender or by third parties that excuses or justifies the negative action (M. R. Scott & Lyman, 1968). A grievant may forgive an offender when the latter proffers an apology or offers to make restitution. Because these remedial actions may limit the expected costs to the offender, they are frequently used to defuse or forestall coercive episodes.

Accounts

Excuses are explanations that deny or mitigate responsibility for an offending act. Among the types of excuses identified by Tedeschi and Riess

---

[11]But as we show in chapter 9, third parties who choose not to act as mediators may also contribute to an escalation of conflict.

(1981) are accidents, mistakes, and assertions that the actor could not control behavior because of temporary states induced by alcohol, drugs, illness, insanity, or coercion. In general, excuses attempt to direct the attributions of observers to external causes of behavior (Weiner, Amirkhan, Folkes, & Verette, 1987). If the grievant is convinced by the excuse, then the blame attributed to the target will be mitigated and the grievance will be weakened or withdrawn.

When offenders provide justifications, they accept responsibility for the negative action but claim it was acceptable under the circumstances. Justifications are reasons why a negative action was the correct or at least the necessary thing to do in a particular situation. Justifications must refer to social norms to make the actions appear acceptable (Hewitt & Stokes, 1975). Justifications may stipulate that the good accomplished outweighed the harm done (i.e., the principle of utility), claim that a higher authority mandated the action, or blame the victim as someone who deserved the negative consequences (Ryan, 1971; G. Sykes & Matza, 1957).

Actors who provide accounts for their offenses are likely to be punished less severely than actors who do not. Dedrick (1978) found that sanctions were less severe for a boy who behaved in an arrogant, unfriendly manner if he offered an account afterward. P. W. Blumstein et al. (1974) found that the account given for a minor infraction was more important than the nature of the violation in predicting subjects' judgments about an offender.

The multiple functions of accounts were demonstrated in a study carried out by Weiner et al. (1987). A social transgression was produced by delaying the arrival of one subject, thereby making another subject wait for 15 minutes to begin the experiment. The delayed subject offered an account for being late. It was found that, in comparison with unacceptable explanations for behavior, acceptable accounts mitigated the perceived responsibility of the transgressor and reduced the listener's anger, maintained the positive self-image of the excuse giver, and enhanced the relationship between the two strangers.

Apologies and Forgiveness

An offender may actively seek forgiveness by offering an apology for negative behavior. A full apology contains three components: (a) a confession of responsibility for the negative event, (b) an expression of remorse that may include reaffirmation of the norm that was violated and a promise not to violate the norm again, and (c) an offer to provide some form of restitution (Goffman, 1971; Schlenker, 1980). Any particular apology may include any or all of these components.

Research has shown that apologies can be very effective in ameliorating negative impressions, removing grievances, and reducing punitive actions directed toward the offender (Riordan, Marlin, & Kellogg, 1983; Schlenker

& Darby, 1981; Schwartz, Kane, Joseph, & Tedeschi, 1978). Apologies may be simple—as in "I'm sorry"—or may consist of complex elements of confession, remorse, guilt, and desire to make restitution (Goffman, 1971; Schlenker & Darby, 1981). Complex apologies have been found to be more effective than simple apologies (Braaten, Cody, & Bell, 1990; Holtgraves, 1989).

Remorseful offenders are perceived as less responsible for their behavior than are offenders who are not remorseful (Bramel, Taub, & Blum, 1968; N. M. Shields, 1979). Offenders who express remorse are also less likely to be punished by victims (Harrell, 1980; Harrell & Hartnagel, 1979) or by third-party observers (Rumsey, 1976; Savitsky, Czyzewski, Dubord, & Kaminsky, 1976). Alternatively, convicted offenders who denied their guilt were likely to receive more severe sentences than those who admitted it (R. B. Felson & Ribner, 1981). A regression analysis showed that when an apology was perceived as sincere there was a reduction of blame and reduced retributive behavior (Ohbuchi, Kameda, & Agarie, 1989).

An apology may lead the grievant to forgive the offender. To forgive is to pardon an offender and to give up claims for retribution. Forgiving the offender allows the grievant to mend the disrupted relationship and removes the need to engage in actions intended to restore justice, which can in some cases be dangerous and costly. Forgiveness can also allow the grievant to avoid the psychic costs of harboring resentment. Unresolved grievances may be associated with depression and feelings of powerlessness. A central issue for patients in psychotherapy is the experience of injustice, betrayals of trust, abuse of the weak by the strong, and feelings of rage (Hope, 1987, p. 241). Still, people often find it difficult to put aside their resentment and humiliation and forgive others. The aggrieved person may believe that forgiving the offender may be perceived as a sign of weakness. The refusal to forgive an offense can be a defensive self-presentation tactic aimed at preventing the grievant from further mistreatment by the offender. Such a defensive strategy can lead to a withdrawal from an intimate relationship. Vogel and Lazare (1990) found this defensive strategy to be a central factor in divorce actions.

To forgive an offense does not imply removal of blame. Forgiveness is more like parole in the criminal justice system. Any removal of blame is provisional and depends on future good conduct. Thus, although an aggrieved person may forgive an offender, the incident is not forgotten. People may be viewed as moral accountants, who keep ledgers and record debits and credits for each person they know. Forgiveness does not expunge a debit, but rather inactivates it so that it does not affect subsequent interactions with the offender. If the offender performs another blame-worthy action, the intensity of the new grievance will be greater than would have been the case if the forgiven incident had never occurred because the moral ledger has a larger negative balance. This cumulative effect of forgiven but reactivated transgressions may be particularly strong if the new transgression violates the same norm as the previous one. Recidivism reveals the insincerity of the perpetrator and may also violate a promise embedded in a previous apology. In the latter instance, the new transgression is both an antinormative action and a betrayal of the offender's prior promise—a case of two offenses bundled in one action. The straw that broke the camel's back phenomenon may occur in such cases because the grievant reacts to the total amount of injustice suffered and not only to the last transgression. Thus, a disproportionate punitive reaction to a particular transgression may represent retribution for a series of transgressions, some of which had been forgiven in the past.

It is not unusual for an accused to remind the accuser of past offenses. A backlog of forgiven offenses may provide the person with a shield against new complaints from the other person. When a complaint is made and the offender reminds the accuser of past faults, the accuser may perceive the countercomplaint as unfair and irrelevant to the present situation. The cycle may escalate if the accuser then expresses additional grievances and becomes more angry. In this way, a small offense can lead to a major confrontation between two people. Instead of arguing about who should have washed the dishes, they end up questioning each other's integrity, commitment to the relationship, and character.

Development of Disputes

Research on the social interaction involved in disputes has demonstrated how grievances and attempts at social control develop into coercive incidents. Schönbach (1990) and Schönbach and Kleibaumhüter (1990) focused on the early stages of disputes in their discussion of account episodes. They viewed account episodes as involving four phases. First, the actor performs an offensive act or fails to fulfill an obligation. Second, a reproach either occurs or is expected. Third, an excuse, justification, concession, or refusal to offer an account occurs. Finally, audiences evaluate the actor in terms of the offending act and the actor's reaction to the reproach. Successful accounts terminate the episode. An unsatisfactory response to a reproach may lead to conflict and possible escalation of hostilities between the two parties.

Studies of the sequence of events in serious verbal disputes and physically violent disputes have shown the importance of grievances early in the encounter (R. B. Felson, 1984; R. B. Felson & Steadman, 1983; Luckenbill, 1977). Felson (1984) obtained data on coercive incidents from the self-reports of former criminal offenders, former mental patients, and a representative sample of the adult population of a northeastern city in the United States. Respondents were asked to describe in detail bad arguments and physically violent incidents in which they had been involved. A coding scheme was developed that allowed a description of the sequence of events that occur in various types of coercive interactions. Most of the incidents began with a social control process in which someone was punished for violating a rule or not complying with an order. Reproaches, rule violations, and accounts occurred with great frequency in these incidents, particularly at the beginning of the encounter. Physical violence was more likely when the transgressor failed to give an account. Accounts tended to be given after an antagonist was reproached and not in anticipation of the challenge. Perhaps, if antagonists had given more accounts prior to reproaches—what Hewitt and Stokes (1975) called *disclaimers*—the conflicts would have been less likely to have a coercive outcome. Instead in these incidents reproaches were given and retaliation occurred in the form of insults and threats. The aggrieved party was usually the first to engage in a verbal attack. These initial attacks usually were reciprocated and the altercation became more intense as the incident progressed, sometimes resulting in physical assaults.

Retributive Justice

Once a decision is made to punish someone, the actor must decide the level of punishment that the offender deserves. The level of punishment is a function of the level of blame, the importance of the rule that was violated, and the degree of harm experienced. The level of blame, as discussed above, is a function of perceptions of intent, legitimacy, and foreseeability. In general, an offender will be assigned greatest blame and given the most severe punishment for offenses that are intentional, controllable, and illegitimate. Unintentional offenses that produce harms that were foreseeable (i.e., negligent and reckless acts) should lead to the lowest level of blame. These distinctions are codified in the sentencing structure of criminal law.

Retributive justice stipulates that the amount of suffering inflicted on offenders should be proportional to the amount of harm done by them. The ancient rule of justice, *lex talionis*, is represented in the Old Testament as "an eye for an eye, and a tooth for a tooth." People appear to be aware that this rule motivates some of their actions. Muir and Weinstein (1962) found that respondents reported that norms of retribution influenced their behavior.[12]

The proportionality rule of retributive justice has been supported in a number of experiments.[13] When subjects were asked to assign a level of

---

[12]Some scholars have referred to proportional retaliation to attacks in terms of a negative norm of reciprocity (cf. Patchen, 1993).

[13]Donnerstein and Hatfield (1982) provided a reinterpretation of much of the laboratory research on aggression in terms of retribution for experienced inequity.

punishment to an agent who harmed a victim, more severe punishments were recommended when greater harm was done (Horai & Bartek, 1978; Landy & Aronson, 1969). Subjects who had been shocked one, five, or nine times by a confederate reciprocated with roughly equivalent number of shocks (Helm, Bonoma, & Tedeschi, 1972). Similar experimental results were obtained by Greenwell and Dengerink (1973). When the form of harm involved in attack and retaliation are different, the retaliation has been found to be less than when the form of harm is the same for both attack and retaliation (McDaniel, O'Neal, & Fox, 1971). One explanation for this cross-punishment effect is that people generally follow the law of *lex talionis*, but they do not want to precipitate an escalation of hostilities. When they are not sure of the equivalence of retaliation, they opt for giving too little rather than too much.

Punishment is likely to be more severe when the offense violates rules that are perceived as more important. There is some consensus, in the United States at least, about the seriousness of various criminal violations. Rossi et al. (1974) found high levels of agreement in the rank ordering of the seriousness of 140 criminal violations. Violence against people, actions against the police, actions against strangers, and selling drugs were ranked as serious violations. There were high levels of consensus between Blacks and Whites, men and women, and educated and uneducated respondents.

Ideas of right and wrong are based on abstract and general principles, and their application to specific circumstances is often not straightforward. Ambiguities of interpretation can lead reasonable people to different judgments, especially when they have opposing interests. From the perspective of the grievant, retribution in the form of punishment redresses injustice, but the recipient is apt to have a different interpretation of the coercive interaction. The recipient may perceive the punishment as unjustified or excessive and may blame the grievant for performing an antinormative, harmful action. A countergrievance may then be formed, and the recipient may retaliate as a way of restoring justice or deterring future attacks.

The means that people use to punish offenders can be quite varied. Black (1983) suggested that many burglaries, robberies, vandalism, and arson involve grievances. A study of arson in Houston, Texas, for the period from 1978 to 1979 found that 59% of all arsons were committed as revenge following a verbal argument or physical confrontation (Pettiway, 1987). The reasons given for the arsons included being barred or evicted from an establishment, being "ripped off," separations or divorces, and sexual rivalry.

Some forms of vandalism can be interpreted as attempts by youth to punish adults generally. In this case, punishment is directed at targets with whom the offender has no personal grievance. Targets are punished because they share some social category with others with whom the offender does have a grievance. Here, there is some notion of collective liability or guilt by association, where an aggrieved party blames the entire group for the misbehavior of one member (Tedeschi & Norman, 1985b).

Negative Equity and Redistributive Justice

When individuals decide that the distribution of rewards and costs is unfair, they may attempt to restore equity by harming the person perceived as privileged, even when that person is not held responsible for the injustice. By increasing the costs or reducing the rewards of the overbenefited person, they can produce equity (see Donnerstein & Hatfield, 1982; Tedeschi & Norman, 1985b). Acts of redistributive justice are probably much less frequent than acts of retributive justice. When people feel they have been unjustly treated, they usually attack the person they blame for the injustice not the person who has benefited from the inequity. Typically, the over-benefited party and the party perceived as blameworthy are the same person, but this is not always the case.

Some of the findings obtained in studies of displaced aggression can be reinterpreted in terms of negative equity and redistributive justice (Tedeschi & Norman, 1985b).[14] An example is a study by D. S. Holmes (1972), in which subjects waited either 5 or 30 minutes for a second person (a confederate) to arrive before beginning the experiment. According to frustration–aggression theory, the longer subjects waited, the more frustrated they would be and the more shock they would give when provided with the opportunity. Subjects did give more shocks in the 30-minute condition than in the 5-minute condition. Furthermore, subjects in the 30-minute condition also gave more shocks to a person who was conscripted as a substitute for the tardy person.

Although D. S. Holmes (1972) interpreted the latter finding as evidence for displaced aggression, Tedeschi and Norman (1985b) noted that subjects had incurred the costs of waiting, whereas the confederate (whether responsible or not) had not. Subjects typically expect that all participants will receive equal credit for participation in an experiment. If so, then the prompt person and the late person would receive equal credit. The longer subjects had to wait, the greater the inequity between them and the other person. The use of shocks by subjects may have had the purpose of reducing the negative inequity that existed in the situation by producing an amount of discomfort for the confederate to equal the amount suffered by them through waiting.

To test the justice-restoring hypothesis, Nacci and Tedeschi (1977) replicated D. S. Holmes's (1972) study and added two new conditions. In

---

[14]Displaced aggression is usually interpreted in terms of the frustration–aggression hypothesis (e.g., Berkowitz, 1989; Dollard et al., 1939). Tedeschi and Norman (1985b) proposed alternative explanations of experimental studies showing displaced aggression effects (see chap. 12).

these new conditions, when subjects arrived for the experiment they were told by Experimenter A that their partner had not yet arrived. Almost immediately afterward a second person arrived in the same general area, was met by Experimenter B, and was told that his partner had not yet arrived. After 5 or 30 minutes, Experimenter A asked Experimenter B to allow him to use Experimenter B's subject so that at least one of them could complete their study. In these two conditions, then, both persons had waited for an equal amount of time for a partner who did not show. The results obtained by Holmes were replicated for the original four conditions, but the amount of shocks given by subjects in the new 5- and 30-minute conditions were not different from the replicated 5-minute conditions. These results appear to support the justice-restoring interpretation for a displaced aggression effect.

SUMMARY AND CONCLUSIONS

People are socialized to believe that blameworthy actions should be punished and are motivated by this value to maintain justice between themselves and others. The belief in retributive justice sometimes leads people to punish those against whom they have a grievance. Because violations of norms are common—whether they be distributive, procedural, or interactional—grievances are common in social life. Grievances are often accompanied by anger, which can disrupt cognitive functioning, reduce social skills, and energize behavior. This in turn may exacerbate conflicts and increase the likelihood that coercion will be used.

The first step in the formation of a grievance is the belief that a norm has been violated. Actors evaluate the behavior of others in comparison with their expectations about how people should behave. Thus, the same behavior may be judged differently depending on the evaluator's expectations. Once a negative judgment occurs, actors attempt to determine whether the offender is blameworthy. The attribution of blame depends on whether the offender's actions are perceived as foreseeable and controllable or as intentional and malevolent. The fixation of blame is tantamount to a judgment of injustice. The victim of that injustice then has a grievance against the offender.

Grievances are often not communicated to the offender because of the expected costs of doing so. A failure to restore justice may leave resentment and a readiness to punish the offender when an opportunity to do so occurs. When grievances are expressed, they take a variety of forms. Grievants may demand an explanation and give offenders an opportunity to give an account and mitigate blame. Sometimes the grievant will absolve the other person of blame, and in this way perceived justice is restored. Grievants may reproach the offender or demand restitution or an apology.

If offenders engage in remedial actions, blame may be removed or they may be forgiven, although the offense will not be forgotten.

A claim for restitution may be met by compliance, a counteroffer, or a refusal. Compliance restores justice, but counteroffers and refusals in a dispute process have the potential to escalate into coercive episodes. The availability of third parties as mediators can keep disputes from erupting into exchanges of threats and punishments.

Finally, grievants may administer retributive justice by punishing offenders. The level of punishment administered will be a function of the level of blame, the level of harm, and the importance of the norm that has been violated. Because of self-serving biases, the fundamental attribution error, and other factors that affect attributions of blame, targets of punishment often see themselves as undeserving victims. They may view the punishment as an illegitimate attack or as excessive and may then form a countergrievance. Their belief in retributive justice may lead them to retaliate. When each party feels aggrieved by the actions of the other, a vicious cycle of escalation is likely to occur. In addition to concerns about justice, both parties are likely to retaliate to maintain a favorable identity. It is to this process that we turn next.

9

SOCIAL IDENTITIES AND COERCIVE ACTIONS

The importance of impression management or saving face as a factor in coercive interactions has been recognized by many scholars (Goffman, 1955; W. B. Miller, 1958; Toch, 1969; Wolfgang & Ferracuti, 1967). People value particular social identities and are motivated to assert and defend them. Theories of impression management focus on the types of social identities people value and the tactics and strategies they use to attain or defend desired identities (e.g., Schlenker, 1980; Tedeschi & Lindskold, 1976). Coercive interactions are public affairs involving at least the two parties in conflict. Furthermore, third parties often are present and serve as audiences or participants in the interaction episode. The public nature of social interactions invokes self-presentation concerns that under certain conditions may be the primary motivation for using threats, punishments, or bodily force against another person.

In this chapter, we examine the role of self-presentation in coercive actions. We adopt a general distinction between assertive and protective self-presentations (Arkin, 1981). Assertive self-presentations are attempts to establish particular social identities, whereas protective self-presentations are face-saving actions performed when a person believes a valued identity is threatened. Coercion exercised for assertive self-presentation tends to be predatory in nature. The actor may attack someone who has done nothing provocative or sets up situations to justify attacking others, for the purpose of establishing a desired identity. Coercion involving protective self-presentation is typically a reaction to a perceived attack from another person and has the purpose of restoring respect and status. Less often it involves an attempt to recover status after failure and embarrassing situations.

We also describe a number of conditions that facilitate or inhibit the performance of coercive actions in situations where the individual actively considers such actions. The presence of third parties can facilitate by increasing self-presentation concerns and making it more likely that coercion will be used to protect identities. A third party may also act as a mediator and serve to reduce the likelihood that coercive actions will be performed.

MOTIVES FOR SELF-PRESENTATION

Individuals' public identities are not fixed but depend both on their own actions and on the social definitions of audiences. Among the many social identities that are valued by actors are those associated with competence, attractiveness, status, physical strength and courage, and moral righteousness. Cross-cultural research on the perception of people measured by the Semantic Differential Scale has indicated that connotative meanings of people are organized around evaluative and power dimensions (Kemper, 1978; C. E. Osgood, May, & Miron, 1975; Triandis, 1972).

According to the Chinese conception of social identities, moral character is distinguished from competence, and power is thought to follow from competence (Hu, 1944). Thus, *lien* refers to the confidence of society in the integrity of an individual's moral character, whereas *mien-tzu* is "a reputation achieved through getting on in life, through success and ostentation" (Hu, 1944, p. 45). *Mien-tzu* influences a person's power because a person who has *mien-tzu* is in a position to exercise considerable influence over others. Others feel compelled to comply with his or her wishes out of fear of adverse consequences. As we show, the use of coercion often involves concerns for the interrelated dimensions of power and competence.

The desire of individuals for the approval and affection of others is one basis for self-presentation. This affiliative motive may underlie the concern for appearing moral, just, cooperative, well behaved, kind, friendly, and merciful. These identities, which are relevant to moral character, will sometimes be associated with the use of coercion. The desire to foster an identity as a morally good person may be associated with a general reluctance to use physical violence. A parent may not spank a child in public for misbehaving, but once they are in the privacy of their home the spanking is administered. Alternatively, a person may publicly harm another person to establish an identity as morally righteous. The actions of vigilantes such as the Guardian Angels against criminal offenders can be interpreted in terms of this form of self-presentation.

The desire of individuals to acquire and exercise social power is a second basis for self-presentations (Tedeschi, 1989). Social power is not well understood by social psychologists. Much of the available research focuses on a typology of power bases. French and Raven (1959) proposed that certain characteristics of the source of influence enhance the effectiveness of influence attempts. Among such characteristics are expertise, legitimate power, and referent power. Tedeschi et al. (1973) have added other power-related identities to the typology, including trustworthiness, credibility, and prestige. They proposed that because these characteristics increase the power of people, individuals will be motivated to achieve and defend such identities. Any aspersion on any of these desired identities may bring about some form of protective action.

Individuals are sometimes willing to accept audience disapproval if it enables them to gain influence. Jellison and Gentry (1978) demonstrated that subjects would present themselves in a socially negative way when it was to their advantage to do so. Subjects were asked to play the role of interviewee for a job and were told either that the personnel manager hired people he personally liked or that he hired people he personally disliked. Subjects responded in a way that would obtain the job even if this required a negative self-presentation. Similar results have been obtained by Pellegrini, Hicks, and Meyers-Winton (1978). In other instances, individuals may behave in a particular way in spite of the disapproval of an audience because some other audience, whose opinion matters more to them, approves of their behavior. An example is the use of physical violence by gang members, which is positively valued by other gang members but is disapproved of by most people (Horowitz & Schwartz, 1974).

Individuals learn to value identities associated with moral character and power through the socialization process. Concern with social identities does not necessarily involve impression management for an external audience. Social behavior may reflect concern about private identities as well (Schlenker, 1980; Tetlock & Manstead, 1985). That is, people behave in ways that confirm, demonstrate, or express the identities they have internalized and value. The research literature focuses on the effects of public identities—by examining effects of an audience, for example—probably because it is easier to do so. In general, we do not attempt to distinguish between private and public identities.

ASSERTIVE SELF-PRESENTATION AND COERCION

We examine two forms of assertive self-presentation that involve the use of coercion: intimidation and self-promotion. Individuals may engage in intimidation tactics to inspire fear in others, to enhance the believability of threats, or to show their resolve. Coercion may also be used as a form of self-promotion to win respect and demonstrate the actor's power and competence.

Intimidation Tactics

In chapter 7, we examined the use of coercion to achieve influence. When threats are used to demand compliance from a target person, auxiliary self-presentation behaviors can inspire fear and increase the probability of successful influence. When police officers conduct a raid on suspects considered to be dangerous, they typically display weapons, shout commands and threats as loud as they can, and use profanity. All of these self-presentation behaviors contribute to the image of people ready and willing to harm anyone who would resist.

Jones and Pittman (1982) described all attempts to inspire fear in others as intimidation tactics. Threats, bursts of outrage, insults, displays of weapons or fists, and many other forms of coercion may establish an identity as powerful and dangerous, which in turn may serve to intimidate others. In addition to enhancing the effectiveness of threats, intimidation tactics may deter other people from engaging in coercive actions against the intimidator. When used to establish trans-situational identities, such behaviors are sometimes referred to as *strategic* rather than *tactical* (Tedeschi & Melburg, 1984).

Intimidation tactics are apparent in male violence among the Yanomamo of South America (Chagnon, 1977). These people have been characterized as the most violent in the world. Male children are socialized to present themselves as fierce, dangerous, and courageous. Boys are encouraged to physically hit each other, and even toddlers are rewarded for swatting at other people. Men often beat their wives in public to display their fierceness. Chagnon described such reputation building:

> Each individual sooner or later has to show that his bluffs and implied threats can be backed up. I suspect that the frequency of wife beating is a component of this syndrome, since men can display ferocity and show others they are capable of violence. . . . The important thing is that the man has displayed his potential for violence and the implication is that other men better treat him with respect and caution. (1977, p. 9)

Intimidation is practiced by professional boxers who make disparaging statements about each other in press conferences and stare fiercely into each other's eyes during instructions from the referee just before a fight. In sidewalk behavior, long eye contact between young men may be interpreted as a challenge to a fight. In a field study, Ellsworth, Carlsmith, and Henson (1972) found that motorists sped away from red lights faster when scooter riders stared at them than when there was no staring. Exline and Winters (1965) found that subjects avoided looking at a hostile interviewer. There may be an evolutionary basis for the effects of staring. Among chimpanzees, staring is known to be a form of intimidation (Altmann, 1967). Gaze aversion is characteristic of the subordinate of two animals and is an expression of submission. How nonverbal behaviors, such as gaze aversion and staring, are interpreted among humans depends on the nature of the relationship between the interactants and the social context (cf. Altmann, 1967).

Intimidation tactics are frequently used in bargaining situations. Most subjects in bargaining experiments display a pattern of behavior—including high demands, few concessions, and frequent use of bluffs—to create an identity of "toughness." On the one hand, toughness decreases the chances of reaching agreement but enhances outcomes when the tactic is successful (Bartos, 1966). On the other hand, yielding encourages the opponent to take a tough bargaining stance. Bargainers who initially make a fair offer and then hold to their positions are perceived as giving too much too soon, and those who make noncontingent and consistent concessions are perceived as weak and encourage the opponent to hold firm and wait for the bargain to sweeten (Komorita & Brenner, 1968). The participants thus face a bargainer's dilemma. If neither makes concessions, then no agreement can be reached. If one makes concessions and the other does not, then a solution will favor the tough bargainer.

Bargainers often threaten one another. Representatives of management and labor threaten lockouts and strikes, or a child threatens not to let a sibling play with a toy unless there is a trade of television programs. Threats may succeed in bringing an adversary to agreement, or they may start an escalatory process ending in costs to all parties. In addition to direct influence purposes, however, the use of threats displays toughness as a bargainer and commitment to a particular position.

Self-Promotion

Whereas the intimidator seeks to instill fear, the self-promoter wants respect. Actors who use coercive actions to promote themselves are attempting to demonstrate prowess, skill, and competence (see Jones & Pittman, 1982). The successful use of coercion—like success in any endeavor—can bring prestige, at least among some audiences. In American culture, skill at physical fighting is often admired among young men. Skill at verbal insults may also be respected. Note, however, that actions oriented toward respect are not necessarily oriented toward approval.

In a study of violent incarcerated men, Toch (1969) described some of them as *self-image promoters*. They initiated fights with strangers without provocation for the purpose of "rep building." These fights occurred in front of audiences so that the desired reputation could be publicized. Rep builders habitually precipitated incidents in which they could legitimate demonstrations of their fighting ability and physical courage. In some cases, as in a movie western where young gunslingers seek out the "fast gun," self-image promoters may deliberately provoke one another. It is important to precipitate incidents to keep their reputations fresh in the memories of observers. Violence motivated by rep building may also be an attempt to intimidate others.

An example of rep building involving the use of coercion is the behavior of bullies. The bully's strategy is to dominate a vulnerable low-status target, who is generally from 1 year to 2 years younger and physically weaker than the bully (Olweus, 1978). Furthermore, the victims are usually unpopular, physically unattractive, and physically uncoordinated children. The role of self-presentation is suggested by the evidence that bullies tend to seek out situations where their behavior can be witnessed by their peers (Wachtel, 1973).

Self-promotion may take the form of a single dramatic action, such as an assassination. Arthur Bremer, who shot and paralyzed Governor George Wallace of Alabama in an assassination attempt, had at one time or another also stalked Richard Nixon, George McGovern, and Hubert Humphrey before shooting Wallace. Bremer did not care who he shot, as long as the victim was a nationally recognized political figure. As he was being escorted from the scene of the crime, Bremer asked the police officers how much they thought he would be offered for his memoirs. John Hinckley, who shot President Reagan and several other people, was motivated by a desire to gain the affection of Jody Foster, a movie actress, with whom he was infatuated.

Presidential assassins are often characterized by a need to bring public attention to themselves (Kirkham, Levy, & Crotty, 1970). A motivation for attention has also been offered as an explanation for the misbehavior of children. We are skeptical that individuals simply want to be noticed. We suspect that to the extent that presidential assassins are oriented toward an audience, their motive is to gain respect or other favorable responses. Of course, they may be deluded about what the response will be. Similarly, children who misbehave in school may be motivated to establish positive identities in the eyes of their peers and may disregard the negative response of the teacher.

The cultural definition of what it means to be masculine probably has an important effect on the way a man will present himself to others. A series of surveys of sex-role stereotypes carried out in the United States throughout the past 2 decades indicated that the typical man is seen as different from the typical woman by both men and women. Men are more likely to be seen as strong and competitive, whereas women are more likely to be characterized as submissive, gentle, and weak (Broverman, Vogel, Broverman, Clarkson, & Rosenkrantz, 1972; Helmreich, Spence, & Gibson, 1982; Rosenkrantz, Vogel, Bee, Broverman, & Broverman, 1968). In addition, there is a persistent belief that men and women are fundamentally different in terms of aggressiveness and dominance (Ruble, 1983).

The gender identity of some men involves a constellation of factors— sometimes collectively described as *machismo*—that are apt to result in the use of coercion against others. Among Latinos, *macho man* is a very positive description and refers to a man who is strong and brave. But machismo has taken on a more negative meaning both in social science and in Latino cultures by its association with violence and chauvinistic attitudes toward women.

In the extreme, some men might want to be viewed as aggressive, tough, dangerous, bad tempered, or as a "bad ass" (Katz, 1988). Such people may be particularly likely to use physical forms of coercion. Such actions are likely to precipitate identity contests with other men, who are also motivated to foster, maintain, and protect a masculine identity. Thus, evidence shows that verbal disputes are much more likely to escalate into physical violence when the antagonists are both males.

Evidence that gender identities help explain why boys are more likely to use physical means of coercion than girls came from a study of junior high school children (R. B. Felson & Liska, 1984). Respondents were asked to rate themselves on adjective pairs, such as sensitive–unfeeling, cowardly– brave, and rough–smooth. Sociometric ratings were used to determine which children in the class fought the most. Regression analyses indicated that a strong gender difference in frequency of fighting was greatly reduced when self-ratings of gender-relevant identities were controlled. It may be concluded that boys are more likely to use physical means of coercion than girls, partly because of their gender role–identities.

Male concern for demonstrating power has been proposed as one reason for rape and other forms of sexual coercion. It has been argued that men engage in sexual coercion because it gives them a feeling of power, control, or dominance over female victims (e.g., Deming & Eppy, 1981). Although there is little or no evidence to support such an explanation, it is certainly plausible. The advantage of a social interactionist approach is that it can incorporate such an explanation into a general theory of coercive actions.

Women are more likely than men to avoid acts that threaten the identities of others (P. Brown, 1980; Connor-Linton, 1986). In contrast, men are more likely to seek to dominate adversaries and to win conflicts. Observation of over 1,000 quarrels among 5- to 7-year-old American children indicated that boys predominantly pursued their own agendas whereas girls showed more concern for maintaining interpersonal harmony (P. Miller, Danaher, & Forbes, 1986). Whereas boys frequently used threats and physical force to attain their objectives, girls more often used strategies—such as compromise, acquiescence, and clarification of intentions—to mitigate conflict.

PROTECTIVE SELF-PRESENTATION AND COERCION

According to self-presentation theory (Schlenker, 1980), individuals find themselves in a predicament when their desired identities are challenged or threatened. To protect, maintain, or reestablish identities that have been questioned, they engage in protective self-presentation, a type of remedial action (Goffman, 1972). Whereas assertive self-presentation is more concerned with appearing powerful, protective self-presentation is more concerned with avoiding the appearance of weakness. The motive to avoid the appearance of weakness is probably much more common than the tendency to use coercion to demonstrate strength. There are many men for whom being a tough guy is unimportant but relatively few who are comfortable with being labeled a *coward*, a *wimp*, a *weakling*, or a *pansy*.

There are two types of predicaments associated with the use of coercion: attacks by others and public failures. The main type of predicament that leads to coercion is a perceived intentional attack by another person. When people believe that their identities have been attacked, they often experience a loss of status and power, which is accompanied by humiliation. These attacks may be deliberate, as in the case of an explicit insult or threat. They may be inadvertent, as when an individual offends someone by violating some politeness norm. People expect others to show respect for them and not to violate their autonomy, and when others fail to act accordingly, they may perceive that their identities have been attacked. We discuss both deliberate and inadvertent attacks on identity below.

Predicaments associated with public failures or incompetent performance sometimes lead to coercive actions. Failure-based predicaments cause the individual to lose face and experience embarrassment, a self-reflective emotion indicating that a desired identity has been endangered by a precipitating event (Goffman, 1959; Leary & Schlenker, 1981). Under special circumstances delineated below, this type of predicament can instigate coercive behavior.

Predicaments, Identities, and Coercion

When people think that another person has intentionally harmed them, they are likely to retaliate. Experimental research has shown that perceived intentional attack is the most reliable elicitor of coercive action. Thus, evidence reviewed in chapter 2 indicated that attack, not failure, is the major determinant of shock delivery by subjects in laboratory studies (e.g., A. H. Buss, 1963; Epstein & Taylor, 1967). Observational studies of children and self-report studies of adults have found that attack is strongly related to counterattack (R. B. Felson, 1982; Rausch, 1965). We argued in chapter 8 that an attack is likely to be perceived as wrongdoing by the target and creates a grievance. Motivated by a sense of justice, the target is likely to retaliate to punish the offender. In addition, the target of an attack may retaliate to deter his or her tormentor from further attack (see chap. 7).

An explanation for why people retaliate cannot be fully provided by either a justice motive or concern for deterrence. A justice motive cannot explain why individuals are more likely to use coercion when they are personally attacked than when they observe attacks on others. In justice-restoring situations, punishment is measured to match the seriousness of the offense. However, retaliatory acts are often disproportionate. A justice motive cannot explain why antagonists attempt to win rather than produce a just outcome. Furthermore, people sometimes retaliate—both in experiments and in naturally occurring situations—when deterrence is not a factor. They sometimes retaliate against people they never expect to see again.

An explanation of the tendency of people to retaliate requires an understanding of the implications of attacks for the target's identity. An attack casts the target into a negative identity by making the target appear weak and ineffectual. The target can nullify that image (i.e., restore face) with a counterattack. By retaliating, targets show they are neither weak nor incompetent; they show that they have honor (i.e., that they cannot be taken lightly or treated with disrespect).[1] A review of the literature on the impact of social identities in conflict situations concludes that actors value an image of strength and are motivated to avoid appearing weak (Tjosvold, 1983). Indeed, Rollo May (1953, 1972) argued that violence is the end product of power deprivation.

An attack on an identity initiates a "character contest," in which the antagonists compete for favorable identities in terms of power and competence (see Goffman, 1955; Luckenbill, 1977). Coercive actions cast the other into a negative identity and allow the actor to move "one up." Goffman (1955) described this process as follows:

> In aggressive interchanges the winner not only succeeds in introducing information favorable to himself and unfavorable to the others, but

---

[1]Heider (1958) noted that arbitrarily harming another person is not confined to physical and material consequences. An offender is often viewed as demonstrating contempt for the harmed person, displaying superior power, or promoting the superiority of the offender's beliefs and values. Punishing the offender may be a means of reasserting one's identity, status, belief, and values.

also demonstrates that as an interactant he can handle himself better than his adversaries. Evidence of this capacity is often more important than all the other information the person conveys in the interchange. (p. 25)

If the target makes a successful riposte,

> the instigator of the play must not only face the disparagement with which the others have answered him but also accept the fact that his assumption of superiority in footwork has proven false. He is made to look foolish; he loses face. Hence, it is always a gamble to make a remark. (p. 25)

Because a counterattack casts its target into a negative identity, it often motivates a counter-counterattack, which creates a "conflict spiral." These attacks can become more serious as the episode progresses, sometimes resulting in physical assaults and homicide (R. B. Felson & Steadman, 1983; Luckenbill, 1977). Thus, identities play an important role in the escalation of coercive encounters.

The person losing a verbal conflict may turn to physical violence as a face-saving move. This is consistent with evidence that homicide offenders tend to have lower scores on intelligence tests and lower school achievement than other types of criminal offenders (Berg & Fox, 1947) and that they also tend to be heavier and taller than the general population (Hooton, 1939). If intelligence is correlated with success in verbal battles and size is correlated with success in physical battles, then large antagonists with lower intelligence would be more likely to use physical means of attack.

Losing a fight may lower status, but status loss can be minimized by putting up a good fight. The loser of a fight can still project an identity as resolute, courageous, and tough. Thus, Short and Strodtbeck (1965) reported incidents of fights between members of different gangs in which both antagonists enhanced their reputations. An identity of being tough may discourage others from attacking a person again.

The actions taken to restore face after affronts take culturally defined forms. Among the Kwakiutl Indians of the Pacific Northwest, responses to insults take the form of a potlatch, which consists of giving so many possessions to the provocateur that the latter cannot repay and consequently loses face within the tribe (M. D. R. Gil & Brown, 1981). In American culture, this might be described as "killing with kindness."

Role of Emotion in Identity Attacks

Attacks on identities often produce a strong emotional response. When targets believe the antagonist has belittled and demeaned them, they are likely to feel humiliated. By retaliating, the target can nullify that negative identity and reduce humiliation. Vogel and Lazare (1990) described the emotional experience of humiliation and how it develops:

> Humiliation refers to an interaction between two or more people, in the course of which one perceives oneself as having suffered an insult which substantially offends one's sense of self-worth; it is experienced by the recipient as an affront, possibly undeserved, which is delivered with hostile intent, even though the offending party may have no awareness of having been hostile or insulting. (p. 141)

Identity attacks may elicit emotional reactions other than humiliation, such as fear, embarrassment, and anger. When physical attacks have occurred or are anticipated, the target may experience fear. Attacks on identities may embarrass the target (and anyone else present) because the interaction ritual has broken down and the target may not know how to respond (Goffman, 1982). College students identified insults as one type of situation that caused embarrassment (Metts & Cupach, 1989). Identity attacks are also likely to produce anger, because they are usually perceived as unjust and antinormative. Anger is associated with a justice motive, whereas humiliation accompanies a protective self-presentation motive. Emotion theorists have noted that anger often accompanies humiliation (Kemper, 1978; Scheff, 1988).

In chapter 8, we proposed that anger is directly related to the use of coercion in several ways. It causes cognitive deficits, and it energizes and amplifies whatever behaviors the angry actor chooses. Humiliation may have similar effects. It tends to narrow the attention of the victim to social comparisons between self and perpetrator, brings about cognitive deficits, and energizes behavior. The intensity of total emotional experience may be amplified by the addition of other motives associated with anger and fear. In addition, the emotional reaction to a provocation late in an escalation cycle can build on reactions to earlier provocations.

Deliberate Insults

Insults are linguistic or paralinguistic acts that show disrespect or contempt for others. Such acts directly altercast a target person into a negative identity. An insult often leads to escalation and the development of a *character contest*. Research on the sequence of events in incidents of verbal and physical coercion has shown that insults tend to lead to counterinsults (R. B. Felson, 1984). The insult casts its target in a negative identity and motivates a counterattack, which motivates a counter-counterattack and results in a conflict spiral.

Insults include obscene words and gestures, jokes, or demeaning statements about the target or groups to which the target belongs. The effect of an insult is often to spoil the identity of the target person and to lower his or her status. Insults may include dirty words referring to body parts, processes, or products; animal terms; social deviations; ethnic or racial slurs; or slights on level of maturity, intelligence, or personality. Among the Utku people, the strongest insult is to call someone *nutataqpaluktug*, which means "a small child without sense or reasoning ability" (Briggs, 1970). The social ideal among these people is to display an ability to reason and adult social responsibility. When an adult is called *nutataqpaluktug*, he or she is altercasted in an identity for which there is strong disapproval in that culture.

Insults, like other forms of punishment, can have pedagogical and social control functions (Lallemand, 1975). Their purpose is often to curtail or change some behavior of the target person. The implication is that if targets understand how their actions are associated with negative typifications, they will desist from engaging in them. Insults may also be used as a means of restoring justice by punishing the target for an antinormative action.

Instances of intergang violence in a Mexican-American community have been attributed to insults. Violence was apt to occur when a member of one gang impugned the honor of a member of a second gang. Such violation of interpersonal respect required gang members to retaliate in kind. Horowitz and Schwartz (1974) described this process:

> Any act or statement that challenges a gang member's "right" treatment in face-to-face relations is interpreted as an insult and hence as a potential threat to his manhood. For these youth honor revolves around a person's capacity to command deferential treatment (i.e., "respect") from others who are, in other respects, like themselves . . . In all honor based cultures or subcultures . . . the possibility of insult inheres in any transaction between persons who are not exempted by kinship or close friendship from the constant effort to determine whether another person shows sufficient respect for one's person and position in the community. (pp. 240–241)

Horowitz and Schwartz (1974) suggested that honor is an issue that arises primarily between men of similar social status in nonintimate relations. They would predict that insults from those who are similar in status are more likely to lead to retaliation than are insults from those who have higher or lower status. Alternatively, retaliation against a person of lower status is likely to be less costly than retaliation against someone of equal or higher status. We are not aware of any research that examines these hypothetical effects of status and intimacy on the likelihood of retaliating for an insult.

Insults are sometimes given in a ritualistic manner, according to a prescribed procedure. The ritualistic use of insults can be illustrated in the game *the dozens*. This insult game is common among Black youth in America and has origins in Africa (Dollard, 1957; Kochman, 1983; Lefever, 1981).

Playing the dozens consists of exchanges of verbal insults between two adolescent men, usually in a street or public setting, in which each attempts to win by delivering insults in the form of one-liners or rhyming sentences. The audience evaluates the insults and urges the antagonists on. One of the parties may become physically violent if he is unable to come up with an adequate riposte. In some groups, the antagonist who first turns to violence is viewed as weaker because he did not have an effective verbal retort and could not keep his "cool." In some other instances, the antagonists might be urged to fight. Physical altercations are more likely when the antagonists are from different groups.

The use of ritualistic insults is also illustrated by the use of song duels to handle disputes among Eskimos living in the Arctic (Hoebel, 1954). Each antagonist ridicules the other in a highly conventionalized singing style but with as much skill as possible. The person who receives the greatest applause is the winner of the song contest and gains prestige. Sometimes the song duels are accompanied by regulated physical combat, such as head butting and wrestling. Grievances, disputes, and identity contests may be settled in this way, but trial by verbal combat, not abstract standards of justice, apply. In a song duel, there is a transformation from a justice process to an identity contest. This process is not unlike the more informal and less ritualized transformation of coercive incidents that begin with a grievance and develop into escalating conflicts over identities that occur in American society (R. B. Felson, 1984; Luckenbill, 1977).

Jay (1980) conducted a survey among college students about when they would respond to verbal insults by fighting. He found that male subjects said they were more apt to retaliate to strong language and implications of homosexuality, whereas female subjects reacted most strongly to words that indicated sexual promiscuity. Although there are important shortcomings of this kind of study with regard both to method and to the restricted sample of middle-class young people, the findings appear to be reliable. Preston and Stanley (1987) found that male and female college students shared a common vocabulary of insults that tended to be gender specific and to display a double standard of sexual conduct. They also found that insults directed toward men tended to focus on homosexuality, whereas those directed toward women focused on sexual promiscuity.

These findings are consistent with Stryker's (1968) view that individuals are different with respect to which identities are salient and important to them. The above studies show that insults attacking gender identity are important to college students. In other words, there is a relationship between the content of an insult, the value of particular identities to the target individual, and reactions to the insult. A man who values an identity as "macho" is more likely to respond to insults challenging his courage or heterosexual preference than is a man for whom such an identity is neither salient nor important.

The salience of social identities has been shown to affect retaliation in response to an insult in a reaction-time game (Richardson, Leonard, Taylor, & Hammock, 1985). Male subjects received information that they had performed poorly or at an average level on a test of physical strength and then were either insulted or not by a woman about that performance. The subjects delivered greater shock to the woman who had insulted them when they had performed poorly on a test of physical strength.

The types of insults that are used and the way target persons react to them are affected by culture. Semin and Rubini (1990) examined insults in northern Italy, which is characterized by individualism, and in southern Italy, which is a more collectivistic culture. Insults in the north were chiefly directed at some characteristic or identity of the individual, whereas those in the south frequently referred to members of the target person's family. Bond and Venus (1991) examined the reactions of Chinese students to insults in the collectivist culture of Hong Kong. Male students were more likely to directly retaliate with some form of negative verbal statement or to indirectly retaliate by giving the antagonist a negative rating when the insult referred to their group identity and occurred in front of third parties than when the insult referred to them as individuals. In the latter case, the individual is expected to show restraint and humility; retaliation would reveal too much self-concern.

An anthropological study of three tribes of West Cameroon indicated that any sexual insult by men directed at a woman (usually referring to genitalia) is considered as an affront to all women (Ardener, 1973). The insulted woman tells other women in the tribe about the incident, and they collectively seek out the offender and publicly humiliate him. If the insulted woman can produce witnesses who heard the insult, the offender is required to pay damages in animals or cash. This restitution is divided among all the women of the tribe, including the female children.

Threats, Identities, and Coercive Influence

In chapter 7, we discussed the importance of threats in incidents involving coercive influence. Threats also have strong implications for social identities. Threats can imply weakness for either of the parties in a coercive interaction. Compliance by a target may give an appearance of appeasement and weakness. If the target does not comply, the source may appear to be irresolute and weak (Deutsch, 1960).

If only costs and gains associated with material outcomes were involved, targets would yield much more frequently than they do. The implications for reputation are so negative that much weaker parties often resist threats from strong adversaries, even when material costs to self are greater than those to the opponent. The use of threats may also be perceived as antinormative. This is why the use of threats tends to make targets angry (Heilman & Garner, 1975).

When a source's contingent threat is defied by a target, the source is faced with a decision that has implications for an identity as a strong and credible person. When a threat fails, the source has obtained nothing and, indeed, at that point has lost little. Punishment, as we saw in chapter 7, is frequently costly to administer—requiring time, effort, and resources to impose—and is apt to bring about retaliation, dislike, and avoidance by the target. Delivering the punishment will not bring about the compliance that has already been withheld. The temptation is to let the matter pass without carrying out the threat and punishing the target. However, failure to punish would reveal the source as bluffing, weak, and lacking in credibility, which undermines the effectiveness of future threats. These considerations provide strong motivation for the source to accept the costs and to deliver the threatened punishment, thus maintaining an identity as strong and credible (Tedeschi et al., 1970). The costs may be considered an investment in the effectiveness of future influence.

Inadvertent Attacks: Violations of Politeness Norms

There are a wide range of behaviors that can cast a person in a negative identity and provoke retaliation. Some of these involve the violation of norms that protect social identities, that is, politeness norms (P. Brown & Levinson, 1987). In their theory of politeness, Brown and Levinson distinguished between threats to negative face and threats to positive face. *Negative face* represents a desire to maintain autonomy and not be interfered with by other people; it refers to a "basic claim to territories, personal preserves, rights to non-distraction—i.e., to freedom of action and freedom from imposition" (P. Brown & Levinson, 1987, p. 61). Acts that threaten a person's autonomy include dares, orders, threats, and warnings. Negative politeness consists essentially of avoiding doing anything that would interfere with the other's perceptions of self-determination and is characterized by restraint, formality, and self-effacement.

Positive face refers to the identities claimed by the individual. Positive face represents a desire to gain approval for one's identities and possessions. There are a large number of acts that may threaten positive face:

> expression of disapproval, criticism, contempt or ridicule, complaints and reprimands, accusation, insults, contradictions or disagreements, challenges . . . blatant non-cooperation in an activity, disruptive, interruptions or other signs of nonattention. (P. Brown & Levinson, 1987, p. 66)

P. Brown and Levinson noted that certain behaviors directed toward achieving personal goals are intrinsic face-threatening acts (FTAs). In other words, they have some inherent potential for casting a negative identity. Threats, orders, and requests are intrinsic FTAs for a target's autonomy, whereas expressions of criticism, complaints, reprimands, and accusations are intrinsic FTAs related to the target's desire for approval.

P. Brown and Levinson's (1987) theory shows how easily common speech acts may inadvertently result in attacks on identity. The avoidance of attack on identities requires considerable effort and skill. It is difficult to have extended interactions with other people and not inadvertently offend them. When people feel their autonomy has been constrained or their positive claims about themselves challenged, they may believe they have been intentionally attacked. Violations of politeness norms not only create grievances (like other norm violations) but also attack identities and, thus, elicit protective self-presentation.

Many inadvertent attacks develop from attempts at informal social control. Studies of the sequence of events in verbal and physical coercive incidents among adults have shown that incidents usually begin with attempts at social control (R. B. Felson, 1984; Luckenbill, 1977). One party admonishes another for some alleged wrongdoing and gives an order or makes requests, and the other takes offense.

It is apparent that the manner in which criticism is given is important in determining whether identities are attacked. This was demonstrated in a study of the response of subjects to "constructive criticism" versus "destructive criticism" from subordinates, peers, or supervisors (R. A. Baron, 1988). All groups received identical, negative ratings of their performance, but subjects in the destructive criticism condition received additional criticisms that were general, were inconsiderate in tone, and attributed poor performance to internal causes. The results showed that destructive criticism made the subjects angry, particularly when it came from a subordinate. However, in the negotiation session that immediately followed, subjects were apparently intimidated by the confederates who gave destructive criticism, because they made more concessions to them. In a study of sources of conflict among 108 white-collar employees in a food-processing plant, "poor use of criticism" was identified as the fifth most likely source of conflict, after "poor communication," "interdependence," "feelings of being treated unfairly," and "ambiguity of responsibility" (R. A. Baron, 1988).

Verbal disagreements can easily develop into arguments in which identities are attacked. When someone challenges the validity of another person's argument, it may be perceived as an attack on their competence rather than simply as a difference in opinion. As the pace quickens and emotions are aroused, the participants may find it increasingly difficult to monitor their behavior carefully. As participants attempt to take and hold their turns, violations of rules of turn taking may occur. In response to interruptions and overlap in conversation, there may be an increase in volume. Interruptions and shouting are likely to be perceived as rule violations and personal attacks (Frick, 1985).

The tendency for people to experience discomfort when their freedom is constrained has been described as *psychological reactance* (Brehm & Brehm, 1981). According to reactance theory, individuals are likely to resist when their autonomy is questioned. To reduce reactance, they engage in actions to demonstrate their right to choose freely (Heilman & Garner, 1975). Reactance was reinterpreted as an attack on identity by Tedeschi, Schlenker, and Bonoma (1971). They argued that challenges to autonomy were resisted because acquiescence would be perceived as appeasement and would encourage further encroachments by others. Resistance to threats was therefore mediated by concerns for face. The fact that reactance appears to be much stronger in public than in private conditions (Baer, Hinkle, Smith, & Fenton, 1980) suggests that the concern for the appearance of autonomy is more important to the individual than a private need to defend freedom in producing resistance to threats.

Individuals acting as agents of social control may violate norms of autonomy when they constrain the behavior of others. Many instances of barroom violence begin when the bartender refuses to serve a customer, because the customer is either too intoxicated or underage (R. B. Felson et al., 1986). Violence sometimes results when the customer perceives this constraint on his or her behavior as an affront.

Some people in their official roles have the responsibility of evaluating the performances of other people. When evaluations are critical or negative, they may be interpreted by the person under evaluation as attacks on identity. A teacher must evaluate and correct the work of students, and the evaluation may be perceived as an attack on identity. An extreme case is illustrative: Some years ago, a disgruntled graduate student at Stanford University murdered a math professor he perceived as preventing him from obtaining his degree. Sometimes all attempts to divorce the behavior criticized from the worth or identity of the individual fail and give offense. Because groups require social control and individuals are protective of valued identities, there are likely to be many incidents in which evaluative comments are misinterpreted as personal attacks.

Challenges to Authority

Insubordination or disrespect for an authority may undermine the legitimacy of that authority. Attempts by an authority to placate or accommodate a dissident may be perceived by audiences as weakness and may legitimate the disruptive behavior. A public display of punishment serves the purpose of showing that the authority cannot be disobeyed without costs. Stotland (1976) interpreted the gratuitous violence used against prisoners by troopers and guards after the rebellion at Attica Prison as partly due to the perception that the prisoners had challenged their authority and competence. The use of coercion may also compel the insubordinate person to submit to the authority.

Toch (1969) found that assaults against police officers often occurred because of altercations precipitated by challenges to their authority. He described an incident in which a person standing on a street corner was told to move on by a policeman. The person perceived the officer's command as arbitrary and unfair because he was not doing anything to violate the law. To use the language of P. Brown and Levinson (1987), the officer "violated a negative politeness norm." Toch (1969) described the ensuing escalation process as follows:

> When the man indicates his unwillingness to comply, the officer ignores his protests and thereby converts the situation (as the person sees it) into a confrontation between two hostile parties. The officer responds by placing the individual under arrest, thereby demonstrating his own authority and power. The person now feels his powerlessness and also reacts by requesting that the officer encounter him on a "man-to-man" basis. This type of incident is an almost inevitable consequence of the exercise of police authority in a context where its legitimacy is not taken for granted. (p. 48)

Westley's (1970) research on the use of illicit force by police found that the most frequent justification police gave for using force was in response to disrespect. A prisoner might be hit "to make him show a little respect" or "when he is trying to make a fool of you in front of everybody else." Violence may also be used to obtain information, instill fear, or increase compliance or as a form of punishment for someone the officer perceives to be guilty of an illegal act.

Perceptions of disrespect by both parties are a source of conflict in interactions between police and civilians, according to an observational study by R. E. Sykes and Clark (1975). Because police are of higher status than many of the citizens with whom they interact, they expect deference from citizens. As a result of this expectation, the police are more likely to be disrespectful than citizens, particularly when the citizen has low status. Ethnic minorities often perceive police behavior as prejudicial and arbitrary, and as a result, they withhold respect. Police then perceive minority resistance as a rejection of their authority and status. In such circumstances, the chances for an altercation are quite good.

There is evidence that suspects' demeanor affects the likelihood that they will be arrested (e.g., Black & Reiss, 1970; D. Smith & Visher, 1981). Kipnis and Misner (1972) found disrespect to be an important cause for the arrests of offenders on charges of disorderly conduct. Interviews with police officers indicated that it was not the nature of the criminal action by the offender that led to the arrest but, rather, verbal abuse and other signs of disrespect for the authority of the police.

The studies by Westley (1970) and R. E. Sykes and Clark (1975) have indicated that misunderstandings stemming from the social control function of police are critical in their conflicts with civilians. Civilians and police often interpret police actions differently. Officers ask questions, give orders, and make accusations, and civilians do not always cooperate and interpret these actions as required by the officers in doing their jobs (Brent & Sykes, 1979). Civilians sometimes view these control behaviors as disrespectful or as attacks on their freedom of action.

The nature of police work makes some degree of conflict inevitable, no matter how deferent or civil the parties are. In a study of complaints of alleged police misconduct, Hudson (1970) found that civilians were likely to challenge police authority when they were unable to get the officer to explain why a particular action was being taken. Citizens were unwilling to accept the role of suspect or violator until the situation had been explained to their satisfaction (see also Wiley & Hudik, 1974). Brent and Sykes (1979) found that confrontations resulted when civilians refused to accept the officer's attempts at control, but that incivility by either officer or civilian was quite rare. These results are consistent with studies of the role of inadvertent attacks on identity in the development of coercive incidents generally: Social control behavior by one party is interpreted as an identity attack by the other party.

Coercive actions to defend a position of authority are not confined to police officers or prison guards. Challenges to the authority of subjects acting as supervisors were manipulated in simulated work settings by Kipnis and Consentino (1969). Supervisors were more likely to use coercive means against workers who lacked motivation than against those who lacked the skill to do a good job. When a worker's resistance to the supervisor's attempts at better production was attributed to a bad attitude ("I refuse") rather than to lack of ability ("I don't know how"), the supervisor relied on threats and punishments to change the worker's behavior. Thus, coercion maintains authority and deters unwanted behavior.

Parents may also use coercion when their authority is challenged by their children (see chap. 10). Like other authorities, parents use coercion for purposes of deterrence (see chap. 7). A disobedient child is also a challenge to parental authority—to their right to command. Once parents give an order they may expect compliance, even if they realize that the particular behavior in question is trivial.

Effects of Failure on the Use of Coercion

Individuals may react negatively to any challenge to their competence. Public failure has been shown to be associated with an increase in coercive actions. In an experiment, some subjects were provided with feedback that they had performed well on an intelligence test, whereas other subjects were unable in several tries to complete the test (Tedeschi, 1979). Subsequently, all subjects were given the capability of sending threats and punishing noncompliance in the context of a modified prisoner's dilemma game. There was no difference with regard to the number of threats sent during the game, but subjects who had performed poorly on the tests delivered more punishments and established higher credibility than did subjects who had performed well on the tests. Thus, subjects who had been ineffective in the prior task could save face by showing that they would not tolerate noncompliance by the target and that they could use coercion effectively. Making threats without backing them up would not communicate effectiveness.

Coercion can be used in anticipation of a predicament as a preventive action. Preemptive face saving was suggested indirectly by two studies performed by D. S. Holmes (1971). These studies suggested that men may submit to pain or attempt to display physical strength when masculine identities are threatened. In the first experiment, some male college students were told that they would later be asked to suck on a baby's bottle, a pacifier, a breast shield, and a baby's rattle. Other subjects were told they would feel the texture of various kinds of surfaces, such as sandpaper. All subjects were then told that in the second part of the experiment they would experience electric shocks and were asked to indicate the maximum level of shock they would accept. Subjects who anticipated an embarrassing experience (i.e., sucking on various objects) indicated that they would accept higher shocks than did the other subjects. In the second experiment, subjects received the same instructions, but the second phase was described as squeezing a hand dynamometer—an exercise device that measures the pressure of a grip response. Subjects who anticipated an embarrassing experience indicated a willingness to expend more effort than did those who did not anticipate a predicament. We can conclude that in these studies college men attempted to display either courage or physical strength in anticipation of a challenge to their masculine identities. Although coercion was not examined in this study, its use can also be a means of displaying courage and physical strength.[2]

Downward Comparison and Coercion

One way to put oneself "up" is to put others "down." Wills (1981) referred to this process as *downward comparison*. Sometimes downward com-

---

[2]This interpretation of the findings assumes that women would not react in the same way as men to the prospect of sucking on baby-related objects. An alternative interpretation would be that the subjects' identity as adults was threatened and that both men and women might under the circumstances be motivated to appear strong.

parison is achieved by engaging in some coercive action that lowers the standing of the target on some dimension, thereby providing a favorable comparison for the actor. Wills proposed downward comparison as an alternative explanation for the displacement effects obtained in experiments testing frustration–aggression theory. He noted that investigations of displaced aggression, scapegoating, and hostility generalization have in common two important elements: (a) There is some challenge to the subjects' identities, and (b) subjects are given an opportunity to provide a general impression of a target person. Under these conditions, subjects typically derogate. In the studies described below, downward comparison is elicited by causing a subject to fail. However, the process can also be instigated by an attack or, in the case of assertive self-presentation, without any provocation.

Downward comparison in the form of verbal derogation was found in a field study at Arizona State University (Cialdini & Richardson, 1980). Students who had experienced a public personal failure rated a rival state university more negatively and their own university more favorably than did other students. This "blasting" effect was interpreted as a way of saving face after failure. By negatively evaluating a rival institution and enhancing their own, students were able (by association) to increase their own relative status.

Melburg and Tedeschi (1989) demonstrated downward comparison in the laboratory. In Phase 1 of the procedure, subjects were individually paired with a confederate, and both were asked to solve identical sets of difficult anagrams. In one condition, the confederate performed better than the subject, and in the other condition, performance was equal. Also, during the anagrams task half of the subjects in each of these conditions were annoyed by friendly talk by the confederate, whereas the remainder were not annoyed. Subsequently, subjects were paired with either the same or a different confederate and were given an opportunity to evaluate the other person by giving electric shocks; a greater number of shocks indicated poor performance. Subjects gave more shocks when they had previously suffered from a negative social comparison with another person than when performance had been the same. A target substitution or displacement effect was obtained because subjects shocked the different confederate as much as they did the same confederate. Annoyance did not affect the amount of physical punishment administered by subjects. Thus, when subjects suffered an unfavorable social comparison and had an opportunity to engage in active downward comparison, they did so.[3]

According to Wills (1981), the mechanism underlying the downward

---

[3]Frustration–aggression theory might be used to interpret these findings. It could be argued that friendly annoyance is not aversive, but unfavorable social comparison is frustrating and aversive. The aversive situation then would lead subjects to display reactive aggression against either confederate. This post hoc explanation was examined in a path analysis of the data. Feelings of frustration were strongly related to negative social comparison, but there was no relationship between frustration and the frequency of shocks delivered to the confederate (i.e., aggression).

comparison process is a self-esteem (or self-enhancement) motive. When a person's self-esteem is lowered, a motive to restore positive self-evaluation is activated, and downward comparison is one kind of action that can satisfy this motive. An alternative (or perhaps complementary) view is that the motive of the individual is to establish a positive public identity in the eyes of audiences.

Experimental subjects placed in a predicament may engage in coercive behavior because they are not given the opportunity to provide accounts or engage in other forms of protective self-presentation. Outside the laboratory, coercive behavior is an unusual response to predicaments involving some type of failure. More common responses were shown in a study in which college students were asked to describe an embarrassing event, what they did to reduce embarrassment, and what other people did to reduce embarrassment (Metts & Cupach, 1989). Analyses of different types of predicaments indicated that students were more apt to use excuses in mistake situations, justifications when they made social blunders, and humor and restitution in accident situations. The only predicaments that led to aggression were those situations when they were insulted by others. This suggests that it is primarily humiliation induced by attacks from others, rather than embarrassment induced by other types of predicaments, that elicits coercive responses.[4]

FACILITATORS AND INHIBITORS ASSOCIATED WITH SELF-PRESENTATION

A number of factors make it more or less likely that coercive actions will be performed by individuals who are motivated to seek compliance, justice, or desired identities. We refer to factors that increase the likelihood or severity of a coercive action as *facilitators*. When the expectation of costs induces a person to decide not to engage in a contemplated coercive act, we refer to *inhibition*. However, when a person has strong moral (or procedural) values that oppose the use of coercion, it is likely that negative actions will not be contemplated and, hence, are not actively rejected. In this case, it would be inappropriate to refer to inhibition because the person did not consider the prohibited act as a decision alternative, and thus there was no impulse or act that was rejected. Because most people never consider engaging in armed robbery,[5] it would be misleading to say that they con-

---

[4]Humiliation is an emotion experienced as a result of actions by others perceived as intended to spoil the person's face. Embarrassment is a negative emotion that is experienced when a desired identity is thrown into question by a person's own actions, accidents, or by the unintended consequences of acts by other people.

[5]It may be that when people make an overall prior decision to obey the law, the whole class of illegal actions is removed from their repertoire of actions.

template robbery and are then inhibited by the anticipated costs. In other words, inhibitions are only relevant when there is temptation. A similar analysis is appropriate to facilitators, which add positive valence to a choice of coercive action by a decision maker who is motivated by other factors to engage in such an action.

In chapter 7, the role of inhibitions was considered in the discussion of the costs of coercion. We now consider five factors that are associated with social identities and that either facilitate or inhibit the use of coercion, including (a) norms of politeness that inhibit attacks on the identities of other people; (b) the legitimations individuals give to justify their coercive behavior; (c) the role of third parties who may mediate, instigate, or even join in the conflict; (d) the effects of cues that direct attention to identities; and (e) the effects of anonymity on coercion.

Norms of Politeness

A central rule of social interaction prescribes polite and friendly exchange, with a show of mutual support (Goffman, 1959). People who disapprove of one another often refrain from expressing their negative evaluations. A "working consensus" protects sacred but vulnerable selves during social interaction. Interacting persons typically accept and support each other's identity claims in public. They smile at people they dislike and avoid actions that can be interpreted as violating rules of deference and politeness. They avoid actions that appear to constrain the freedom of others, unless they have the authority to do so. Conformity with politeness norms (P. Brown & Levinson, 1987) is an important reason why coercive interactions are relatively infrequent in everyday life. Recall from chapter 8 Averill's (1983) finding that anger-producing incidents seldom led to coercive interactions and Baumgartner's (1988) finding that avoidance of conflict was the dominant response to grievances in suburbia.

Any event that affects the propensity or ability of individuals to be polite should affect the likelihood of coercion. People who are intoxicated are less skilled at cooperative "face work." People who drink are less attentive to external cues and are less articulate in using language (Hull, 1981). Also, negative emotions and moods focus attention on internal states and make the individual less attentive to politeness norms. R. B. Felson (1991) argued that people more often violate rules of deference when they are distressed or upset. They may find it difficult to feign positive emotions, and their mood may reduce interest in showing deference, which disinhibits behavior that others may consider inappropriate or even aggressive. If others are offended, coercive interactions can result. Such a scenario is suggested by the finding (R. B. Felson, 1991) that stress is related to being the target of physical coercion and that being targeted mediates the relationship between stressful life events and physical coercion.

A similar process apparently occurs with the experience of depression, a mood that may be induced by stress. Depressed people display social skill deficits, expect to be and are rejected by others, more often communicate their negative thoughts to others, and tend to elicit hostility from others (Blumberg & Hokanson, 1983; Coyne, 1976; Gotlib & Asarnow, 1979; Hammen & Peters, 1978; Strack & Coyne, 1983). Depression may also be associated with a hostility bias in making attributions about the reasons for the actions of other people. These cognitive and behavioral tendencies in depressed people may lead to coercive episodes.

Legitimations and Coercive Actions

An action is labeled *aggressive* and *bad* when observers believe the action is intended to harm someone and when there is no justification or excuse for doing so (Tedeschi et al., 1974). There are perceived costs associated with being labeled as an aggressor. In addition to possible re-taliation, actors who illegitimately use coercion are apt to gain a negative reputation and to suffer deterioration in their social relationships. Individ-uals can avoid these potential costs if they can excuse or justify their coercive actions. Thus, legitimations facilitate (but do not motivate) the use of coercion (see chaps. 7 and 8).

In social psychological experiments on aggression, procedures almost always include cover stories that legitimize the use of physical punishments by subjects. Subjects may be asked to punish a confederate to facilitate learning in the teacher–learner paradigm or to deliver noxious stimuli as a means of evaluating the task performance of another person (see chap. 2). The motivation to use coercion is provided by insulting or otherwise at-tacking the subjects, and they are then given an opportunity to punish the provocateur under legitimizing conditions. When legitimacy is decreased, there is less use of coercion by subjects (Milgram, 1974). Lack of legiti-mation serves to inhibit the use of physical punishments, presumably be-cause subjects who are otherwise motivated to retaliate for a provocation believe that coercive actions will project a negative identity to the exper-imenter.

A person may be proud of an identity as a morally principled person and, hence, be motivated to maintain and enhance that identity. Moral values, however learned or instilled and whatever the motivation that sustains them, sometimes reduce the use of coercion. Conversely, as was shown in chapter 8, moral righteousness and the desire to maintain justice may serve as the motivation for the use of intense punishment of other people. A concern for an identity as a just and norm-abiding citizen may facilitate the use of punishments against norm violators. However, such values may also inhibit the use of antinormative forms of punishment.

The legitimacy of an act of coercion is likely to be affected by the social characteristics of the antagonists and their role relationship. The moderate use of coercion by parents against children is viewed favorably, whereas the use of coercion by children against parents is viewed unfavorably (Stark & McEvoy, 1970). In general, people perceived as deviant or of lower status are more likely to be considered legitimate targets. Recall the evidence that bullies usually attack children who are unpopular, physically unattractive, and physically uncoordinated (Olweus, 1984). Bullies may also target gay males and lesbians and members of different ethnic groups. These attacks may be labeled *hate crimes* even though the attack may be facilitated rather than motivated by prejudice.

The legitimations that individuals give to explain behaviors that are subject to moral challenge are referred to as *accounts*. The use of accounts by the target of a grievance to ward off punishment was discussed in chapter 8. We now consider the use of accounts by individuals who are contemplating the use of coercion or have already engaged in such actions. When accounts are considered prior to action, they may serve as facilitators of coercion. If actors believe they can legitimate their coercive behavior, they are more likely to engage in the behavior. As indicated in chapter 8, accounts may involve excuses, which attempt to deny or mitigate personal responsibility, or justifications, which admit responsibility but give a reason that implies that the act is not wrong in the present context because of some overriding norm, value, or authority (A. R. Buss, 1978; M. R. Scott & Lyman, 1968; G. Sykes & Matza, 1957; Tedeschi & Riess, 1981). Successful legitimations would eliminate or mitigate negative reactions by others to the actor's use of coercion, thereby reducing probable costs. The expectation that legitimations will be successful therefore disinhibits coercive actions. The degree of disinhibition is directly related to the value of costs avoided by successful legitimation and the probability that the legitimation will be successful.

Schönbach and Kleibaumhüter (1990) have postulated a similar process regulated by self-esteem and control needs in individual actors. Derogation of an individual lowers self-esteem and reduces the perception of control, which motivates the individual to act to restore control and positive self-esteem. The greater the severity of a reproach, the more motivated the individual will be to regain control. Furthermore, the greater the person's habitual need for control, the greater the intensity of reactions to reproaches from other people. This conceptualization of the accounting process and its motivational basis in concern for social power and social identity is parallel to our view of protective self-presentation and identity contests.

Averill (1993) proposed that expressions of anger are attempts to legitimate aggression. Anger excuses aggression because it suggests that individuals are not in full control of their behavior; thus, crimes of passion are treated more leniently than calculated actions. Anger also justifies aggression because it identifies the behavior as a response to the target's misdeeds. That is, anger involves the claim that the individual has been treated unjustly by another person. The claim is likely to be accepted when the behavior is consistent with social norms (or "folk theories") that specify when a person should be angry.

Toch (1993) examined the accounts that individuals give to legitimate extremely violent behavior. In their self-portraits, violent actors must explain the disproportionality of their response to provocation and their tendency to lose control of themselves. Defensive accounts are likely to be used in official circumstances, but more assertive stories may be told to intimates, who share the actor's values. Defensive accounts are meant to deny, excuse, or justify the action in question and avoid blame or retribution. For example, actors may cite intense pressures, stress, or other environmental factors to explain their violent behavior. Studies that show a correlation between aversive stimuli and aggression may be partially explained by the disinhibitory effect of having an available excuse for engaging in such behavior. In addition, successful accounts increase the social distance between the listener and the victim with the consequence of reducing empathy for the victim. In assertive self-portraits, actors boast about their violent behavior. In their war stories, storytellers present themselves as heros in a "morality play" by emphasizing the victim's provocations and their own honorable motives and heroic struggle. They are only countering bad violence from nasty aggressors who pick on innocent victims.

In two studies, the accounts that male offenders gave to criminal justice officials for homicide and assault were examined. In one, the offender's version of the circumstances leading up to the crime was compared with the official version in terms of the frequency of various types of actions (R. B. Felson, Baccaglini, & Ribner, 1985). In comparison with the official version, offenders' versions attributed more physical attacks but not verbal attacks to victims. Presumably, the offender believed that only the victim's physical attacks could justify his action. Offenders attempted to excuse their behavior by not mentioning their own verbal attacks (threats and insults) because such actions might suggest a high degree of intent. A second study examined the shorthand explanations offenders gave for their crime (R. B. Felson & Ribner, 1981). Offenders were more likely to give justifications (e.g., self-defense and wrongful acts by the victim) than excuses (e.g., accidents and drinking). Note that when offenders focused on victim wrongdoing to justify their coercion, they neglected to explain the disproportionality of their response (Toch, 1993).

Third Parties, Identities, and Coercive Actions

The presence of third parties increases the salience of social identities in coercive interactions. An audience may exacerbate the conflict because it magnifies the humiliation associated with affronts or challenges to authority. The presence of an audience may increase a person's motivation to win in competitive situations and may thereby increase the likelihood that coercion will be used to gain competitive advantage. Borden and Taylor (1973) found that subjects delivered more intense shocks in a competitive reaction-time task when an audience was present, whether they had been provoked or not. D. Smith and Visher (1981) found that police were more likely to arrest a suspect if there were bystanders present, controlling for whether anyone requested that an arrest be made.

What effect the audience will have depends in part on the attitude of the audience toward coercion, as perceived by the antagonists. Borden (1975) found that college men delivered more intense shocks to a moderately aggressive antagonist when they were observed by men than when they were observed by women. Presumably, they assumed that men would be more favorable to shock delivery than women. When left alone in subsequent trials, subjects who had been observed by men reduced their shock levels, whereas subjects who had been observed by women increased their shock levels slightly. In a second study, the gender and the values of observers were orthogonally manipulated. Observers were presented as members of either a pacifistic organization or a karate club. In this study, shock intensities were related to the values of the observer but not to their gender. Again, when the observers departed, the shock intensities in the aggressive-observer condition declined, whereas the shock intensities in the pacifistic-observer condition slightly increased. Thus, subjects changed the intensity of their punitive behavior to conform to the values of the audience, presumably because they wanted to gain approval.

The expectations of high school hockey players about the reactions of various audiences to fighting were examined by M. D. Smith (1979). The hockey players believed that their fathers and coaches approved of retaliation when they were provoked by an opposing player. They believed that their teammates and peers approved of starting fights as well as retaliation for provocations. Only mothers were described in the survey data as negatively evaluating fighting under all circumstances.

People tend to make assumptions about the kinds of identities and behaviors that will gain approval. R. A. Baron (1971) found that the presence of an audience decreased the magnitude of punishment used by subjects. He suggested that these subjects were motivated to avoid appearing vengeful. However, there are some people whose use of coercion is relatively unaffected by the values of audiences (S. P. Taylor, 1970). In a competitive reaction-time game, subjects with low concerns for social approval responded with consistently high levels of shock, no matter what their opponent's strategy. Subjects with strong or moderate concerns for approval tended to match the strategy of their opponents.

Third parties can influence people to engage in coercion even when the behavior will be costly to them. This was demonstrated in an experiment in which adolescent male subjects participated against a programmed adversary in a trucking game (B. R. Brown, 1968). The programmed player had control over the gate during the first half of the game and used it quite often to penalize subjects and to handily win the game. Subjects were told that a group of peers were observing the game through a one-way mirror. After the first half of the game, subjects were either told that their peers viewed them as poor bargainers and as "weak," a "sucker," and "pretty bad" or they were told that all things considered they looked good because they had tried hard and played fair. After receiving this bogus information, the subjects were given the power to choose from a toll schedule (low, moderate, or high) how much they wanted to charge the programmed player to pass through the gate and were given control over the gate. Subjects were charged substantial opportunity costs whenever they charged the highest toll. Thus, subjects were provided with the opportunity to either maximize their own outcomes by charging moderate tolls at little cost to themselves or save face by hurting the opponent but at a high cost to self. Half of the subjects believed their opponent knew precisely what their opportunity costs were, and the other half thought that the opponent did not know their cost schedule.

The results indicated that subjects who felt they had looked foolish earlier charged much higher tolls than did the subjects who felt they had looked good. They imposed costs on the opponent despite the costs to themselves. These results suggest that a person will make sacrifices to avoid a negative response from an audience. Additionally, self-damaging retaliation was more frequent when the opponent was said not to know the subjects' costs than when the costs were known. The opponent's awareness that the subject was harming himself to gain revenge suppressed the use of self-damaging tactics.

The most dramatic evidence of the effect of third parties on coercion comes from Milgram's classic studies of obedient aggression. Milgram (1974) found that subjects were willing to deliver extremely high levels of shock if the behavior was legitimated by the experimenter. The experimenter's verbal persuasion, coupled with the authority associated with a scientific experiment in a high prestige university, led subjects to deliver shock levels that produced cries of pain by the recipient. The conditions that legitimized the use of physical punishment in these studies of obedience are not unlike those that are involved in military units during wars. Young people are trained to use deadly force under the direction of legitimate authorities. The massacre at My Lai in Vietnam, in which over 200 women and children were shot by American soldiers, indicates that many young men will follow orders even when their actions violate social norms they have been taught since childhood.

In a survey of persons involved in coercive incidents involving physical violence, R. B. Felson (1982) found that the presence of third parties increased the likelihood that verbal arguments would escalate into physical violence when the antagonists were of the same sex. Presumably, the presence of third parties increased the salience of identities, which in turn increased the tendency for antagonists to retaliate. The presence of third parties inhibited escalation when the antagonists were of the opposite sex. Because male violence against women is proscribed, men were apparently unwilling to engage in a physically violent incident with women when there was an audience present.

The presence of a third party to mediate conflicts can be effective in preventing identity contests or in allowing them to end. The mere presence of a third party may curtail the use of threats, hollow promises, lies, insults, and other negative actions by the parties to the conflict. When third parties attempt to resolve the conflict between the opponents, they are referred to as *mediators* (Pruitt & Rubin, 1986).

One reason mediators can be effective is that they allow both sides to back down without losing face. The concern for appearing tough in conflict situations can be defused because all offers and concessions can be channeled through a third party. In addition, the offers and concessions mediated by a third party appear more fair than would otherwise be the case. The effectiveness of a mediator was shown in an experiment by Pruitt and Johnson (1970). They found that bargainers made substantially greater concessions when a mediator was present than when they bargained on a face-to-face basis. Subjects who made concessions reported feeling weak only when there was no mediator.

The likelihood of a third party taking a mediating role in conflicts is a function of group memberships, interpersonal relationships, obligations and commitments, ulterior motives, and other factors. In a study of assaults and homicides, R. B. Felson, Ribner, and Siegel (1984) found that third parties frequently entered into confrontations on the side of one of the contestants, especially among the younger offenders. Furthermore, there was medical evidence that offenders delivered more blows and inflicted more physical damage when third parties entered the fray but fewer blows when the third parties took a mediating role.

Third parties play a critical role in ritualized conflicts. Recall from our discussion of the dozens and song duels that the audience evaluates each insult and urges the antagonists on. Fox (1989) emphasized the role of third parties in his observations of fights on an island in Ireland. The fights usually involved two men with a history of antagonistic relations between themselves or between members of their families. A fight would not start unless close kin of each antagonist and kin related to both antagonists were present. When the two antagonists squared off, the close kin would restrain them while the common kin would act as negotiators. The antagonist's attitude was always "Hold me back or I'll kill him." The fight would end without anyone hurt when the mother of one of the antagonists, or some other female relative, would plead with him to stop fighting. A "proper fight" involved two men who stood up to each other and showed they were willing to fight. If there were few people around, they sometimes came to blows, but rarely was anyone injured. However, it was unusual for two men to start a fight with no audience around, and when this occurred, there was universal condemnation.

Interviews of 71 Scottish men convicted of violent assault revealed effects of third parties (Berkowitz, 1986). Very few offenders said that their motive was to protect their reputation or obtain approval, whether there were third parties present or not. Because offenders behaved similarly when third parties were present, Berkowitz argued that impression management was not involved. Instead he claimed that these men impulsively struck out in rage in response to aversive stimuli, without a concern for long-range consequences.

For a variety of reasons, we do not find this study convincing. First, it contradicts the experimental, survey, and ethnographic studies described above. Second, the survey studies—which are directly comparable to this study—are based on more rigorous methodology. Berkowitz (1986) used a small sample for survey analysis and did not report statistical significance. He used self-reports by convicted felons about their motives, which may not have been reliable. The research cited above, alternatively, examines the effect of third parties on actual behavior. Third, Berkowitz did not examine the behavior or perceived values of the third parties who were present during the offense. Research cited above shows that the effect of third parties on coercion depends on whether they approve of a coercive response and whether they mediate or instigate the conflict. Finally, Berkowitz reported some evidence of third-party effects. When third parties were present, respondents were more likely to say they had wanted to hurt their opponent and were less likely to say they were motivated by a concern for safety.

Self-Awareness and Coercion

At any given time an individual may be focused on external cues or on internal values. According to self-awareness theory (Wicklund, 1975), the internal or external focus of the individual will be important in determining behavior, particularly when the implications of these two loci are contradictory. When the focus is inward (i.e., the individual is self-aware), behavior is more likely to conform to internal values or standards. When the focus is external, and there is an audience present, the individual is more likely to conform to the expectations of that audience.

Cues that affect self-awareness may facilitate or inhibit coercive actions, depending on the values of the individual. Experimental research has shown that the presence of a mirror, which is a cue that increases self-awareness, inhibits the delivery of shocks to female targets by male subjects (Carver, 1974; Scheier, Fenigstein, & Buss, 1974). In American culture, it is a general norm that men should not physically attack women, and it can be assumed that most men internalize the norm. It is assumed that, when presented with a self-awareness cue, male subjects focus their attention on internal standards and act accordingly. In another condition of these experiments, male subjects were provided with legitimizing instructions to the effect that delivery of shocks would help eliminate errors and improve the performance of male learners. Under these legitimizing instructions, the subjects delivered more intense shocks when the mirror was present than when no self-awareness cue was present. These experimental findings indicate that self-awareness cues may either inhibit or facilitate the use of coercion, depending on external norms, legitimizations, and degree of self-awareness.

The relationships of internal standards, evaluative audiences, and the use of physical punishments were convincingly demonstrated in two experiments carried out by Froming, Walker, and Lopyan (1982). In the first experiment, college students were selected who opposed the use of physical punishments but believed that most other people were favorable to the use of physical punishments. In a teacher–learner situation, the presence of a mirror inhibited the use of shocks, but the presence of an evaluative audience facilitated coercive behavior.

In the second experiment, the criterion for selection of subjects was reversed. Only students who were favorable to the use of physical punishments but believed most others were unfavorable were selected. The results were exactly the opposite of those found in Experiment 1. When a mirror was present, subjects gave more shocks than control subjects, and the presence of an evaluative audience decreased the use of coercion.

In most cases the internalized procedural values of an individual and those of audiences coincide. Individuals tend to associate with other people who have similar values (cf. Byrne, 1971). When individual and audience values coincide, then self-awareness cues and the presence of an evaluative audience should have similar effects on the use of physical punishments. Thus, Fenigstein, Scheier, and Buss (1975) found that men in either mirror or audience conditions delivered less intense shocks to women in a teacher–learner situation than did men in a control condition.

Disinhibition and Coercion

Disinhibition of coercive actions occurs when conditions that typically inhibit their use are removed or are absent. Many of the disinhibiting factors have been identified by investigators studying deindividuation. According to deindividuation theory (e.g., Zimbardo, 1970), there are a variety of conditions in which people lose their individual identities. Zimbardo (1970) proposed that anonymity, focus on the present to exclusion of past and future, altered states of consciousness due to ingestion of drugs and alcohol, and group membership reduce concern about self-evaluation and evaluations by others. When individuals are deindividuated, their ability to inhibit violent and aggressive impulses is lessened. A number of criticisms have revealed conceptual problems with deindividuation theory and interpretative problems with the research (cf. Dipboye, 1977; Lindskold & Propst, 1981). Nevertheless, the research has been useful in suggesting factors that may disinhibit coercive actions when the individual is motivated to use coercion.

Deindividuating factors are especially important as disinhibitors of coercive actions when engaging in such actions is likely to produce unwanted negative identities—a negative secondary outcome associated with using coercion. It would be expected that deindividuating conditions, such as anonymity and altered states of consciousness, would reduce concerns about secondary costs associated with negative identities that might result from the use of coercion. When any of these conditions is present and the individual is motivated to use coercion, it is more likely that the individual will engage in coercive action.

SUMMARY AND CONCLUSIONS

Coercive actions are sometimes motivated by a desire to assert or to protect the identities of the actor. Particular identities are valued by the actor because they gain the approval and affection of others or because they serve as bases of power that enhance the ability of the actor to influence others. Self-presentations may be assertive or they may be protective. Two kinds of assertive self-presentational uses of coercion are intimidation and self-promotion. Intimidation tactics have the intent to inspire fear in the target person, which in turn may make the target more apt to comply to threats, orders, commands, or requests. Coercion is a form of self-promotion when its purpose is to establish an identity as tough, resolute, or courageous.

Protective self-presentation is typically elicited by a perceived aspersion or attack by another person on a valued identity. A perceived attack on identity is a type of social predicament. Predicaments are associated with lowered status and the emotional reaction of humiliation. A person experiencing humiliation is motivated to restore status. A prominent way to restore status is to spoil the identity and lower the status of the offending person. Retaliation places the offender in a predicament, and a character contest is likely to ensue. Escalation cycles typically occur in character contests and may result in some form of physical coercion if there is no situational factor to stop the process.

Predicaments may be classified in terms of violations of politeness norms, which protect both positive face and negative face. Positive face refers to desired identities proferred by actors; they are typically deferred to by others who wish to avoid conflicts and to maintain smooth interactions. Insults, criticisms, negative evaluations, and slights are violations of positive face that place the target person in a predicament. People in positions of authority are particularly likely to use coercion against people of lower status when their authority is the focus of an identity attack. Attacks on positive face may be inadvertent and are particularly likely to occur when an offender is under great stress, experiences strong emotions, is inebriated, or has responsibility for evaluating the performance of another person.

Negative face refers to the individual's desire to maintain autonomy and control over his or her own actions. Some forms of social influence and control intrinsically threaten negative face. Threats, orders, bribes, and other attempts to control the person are perceived as attempts to restrict the freedom of the individual and are likely to produce reactance by the person experiencing the predicament.

Politeness norms may be interpreted as inhibitors of coercive actions. The knowledge that lack of deference or respect will elicit coercive reactions from others inhibits violations of politeness norms. The presence of third parties can facilitate or inhibit the use of coercion. The assumed values of the audience affect coercive actions. If it is believed that the audience approves of and gives status to people who use coercion, then the actor is more likely to use coercion. When third parties are believed to have more pacifistic values, their presence will inhibit the use of coercion. On the one hand, the provision of accounts or apologies by offending parties aborts the escalation cycle associated with character contests and, hence, may be viewed as an inhibiting factor. On the other hand, an actor's belief that accounts given after an attack will inhibit retaliation by the other person may facilitate the actor's own use of coercion. Disinhibitors generally are factors that lower the expected costs of engaging in coercion. Among factors that reduce the expectation of costs for coercive action are anonymity and acting within the context of a larger group.

III

TWO APPLICATIONS
OF SOCIAL
INTERACTIONIST THEORY

INTRODUCTION

TWO APPLICATIONS OF SOCIAL
INTERACTIONIST THEORY

A social interactionist approach is applicable to all forms of coercive actions. Some applications were briefly discussed in chapters 7–9. There was some discussion of domestic violence between husbands and wives and between siblings. In the area of criminal violence, we reviewed some of the research on homicide, assault, and robbery. In chapters 10 and 11, we provide a much more extended discussion of two forms of coercion that were only mentioned in passing in earlier chapters. In each case, we attempt to show the utility of a social interactionist approach.

In chapter 10, we apply our social interactionist theory to the literature on child rearing and child abuse. Other scholars have, in fact, already presented what they describe as a "social interactionist approach to child abuse" that is similar in many ways to the approach presented in this book. However, our view embraces all forms of coercion used against children by parents, and what has been characterized as abuse is simply the most extreme form of physical punishment used in social control situations. As agents of social control, parents use a variety of coercive and noncoercive techniques to change the attitudes, values, and behavior of children. Research indicates that most severe punishment—sometimes labeled *child abuse*—occurs during disciplinary situations and is a response to the child's misbehavior. The punishment, then, is a form of social control. We review the research that has examined the social interaction between parents and children in disciplinary situations as well as how these coercive incidents escalate until extreme forms of punishment are used.

The characteristics of both children and parents affect the likelihood of severe punishment. Children with behavioral problems—because of temperament or poor parenting—are likely to be targets of coercion and severe punishment. Parents who are punitive or who lack influence on their children with either noncoercive means or mild forms of coercion are more likely to use severe punishment.

In chapter 11, we apply our approach to the study of sexual coercion. Theories of aggression and violence are not usually applied to this sensitive topic. Unfortunately, this area of research has been a battleground of ideological and political conflict, and theoretical assertions have served as slogans rather than as testable hypotheses. It has been assumed that sexual coercion must be motivated by hatred for women or an assertion of domination by men over women. The possibility that some sexual coercion is sexually motivated has been rejected out of hand by some feminists. Although we examine the feminist perspective, our strategy is to avoid taking an ideological position regarding any hypothesis. Instead, we examine all of the theoretical statements, including sociobiological hypotheses, in terms of the available empirical evidence.

The evidence indicates that sexual motivation plays a major role in many incidents of sexual coercion. Because the hypotheses about the role of power and hatred for women in sexual coercion are vague and apparently untestable, we reinterpret these factors in terms of social identities and grievances. These motives may also contribute to sexual coercion. Finally, we examine the question of whether men who engage in sexual coercion lack inhibitions about the use of coercion in general. It is possible that it is not hatred of women but, rather, the proclivity to use coercion as the means of gaining compliance from others that is an important individual-differences factor contributing to sexual coercion.

10

PARENTS AND CHILDREN

Perhaps adults' most frequent target of coercive behavior is their own children. People who rarely if ever use coercion with others make an exception in the case of their children. When these coercive actions are severe, they are often referred to as *child abuse*. However, less severe forms of parental coercive behavior are usually perceived as appropriate responses to children's misbehavior. Laypersons refer to most parents' harmdoing as *punishment* rather than *aggression* because they view it as desirable. Thus, our use of the term *punishment* in this chapter coincides with common usage.

We begin the chapter with a discussion of the relationship between our approach to coercion and the literature on child abuse. We compare our approach with the already established social interactionist approach to child abuse. We then consider the use of coercion as a method of social control and compare it with other methods. In later sections, we shift our attention to the more severe forms of physical punishment that are commonly labeled *child abuse*. We first consider the causal role of children and then individual differences between parents. In the final section, we consider the impact of third parties on severe forms of punishment.

COERCION AND CHILD ABUSE

Most research on the use of coercion by parents focuses on child abuse in its most extreme form. Unfortunately, the definition of what behaviors are abusive is vague and depends on the observer's values (Gelles, 1982; Giovannoni & Becerra, 1979). Disagreement about what is abusive is particularly high for less extreme forms of punishment (Giovannoni & Becerra, 1979). Observers generally use the term *abuse* the way they use the term *aggression*—to describe behaviors that they disapprove of or view as too severe (see chap. 6).[1] The values inherent in judgments of abuse are revealed by the evidence that an act that is considered too severe in one culture may not be considered so in another culture (Korbin, 1981). Judgments of the severity of a punishment depend in part on judgments about whether it was deserved. The same punishment may be considered severe if it is in response to a minor infraction and mild if it is in response to a more serious violation. Furthermore, physical punishment is not always perceived as more severe than verbal punishment.

Some observers label any form of physical coercion *child abuse*. Evidence that most Americans approve of physical punishment of children shows that this view is not common (Blumenthal et al., 1972; Stark & McEvoy, 1970). A national survey of 10,000 middle-class families showed that 77% of respondents thought "children should be disciplined by physical punishment whenever necessary" (Stark & McEvoy, 1970). More recently, C. G. Ellison and Sherkat (1993) found that about 80% of respondents from a national survey either agreed or strongly agreed that "it is sometimes necessary to discipline a child with a good, hard spanking."

In some cases of child abuse, parents unintentionally injure their children. When engaging in physical punishments, parents may miscalculate their effects. One reason younger children are at a higher risk for abuse than older children may be that they are more vulnerable to physical injury (Straus et al., 1980). Parents may ignore the fact that young children are smaller and weaker than adults and more vulnerable to injury.

Because it is value laden and ambiguous, we avoid the term *abuse* wherever possible. We focus instead on the determinants of coercion and the severity of (primarily physical) punishment.[2] It is more realistic to consider severity of punishment as a continuous variable (B. Weiss, Dodge, Bates, & Pettit, 1992). When describing particular studies we sometimes speak of *abuse* because this term is used in the research we cite. Unless otherwise indicated, the term refers to the physical injury of children.

---

[1]At the time of this writing, there appears to be some hysteria about physical and sexual abuse in the United States, with many false charges and exaggerated statistics (see Gilbert, 1991).

[2]Measuring severity can be difficult because judgments of severity depend on context and on value judgments.

Some discussions of child abuse include the sexual abuse of children. However, although children may be harmed by sexual relations with adults, coercion is not necessarily involved. Adults may use persuasion, bribery, and other methods to influence children to engage in sexual behavior. Coercion is involved when threats or bodily force are used to get children to comply or to discourage them from reporting to third parties. Because these threats may be implicit, it is sometimes difficult to determine when sexual abuse involves coercion.

Many discussions of child abuse also include discussions of other forms of maltreatment of children, such as neglect. We do not consider neglect coercive unless it is being used to punish or force compliance. Thus, parents may mistreat or harm their children in a variety of ways that are not coercive. We are only concerned with actions whose intent is to impose harm or to force compliance.

SOCIAL INTERACTIONIST APPROACHES TO CHILD ABUSE

A number of scholars have applied a "social interactional model" to child abuse (e.g., Kadushin & Martin, 1981; Parke & Collmer, 1975; Patterson, 1982; Reid, Taplin, & Loeber, 1981; Wolfe, 1985). These theorists rely on research suggesting that child abuse develops out of attempts by parents to discipline their children (e.g., D. Gil, 1970; Herrenkohl, Herrenkohl, & Egolf, 1983). They focus on the social interaction between the parent and child, rather than on the parent alone, recognizing that parents and children influence each other. When parents use coercion in response to a child's misbehavior, the conflict can escalate until the child is injured.

An emphasis on social interaction leads to a recognition of a causal role for the child in child abuse. These scholars show how child abuse is in part a parental reaction to a child's misbehavior and that misbehavior is a function of the child's temperament as well as of environmental factors.

Scholars in this tradition do not neglect the role of parental characteristics. They recognize that the behavior of children can be affected by how they have been treated by parents. They emphasize in particular the roles of parental expectations, parental competence, and social learning. However, these factors alone do not result in parents harming their children. Rather, child-aversive behavior and a stress-filled environment are precipitating conditions that produce intense physical punishment by parents who lack competence and have unrealistic expectations (Wolfe, 1985).

Our discussion of parental coercion borrows heavily from those who take a social interactionist approach. However, we differ in our interpretation of why the child's behavior results in physical punishment by parents. Most of the theorists associated with this approach rely on a frustration–

aggression mechanism that treats parental coercion as an emotional outburst produced by stress. From our point of view, stress can facilitate coercive actions (see chap. 7), but it does not instigate them.

Instead, we interpret severe forms of punishment (child abuse) and other forms of parental coercion as goal-oriented behavior, designed to influence children, promote retributive justice, and assert and defend favorable identities. We emphasize the social control function, that is, the attempt to deter misbehavior and encourage desirable behavior. If parents believe a child has misbehaved, they may respond with threats and punishments to deter future wrongdoing. They may use bodily force with young children, carrying them off to bed or physically restraining them. Retributive justice also plays a role in parental punishment in that parents believe that children deserve to be punished for wrongdoing. Furthermore, if children defy them or retaliate, then parents' own identities are threatened, and they may counterattack. Continued defiance involves a challenge to parental authority and therefore involves an attack on the parent's identity. In summary, parental punishment is used to produce compliance, but it is also affected by concerns for identity and justice.

Some forms of parental coercion appear spontaneous and uncontrolled by cognitive processes. The child misbehaves, and the parent explodes in anger. However, as indicated in chapter 7, we consider these coercive actions to reflect choices rather than involuntary responses. We recognize that some parental coercion may be scripted and that what originally was an instrumental action can become a habitual response that is used without much consideration of alternatives or consequences.

Reid et al. (1981) took a stance similar to our own (see also Patterson, 1982). They postulated that a major cause of abuse is lack of parental skill in teaching children appropriate behavior and in handling discipline situations. Parents perceive correctly that they have lost control of their child and consequently feel dominated by them. Reid et al. suggested that child abuse reflects a futile attempt by parents to control their children.

COERCION AS A METHOD OF SOCIAL CONTROL

In this section we consider parents' use of coercion and other techniques to control their children. We first present data showing that parents are frequent users of coercion, and then we suggest why this is so. Then we examine factors that affect its use relative to other methods of social control.

Frequency of Coercion Against Children

Studies of parent–child interaction in American families reveal high levels of coercive behavior, including bodily force, verbal and physical punishment, physical isolation, and deprivation of resources (e.g., Grusec & Kuczynski, 1980; Trickett & Kuczynski, 1986). Research has focused on the prevalence of physical punishment. In one national survey of the United States, parents of children 3 to 17 years old were asked about their behavior toward a referent child (Gelles, 1978). Sixty-three percent reported that they had engaged in at least one violent act toward that child in the survey year. Stark and McEvoy (1970) found that 93% of American parents use physical punishment. Physical force is used more often against younger children than older children (Straus et al., 1980). However, more than half of a sample of adolescents reported they had experienced actual or threatened physical punishment by parents in their senior year of high school (Straus, 1971).

The use of physical punishment and other forms of coercion varies considerably across cultures. Chinese parents use physical punishment less frequently than do American parents (Niem & Collard, 1971). Physical punishment is rare among the Arapesh and the Tahitians (Levy, 1973; Mead, 1935). In Sweden and Finland, physical punishment of children is forbidden by law. Child-rearing practices across cultures reveal that physical punishment is used by parents and other caretakers in about 75% of the societies studied (H. Barry, Josephson, Lauer, & Marshall, 1980; Levinson, 1989).

Given the love most parents feel toward their children, the frequency of coercion might seem surprising. The high rate of parental coercion against children is directly related to the parent's role as an agent of social control. Agents of social control are likely to engage in a high number of coercive acts against their charges either to compel them to engage in desired behaviors or to deter their misbehavior. Research shows that coercion is an effective technique for producing short-term compliance in children (Chapman & Zahn-Waxler, 1982; Lytton & Zwirner, 1975). Success in gaining compliance provides an immediate reward to parents and increases the likelihood they will use coercion again.

There are other reasons why parents use coercion so frequently. First, children often behave in ways that their parents find offensive and intolerable. Noncompliance by children in response to parental directives is common (Forehand, 1977). Patterson and Forgatch (1982) estimated noncompliance rates as high as 40% to 50% for 10- to 11-year-old boys. Noncompliance is likely to elicit punishment and other forms of coercion.

Second, the interdependence of parents and children provides many opportunities for conflict. Parents have a critical interest in controlling their children's behavior because that behavior strongly affects their own outcomes. For example, the way children treat family possessions and their performance of chores in the home affects parental outcomes. In addition, the behavior of children reflects on their parents' social identities, because parents are to some extent held responsible for their children's behavior.

Third, parents are likely to use coercion because they have more power than their children (see chap. 7). Parents control the financial and material resources in the family and can deprive children of these resources as a form of punishment. In the case of younger children, parents have superior size and strength as well. Parental use of coercion is supported normatively and legally by the larger society. Normatively, parents are expected to use some level of coercion with their children (e.g., Stark & McEvoy, 1970). Not only are such actions perceived as legitimate behavior for parents, but a parent who fails to use punishment when appropriate may be perceived as too permissive or as spoiling the child. The state also provides legal supports for parents in their use of coercion (Goode, 1971). The state backs up parental authority over children with its own coercive powers; thus, parents of defiant children can get assistance from juvenile courts.

Finally, the frequency of coercion is a function of the frequency of interaction between parents and children. The more time people spend together, the more opportunities for conflict and coercion, according to a routine activity approach (see chap. 5). Contact also prevents people from avoiding each other when they have a conflict (Baumgartner, 1988).[3] Living conditions and architectural arrangements that produce greater contact should therefore lead to more coercion. A study in Hong Kong shows that coercion is more frequent in families that live in upper floors of high-rise apartment buildings than those who reside in lower floors (Mitchell, 1971). Presumably, the easier outside access of residents of lower floors results in less contact between family members, which lowers the frequency of conflict and makes it easier to escape those conflicts.

Coercion Versus Other Methods of Social Control

Coercion, or *power assertion*, as it is often referred to in the literature, is one of several methods that parents use to influence their children. It is not a popular method among some experts on child care. Most experts recommend reasoning or persuasion as methods of control (e.g., Marion, 1983).[4] Presumably, persuasion leads children to internalize the message and thus has long-term effects on compliance (e.g., M. L. Hoffman, 1970). Many parents apparently recognize this benefit as indicated by evidence that parents are more likely to use reasoning when they wish to exert a long-term influence on their children than when they are in situations in which they want to elicit immediate compliance (Kuczynksi, 1984).

---

[3]In addition, when people spend much time together, rules of politeness are relaxed, and grievances are likely to be expressed openly (see chap. 9).

[4]Behavior modification researchers recommend the use of nonphysical punishment, such as time-out or deprivation of privileges, to produce immediate compliance. These forms of punishment are not necessarily used as substitutes for physical punishment, abusive parents use them as well (Trickett & Kuczynski, 1986).

Parents may not use persuasion because of the effort and patience (opportunity costs) and the verbal skills that it requires. Furthermore, children do not always respond to persuasion, particularly when they are very young. Straus et al. (1980) suggested that the potential for parental violence arises because of the younger child's inability to reason and the older child's refusal to reason.

Even when persuasion is used, children may be aware that parents will use coercion if necessary. Persuasion is probably more effective when it is backed by the threat of force. Evidence indicates that coercion combined with persuasion is the most effective strategy for achieving short-term compliance (Crockenberg & Litman, 1990). In some cases, persuasion can be interpreted as the parents' account or explanation for their coercive behavior. After parents force compliance, they then explain to children why they must comply. Grusec and Kuczynski (1980) found that parents frequently reported that they would use coercion in response to a child's misbehavior and then explain why compliance was necessary.

Studies show that the use of coercion versus persuasion depends highly on the nature of the child's transgression (Nucci & Turiel, 1978; Zahn-Waxler & Chapman, 1982). Parents of children ages 4 to 6 years and 7 to 8 years reported that they were more likely to use power assertion than reasoning for most of the misbehaviors studied (Grusec & Kuczynski, 1980). Only when the child engaged in acts that resulted in some psychological harm were parents more likely to use persuasion than coercion.

Dix, Ruble, and Zambarano (1989) found that the greater the competence required to act appropriately, the more parents favored using persuasion and the less they favored using coercion. Parents also indicated that they were more likely to use coercion and less likely to use persuasion when children understood the rules that they had violated. Parents attributed more blame to children who were competent enough to understand what they had done wrong. As a result, they were more likely to think coercion was appropriate for older children.

Promises are another method of social influence and control. Parents may avoid promises because they are costly: A reward must be provided if the child complies (see chap. 7, on opportunity costs). Furthermore, such an exchange implies that future compliant behavior will also be rewarded, which entails additional costs. Finally, promises leave it up to the child to comply and therefore may not be perceived as adequate to secure compliance.

Parents frequently give commands to children to engage in or desist from engaging in certain behaviors. Commands vary in their effectiveness. Precise commands that specify a concrete behavior are more effective than vague commands (e.g., "quit bugging me") that do not refer to a specific behavior (Houlihan, Sloane, Jones, & Patten, 1992). Commands that are accompanied by positive affect may also be more effective. One way to express a command positively is to use the form of a request. Because compliance is obligatory—the child is not given a choice—this type of request is intended and understood as a command. Lytton and Zwirner (1975) found that suggestions led to greater compliance than commands, possibly because they tended to be used in less conflict-laden situations.

Commands are often supported by an implied threat. Nevertheless, parental commands may be ignored if the child's experience shows that commands are often forgotten or not followed up by coercion. Children will comply with commands when they anticipate punishment following noncompliance. When they comply in response to the command, threats and punishments are unnecessary.

Goode (1971) emphasized the notion of implicit threats in his discussion of coercion in the family. He suggested that there is always an element of coercion in parent–child relations, even when no overt act of coercion has taken place. Furthermore, when punishment is actually administered, it implies that the threat of punishment was not sufficient to ensure compliance. An explicit threat may not be necessary if children are led to believe that force will be used if they disobey parental commands.

Children may ignore commands unless parents express anger or sternness in their voices. Commands issued in anger communicate an implicit threat that punishment will follow noncompliance (see chap. 6). Anger and sternness also communicate the parent's resolve and commitment.

Children often perceive the control attempts of parents and other authorities as coercive. They believe that resistance to control attempts will be followed by some form of coercion (Braine, Pomerantz, Lorber, & Krantz, 1991). They also recognize the legitimacy of parental authority. They see adults as having the right to make and enforce rules, although they see that authority as limited. For example, children do not believe that parents have the authority to compel immoral acts, and they believe that certain behaviors—such as choosing their friends—are outside the boundaries of parental authority. The scope of legitimate parental authority decreases during adolescence (for a review, see Braine et al., 1991).

HOW CHILDREN AFFECT THE SEVERITY OF PUNISHMENT

We have suggested that well-behaved children require fewer attempts at influence and are more easily influenced by noncoercive techniques. As a result, they are less likely to elicit coercive behavior from parents (Trickett & Kuczynski, 1986). Well-behaved children also comply when faced with mild forms of coercion, which makes more intense forms of coercion unnecessary. On the other hand, children with behavior problems create conflicts between parent and child that sometimes lead to severe punishment. They may openly defy their parents or retaliate when parents use coercion, which may then lead parents to use severe forms of punishment.

The discussion that follows examines how the child's behavior and characteristics affect the severity of parental punishment. We first review studies that describe the behavior of children that precipitates incidents of severe punishment and injury. We then review studies that examine how abused children are different from other children. Finally, we describe studies of the escalation process and focus on how children respond to initial acts of parental coercion.

The Child's Behavior as a Precipitant

Research has shown that incidents in which parents engage in severe forms of punishment develop out of attempts to discipline children. Libbey and Bybee (1979) found that most of the cases of abuse that they studied were preceded by disobedience or arguments with parents. In some instances where parents use severe punishment, they may be responding to earlier misbehavior; not all severe punishment is immediately preceded by a child's misbehavior.

Kadushin and Martin (1981) examined the exact nature of the child's offense. They found that the precipitating factors for abuse included aggression (21%), stealing and lying (9%), and nine other less frequent misbehaviors. Herrenkohl et al. (1983) examined the types of child behaviors that lead to severe punishment in a sample of physically abused children and their parents. Parental response ranged from mild discipline to severe discipline. Children who refused to talk, eat, or listen or who talked back to their parents were likely to receive more severe punishment than children who did not commit these offenses. Children who engaged in fighting or in dangerous or immoral behavior were also punished more severely.

In young children, crying can precipitate coercive episodes resulting in severe punishment. Weston (1968) found that 80% of parents who abused infants less than 1 year old gave excessive crying as the reason for abuse. Parents may use violence because they believe children can control their crying and that punishment will deter them. They may blame the infant because they fail to adequately consider the usual criteria for assigning blame, such as intent. No one, to our knowledge, has examined these factors as they relate to the child's behavior and the severity of punishment.

Infants who are irritable and difficult to console are more likely to be mistreated by parents (Egeland & Brunnquell, 1979). There is plenty of evidence that severe punishment, including physical punishment, is more likely to be directed at children with behavior problems (for reviews, see Ammerman, 1991; W. N. Friedrich & Boriskin, 1976; Frodi, 1981; Wolfe, 1985).

It is not clear from these studies whether misbehavior results in severe punishment or severe punishment leads to misbehavior. We suspect that these variables are reciprocally related. Some children are difficult to control because of either temperament or inadequate parenting. Parents are ineffective in their use of more mild forms of coercion against these children. In response to the child's noncompliance or defiance, parents turn to more severe forms of coercion. Although this punitive behavior may result in immediate compliance, in the long run it can lead to behavioral problems. Thus, severe punishment by parents (along with other forms of mistreatment) is associated with various forms of misbehavior engaged in by children when they become adults (see chap. 4).

If children's characteristics affect the likelihood of severe punishment, then one would expect the same parents to respond differently to different children. A number of studies have shown that typically only one child is abused in multichild families (e.g., D. Gil, 1970; see also W. N. Friedrich & Boriskin, 1976). In addition, there is evidence that the same child tends to be abused in consecutive foster homes (Milowe & Lourie, 1964; see also Morse, Sahler, & Friedman, 1970).

If children have a history of misbehavior, parents may resent them and respond more intensely when a violation occurs. Severe punishment may reflect an accumulation of grievances. The precipitating behavior may be the straw that broke the camel's back (see chap. 8). The effects of children's reactions to discipline on later parental responses to misbehavior have been examined experimentally (Parke, Sawin, & Kreling, 1974, as cited in Parke & Collmer, 1975). The children either ignored the adults who punished them, made reparations, pleaded with the adults, or behaved in a defiant manner. When the children misbehaved on a later occasion, the adults gave the most severe punishment to children who had earlier been defiant and the least severe punishment when the children had made reparations.

A study by Anderson, Lytton, and Romney (1986) showed the causal role of the child in producing coercive behavior. Mothers of children with conduct disorders and mothers of normal children interacted with either their own children or other children on a series of tasks. Children with conduct disorders elicited more negative responses and commands from both types of mothers. Mothers of children with conduct disorders did not differ in their behavior from mothers of normal children. However, mothers of difficult children were more negative toward their own children than toward other difficult children, presumably because of their past history of conflict.

There is some evidence suggesting that children with congenital defects, mental retardation, or low birth weight and those born prematurely are more likely to be the targets of severe punishment (see reviews by Ammerman, 1991; W. N. Friedrich & Boriskin, 1976; Starr, 1988). Such

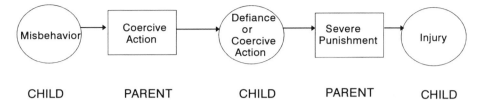

Figure 10.1. Escalation in a typical incident resulting in injury to a child.

infants may exhibit behaviors that precipitate coercive incidents (for a review, see Parke & Collmer, 1975). Premature infants with low birth weights have more feeding disturbances, cry more frequently, and have irritating cries (Frodi, Lamb, Leavitt, & Donovan, 1978).

Not all studies find an association between abuse and congenital abnormalities (Ammerman, 1991; Starr, 1988). The inconsistent evidence suggests that if there is a causal effect, it is probably small and contingent on other factors.[5] It may be that parents have lower expectations for children with handicaps and greater toleration for substandard behavior (Starr, 1988). The parents of handicapped children may not view their children's misbehavior as intentional or otherwise blameworthy but, instead, may attribute it to their impairment. Such parents may be less likely to abuse their children than parents of children with attention deficits, hyperactivity, and other abnormalities with less apparent external causes (Martin & Beezley, 1974). Punishment is likely to be more severe when parents attribute misbehavior to internal causes.

The Child's Role in Escalation

The severity of punishment often depends on the child's response to an initial and usually less severe form of coercion. Sometimes children do not comply with their parents directives even when parents threaten or punish them. Parents may engage in more severe punishment in response to this defiance. Studies find that abused children exhibit higher rates of defiance than other children (e.g., Oldershaw, Walters, & Hall, 1986; Reid et al., 1981; Trickett & Kuczynski, 1986). The escalation process is depicted in Figure 10.1, which shows how a child's misbehavior ultimately can lead to the child's injury.

The skill that children display when they resist compliance is likely to affect the parent's response. Some children negotiate with their parents to persuade them to modify their requests or commands. Others are openly

---

[5]It is possible that the separation of premature infants from their mothers at birth negatively influences their relationship (Klaus & Kennell, 1970). It is also possible that prematurity is the result of poor prenatal care. Parents who give poor prenatal care may also engage in more severe punishment. However, Egeland and Vaughn (1981) found that abuse was not associated with quality of prenatal care.

defiant. Evidence suggests that mothers' use of persuasion is associated with children's use of negotiation, whereas mothers' use of coercion is associated with children's open defiance (Kuczynski, Kochanska, Radke-Yarrow, & Girnius-Brown, 1987). Children who are unskilled in their resistance are more likely to be reported by their mothers to have behavior problems later on (Kuczynski & Kochanska, 1990).

Some children not only defy their parents but also retaliate when disciplined.[6] Children who retaliate are particularly likely to be the target of severe forms of punishment. Patterson (1976) found that parental punishment resulted in an escalating cycle of attack and counterattack in abusive families. Anderson and Burgess (1977) found that children in abusive families are more likely to reciprocate their parents' aversive behaviors than are children in matched control families (see also Loeber, Felton, & Reid, 1984). Finally, Trickett and Kuczynski (1986) found that abused children were more likely than controls to accompany their noncompliance with verbal refusals, anger, and other forms of overt opposition.

In some instances, a child's counterattack may decrease the likelihood of further parental attack. Children can make punishment costly for parents by retaliating or, in the case of younger children, crying. As children, particularly boys, get older, their relative physical power increases, and parents may no longer be able to attack them with impunity.

When parents respond to defiance or retaliation with severe punishment and children finally comply, the children may be reinforcing the parents' behavior. Patterson and Cobb (1971) suggested that there are many women with no past history of violence who are shaped by interactions with their children. The mother learns that violence terminates the aversive behavior of children: "A young woman, unskilled in mothering, is trained by her own children to carry out assaults that result in bodily injury to her trainers" (Patterson & Cobb, 1971, p. 124). In summary, interactions involving severe physical punishment are usually the culmination of a cycle of aversive behavior in which children are active participants.

PARENTAL DIFFERENCES AND SEVERITY OF PUNISHMENT

Most if not all parents use coercion against their children. However, there are strong individual differences between parents in their tendency to engage in severe forms of punishment. A scheme that attempts to represent how child and parental factors result in severe levels of punishment is presented in Figure 10.2. The figure indicates that those who lack parenting skills are likely to produce children who misbehave. The tempera-

---

[6]Children are sometimes the first to use coercion. For example, a child may find that throwing a temper tantrum is useful in gaining compliance from parents.

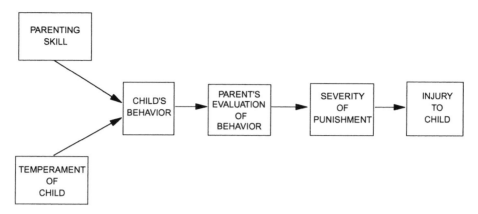

Figure 10.2. The path from parental and child characteristics to injury or abuse.

ment of children also affects whether they engage in misbehavior, as was discussed in the last section. Children's behavior then affects how parents respond to them. However, the parents' own characteristics also affect how they evaluate their children's behaviors. Those who evaluate these behaviors more harshly are likely to punish children more severely. These severe punishments can result in injuries to the children.

We first discuss the relationship of parenting skills to the use of coercion against children. Then we discuss individual-differences factors that affect parents' tendencies to evaluate children's behavior negatively and to respond punitively, including the parents' attitudes toward their children. Finally, we consider how parents' sociodemographic characteristics affect their tendency to use severe forms of punishment.

Parenting Skills and Effective Social Control

The social control of children requires child management skills. Parents who lack these skills are less successful in controlling their children using noncoercive means, and their efforts at mild forms of coercion are more likely to be ineffectual. When parents are unable to control their children by using other means, conflict may escalate, and they may inflict severe physical punishment. As Wolfe (1985) put it:

> Abusive parents fail to use effective contingencies that would serve to reduce problems with their child and fail to use positive methods to teach their child desirable behaviors . . . As a result of such indiscriminant methods, the parent and child engage in a cycle of aversive behavior that may culminate in harm to the child. (p. 493)

Abusive parents do not differ from nonabusive parents in their beliefs about the value of spanking or in their tendency to use physical punishment (Trickett & Susman, 1988). They are more likely to use more severe forms of punishment, however, such as striking the face, hitting with an object, or pulling hair (Trickett & Kuczynski, 1986). They are also more likely to use social punishments and resource deprivation (Trickett & Susman, 1988).

Parents who use severe forms of punishment are unlikely to use non-coercive strategies in discipline situations. A study based on daily reports of disciplinary incidents revealed that both abusive parents and nonabusive parents used punishment in almost all of the incidents (Trickett & Kuczynski, 1986). However, abusive parents used persuasion in 16% of the incidents, whereas nonabusive parents used persuasion in 38% of the incidents (see also Trickett & Susman, 1988). The difference between abusive and control parents in these incidents was not in their use of coercion but in whether persuasion accompanied coercive behavior. Evidence also shows that abusive parents are much less likely to accompany their commands with positive affect than are nonabusive parents (Oldershaw et al., 1986).[7]

Abusive parents are aware of noncoercive strategies for influencing children but use them infrequently and ineffectively (Oldershaw et al., 1986). They may have learned coercive scripts for handling children that they enact without much consideration of alternatives. This is suggested by the finding that abusive parents tend to be inflexible in their use of control strategies (Oldershaw et al., 1986). Abusive parents tended to repeat failing strategies, whereas parents in a control group tried something different when a strategy failed.

Parents who use severe forms of punishment with their children are also likely to be "disorganized" in the way they treat their children (Elmer, 1967). They are unlikely to have clear and consistent expectations for their children or clearly defined household responsibilities (Young, 1964). As a result of poor management, children are more likely to misbehave, and coercive behavior by parents is likely to follow.

One reason parental coercion may lead to escalation rather than deterrence is that it is applied inconsistently. Parents who engage in child abuse tend to be inconsistent in the way they discipline their children (for a review, see Parke & Collmer, 1975). Either they are inconsistent in their punishment of particular behaviors or they make contingent threats that they fail to back up (Patterson, 1976). Because of these parents' low credibility, children do not comply. When children continue to misbehave in the face of inconsistent treatment, parents may intensify their punishment to control them.

In a laboratory study, Deur and Parke (1970) found that coercive behavior that has been punished intermittently is more likely to persist than coercive behavior that has been consistently punished.[8] Because in-

---

[7]They also give many more commands.

[8]Inconsistent discipline has also been associated with delinquency in field studies (McCord, 1986).

consistent discipline is associated with low levels of compliance, the coercive behavior of parents is only intermittently reinforced with compliance, and the negative behaviors of the children are only intermittently punished. The eventual outcome of such a pattern of interaction may be escalation by parents to more severe forms of punishment.

The positive affection and empathy that parents feel toward their children may make it difficult for them to carry out their threats and lead them to be inconsistent in their use of punishment. In general, agents of social control may be able to use coercion most effectively when they have no emotional attachment to their charges. It is ironic that a positive attitude toward a child could eventually lead to more severe punishment for misbehavior or noncompliance.

Some research shows a relationship between parents' experience of stressful life events and their tendency to engage in severe physical punishment (for a review, see Starr, 1988). Some researchers interpret stress effects with a frustration–aggression mechanism. From our point of view, stress interferes with parental competence (see also Wolfe, 1985). Parents are less likely to be effective when they are under stress. Distressed parents are likely to experience depression and health problems that impair their ability to effectively influence their children. Also, stress may affect the decision-making process, which leads to the failure to consider alternatives to coercion or its costs. Distressed parents may instead rely on the most available script, which may involve coercion.

Differences in Parental Punitiveness

Unless a parent evaluates a child's behavior negatively there should not be an attempt to control it. Parents are likely to differ in their evaluation of children's behavior. A behavior that is ignored by one parent may be intolerable to another. The effect of children's actual behavior on parental coercion is not likely to be strong if it is mediated by the parents' subjective evaluations of the behavior (see Figure 10.2).

There is some evidence that parental perceptions of children's behavior are more important than actual behavior in predicting severe punishment. Mash, Johnston, and Kovitz (1983) found a discrepancy between parents' reports and direct observations of children's behavior. Abusive mothers were more likely than controls to report that their children had behavior problems. However, when interactions between children and mothers were observed, the abused children did not reveal more behavior problems than did controls (see also Reid, Kavanagh, & Baldwin, 1987).

The parents' evaluation of behavior depends in part on their expectations. Parents who have unrealistic expectations for their children should be more likely to find their children's behavior disappointing or objectionable. Evidence that parental expectations are associated with severe punishment is mixed (for a review, see Starr, 1988). Some studies find that abusive parents expect their children to perform various tasks at earlier ages than do control parents, whereas others do not. One reason these studies show inconsistent results is that they do not control for the level of the child's conduct. The child's conduct is likely to affect expectations and punishment in opposite directions (see Figure 10.3). In general, children who behave themselves are likely to be punished less. However, parents are likely to have higher expectations for better behaved children. These effects are likely to suppress any positive correlation between expectations and punishment. In addition, the correlation between children's conduct and the level of punishment they receive is suppressed because of differential expectations.

Parental use of coercion and severe forms of punishment also depends on the degree of blame they assign to their children for misbehaviors. Parents who have a hostility bias—that is, who more readily interpret their children's misbehavior as intentional, malevolent, or reckless—are likely to attribute high levels of blame and punish severely (see chap. 8). Mothers with an authoritarian ideology prefer coercive discipline because they attribute greater blame to misbehaving children (Dix et al., 1989). Evidence shows that child abusers are more likely to attribute their children's misbehavior to internal, stable characteristics than are other parents (Larrance & Twentyman, 1983).

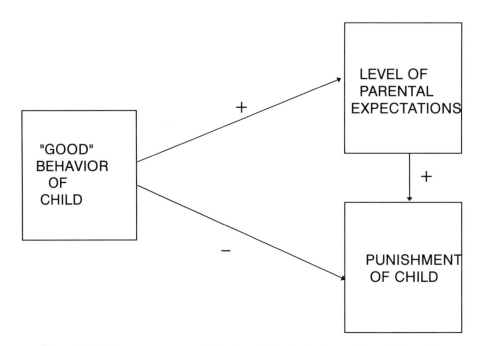

Figure 10.3. The suppressor effect of a child's behavior on the relationship between expectations of the parent and punishment of the child.

Parental punitiveness is not just a function of how parents evaluate their child's behavior. Parents may also differ in their beliefs about the level of punishment that is appropriate for a given offense. Some may endorse low levels of punishment for an offense, whereas others are quite harsh. For example, parents with conservative Christian religious beliefs tend to be more punitive toward children (e.g., C. G. Ellison & Sherkat, 1993). Parents may also differ in the procedural value they assign for different forms of punishment (Stark & McEvoy, 1970). They may assign a low value to physical punishment and show a preference for deprivation of resources and social punishments.

Abusive parents may have stronger emotional reactions to their children's behavior (Wolfe, 1985). Emotional arousal may affect the decision-making process by interfering with concerns about costs, or it may increase the intensity of the response (see chap. 7). Experimental studies show that abusive parents are more likely than other parents to be physiologically aroused when shown videotapes of aversive child behaviors (Disbrow, Doerr, & Caulfield, 1977; Frodi & Lamb, 1980; Wolfe, Fairbank, Kelly, & Bradlyn, 1983). Abusive parents were also more likely than controls to report that they were angry during disciplinary incidents (Trickett & Kuczynski, 1986). However, it is unclear whether the anger was a consequence of the lower compliance of abused children or reflected a proneness to anger among abusive parents because compliance was not controlled.

Parent–Child Relationships

Parents are more likely to use coercion and severe forms of punishment when they have a negative relationship with their children. Parents who feel negatively toward their children may attribute higher levels of blame to them when they misbehave. They may also have a history of grievances against their children (see chap. 8). A negative relationship between parents and children may also decrease the effectiveness of noncoercive means of influence (see chap. 7).

A number of studies show that parents who have poor relationships with their children are more likely to use severe forms of punishment. Abusive parents are less likely to show positive affect during interactions with their children (see Wolfe, 1985). They tend to respond less positively to children's talking and will ignore children who ask questions (Kavanagh, Youngblade, Reid, & Fagot, 1988). This lack of encouragement may explain why abused children talk less to their abusive parents than other children do. Abusive parents also tend to derogate their children (Young, 1964). They are much more likely than parents who neglect their children to speak of the child in highly negative terms. A number of studies have shown that parents with insecure attachments with infants are more likely to abuse them (Cicchetti, 1987; Egeland & Sroufe, 1981). However, as in many of these studies, it is unclear whether a poor parent–child relationship leads to severe punishment or severe punishment interferes with the relationship.

Numerous studies have shown that ordinary social interaction between parents and children are different in abusive families. A consistent finding is that the level of positive interactions in abusive families is lower (for a review, see Wolfe, 1985). Family members in abusive homes interact with one another at a much lower rate (R. L. Burgess & Conger, 1978). The evidence in observational studies for greater levels of negative interaction in abusive families is inconsistent (Wolfe, 1985). It may be that coercion is also common in nonabusive families but that it does not escalate. It is also possible that coercive behaviors in abusive families are hidden from observers.

Parents may be less likely to severely punish their children when their predispositions are complementary (Kadushin & Martin, 1981). When there is a good fit between a particular parent and a particular child, the child's behavior is likely to be rewarding to the parent. Mismatches may occur, as when infants desire less physical contact than their parents do or when they are less responsive or less active than the parents would like (see B. F. Steele & Pollock, 1968). If parent and child are out of sync, conflict, coercion, and severe punishment are more likely to occur.

Parents' Sociodemographic Characteristics

Parents' use of severe forms of punishment is associated with their sociodemographic characteristics. Younger parents are more likely to engage in severe punishment than are older parents (Wolfe, 1987). This age effect is consistent with the pattern observed for age effects on other forms of violent behavior (see chap. 5).

Parental use of coercion and severe forms of punishment is associated with ethnicity and social class. D. Gil (1970) found much higher rates of physical violence by Black parents against children than by White parents. In a large national survey, parents with incomes above $20,000 were half as likely to use physical punishment as those earning less that $5,999 (Straus et al., 1980; see also D. Gil, 1970). It may be that parents with low socioeconomic status are less effective in using noncoercive techniques to influence their children. Middle-class parents are more likely to use persuasion, and working-class parents are more likely to use coercion in disciplining their children (Bronfenbrenner, 1958).

Mothers are more likely than fathers to use physical punishment against their children (Straus et al., 1980). This gender reversal can be attributed to the fact that mothers are usually the primary caretakers. Estimates of the rate of severe violence for single fathers (189 per 1,000) are substantially greater than the estimates for single mothers (130 per 1,000;

Gelles, 1987; see also, Pagelow, 1984). Thus, when time spent caretaking is controlled, fathers are more violent than mothers.

THIRD PARTIES AND PARENTAL USE OF COERCION

Parental use of coercion and severe punishment are affected by third parties who either observe an event or find out about it later. Third parties can be another parent, extended family, other children, neighbors, and government authorities. However, the privacy of the family and the household setting to some extent prevent the interference of outsiders. Even when misbehavior occurs in public, parents may wait until they are alone with children to use coercion. Government agencies only intervene in extreme instances.

There is more violence against children in single-parent families (D. Gil, 1970).[9] Violence is also more likely when the nuclear family is isolated from extended family and when families are geographically mobile (D. Gil, 1970). Abusive mothers meet less often with friends and relatives than do controls (Kotelchuk, 1982; Starr, 1982). One explanation of these isolation effects is that third parties (e.g., spouses or extended family members) serve as guardians in preventing violence. Third parties may also reduce the level of violence by assisting in child care and providing other support (Garbarino & Sherman, 1980). Recall from chapter 5 that the routine activities theory stresses the importance of guardians in the prevention of crime.

Problems of control may explain why child abuse is more prevalent in large families (D. Gil, 1970; Light, 1973). The greater the number of children in a family, the greater the problem of social control. Social control is facilitated when the ratio of agents to targets of control is higher. However, the rate of abuse declines in families with more than five children, perhaps because older children help with child care (Straus et al., 1980). The social control ratio may also explain why abuse is more prevalent in single-parent families.

SUMMARY AND CONCLUSIONS

Parents use a variety of coercive and noncoercive techniques to control their children. Sometimes coercive and noncoercive techniques are used simultaneously, and sometimes coercion is used as a last resort. When

---

[9]It is possible that this relationship is spurious because of the effect of marital discord on divorce and on the use of severe punishment. Marital discord has been shown to be associated with child abuse (e.g., Green, 1976).

noncoercive techniques fail to deter noncompliance, coercive techniques are likely to be used. When mild coercive techniques fail, more severe forms of coercion are likely. Severe forms of punishment, sometimes characterized as child abuse, usually occur during attempts at discipline. Lack of compliance by children in discipline situations is an important factor in determining the severity of punishment.

Characteristics of both parents and children affect the likelihood of severe forms of punishment. Parents who are more skillful in controlling children encounter less disobedience and are less likely to engage in severe punishment. Some parents are more punitive than others because they evaluate their children's misbehavior more harshly or because they endorse severe sanctions. Children who are difficult because of temperament, ineffective parenting, disabilities, or other factors are more likely to be the targets of severe punishment. They do not comply or are unable to comply when faced with mild forms of coercion, and they may openly defy their parents or retaliate. The conflict then may escalate, leading some parents to use more extreme forms of coercion.

Parent–child interaction is a useful arena for studying coercive actions. Because parents use coercion frequently against their children and because it is socially acceptable, it is more readily observed in natural settings than most other forms of coercion. As a result, a significant amount of research has been done that focuses on the social interaction between parent and child during conflicts. This research provides a better picture of the escalation process and a greater appreciation of the importance of social interaction processes.

11

SEXUAL COERCION

Sexual coercion involves the use of contingent threats or bodily force to compel a person to engage in sexual activity. In the case of contingent threats, the source threatens to harm the target unless he or she engages in sexual relations. For example, to obtain sexual compliance, a man may threaten to physically harm a woman, to fire an employee, to leave his date stranded, or to leave the relationship. In the case of bodily force, a man may use superior strength to physically force sexual activity on an unwilling woman. Or he may impose sexual relations when the target is unconscious or in a condition where consent is impossible. Note that some of these behaviors are illegal and some are not. Incidents may be legally classified as *attempted* or *completed rape, sexual assault,* or *sexual harassment,* depending on the outcome of the incident, as well as other factors. In this chapter we focus on the use of sexual coercion as a type of social behavior, ignoring legal classifications and avoiding moral judgments. Much of our discussion is about rape, not because it is the most prevalent form of sexual coercion (it probably is not) but because much of the research on sexual coercion has focused on rape.

It is important to distinguish sexual coercion from noncoercive means that a source may use to influence a target who is unwilling or hesitant to engage in sexual relations. The source may use persuasion, deception, exchange of rewards, or various forms of self-presentation. A man may ingratiate himself, or he may devote extra effort to improving his appearance. He may express love for the woman, whether he feels it or not. He may treat her to an expensive dinner or promise some future reward. He may attempt to increase the woman's interest by creating a romantic atmosphere or with foreplay. Such techniques are primarily used when source and target know each other.

In our view, sexual coercion, including rape, is similar to the use of coercion to achieve other types of values. Sexual coercion may be used as a form of influence to obtain sexual satisfaction, to punish a person for some perceived wrong, to establish or protect desired social identities, or for all of these reasons. Although an offender may have multiple goals, we assume that for a given incident of sexual coercion, one goal is primary. The evidence we present indicates that the most prevalent motivation for the use of sexual coercion is to produce sexual compliance and to gain sexual satisfaction.

As was indicated in chapter 7, terminal values are not the only factors involved in decisions to engage in coercion. External costs, attitudes (or procedural values) regarding coercion, internal inhibitions, and expectations of success are also important. If a man is tempted for some reason to engage in sexual coercion, he may refrain because he fears punishment or because it violates his moral standards. On the other hand, if he is intoxicated, he may not weigh the costs or he may use the alcohol as an excuse. Also, a negative attitude toward the target or toward women generally may facilitate his use of sexual coercion. In addition to the primary goal or value sought, there may be secondary gains. For example, an aggrieved actor may seek to punish the target, and sexual satisfaction could be an added incentive.

The decision to use coercion may or may not be impulsive. Amir (1971) presented evidence, based on offenders' reports, that most rapes reported to the police are planned; however, it is unclear how he made this determination (for a contradictory claim, see B. C. Glueck, 1956). It is often assumed that men choose methods, targets, and situations that increase their likelihood of success. Apparently, these calculations are often incorrect. In many instances of rape, as well as milder forms of sexual coercion, the offender is unsuccessful in gaining compliance (Koss, Gidycz, & Wisniewski, 1987; McDermott, 1979). Approximately one out of three attempted rapes actually result in intercourse, according to the National Crime Survey (McDermott, 1979). Offenders fail because victims resist and for a variety of other reasons (Lizotte, 1986).

Social scientists are concerned with the causes of sexual coercion, not with establishing blame (R. B. Felson, 1991). Evidence indicating that some characteristic or behavior of the victim is a causal factor in sexual coercion does not imply that the victim is to blame for the incident. An event has many causes, and only some imply blame. Even if an action appears blameworthy (e.g., the victim walks alone at night in a neighborhood she knows to be dangerous), it does not exonerate the offender. Studies of reactions to rape indicate that although rape victims are sometimes assigned a causal role in the crime, most of the blame is assigned to the offender (for a review, see Allison & Wrightsman, 1993). At any rate, we consider it inappropriate to alter scientific theory to protect the image of victims or to vilify offenders. Actually, the political and legal implications of our position are ambiguous. A rapist may seem less blameworthy to some if he is motivated by commonplace sexual desire rather than by hatred and hunger for power. However, it can also be argued that treating sexual coercion as an instrumental action (rather than an involuntary outburst) makes the offender appear more blameworthy.

This chapter is divided into seven sections. In the first section, we discuss sex differences in sexuality and examine the sociobiological argument about their source. Whether these sex differences are due to biological or cultural factors, we suggest that sex differences in sexual selectivity produce the conflict that results in most sexual coercion. Second, we examine the issue of sexual motivation, reviewing evidence suggesting that as sexual incentives increase, the likelihood of sexual coercion increases. The third section focuses on sexual coercion involving people who know each other. We discuss the role of sexual scripts in consensual sexual activity and how they sometimes result in sexual coercion by sexually motivated men. In the fifth and sixth sections we consider alternatives to sexual motivation. In the fifth section, sexual coercion as a form of social control is examined. The focus is on sexual coercion as an expression of grievances, but we also consider the hypothesis that sexual coercion reflects a method of controlling women. In the sixth section, we discuss the role of social identities in sexual coercion and consider the possibility that sexual coercion is a means through which men demonstrate power. In the final section, we examine the role of factors that might facilitate and inhibit the use of sexual coercion, such as attitudes toward women and attitudes toward coercion.

SEX DIFFERENCES IN SEXUAL SELECTIVITY

Sexual coercion is overwhelmingly committed by men. In the case of rape, data from the National Crime Survey have indicated that less than 1% of offenders are women. Some men use coercive techniques to force sexual relations with other men. Although some of these incidents occur in prison settings (e.g., Lockwood, 1980), they are more frequent outside of prison than is generally realized. According to the National Crime Survey, 7.3% of the victims of rape are male (R. B. Felson & Krohn, 1990). Presumably, the offenders in these incidents are homosexuals. Actually, this figure may underestimate the percentage of rapes that involve male victims if males are less likely to report these victimizations to interviewers than are females. Rapes are embarrassing to female victims, but they may be more embarrassing to male victims, given the stigma of homosexuality in American society.

The sex difference in committing rape partly reflects sex differences in the use of physical coercion in general. It may also be difficult for a woman to force a man to engage in intercourse because it requires him to be aroused. However, male victims can be aroused involuntarily during rape (Groth & Burgess, 1980; Sarrel & Masters, 1982), and they can be forced to engage in noncoital forms of sexual activity. Sex differences in physical strength may also play a role in sex differences in sexual coercion, but some women are stronger than men, and weapons would provide potential female offenders with the necessary force. There must be some other reason why rape is almost exclusively a male activity. We can think of no other type of coercive behavior, and few other noncoercive behaviors, in which the sex difference is so strong.

Sex differences in sexuality may be important in explaining why women almost never commit rape. Research on permissive sexual behavior reveals dramatic differences between men and women. Eysenck (1976) found that 61% of men and only 4% of women reported that they would take part in an orgy. In an experimental study, 69% of male subjects agreed when they were asked by a confederate of the opposite sex to engage in sexual relations, yet none of the female subjects were willing (R. D. Clark, 1990). Research on the conflicts of couples suggests that men are more likely to complain about the unwillingness of women to engage in sexual relations, whereas women are more likely to complain about the sexual aggressiveness of men (D. M. Buss, 1989a). The fact that people with sexual fetishes are almost exclusively male also indicates a strong sex difference in the ability to disassociate sexual response from interpersonal relationships (Gregor, 1990). Finally, there are strong sex differences in sexual fantasies. Reviewing the empirical literature, B. J. Ellis and Symons (1990) concluded that "male sexual fantasies tend to be more ubiquitous, frequent, visual, specifically sexual, promiscuous, and active. Female sexual fantasies tend to be more contextual, emotive, intimate, and passive" (p. 529).

An examination of the sexual behavior of lesbians and gay men is informative about male and female sexuality, because these liaisons do not involve a compromise between the sexes (Symons, 1979). Comparisons reveal dramatic differences between gay males and lesbians in sexual behavior. A study of 151 lesbians and 581 gay men in Germany found that only 1% of the lesbians had had sex with more than 10 partners, whereas 61% of the gay men had (Schafer, 1977).

These studies show that men are more likely than women to be indiscriminate and casual in their attitudes toward sexual relations. Women, on the other hand, are more likely to insist on some commitment or closeness before engaging in sexual relations (Simpson & Gangestad, 1991). They are more likely than men to interpret sexual activity as romance rather than recreation (Gagnon & Simon, 1973). Reiss (1986) described male sexuality as body centered and female sexuality as person centered.[1]

Sex differences in sexuality should lead to conflict between the sexes. If men are less discriminating in choosing sexual partners, then they should be more likely to attempt to influence women to have sex, using a variety of techniques, including coercion. On the other hand, women may use sexual relations to reward men or may withhold them as a form of punishment. Some women may engage in sexual relations to gain advantages in social exchanges, and some may deny consent for sexual relations when they feel aggrieved with their partner.

A sociobiological approach attributes sexual coercion to biological differences between the sexes in sexual behavior (L. Ellis, 1989; Shields & Shields, 1983; Symons, 1979; Thornhill & Thornhill, 1983). In all mammals, males and females have evolved different orientations toward the task of reproduction. Males are less discriminating, more promiscuous, and more assertive in their attempts to copulate than females are. Males are physically able to produce an almost unlimited number of offspring, and therefore they have a relatively small investment in each. They may also have a low investment in each offspring because of their uncertainty about parentage. They can increase their reproductive potential by copulating with as many females as possible. As a result of selection, traits evolve in males that increase their chances of inseminating large numbers of females. These traits may explain why polygamy (multiple wives) is the most common marital arrangement (84% of cultures) whereas polyandry (multiple husbands) is almost never practiced (Ford & Beach, 1951).

Females have a strong investment in each offspring because of limitations in the number they can physically produce. Because of their limited fertility, females must be careful in choosing who will father their offspring. They prefer males who will remain with them and help care for and protect their young. They will not usually respond sexually until males exhibit evidence that they are willing to commit themselves. Females can increase the chances that their offspring will survive if they find males willing to make a parental "investment." This investment is particularly important

---

[1]Note also that most women are not promiscuous even though their opportunities for promiscuity are virtually unlimited.

to females in the human species because of the long period of infant dependency.

According to sociobiologists, the biological differences in sexual orientation create conflict between males and females. Tension is produced because of the disparity in reproductive interests, that is, the conflict between the male's desire for partners and the female's desire for commitment. The result is a high degree of deception, negotiation, and compromise during courtship. Males use various means, including coercion and feigned commitment, to influence females to have a sexual relationship. Females often resist, wanting some form of commitment before engaging in sexual relationships.

Sociobiologists propose that males prefer females at ages when female reproductive potential is highest (Thornhill & Thornhill, 1983). This preference explains why men are more sexually attracted to young women. The association between youth and sexual attractiveness of women is apparently a universal. In all 34 cultures studied by D. M. Buss (1989b), men generally showed a preference for younger women (see also Thornhill & Thornhill, 1983).

A sociobiological approach also suggests that rape should be most likely at the ages prior to the usual age of marriage, when competition for women is most intense. In support of this prediction, Thornhill and Thornhill (1983) cited data showing that the median age of rape offenders ranges from 20 to 23 years. They also found a significant positive correlation between the median marriage age and the median age of rape offenders from 1957 to 1978.

Because heterosexual relations obviously require a partner, the mean number of partners must be the same for sexually active people of both sexes. There may be sex differences in the variance in number of partners, however. It may be that most women have a limited number of partners, whereas a few have many partners. Greater variance in promiscuity among women may account for the stereotypes about "good girls" and "bad girls." Such a pattern must exist, given that a higher proportion of men than women engage in premarital and extramarital sexual behavior (Marshall & Suggs, 1971).

Sociobiology does not indicate exactly what is programmed into the genes to explain sex differences in sexuality or the propensity to rape. It does not specify the relevant traits that are selected or the mechanism through which they affect sexual behavior (see Palmer, 1991). It seems unlikely that rape itself—a social behavior—is programmed in the genes. Perhaps there are sex differences in sexual arousal that account for this difference. Young men are much more likely than young women to report that they think a lot about sex and are easily aroused (Eysenck, 1976). In addition, it seems likely that evolution plays a role in sex differences in sexual response. Sex differences in sexual response are likely to have important implications for reproductive potential, and so one might expect them to become encoded into human genes. Thus, rape is more likely to be a by-product of evolved sex differences in sexuality and not an adaptation itself (Palmer, 1991; Symons, 1979).

Sex differences in sexual response have also been attributed to greater learned inhibitions among women. The evidence does not support this socialization explanation (for a review, see B. Singer, 1985). Sex differences in masturbation rates and sexual functioning remain even when level of inhibitions about sex are controlled. Women usually attribute their low masturbation rates to lack of desire, not to guilt (LoPiccolo, 1980).

SEXUAL MOTIVATION

Given that there can be conflict over sexual relations—for example, a man may desire sex and a woman may be unwilling—and given that some people use coercion to get what they want, it is plausible that sexual satisfaction is the incentive (or terminal value) for at least some sexual coercion. The source uses threats or bodily force to gain compliance so that he can achieve sexual satisfaction. Although a sexually motivated offender dominates the victim and accepts the victim's suffering as a consequence of his actions, domination and punishment are not what is valued.

Since the 1970s, most researchers have rejected the idea that the goal of rape and other forms of sexual coercion is sexual. This counterintuitive idea is stated repeatedly and in the strongest possible terms, without any reasonable evidence to support it. We can think of no other assertion in the social sciences that has achieved such wide acceptance on the basis of so little evidence.

Palmer (1988) has reviewed and criticized the arguments that have been made against the idea that rape is sexually motivated (see also Hagen, 1979; W. M. Shields & Shields, 1983; Symons, 1979; Thornhill & Thornhill, 1983). In general, these arguments are based on spurious reasoning and the misreporting of evidence, in those few instances when evidence is reported. The facts that force is used, that some rapes are premeditated, that some rapists experience sexual dysfunction, and that victims are not always young have all been cited as evidence against sexual motivation. As Palmer pointed out, these facts say little or nothing about the motivation for rape. In regard to sexual dysfunction, N. A. Groth and Birnbaum (1979) reported that 16% of the rapists in their sample experienced some degree of erective inadequacy during the incident, usually during the initial stage of the assault. However, some occurrences of sexual dysfunction should be expected because of the victim's resistance and because of the offender's anxiety while engaging in a criminal act.[2]

In the discussion that follows, we review evidence regarding the sexual motivation for sexual coercion. The focus is on factors that increase the incentives for a man with a sexual goal to engage in coercion. As we proposed in chapter 7, the greater the incentive for using coercion, the greater the likelihood of coercion. Among the factors that increase the value of sexual activity and, thus, the incentive for using coercion is the strength of sexual desire of the actor, as affected by sexual deprivation, age, castration, sexual arousal, and the attractiveness of the target person. We also consider whether some offenders value coercion itself and prefer coercive to consensual sexual relations.

Sexual Deprivation

Sexual interest may be higher among men who are sexually deprived. Men who have not experienced recent sexual relations might be more likely than men with many sexual outlets to use sexual coercion.[3] Contrary to this hypothesis, Kanin (1967) found a positive relationship between the use of coercion and frequency of sexual experience among college men: Men who engaged in sexual coercion had more sexual experience. The men who used coercion also used noncoercive techniques more frequently than other men did to obtain sexual relations. These results suggest that men who engage in more effort to obtain sexual experiences are sometimes successful and that this leads to higher levels of sexual activity.[4] Thus, men who have more frequent sexual relations and may have higher levels of expectation may engage in more sexual coercion, but the relationship of deprivation to sexual coercion is unclear.

Some researchers have examined the effect of sexual deprivation on physical coercion indirectly by examining the marital status of rapists. It is assumed that married men are likely to engage in sexual relations more frequently than single men and, therefore, that married men should experience less deprivation. The evidence shows that rapists are more likely than the general population to be single but that their marital status is similar to that of other criminal offenders (Alder, 1984; Amir, 1971). We do not view this evidence as informative about the motivation for sexual coercion. First, marriage is only weakly correlated with the frequency of

---

[2]If men continue to attempt rape when they have been unable to perform successfully in their past attempts, it is unlikely that their motive is to demonstrate power. The condition in which men are unable to perform sexually is called *impotence*—a term that probably describes their self-perception when this occurs as well.

[3]This assumes that sexual interest is not completely satisfied by masturbation.

[4]The longitudinal data needed to evaluate a possible reciprocal relationship between sexual deprivation and sexual coercion are not presently available.

sexual relations. Second, husbands engage in other sexually motivated behavior not involving their wives. If some married men masturbate and some engage in extramarital affairs, then it should not be surprising that some married men rape. In addition, as Symons (1979) suggested, "Most patrons of prostitutes, adult bookstores, and adult movie theatres are married men, but this is not considered evidence for lack of sexual motivation" (p. 279). Third, because many women are reluctant to have relationships with married men, married men may have less access to consensual relationships outside their marriage than single men do.

Research on the relationship between rape rates and access to alternative sexual outlets such as prostitutes provides an indirect way to assess the effect of deprivation. In a longitudinal study, Barber (1969) found that the rate for rape and attempted rape increased substantially following the closure of brothels in Australia. The increase was 3 times the rate increase for other violent crimes.[5]

One place where heterosexual sexual access is either forbidden or severely restricted is in prison. Because many inmates are young and at the height of their sexual interest, it is not surprising that some heterosexual men engage in homosexual relations while in prison. The use of coercion in part reflects the fact that prisons are filled with men who frequently use coercion to get their way with others. The use of coercion may also reflect the reluctance of many heterosexual men to take the passive role in homosexual sex. Because there are many inmates willing to play the active role and relatively few willing to play the passive role, it is probably difficult to find partners to engage in consensual sexual activity. Powerful inmates who seek sexual satisfaction are likely to force weaker inmates to play this role. This conflict is similar in some respects to the situation outside prison, where there is a surplus of men and a scarcity of women interested in casual sex. Coercion is likely to be frequent in circumstances where the demand for an activity is high and the supply of that activity is low.

Sexual deprivation plays a role in sexual coercion among the Gusii of southwestern Kenya (R. A. Levine, 1959). The sexuality of young men is limited because of rules against sex within their own clan. Adultery and masturbation are forbidden, and bestiality is only permitted for the very young. Because of these restrictions, young men turn to unmarried women in other clans. When a Gusii man does not have the economic means, the attractiveness, or social skill to acquire a wife, he may abduct a woman from another clan. In this case, men use coercion as a last resort when they lack the resources to influence women and their families. Furthermore,

---

[5]Rape rates are not likely to be negatively associated with prostitution and pornography in a cross-sectional design. More tightly controlled societies are likely to restrict nonmarital consensual sexual activity as well as criminal behavior. For example, in Muslim countries like Saudi Arabia, there are low rates of rape and other forms of violent crime as well as strict laws against prostitution and pornography.

inflation in the bride-wealth price (the number of cattle transferred from the father of the groom to the father of the bride) may have resulted in an increase in the incidence of rape. As suggested in chapter 7, an increase in the cost of noncoercive means leads to an increase in the use of coercion.

Sexual Aspirations

Physical pleasure is only one of the reasons people value sexual activity. The motivation for sex—whether coercive or consensual—is at least partly based on nonsexual motives (Gagnon, 1977). Both coercive and consensual sexual activity could ultimately reflect quests for power, status, or self-esteem. And sexual activity can bring these rewards for women as well as men. Because sexuality in human beings is a social psychological as well as a biological process, it might be better to describe the goal of sexual coercion as "sociosexual" rather than sexual (R. B. Felson & Krohn, 1990).

If social factors are involved in sexual relations, then sexual desire is not likely to be related in any simple way to sexual deprivation. Although there is an obvious short-term relationship between sexual orgasm and desire in men, we are not aware of any evidence concerning the longer-term effect of the recency of sexual relations on sexual desire. Individual differences in expectations probably reduce the relationship between deprivation and desire, because those who have sexual relations infrequently have lower expectations than those who engage in sexual relations more frequently.

Kanin (1965, 1967) found that "sexual aspirations"—subjective sexual deprivation rather than frequency of sexual activity—are positively correlated with the use of sexual coercion among college men. College men who were dissatisfied with the frequency of their sexual activity were more likely to engage in both coercive and noncoercive sexual behavior than those who were satisfied. Also, men who indicated that they needed a high frequency of orgasms during a week to be sexually satisfied were more likely to use coercion than were those who required fewer orgasms. These men also used noncoercive techniques more frequently than did men with lower sexual aspirations. And, as indicated earlier, those who used sexual coercion were likely to have more sexual experience, presumably because they engaged in more effort to obtain partners. Thus, Kanin (1967) found that high school and college-aged males who used sexual coercion were much more likely to initiate necking and petting during the course of dating than were noncoercive males. Similarly, rapists who have been married reported a higher frequency of marital intercourse and extramarital affairs than did married men generally (Gebhard, Gagnon, Pomeroy, & Christenson, 1965; M. J. Goldstein, 1973; Le Maire, 1956).

Kanin (1967) found that young men devote considerable effort to finding women who will engage in sexual relations. Access to willing, attractive women, even in a permissive sexual atmosphere, is restricted for most men. The fact that some men are willing to pay a high price to engage a prostitute indicates that there are strong barriers to sexual access. On the other hand, men willing to use coercion have an almost unlimited choice of sexual partners.

Sexual aspirations are influenced by social pressures. Thus, Kanin (1967) found that the use of coercive sexual behavior was related to peer-group pressure to have sexual experience. College men who used coercion reported more pressure from friends to find new sexual experience than did men who did not use coercion. The men who used sexual coercion were also more likely to indicate that an admission of virginity would involve a loss of status with their friends.

Sexual aspirations vary across situations as well as individuals. Because a sexually stimulated man has high sexual aspirations, sexual coercion should frequently occur during consensual sexual encounters when a woman attempts to limit sexual activity. A study of 71 college students who had committed rape indicated that this is the case (Kanin, 1985). In every instance, the rape occurred on a date during an intensive consensual sexual encounter, most commonly involving oral–genital sex. If date rape occurs when men are sexually aroused, it suggests that a sexual goal is involved. Evidently, date rapes generally occur as a result of a conflict between men who are interested in intercourse and women who are interested in sexual activity short of intercourse.

Research on the effect of castration on sexual coercion permits an examination of the effect of indirectly lowering sexual aspirations. Castration decreases the sexual interest of at least some adult men who have the operation (Ford & Beach, 1951). Palmer (1988) cited evidence that castration dramatically affects the likelihood that sexual offenders continue to engage in sexual offenses. One study in Denmark showed that 15.6% of castrated sexual offenders, including rapists, continued these offenses in comparison with 80.2% of offenders who were not castrated (Sturup, 1960).[6]

Is There a Preference for Physical Coercion?

Sexually motivated offenders should not have a special attraction or preference for coercive tactics. Rather, one would expect them to use a variety of means to achieve their sexual goals. When they know the target, they should use coercion as a last resort, after other methods of influence have failed.[7] Thus, high school and college-aged males who used sexual coercion were more likely than other males to use various methods to encourage sexual relations, such as falsely professing love or attempting to get a female drunk (Kanin, 1967). Lockwood (1980) found evidence that

---

[6]There may also be a slight effect on nonsexual offenses.
[7]Coercion is used as a first resort with strangers, because noncoercive tactics are not effective.

inmates tried noncoercive as well as coercive means to influence other men to engage in sexual activity in male prisons. The results indicated that men who use sexual coercion may have no special attraction for coercive tactics because they also use other means to get what they want.

For some men physical violence itself may be sexually arousing. These offenders have a sexual goal, but physical coercion may add to the excitement and thus has greater value than consensual sexual behavior. Evidence from laboratory research has not supported this hypothesis (e.g., Abel, Barlow, Blanchard, & Guild, 1977; Quinsey, Chaplin, & Varney, 1981). In these studies, films of violent and consensual sex were shown to convicted rapists and to control groups, and penile tumescence was measured. Rapists were no more likely to be sexually aroused by depictions of rape than they were by depictions of consensual sexual acts. The control group of non-rapists, on the other hand, was less aroused by depictions of rape than by depictions of consensual sex. When inhibitions were experimentally lowered in another study, the arousal levels of nonrapists to depictions of violent sex was increased (e.g., Sundberg, Barbaree, & Marshall, 1991). These results indicate that rapists differ from other men in terms of their inhibitions regarding rape, not in their preference for sexual violence (W. L. Marshall & Barbaree, 1984).

It is possible that rapists are more aroused than nonrapists by engaging in violent sex but not merely by watching it. Furthermore, if a small percentage of rapists were aroused by violence it would not necessarily be revealed in the arousal studies, because they are based on relatively small samples. Interviews with rapists and victims have indicated that between 4% and 6% of rapists are aroused by violence itself (A. N. Groth, Burgess, & Holmstrom, 1977). Thus, at most, a small percentage of men who use sexual coercion derive sexual pleasure from the coercive aspect of these encounters.

Target's Attractiveness

If sexual coercion is sexually motivated, then the incentive for using sexual coercion should be greater when the target is more attractive, and physically attractive women should be preferred when there is a choice. The relationship between attractiveness and the likelihood of being the victim of sexual coercion has never been directly examined.[8] The effect of physical attractiveness may be indirectly tested by examining the age of victims of rape, because young women tend to be viewed as more sexually desirable than older women.

---

[8]Forced sexual activity is dependent on opportunity and access as well as the offender's preferences. A man with limited resources to attract women is unlikely to have access to attractive women in dating situations and, therefore, would not have the opportunity to use sexual coercion.

Research has shown that there is a strong relationship between age and the likelihood of being the victim of rape. According to the U.S. National Crime Survey, 89% of female rape victims were under 35 (vs. 55.8% of the female population in 1980), and 96% were under 50 (vs. 71.8% of the female population; BJS, 1985). This same pattern is apparent in the rape of male victims.[9] Note that older men and women are not frequently victimized, even though they are not as strong as younger targets and are thus more vulnerable.

It is possible that victims of rape tend to be young because of the routine activity patterns of youth (L. E. Cohen & Felson, 1979). Young women are more likely to go out at night and to date; their greater contact with a variety of men may put them at greater risk (Ploughman & Stensrud, 1986). Although differential opportunity may be a factor, there is evidence that it is only a partial explanation of the age-victimization relationship. This has been indicated by research in which attempts have been made to control for differential opportunity by comparing crimes of robbery with crimes in which rape is committed in conjunction with robbery (R. B. Felson & Krohn, 1990). During the robbery of a woman, an offender sometimes has the opportunity to rape her as well. The evidence shows that during a robbery involving a male offender and a female victim, a rape is more likely to occur if the victim is young. The average age of female robbery victims is 35, whereas the average age of female robbery–rape victims is under 28. Female rape victims also tend to be younger than female victims of homicide, aggravated assault, and property crimes (Ennis, 1967; Thornhill & Thornhill, 1983). These differences indicate that rapists have a preference for young women and that they prefer physically attractive victims.[10]

Rapists have reported in interviews that attractiveness is an important factor in their selection of victims (Ageton, 1983; Queen's Bench Foundation, 1976). Chappell and James (1976) found that rapists preferred victims who were nice, friendly, young, pretty, and middle-class. Scully and Marolla (1985) found that some rapists preferred somewhat older women who they assumed were more sexually experienced. Thus, even men who rape older women may be sexually motivated. Attractiveness may also explain choice of male rape victims in prisons. Lockwood (1980) found that most victims of prison rapes were young, slim, White males. Interviews with inmates suggested that men who were young and slim were preferred because they were viewed as more attractive and as most highly resembling women.

---

[9]Gay men also show a strong sexual preference for young adults (A. P. Bell & Weinberg, 1978).
[10]Sexual relations with younger victims might also enhance the offender's status, although this seems more likely for consensual relations. However, the sexual preference for the young is also apparent in the private act of masturbation: The models in pornography are almost always young. The reason that a consensual sexual relationship with a young woman is status enhancing for a man is that she is perceived as desirable.

SEXUAL COERCION BETWEEN PEOPLE WHO KNOW EACH OTHER

According to the National Crime Survey, about one third of rapes involve people who know each other (R. B. Felson & Krohn, 1990). In more than half of the incidents involving a person known to the victim, the person was well known; the rest were casual acquaintances.[11] For milder forms of sexual coercion, the likelihood that the offender is known is much higher (Koss et al., 1987). Sexual coercion between people who know each other is usually very different from sexual coercion involving strangers.[12] Men who use coercion against women they know are more likely to use bodily force rather than threats or punishments, and weapons are rarely used. Frequently, there is a limited level of coercion and the target is likely to feel pressured rather than endangered (Gilbert, 1991). The incident may occur on a date, and the coercive behavior may occur during consensual activity. Recall that Kanin (1985) found that every date rape he studied occurred during intensive consensual sexual activity.

To explain sexual coercion involving people who know each other it is necessary to consider the norms of sexual interaction. We describe these norms in American society and compare them with norms in tribal societies. We then present evidence showing that when men use coercion, they use it along with other influence techniques to encourage sexual relations, usually as a means of last resort. Miscommunication and false expectations about women's sexual interest can contribute to the use of coercion. Finally, we show how the difficulty in distinguishing between coercive and non-coercive methods of influence in sexual encounters creates a problem in estimating the frequency of coercion.

Sexual Scripts

A *sexual script* refers to expectations about the proper sequence of behavior in a sexual interaction (Gagnon, 1977). According to the sexual script of heterosexuals in American society, men initiate each level of sexual activity, usually without making any verbal request, and women either comply or resist. Men then proceed to higher levels of intimacy according to a prescribed sequence, until they meet resistance.

Broude and Greene (1976) provided some information on sexual scripts across cultures based on ethnographic data. In 50% of the 34 tribal

---

[11]The National Crime Survey probably underestimates the number of offenders who are well known to the respondent.

[12]We avoid using the term *date rape* because rape is usually not involved and because the incidents do not necessarily occur on dates.

societies in which information was available, men either always or usually take the initiative in sexual encounters. In 17.6% of the societies, women take the initiative, and in 32.4% both sexes take the initiative with equal frequency. In 77% of a larger sample of societies ($N = 65$), men are described as either verbally or physically aggressive in their sexual advances.

Some sexual encounters involve a negotiation in which men pursue and women comply after initial resistance. Men may treat initial resistance as an opening bargaining position rather than as a final offer. This perception is not necessarily inaccurate, as indicated by reports from women that they sometimes engage in "token resistance," that is, they resist initially when they are actually interested in sexual activity (Muehlenhard & Hollabaugh, 1988). G. D. Johnson, Palileo, & Gray (1992) found that 17% of the college women in their sample indicated that they always said no to sexual activity when they actually meant yes. One reason why women may engage in token resistance is that they can increase their power and status by not giving in too easily. The phrase "playing hard to get" describes this strategy. In addition, women may wish to shift responsibility for the episode to the man or, at least, to present themselves as not responsible. Knowing that women sometimes use these strategies, some men may continue sexual activity in the face of resistance.

A man may continue sexual initiatives when faced with resistance because he believes the woman will become sexually stimulated and change her mind. This strategy is likely to be effective when women are ambivalent about whether to engage in sexual relations, which is often the case (Muehlenhard & Hollabaugh, 1988).

If men become sexually aroused during consensual sexual activity or during the "negotiation process," their inhibitions about using coercion may be lowered. They may give less attention to the feelings of their partner or to the long-range implications of the behavior and thus may fail to consider its costs or its moral implications. Although we reject the idea that sexual arousal causes men to lose control of themselves, the evidence presented in chapter 3 suggests that arousal does affect information processing and restrict one's focus of attention. Decisions made in the heat of passion may focus on the ends to be achieved and may disregard concerns for the morality of the means used.

The sexual scripts among the Gusii of southwestern Kenya also contribute to the use of sexual coercion (R. A. Levine, 1959). Unmarried young men and women from different clans often meet at the marketplace. Frequently, young men use their social and musical skills to seduce young women. Gifts and flattery are provided in hopes of influencing the young women to have sexual relations. The young women may behave provocatively and encourage young men in the early stages of courtship in order to enjoy their gifts and attention, but they may have no desire to have a sexual relationship. The women often make provocative and hostile sexual comments and attempt to prolong the period of pursuit. The men assume that the women will resist even if they are interested in intercourse. This sexual script may lead to rape and claims of rape. Such token resistance typically offered by a woman leads to misunderstandings: He may not know that she is actually unwilling.

Legitimate marital encounters among the Gusii are aggressive contests in which the men use force and attempt to inflict pain and the women resist and sometimes attempt to humiliate their husbands. The hostile relations are partly a pretense and partly reflect the fact that the husband and wife are from different clans. On the wedding night, the groom and his clansmen force the bride to engage in sexual intercourse. She is determined to put him to a severe test and takes magical measures to thwart his performance and positions her body to prevent penetration. Brides take pride in the length of time they can deter their husbands. If a new wife fails to resist, she is thought to be promiscuous. In marital relations, wives never initiate sexual intercourse, and they generally engage in token resistance.

Men initiate most sexual interactions among the Mehinaku Indians of Brazil (Gregor, 1990). Men show a much stronger proclivity than women to engage in sexual activity; they describe unwilling women as "stingy with their genitals." The men attempt to encourage women to engage in sexual relations frequently by offering fish in exchange. Although there is a high level of promiscuity in the tribe, the women sometimes refuse. On these occasions, the men may use some level of coercion, described vaguely as "pulling," to force the women into the bush.

Frequency of Coercive Versus Noncoercive Methods of Influence

A good deal of the literature on sexual coercion is concerned with the frequency of rape. According to the National Crime Survey, in 1983, 1 out of every 600 females in the United States, 12 years of age and older, reported that she had been the victim of rape or attempted rape (BJS, 1985). Much higher frequencies of rape have been reported in some studies (e.g., Koss et al., 1987; Russell, 1984). According to Gilbert (1991), feminist researchers have grossly exaggerated the frequency of rape, creating what he describes as a "phantom epidemic." These "advocacy numbers" are useful for those who wish to demonstrate high levels of victimization of females by males (see also Gutmann, 1990).[13] Gilbert pointed out that in 73% of the incidents defined as rape in one well-known study (Koss et al., 1987), the target did not view herself as a rape victim (see also Johnson et al., 1992). In 42% of the cases, the target had sex at a later time with

---

[13]It may also be useful in promoting careers, because the work of researchers seems more important if the behavior they study is pervasive.

the person who supposedly raped her. Rejecting the notion that the discrepancy is due to the target's ignorance, he suggested that "if reasonable people feel confusion rather than outrage, perhaps there is something to be confused about" (Gilbert, 1991, p. 60).

One problem in estimating frequencies of sexual coercion is a tendency by researchers to describe methods of influence that they find personally objectionable as *coercive* or *assaultive*. These classifications reflect value judgments rather than scientific analysis. As indicated in chapter 6, one must be careful to avoid value judgments in defining coercive actions. False promises of love and badgering may be obnoxious or morally repugnant, but they are not coercive. Giving alcohol to someone is not coercive, although coercion may follow if sexual relations are forced on a person who is incapacitated or unconscious. Coercion is involved when a man threatens to leave his wife because she refuses to have sexual relations, but such a threat does not involve violence and is not a criminal action.

Determining whether coercion is involved in an incident is particularly difficult when there is a power differential between source and target. Consider sexual relationships between male faculty and female students. A female student may be attracted to a male professor because of his high occupational status, and she appeals to him because of her youth. Or she may be motivated to reap some benefit, such as a recommendation or a better grade. Either person may initiate this voluntary exchange. When he initiates, there may be an implicit threat of negative consequences if she does not comply. She may feel threatened whether it is his intent to threaten her or not. Only when he intends for her to feel threatened is he engaged in a coercive action. Estimates of frequency of sexual coercion are usually based on the accounts of female victims. These are much higher than estimates that are based on self-reports from men. Perhaps men underreport coercive incidents because they are unwilling to acknowledge that they have engaged in antisocial behaviors. It is also possible that females overreport. To some degree, these differences may be due to differences in interpretation of sexual episodes.

Whether an intimate touch is perceived as coercive by targets will depend in part on whether they see the behavior as legitimate. The behavior will be labeled differently depending on whether or not it is performed by someone perceived as having a right to make a sexual bid. The same behavior may be considered normal lovemaking, an annoyance, or a sexual assault, depending on the context. Furthermore, women are likely to differ in their tolerance of persistence and pressure. When a woman believes a man has pushed too far, she is likely to feel that she is being coerced or assaulted. In addition, labeling a sexual episode *coercive* may also help women avoid any blame for behavior that they regret afterward. These factors may lead women to report incidents that were not coercive, given the man's intentions. Recall from chapter 6 that it is the actor's point of view that is crucial in defining coercive actions.

A number of studies have described the methods people use to influence others to have sexual relations. In one study (Sorenson, Stein, Siegel, Golding, & Burnam, 1987), data were obtained from 3,132 adult residents in Los Angeles. Men and women were asked whether anyone had tried to pressure or force them to have sexual contact. About 17% of the women and 9% of the men reported that they had been pressured or forced to have sex during their lives. The most recent incident typically involved someone they knew (79%). Persuasion—a noncoercive method—was most frequently used. Men were more likely to be targets of persuasion, whereas women were much more likely to be targets of coercive behaviors, such as threatened harm and physical restraint.[14]

Koss et al. (1987) conducted a study of sexual coercion among a large national sample of college students. Respondents were questioned about sexual experiences they had had since they were 14 years old. About 44% of the college women reported that they had "given in to sex play (fondling, kissing, or petting, but not intercourse) when you didn't want to because you were overwhelmed by a man's continual arguments and pressure" (p. 167). As indicated above, these incidents more often involve persuasion than coercion. A smaller percentage of college women (13%) reported having engaged in an incident of sex play "because a man threatened or used some degree of physical force (twisting your arm, holding you down, etc.) to make you." Nine percent reported that they had engaged in sexual intercourse in response to physical force.

The fact that the respondents were asked about "unwanted sexual relations" may have led to the inclusion of both coercive and noncoercive incidents. Women's resistance in most cases of unwanted sexual activity is minimal (Murnen, Perot, & Byrne, 1989). Thus, the level of coercion in the incidents involving bodily force may be low. In addition, women who would have preferred to abstain may have decided to comply for various other reasons. They may have wished to avoid a scene, may have felt some obligation, or may have wished to satisfy their partner. People do many things out of obligation that they would prefer not to do. According to an unpublished study, how women respond to items measuring unwanted sexual activity depends on the wording of the question and the context provided (Leonard Martin, personal communication, 1993). Women were much more likely to respond affirmatively to a question about whether they engaged in unwanted sex when the question was placed with items about doing favors for people than when the question was placed with items about

---

[14]Unfortunately, Sorenson, Stein, Siegel, Golding, and Burnam (1987) did not provide information on the gender of the person who engaged in these behaviors, so it is unclear from the data whether women sometimes used coercion against men.

coercion. The placement of the item did not affect men, many of whom had also engaged in unwanted sex.[15] In fact, Muehlenhard and Cook (1987) found that men were as likely as women to report that they had engaged in unwanted sexual activity.

Ambiguities regarding whether coercion is involved in sexual relations prevent one from having much confidence in estimates of rates of rape or sexual coercion among people who know each other. It is likely that the National Crime Survey underestimates the frequency of rape but that Koss (1992) and others grossly overestimate it. Future research should elicit more detailed information on the context of these incidents.

Miscommunication About Female Sexual Interest

To some degree, sexual coercion may result from miscommunications about female sexual interest. Research has shown that men who engage in sexual coercion are less able to discriminate friendly from seductive behavior (Lipton, McDonel, & McFall, 1987; Murphy, Coleman, & Haynes, 1986). Research also has indicated that men overestimate women's interest in sex. This leads men to inaccurately interpret women's friendliness as sexual interest (Abbey, 1982; Muehlenhard, 1988; L. Shotland & Craig, 1988).[16] L. Shotland and Craig attributed the gender difference in the perception of sexual intent to "male's greater sexual appetite, which the male uses as a model for the attribution of the appetites of others" (1988, p. 66).

Miscommunication is likely to occur in dating situations when a man expects that a woman is interested in consensual sexual activity and she is not. Thus, Koss, Dinero, Seibel, and Cox (1988) found that slightly over 50% of incidents that they described as acquaintance rape and 20.5% of stranger rapes were described by the victims as involving miscommunication. Miscommunications occur in part because men and women do not openly communicate about the level of sexual activity desired (Weis & Borges, 1973). Misunderstandings also arise because women sometimes engage in token resistance. Also, a woman may avoid expressing a firm refusal because she does not want to insult a man. Thus, the interaction ritual described by Goffman (1955) may result in miscommunication and coercion.

---

[15]Another potential problem is the sponsorship of the study by Ms. magazine, which was mentioned on the cover page of the survey. Perhaps the feminist sponsor led men to underreport incidents or women to exaggerate the level of coercion that they experienced or to reinterpret noncoercive incidents as coercive.

[16]Some convicted rapists reported that their victims wanted to engage in sexual relations (Scully & Marolla, 1985). If these rapists really believed that the women were willing, then they were not engaged in coercion. However, the excuses and justifications offered by criminal offenders are unreliable. Why would an offender use weapons and physical force if the victim actually was a willing participant?

Miscommunications may lead women to perceive a given sexual episode as aggressive and illegitimate, whereas men may believe it was consensual. If a man does not view his own behavior as aggressive, then the usual inhibitions about the use of coercion will not be activated. However, if the woman continues to resist strongly, it seems likely that he would realize that she is unwilling.

The expectations of men play an important role in miscommunication. Men are more likely to use coercion when they expect a woman to engage in sexual activity and she resists. Therefore, attitudes or situational factors that lead men to expect sexual activity may result in sexual coercion. Goodchilds and Zellman (1984) and Muehlenhard (1988) found that male adolescents expected female adolescents to engage in sex if they had a reputation for having had sex with others, if they wore provocative clothing, or if they agreed to go to certain settings. Male adolescents also assumed a female adolescent was interested in sex if she talked about sex or commented on her date's appearance. These sexual signals had similar meanings for male and female adolescents.

Male expectations may help explain why sexual coercion is more likely to occur when some sexual activity has occurred but the woman attempts to limit it. Expectations may also be affected by exchange processes. Some men are likely to expect sexual activity when they have spent a large amount of money on a date or when they have given women gifts.

If women who are uninterested in sexual activity give sexual signals or engage in sexually provocative behavior, men are more likely to engage in sexual coercion. Evidence for this relationship was found in a study in which college women were asked whether they had ever been sexually aggressive and offended a male companion by their "forward or provocative behavior" (Kanin & Parcell, 1977). Approximately one out of four women answered affirmatively, and those who did were more likely to report having been the target of sexual coercion by men.

GRIEVANCES, SOCIAL CONTROL, AND SEXUAL COERCION

In chapter 8 we examined the development of grievances and the conditions under which they lead to coercive actions. The grievant attributes blame to another person for an antinormative action and may attempt to restore justice by punishing the offender. From the point of view of the offender, the victim has committed some wrongful act and deserves to be punished: The punishment is an act of personal justice and the harm to the victim just desserts.

To test the personal grievance explanation, it is necessary to determine whether men who commit acts of sexual coercion feel aggrieved toward the victim prior to the act. Men who engage in sexual coercion for this reason are likely to have been involved in a conflict with the victim beforehand. The social interaction is likely to be similar to interactions leading to homicides and assaults, in which verbal conflict escalates, culminating in physical and sexual attacks. It is also possible that men feel aggrieved when women resist their noncoercive attempts to encourage sexual activity and then use sexual coercion as punishment.

In chapter 8 we showed that grievances are much more likely to arise in coercive incidents involving people who know each other than in incidents involving strangers. If sexual coercion is a form of retribution, then it should be associated with conflict between couples who are married, estranged, or involved in a romantic or sexual relationship. Sexual coercion could be expected to be particularly common among estranged couples where the woman is no longer receptive to a sexual relationship. Men may also use sexual coercion to punish women for some insult, for ending their relationship, for some alleged infidelity, or for some petty grievance.

In this section, we examine the hypothesis that sexual coercion involves grievances and social control. We consider the offender's use of force during incidents of sexual coercion to understand his motivation. We then consider whether sexual coercion involves grievances against women generally or against some other social category. Finally, we examine whether sexual coercion may be condoned by society as a method for controlling all women.

Punishment Versus the Tactical Use of Force

The tactical use of force—or coercion oriented toward immediate compliance—is involved in all incidents of sexual coercion. The offender uses contingent threats or bodily force, and, if the victim complies, no further force is necessary.[17] One would expect men whose goal is sexual compliance to use only tactical force. They would not physically attack the victim or engage in any act of punishment unless it was useful for achieving compliance. On the other hand, if offenders punish victims during incidents of sexual coercion for reasons that are not tactical, it suggests that they feel aggrieved and that they value harm and not compliance.[18] In other words, the motive of retributive justice is revealed when the level of punishment during the incident is greater than is necessary to gain compliance.

There are a variety of tactical reasons why an offender physically attacks victims. The offender may attack victims who resist or may engage

---

[17]The strategy may also involve noncoercive elements. For example, the offender may use various techniques to gain the confidence of the target and give himself an opportunity to use coercion (A. W. Burgess & Holstrom, 1974).

[18]It is possible that aggrieved men limit their punishment to sexual coercion. Nevertheless, a grievance hypothesis would predict that nontactical violence is more likely when the offender values punishment rather than compliance.

in a preemptive attack to increase the credibility of their threat.[19] Physical attacks may be used to frighten the victim and deter the victim from reporting the crime to the police. In some instances, the victim may be killed to prevent her from testifying in criminal proceedings.

These tactics are similar to the tactics described for robbery in chapter 7. There are some tactical differences between rape and robbery, however.[20] First, a rape requires more time, closer proximity, and more bodily exposure than a robbery. The rapist therefore has a greater risk of being identified than a robber, who "takes the money and runs." Second, rape requires compliance from the victim for a series of acts, whereas robbery requires a single act of compliance. Rape offenders sometimes use violence to force victims to take a more active role during the rape (MacDonald, 1971). The evidence suggests that rape victims often engage in passive resistance. Koss et al. (1988) found that over 70% of rape victims reported that they resisted the rape by "turning cold" during the incident.

In general, the evidence indicates that violence is used sparingly in incidents of sexual coercion (Amir, 1971). Ageton (1983) found that only a small proportion of adolescents use much physical force during incidents of sexual coercion. Studies of the National Crime Survey also indicated that rapes produce relatively few serious physical injuries (BJS, 1985). Finally, sexual coercion among college students rarely involves a physical attack (Koss et al., 1987). These studies suggest that most men who engage in sexual coercion do not feel angry and aggrieved.

If nontactical violence reflects an expression of grievances, then it should be more frequent during incidents of sexual coercion among estranged couples and others who know each other. A number of studies have provided support for this hypothesis (e.g., Koss et al., 1988). R. B. Felson and Krohn (1990) found that victims were more likely to be physically injured in rapes involving married couples. In most of these rapes, the husband and wife were separated (Finklehor & Yllo, 1985). Presumably, the offender rapes and beats up his ex-wife or girlfriend as an act of punishment.

Rapes involving older offenders more often involve nontactical violence (R. B. Felson & Krohn, 1990). The positive association between age and violence is striking given that youth are much more violent during other crimes and in other contexts (Gottfredson & Hirschi, 1990). A plausible explanation is that grievances are more likely to play a role in rapes involving older offenders, whereas a sexual goal is more likely in rapes

---

[19]Recall that in robbery, a victim is less likely to be injured if the offender has a weapon (and presumably, a credible threat). In rape, however, victims are more likely to be injured if the offender is armed (R. B. Felson & Krohn, 1990).

[20]An offender usually does not injure the victim so much that she is incapable of complying with his orders. In robbery, offenders who require compliant actions by a victim—to open a safe, for example—also limit their use of force (Luckenbill, 1980).

involving younger offenders. Thus, incidents involving younger offenders with presumably greater sexual interests tend to involve less nontactical violence.

Offenders with sexual goals should choose younger victims because they are more likely to be physically attractive. Thus, the level of nontactical violence should be higher against older victims than younger victims. In support of this line of reasoning, R. B. Felson and Krohn (1990) found that older victims were more likely to be physically injured during a rape than younger victims.

An offender motivated by a grievance might be expected to express his anger by insulting, humiliating, and mistreating the victim in a variety of ways, even when she is in full compliance. No one has ever examined how men who engage in sexual coercion behave toward compliant female victims. Holmstrom and Burgess (1979) reported 20 instances of "obscene names or racial epithets" and instances of "sexual put-downs" in a study of 115 female victims of rape but did not obtain information on whether these were reactions to the victim's behavior. In 19 instances, offenders either apologized, socialized, or attempted to help the victim after raping her. MacDonald (1971) also reported incidents in which rape offenders engaged in acts of tenderness normally associated with consensual sex. In some rape incidents, offenders force victims to engage in oral–genital sex and repeated intercourse—acts that Amir (1971) referred to as *humiliating*. However, there is no reason to believe that offenders engage in these behaviors to humiliate the victim—these are common sexual practices. In 91% of the rapes studied by Amir, offenders let the victim go immediately after the rape; in the other cases, victims were usually held captive for tactical reasons.

An offender might become aggrieved during a crime. The victim's behavior during the interaction could anger the offender and lead him to additional attacks. When rapists are asked how a victim made them angry, the most frequent responses were negative references to their masculinity (15%), threats to call the police (8%), threatened physical harm (6%), and sympathetic talking (5%; Chappell & James, 1976). Some of these responses are likely to lead rapists to retaliate to restore their sense of justice and defend their social identities.

Generalized Grievances Against Women and Other Groups

It is possible that men who use sexual coercion have grievances against a woman other than the target and that the incident is an instance of displacement or target substitution. A rapist could be angry at his mother, his wife, or his girlfriend and displace his attack onto another woman. But why would the men displace their aggression rather than attack the source of their grievance? Perhaps high costs would be associated with attacks on the women they know. Scully and Marolla (1985) reported that some of the male rapists they interviewed attributed their attack on a stranger to their anger with a girlfriend (see also N. A. Groth & Birnbaum, 1979). It is difficult to evaluate this type of evidence because we do not know how frequently convicted rapists give this explanation.

Men may have generalized grievances against the social category of which the female victim is a member. In other words, they may be angry at women generally, and they may express their grievances through sexual coercion. The evidence is mixed concerning the relationship between male sexual coercion and hostility toward women (A. H. Buss & Durkee, 1957; Craig, Kalichman, & Follingstad, 1989; Koss & Dinero, 1987; Rada, Laws, & Kellner, 1976; Scully & Marolla, 1985). However, even if a relationship between hostility toward women and rape were found, it would not necessarily imply that sexual coercion is an expression of general hostility toward women. Negative attitudes toward women may reduce men's inhibitions about using sexual coercion rather than instigate the coercive behavior (Malamuth, 1986). The hypothesis that a man with a sexual goal might use coercive means because he lacks concern for women is discussed further below.

We are generally skeptical of explanations of interpersonal violence that emphasize hatred for groups. Most homicides and assaults are committed against victims whom offenders believe have engaged in some provocation. In spite of recent emphasis on bias crimes (crimes based on group prejudice), such incidents are quite rare (Bureau of Justice Statistical Services, 1993). If bias toward out-groups was associated with the use of coercion, then one might expect a high level of interracial crime based on group prejudices. Most crimes in the United States, however, including rape, are intraracial.

If interracial rapes reflect prejudice, then one would expect that White men would frequently rape Black women. However, the incidence of Whites raping Blacks is extremely rare: About 3% of rapes committed by White men target Black women, according to the National Crime Survey (South & Felson, 1990). Its rarity suggests the possibility that prejudice leads Whites to avoid sexual relations with Blacks. Alternatively, about 40% of rapes committed by Black men target White women. It has been suggested in the literature that interracial rapes by Blacks reflect hatred for Whites (e.g., O'Brien, 1987). This work usually cites the admission of the radical Black author and activist Eldreage Cleaver that he raped White women when he was a young man to obtain vengeance against White men (Cleaver, 1968). The evidence does not support the idea that such motivation is common among Blacks. South and Felson (1990) found that the level of interracial rape was unrelated to the level of interracial conflict or inequality in metropolitan areas (see also O'Brien, 1987). Rather, the racial patterning of rape was related to the opportunities for personal contact between Blacks and Whites.

Sexual Coercion as Generalized Social Control

Some feminists have argued that the function of sexual coercion is to control women and keep them in traditional roles. A patriarchal social context supposedly encourages coercive behavior against women. Brownmiller (1975) argued that rape is "a conscious process of intimidation by which all men keep all women in a state of fear" (p. 5). The male genitals were the vehicle of man's original conquest of women, according to Brownmiller. Because of their fears of an open season of rape, women became dependent and were "domesticated" by protective mating. In exchange for protection, women became the property of men and men passed laws against rape to protect their property. Just as Samson's hair was the source of his power, for Brownmiller, male genitals are the source of their power over women. Men use this "weapon" in rape, whereas women are disadvantaged because they cannot retaliate in kind.[21]

For any form of punishment to act as a social control mechanism, there must be clear rules about its application. If sexual coercion is to serve as a sanction, it must be directed at the rule violator, not randomly at all women. Otherwise, it cannot be used as a deterrent to proscribed behaviors. In addition, the fact that women restrict their activities because of fear of rape does not necessarily imply that rape was somehow designed for this purpose. Men also restrict their activities to avoid criminal victimization.

Brownmiller (1975) does not explain how patriarchy leads an individual rapist to do his job. For rape to operate as social control, its use must be legitimated, at least among men, and it must not be viewed as a criminal act deserving of severe punishment. Group rape is perceived as legitimate in the societies described above and is prescribed as a social control mechanism. That such a pattern is rarely observed in most societies suggests that rape is generally not a social control mechanism developed by men to control women. The societies that use group rape are exceptions that prove the rule.

SEXUAL COERCION AND SOCIAL IDENTITIES

In chapter 9 we emphasized the role of power in discussing the effect of social identities on coercion. We suggested that those who engage in coercion sometimes seek to display power. In the case of sexual coercion, a man may seek to demonstrate power by dominating a woman. The idea that men use sexual coercion because it gives them a feeling of power, control, or dominance over women is a popular one (e.g., Allison &

---

[21]For a review of criticisms of Brownmiller's (1975) conspiracy theory, see Geis (1977).

Wrightsman, 1993; Deming & Eppy, 1981; N. A. Groth & Birnbaum, 1979).[22]

Sexual coercion could involve either an assertive or a protective form of self-presentation. In the case of assertive self-presentation, a man may attempt to impress some audiences with his power by bullying women or he may demonstrate power to the woman he is bullying. For most audiences, this attempt at self-promotion is not likely to be effective. Men who attack women are likely to be perceived as cowardly rather than powerful.[23] In the case of protective self-presentation, a man who perceives that he has been attacked by a woman may use sexual coercion in retaliation. For example, when women reject a sexual overture, some men may perceive it as an attack on their identity and may counterattack by using sexual coercion.[24]

To display power, a person must influence the target to do something they would not do otherwise. Therefore, sexually coercive men who are power oriented should show a preference for using coercion and overcoming resistance. They should initiate sexual activity with women who they expect will resist. When initiating sexual relations with someone they know, these men should use coercive techniques as a first rather than a last resort. However, the evidence cited earlier shows that coercion is used along with noncoercive techniques in incidents involving people who know each other and that coercion is probably not used as a first resort. The evidence is more consistent with the hypothesis that most men in coercive incidents value sexual satisfaction, not power.

N. A. Groth et al. (1977) classified 65% of their sample of convicted rapists as motivated by power, but they gave no evidence to distinguish power from sexual motivation (see Palmer, 1988, for a critique of their classification). Malamuth (1986) found a relationship between scores on a sexual dominance scale and self-reported sexual coercion, but it was weak and only appeared when complex interaction terms were included in the regression equation. In addition, the items in the measure of sexual dominance appeared to refer to sexual pleasure associated with dominance rather than to social identities (e.g., "I enjoy the feeling of having someone in my grasp").

Interviews with male rapists have indicated that they generally prefer acquiescence once they have made their intent known (Chappell & James, 1976). The overwhelming majority (78%) indicated that they desired the

---

[22]By definition, all acts of coercion involve power and domination. When individuals impose outcomes on other people they are exercising power, and, if they are successful, they dominate their antagonists. However, the description of an action is not the same thing as its goal or motive.

[23]Retaliation may also be an attempt to recover self-esteem, which would not be affected by the presence of an audience.

[24]Recall from chapter 8 that retaliatory attacks may also be motivated by retributive justice and deterrence.

victim "to give up and agree to anything." In addition, most rapists did not mention dominance as their motivation for committing the crime (Feild, 1978; Yegidis, 1986). Rapists were much more likely to mention sexual motivation or the desire for excitement. However, in Scully and Marolla's (1985) study, some rapists reported that they enjoyed the power they exercised over their victims. In Chappell and James's (1976) study, 12% said that they preferred a woman to plead during the rape.

Power could be defined more broadly to refer to the male pursuit of many sexual partners. Men could view their ability to attract women as an accomplishment or an achievement. This type of thinking is reflected in the concepts of "scoring" and the use of baseball metaphors to represent levels of sexual activity: for example, "getting to first base," "second base," and so on. In this context, it seems likely that men would view consensual rather than coercive sexual activity as an accomplishment. A man does not demonstrate his attractiveness to women if he must use coercion to find sexual partners.[25]

The achievement aspect of sexual relations for men is probably related to gender differences in sexuality. Because most women require some positive feeling or evaluation for a man before engaging in sexual activity, their decision to engage in sexual relations reveals their positive evaluation of him. By engaging in sexual behavior, a woman confers a special status on a man. A man is thus able to increase his status by having sexual relations with attractive women. This strategy is not as useful for women, because men are much less discriminating about sexual partners. When a man has a sexual liaison with a woman, it does not necessarily imply that he holds her in high regard.[26]

In summary, although the evidence is extremely limited, it is plausible that sexual coercion is sometimes motivated by a desire for power or a desire to appear powerful. In several accounts, a relatively small percentage of rapists indicated that power played a role in their crime. In addition, if power is a value in some incidents of nonsexual coercion, then it seems likely that it is a value in at least some incidents of sexual coercion as well.

FACILITATORS AND INHIBITORS

Most men have sexual interests, are concerned for their identities, and have at least an occasional grievance with a woman, yet relatively few engage in sexual coercion. As was suggested in previous chapters, other situational and individual factors contribute to a decision to use coercion.

---

[25]A man could report a sexual liaison to his friends and fail to mention the coercive aspect. But then, if he is going to lie about the coercion, he could just as easily lie about the sexual activity, saying it occurred when it did not.

[26]However, both men and women may get some ego gratification from sexual relations.

In this section we examine situational factors, such as the costs of sexual coercion for the perpetrator and the opportunities he has to engage in the behavior. We include a discussion of research purporting to show what men would do if there were no costs. Then we consider individual factors, including attitudes toward women, attitudes toward coercion, and more general predispositions that disinhibit various forms of criminal and deviant behavior generally. In this discussion, we evaluate the question of whether men who engage in sexual coercion are specialists who target women or are generalists who use coercion against targets of both sexes.

Costs of Sexual Coercion

In chapter 7 we noted that the target may impose costs on a coercive actor. Because the perpetrator in sexual coercion is likely to have superior coercive resources—either a weapon or greater physical strength—the costs to the perpetrator of direct retaliation by the target are usually low. Although women often resist rape, their actions appear to be oriented toward avoiding victimization rather than harming the offender (McDermott, 1979). When a man targets a woman he knows, he may destroy their relationship, and this may be perceived as a cost. However, recall the evidence that in many instances men and women continue to have a sexual relationship after an incident of sexual coercion. If women respond mildly to certain forms of sexual coercion, then the cost for male perpetrators is low.

Costs can be imposed on perpetrators by third parties, such as kin or the criminal justice system. In some cultures, when a man physically assaults a woman, she can rely on other men, usually her kin, to punish the perpetrator on her behalf (Baumgartner, 1993). The anticipation of such costs should inhibit coercive actions by men against women. R. A. Levine (1959) attributed an increase in rape among the Gusii of southwestern Kenya in part to the intervention of British law, which led to less severe penalties for interclan rape. Where formerly a rape or abduction might have resulted in a feud, bringing possible death to the offender and his clansmen, British law brought an assault charge carrying a fine. Likewise, the high frequency of rape of civilians in war zones may be due to its low cost; soldiers may be able to engage in rape without fear of punishment from authorities.

In most societies, rape is punished severely. A cross-cultural survey of 110 societies from the Human Relations Area Files showed that rape is one of the three most heavily punished crimes, with punishment ranging from payment of compensation to death (J. S. Brown, 1952). At the present time, sentences for rape in the United States are at least as severe as sentences for homicide and other violent crimes.

Brownmiller (1975) has provided evidence suggesting that historically it has been difficult to prosecute men who have been accused of rape. She interprets this difficulty as due to the issue of consent. The accused may admit to sexual relations but may claim it was consensual. There may be no eye witnesses, physical injury, or other corroborative evidence. The difficulty in prosecuting rape may reflect the nature of the crime rather than male attitudes toward women: It is often her word against his.

Many of these difficulties exist in the prosecution of other types of crimes. Actually, the arrest and conviction rates for rape are comparable to the arrest and conviction rates for other crimes in the United States. About 52% of rapes known to the police in 1991 resulted in arrests (BJS, 1993). Only arrest rates for homicide and assault were higher than arrest rates for rape. In large, urban counties in 1990, 56% of rape defendants were convicted (BJS, 1993). This conviction rate was slightly lower than conviction rates for murder and robbery but was higher than rates for assault. The evidence points to the difficulty in prosecuting crime in general in American society, not to a tolerance of rape among male officials of the criminal justice system.

Many rapes are not reported to the police, particularly when they involve people who know each other. However, rapes are reported to the police more often than some other crimes. According to the National Crime Survey, rape is more likely to be reported to the police than robbery without injury or simple assault with injury (BJS, 1983). Victims give a wide variety of reasons for not reporting rape to the police; many of the reasons are the same as those given by victims of other crimes.[27] Whatever the reason, men who rape are as likely to avoid prosecution as men who commit other crimes. The expectation of low costs increases the likelihood of all crimes.

What If There Were No Costs for Rape?

Malamuth (1981) argued that many men have a proclivity to rape and are only inhibited by the anticipated costs. He based this conclusion on a series of studies in which men (mostly college students) were asked to estimate the likelihood that they personally would rape if they could be assured of not being caught and punished. Subjects responded on a 5-point scale ranging from *not at all likely* (1) to *very likely* (5). Across studies, Malamuth and his colleagues found that an average of 35% of college men answered 2 or above and 20% answered 3 or above. Because a fair number of men did not absolutely rule out the possibility that they could commit this crime, Malamuth claimed that the data showed that many men have a proclivity to rape.

A measure based on respondents' estimations of how they would behave under hypothetical and unrealistic conditions must be viewed with

---

[27]The three most common reasons given by the victim for not reporting are (a) the rape was a private matter, (b) nothing could be done or there was a lack of proof, and (c) fear of reprisal.

great skepticism. Scores on these measures were either uncorrelated or only slightly correlated ($r = .15$) with a self-report measure of sexual aggression (Greendlinger & Byrne, 1987; Malamuth & Check, 1981).[28] In addition, there was no attempt to compare the likelihood measure for rape with likelihood measures for other crimes, to see if some men have a special proclivity to rape. Finally, it is unclear how subjects may have interpreted the question. Martin (personal communication, 1993) found that responses to the likelihood measure depended on the context in which it is presented. He was able to replicate Malamuth's results when he placed the likelihood measure after items concerning sexual activity. When the measure was placed after items focusing on aggression and force, fewer respondents indicated any likelihood of engaging in rape.

The results given above may be intrepreted as indicating that a fair number of men—perhaps not as many as Malamuth suggested—are not so mortified by the thought of rape that they would rule it out completely. In fact, rape is not so repugnant to some men and women that they do not fantasize about it. Loren and Weeks (1986) found that about 39% of college students of both genders reported that they fantasized about forced sexual activity. We think it would be a mistake to take fantasies or responses to fantasy situations seriously as evidence about human behavior.

Opportunities for Sexual Coercion

According to the routine activity approach, discussed in chapter 5, crime is more likely when routine activities draw together motivated offenders and suitable targets in the absence of capable guardians (L. E. Cohen & Felson, 1979). Variation in crime rates over time and across space are traced to factors that produce contact between potential offenders and victims and reduce surveillance.[29] On the basis of this theory, sexual coercion should be more likely when there is greater contact between young men and women and when adults are not present to chaperone. Thus, women who "date around" are considerably more likely to be targets of sexual coercion (Kanin & Parcell, 1977). During consensual, noncoital sex there may be a greater opportunity for coercion because women may attempt to limit the level of intimacy.

The availability of cars provides opportunities for both consensual and coercive sexual encounters. Activities that draw women outside the home, particularly at night, may put them at risk. Thus, McDermott (1979) found much higher rates of rape victimization among women who spend much of their time outside the home than among women who are homemakers.

---

[28]They also correlate slightly with laboratory and self-report measures of aggression against women.
[29]Surveillance also increases the likelihood of costs to the perpetrator.

Amir (1971) found that the street is most frequently the contact point for rapists and victims and that most rapes occur at night.

According to R. A. Levine (1959), spatial segregation of the sexes and lack of privacy are important inhibitors of rape. Chaperonage, veiled seclusion of women, and separate schooling inhibit both consensual and coercive sexual relations. Levine attributed the increase in rape among the Gusii not only to low penalties but also to increased contact between unmarried people of different clans, because of rapid population growth and British pacification. He suggested that when structural barriers preventing contact between men and women are lowered, socialized inhibitions become more important. If both men and women are uninhibited, then promiscuity results. If only women are inhibited, then rape is more likely to occur.[30]

In cultures where women are sexually uninhibited and there is promiscuity, women will still avoid sexual relations with some men, creating an incentive for coercion. High levels of promiscuity do not necessarily imply that women are as indiscriminate as men in their sexual relations. In addition, male expectations for sexual activity may be higher in cultures with high levels of promiscuity, which may increase the likelihood of coercion when women are resistant. Finally, consensual sexual activity creates opportunities for sexual coercion, as we indicated earlier.

Attitudes Toward the Target

In chapter 8 it was suggested that a negative attitude toward the target is likely to facilitate or disinhibit the use of coercion when an actor is motivated to engage in coercion. Thus, one might expect that a sexually motivated man might use sexual coercion against a target he does not respect.[31] There is some evidence that men are more likely to use sexual coercion against women that they consider to be deviant. Amir (1971) found that about 20% of the rape victims he studied had "bad reputations," whereas another 20% had police records, many of them for sexual misconduct. It may be that women with bad reputations are more likely to have contact with potential rape offenders. However, Kanin (1985) found evidence that deviant targets are preferred over other targets. Relatively few men (7%–9%) believed that their best friends would respond favorably if they knew that the respondent attempted to coerce a "more or less regular date" to have sexual intercourse. On the other hand, the percentages were much higher for "bar pick-ups," "known teasers," "economic exploiters,"

---

[30]Levine (1959) assumed that there are no cultures in which women are uninhibited and men are inhibited.

[31]It could also be argued that if he dislikes her, he is less likely to find her attractive and, therefore, less likely to want sexual relations with her.

and women with "loose reputations." Eighty-one percent of rapists and 40% of a control group indicated that they would get a positive response from their friends if the woman was a known teaser.

Note that these deviant categories are all at least indirectly related to sexual behavior. It may be that women who violate sexual norms are more likely to be targeted as rape victims.[32] Some men may believe that rape is justifiable against women who violate sexual norms. They may have lower respect for promiscuous women, they may wrongly assume that these women are willing to engage in sexual relations, they may be insulted when their advances are resisted, and they may use the target's bad reputation to justify their behavior. The costs of harming deviant women may be lower than the costs of harming other women because the reactions of third parties—including the reaction of the criminal justice system—are likely to be less severe. Whatever the reason, there is evidence that women who violate sexual norms tend to be preferred as targets of sexual coercion.

There is an alternative explanation for why deviant targets are preferred. It may be that some men feel personally aggrieved against deviant women and attempt to punish them for their alleged wrongdoing. In this case, the actor values harm, and his attitude toward the target plays a instigating role rather than a facilitative role. This explanation is inconsistent with the evidence that men do not usually engage in nontactical violence and that sexual goals are important in sexual coercion.

Attitudes Toward Women

In the section on grievances, we discussed the possibility that men with negative attitudes toward women generally feel aggrieved and might use sexual coercion as a form of punishment. Another possibility is that men with sexual goals are disinhibited about using coercion if they have negative attitudes toward women. They may have a lack of concern for women, a tendency to view women as sex objects, a belief that women want to be raped, or some other attitude related to women. The evidence that so-called sexist attitudes affect sexual coercion is inconsistent. Some studies found that rape offenders and college men who either engaged in sexual coercion or indicated a likelihood of engaging in rape were more likely than other men to have callous attitudes toward women, to accept rape myths, and to believe in a double standard for male and female sexual behavior (Kanin, 1969; Malamuth, 1986; see Koss & Leonard, 1984; Malamuth, 1981, for reviews). Other studies did not find that men who had committed date rape subscribed to more rape myths or had more traditional

---

[32]The category that seems the least likely to be related to sexual behavior is the "economic exploiter." However, these young, unmarried respondents may have interpreted this category to mean a woman who feigns sexual interest to encourage men to spend money on her.

attitudes toward sex roles (Ageton, 1983; Craig et al., 1989; Rapaport & Burkhart, 1984). In addition, convicted rapists are similar to men convicted of other offenses in their attitudes toward women and women's rights (Howells & Wright, 1978; Kozma & Zuckerman, 1983) and in their belief in rape myths (E. R. Hall, Howard, & Boezio, 1986).

There are measurement problems with the items in the scale measuring belief in rape myths. Myths are false but widely held beliefs, and it is not clear from the research which of the beliefs are widely held (Burt, 1980). Furthermore, not all of the beliefs included in these scales are false (L. Ellis, 1989). For example, there is evidence that both men and women believe that a woman who goes to a man's home on a date where they will be alone is giving a signal that she is willing to have sex (Goodchilds & Zellman, 1984). Finally, the scale was not unidimensional. Briere, Malamuth, and Check (1985) identified four factors in this scale through factor analysis and labeled the two dominant ones *Disbelief of Rape Claims* and *Victim Responsible for Rape.* It is unclear which, if any, of these factors is associated with sexual coercion.

Feminists and others have argued that sexist attitudes are partially learned from pornography (e.g., Dworkin, 1981; MacKinnon, 1984). Exposure to pornography supposedly leads to negative attitudes toward women, which, in turn, affects the likelihood of sexual coercion. Recall that the evidence from chapter 3 does not support this conclusion. The experimental evidence indicates that exposure to nonviolent pornography has no effects on behavior toward women. Effects of violent pornography have been reported in laboratory experiments, but they occur only under highly circumscribed conditions. As we suggested earlier, if violent pornography is shown to affect sexual coercion outside the laboratory, then it probably is due to the violence and not the sexual content of the pornography. Finally, correlational data have indicated that men who are interested in pornography have more (not less) liberal attitudes toward gender roles (Reiss, 1986).

One problem in the attitude research is the assumption that traditional attitudes about gender roles and negative attitudes toward woman are equivalent. Men who believe in a traditional division of labor do not necessarily hold women in low regard. Such people are likely to have religious and other traditional views that inhibit sexual coercion and sexual relations outside of marriage in general. Rape rates are twice as high at private colleges and major universities than they are at religiously affiliated institutions (Koss et al., 1987).

Even if a correlation between certain attitudes regarding women and sexual coercion could be established, the causal interpretation would be unclear. One interpretation is that men express certain beliefs to justify coercive behavior already performed (Koss, Leonard, Beezley, & Oros, 1985). It is well known that people who engage in deviant behavior usually provide accounts for the behavior afterward (e.g., G. Sykes & Matza, 1961):

A rapist's report that the victim "enjoyed it" serves to justify his behavior. The problematic causal interpretation is well known in the attitude–behavior literature. Longitudinal research is necessary to determine whether such beliefs do in fact have a causal impact on coercive sexual behavior.

If attitudes toward women do affect sexual coercion, then it is not clear whether they act as instigators or as disinhibitors. If a man who feels aggrieved toward women uses sexual coercion to punish them, then his hostility instigates the attack. Alternatively, a man may have a sexual or identity-related goal, and he may feel justified in using coercion because of his hostility toward women (Malamuth, 1986). If hostility toward women facilitates sexual coercion, then one would expect to find statistical interactions between attitudes and goals in their effect on behavior (Malamuth, 1986). For example, one might predict the relationship between sexual aspirations and sexual coercion to be stronger when men have negative attitudes toward women. Conversely, if attitudes toward women have only main effects on sexual coercion, then hostility probably instigates rather than disinhibits. Support for the interaction model comes from work by Malamuth (1986), who found that the effect of sexual arousal to rape scenes on sexual coercion depended on various attitudes of the subjects.

Aggregate Data

Using aggregate data, some researchers have examined the relationship between attitudes toward women and the frequency of rape. Sanday (1981) coded 95 tribal societies according to the frequency of rape. She found that societies with a high frequency of rape tended to be characterized by a high level of male dominance. When women had political or economic power, had public influence, or were respected as citizens, rape rates tended to be lower. Reiss (1986) also reported a correlation between a belief in the inferiority of women and the frequency of rape across cultures.[33] These studies indicate that gender roles and the status of women do have effects on the incidence of sexual coercion, at least in tribal societies. Whether the low status of women is a disinhibitor or instigator of sexual coercion is still unclear, however.

Other researchers have used aggregate analyses to examine the effect of gender inequality on the frequency of rape in the United States. If gender inequality is associated with the subordination of women, then one would expect it to predict rapes and other forms of male violence against women. L. Baron and Straus (1987) found that states with high gender inequality were more likely to have high incidents of rape. Gender inequality was measured by a variety of indicators, such as the ratio of the median income

---

[33]Whether there is a cross-cultural correlation between the rape rate and the rates of other types of violence appears to depend on the measure used (Reiss, 1986; Sanday, 1981). The presence or absence of such a correlation does not reveal information about the motivation for rape.

of women to the median income of men and the percentage of women in the state legislature.

Results from two other studies cast doubt on L. Baron and Straus's (1987) conclusions. First, L. Ellis and Beattie (1983) found that rape rates in American cities were unrelated to sex disparities in education and oc-cupational status. Second, Messner (1991) replicated L. Baron and Straus's methods, substituting a state's homicide rate for the rape rate. If gender inequality is associated with efforts to subordinate women, then one would expect it to also predict homicides involving male offenders and female victims. Messner found that the level of gender inequality within a state predicted the homicide rate for homicides involving all gender combina-tions: male offenders–male victims, male offenders–female victims, female offenders–male victims, and female offenders–female victims. The strongest effect was observed for intragender homicides involving females. These results are inconsistent with the gender-inequality hypothesis.

Versatility of Rapists

If attitudes toward women play a role in rape, then one would expect rapists to have a history of crimes against women. However, the criminal records of those who have been convicted of rape tend to be similar to the criminal records of those convicted of other crimes (Alder, 1984; Krutt-schnitt, 1989). Most rapists do not specialize in rape or in violent crime. These findings are consistent with the evidence reviewed in chapter 5 showing that repeat offenders rarely specialize. Furthermore, the variables that predict sexual assault are the same variables that predict involvement in criminal behavior generally. Thus, the sociodemographic characteristics and family backgrounds of rapists tend to be similar to those of other types of offenders (Alder, 1984; Kruttschnitt, 1989). Ageton (1983) found that boys who commit sexual assault are more likely to associate with delinquent peers and are less likely to have close ties to their families. She also found that adolescents who engaged in sexual coercion engaged in other types of deviant and criminal behavior.

The versatility of rapists suggests that their crime has little or nothing to do with their attitudes toward women. Rape offenders engage in a wide variety of deviant and criminal behaviors. They use coercion, fraud, and other techniques to get what they want without consideration for people of either sex. The individual factors associated with rape may be the same individual factors associated with other forms of deviance and crime. Rapists may lack self-control, may value risk taking, or may lack certain moral inhibitions (see Gottfredson & Hirschi, 1990). Thus, E. R. Hall et al. (1986) found that men convicted of sexual assault were similar to men convicted of assault and armed robbery in having more antisocial attitudes than a control group (see also Rapaport & Burkhart, 1984).

Even if it turns out that attitudes toward women affect sexual coercion, this does not necessarily support the argument that rapists are specialists. Perhaps men who have negative attitudes toward women are likely to treat people more harshly, no matter what their gender. Evidence that negative attitudes toward a group are associated with the tendency to use coercion generally comes from the literature on how prejudice toward Blacks affects coercion (see chap. 8). Subjects who were prejudiced toward Blacks tended to give higher levels of shocks than subjects who were not prejudiced, whether the target was White or Black (Leonard & Taylor, 1981).

Men who use sexual coercion tend to have a more favorable attitude toward violence in general (e.g., Burt, 1980; Malamuth, Check, & Briere, 1986). Some researchers interpret this relationship as supporting the idea that the goal of sexual coercion is to harm or dominate the victim (e.g., Burt, 1980; Malamuth et al., 1986). However, attitudes toward coercion involve an attitude toward means (or procedural values) rather than an attitude toward goals. Thus, a man with a sexual goal and positive attitudes toward the use of force may be more likely to use coercion to influence others to have sexual relations.

Although versatility may be the rule, there are likely to be some men who specialize in particular forms of coercion. For those who specialize in sexual coercion, attitudes toward women may be a factor. Given the degree of body contact in sexual scripts, one might expect that there are men who engage in mild forms of bodily force who do not use coercion in other circumstances and do not engage in other forms of crime and deviance. Note that the evidence for versatility involves serious sexual assaults and does not necessarily apply to nonphysical forms of coercion.

SUMMARY AND CONCLUSIONS

There is considerable evidence that the goal of most acts of sexual coercion is to gain sexual gratification. Offenders have high sexual aspirations and almost always choose young women. When they know the victim, they use sexual coercion as a last resort after noncoercive techniques have failed. Some men may persist when women resist them because they believe that women are ambivalent or that they are engaged in token resistance.

Sexual coercion undoubtedly has goals other than sexual gratification. The hypothesis that men use sexual coercion to demonstrate their power is plausible, given the general evidence that coercion is sometimes motivated by concern for social identities (see chap. 9). However, at the present time there is a lack of evidence for such a process. There is at least indirect evidence that some sexual coercion involves the expression of grievances. The use of nontactical violence during some incidents—particularly those involving estranged couples—implies that some men seek to punish their victims.

Sexual coercion occurs in part because women are more sexually selective than men, which leads to a conflict between the genders over sexual behavior. This conflict leads men to use a variety of methods to influence women to have sexual relations. As in other social conflicts, coercion is one of those methods.

Men are more likely to engage in sexual coercion when the costs are low, when they view the target as having a deviant status, and when they lack moral values that would inhibit such behavior. The evidence on the versatility of rapists suggests that attitudes toward women play, at most, a minor role in rape. Rather, the individual-differences factors associated with rape are likely to be the same ones that are associated with other crimes.

IV

EPILOGUE

12

COERCIVE ACTIONS
AND AGGRESSION

We have critically reviewed numerous theories of aggression and violence, as well as a voluminous research literature. The inadequacies of current definitions of *aggression* and *intention* have been described, and an alternative theoretical language of coercive actions has been proposed. A theory of coercive actions was promulgated to provide an integration of what are currently separate literatures of conflict, aggression, justice, power and influence, and social identities.

In the first section of this chapter, we provide an overview of our theory, describing the language of coercive actions, the decision-making process, and the goals of coercive action. We consider incidents in which actors believe they have been provoked and incidents in which there is no perceived provocation.

In the second section of the epilogue, we consider the role of individual differences, biological factors, and demographic characteristics in coercive actions from a social interactionist point of view. Examination of these topics has been scattered through chapters 7–9, but until now we have not provided a focused discussion of them.

In the third and last section of the chapter, we indicate similarities and differences between traditional theories of aggression and the social interactionist theory of coercive actions. We examine the issue of whether aggression consists of a special system of behaviors, requiring a separate theory, or whether it is fundamentally no different from other types of social behavior and can be incorporated within a more general theory. Those who take a frustration–aggression approach have proposed that aggression is a special system of behavior. The evidence they provide for a system of aggressive behavior includes catharsis, displacement, the role of aversive stimuli (or frustration), and environmental cues, as discussed in chapter 2. In this concluding discussion, we evaluate the overall claims of frustration–aggression and reactive aggression theories. Finally, we point to the affinity of our social interactionist theory to social learning theory and to theories of criminal behavior.

SOCIAL INTERACTIONIST THEORY OF COERCIVE ACTIONS

Fundamental to social interactionist theory is the assumption that coercive action is one form of social influence. Coercive actions are instrumental: They are means to various ends. Such actions are intended to change target persons in some way—to compel behavior, to deter behavior, to inflict discomfort, to lower status, to change dispositions, and so on. These changes in the target are perceived as instrumental to achieving other terminal values.

The first step in developing the social interactionist theory was to define various types of coercive actions and explicate the concept of "intent." The chief task of the theory is to explain why actors choose to perform coercive actions. A decision model was adopted in which the actor is viewed as typically examining alternative means of achieving social goals. Three major goals were postulated as important for explaining the choice to perform coercive actions: (a) to control the behavior of others, (b) to restore justice, and (c) to assert and protect identities.

Language of Coercive Actions

A coercive action is an action taken with the intent of imposing harm on another person or forcing compliance. Threats, bodily force, and punishments are the three types of coercive actions. A threat is a communication of an intent to do harm. With a contingent threat, a source issues a demand and warns that punishments will result from noncompliance. Bodily force is the use of physical contact to compel or constrain behaviors of another person. Punishment is an act that is intended to do harm.

In the traditional literature, aggression is typically defined as the intent to do harm, but *intent* is never explicitly defined. This vagueness allows frustration–aggression theorists to interpret reactive aggression as both intentional and involuntary. In our scheme, intention is defined in the context of decision making by the actor and refers to the expected value associated with a chosen act. An intentional action is performed with the expectation that it will produce a proximate outcome of value to the actor. The proximate outcome is valued because of its perceived causal relationship to some valued terminal outcome. The valued terminal outcome is referred to as the *motive*. The proximate outcome, or goal, of a contingent threat is compliance. Compliance is valued because it brings money, safety, sexual gratification, or something else of value.

Harm is the expected proximate outcome in the case of punishment, but harm has no intrinsic value.[1] Harming another person is instrumental in attaining other values, such as deterrence, justice, and desired social identities. It is proposed that there are three qualitatively distinct forms of harm. Physical punishments involve manipulation of physical stimuli to impose bodily discomfort or biological damage on a target person. Deprivations refer to attempts to restrict opportunities or take away values possessed or expected by the target. Finally, social harm involves damage to the social identity of target persons and a lowering of their power or status.

For a variety of reasons, we have introduced a vocabulary of coercive actions rather than adopt the traditional vocabulary of aggression or violence. First, the language of coercive actions links other literatures to the aggression literature. In particular, it ties in the literature on conflict, social justice, social control, and other forms of social influence. Second, the language of coercion focuses attention on the social goals of actors who use coercion to gain their interpersonal objectives. Conversely, the language of aggression focuses on biological or psychological processes within the person, such as hormones, drives, or arousal states, and tends to ignore the social causes and functions of the relevant behavior. Third, coercion is used in an attempt to gain compliance or to administer harm, whereas aggression refers only to acts intended to do harm. In the traditional literature, threats are sometimes referred to as *instrumental aggression* even though the intent of a contingent threat is to gain compliance, not to inflict harm. Finally, descriptions of coercive actions are more evaluatively neutral than descriptions of aggression. Coercive actions refer not only to criminal violence but also to the judge's sentencing of the criminal to a jail term, and not only to physical abuse of children but also to deprivations or admonishments

---

[1] It is possible that harm can become a secondary or generalized reinforcer by frequent association with positively valued distal outcomes, especially in the process of retributive justice. In the latter case, the imposition of harm and the satisfaction experienced when justice is reestablished typically occur together. If classical conditioning occurs, and the person learns to take pleasure in the harming and not just in the goal accomplished through harming, it derives from an instrumental learning process, which is just the opposite process to that postulated by Berkowitz (1993).

of parents who punish the misbehavior of their children. The tendency of aggression theorists is to focus on events that are evaluated negatively by most people within a given culture. Social interactionist theory proposes to explain all forms of coercion, whether justified or not and no matter the type of harm that is attempted, threatened, or accomplished.

Decision-Making Model

We argued in chapter 7 that a coercive action, no matter how impulsive it appears, involves a series of decisions. An actor must decide whether to use coercion or perform some other action, and if coercion, what type and magnitude, and then when and how to carry it out. The basic elements involved in a decision include the value of the outcome, expectations about success in achieving that outcome, expectations about incurring costs, and the negative value of the costs. The greater the expected value and the lower the expected cost for performing a coercive act, the greater the likelihood that it will be performed. Note that even frustration–aggression theorists recognize that decisions about costs may inhibit reactive aggression. We differ from them in interpreting both instigation and inhibition in terms of factors affecting decision making.

A weak form of rationality is relevant in many coercive interactions because these encounters often involve strong emotions, quick decisions, and scripted behaviors. In some instances, individuals may use a satisficing principle. They may consider only one solution, and because it appears satisfactory, they do not consider alternatives. The behavior may appear to be impulsive and mindless, but individuals are able to inhibit their behavior, if they expect the costs to be high. Sometimes there is a failure to consider costs, particularly when the person is intoxicated or is very angry. Although there is variation in the amount of thought given to decisions about whether to use coercion, decisions are always involved.

Individuals attach value to both outcomes (terminal values) and means for achieving those outcomes (procedural values). Terminal values serve as incentives for behavior. Coercion is more likely when there are conflicts over terminal values with other people, particularly when there is scarcity and the rules of distribution are unclear. For example, siblings fight because they are in conflict over the use of material goods and the division of labor in the home and because the rules concerning the distribution of goods and chores are often unclear.

Procedural values may inhibit or facilitate the use of various forms of coercion. Although some people consider the use of physical punishment as a last resort because it violates their moral values, other people have found that threatening or using physical harm is a useful and reliable means of achieving their social goals and have no moral qualms about using such means. Thus, both means and ends have values, and these values enter into the decision making of the actor.

Principles of inhibition in aggression theories assert that the greater the expected costs for engaging in harmdoing behavior, the less apt the individual is to perform such behavior (e.g., Dollard et al., 1939). Opportunity costs, target-imposed costs, and costs imposed by third parties all contribute to inhibition of coercion. Thus, the potential costs of enforcing threats, the possible deterioration of social relationships, and the likelihood and magnitude of possible retaliation reduce the probability that coercive actions will be performed by an actor. On the other hand, even great costs for engaging in coercive actions will be accepted by an actor in a least-of-evils situation, when the costs of noncoercion are expected to be greater than coercion.

Terminal Values (Goals) and Coercive Actions

Coercive actions are performed to achieve valued outcomes. Some of these valued outcomes can be mediated by the compliant behavior of target people. Compliance may provide services, commodities, safety, and many other values. Valued outcomes may also be achieved by directly harming the target person. Harmdoing may be motivated to achieve future compliance, but it is also frequently used to redress injustices and to enhance and protect social identities. The processes related to gaining compliance, redressing injustice, and protecting identities are somewhat different, although any given real-world incident may involve all of these processes.

Compliance

The use of coercion to force compliance is associated with a variety of terminal values, including material gain, safety, sexual satisfaction, and services. There are many ways of influencing others. The actor can use persuasion, promises, modeling, cue control, and many other tactics. One might ask why an actor chooses to use coercion rather than more benign forms of influence to gain compliance. According to a decision-making model, an analytic actor evaluates which technique is likely to be more successful and which has lower expected costs. A nonanalytic decision maker may act after examining only a single alternative. In general, when individuals are pessimistic about the success of noncoercive forms of influence they are more likely to use coercive actions.

People who possess greater relative power than others may be encouraged to use coercion because they expect to be successful and to incur little cost. However, the relationship between power and coercion is complex. Weaker parties who expect to be attacked by powerful adversaries may engage in preemptive threats or punishments to communicate to the more powerful target a resolve to resist intimidation. Although costs may be incurred, from the weak party's perspective there would be greater costs if preemptive coercive actions were not performed.

Coercion is more likely to be used to achieve compliance when there is social conflict. When interests diverge, each contender may be tempted to use coercive techniques to force the other to act against his or her own interest. Noncoercive forms of influence, such as persuasion or inducements, are not very effective in a conflict situation because communications are viewed as self-serving and manipulative. Escalation may occur when each antagonist meets resistance from the other and when the motives to defend social identities and mete out justice are salient. Levels of harm may be inflicted that outweigh any tangible benefits that could be expected by either person.

The Justice Motive and the Expression of Grievances

The formation of a grievance is based on the attribution of blame to an offender. The attribution of blame depends on judgments of whether the offensive behavior was intentional, controllable, and unjustified. The scope of blame may incorporate both the antinormative action of the offender and all of the subsequent negative outcomes the victim causally links to that action.

The perspective of the person is important for understanding reactions to events. A person may attribute blame when none is warranted. Individuals tend to overattribute blame to others because of a tendency to attribute the behavior of others to internal factors and to ignore situational factors (i.e., the fundamental attribution error). Blaming others can be a way of deflecting blame from oneself when cooperative effort produces negative outcomes. Blaming others may provide an explanation of events that are otherwise difficult to understand. Divergences in perspectives occur because perpetrators underestimate the harm they do and offer excuses and justifications for their behavior, whereas victims tend to exaggerate the harm done and the injustice of the action.

Attribution of blame and the perception of injustice causes the individual to experience anger. The experience of anger affects cognitive and behavioral functioning in ways that increase the likelihood of coercive actions. Social skills and argumentative skills suffer deterioration. As a result, accusations and insults may replace discussion and a coercive interaction may occur.

Anger causes the individual to focus attention on the negative event to the exclusion of future consequences. Such an existential focus on the present may disinhibit the individual from performing coercive actions because he or she fails to consider the future costs of such actions. The energizing effect of anger may produce more intense behavior. The expression of anger, as distinct from its experience, has a number of social goals, including communication of perceived injustice and blame, showing commitment to resolving the grievance, intimidation of the target, and so on.

A perceived injustice is the basis of a grievance. People who have grievances are motivated to restore justice. Nevertheless, many grievances are never openly expressed to the offender. Inaction may occur because the grievant lacks confidence that any action will restore justice or will deter future offenses. The grievant is also likely to do nothing when the offense is minor or when the expected costs of expressing grievances are high. Embarrassment is one such cost, because the expression of grievances violates rules of politeness.

The expression of grievances may involve a reproach or criticism of the offender's behavior or person. Sometimes the grievant may make a claim for some remedial action by the wrongdoer. In the claim they may demand an apology or explanation for the wrongdoer's conduct, or they may seek a remedy or restitution. The grievant may punish the miscreant as a form of retributive justice. The intensity of punishment will be directly related to the severity of the offense that led to the grievance. Intensity of punishment may also be affected by a desire to reform the wrongdoer and to deter further offenses—both of which are social control objectives.

The course of interaction subsequent to the expression of a grievance depends on the reaction of the offender. In some cases, the two parties negotiate a solution. If offenders provide satisfactory accounts or apologies, they may be forgiven. If they provide adequate restitution, justice will be restored. In other cases, the claim may be rejected by the offender. This type of situation is ripe for an escalation of hostilities between the two parties and increases both the likelihood and intensity of coercive actions. In general, it could be expected that the greater the demands made by the grievant, the more likely that the harmdoer will resist and, hence, the more probable that a coercive interaction will occur.

Another factor that affects intensity of punishment is the number of prior offenses committed by the wrongdoer. The frequency and severity of past offenses will add to the intensity of punishment meted out by the grievant for the last offense. Even past offenses that have been forgiven may affect punishment, because they are not necessarily forgotten. If the wrongdoer engages in some further blameworthy action, the intensity of the grievance brought about by the new transgression will be greater than would have been the case if the forgiven action had never occurred. People apparently keep ledgers of the transgressions that have been committed against them. The level of a particular grievance may also be affected by accumulated experiences of injustice perpetrated by other people, especially when they share a particular social category. As transgressions accumulate, the grievant's resentment intensifies, leading to stronger actions that appear out of all proportion to the triggering incident.

Sometimes grievants seek the aid of third parties to either mediate the dispute or punish the offender. Black (1983) emphasized this alternative in his discussion of "crime as social control." He suggested that some people use the police and the courts to satisfy their grievances, whereas others engage in self-help and punish the violator themselves. Thus, many acts of criminal violence reflect decisions of offenders to settle grievances themselves when they perceive that police are unavailable or ineffective.

An alleged offender may not passively accept punishment, particularly if punishment is perceived as illegitimate or disproportionate, but may retaliate by punishing the grievant. The alleged offender is now also aggrieved. The retaliation may further enrage the grievant, leading to escalation. Escalation is particularly likely to occur because of the involvement of social identities.

Social Identities

In general, people have strong concerns about the images of themselves that they project in a situation. These social identities play an important role in coercive interactions. Actors can use both assertive and protective strategies to achieve a valued identity (Arkin, 1981).

An actor may use coercion as an intimidation tactic to inspire fear in others, to demonstrate commitment to a course of action, and to enhance the credibility of future threats. A strategic goal of establishing a reputation as tough may motivate an assertive and unprovoked use of coercion. Such an identity is more likely to be valued by men and may help to explain gender differences in violent behavior.

Violations of norms of politeness and insulting behavior by others casts the target into a negative identity and motivates the target to "save face." By retaliating, targets can lower the status of the norm violator and can demonstrate their own power, courage, and competence. By putting the antagonist down, retaliators put themselves "one up" and restore their status. A conflict spiral may ensue, with the incident becoming more serious as it progresses. In some instances, the person losing the verbal battle may turn to physical violence as a face-saving move.

Our social interactionist approach predicts strong audience effects on the use of coercion. In general, the presence of an audience increases identity concerns and the likelihood of retaliation. On the other hand, an actor who attributes more pacifistic values to the audience may inhibit retaliation. The effects of the audience may depend on whether its members attempt to mediate the conflict or urge the antagonists on. At least one reason that mediators are important is that they allow both sides to back down without losing face.

The Relationship Between Motives

Many coercive actions have more than one motive. The grievant's act of punishing an offender may be motivated by both justice and deterrence. Many acts of formal and informal social control involve both of these motives. When a coercive action is carried out, it is likely to activate multiple motives for retaliation in the target. The target is likely to retaliate to deter future attacks. The target will probably perceive the source's action as unjust and therefore deserving of punishment. Finally, the coercive action is likely to be perceived as an identity attack and should motivate retaliation in order to save face.

Retribution, deterrence, and social identities may all be involved in the coercive behavior that sometimes occurs in love triangles. When a partner is found to be cheating, the offended party may threaten either the partner or the rival to deter future dalliances. Research has indicated that the offended party is more likely to blame the partner than the rival and that the partner is more likely to be the target of attack (Paul, Foss, & Galloway, 1993). The partner is usually the main person who has betrayed a trust, unless perhaps the rival is a friend. Both the partner and rival have lowered the social identity of the offended party, and either may be attacked in the partner's attempt to save face.[2]

In chapters 7–9, we artificially separated motives that frequently jointly cause coercive actions. Individuals who seek personal gain through coercion may get involved in disputes that cause others to form grievances against them. During the course of disputes, identity concerns may become salient, and the conflict may take on the form of a character contest. Although the relationships between these three motives may take other forms as well, it is important to stress how self-presentation concerns differ from motives to gain compliance or to restore justice.

Influence and Self-Presentation

Social influence is an attempt to achieve some interpersonal goal through changing another person. In chapter 7, we focused on the use of coercion to gain compliance from target individuals. This is a very direct means of attempting influence. Self-presentations are also attempts to influence other people, but the goal is more directed toward changing the

---

[2]In contrast with the predictions of sociobiologists (Daly & Wilson, 1988), evidence suggests that females are more likely to use coercion in response to an infidelity than males (Paul, Foss, & Galloway, 1993).

cognitive or emotional states of the target (or third parties) than toward gaining compliance. One goal of self-presentation may be to create inner states in the target that increase the likelihood that other, more direct modes of influence will gain compliance. For example, intimidation tactics, such as expressing great anger when issuing a threat, make it more likely that a target will comply to the threatener's demands.

A distinction between tactical and strategic self-presentations is useful in examining the relationships between attempts to gain compliance and self-presentation (Tedeschi & Melburg, 1984). Self-presentation tactics are intended to have specific, if indirect, effects on a target's behavior. In our example, intimidation tactics are expected to inspire fear, which in turn is expected to mediate compliance by the target. Strategic self-presentations are intended to foster long-term reputations. Cross-situational identities, such as competence, attractiveness, status, trustworthiness, and credibility, increase the effectiveness of threats, promises, and persuasion (Tedeschi et al., 1973).

One implication of the relationship of strategic identities to social influence is that aspersions on these identities are perceived as attempts to reduce one's power (or status). Tolerance of such attacks is equivalent to giving up power and future influence. The prospects of such open-ended and unknown costs are sufficient to motivate the individual to engage in face-saving actions directed toward restoring and even bolstering status.

Justice and Self-Presentation

As we saw in chapter 8, when a blameworthy action is performed, the victim may be motivated to restore justice in the situation. When unjust actions convey disrespect and lower status, it is likely the victim will be motivated to save face. Although the motives to restore justice and save face frequently coexist, one may be more salient than the other. In such cases, the motives have different implications for coercive actions.

A person who administers punishments to restore justice is guided by a negative norm of reciprocity, or *lex talionis*. The level of punishment should be proportional to the amount of blame attributed to the perpetrator. When the precipitating action is an affront, the person will attempt to restore status by putting the other person down. Although the goal of justice is to get even, a person motivated to restore or save face values winning. The implication is that affronts are likely to lead to more punitiveness than do other types of unjust actions.

Another difference between the motives of justice and self-presentation involves preferences about the way punishments are administered. A person with a grievance should be satisfied when the offender gets just desserts, even when the punishment is administered by someone else. Those motivated by face saving prefer carrying out the punishment themselves.

They also prefer that the target knows at whose hands they suffer, unless the costs of openness are too great. Worchel, Arnold, and Harrison (1978) provided experimental evidence that identity concerns were involved in the procedural preference of a person subject to an attack. Subjects either were insulted by a confederate or were not insulted. Subsequently, they participated as the teacher in a teacher–learner aggression procedure. The learner either did or did not know the identity of the subjects. Subjects delivered more shocks in the insult condition than in the no-insult condition. In addition, subjects who were insulted gave more intense shocks to the learner when they were identifiable than when they were anonymous. The latter finding indicates that subjects wanted their antagonist to know that they had imposed the harm.

The motives for justice and self-presentation imply different reactions to unsuccessful attacks. Unsuccessful attacks on a person's identity often do not instigate character contests. A clumsy verbal joust or other identity attack that fails may spoil the identity of the attacker more than that of the target person. Through social comparison, the failed attack of a denigrator may actually enhance the status of the intended victim. Conversely, a physical attack is likely to be perceived as antinormative and unjust whether it is successful in inflicting harm or not. The intent of the attacker and the act performed are the bases for punitive measures. Recall that the magnitude of retaliation by subjects in a competitive reaction-time game was closer to the shock levels preset by their opponent than to the actual shock levels administered by their opponent (Shuck & Pisor, 1974). The response to intent rather than to the infliction of harm suggests that the justice motive was involved.

Finally, a grievant may want to parade and showcase injuries or losses to others as a way of maximizing the legitimacy of subsequent claims or gaining sympathy and support of others. Alternatively, a person who suffers from a spoiled identity is apt to try to hide his or her "injuries" from others. If a person admits to being humiliated, then it is an admission that the antagonist has won. This difference between the motives for justice and self-presentation may disappear after successful punitive reactions are taken. Victims of humiliating actions may then reveal their social wounds to provide justification for their punitive actions.

Secondary Gains for Coercive Actions

When a person considers whether to use coercive actions for one reason, the prospect of also achieving other desired outcomes should facilitate the choice of coercion. Thus, we suggested in chapter 8 that a person who punishes a wrongdoer may also believe that the punishment will deter further wrongdoing. Similarly, when a person is motivated to use coercion to protect identity, beliefs about justice may facilitate a coercive response. For the person who is motivated by identity concerns, justice is an added value or a secondary gain. In this case, one might speak of "justice in the service of revenge."

When a person considers whether to use coercive actions to gain compliance or to restore justice, the prospect of incidentally achieving positive consequences for identity should also facilitate the choice of coercion. In such cases, the added value or secondary gain associated with enhanced identity will increase the likelihood that the person will perform the coercive action. A man who is provoked may retaliate to restore status, but the probability of retaliation is greater when he believes the coercion will also serve to deter future provocations.

From a decision theory perspective, the creation of multiple goals for a single behavioral alternative should enhance its incentive value. When the conditions for using coercion exist and several goals can be achieved with a single act, the likelihood that coercion will be used will be increased. Even when there is only a single motive for the use of coercion, such as to achieve compliance or to protect a valued identity, a claim about retributive justice may be used to legitimate behavior. When this happens, beliefs about justice might better be described as facilitators or disinhibiting factors, rather than as instigators of coercive behavior.

In summary, although the motives to restore justice and defend identities may both be activated in a particular situation, they have different implications for the subsequent course of interaction. If an aggrieved person decides to inflict retribution, then the punishment is made to fit the severity of the transgression; retributive justice is a matter of getting even. Conversely, the goal in a contest over identities is to win. Thus, the defense of identities is more likely to escalate and involve severe harm than is punitive action intended to administer retributive justice. Indeed, the value for retributive justice may inhibit the severity of punishment because its legitimacy is inextricably bound to fair or equitable punishment. The desire for justice can also be satisfied by the retributive acts of third parties, but people motivated to defend identities prefer to carry out face-restoring punitive acts themselves.

INDIVIDUAL DIFFERENCES IN THE USE OF COERCION

The processes described by social interactionist theory are assumed to be universal, applying to men and women, to young and old, to members of all ethnic groups, and to all cultures. In our exposition of the theory, however, we have not always been specific about the form or severity of coercion that is likely to be used by a person. Why does one person respond to an insult with a verbal retort, whereas another person uses a weapon to harm the antagonist? Individual differences are critical for explaining variation in the use of severe forms of coercion. It is our view that learning experiences, temperament, and other individual-differences factors interact with situational factors to determine the type and magnitude of coercion used. The notion of a person–situation interaction is consistent with Toch's (1969) observation that the violent men in his sample only became violent under certain stimulus conditions.

Most research on individual differences focuses on variables that affect the use of violence or physical forms of coercion. Available evidence strongly supports the conclusion that some people are much more likely to use physical violence than others. Individual differences in violence manifest themselves early in life and tend to be maintained well into adulthood (see chap. 7). It is not known if there are individual differences in other forms of harmdoing, such as the use of deprivations and social punishments. Different coercive influence styles may coalesce around forms of harmdoing.

In the following discussion, we speculate about possible individual differences that are suggested by social interactionist theory. There is little research available with which to evaluate these speculations, but they may stimulate research linking individual-differences factors to the form, frequency, and intensity of coercion used by actors. Differences in the kinds and magnitudes of terminal and procedural values of individuals are probably important in explaining variations in the use of coercion. The characteristic way that a person construes probable costs may serve to disinhibit or inhibit the use of various forms of coercion. Any characteristic of the individual that increases the likelihood of friction and conflict with others, such as a tendency to be easily offended or to insult others, would be associated with the frequency, form, and intensity of coercion that the actor uses and experiences from other people.

Terminal and Procedural Values

Individual differences in terminal values are likely to be associated with the use of coercion. Particularly important from the perspective of social interactionist theory are types of social identities that people seek. A person who believes it is important to appear tough or courageous is more likely to use physical coercion than someone for whom these identities are not important, especially in front of audiences that share these values.

Because coercion can be used to obtain money, sex, and other values, one might predict that those who have high aspirations in these areas are more likely to use coercion to achieve them. Evidence reviewed in chapter 11 showed that young men with high sexual aspirations are more likely to use coercion in pursuit of sexual gratification. However, high aspirations may lead to coercive behavior only when individuals do not expect to achieve these values using other means. Blocked opportunity theory (see chap. 5) emphasizes this discrepancy between goals and means in explaining criminal behavior.

Individual differences in sensation seeking may also be associated with coercive behavior. The risks associated with violence and other forms of coercion generate excitement and stimulation in participants, providing a form of recreation. Psychopaths score high on sensation seeking, as do recreational sky divers (Blackburn, 1978). Some studies show that psychopaths have diminished reactivity to normal stimuli and generally low arousal levels (see J. Q. Wilson & Herrnstein, 1985, for a review). Such people may become bored with school and other conventional activities and engage in coercive actions and other risky behavior for stimulation.[3] Sensation seeking could be one reason for the versatility of deviant conduct by criminals. Smoking, drinking, gambling, fighting, and committing crimes may provide excitement and stimulation for people.

Some people learn to give procedural value to coercive actions because of their past utility in achieving interpersonal goals. Other people learn that some forms of coercive actions are morally wrong and give negative procedural value to their use. Values such as pacifism, respect for law, and respect for human life are moral values that inhibit the use of physical forms of coercion. Thus, individual differences in procedural values may serve to facilitate or inhibit particular coercive actions. Individuals are also likely to differ in their beliefs about appropriate punishment for particular offenses. Those who are more punitive are likely to engage in more severe forms of punishment.

Individuals may vary in the extent to which their values affect their behavior. Those who can neutralize or rationalize their behavior to themselves should be more likely to engage in antinormative coercive behavior. Individuals who tend to be objectively self-aware—their attention is focused on their own thoughts—are more likely to behave according to their procedural values. A person who has a positive value for physical coercion should be more apt to use it when self-aware than when not self-aware. Similarly, a person who has a negative value for using physical coercion would be more inhibited when self-aware than when not self-aware.

Evaluation of Costs

Violence and other forms of coercion are less likely to be used when actors expect them to be costly. Individuals are likely to differ in their estimates of the probability of costs, in their perceptions of the negative value of costs, and in their tendency to even consider costs. Those who are optimistic about avoiding costs, who underestimate costs, or who fail to consider costs are more likely to perform coercive actions. Such people are sometimes described as risk takers. In general, risk takers are more likely

---

[3]The most common explanation given by delinquents for disliking school is that school is boring (S. Glueck & Glueck, 1950).

to engage in coercion than those who are risk aversive. People who act quickly without thinking of alternatives or risks are sometimes referred to as *impulsive*. Evidence shows that impulsive individuals are more likely to engage in coercive behavior (e.g., Hynan & Grush, 1986). The impulsive use of coercion may be more likely when individuals have learned coercive scripts. Impulsive people may choose a coercive action with little or no consideration of costs.

Risk aversiveness may be displayed when individuals experience high levels of fear and anxiety in a situation with potentially high costs. People who are more fearful or socially anxious may avoid the use of coercion because they are preoccupied with probable costs, because they are pessimistic about avoiding costs, or because they exaggerate the costs. Alternatively, protracted fear or a least-of-evils situation may induce a strong preemptive attack by a fearful individual.

One reason that young people engage in more violence and other forms of coercion is their tendency to take risks. Youth are less likely to consider the costs of their behavior (i.e, they tend to be impulsive), and when they do consider the probability and level of costs, they are more likely to underestimate them. Young men may value risk taking for identity reasons or to generate excitement.

The costs of violent behavior may be lower for young people than for adults. Youth are less vulnerable to physical injury. Adult commitments, such as to job and family, increase the costs of engaging in any illegal behavior (see chap. 5). People with stronger ties to conventional others are likely to have a greater stake in conformity and to have more to lose if they engage in illicit activities.

Coercive and Noncoercive Power

In general, individuals with greater coercive power should be more likely to engage in coercion than those with less power. Superiority in physical size, strength, and fighting skills may make it more likely that an individual will engage in physical violence. Recall that bullies tended to be bigger than their victims. These relationships may be obscured in research because of the complex interaction of these factors with target perceptions and situational factors. For example, targets may be more compliant to noncoercive forms of influence because they perceive an implied threat from those who possess superior coercive power. Possession of coercive power may make its actual use unnecessary.

Lack of an ability to achieve influence by noncoercive means increases the likelihood that a person will become involved in a coercive interaction. Thus, individuals with greater noncoercive power should be less likely to engage in coercion than those who lack such power. Those who have expertise, high credibility, and good social skills should be less likely to use coercion than those who have do not have these characteristics. These skills and reputational characteristics are probably affected by both genetically inherited factors, such as intelligence and verbal ability, and environmental factors, such as educational opportunity, social models, and child-rearing practices.

Taking and Giving Offense

Any characteristic that leads a person to become involved in conflict should increase the likelihood of a coercive episode. A person who consistently violates distributive, procedural, or interactional rules (see chap. 8) is likely to be a frequent target of grievants seeking retributive justice. People who can state grievances and criticize without offending the target and who can give adequate accounts for their own misbehavior are less likely to become involved in coercive episodes. Poor performance and deviant conduct may elicit social control behaviors from others, including the use of threats and punishments. People who are impolite, outspoken, or dogmatic or who have strong opinions will offend others, elicit grievance-related actions from them, and, in turn, may retaliate as the conflict escalates in intensity of harmdoing. The tendency of young people to violate rules may generate grievances against them, leading to their frequent involvement in coercive interactions.

Hostility biases affect the formation of grievances and reactions to norm violators (see chap. 8). Such people tend to interpret the behavior of others as hostile even when it is not. A paranoid style of making attributions, particularly in situations where the intentions of others are ambiguous, may induce preemptive attacks or deterrent threats. Individuals with low self-esteem may have a greater tendency to be "thin-skinned" than individuals with high self-esteem. Their insecurity about themselves may lead them to be sensitive to any slight and to take an attack on their identity very seriously. People with low self-esteem may be more envious of others if they see their own outcomes as relatively impoverished, and they may attempt to lower the outcomes of others to produce redistributive justice.[4]

People who weight negative information more heavily than positive information about a person may be more likely than less misanthropic people to assign blame and form grievances when negative actions occur under

---

[4]Baumeister, Tice, and Hutton (1989) suggested that self-esteem is related to assertive self-presentation and protective self-presentation in different ways. Their approach implies that people with high self-esteem are more likely to engage in coercion that involves assertive forms of self-presentation because they tend to take more risks and want to be the center of attention. People with low self-esteem, on the other hand, are risk aversive and are more likely to use coercion to protect their image.

ambiguous circumstances. Perhaps individuals who are extreme in their evaluations of negative events react more strongly to provocations.

On the more positive side of individual differences in judging other people are people with the ability to decenter and take the viewpoint of others when forming judgments about them. Empathy with others inhibits the use of coercion, whereas egocentrism should facilitate its use. Individuals who consider the point of view of others are better able to accept excuses and justifications for an offense and to forgive transgressions. Empathy for a victim who is suffering may inhibit further attack from an actor. One reason for differences between the sexes in the use of physical coercion may be the greater empathy that women have for other people.

Role of Biological Factors

Sociobiologists have breathed new life into research trying to establish a connection between genetic profile and aggressive behavior. The new interest in biological characteristics is most apparent in the areas of personality and social behavior. Family resemblance studies, reviewed in chapter 1, indicate that genes may have an impact on coercive behavior. However, it is a giant conceptual leap between biochemical transfers of information at conception to a specific threat or punishment made by a person in a particular situation years later. It is fair to ask the biologically oriented theorist what the causal chain is that leads from a "gene for aggression" to the specific action. No existing theory proposes such a causal sequence.

Nevertheless, it would be unwise to conclude that biological factors play no role in the performance of coercive actions. Surely they do. Our view is that factors that may have a heritability component facilitate or inhibit coercive acts or affect them indirectly. Biologically based individual differences may indirectly affect the decision-making process and the effectiveness of socialization in producing normative conduct. Among the individual characteristics that are associated with the use of physical coercion and have a heritability component are intelligence, extraversion–introversion, impulsiveness, emotionality, conditionability, fearfulness, activity level, arousal level, tolerance of pain, size, strength, and sexual drive. Some of these characteristics may help explain gender and age differences in violence.

SOCIAL INTERACTIONIST THEORY AND THEORIES OF AGGRESSION

Some traditional theories have proposed that aggression is a special class of behaviors that operate under somewhat different principles than other types of behavior. Traditional frustration–aggression theory and Berkowitz's (1982) system of reactive aggression assume that aggressive drive is biologically tied to certain classes of stimuli and that drive causes the individual to hurt other people.

Bandura (1973) has argued that aggressive behavior is just another means of attaining rewards or avoiding punishments and does not differ fundamentally from other behavior. Although we would refer to various forms of coercion rather than the term *aggression*, we basically agree with Bandura.

Berkowitz, as the contemporary exponent of frustration–aggression theory, has proposed a distinction between reactive and instrumental aggression (see chap. 2). According to him, aggressive behavior based on "a desire to hurt" a victim is fundamentally different from harmdoing that is instrumental to achieving some other goal. In other words, reactive aggression is intrinsically rewarding, whereas instrumental aggression is only a means to attaining other rewards.

A claim for a system of behavior that is fundamentally different from other kinds of behavior is one that requires substantial justification. Frustration–aggression theorists viewed the processes of catharsis and displacement as indicators of a separate system of aggressive behavior. In his revision of frustration–aggression theory, Berkowitz proposed a number of evidential grounds to establish a system of reactive aggression, including reflex fighting, the effects of aversive stimuli and stress, reactions to pain cues, and the effects of the presence of aggressive stimuli (particularly weapons) on aggressive behavior. We briefly review this evidence and offer alternative interpretations where relevant. In our view, the evidence does not provide sufficient grounds for positing a special system of reactive aggression.

After considering issues raised by drive theories in general and by Berkowitz's theory of reactive aggression in particular,[5] we discuss the relationship of our approach and social learning theory with various theories of violent crime. The social interactionist theory presented in chapters 6–11 is consistent with these theories and borrows many concepts and processes from them.

Catharsis and Displacement

Classic frustration–aggression theory postulated that a special class of events, defined as frustration, is biologically linked to the arousal of aggressive drive, which in turn activates aggressive responses in the organism. Aggressive behavior reduces drive and is therefore self-reinforcing. The aggressive discharge of the aggressive drive is referred to as *catharsis*; when

---

[5]We find many areas of agreement between our theory and Berkowitz's (1993) theory when he discusses instrumental aggression.

the aggression is discharged on someone other than the frustrating agent, displacement is involved. The establishment of catharsis and displacement processes would support the assumption that there is a special system of aggressive behavior.

All reviewers who have examined the evidence regarding catharsis have drawn the same conclusion. Performance of aggressive behavior in laboratory studies does not reduce the likelihood of subsequent aggressive behavior and sometimes increases its likelihood and intensity. Conversely, a reliable displacement effect has been demonstrated, according to the only review of experimental research in the area (Tedeschi & Norman, 1985b).

The question is, Why does displacement occur? According to frustration–aggression theorists, displacement occurs because the dominant aggressive response to the frustrating agent is inhibited. The pent-up aggressive energy must find release and does so through displacement. In other words, displacement occurs because the organism needs catharsis. However, because the evidence does not support the notion of catharsis—the engine that supposedly produces displacement—an alternative explanation is needed.

A social interactionist approach suggests some mechanisms that can produce displacementlike effects, which we refer to as *target substitution*.[6] First, target substitution may be the result of beliefs in redistributive justice. A person who is disadvantaged in a distribution of rewards and is inhibited from expressing a grievance against the person who distributed rewards may attempt to impose costs on the advantaged party. Equity is restored when advantaged others are made to suffer because the costs imposed decrease the net gains of the advantaged people. A redistributive punitive action fits the definition of displacement because the person who is attacked is not the frustrating agent and has done nothing to provoke the punitive actor.

Second, target substitution may reflect protective self-presentation after a failure or an attack. Displaced aggression in the laboratory has been shown to involve active downward comparison for the purpose of restoring favorable social identities (Melburg & Tedeschi, 1989). Subjects who were made to appear relatively inferior to a confederate on some task gave more shocks to indicate a negative evaluation of the confederate than did subjects who had not suffered an unfavorable comparison. This kind of downward comparison occurred when the confederate was the one who had received the more favorable evaluation as well as when the confederate was new to the experiment. By putting the other person down, the subjects put themselves one up.

---

[6]In some of the experiments demonstrating displacement effects, results were probably due to demand cues introduced inadvertently by experimenters (see Tedeschi & Norman, 1985b).

Protective self-presentation may also be involved when a person is attacked but either does not have the opportunity to retaliate against the person who provoked him or her or is inhibited because the anticipated costs are too high. A successful attack against a third party may help the person restore, at least to some extent, an identity as tough or competent.[7] By changing competitors, the actor shifts to a contest that is winnable: "If you can't beat 'em, beat someone else."

Finally, target substitution may be due to guilt by association or collective guilt when the original antagonist and the innocent third party are members of the same social category. Any member of a particular category might be held responsible for the blameworthy action of another member and so might be punished. From the aggrieved actor's point of view, the attack against the third party is not displacement but, rather, the legitimate punishment of a guilty party. Blood feuds, bias crimes, and, perhaps, some rapes are examples of punishments carried out against members of a social category.[8]

Aversive Stimulation and Reactive Aggression

According to Berkowitz (1993), any type of aversive stimulation causes "a desire to hurt" in the person and will, in the absence of learned inhibitions, lead to physical aggression. A large number of experiments have associated aversive stimulation in the form of noise, heat, physical discomfort, and pain to increases in the intensity of retaliation to an attack. According to Berkowitz, it is the negative affective experience that causes aggression. However, the preponderance of research indicates that aversive stimuli intensify aggression against a provoker but have little or no effect on aggressiveness toward people who have not provoked the actor (see Zillmann, 1983). If aversive stimulation instigates aggression, then provocation should not be necessary to produce an effect. It might be argued that aversive stimuli instigate aggression but that an additional provocation is necessary to release inhibitions in the laboratory. However, the effect of provocation is more reliable, much stronger, and occurs in the absence of aversive stimuli.

Physical pain and discomfort are aversive experiences. Despite Berkowitz's claim (1993, p. 76) that pain elicits reflex fighting in animals and more intense retaliatory use of noxious stimuli by humans, the evidence does not support such a relationship. As we argued in chapter 2, the

---

[7]These actions may involve self-presentation to an audience or attempts to restore self-esteem.
[8]Mistreatment by an experimenter may create a general negative attitude toward participation in research, leading to an increase in the probability and degree of negative behavior by subjects. It has been shown that subjects exposed to a failure–insult procedure expressed more deviant attitudes, including expressions of racial prejudice (N. E. Miller & Bugelski, 1948; Silverman & Kleinman, 1967). These are not coercive actions, however.

evidence (cf. R. N. Johnson, 1972) indicates that pain-elicited fighting is not a normal response of subhuman animals and is probably not a reflex. Furthermore, there is no evidence that pain elicits fighting in humans. Studies of the effect of physically uncomfortable temperatures on aggression in the laboratory have yielded inconsistent results (see chap. 2).

Sadness, depression, guilt, and other forms of psychological pain are aversive experiences. Longitudinal analyses of survey data suggest that these psychological states do not lead to increases in coercive behavior (R. B. Felson, 1992). Although some correlational studies have found that people who have experienced stressful life events are more likely to engage in interpersonal violence, recent research indicates that the relationship is not mediated by frustration or negative affect (R. B. Felson, 1992). The death of a loved one is a very negative experience. Yet, coercive behavior rarely occurs at funerals or other situations involving mourning.

When aversiveness is perceived as intentionally imposed by another person and the target attributes blame to the actor, the likelihood of a coercive reaction is increased.[9] Thus, subjects tend to retaliate for intended attacks even when those attacks are never carried out (Epstein & Taylor, 1967). However, aversiveness that is not associated with a blameworthy action of another does not instigate the use of coercion. Recall (from chap. 2) that it is primarily arbitrary or unjustifiable frustrations that lead to a coercive response.

In our view, aversive stimuli can indirectly affect the likelihood of coercive actions because they tend to impair performance. Distressed people may act impulsively without considering costs or alternative choices. Aversive stimuli may induce depression, which is known to reduce social competence and increases the likelihood that others will reject the person (Pietromonaco & Rook, 1987). Stress and other aversive stimuli may make a person less attentive to politeness norms, more irritable, less empathic, and more egocentric in interactions with other people. Interaction partners may be angered by the actor's insensitive behavior, irritability, or poor performance, and a coercive episode may ensue.

Our conclusion is that there is no automatic relationship between aversive stimuli and aggression. Aversive experiences produce changes in the cognitive and affective processes of the individual, which in turn may facilitate coercive choices or lead to behaviors that elicit coercive reactions from other people. In our view, aversive experiences that are not attributed to the actions of other people have only a minor role in producing coercive

---

[9]Human agency and blame are critical factors in determining whether aversive stimuli lead to coercive actions. Studies have shown that subjects are more likely to retaliate when a person is the source of punishment than when the costs are imposed by a preprogrammed machine or are otherwise fixed (Sermat, 1967; Tedeschi, Bonoma, & Novinson, 1970). An aversive experience that is attributed to another person elicits greater harmdoing than the same kind of aversive experience that is attributable to other circumstances.

behavior. The tendency to view aversive stimuli as inducing reactive aggression has prevented researchers from going beyond looking at the coercive episodes as simple stimulus–response sequences to examine factors related to decision making and the social goals of the actor.

External Cues and Reactive Aggression

Berkowitz (1993) postulated that the goal of a person who has experienced aversive stimulation is to hurt others and that indications of pain by the victim will heighten the attack. As our review in chapter 2 indicated, evidence of pain-cue effects on aggressive behavior is inconsistent. Even if it could be reliably shown that pain cues lead to repeated or intensified attack, this would not be evidence for reactive aggression. The fact that individuals value harm in certain instances does not necessarily imply that it has intrinsic value for them. We would argue that harm has extrinsic value: They value harm because it is a means to some end, such as deterrence or retributive justice.

In our view, the effect of pain cues on the subsequent use of coercion is rather complex. Any type of goal-oriented behavior is less likely to be immediately repeated if the goal is accomplished. Performance of a coercive action should decrease the probability of subsequent coercion if it succeeds in carrying out its goal. An actor who makes an effective riposte is winning an identity contest and does not need to attack further. Adequate punishment restores justice, making it unnecessary to repeat the attack. If a certain level of physical pain is viewed as adequate punishment, then the victim's expression of that level of pain should terminate the attack—justice has prevailed.

Pain cues may elicit empathy in the actor for the victim and decrease punitive behavior (Ohbuchi et al., 1993). Alternatively, if the pain cues only indicate that events are headed in the right direction but the goal has not been accomplished, they should spur the actor to use even more punishment. Individuals who engage in coercive actions may exaggerate the extent to which the target has misbehaved to justify their attack and to convince themselves that further punishment is needed. Also, an actor's coercive actions often lead to retaliation from the target, which may then induce the actor to attack again.

The classic weapons-eliciting effect on aggressive behavior is still another basis for believing that aggressive behavior can be elicited involuntarily by environmental stimuli. According to Berkowitz (1993), the presence of aggressive cues may heighten the desire to hurt and, hence, contribute to reactive aggression. Aggressive cues, such as weapons, induce such a strong internal state in the individual that aggressive behavior is pushed out.

Frequent failures to replicate the weapons effect, coupled with findings of the opposite effect in some studies, have provided little justification for Berkowitz's (1981b) statement that sometimes "the trigger pulls the finger." Our review in chapter 2 of this research indicated that there is no reliable weapons effect.

Conclusions: A System of Reactive Aggression

The evidence does not provide a strong foundation for believing in a distinctive system of reactive aggression. There is no direct evidence showing that there is reflexive fighting in humans. Human agency and blame are critical factors in determining whether aversive stimuli lead to coercive actions. Aversive stimuli unrelated to blame may play some role in heightening aggressive behavior in the laboratory, but it appears to be confined to situations where the actor has first been provoked by an attack from another person. The cognitive and social effects of stress probably account for a stress–violence relationship. The complex relationship of pain cues to the incitement of further immediate aggression requires analysis of the goals of the actor, empathy, and numerous other factors. Finally, the unreliability of a weapons effect undermines Berkowitz's belief that intense internal forces can push out aggression in the absence of plans, intentions, attributions, or social motives.

Social Learning Theory

An instrumental view of behavior assumes that all behavior is learned. We like a lot that is said about learning in Bandura's social learning theory, and we have borrowed from it. Expectancies, incentives, and inhibitions are central to social learning theory, as they are to our own approach.[10] Various scholars working in the context of social learning theory have suggested modifications that include more elaborate cognitive mechanisms, such as scripts (Huesmann, 1988) and hostile attribution biases (Dodge & Coie, 1987). We have adopted these innovative ideas in our theory.

Social learning theory elucidates the processes through which people develop expectations and values, scripts, and coercive influence styles. The learning history of the individual provides information that allows predictions about individual differences in coercive behavior. However, the theory is not very informative about the situational factors that elicit coercion. There is no reference in social learning theory to motives associated with justice and identity. The social interaction in coercive episodes is also ignored. Internal representations of past learning in a single individual are not enough to make predictions about coercive actions. An adequate theory

---

[10]Indeed, a strong case has been made for the conceptual compatibility of social learning and rational-choice theories (Akers, 1990).

must include interaction sequences between the actor, the target, and third parties. The statuses and relationships between people, their perceptions of each other, their social goals—including the potential for cooperation and conflict—and many other social factors define the social context of behavior and set the stage for coercive actions.

Criminological Theories

In chapter 5, we discussed some of the evidence and theoretical controversies associated with sociological theories of violence and crime. Some criminologists believe an integration of these theories is possible, whereas others argue that their assumptions are incompatible. Whether the theories, in their entirety, can be integrated is not our concern here. We have borrowed from each of these theories those ideas that are compatible with a decision-making approach.

Control theory contributes to an understanding of the costs of using violent forms of coercion. Internal controls, which we have discussed primarily in terms of procedural values, inhibit the use of violence. Lack of self-control, which we have discussed in terms of the decision-making process, refers to the tendency to consider the short-term benefits of coercion and to ignore or disregard its long-term costs. External controls, which we discussed in terms of costs imposed by third parties, are also important inhibitors of the use of violence. Social bonds with conventional people increase the costs of engaging in violence and thereby inhibit its use. When children are subjected to harsh and erratic disciplinary techniques, they develop weak bonds with their parents and become more likely to engage in violence and other forms of delinquency.

The routine activities of daily life create opportunities for violent incidents to occur. When circumstances bring violence-prone people together—such as young men—violence is more likely. Violence is more likely to occur when third parties who might impose costs on the participants are absent. Violence feeds on routine, nonviolent forms of social control because it is an alternative when routine social control fails. Thus, parental violence toward children occurs during disciplinary situations. Rule breaking or any other routine activity leading to grievances or interpersonal conflict is likely to increase the likelihood of violence.

In agreement with cultural theories, we think it is likely that there are group differences in values relevant to violent behavior. Values related to violence are likely to be different in different societies. There are also likely to be differences among small groups. In gangs of young men, a macho identity is valued, and concern for appearing tough and courageous is likely to lead to violence. People may self-select into violent-prone groups, but differential association may accentuate behavioral differences that already exist between members of different groups. The important role of self-presentation in coercive behavior ensures that groups are likely to have an impact. It is uncertain, however, whether values can help explain the high levels of violence and crime among minorities and lower-class people in the United States.

In agreement with blocked opportunity theory, we think that violence can be a way of obtaining values when other means are ineffective. Violence can be used to obtain money or status when legitimate opportunities are unavailable because of discrimination or the individual's own limitations. We are uncertain whether high ambition can lead to the use of coercive methods or whether blocked opportunities can help explain class and race differences in violence. Consistent with self-help theory, we believe that violence is more likely to be used to obtain justice when the legal system is perceived as unavailable.

Rational choice perspectives represent a promising development in the study of crime (e.g., Cornish & Clarke, 1986). However, scholars using that approach do not usually apply it to emotionally charged acts of criminal violence. We have attempted to show that a rational-choice perspective is applicable to such crimes if a broader range of incentives is considered.

SOME FINAL WORDS

For the social interactionist theory of coercive actions propounded in this book, we have borrowed heavily from traditional theories of aggression and criminal violence. There is plenty of skepticism by scholars in the area about viewing aggression as a special system of behavior. The instrumental use of aggression is discussed throughout these literatures, but the material has never been integrated into a comprehensive theory. We have attempted to provide such an integration here.

The general nature of the theory allows an integration of many areas of research that heretofore have not been systematically related to theories of aggression and violence. Thus, we have brought together propositions from the literature on power and influence, conflict and competition, retributive and redistributive justice, self-presentation, social learning theory, attribution and other cognitive theories, and criminal violence. We have attempted to organize many studies from diverse areas of research with this social interactionist theory. One might argue that the integrative power of social interactionist theory is based in large part on post hoc interpretations. However, a "hindsight is 20–20" syndrome is avoided if the theory generates many new hypotheses to be tested. There can be little doubt that social interactionist theory does propose many new empirical relationships and, hence, should stimulate much new research.

REFERENCES

Abbey, A. (1982). Sex differences in attributions for friendly behavior: Do males misperceive females' friendliness? *Journal of Personality and Social Psychology, 42,* 830–838.

Abel, G. G., Barlow, D. H., Blanchard, E. B., & Guild, D. (1977). The components of rapists' sexual arousal. *Archives of General Psychiatry, 34,* 895–903.

Abelson, R. P. (1976). Script processing in attitude formation and decision making. In J. S. Carroll & J. W. Payne (Eds.), *Cognition and social behavior* (pp. 33–46). Hillsdale, NJ: Erlbaum.

Adams, D. B. (1979). Brain mechanisms for offense, defense and submission. *Behavioral and Brain Sciences, 2,* 201–241.

Adams, J. P., Jr., & Dressler, W. W. (1988). Perceptions of injustice in a Black community: Dimensions and variation. *Human Relations, 41,* 753–767.

Affleck, G., Allen, D. A., Tennen, H., McGrade, B. J., & Ratzan, S. (1985). Causal and control cognitions in parent coping with a chronically ill child. *Journal of Social and Clinical Psychology, 3,* 369–379.

Affleck, G., Pfeiffer, C., Tennen, H., & Fifield, J. (1987). Attributional processes in rheumatoid arthritis. *Arthritis and Rheumatism, 30,* 927–931.

Ageton, S. (1983). *Sexual assault among adolescents.* Lexington, MA: Lexington Books.

Aguinis, H., Nesler, M. S., Hosoda, M., & Tedeschi, J. T. (in press). The use of influence tactics and the "persuade package." *Journal of Social Psychology.*

Akers, R. (1990). Rational choice, deterrence, and social learning theory in criminology: The path not taken. *Journal of Criminal Law and Criminology, 81,* 653–676.

Alder, C. (1984). The convicted rapist: A sexual or a violent offender? *Criminal Justice and Behavior, 11,* 157–177.

Aldis, O. (1975). *Play fighting.* San Diego, CA: Academic Press.

Allison, J. A., & Wrightsman, L. S. (1993). *Rape: The misunderstood crime.* Newbury Park, CA: Sage.

Altman, I. (1975). *The environment and social behavior.* Monterey, CA: Brooks/Cole.

Altmann, S. A. (1967). The structure of primate communication. In S. A. Altmann (Ed.), *Social communication among primates* (pp. 325–362). Chicago: University of Chicago Press.

Amir, M. (1971). *Patterns in forcible rape.* Chicago: University of Chicago Press.

Ammerman, R. T. (1991). The role of the child in physical abuse: A reappraisal. *Violence and Victims, 6,* 87–101.

Amsel, A. (1958). The rule of frustrative non-reward in non-continuous reward situations. *Psychological Bulletin, 55,* 102–119.

Anderson, E. A., & Burgess, R. L. (1977, December). *Interaction patterns between same- and opposite-gender parents and children in abusive and nonabusive families.* Paper presented at the annual meeting of the Association for the Advancement of Behavior Therapy, Atlanta, GA.

Anderson, K. E., Lytton, H., & Romney, D. M. (1986). Mothers' interactions with normal and conduct-disordered boys: Who affects whom? *Developmental Psychology, 22,* 604–609.

Andison, F. S. (1977). TV violence and viewer aggression: A cumulation of study results: 1956–1976. *Public Opinion Quarterly, 41,* 314–333.

Appel, J. B. (1963). Punishment and shock intensity. *Science, 141,* 528–529.

Ardener, S. G. (1973). Sexual insult and female militancy. *Man, 8,* 422–440.

Ardrey, R. (1966). *The territorial imperative.* New York: Atheneum.

Arkin, R. M. (1981). Self-presentation styles. In J. T. Tedeschi (Ed.), *Impression management theory and social psychological research* (pp. 311–334). San Diego, CA: Academic Press.

Asch, S. E. (1951). Effects of group pressure on the modification and distortion of judgments. In H. Guetzkow (Ed.), *Groups, leadership and men* (pp. 177–190). Pittsburgh, PA: Carnegie Press.

AuBuchon, P. G., & Calhoun, K. S. (1985). Menstrual cycle symptomatology: The role of social expectancy and experimental demand characteristics. *Psychosomatic Medicine, 47,* 35–45.

Austin, J. L. (1961). *Philosophical papers.* New York: Oxford University Press.

Averill, J. R. (1982). *Anger and aggression: An essay on emotion.* New York: Springer-Verlag.

Averill, J. R. (1983). Studies on anger and aggression: Implications for theories of emotion. *American Psychologist, 38,* 1145–1160.

Averill, J. R. (1993). Illusions of anger. In R. B. Felson & J. T. Tedeschi (Eds.), *Aggression and violence: Social interactionist perspectives* (pp. 171–192). Washington, DC: American Psychological Association.

Azrin, N. H. (1960). Effects of punishment intensity during variable-interval reinforcement. *Journal of the Experimental Analysis of Behavior, 3,* 123–142.

Azrin, N. H. (1970). Punishment of elicited aggression. *Journal of the Experimental Analysis of Behavior, 14,* 7–10.

Azrin, N. H., Hutchinson, R. R., & Hake, D. F. (1963). Pain-induced fighting in the squirrel monkey. *Journal of the Experimental Analysis of Behavior, 6,* 620.

Azrin, N. H., Hutchinson, R. R., & Hake, D. F. (1967). Attack, avoidance, and escape reactions to aversive shock. *Journal of the Experimental Analysis of Behavior, 10,* 131–148.

Bachrach, R. S. (1986). The differential effect of observation of violence on kibbutz and city children in Israel. In L. R. Huesmann & L. D. Eron (Eds.), *Television and the aggressive child: A cross-national comparison* (pp. 201–238). Hillsdale, NJ: Erlbaum.

Baenninger, R., & Grossman, J. C. (1969). Some effects of punishment on pain-elicited aggression. *Journal of the Experimental Analysis of Behavior, 12,* 1017–1022.

Baer, R., Hinkle, S., Smith, K., & Fenton, M. (1980). Reactance as a function of actual versus projected autonomy. *Journal of Personality and Social Psychology, 38,* 416–422.

Ball-Rokeach, S. J. (1973). Values and violence: A test of the subculture of violence thesis. *American Sociological Review, 38,* 736–749.

Bandura, A. (1971). *Social learning theory.* New York: General Learning Press.

Bandura, A. (1973). *Aggression: A social learning analysis.* Englewood Cliffs, NJ: Prentice Hall.

Bandura, A. (1977). *Social learning theory.* Englewood Cliffs, NJ: Prentice Hall.

Bandura, A. (1983). Psychological mechanisms of aggression. In R. G. Geen & E. I. Donnerstein (Eds.), *Aggression: Theoretical and empirical reviews* (Vol. 1, pp. 1–40). San Diego, CA: Academic Press.

Bandura, A. (1986). *Social foundations of thought and action: A social cognitive theory.* Englewood Cliffs, NJ: Prentice Hall.

Bandura, A., Ross, D., & Ross, S. (1963). Vicarious reinforcement and imitative learning. *Journal of Abnormal and Social Psychology, 67,* 601–607.

Bandura, A., & Walters, R. H. (1959). *Adolescent aggression.* New York: Ronald Press.

Bandura, A., & Walters, R. H. (1963). *Social learning and personality development.* New York: Holt, Rinehart & Winston.

Barber, R. N. (1969). Prostitution and the increasing number of convictions for rape in Queensland. *Australian and New Zealand Journal of Criminology, 2,* 169–174.

Baron, J. N., & Reiss, P. C. (1985). Same time next year: Aggregate analyses of the mass media and violent behavior. *American Sociological Review, 50,* 347–363.

Baron, L., & Straus, M. A. (1987). Four theories of rape: A macrosociological analysis. *Social Problems, 34,* 467–489.

Baron, R. A. (1971). Magnitude of victim's pain cues and level of prior anger arousal as determinants of adult aggressive behavior. *Journal of Personality and Social Psychology, 17,* 236–243.

Baron, R. A. (1973). Threatened retaliation from the victim as an inhibitor of physical aggression. *Journal of Research in Personality, 21,* 183–189.

Baron, R. A. (1974a). The aggression-inhibiting influence of heightened sexual arousal. *Journal of Personality and Social Psychology, 30,* 318–322.

Baron, R. A. (1974b). Sexual arousal and physical aggression: The inhibiting influence of "cheesecake" and nudes. *Bulletin of the Psychonomic Society, 3,* 337–339.

Baron, R. A. (1977). *Human aggression.* New York: Plenum.

Baron, R. A. (1979). Effects of victim's pain cues, victim's race, and level of prior instigation upon physical aggression. *Journal of Applied Social Psychology, 9,* 103–114.

Baron, R. A. (1988). Negative effects of destructive criticism: Impact on conflict, self-efficacy, and task performance. *Journal of Applied Psychology, 73,* 199–207.

Baron, R. A., & Bell, P. A. (1973). Effects of heightened sexual arousal on physical aggression. *Proceedings of the 81st Annual Convention of the American Psychological Association, 8,* 171–172.

Baron, R. A., & Bell, P. A. (1975). Aggression and heat: Mediating effects of prior provocation and exposure to an aggressive model. *Journal of Personality and Social Psychology, 31,* 825–832.

Baron, R. A., & Bell, P. A. (1976). Aggression and heat: The influence of ambient temperature, negative affect, and a cooling drink on physical aggression. *Journal of Personality and Social Psychology, 33,* 245–255.

Baron, R. A., & Bell, P. A. (1977). Sexual arousal and aggression by males: Effects of type of erotic stimuli and prior provocation. *Journal of Personality and Social Psychology, 35,* 79–87.

Baron, R. A., & Kepner, C. R. (1970). Model's behavior and attraction toward the model as determinants of adult aggressive behavior. *Journal of Personality and Social Psychology, 14,* 335–344.

Baron, R. A., & Richardson, D. (1993). *Human aggression.* (2nd ed.). New York: Plenum.

Barry, H., III, Josephson, L., Lauer, E., & Marshall, C. (1980). Agents and techniques for child training: Cross-cultural codes, 6. In H. Barry III & A. Schlegel (Eds.), *Cross-cultural samples and codes* (pp. 237–276). Pittsburgh, PA: University of Pittsburgh Press.

Bartos, O. J. (1966). Concession-making in experimental negotiations. *General Systems, 10,* 145–156. (SSRI Preprint No. 6)

Baumeister, R. F., Stillwell, A., & Wotman, S. R. (1990). Victim and perpetrator accounts of interpersonal conflict: Autobiographical narratives about anger. *Journal of Personality and Social Psychology, 59,* 994–1005.

Baumeister, R. F., Tice, D. M., & Hutton, D. G. (1989). Self-presentational motivations and personality differences in self-esteem. *Journal of Personality, 57,* 547–579.

Baumgartner, M. P. (1988). *The moral order of a suburb.* New York: Oxford University Press.

Baumgartner, M. P. (1993). Violent networks: The origins and management of domestic conflict. In R. B. Felson & J. T. Tedeschi (Eds.), *Aggression and violence: Social interactionist perspectives* (pp. 209–231). Washington, DC: American Psychological Association.

Beach, F. A. (1974). Behavioral endocrinology and the study of reproduction. *Biology of Reproduction, 10,* 2–18.

Beach, L. R., & Mitchell, T. R. (1978, July). A contingency model for the selection of decision strategies. *Academy of Management Review,* 439–449.

Beeman, E. A. (1947). The effect of male hormone on aggressive behavior in mice. *Physiological Zoology, 20,* 373–405.

Bell, A. P., & Weinberg, M. S. (1978). *Homosexualities: A study of diversity among men & women.* New York: Simon & Shuster.

Bell, P. A., & Baron, R. A. (1976). Aggression and heat: The mediating role of negative affect. *Journal of Applied Social Psychology, 6,* 18–30.

Bell, P. A., & Baron, R. A. (1977). Aggression and ambient temperature: The facilitating and inhibiting effects of hot and cold environments. *Bulletin of the Psychonomic Society, 9,* 443–445.

Berg, I., & Fox, V. (1947). Factors in homicides committed by 200 males. *Journal of Social Psychology, 26,* 109–119.

Berkowitz, L. (1962). *Aggression: A social psychological analysis.* New York: McGraw-Hill.

Berkowitz, L. (1964). Aggressive cues in aggressive behavior and hostility catharsis. *Psychological Review, 71,* 104–122.

Berkowitz, L. (1965a). The concept of aggressive drive: Some additional considerations. In L. Berkowitz (Ed.), *Advances in experimental social psychology* (Vol. 2, pp. 301–330). San Diego, CA: Academic Press.

Berkowitz, L. (1965b). Some aspects of observed aggression. *Journal of Personality and Social Psychology, 2,* 359–369.

Berkowitz, L. (1981a). The goals of aggression. In D. Finkelhor, R. J. Gelles, G. T. Hotaling, & M. A. Straus (Eds.), *The dark side of families* (pp. 166–180). Beverly Hills, CA: Sage.

Berkowitz, L. (1981b, June). How guns control us. *Psychology Today,* pp. 11–12.

Berkowitz, L. (1981c). On the differences between internal and external reactions to legitimate and illegitimate frustration: A demonstration. *Aggressive Behavior, 7,* 83–96.

Berkowitz, L. (1982). Aversive conditions as stimuli to aggression. In L. Berkowitz (Ed.), *Advances in experimental social psychology* (Vol. 15, pp. 3–15). San Diego, CA: Academic Press.

Berkowitz, L. (1983a). Aversively stimulated aggression: Some parallels and differences in research with animals and humans. *American Psychologist, 38,* 1134–1144.

Berkowitz, L. (1983b). The experience of anger as a parallel process in the display of impulsive, "angry" aggression. In R. G. Geen & E. I. Donnerstein (Eds.), *Aggression: Theoretical and empirical reviews* (Vol. 1, pp. 103–133). San Diego, CA: Academic Press.

Berkowitz, L. (1984). Some effects of thoughts on anti- and prosocial influences of media events: A cognitive-neoassociation analysis. *Psychological Bulletin, 95,* 410–427.

Berkowitz, L. (1986). Some varieties of human aggression: Criminal violence as coercion, rule-following, impression management, and impulsive behavior. In A. Campbell & J. J. Gibbs (Eds.), *Violent transactions* (pp. 87–103). Oxford, England: Basil Blackwell.

Berkowitz, L. (1988). Frustrations, appraisals, and aversively stimulated aggression. *Aggressive Behavior, 14,* 3–11.

Berkowitz, L. (1989). The frustration–aggression hypothesis: An examination and reformulation. *Psychological Bulletin, 106,* 59–73.

Berkowitz, L. (1993). *Aggression: Its causes, consequences, and control.* New York: McGraw-Hill.

Berkowitz, L., & Alioto, J. T. (1973). The meaning of an observed event as a determinant of its aggressive consequences. *Journal of Personality and Social Psychology, 28,* 206–217.

Berkowitz, L., Cochran, S. T., & Embree, M. C. (1981). Physical pain and the goal of aversively stimulated aggression. *Journal of Personality and Social Psychology, 40,* 687–700.

Berkowitz, L., Corwin, R., & Heironimus, M. (1962). Film violence and subsequent aggressive tendencies. *Public Opinion Quarterly, 27,* 217–229.

Berkowitz, L., & Geen, R. G. (1966). Film violence and the cue properties of available targets. *Journal of Personality and Social Psychology, 3,* 525–530.

Berkowitz, L., & Geen, R. G. (1967). Stimulus qualities of the target of aggression: A further study. *Journal of Personality and Social Psychology, 5,* 364–368.

Berkowitz, L., & LePage, A. (1967). Weapons as aggression-eliciting stimuli. *Journal of Personality and Social Psychology, 7,* 202–207.

Berkowitz, L., & Rawlings, E. (1963). Effects of film violence: An inhibition against subsequent aggression. *Journal of Abnormal and Social Psychology, 66,* 405–412.

Berkowitz, L., & Thome, P. R. (1987). Pain expectation, negative affect, and angry aggression. *Motivation and Emotion, 11,* 183–193.

Berne, E. (1964). *Games people play.* New York: Grove Press.

Bernstein, I. S., Gordon, T. P., & Rose, R. M. (1983). The interaction of hormones, behavior, and social context in nonhuman primates. In B. Svare (Ed.), *Hormones and aggressive behavior* (pp. 535–562). New York: Plenum.

Bernstein, I. S., & Mason, W. A. (1963). Group formation by rhesus monkeys. *Animal Behavior, 11,* 28–31.

Best, A., & Andreasen, A. R. (1977). Consumer responses to unsatisfactory purchases: A survey of perceiving defects, voicing complaints, and obtaining redress. *Law and Society Review, 11,* 701–742.

Bies, R. J. (1986, August). *Identifying principles of interactional justice: The case of corporate recruiting.* Paper presented at the annual meeting of the National Academy of Management, Chicago.

Bies, R. J., & Moag, J. S. (1986). Interactional justice: Communications criteria of fairness. In R. Lewitzki, M. Bazerman, & B. Sheppard (Eds.), *Research on negotiation in organizations* (Vol. 1, pp. 43–55). Greenwich, CT: JAI Press.

Bisanz, G. L., & Rule, B. G. (1989). Gender and the persuasion schema: A search for cognitive invariants. *Personality and Social Psychology Bulletin, 15,* 4–18.

Bjorkqvist, K., Lagerspetz, K. M. J., & Kaukiainen, A. (1992). Do girls manipulate and boys fight? Developmental trends in regard to direct and indirect aggression. *Aggressive Behavior, 18,* 117–127.

Black, D. J. (1970). Production of crime rates. *American Sociological Review, 35,* 733–748.

Black, D. J. (1983). Crime as social control. *American Sociological Review, 48,* 34–45.

Black, D. J., & Reiss, A. H. (1970). Police control of juveniles. *American Sociological Review, 35,* 63–77.

Blackburn, R. (1978). Psychopathy, arousal, and the need for stimulation. In R. D. Hare & D. Schalling (Eds.), *Psychopathic behavior: Approaches to research* (pp. 157–164). New York: Wiley.

Block, J. (1983). Differential premises arising from differential socialization of the sexes: Some conjectures. *Child Development, 54,* 1335–1354.

Blumberg, S. R., & Hokanson, J. E. (1983). The effects of another person's response style on interpersonal behavior in depression. *Journal of Abnormal Psychology, 92,* 196–209.

Blumenthal, M., Kahn, R. L., Andrews, F. M., & Head, K. B. (1972). *Justifying violence: Attitudes of American men.* Ann Arbor, MI: Institute for Social Research.

Blumstein, A., & Cohen, J. (1979). Estimation of individual crime rates from arrest records, *Journal of Criminal Law and Criminology, 70,* 561–585.

Blumstein, P. W., Carssow, K. G., Hall, J., Hawkins, B., Hoffman, R., Ishem, E., Maurer, C. P., Spens, D., Taylor, J., & Zimmerman, D. L. (1974). The honoring of accounts. *American Sociological Review, 39,* 551–566.

Bober, J. (1991). *Begehen und Unterlassen. eine experimentelle Ueberpruefung der Beurteilung ihres aggressiven Gehalts* [Action and inaction: An experimental study of perceived aggression]. Münster, Germany: Lit-Verlag.

Boelkins, C. R., & Heiser, J. F. (1970). Biological bases of aggression. In D. N. Daniels, M. F. Gilula, & F. M. Ochberg (Eds.), *Violence and the struggle for existence* (pp. 15–52). Boston: Little, Brown.

Boldizar, J. P., Perry, D. G., & Perry, L. C. (1989). Outcome values and aggression. *Child Development, 60,* 571–579.

Bolles, R. C. (1967). *Theory of motivation.* New York: Harper & Row.

Bond, M. H., & Venus, C. K. (1991). Resistance to group or personal insults in an ingroup or outgroup context. *International Journal of Psychology, 26,* 83–94.

Borden, R. J. (1975). Witnessed aggression: Influence of an observer's sex and values on aggressive responding. *Journal of Personality and Social Psychology, 31,* 567–573.

Borden, R. J., & Taylor, S. P. (1973). The social instigation and control of physical aggression. *Journal of Applied Social Psychology, 3,* 354–361.

Bornerwasser, M., & Mummendey, A. (1982). Effects of Arbitrary provocation and arousal on aggressive behavior. *Aggressive Behavior, 8,* 229–232.

Boulding, K. E. (1965). Reality testing and value orientation. *International Social Science Journal, 17,* 404–416.

Boulding, K. E. (1968). Am I a man or a mouse—or both? In A. Montagu (Ed.), *Man and aggression* (pp. 168–175). New York: Oxford University Press.

Braaten, D. O., Cody, M. J., & Bell, K. (1990, June). *Account episodes in organizations: Remedial work and impression management.* Paper presented at the annual meeting of the International Communication Association, Dublin, Ireland.

Brain, P. H. (1984). Biological explanations of human aggression and the resulting therapies offered by such approaches: A critical evaluation. In R. J. Blanchard & D. C. Blanchard (Eds.), *Advances in the study of aggression* (Vol. 1, pp. 63–102). San Diego, CA: Academic Press.

Braine, L. G., Pomerantz, E., Lorber, D., & Krantz, D. H. (1991). Conflicts with authority: Children's feelings, actions, and justifications. *Developmental Psychology, 27,* 829–840.

Bramel, D. (1969). Interpersonal attraction, hostility, and perception. In J. Mills (Ed.), *Experimental social psychology* (pp. 1–120). New York: Macmillan.

Bramel, D., Taub, B., & Blum, B. (1968). An observer's reaction to the suffering of his enemy. *Journal of Personality and Social Psychology, 8,* 384–392.

Brand, P. A., & Kidd, A. H. (1986). Frequency of physical aggression in heterosexual and female homosexual dyads. *Psychological Reports, 59,* 1307–1313.

Brantingham, P. J., & Brantingham, P. L. (Eds.). (1990). *Environmental criminology.* Prospect Heights, IL: Waveland.

Brehm, S. S., & Brehm, J. W. (1981). *Psychological reactance: A theory of freedom and control.* San Diego, CA: Academic Press.

Brennan, P., Mednick, S., & John, J. R. (1989). Specialization in violence: Evidence of criminal subgroup. *Criminology, 27,* 437–453.

Brent, E. E., & Sykes, R. E. (1979). A mathematical model of symbolic interaction between police and suspects. *Behavioral Science, 24,* 388–402.

Briere, J., Malamuth, N., & Check, J. V. P. (1985). Sexuality and rape-supportive beliefs. *International Journal of Women's Studies, 8,* 398–403.

Briggs, J. L. (1970). *Never in anger: Portrait of an Eskimo family.* Cambridge, MA: Harvard University Press.

Brockner, J., Rubin, J. Z., Fine, J., Hamilton, T. P., Thomas, B., & Turetsky, B. (1982). Factors affecting entrapment in escalating conflicts: The importance of timing. *Journal of Research in Personality, 16,* 247–266.

Bronfenbrenner, U. (1958). Socialization and social class through time and space. In E. E. Maccoby, T. M. Newcomb, & E. L. Hartley (Eds.), *Readings in social psychology* (3rd ed., pp. 400–424). New York: Holt, Rinehart & Winston.

Broude, G. J., & Greene, S. J. (1976). Cross-cultural codes on twenty sexual attitudes and practices. *Ethnology, 15,* 409–429.

Broverman, I. K., Vogel, S. R., Broverman, D. M., Clarkson, F. E., & Rosenkrantz, P. S. (1972). Sex-role stereotypes: A current appraisal. *Journal of Social Issues, 28,* 59–78.

Brown, B. R. (1968). The effects of need to maintain face in interpersonal bargaining. *Journal of Experimental Social Psychology, 4,* 107–122.

Brown, J. S. (1952). A comparative study of deviations from sexual mores. *American Sociological Review, 17,* 135–146.

Brown, J. S., & Farber, I. E. (1951). Emotions conceptualized as intervening variables with suggestions toward a theory of frustration. *Psychological Bulletin, 48,* 465–495.

Brown, P. (1980). How and why are women more polite?: Some evidence from a Mayan community. In S. McConnell-Ginet, R. Borker, & N. Furman (Eds.), *Women and language in literature and society* (pp. 111–136). New York: Praeger.

Brown, P., & Elliott, R. (1965). Control of aggression in a nursery school class. *Journal of Experimental Child Psychology, 2,* 103–107.

Brown, P., & Levinson, S. C. (1987). *Politeness: Some universals in language usage.* New York: Cambridge University Press.

Brown, R. (1965). *Social psychology.* New York: Free Press.

Brown, R. C., Jr., & Tedeschi, J. T. (1976). Determinants of perceived aggression. *Journal of Social Psychology, 100,* 77–87.

Brown, S. A., Goldman, M. S., Inn, A., & Anderson, L. R. (1980). Expectations of reinforcement from alcohol: Their domain and relation to drinking patterns. *Journal of Counseling and Clinical Psychology, 48,* 419–426.

Brownmiller, S. (1975). *Against our will: Men, women and rape.* New York: Simon & Schuster.

Brunn, K., Markkanen, T., & Partanen, J. (1966). *Inheritance of drinking behavior, a study of adult twins.* Helsinki, Finland: Finnish Foundation for Alcohol Research.

Bryant, J., & Zillmann, D. (1979). Effect of intensification of annoyance through unrelated residual excitation on substantially delayed hostile behavior. *Journal of Experimental Social Psychology, 15,* 470–480.

Buck, R. (1985). Prime theory: An integrated view of motivation and emotion. *Psychological Review, 92,* 389–413.

Buehler, R. E., Patterson, G. R., & Furniss, J. M. (1966). The reinforcement of behavior in institutional settings. *Behavior Research and Therapy, 4,* 157–167.

Bureau of Justice Statistical Services. (1993, December). *New York State bias crime incident reporting program: Data from 1992 report.* Albany: New York State Division of Criminal Justice Services.

Bureau of Justice Statistics. (1983). *Report to the nation on crime and justice: The data.* Washington, DC: National Institute of Justice.

Bureau of Justice Statistics. (1985). *The crime of rape.* Washington, DC: U.S. Department of Justice.

Bureau of Justice Statistics. (1993). *Sourcebook of criminal justice statistics—1992.* Washington, DC: U.S. Department of Justice.

Burgess, A. W., & Holstrom, L. L. (1974). *Rape: Victims of crisis.* Bowie, MD: Robert J. Brady.

Burgess, R. L. (1979). Child abuse: A social interactional analysis. In B. D. Lahey & A. E. Kazdin (Eds.), *Advances in clinical child psychology* (Vol. 2, pp. 142–172). New York: Plenum.

Burgess, R. L., & Conger, R. D. (1978). Family interactions in abusive, neglectful, and normal families. *Child Development, 49,* 1163–1173.

Burt, M. R. (1980). Cultural myths and support for rape. *Journal of Personality and Social Psychology, 38,* 217–230.

Buss, A. H. (1961). *The psychology of aggression.* New York: Wiley.

Buss, A. H. (1963). Physical aggression in relation to different frustrations. *Journal of Abnormal and Social Psychology, 67,* 1–7.

Buss, A. H. (1966a). The effect of harm on subsequent aggression. *Journal of Experimental Research in Personality, 1,* 249–255.

Buss, A. H. (1966b). Instrumentality of aggression, feedback, and frustration as determinants of physical aggression. *Journal of Personality and Social Psychology, 3,* 153–162.

Buss, A. H. (1971). Aggression pays. In J. L. Singer (Ed.), *The control of aggression and violence* (pp. 7–18). San Diego, CA: Academic Press.

Buss, A. H., Booker, A., & Buss, E. (1972). Firing a weapon and aggression. *Journal of Personality and Social Psychology, 22,* 296–302.

Buss, A. H., & Durkee, A. (1957). An inventory for assessing different kinds of hostility. *Journal of Consulting Psychology, 21,* 343–349.

Buss, A. H., & Plomin, R. (1984). *Temperament: Early developing personality traits.* Hillsdale, NJ: Erlbaum.

Buss, A. R. (1978). Causes and reasons in attribution theory: A conceptual critique. *Journal of Personality and Social Psychology, 3,* 153–162.

Buss, D. M. (1989a). Conflict between the sexes: Strategic interference and the evocation of anger and upset. *Journal of Personality and Social Psychology, 56,* 735–747.

Buss, D. M. (1989b). Sex differences in human mate preferences: Evolutionary hypotheseses in 37 cultures. *Behavioral and Brain Sciences, 12,* 1–49.

Byrne, D. (1971). *The attraction paradigm.* San Diego, CA: Academic Press.

Cahalan, D. (1978). Implications of American drinking practices and attitudes for prevention and treatment of alcoholism. In G. A. Marlatt & P. E. Nathan (Eds.), *Behavioral approaches to alcoholism* (pp. 6–26). New Brunswick, NJ: Rutgers Center for Alcohol Studies.

Cahn, E. (1949). *The sense of injustice.* Bloomington: Indiana University Press.

Cairns, R. B., Cairns, B. D., Neckderman, H. J., Gest, S. D., & Gariepy, J. (1988). Social networks and aggressive behavior: Peer support or peer rejection? *Developmental Psychology, 24,* 815–823.

Camp, D. S., Raymond, G. A., & Church, R. M. (1967). Temporal relationship between response and punishment. *Journal of Experimental Psychology, 74,* 114–123.

Canter, S. (1973). Personality traits in twins. In G. Claridge, S. Canter, & W. I. Hume (Eds.), *Personality differences and biological variations* (pp. 21–51). Elmsford, NY: Pergamon Press.

Cantoni, L. (1981). Clinical issues in domestic violence. *Social Casework: The Journal of Contemporary Social Work, 62,* 3–12.

Caprara, G. V., Renzi, P., D'Augello, D., D'Imperio, G., Rielli, I., & Travaglia, G. (1986). Interpolating physical exercise between instigation to aggress and aggression: The role of irritability and emotional susceptibility. *Aggressive Behavior, 12,* 83–91.

Carlson, B. (1992). Questioning the party line on family violence. *Affilia, 7,* 94–110.

Carlson, M., Marcus-Newhall, A., & Miller, N. (1990). Effects of situational aggression cues: A quantitative review. *Journal of Personality and Social Psychology, 58,* 622–633.

Carpenter, C. R. (1940). A field study in Siam of the behavior and social relations of the gibbon. *Comparative Psychology Monographs, 16,* 1–212.

Carroll, D., & O'Callaghan, M. A. J. (1981). Psychosurgery and the control of aggression. In P. F. Brain & D. Benton (Eds.), *The biology of aggression* (pp. 457–472). Alphen aan den Rijn, The Netherlands: Noordhoff/Sijthoff.

Carroll, J. S. (1978). A psychological approach to deterrence: The evaluation of crime opportunities. *Journal of Personality and Social Psychology, 36,* 1512–1520.

Carver, C. S. (1974). Physical aggression as a function of objective self-awareness and attitudes toward punishment. *Journal of Experimental Social Psychology, 11,* 510–519.

Cattell, R. B. (1972). The nature and genesis of mood states: A theoretical model with experimental measurements concerning anxiety, depression, arousal, and other mood states. In C. D. Spielberger (Ed.), *Anxiety: Current trends in theory and research* (pp. 115–183). San Diego, CA: Academic Press.

Cederlöf, R., Friberg, L., Jonsson, E., & Kaij, L. (1961). Studies on similarity diagnosis with the aid of mailed questionnaires. *Acta Genetica et Statistica Medica, 11,* 338–362.

Chagnon, N. A. (1977). *Yanomamo, the fierce people.* New York: Holt, Rinehart & Winston.

Chapman, M., & Zahn-Waxler, C. (1982). Young children's compliance and noncompliance to parental discipline in a natural setting. *International Journal of Behavioral Development, 5,* 81–94.

Chappell, D., & James, J. (1976, September). *Victim selection and apprehension from the rapist's perspective: A preliminary investigation.* Paper presented at the Second International Symposium on Victimology, Boston.

Chasdi, E. H., & Lawrence, M. S. (1955). Some antecedents of aggression and effects of frustration in doll play. In D. McClelland (Ed.), *Studies in motivation* (pp. 517–528). New York: Appleton-Century-Crofts.

Chiricos, T. G., & Waldo, G. P. (1975). Socioeconomic status and criminal sentencing: An empirical assessment of a conflict proposition, *American Sociological Review, 40*, 753–772.

Christiansen, K. O. (1974). The genesis of aggressive criminality: Implications of a study of crime in a Danish twin study. In J. de Wit & W. W. Hartup (Eds.), *Determinants and origins of aggressive behavior* (pp. 233–253). The Hague, The Netherlands: Mouton.

Cialdini, R. B., & Richardson, K. D. (1980). Two indirect tactics of image management: Basking and blasting. *Journal of Personality and Social Psychology, 39*, 406–415.

Cicchetti, D. (1987). Developmental psychopathology in infancy: Illustration from the study of maltreated youngsters. *Journal of Consulting and Clinical Psychology, 55*, 837–845.

Claerhout, S., Elder, J., & Janes, C. (1982). Problem-solving skills of rural battered women. *American Journal of Community Psychology, 10*, 605–613.

Clark, R. D., III. (1990). The impact of AIDS on gender differences in willingness to engage in casual sex. *Journal of Applied Social Psychology, 20*, 771–782.

Clark, W. B., & Midanik, L. (1982). Alcohol use and alcohol problems among U.S. adults: Results of the 1979 National Survey. In *Alcohol consumption and related problems* (Alcohol and Health Monograph 1, pp. 3–52, DHHS Publication No. ADM 82-1190). Washington, DC: U.S. Government Printing Office.

Claster, D. S. (1967). Comparison of risk perception between delinquents and nondelinquents. *Journal of Criminal Law, Criminology, and Police Science, 58*, 80–86.

Cleaver, E. (1968). *Soul on ice.* New York: Dell-Delta/Ramparts.

Cline, V. B., Croft, R. G., & Courrier, S. (1973). The desensitization of children to television violence. *Journal of Personality and Social Psychology, 27*, 360–365.

Cloninger, C. R., & Gottesman, I. I. (1987). Genetic and environmental factors in antisocial behavior disorders. In S. A. Mednick, T. E. Moffitt, & S. A. Stark (Eds.), *The causes of crime: New biological approaches* (pp. 92–109). New York: Cambridge University Press.

Cloward, R. A., & Ohlin, L. E. (1960). *Delinquency and opportunity: A theory of delinquent gangs.* New York: Free Press of Glencoe.

Coccaro, E. F., Bergeman, C. S., & McClearn, G. E. (1993). Heritability of irritable impulsiveness: A study of twins reared together and apart. *Psychiatry Research, 48,* 229–242.

Cody, M. J., & Braaten, D. O. (1992). The social-interactive aspects of account-giving. In M. L. McLaughlin, M. J. Cody, & S. J. Read (Eds.), *Explaining oneself to others: Reason-giving in a social context* (pp. 225–243). Hillsdale, NJ: Erlbaum.

Cody, M. J., & McLaughlin, M. L. (1988). Accounts on trial: Oral arguments in traffic court. In C. Antaki (Ed.), *Analyzing everyday explanation: A casebook of methods* (pp. 113–126). London: Sage.

Cohen, A. (1955). *Delinquent boys.* New York: Free Press of Glencoe.

Cohen, A. R. (1955). Social norms, arbitrariness of frustration, and status of the agent of frustration in the frustration–aggression hypothesis. *Journal of Abnormal and Social Psychology, 51,* 222–226.

Cohen, D. J., Dibble, E., Grawe, J. M., & Pollin, W. (1973). Separating identical from fraternal twins. *Archives of General Psychiatry, 29,* 465–469.

Cohen, L. E., & Felson, M. (1979). Social change and crime rate trends: A routine activity approach. *American Sociological Review, 44,* 588–608.

Cohen, L. E., Kluegel, R., & Land, K. (1981). Social inequality and predatory criminal victimization: An exposition and test of a formal theory. *American Sociological Review, 46,* 505–524.

Cohen, S. (1980). After-effects of stress on human performance and social behavior: A review of research and theory. *Psychological Bulletin, 88,* 82–108.

Cohen, S., Evans, G. W., Krantz, D. S., & Stokols, D. (1980). Physiological, motivational and cognitive effects of aircraft noise on children: Moving from the laboratory to the field. *American Psychologist, 35,* 231–243.

Coie, J., & Dodge, K. A. (1983). Continuities and changes in children's social status: A five-year longitudinal study. *Merrill-Palmer Quarterly, 29,* 261–282.

Coleman, K. H. (1980). Conjugal violence: What 33 men report. *Journal of Marital and Family Therapy, 6,* 207–213.

Collins, W. A., Berndt, T. J., & Hess, V. L. (1984). Observational learning of motives and consequences for television aggression: A developmental study. *Child Development, 45,* 799–802.

Conklin, J. E. (1972). *Robbery and the criminal justice system.* New York: Lippincott.

Connor, R. L., & Levine, S. (1969). Hormonal influences on aggressive behaviour. In S. Garanttini & E. B. Sigg (Eds.), *Aggressive behaviour* (pp. 150–163). New York: Wiley.

Connor-Linton, J. (1986). Gender differences in politeness: The struggle for power among adolescents. In J. Connor-Linton, C. J. Hall, & M. McGinnis (Eds.), *Southern California Occasional Papers in Linguistics, 11,* 64–98.

Cook, P. J., & Nagin, D. (1979). *Does the weapon matter?* Washington, DC: Institute of Law and Social Research.

Cook, T. D., Kendzierski, D. A., & Thomas, S. V. (1983). The implicit assumptions of television: An analysis of the 1982 NIMH Report on Television and Behavior. *Public Opinion Quarterly, 47,* 161–201.

Cornish, D., & Clarke, R. (Eds.). (1986). *The reasoning criminal: Rational choice perspectives on offending.* New York: Springer-Verlag.

Cotton, J. L. (1981). A review of research on Schachter's theory of emotion and the misattribution of arousal. *European Journal of Social Psychology, 11,* 365–397.

Cowan, P. A., & Walters, R. H. (1963). Studies of reinforcement of aggression: Part I. Effects of scheduling. *Child Development, 34,* 543–551.

Coyne, J. C. (1976). Depression and the response of others. *Journal of Abnormal Psychology, 85,* 186–193.

Craig, M. E., Kalichman, S. C., & Follingstad, D. R. (1989). Coercive sexual behavior among college students: Relationship characteristics and affective experiences. *Archives of Sexual Behavior, 18,* 421–434.

Crockenberg, S., & Litman, C. (1990). Autonomy as competence in 2-year-olds: Maternal correlates of child defiance, compliance, and self-assertion. *Developmental Psychology, 26,* 961–971.

Crowe, L. C., & George, W. H. (1989). Alcohol and human sexuality: Review and integration. *Psychological Bulletin, 105,* 374–386.

Cusson, M., & Pinsonneault, P. (1986). The decision to give up crime. In D. Cornish & R. Clarke (Eds.), *The reasoning criminal: Rational choice perspectives on offending* (pp. 72–82). New York: Springer-Verlag.

Dahl, R. A. (1957). The concept of power. *Behavioral Science, 2,* 201–218.

Dahlbäck, O. (1978). *Risktagande* [Risk-taking]. Unpublished doctoral dissertation, University of Stockholm, Sweden.

Dalton, K. (1964). *The premenstrual syndrome.* Springfield, IL: Charles C Thomas.

Dalton, K. (1982). Premenstrual tension: An overview. In R. C. Friedman (Ed.), *Behavior and the menstrual cycle* (pp. 217–242). New York: Dekker.

Daly, M., & Wilson, M. (1988). *Homicide.* New York: Aldine.

Darwin, C. (1936). *The origin of the species.* New York: Modern Library. (Original work published 1859)

Davitz, J. R. (1952). The effects of previous training on post-frustration behavior. *Journal of Abnormal and Social Psychology, 47,* 309–315.

Dedrick, D. K. (1978). Deviance and sanctioning within small groups *Social Psychology, 41,* 94–105.

Deming, M. B., & Eppy, A. (1981). The sociology of rape. *Sociology and Social Research, 64,* 357–380.

Dengerink, H. A. (1976). Personality variables as mediators of attack-instigated aggression. In R. G. Geen & E. C. O'Neal (Eds.), *Perspectives on aggression* (pp. 61–98). San Diego, CA: Academic Press.

Dengerink, H. A., & Levendusky, O. G. (1972). Effects of massive retaliation and balance of power on aggression. *Journal of Experimental Research in Personality, 6,* 230–236.

DeRidder, R. (1985). Normative considerations in the labeling of harmful behavior as aggressive. *Journal of Social Psychology, 125,* 659–666.

DeRidder, R., Schruijer, S. G. L., & Tripathi, R. C. (1992). Norm violation as a precipitating factor of negative intergroup relations. In R. DeRidder & R. C. Tripathi (Eds.), *Norm violation and intergroup relations* (pp. 3–37). Oxford, England: Clarendon Press.

DeRidder, R., & Syroit, J. (1992, May). *Laypersons' view on aggression and injustice.* Paper presented at the East–West Meeting of the European Association of Experimental Social Psychology, Münster, Germany.

Deshields, T. L., Jenkins, J. O., & Tait, R. C. (1989). The experience of anger in chronic illness: A preliminary investigation. *International Journal of Psychiatry in Medicine, 19,* 299–309.

Deur, J. L., & Parke, R. D. (1970). The effects of inconsistent punishment on aggression in children. *Developmental Psychology, 2,* 403–411.

Deutsch, M. (1960). Trust, trustworthiness, and the F-scale. *Journal of Abnormal and Social Psychology, 61,* 138–140.

Deutsch, M. (1969). Socially relevant science: Reflections on some studies of interpersonal conflict. *American Psychologist, 24,* 1076–1092.

Deutsch, M., & Krauss, R. M. (1960). The effect of threat upon interpersonal bargaining. *Journal of Abnormal and Social Psychology, 61,* 181–189.

Deutsch, M., & Krauss, R. M. (1962). Studies of interpersonal bargaining. *Journal of Conflict Resolution, 6,* 52–76.

DiLalla, L. F., & Gottesman, I. I. (1991). Biological and genetic contributors to violence—Widom's untold tale. *Psychological Bulletin, 109,* 125–129.

Dion, K. K. (1972). Physical attractiveness and evaluation of children's transgressions. *Journal of Personality and Social Psychology, 24,* 207–213.

Dipboye, R. L. (1977). Alternative approaches to deindividuation. *Psychological Bulletin, 84,* 1057–1075.

Disbrow, M. A., Doerr, H., & Caulfield, C. (1977). Measuring the components of parents' potential for child abuse and neglect. *Child Abuse and Neglect, 1,* 279–296.

Dix, T., Ruble, D. N., & Zambarano, R. J. (1989). Mother's implicit theories of discipline: Child effects, parent effects and the attribution process. *Child Development, 60,* 1373–1391.

Dobash, R. P., Dobash, R. E., Wilson, M., & Daly, M. (1992). The myth of sexual symmetry in marital violence. *Social Problems, 39,* 71–91.

Dodge, K. A., & Coie, J. D. (1987). Social-information-processing factors in reactive and proactive aggression in children's peer groups. *Journal of Personality and Social Psychology, 53,* 1146–1158.

Dodge, K. A., & Crick, N. R. (1990). Social-information-processing bases of aggressive behavior in children. *Personality and Social Psychology Bulletin, 16,* 8–22.

Dodge, K. A., & Newman, J. P. (1981). Biased decision-making processes in aggressive boys. *Journal of Abnormal Psychology, 90,* 375–379.

Dodge, K. A., & Somberg, D. R. (1987). Hostile attributional biases among aggressive boys are exacerbated under conditions of threats to self. *Child Development, 58,* 213–224.

Dollard, J. (1957). *Caste and class in a southern town* (3rd ed.). Garden City, NY: Doubleday.

Dollard, J., Doob, N., Miller, N. E., Mowrer, O. H., & Sears, R. R. (1939). *Frustration and aggression.* New Haven, CT: Yale University Press.

Donnerstein, E. (1980). Aggressive erotica and violence against women. *Journal of Personality and Social Psychology, 39,* 269–277.

Donnerstein, E., & Barrett, G. (1978). The effects of erotic stimuli on male aggression toward females. *Journal of Personality and Social Psychology, 36,* 180–188.

Donnerstein, E., & Berkowitz, L. (1981). Victim reactions in aggressive erotic films as a factor in violence against women. *Journal of Personality and Social Psychology, 41,* 710–724.

Donnerstein, E., & Donnerstein, M. (1973). Variables in interracial aggression: Potential ingroup censure. *Journal of Personality and Social Psychology, 27,* 143–150.

Donnerstein, E., Donnerstein, M., & Evans, R. (1975). Erotic stimuli and aggression: Facilitation or inhibition. *Journal of Personality and Social Psychology, 32,* 237–244.

Donnerstein, E., Donnerstein, M., Simon, S., & Ditrichs, R. (1972). Variables in interracial aggression: Anonymity, expected retaliation, and a riot. *Journal of Personality and Social Psychology, 22,* 236–245.

Donnerstein, E., & Hallam, J. (1978). The facilitating effects of erotica on aggression toward females. *Journal of Personality and Social Psychology, 36,* 1270–1277.

Donnerstein, E., & Hatfield, E. (1982). Aggression and inequity. In J. Greenberg & R. Cohen (Eds.), *Equity and justice in social behavior (pp. 309–336).* San Diego, CA: Academic Press.

Donnerstein, E., & Linz, D. (1986). Mass media sexual violence and male viewers. *American Behavioral Scientist, 29,* 601–618.

Donnerstein, E., & Wilson, D. W. (1976). Effects of noise and perceived control on ongoing and subsequent aggressive behavior. *Journal of Personality and Social Psychology, 34,* 774–781.

Doob, A. N., & Wood, L. (1972). Catharsis and aggression: The effects of annoyance and retaliation on aggressive behavior. *Journal of Personality and Social Psychology, 22,* 156–162.

Dreiser, T. (1929). *An American tragedy*. New York: Liveright.

Dretske, F. I. (1988). *Knowledge and the flow of information*. Cambridge, MA: MIT Press.

DuBois, C. (1961). *The peoples of Alor*. New York: Harper & Row.

Duncan, B. L. (1976). Differential social perception and attribution of intergroup violence: Testing the lower limits of stereotyping Blacks. *Journal of Personality and Social Psychology, 34,* 590–598.

Dworkin, A. (1981). *Pornography: Men possessing women*. New York: Putnam.

Dyck, R. J., & Rule, B. G. (1978). Effects on retaliation of causal attributions concerning attack. *Journal of Personality and Social Psychology, 36,* 521–529.

Eagly, A. H., & Steffen, V. J. (1986). Gender and aggressive behavior: A meta-analytic review of the social psychological literature. *Psychological Bulletin, 100,* 309–330.

Edney, J. (1974). Human territoriality. *Psychological Bulletin, 12,* 959–975.

Edney, J. (1975). Territoriality and control: A field experiment. *Journal of Personality and Social Psychology, 31,* 1108–1115.

Egeland, B., & Brunnquell, D. (1979). An at-risk approach to the study of child abuse. *Journal of the American Academy of Child Psychiatry, 18,* 219–236.

Egeland, B., & Sroufe, L. A. (1981). Attachment and early maltreatment. *Child Development, 52,* 44–52.

Egeland, B., & Vaughn, B. (1981). Failure of "bond formation" as a cause of abuse, neglect, and maltreatment. *American Journal of Orthopsychiatry, 51,* 78–84.

Egger, M. D., & Flynn, J. P. (1963). Effect of electrical stimulation of the amygdala on hypothalamically elicited attack behavior in cats. *Journal of Neurophysiology, 26,* 705–720.

Elias, M. (1981). Serum cortisol, testosterone and testosterone binding blobulin responses to competitive fighting in human males. *Aggressive Behavior, 7,* 215–224.

Eliasz, H. (1981). Effect of empathy, reactivity level and anxiety on intensity of aggression. *Studia Psychologiczne, 20,* 73–86.

Eliot, R. (1964). Physiological activity and performance: A comparison of kindergarten children with young adults. *Psychological Monographs, 78*(10, Whole No. 587).

Elliot, D., Huizinga, D., & Ageton, S. (1985). *Explaining delinquency and drug use*. Beverly Hills, CA: Sage.

Elliot, D., & Voss, H. (1974). *Delinquency and dropout*. Lexington, MA: Heath.

Ellis, B. J., & Symons, D. (1990). Sex differences in sexual fantasy: An evolutionary psychological approach. *Journal of Sex Research, 27,* 527–555.

Ellis, D., & Austin, P. (1971). Menstruation and aggressive behavior in a correctional center for women. *Journal of Criminal Law and Police Science, 62,* 388–395.

Ellis, D. P., Weiner, P., & Miller, L. (1971). Does the trigger pull the finger? An experimental test of weapons as aggression-eliciting stimuli. *Sociometry, 34,* 453–465.

Ellis, L. (1989). *Theories of rape: Inquiries into the causes of sexual aggression.* New York: Hemisphere.

Ellis, L., & Beattie, C. (1983). The feminist explanation of rape: An empirical test. *Journal of Sex Research, 19,* 74–93.

Ellison, C. G., & Sherkat, D. E. (1993). Conservative protestantism and support for corporal punishment. *American Sociological Review, 58,* 131–144.

Ellison, G. D., & Flynn, J. P. (1968). Organized aggressive behavior in cats after surgical isolation of the hypothalamus. *Archives of Italian Biology, 106,* 1–20.

Ellsworth, P. C., Carlsmith, J. M., & Henson, A. (1972). The stare as a stimulus to flight in human subjects: A series of field experiments. *Journal of Personality and Social Psychology, 21,* 302–311.

Elmer, E. (1967). *Children in jeopardy: A study of abused minors and their families.* Pittsburgh, PA: University of Pittsburgh Press.

Ennis, P. H. (1967). *Criminal victimization in the United States: A report of a national survey* (University of Chicago, National Opinion Research Center). Washington, DC: U.S. Government Printing Office.

Epstein, S. (1965). Authoritarianism, displaced aggression and social status of the target. *Journal of Personality and Social Psychology, 2,* 585–589.

Epstein, S., & Taylor, S. P. (1967). Instigation to aggression as a function of degree of defeat and perceived aggressive intent of the opponent. *Journal of Personality, 35,* 265–289.

Erlanger, H. S. (1974). The empirical status of the subculture of violence thesis. *Social Problems 22,* 280–291.

Erlanger, H. S., & Winsborough, H. H. (1976). The subculture of violence thesis: An example of a simultaneous equation model in sociology, *Sociological Methods and Research, 5,* 231–246.

Eron, L. D., Huesmann, L. R., Lefkowitz, M. M., & Walder, L. O. (1972). Does television violence cause aggression? *American Psychologist, 27,* 253–263.

Ervin, F. R., Mark, V. H., & Stevens, J. (1969). Behavioral and affective response to brain stimulation in man. In J. Zubin & C. Shogass (Eds.), *Neurobiological aspects of psychopathology* (pp. 54–65). New York: Grune & Stratton.

Estes, W. K. (1969). Outline of a theory of punishment. In B. A. Campbell & R. M. Church (Eds.), *Punishment and aversive behavior* (pp. 57–82). New York: Appleton-Century-Crofts.

Exline, R. V., & Winters, L. C. (1965). Affective relations and mutual glances in dyads. In S. Tomkins & C. Izard (Eds.), *Affect, cognition and personality* (pp. 319–330). New York: Springer.

Eysenck, H. (1976). *Sex and personality.* London: Open Books.

Farnsworth, M., & Leiber, M. J. (1989). Strain theory revisited: Economic goals, educational means, and delinquency. *American Sociological Review, 54,* 263–274.

Farrington, D. P. (1978). The family backgrounds of aggressive youths. In L. Hersov, M. Berger, & D. Shaffer (Eds.), *Aggression and anti-social behavior in childhood and adolescence* (pp. 73–93). Elmsford, NY: Pergamon Press.

Farrington, D. P. (1989). Early predictors of adolescent aggression and adult violence. *Violence and Victims, 4,* 79–100.

Feeney, F. (1986). Robbers as decision-makers. In D. B. Cornish & R. V. Clarke (Eds.), *The reasoning criminal* (pp. 53–73). New York: Springer-Verlag.

Feild, H. S. (1978). Attitudes toward rape: A comparative analysis of police, rapists, crisis counselors and citizens. *Journal of Personality and Social Psychology, 36,* 156–179.

Felson, M. (1986). Routine activities, social controls, rational decisions and criminal outcomes. In D. Cornish & R. Clarke (Eds.), *The reasoning criminal: Rational choice perspectives on offending* (pp. 119–128). New York: Springer-Verlag.

Felson, M. (1993). *Crime and everyday life: Insights and implications for society.* Thousand Oaks, CA: Pine Forge.

Felson, R. B. (1978). Aggression as impression management. *Social Psychology, 41,* 205–213.

Felson, R. B. (1982). Impression management and the escalation of aggression and violence. *Social Psychology Quarterly, 45,* 245–254.

Felson, R. B. (1983). Aggression and violence between siblings. *Social Psychology Quarterly, 46,* 271–285.

Felson, R. B. (1984). Patterns of aggressive interaction. In A. Mummendey (Ed.), *Social psychology of aggression: From individual behavior to social interaction* (pp. 107–126). Berlin, Germany: Springer-Verlag.

Felson, R. B. (1991, spring). Blame analysis: Accounting for the behavior of protected groups. *American Sociologist,* 5–23.

Felson, R. B. (1992). "Kick 'em when they're down": Explanations of the relationship between stress and interpersonal aggression and violence. *Sociological Quarterly, 33,* 1–16.

Felson, R. B., Baccaglini, W., & Gmelch, G. (1986). Bar-room brawls: Aggression and violence in Irish and American bars. In A. Campbell & J. J. Gibbs (Eds.), *Violent transactions* (pp. 153–166). Oxford, England: Basil Blackwell.

Felson, R. B., Baccaglini, W., & Ribner, S. (1985). Accounting for criminal violence: A comparison of official and offender versions of the crime. *Sociology and Social Research, 70,* 93–95.

Felson, R. B., & Krohn, M. (1990). Motives for rape. *Journal of Research in Crime and Delinquency, 27,* 222–242.

Felson, R. B., & Liska, A. E. (1984). Explanations of the sex-deviance relationship. *Deviant Behavior, 5,* 1–10.

Felson, R. B., Liska, A., South, S., & McNulty, T. (in press). *School subcultures of violence and delinquency. Social Forces.*

Felson, R. B., & Ribner, S. (1981). An attributional approach to accounts and sanctions for criminal violence. *Social Psychology Quarterly, 44,* 137–142.

Felson, R. B., Ribner, S., & Siegel, M. (1984). Age and the effect of third parties during criminal violence. *Sociology and Social Research, 68,* 452–462.

Felson, R. B., & Russo, N. (1988). Parental punishment and sibling aggression. *Social Psychology Quarterly, 51,* 11–18.

Felson, R. B., & Steadman, H. J. (1983). Situational factors in disputes leading to criminal violence. *Criminology, 21,* 59–74.

Felstiner, W. L. F., Abel, R. L., & Sarat, A. (1980–1981). The emergence and transformation of disputes: Naming, blaming, claiming. *Law and Society Review, 15,* 631–654.

Fenigstein, A., Scheier, M. F., & Buss, A. H. (1975). Public and private self-consciousness: Assessment and theory. *Journal of Consulting and Clinical Psychology, 43,* 522–527.

Ferguson, T. J., & Rule, B. G. (1981). An attributional perspective on anger and aggression. In R. Geen & R. E. Donnerstein (Eds.), *Perspectives on aggression: Theoretical and empirical reviews* (pp. 41–74). San Diego, CA: Academic Press.

Feshbach, S. (1970). Aggression. In P. H. Mussen (Ed.), *Carmichael's manual of child psychology* (Vol. 2, pp. 159–259). New York: Wiley.

Feshbach, S. (1972). Reality and fantasy in filmed violence. In J. P. Murray, E. Rubinstein, & G. A. Comstock (Eds.), *Television and social behavior: Television and social learning* (Vol. 2, pp. 318–345). Washington, DC: U.S. Government Printing Office.

Feshbach, S., & Malamuth, N. (1978, November). Sex and aggression: Proving the link. *Psychology Today,* pp. 11, 112, 114, 116–117, 122.

Feshbach, S., & Singer, R. (1971). *Television and aggression.* San Francisco: Jossey-Bass.

Feshbach, S., Stiles, W. B., & Bitter, E. (1967). Reinforcing effect of witnessing aggression. *Journal of Experimental Research in Personality, 2,* 133–139.

Fincham, F. D. (1992). The account episode in close relationships. In M. L. McLaughlin, M. J. Cody, & S. J. Read (Eds.), *Explaining oneself to others: Reason-giving in a social context* (pp. 167–182). Hillsdale, NJ: Erlbaum.

Fincham, F. D., & Jaspars, J. M. (1983). A subjective probability approach to responsibility attribution. *British Journal of Social Psychology, 22,* 145–162.

Fincham, F. D., & Shultz, T. R. (1981). Intervening causation and the mitigation of responsibility for harm. *British Journal of Social Psychology, 20,* 113–120.

Fine, M. (1979). Options to injustice: Seeing other lights. *Representative Research in Social Psychology, 10,* 61–76.

Fine, M. (1983). The social context and a sense of injustice: The option to challenge. *Representative Research in Social Psychology, 13,* 15–33.

Fingerhut, L. A., & Kleinman, J. C. (1990). International and interstate comparisons of homicide among young males. *Journal of the American Medical Association, 263,* 3292–3295.

Finklehor, D., & Yllo, K. (1985). *License to rape: Sexual abuse of wives.* New York: Holt, Rinehart & Winston.

Fischer, C. S. (1969). The effect of threats in an incomplete information game. *Sociometry, 32,* 301–314.

Fischer, D. G., Kelm, H., & Rose, A. (1969). Knives as aggression-eliciting stimuli. *Psychological Reports, 24,* 755–760.

Fisher, R., & Ury, W. (1981). *Getting to YES: Negotiating agreement without giving in.* Boston, MA: Houghton Mifflin.

Flanagan, T. J., Van Alstyne, D. J., & Gottfredson, M. R. (1982). *Sourcebook of criminal justice statistics—1981* (U.S. Department of Justice, Bureau of Justice Statistics). Washington, DC: U.S. Government Printing Office.

Flynn, J. P. (1967). The neural basis of aggression in cats. In D. C. Glass (Ed.), *Neurophysiology and emotion* (pp. 40–59). New York: Rockefeller University Press and Sage.

Flynn, J. P., Vanegas, H., Foote, W., & Edwards, S. (1970). Neural mechanisms involved in a cat's attack on a rat. In R. E. Whalen, R. F. Thompson, M. Verzeano, & N. M. Weinberger (Eds.), *The neural control of behavior* (pp. 135–173). San Diego, CA: Academic Press.

Foa, U. G. (1971). Interpersonal and economic resources. *Science, 171,* 345–351.

Folger, R. (1986). A referent cognitions theory of relative deprivation. In J. M. Olson, C. P. Herman, & M. P. Zanna (Eds.), *Relative deprivation and social comparison: The Ontario symposium* (Vol. 4., pp. 33–55). Hillsdale, NJ: Erlbaum.

Folger, R., & Martin, C. (1986). Relative deprivation and referent cognitions: Distribution and procedural justice effects. *Journal of Experimental Social Psychology, 22,* 531–546.

Folger, R., Rosenfield, D., & Robinson, T. (1983). Relative deprivation and procedural justifications. *Journal of Personality and Social Psychology, 45,* 268–273.

Ford, C. S., & Beach, F. A. (1951). *Patterns of sexual behavior.* New York: Harper & Row.

Forehand, R. (1977). Child noncompliance to parental requests: Behavioral analysis and treatment. In M. Hersen, R. M. Eisler, & P. M. Miller (Eds.), *Progress in behavior modification* (Vol. 5, pp. 111–147). San Diego, CA: Academic Press.

Forgas, J. P., O'Connor, K. V., & Morris, S. L. (1983). Smile and punishment: The effects of facial expression on responsibility attribution by groups and individuals. *Personality and Social Psychology Bulletin, 9,* 587–596.

Fox, R. (1989). *The search for society: Quest for a biosocial science and morality.* New Brunswick, NJ: Rutgers University Press.

Fraczek, A. (1986). Socio-cultural environment, television viewing, and the development of aggression among children in Poland. In L. R. Huesmann &

L. D. Eron (Eds.), *Television and the aggressive child: A cross-national comparison* (pp. 119–160). Hillsdale, NJ: Erlbaum.

Freedman, J. L. (1984). Effects of television violence on aggressiveness. *Psychological Bulletin, 96,* 227–246.

French, J. R. P., Jr., & Raven, B. (1959). The bases of social power. In D. Cartwright (Ed.), *Studies in social power* (pp. 150–167). Ann Arbor: University of Michigan Press.

Freud, S. (1933). *New introductory lectures on psychoanalysis.* New York: Norton.

Freud, S. (1938). *Basic writings of Sigmunt Freud* (A. A. Brill, ed. and trans.). New York: Modern Library.

Freud, S. (1950). *Beyond the pleasure principle* (J. Strachey, trans.). New York: Liveright.

Frick, R. W. (1985). Communicating emotion: The role of prosodic features. *Psychological Bulletin, 97,* 412–429.

Friedrich, L. K., & Stein, A. H. (1973). Aggressive and prosocial television programs and the natural behavior of preschool children. *Monographs of the Society for Research in Child Development, 38*(4, Serial No. 151).

Friedrich, W. N., & Boriskin, J. A. (1976). The role of the child in abuse: A review of the literature. *American Journal of Orthopsychiatry, 46,* 580–590.

Friedrich-Cofer, L., & Huston, A. C. (1986). Television violence and aggression: The debate continues. *Psychological Bulletin, 100,* 364–371.

Frodi, A. (1975). The effect of exposure to weapons on aggressive behavior from a cross-cultural perspective. *International Journal of Psychology, 10,* 283–292.

Frodi, A. (1977). Sexual arousal, situational restrictiveness, and aggressive behavior. *Journal of Research in Personality, 11,* 48–58.

Frodi, A. M. (1981). Contribution of infant characteristics to child abuse. *American Journal of Mental Deficiency, 85,* 341–349.

Frodi, A. M., & Lamb, M. E. (1980). Child abusers' responses to infant smiles and cries. *Child Development, 51,* 238–241.

Frodi, A. M., Lamb, M. E., Leavitt, L., & Donovan, W. (1978). Fathers' and mothers' response to infant smiles and cries. *Developmental Psychology, 14,* 490–498.

Frodi, A., Macaulay, J., & Thome, P. (1977). Are women always less aggressive than men? A review of the experimental literature. *Psychological Bulletin, 84,* 634–660.

Froming, W. J., Walker, G. R., & Lopyan, K. J. (1982). Public and private self-awareness: When personal attitudes conflict with societal expectations. *Journal of Experimental Social Psychology, 18,* 476–487.

Furer-Haimendorf, C. von. (1967). *Moral and merit: A study of values and social controls in South Asian societies.* London: Weidenfeld and Nicholson.

Gagnon, J. H. (1977). *Human sexualities.* Glenview, IL: Scott, Foresman.

Gagnon, J. H., & Simon, W. (1973). *Sexual conduct: The social sources of human sexuality.* Chicago: Aldine.

Galef, B. G., Jr. (1970). Target novelty elicits and directs shock-associated aggression in wild rats. *Journal of Comparative and Physiological Psychology, 71,* 87–91.

Gamson, W. A. (1964). Experimental studies of coalition formation. In L. Berkowitz (Ed.), *Advances in experimental social psychology* (Vol. 1, pp. 81–110). San Diego, CA: Academic Press.

Gandelman, R., vom Saal, F. S., & Reinish, J. M. (1977). Contiguity to male fetuses affects morphology and behavior of male mice. *Nature, 266,* 722–724.

Garbarino, J., & Sherman, D. (1980). High-risk neighborhoods and high-risk families: The human ecology of child maltreatment. *Child Development, 51,* 188–198.

Gastil, R. D. (1971). Homicide and a regional subculture of violence, *American Sociological Review, 36,* 412–427.

Gebhard, P. H., Gagnon, J. H., Pomeroy, W. B., & Christenson, C. V. (1965). *Sex offenders: An analysis of types.* New York: Harper & Row.

Gecas, V. (1982). The self-concept. In R. H. Turner & J. F. Short (Eds.), *Annual review of sociology* (Vol. 8, pp. 1–33). Palo Alto, CA: Annual Reviews.

Geen, R. G. (1968). Effects of frustration, attack, and prior training in aggressiveness upon aggressive behavior. *Journal of Personality and Social Psychology, 9,* 316–321.

Geen, R. G. (1970). Perceived suffering of the victim as an inhibitor of attack-induced aggression. *Journal of Social Psychology, 81,* 209–216.

Geen, R. G. (1978). Some effects of observing violence upon the behavior of the observer. In B. Maher (Ed.), *Progress in experimental personality research* (Vol. 8, pp. 49–93). San Diego, CA: Academic Press.

Geen, R. G. (1983). Aggression and television violence. In R. G. Geen & E. I. Donnerstein (Eds.), *Aggression: Theoretical and empirical reviews* (Vol. 2, pp. 103–125). San Diego, CA: Academic Press.

Geen, R. G. (1990). *Human aggression.* Pacific Grove, CA: Brooks/Cole.

Geen, R. G., & Berkowitz, L. (1967). Some conditions facilitating the occurrence of aggression after the observation of violence. *Journal of Personality, 35,* 666–676.

Geen, R. G., & Pigg, R. (1970). Acquisition of an aggressive response and its generalization to verbal behavior. *Journal of Personality and Social Psychology, 15,* 165–170.

Geen, R. G., & O'Neal, E. C. (1969). Activation of cue-elicited aggression by general arousal. *Journal of Personality and Social Psychology, 11,* 289–292.

Geen, R. G., & Quanty, M. B. (1977). The catharsis of aggression: An evaluation of a hypothesis. In L. Berkowitz (Ed.), *Advances in experimental social psychology* (Vol .10, pp. 2–39). San Diego, CA: Academic Press.

Geen, R. G., & Stonner, D. (1971). The effects of aggressiveness habit strength upon behavior in the presence of aggression-related stimuli. *Journal of Personality and Social Psychology, 17,* 149–153.

Geis, G. (1977). Forcible rape: An introduction. In D. Chappell, R. Geis, & G. Geis (Eds.), *Forcible rape: The crime, the victim and the offender* (pp. 1–44). New York: Columbia University Press.

Gelles, R. J. (1978). Violence towards children in the United States. *American Journal of Orthopsychiatry, 48,* 580–592.

Gelles, R. J. (1982). Problems in defining and labeling child abuse. In R. H. Starr, Jr. (Ed.), *Child abuse prediction: Policy implications* (pp. 1–30). Cambridge, MA: Ballinger.

Gelles, R. J. (1987). *The violent home.* Newbury Park, CA: Sage.

Genthner, R., Shuntich, R., & Bunting, K. (1975). Racial prejudice, belief similarity, and human aggression. *Journal of Psychology, 9,* 229–234.

Gentry, W. D. (1970). Effects of frustration, attack, and prior aggressive training on overt aggression and vascular processes. *Journal of Personality and Social Psychology, 16,* 718–725.

Gerbner, G., & Gross, L. (1976). Living with television: The violence profile. *Journal of Communication, 26,* 173–199.

Gibbs, J. (1986). Punishment and deterrence: Theory, research, and penal policy. *Law and the Social Sciences, 4,* 319–325.

Gibbs, J. P. (1975). *Crime, punishment, and deterrence.* New York: Elsmere.

Gil, D. (1970). *Violence against children: Physical child abuse in the United States.* Cambridge, MA: Harvard University Press.

Gil, M. D. R., & Brown, B. (1981). Face saving among West Coast (Kwakiutl) Indians. *Journal of Psychological Anthropology, 3,* 297–308.

Gilbert, N. (1991, spring). The phantom epidemic of sexual assault. *Public Interest,* 54–65.

Ginsburg, H. J., & Miller, S. M. (1982). Sex differences in children's risk-taking behavior. *Social Psychology Quarterly, 47,* 146–159.

Giovannoni, J. M., & Becerra, R. M. (1979). *Defining child abuse.* New York: Free Press.

Glass, D. C., & Singer, J. R. (1972). *Urban stress.* San Diego, CA: Academic Press.

Glueck, B. C., Jr. (1956). *New York final report on deviated sex offenders.* Albany: New York State Department of Mental Hygiene.

Glueck, S., & Glueck, E. (1950). *Unraveling juvenile delinquency.* Cambridge, MA: Harvard University Press.

Goffman, E. (1955). On face-work: An analysis of ritual elements in social interaction. *Psychiatry, 18,* 213–231.

Goffman, E. (1959). *The presentation of self in everyday life.* New York: Doubleday Anchor.

Goffman, E. (1971). *Relations in public.* New York: Basic Books.

Goffman, E. (1972). *Relations in public: Microstudies of the public order.* New York: Harper & Row.

Goffman, E. (1982). *Interaction ritual: Essays on face-to-face behavior.* New York: Pantheon Books.

Goldstein, D., & Rosenbaum, A. (1985). An evaluation of self-esteem of maritally violent men. *Family Relations, 34,* 425–428.

Goldstein, M. J. (1973). Exposure to erotic stimuli and sexual deviance. *Journal of Social Issues, 29,* 197–219.

Goldstein, P. J. (1981). Drugs and violent crime. In N. A. Weiner & M. A. Zahn (Eds.), *Violence: Patterns, causes, public policy* (pp. 295–302). San Diego, CA: Harcourt Brace Jovanovich.

Goodchilds, J. D., & Zellman, G. L. (1984). Sexual signaling and sexual aggression in adolescent relationships. In N. M. Malamuth & E. Donnerstein (Eds.), *Pornography and sexual aggression* (pp. 233–243). San Diego, CA: Academic Press.

Goode, W. J. (1971, November). Force and violence in the family. *Journal of Marriage and the Family,* 624–635.

Goodman, R., & Clary, B. (1976). Community attitudes and action in response to airport noise. *Environment and Behavior, 8,* 441–470.

Goodstadt, B., & Kipnis, D. (1970). Situational influences on the use of power. *Journal of Applied Psychology, 54,* 201–207.

Gotlib, I. H., & Asarnow, R. F. (1979). Interpersonal and impersonal problem-solving skills in mildly and clinically depressed university students. *Journal of Consulting and Clinical Psychology, 47,* 86–95.

Gottesman, I. I., Carey, G., & Hanson, D. R. (1983). Pearls and perils in epigenetic psychopathology. In S. B. Guze, E. J. Earls, & J. E. Barrett (Eds.), *Childhood psychopathology and development* (pp. 287–300). New York: Raven Press.

Gottfredson, M., & Hirschi, T. (1986). The true value of lambda would appear to be zero: An essay on career criminals, selective incapacitation, cohort studies, and related topics. *Criminology, 24,* 213–234.

Gottfredson, M., & Hirschi, T. (1990). *A general theory of crime.* Stanford, CA: Stanford University Press.

Gottfredson, M., & Hirschi, T. (1993). A control theory interpretation of psychological research on aggression. In R. B. Felson & J. T. Tedeschi (Eds.), *Aggression and violence* (pp. 47–68). Washington, DC: American Psychological Association.

Gouze, K. R. (1987). Attention and social problem solving as correlates of aggression in preschool males. *Journal of Abnormal Child Psychology, 15,* 181–197.

Green, A. H. (1976). A psychodynamic approach to the study and treatment of child abusing parents. *Journal of American Academy of Child Psychiatry, 15,* 414–429.

Green, R. G., Stonner, D., & Shope, G. L. (1975). The facilitation of aggression by aggression: Evidence against the catharsis hypothesis. *Journal of Personality and Social Psychology, 31,* 721–726.

Greendlinger, V., & Byrne, D. (1987). Coercive sexual fantasies of college men as predictors of self-reported likelihood to rape and overt sexual aggression. *Journal of Sex Research, 23,* 1–11.

Greenwell, J., & Dengerink, H. A. (1973). The role of perceived versus actual attack in human physical aggression. *Journal of Personality and Social Psychology, 26,* 66–71.

Gregor, T. (1990). Male dominance and sexual coercion. In J. W. Stigler, R. A. Shweder, & G. Herdt (Eds.), *Cultural psychology: Essays on comparative human development* (pp. 477–495). Cambridge, MA: Cambridge University Press.

Groth, N. A., Burgess, A. W., & Holmstrom, L. L. (1977). Rape: Power, anger, and sexuality. *American Journal of Psychiatry, 134,* 1239–1243.

Groth, N. A., & Birnbaum, H. J. (1979). *Men who rape: The psychology of the offender.* New York: Plenum.

Groth, N. A., & Burgess, A. W. (1980). Male rape: Offenders and victims. *American Journal of Psychiatry, 137,* 806–810.

Grusec, J. E., & Kuczynski, L. (1980). Direction of effect in socialization: A comparison of the parent's versus the child's behavior as determinants of disciplinary techniques. *Developmental Psychology, 16,* 1–9.

Grusec, J., & Mischel, W. (1966). The model's characteristics as determinants of social learning. *Journal of Personality and Social Psychology, 4,* 211–215.

Gurr, T. R. (1970). *Why men rebel.* Princeton, NJ: Princeton University Press.

Guthrie, E. R. (1939). *The psychology of learning.* New York: Harper & Row.

Gutmann, S. (1990). It sounds like I raped you. *Reason: Free Minds and Free Markets, 22,* 22–27.

Hackney, S. (1969). Southern violence. *American Historical Review, 74,* 906–925.

Hagan, J. (1985). *Modern criminology: Crime, criminal behavior, and its control.* New York: McGraw-Hill.

Hagen, R. (1979). *The biosexual factor.* New York: Doubleday.

Hall, E. R., Howard, J. A., & Boezio, S. L. (1986). Tolerance of rape: A sexist or antisocial attitude? *Psychology of Women Quarterly, 10,* 101–118.

Hall, E. T. (1959). *The silent language.* New York: Doubleday.

Hamburg, D. A. (1966). Effects of progesterone on behavior. In R. Levine (Ed.), *Endocrines and the central nervous system.* Baltimore: Williams & Wilkins.

Hamburg, D. A., Moos, R. H., & Yalom, I. D. (1968). Studies of distress in the menstrual cycle and the postpartum period. In R. P. Michael (Ed.), *Endocrinology and human behavior.* London: Oxford University Press.

Hammen, C. L., & Peters, S. D. (1978). Interpersonal consequences of depression: Responses to men and women enacting a depressed role. *Journal of Abnormal Psychology, 87,* 322–332.

Hands, J., Herbert, V., & Tennent, G. (1974). Menstruation and behavior in a special hospital. *Medicine, Science, and the Law, 14,* 32–35.

Haner, C. F., & Brown, P. A. (1955). Clarification of the instigation to action concept in the frustration–aggression hypothesis. *Journal of Abnormal and Social Psychology, 51,* 204–206.

Hanratty, M. A., Liebert, R. M., Morris, L. W., & Fernandez, L. E. (1969). Imitation of film-mediated aggression against live and inanimate victims. *Proceedings of the 77th Annual Convention of the American Psychological Association,* 457–458.

Harford, T. C. (1978). Contextual drinking patterns among men and women. In F. A. Seixas (Ed.), *Currents in alcoholism* (Vol. 9, pp. 287–296). San Francisco: Grune & Stratton.

Harford, T. C., & Gerstel, E. K. (1981). Age-related patterns of daily alcohol consumption in metropolitan Boston. *Journal of Studies on Alcohol, 42,* 1062–1066.

Harré, R., & Secord, P. F. (1973). *The explanation of social behavior.* Totowa, NJ: Littlefield, Adams.

Harrell, W. A. (1980). Retaliatory aggression by high and low Machiavellians against remorseful and non-remorseful wrongdoers. *Social Behavior and Personality, 8,* 217–220.

Harrell, W. A., & Hartnagel, T. F. (1979). Aggression against a remorseful wrong-doer: The effects of self-blame and concern for the victim. *Journal of Social Psychology, 107,* 267–275.

Harris, D. M., & Guten, S. (1979). Health protective behavior: An exploratory study. *Journal of Health and Social Behavior, 20,* 17–29.

Hart, H. L. A. (1968). *Punishment and responsibility.* New York: Oxford University Press.

Hartmann, D. P. (1969). Influence of symbolically modeled instrumental aggression and pain cues on aggressive behavior. *Journal of Personality and Social Psychology, 11,* 280–288.

Hartshorne, H., & May, M. A. (1929). *Studies in the nature of character: Vol. 2. Studies in self-control.* New York: Macmillan.

Hartup, W. W. (1974). Aggression in childhood: Developmental perspectives. *American Psychologist, 29,* 336–341.

Harvey, M. D., & Rule, B. G. (1978). Moral evaluations and judgments of responsibility. *Personality and Social Psychology Bulletin, 4,* 583–588.

Haug, M., Brain, P. F., & Kamis, A. B. (1985). A brief review comparing the effects of sex steroids on two forms of aggression in laboratory mice. *Neuroscience and Behavioral Reviews, 10,* 463–467.

Hearold, S. (1986). A synthesis of 1,043 effects of television on social behavior. In G. Comstock (Ed.), *Public communication and behavior* (Vol. 1, pp. 65–133). San Diego, CA: Academic Press.

Heath, R. G. (1981). The neural basis for violent behavior: Physiology and anatomy. In L. Valzelli & I. Morgese (Eds.), *Aggression and violence: A psychol biological and clinical approach* (pp. 176–194). St. Vincent, Italy: Edizioni Saint Vincent.

Heider, F. (1944). Social perceptual and phenomenal causality. *Psychological Review, 51,* 358–374.

Heider, F. (1958). *The psychology of interpersonal relations.* New York: Wiley.

Heilman, M. E., & Garner, K. A. (1975). Counteracting the boomerang: The effects of choice on compliance to threats and promises. *Journal of Personality and Social Psychology, 31,* 911–917.

Helm, B., Bonoma, T. V., & Tedeschi, J. T. (1972). Reciprocity for harm done. *Journal of Social Psychology, 87,* 89–98.

Helmreich, R. L., Spence, J. T., & Gibson, R. H. (1982). Sex-role attitudes: 1972–1980. *Personality and Social Psychology Bulletin, 8,* 656–663.

Hendrick, C., & Taylor, S. P. (1971). Effects of belief similarity and aggression on attraction and counter aggression. *Journal of Personality and Social Psychology, 17,* 342–349.

Hennigan, K. M., Del Rosario, M. L., Heath, L., Cook, T. D., Wharton, J. D., & Calder, B. J. (1982). The impact of the introduction of television on crime in the United States. *Journal of Personality and Social Psychology, 42,* 461–477.

Herrenkohl, R. C., Herrenkohl, E. C., & Egolf, B. P. (1983). Circumstances surrounding the occurrence of child maltreatment. *Journal of Consulting and Clinical Psychology, 51,* 424–431.

Hewitt, J. P., & Stokes, R. (1975). Disclaimers. *American Sociological Review, 40,* 1–11.

Hicks, D. J. (1968a). Effects of co-observer's sanctions and adult presence on imitative aggression. *Child Development, 39,* 303–309.

Hicks, D. J. (1968b). Short and long-term retention of affectively varied modeled behavior. *Psychonomic Science, 11,* 369–370.

Hilgard, E. R., & Bower, G. H. (1975). *Theories of learning* (4th ed.). Englewood Cliffs, NJ: Prentice Hall.

Hindelang, M. J. (1976). *Criminal victimization in eight American cities.* New York: Ballinger.

Hinton, J. W. (1981). Biological approaches to criminality. In P. F. Brain & D. Benton (Eds.), *Multidisciplinary approaches to aggression research* (pp. 447–462). Amsterdam: Elsevier/North-Holland.

Hirschi, T. (1969). *Causes of delinquency.* Berkeley: University of California Press.

Hitchcock, J., & Waterhouse, A. (1979). Expressway noise and apartment tenant response. *Environment and Behavior, 11,* 251–267.

Hobbes, T. (1909). *Leviathan* (reprint of first [1651] ed.). Oxford, England: Clarendon.

Hoebel, E. A. (1954). *The law of primitive man.* Cambridge, MA: Harvard University Press.

Hoffman, L. W. (1985). The changing genetics/socialization balance. *Journal of Social Issues, 41,* 127–148.

Hoffman, M. L. (1970). Moral development. In P. H. Mussen (Ed.), *Carmichael's manual of child psychology* (Vol. 2, pp. 261–359). New York: Wiley.

Hogan, R., & Emler, N. P. (1981). Retributive justice. In M. J. Lerner & S. C. Lerner (Eds.), *The justice motive in social behavior* (pp. 125–143). New York: Plenum.

Hokanson, J. E. (1970). Psychophysiological evaluation of the catharsis hypothesis. In E. I. Megargeee & J. E. Hokanson (Eds.), *The dynamics of aggression.* New York: Harper & Row.

Hokanson, J. E., & Burgess, M. (1962). The effects of status, type of frustration, and aggression on vascular processes. *Journal of Abnormal and Social Psychology, 65,* 232–237.

Hokanson, J. E., & Shetler, S. (1961). The effect of overt aggression on physiological arousal level. *Journal of Abnormal and Social Psychology, 63,* 446–448.

Holmes, D. S. (1971). Compensation for ego threat: Two experiments. *Journal of Personality and Social Psychology, 18,* 234–237.

Holmes, D. S. (1972). Aggression, displacement and guilt. *Journal of Personality and Social Psychology, 21,* 296–301.

Holmes, T. H., & Masuda, M. (1974). Life change and illness susceptibility. In B. S. Dohrenwend & B. P. Dohrenwend (Eds.), *Stressful life events: Their nature and effects* (pp. 45–72). New York: Wiley.

Holmstrom, L. L., & Burgess, A. W. (1979). Rapists talk. *Deviant Behavior, 1,* 101–125.

Holtgraves, T. (1989). The form and function of remedial moves: Reported use, psychological reality, and perceived effectiveness. *Journal of Language and Social Psychology, 8,* 1–16.

Homans, G. C. (1950). *The human group.* New York: Harcourt, Brace.

Homans, G. C. (1961). *Social behavior: Its elementary forms.* New York: Harcourt, Brace & World.

Hooton, E. A. (1939). *Crime and the man.* Cambridge, MA: Harvard University Press.

Hope, D. (1987). The healing paradox of forgiveness. *Psychotherapy, 24,* 240–244.

Horai, J. (1977). Attributional conflict. *Journal of Social Issues, 33,* 88–100.

Horai, J., & Bartek, M. (1978). Recommended punishment as a function of injurious intent, actual harm done, and intended consequences. *Personality and Social Psychology Bulletin, 4,* 575–578.

Horn, J. M., Plomin, R., & Rosenman, R. (1976). Heritability of personality traits in adult male twins. *Behavior Genetics, 10,* 17–30.

Hornstein, H. A. (1965). The effects of different magnitudes of threat upon interpersonal bargaining. *Journal of Experimental Social Psychology, 1,* 282–293.

Horowitz, R., & Schwartz, G. (1974). Honor, normative ambiguity and gang violence. *American Sociological Review, 39,* 238–251.

Houlihan, D., Sloane, H. N., Jones, R. N., & Patten, C. (1992). A review of behavioral conceptualizations and treatments of child noncompliance. *Education and Treatment of Children, 15,* 56–77.

Howells, K., & Wright, E. (1978). The sexual attitudes of aggressive sexual offenders. *British Journal of Criminology 18,* 170–173.

Hoyt, J. L. (1970). Effect of media violence "justification" on aggression. *Journal of Broadcasting, 14,* 455–464.

Hu, H. C. (1944). The Chinese conception of face. *American Anthropologist, 46,* 45–64.

Hudson, J. R. (1970). Police–citizen encounters that lead to citizen complaints. *Social Problems, 18,* 179–193.

Huesmann, L. R. (1982). Television violence and aggressive behavior. In D. Pearl, L. Bouthilet, & J. Lazar (Eds.), *Television and behavior: Ten years of scientific progress and implications for the eighties: Vol. 2. Technical reviews* (pp. 220–256). Washington, DC: National Institute of Mental Health.

Huesmann, L. R. (1988). An information processing model for the development of aggression. *Aggressive Behavior, 14,* 13–24.

Huesmann, L. R., & Eron, L. D. (1986). The development of aggression in American children as a consequence of television violence viewing. In L. R. Huesmann & L. D. Eron (Eds.), *Television and the aggressive child: A cross-national comparison* (pp. 45–80). Hillsdale, NJ: Erlbaum.

Huesmann, L. R., Lagerspetz, K., & Eron, L. D. (1984). Intervening variables in the TV violence–aggression relation: Evidence from two countries. *Developmental Psychology, 20,* 746–775.

Hull, J. G. (1981). A self-awareness model of the causes and effects of alcohol consumption. *Journal of Abnormal Psychology, 90,* 586–600.

Hull, J. G., & Bond, C. F. (1986). Social and behavioral consequences of alcohol consumption and expectancy: A meta-analysis. *Psychological Bulletin, 99,* 347–360.

Hyde, J. S. (1986). Gender differences in aggression. In J. S. Hyde & M. C. Linn (Eds.), *Psychology of gender differences* (pp. 51–65). Baltimore: Johns Hopkins University Press.

Hynan, D. J., & Grush, J. E. (1986). Effects of impulsivity, depression, provocation, and time on aggressive behavior. *Journal of Research in Personality, 20,* 158–171.

Infante, D. A., Chandler, T. A., & Rudd, J. E. (1989). Test of an argumentative skill deficiency model of interspousal violence. *Communication Monographs, 56,* 163–177.

Instone, D., Major, B. R., & Bunker, B. B. (1983). Gender, self-confidence, and social influence strategies: An organizational simulation. *Journal of Personality and Social Psychology, 44,* 322–333.

Isenberg, D. J. (1986). Group polarization: A critical review and meta-analysis. *Journal of Personality and Social Psychology, 50,* 1141–1151.

Jacobs, P. A., Brunton, M., Melville, M. M., & Brittain R. P. (1965). Aggressive behaviour, mental subnormality and the XYY male. *Nature, 208,* 1351–1352.

Jaffe, Y., Malamuth, N., Feingold, J., & Feshbach, S. (1974). Sexual arousal and behavioral aggression. *Journal of Personality and Social Psychology, 30,* 759–764.

James, W. (1950). *The principles of psychology.* New York: Dover.

Jansen, M. A., & Meyers-Abel, J. (1981). Assertive training for battered women. A pilot program. *Social Work, 26,* 164–165.

Jay, T. B. (1980). Sex roles and dirty word usage: A review of the literature and a reply to Haas. *Psychological Bulletin, 88,* 614–621.

Jegard, S., & Walters, R. (1960). A study of some determinants of aggression in young children. *Child Development, 31,* 739–747.

Jellison, J. M., & Gentry, R. A. (1978). A self-presentation interpretation of the seeking of social approval. *Personality and Social Psychology Bulletin, 4,* 227–230.

Johnson, G. D., Palileo, G. J., & Gray, N. B. (1992). Date rape on a southern campus: Reports from 1991. *Sociology and Social Research, 76,* 37–41.

Johnson, R. N. (1972). *Aggression in man and animals.* Philadelphia: W. B. Saunders.

Jones, E. E., & Berglas, S. (1978). Control of attributions about the self through self-handicapping strategies: The appeal of alcohol and the role of under-achievement. *Personality and Social Psychology Bulletin, 4,* 200–206.

Jones, E. E., & Davis, K. E. (1965). From acts to dispositions: The attribution process in person perception. In L. Berkowitz (Ed.), *Advances in experimental social psychology* (Vol. 2, pp. 220–266). San Diego, CA: Academic Press.

Jones, E. E., & McGillis, D. (1976). Correspondent inferences and the attribution cube: A comparative reappraisal. In J. H. Harvey, W. J. Ickes, & R. F. Kidd (Eds.), *New directions in attribution research* (Vol. 1, pp. 389–420). Hillsdale, NJ: Erlbaum.

Jones, E. E., & Pittman, T. S. (1982). Toward a general theory of strategic self-presentation. In J. Suls (Ed.), *Psychological perspectives on the self* (Vol. 1, pp. 231–262). Hillsdale, NJ: Erlbaum.

Joseph, J. M., Kane, T. R., Gaes, G. G., & Tedeschi, J. T. (1976). Effects of effort on attributed intent and perceived aggressiveness. *Perceptual and Motor Skills, 42,* 706.

Joseph, J. M., Kane, T. R., Nacci, P. L., & Tedeschi, J. T. (1977). Perceived aggression: A re-evaluation of the Bandura modeling paradigm. *Journal of Social Psychology, 103,* 277–289.

Josephson, W. L. (1987). Television violence and children's aggression: Testing the priming, social script, and disinhibition predictions. *Journal of Personality and Social Psychology, 53,* 882–890.

Kadow, K. D., & Sprafkin, J. (1993). Television "violence" and children with emotional and behavioral disorders. *Journal of Emotional and Behavioral Disorders, 1,* 54–63.

Kadushin, A., & Martin, J. A. (1981). *Child abuse: An interactional event.* New York: Columbia University Press.

Kagehiro, D. K., & Werner, C. M. (1981). Divergent perceptions of jail inmates and correctional officers: The "blame the other–expect to be blamed" effect. *Journal of Applied Social Psychology, 11,* 507–528.

Kahneman, D., & Tversky, A. (1979). Prospect theory: An analysis of decision under risk. *Econometrica, 47,* 263–291.

Kaleta, R. J., & Buss, A. H. (1973, May). *Aggression intensity and femininity of the victim.* Paper presented at the meeting of the Eastern Psychological Association, Boston.

Kalmuss, S. (1984). The intergeneration transmission of marital aggression. *Journal of Marriage and the Family, 46,* 11–19.

Kalven, H., Jr., & Zeisel, H. (1966). *The American jury.* Boston: Little, Brown.

Kane, T. R., Joseph, J. M., & Tedeschi, J. T. (1976). Person perception and an evaluation of the Berkowitz paradigm for the study of aggression. *Journal of Personality and Social Psychology, 33,* 663–673.

Kanin, E. J. (1965). Male sex aggression and three psychiatric hypotheses. *Journal of Sex Research, 1,* 227–229.

Kanin, E. J. (1967). An examination of sexual aggression as a response to sexual frustration. *Journal of Marriage and the Family, 3,* 429–433.

Kanin, E. J. (1969). Selected dyadic aspect of male sex aggression. *Journal of Sex Research, 5,* 12–28.

Kanin, E. J. (1985). Date rapists: Differential sexual socialization and relative deprivation. *Archives of Sexual Behavior, 6,* 67–76.

Kanin, E. J., & Parcell, S. R. (1977). Sexual aggression: A second look at the offended female. *Archives of Sexual Behavior, 6,* 67–76.

Kanouse, D. E., & Hanson, L. R. (1971). Negativity in evaluations. In E. E. Jones, D. E. Kanouse, H. H. Kelley, R. E. Nisbett, S. Valins, & B. Weiner (Eds.), *Attribution: Perceiving the causes of behavior* (pp. 47–62). Morristown, NJ: General Learning Press.

Kanter, R. M. (1977). *Men and women of the corporation.* New York: Basic Books.

Kaplan, A. (1964). *The conduct of inquiry.* San Francisco: Chandler.

Karli, P. (1956). The Norway rat's killing response to the white mouse: An experimental analysis. *Behaviour, 10,* 81–103.

Karli, P. (1991). *Animal and human aggression.* New York: Oxford University Press.

Karniol, R., & Miller, D. T. (1981). Morality and the development of conceptions of justice. In M. J. Lerner & S. C. Lerner (Eds.), *The justice motive in social behavior* (pp. 73–89). New York: Plenum.

Katz, J. (1988). *Seductions of crime: Moral and sensual attractions of doing evil.* New York: Basic Books.

Kaufmann, H. (1970). *Aggression and altruism.* New York: Holt, Rinehart & Winston.

Kavanagh, K. A., Youngblade, L., Reid, J. R., & Fagot, B. I. (1988). Interactions between children and abusive versus control parents. *Journal of Clinical Child Psychology, 17,* 137–142.

Keane, C., Gillis, A. R., & Hagan, J. (1989). Deterrence and amplification of juvenile delinquency by contact: The importance of gender and risk orientation. *British Journal of Criminology, 29,* 336–352.

Keller, F. S., & Schoenfeld, W. N. (1950). *Principles of psychology.* New York: Appleton-Century-Crofts.

Kelsen, H. (1957). *What is justice?* Berkeley: University of California Press.

Keltikangas-Järvinen, L., & Kangas, P. (1988). Problem-solving strategies in aggressive and nonaggressive children. *Aggressive Behavior, 14,* 255–264.

Kemper, T. D. (1978). *A social interactional theory of emotions.* New York: Wiley.

Kennedy, L. W., & Forde, D. R. (1990). Routine activities and crime: An analysis of victimization in Canada. *Criminology, 28,* 137–152.

Kimmel, M., Pruitt, D. G., Magenau, J., Konar-Goldband, E., & Carnevale, P. J. (1980). The effects of trust, aspiration, and gender on negotiation tactics. *Journal of Personality and Social Psychology, 38,* 9–23.

King, H. E. (1961). Psychological effects of excitation in the limbic system. In D. E. Sheer (Ed.), *Electrical stimulation of the brain* (pp. 58–93). Austin: University of Texas Press.

Kipnis, D. (1976). *The powerholders.* Chicago: University of Chicago Press.

Kipnis, D., & Consentino, J. (1969). Use of leadership powers in industry. *Journal of Applied Psychology, 53,* 460–466.

Kipnis, D., & Misner, R. P. (1972). *Police actions and disorderly conduct.* Unpublished manuscript, Temple University, Philadelphia.

Kipnis, D., & Schmidt, S. M. (1983). An influence perspective on bargaining in organizations. In M. Bazerman & R. Lewicki (Eds.), *Negotiating in organizations* (pp. 303–319). Beverly Hills, CA: Sage.

Kirkham, J. S., Levy, S., & Crotty, W. J. (Eds.). (1970). *Assassination and political violence.* New York: Praeger.

Kirscht, J. P., Haefner, D. P., Kegeles, S. S., & Rosenstock, I. M. (1966). A national study of health beliefs. *Journal of Health and Human Behavior, 7,* 248–254.

Klaus, M., & Kennell, J. (1970). Mothers separated from their newborn infants. *Pediatric Clinics of North America, 17,* 1015–1037.

Klebanov, P. K., & Jemmott, J. B., III. (1992). Effects of expectations and bodily sensations on self-reports of premenstrual symptoms. *Psychology of Women Quarterly, 16,* 289–310.

Kleck, G., & McElrath, K. (1991). The effects of weaponry on human violence. *Social Forces, 69,* 669–692.

Klein, R., & Bierhoff, H. W. (1992). *Responses to achievement situations: The mediating function of perceived fairness.* Manuscript submitted for publication.

Kleinig, J. (1973). *Punishment and desert.* The Hague, Netherlands: Martinus Nijhoff.

Knauft, B. M. (1987). Reconsidering violence in simple human societies: Homicide among the Gebusi of New Guinea. *Current Anthropology, 28,* 457–497.

Knott, P. D., & Drost, B. (1972). Effects of varying intensity of attack and fear arousal on the intensity of counter aggression. *Journal of Personality, 40,* 27–37.

Knutson, J. F. (1971). The effects of shocking one member of a pair of rats. *Psychonomic Science, 22,* 265–266.

Kobrin, S. (1951). The conflicts of values in delinquency areas, *American Sociological Review, 16,* 657–662.

Kochman, T. (1983). The boundary between play and nonplay in Black verbal dueling. *Language in Society, 12,* 329–337.

Kogan, N., & Dorros, K. (1978). Sex differences in risk-taking and its attribution. *Sex Roles, 4,* 755–765.

Komorita, S. S., & Brenner, A. R. (1968). Bargaining and concession-making under bilateral monopoly. *Journal of Personality and Social Psychology, 9,* 15–20.

Konečni, V. J. (1975). The mediation of aggressive behavior: Arousal level versus anger and cognitive labeling. *Journal of Personality and Social Psychology, 32,* 706–712.

Konečni, V. J., & Doob, A. N. (1972). Catharsis through displacement of aggression. *Journal of Personality and Social Psychology, 23,* 379–387.

Korbin, J. E. (1981). Conclusions. In J. E. Korbin (Ed.), *Child abuse and neglect: Cross-cultural perspectives* (pp. 205–210). Berkeley: University of California Press.

Koss, M. P. (1992). The underdetection of rape: Methodological choices influence incidence estimates. *Journal of Social Issues, 48,* 61–75.

Koss, M. P., & Dinero, T. E. (1987, January). *Predictors of sexual aggression among a national sample of male college students.* Paper presented at the New York Academy of Sciences Conference "Human Sexual Aggression: Current Perspectives," New York.

Koss, M. P., Dinero, T. E., Seibel, C. A., & Cox, S. L. (1988). Stranger and acquaintance rape: Are there differences in the victim's experience? *Psychology of Women Quarterly, 12,* 1–24.

Koss, M. P., Gidycz, C. A., & Wisniewski, N. (1987). The scope of rape: Incidence and prevalence of sexual aggression and victimization in a national sample of students in higher education. *Journal of Consulting and Clinical Psychology, 55,* 162–170.

Koss, M. P., & Leonard, K. E. (1984). Sexually aggressive men: Empirical findings and theoretical implications. In N. M. Malamuth & E. I. Donnerstein (Eds.), *Pornography and sexual aggression* (pp. 213–232). San Diego, CA: Academic Press.

Koss, M. P., Leonard, K. E., Beezley, D. A., & Oros, C. J. (1985). Non-stranger sexual aggression: A discriminate analysis classification. *Sex Roles, 12,* 981–992.

Kotelchuk, M. (1982). Child abuse and neglect: Prediction and misclassification. In R. H. Starr, Jr. (Ed.), *Child abuse prediction: Policy implications* (pp. 67–104). Cambridge, MA: Ballinger.

Kozma, C., & Zuckerman, M. (1983). An investigation of some hypotheses concerning rape and murder. *Personality and Individual Differences, 4,* 23–29.

Krauss, R. M. (1966). Structural and attitudinal factors in interpersonal bargaining. *Journal of Experimental Social Psychology, 2,* 42–55.

Kreuz, L. E., & Rose, R. M. (1972). Assessment of aggressive behavior and plasma testosterone in a young criminal population. *Psychosomatic Medicine, 34,* 321–332.

Kruttschnitt, C. (1989). A sociological, offender-based study of rape. *Sociological Quarterly, 30,* 305–329.

Kryter, K. D. (1970). *The effects of noise on man.* San Diego, CA: Academic Press.

Kuczynski, L. (1984). Socialization goals and mother–child interaction: Strategies for long-term and short-term compliance. *Developmental Psychology, 20,* 1061–1073.

Kuczynski, L., & Kochanska, G. (1990). Development of children's noncompliance strategies from toddlerhood to age 5. *Developmental Psychology, 26,* 398–408.

Kuczynski, L., Kochanska, G., Radke-Yarrow, M., & Girnius-Brown, O. (1987). A developmental interpretation of young children's noncompliance. *Developmental Psychology, 23,* 799–806.

Kuhn, T. S. (1962). *The structure of scientific revolutions.* Chicago: University of Chicago Press.

Kuo, Z. Y. (1930). The genesis of the cat's response toward the rat. *Journal of Comparative Psychology, 11,* 1–35.

Lacey, J. I. (1967). Somatic response patterning of stress: Some revisions of activation theory. In M. Appley & R. Trumbell (Eds.), *Psychological stress* (pp. 14–36). New York: Appleton-Century-Crofts.

Lagerspetz, K., & Viemero, V. (1986). Television and aggressive behavior among Finnish children. In L. R. Huesmann & L. D. Eron (Eds.), *Television and the aggressive child: A cross-national comparison* (pp. 81–118). Hillsdale, NJ: Erlbaum.

Lallemand, S. (1975). "Raghead": Insult and pedagogy among the Mosi. *Cahiers d'Etudes Africaines, 15,* 649–668.

Landy, D., & Aronson, E. (1969). The influence of the character of the criminal and his victim on the decisions of simulated jurors. *Journal of Experimental Social Psychology, 5,* 141–152.

Lang, A. R., Goeckner, D. J., Adesso, V. J., & Marlatt, G. A. (1975). Effects of alcohol on aggression in male social drinkers. *Journal of Abnormal Psychology, 84,* 508–518.

Larrance, D. T., & Twentyman, C. T. (1983). Maternal attributions and child abuse. *Journal of Abnormal Psychology, 92,* 449–457.

Laschet, U. (1972). Antiandrogen in the treatment of sex offenders: Mode of action and therapeutic outcome. In J. Zubin & J. Money (Eds.), *Contemporary sexual behavior: Critical issues in the 1970s* (pp. 311–320). Baltimore: Johns Hopkins University Press.

Laughhunn, D. J., Payne, J. W., & Crum, R. (1980). Managerial risk preferences for below-target returns. *Management Science, 26,* 1238–1249.

Lawler, E. J. (1986). Bilateral deterrence and conflict spiral: A theoretical analysis. In E. J. Lawler (Ed.), *Advances in group processes* (Vol. 3, pp. 107–130). Greenwich, CT: JAI Press.

Lawler, E. J., & Bacharach, S. B. (1987). Comparison of dependence and punitive forms of power. *Social Forces, 66,* 446–462.

Lawler, E. J., Ford, R., & Blegen, M. A. (1988). Coercive capability in conflict: A test of bilateral deterrence versus conflict spiral theory. *Social Psychology Quarterly, 51,* 93–107.

Lawson, R. (1965). *Frustration: The development of a scientific concept.* New York: Macmillan.

Lazarus, R. S. (1968). Emotions and adaptation: conceptual and empirical relations. In W. J. Arnold (Ed.), *Nebraska Symposium on Motivation* (pp. 175–265). Lincoln: University of Nebraska Press.

Leary, M. R., & Schlenker, B. R. (1981). The social psychology of shyness: A self-presentation model. In J. T. Tedeschi (Ed.), *Impression management theory and social psychological research* (pp. 335–358). San Diego, CA: Academic Press.

Lefever, H. G. (1981). "Playing the dozens": A mechanism for social control. *Phylon, 42,* 73–85.

Leland, J. (1982). Gender, drinking and alcohol abuse. In I. Al-Issa (Ed.), *Gender and psychopathology* (pp. 201–220). San Diego, CA: Academic Press.

Le Maire, L. (1956). Danish experiences regarding the castration of sexual offenders. *Journal of Criminal Law, Criminology, and Police Science, 47,* 294–310.

Leonard, K. E., & Taylor, S. P. (1981). Effects of racial prejudice and race of target on aggression. *Aggressive Behavior, 7,* 205–214.

Lerner, M. J. (1981). The justice motive in human relations: Some thoughts on what we know and need to know about justice. In M. J. Lerner & S. C. Lerner (Eds.), *The justice motive in social behavior* (pp. 11–35). New York: Plenum.

Lerner, M. J., Miller, D. T., & Holmes, J. G. (1976). Deserving and the emergence of forms of justice. In L. Berkowitz & E. Walster (Eds.), *Advances in experimental social psychology* (Vol. 9, pp. 133–140). San Diego, CA: Academic Press.

Leshner, A. I. (1978). *An introduction to behavioral endocrinology.* New York: Oxford University Press.

Letkemann, P. (1973). *Crime as work.* Englewood Cliffs, NJ: Prentice Hall.

Levenson, R. W., Sher, K. J., Grossman, L. M., Newman, J., & Newlin, D. B. (1980). Alcohol and stress response dampening: Pharmacological effects, expectancy, and tension reduction. *Journal of Abnormal Psychology, 89,* 528–538.

Leventhal, H. (1980). Toward a comprehensive theory of emotion. In L. Berkowitz (Ed.), *Advances in experimental social psychology.* (Vol. 13, pp. 140–208). San Diego, CA: Academic Press.

Levine, J. M., Kramer, G. G., & Levine, E. N. (1975). Effects of alcohol on human performance: An integration of research findings based on an abilities classification. *Journal of Applied Psychology, 60,* 285–295.

Levine, R. A. (1959). Gusii sex offenses: A study in social control. *American Anthropologist, 61,* 189–226.

Levinson, D. (1989). *Family violence in cross-cultural perspective.* Newbury Park, CA: Sage.

Levy, R. I. (1973). *Tahitians: Mind and experience in the Society Islands.* Chicago: University of Chicago Press.

Lewontin, R. C., Rose, S., & Kamin, L. J. (1984). *Not in our genes.* New York: Pantheon Books.

Leyens, J. P., Parke, R. D., Camino, L., & Berkowitz, L. (1975). Effects of movie violence on aggression in a field setting as a function of group dominance and cohesion. *Journal of Personality and Social Psychology, 32,* 346–360.

Libbey, P., & Bybee, R. (1979). The physical abuse of adolescents. *Journal of Social Issues, 35,* 101–126.

Light, R. J. (1973). Abused and neglected children in America: A study of alternative policies. *Harvard Educational Review, 43,* 556–598.

Lindskold, S., & Propst, L. R. (1981). Deindividuation, self-awareness, and impression management. In J. T. Tedeschi (Ed.), *Impression management theory and social psychological research* (pp. 201–222). San Diego, CA: Academic Press.

Lindskold, S., & Tedeschi, J. T. (1970). Self-confidence, prior success, and the use of power in social conflicts. *Proceedings of the 78th Annual Convention of the American Psychological Association, 5,* 425–426.

Lindskold, S., & Tedeschi, J. T. (1971). Self-esteem and sex as factors affecting influenceability. *British Journal of Social and Clinical Psychology, 10,* 114–122.

Lipton, D. M., McDonel, E. C., & McFall, R. M. (1987). Heterosocial perception in rapists. *Journal of Consulting and Clinical Psychology, 55,* 17–21.

Liska, A. (1971). Aspirations, expectations and delinquency: Stress and additive models. *Sociological Quarterly, 12,* 99–107.

Liska, A., Felson, R. B., Chamlin, M., & Baccaglini, W. (1984). Estimating attitude-behavior relations within a theoretical specification. *Social Psychology Quarterly, 47,* 15–23.

Liska, A. E., & Reed, M. D. (1985). Ties to conventional institutions and delinquency: estimating reciprocal effects. *American Sociological Review, 50,* 547–560.

Lizotte, A. J. (1986). Determinants of completing rape and assault. *Journal of Quantitative Criminology, 2,* 203–217.

Lockwood, D. (1980). *Prison sexual violence.* New York: Elsevier Science.

Loeber, R., Felton, D. K., & Reid, J. (1984). A social learning approach to the reduction of coercive processes in child abusive families: A molecular analysis. *Advances in Behavior Research and Therapy, 6,* 29–45.

Loeber, R., & Stouthamer-Loeber, M. (1986). Family factors as correlates and predictors of juvenile conduct problems and delinquency. In M. Tonry & N. Morris (Eds.), *Crime and justice: An annual review of research* (Vol. 7, pp. 29–149). Chicago: University of Chicago Press.

Loehlin, J. C., & Nichols, R. C. (1976). *Heredity, environment, and personality.* Austin: University of Texas Press.

Loew, C. A. (1967). Acquisition of a hostile attitude and its relationship to aggressive behavior. *Journal of Personality and Social Psychology, 5,* 335–341.

Lopes, L. L. (1984). Risk and distributional inequality. *Journal of Experimental Psychology: Human Perception and Performance, 10,* 465–485.

LoPiccolo, L. (1980). Low sexual desire. In S. R. Leiblum & L. A. Pervin (Eds.), *Principles and practices of sex therapy* (pp. 29–64). New York: Guilford Press.

Loren, R. E. A., & Weeks, G. (1986). Sexual fantasies of undergraduates and their perceptions of the sexual fantasies of the opposite sex. *Journal of Sex Education and Therapy, 12,* 31–36.

Lorenz, K. (1966). *On aggression.* New York: Harcourt, Brace & World.

Löschper, G., Mummendey, A., Linneweber, V., & Bornewasser, M. (1984). The judgment of behavior as aggressive and sanctionable. *European Journal of Social Psychology, 14,* 391–404.

Luckenbill, D. F. (1977). Criminal homicide as a situated transaction. *Social Problems, 25,* 176–186.

Luckenbill, D. F. (1980). Patterns of force in robbery. *Deviant Behavior, 1,* 361–378.

Luckenbill, D. F. (1982). Compliance under threat of severe punishment. *Social Forces, 60,* 810–825.

Luckenbill, D. F., & Doyle, D. P. (1989). Structural position and violence: Developing a cultural explanation. *Criminology, 27,* 419–436.

Luengo, M. A., Carrillo-de-la-Peña, M. T., Otero, J. M., & Romero, E. (1994). A short-term longitudinal study of impulsivity and antisocial behavior. *Journal of Personality and Social Psychology, 66,* 542–548.

Lysak, H., Rule, B. G., & Dobbs, A. R. (1989). Conceptions of aggression: Prototype or defining features? *Personality and Social Psychology Bulletin, 15,* 233–243.

Lytton, H., & Zwirner, W. (1975). Compliance and its controlling stimuli observed in a natural setting. *Developmental Psychology, 11,* 769–779.

MacDonald, J. M. (1971). *Rape offenders and their victims.* Springfield, IL: Charles C Thomas.

MacKinnon, C. (1984). Not a moral issue. *Yale Law and Policy Review, 2,* 321–345.

MacLean, G., & Tedeschi, J. T. (1970). *The use of social influence by children of entrepreneurial and bureaucratic parents.* Unpublished manuscript.

Major, B., Mueller, P., & Hildebrandt, K. (1985). Attributions, expectations, and coping with abortion. *Journal of Personality and Social Psychology, 48,* 585–599.

Malamuth, N. M. (1981). Rape proclivity among males. *Journal of Social Issues, 37,* 138–157.

Malamuth, N. M. (1986). Predictors of naturalistic sexual aggression. *Journal of Personality and Social Psychology, 50,* 953–962.

Malamuth, N. M., & Ceniti, J. (1986). Repeated exposure to violent and nonviolent pornography: Likelihood of raping ratings and laboratory aggression against women. *Aggressive Behavior, 12,* 129–137.

Malamuth, N. M., & Check, J. V. P. (1981). The effects of mass media exposure on acceptance of violence against women: A field experiment. *Journal of Research in Personality, 15,* 436–446.

Malamuth, N. M., Check, J. V. P., & Briere, J. (1986). Sexual arousal in response to aggression: Ideological, aggressive, and sexual correlates. *Journal of Personality and Social Psychology, 50,* 330–340.

Malin, H., Wilson, R., Williams, G., & Aitken, S. (1986). 1983 alcohol/health practices. *Alcohol Health and Research World, 10,* 48–50.

Mallick, S. K., & McCandless, B. R. (1966). A study of catharsis of aggression. *Journal of Personality and Social Psychology, 4,* 591–596.

Mandell, A., & Mandell, M. (1967). Suicide and the menstrual cycle. *Journal of the American Medical Association, 200,* 792–793.

Mandler, G. (1979). Emotion. In E. Hearst (Ed.), *The first century of experimental psychology* (pp. 275–322). Hillsdale, NJ: Erlbaum.

Marion, M. (1983). Child compliance: A review of the literature with implications for family life education. *Family Relations, 32,* 545–555.

Marlatt, G. A., & Rohsenow, D. J. (1980). Cognitive process in alcohol use:

Expectancy and the balanced placebo design. In N. K. Mello (Ed.), *Advances in substance abuse: Behavioral and biological research* (pp. 159–199). Greenwich, CT: JAI Press.

Marshall, D., & Suggs, R. (Eds.). (1971). *Human sexual behavior: Variations in the ethnographic spectrum.* New York: Basic Books.

Marshall, G., & Zimbardo, P. G. (1979). Affective consequences of inadequately explained physiological arousal. *Journal of Personality and Social Psychology, 37,* 970–988.

Marshall, W. L., & Barbaree, H. E. (1984). A behaviorial view of rape. *International Journal of Law and Psychiatry, 7,* 51–77.

Martin, H. P., & Beezley, P. (1974). Prevention and the consequences of child abuse. *Journal of Operational Psychiatry, 6,* 67–77.

Maruniak, J. A., Desjardins, C., & Bronson, F. H. (1977). Dominant–subordinate relationships in castrated male mice bearing testosterone implants. *American Journal of Physiology, 233,* 495–499.

Mash, E. J., Johnston, C., & Kovitz, K. (1983). A comparison of the mother–child interactions of physically abused and non-abused children during play and task situations. *Journal of Clinical Child Psychology, 12,* 337–346.

Maslach, C. (1979). Negative emotional biasing of unexplained arousal. *Journal of Personality and Social Psychology, 37,* 953–969.

Mason, S. F. (1962). *A history of the sciences* (Rev. ed.). New York: Collier.

Massey, J. L., & Myers, M. A. (1989). Patterns of repressive social control in post-reconstruction Georgia, 1882–1935. *Social Forces, 68,* 458–488.

Masters, J. C., Felleman, E. S., & Barden, R. C. (1981). Experimental studies of affective states in children. In B. Lahey & A. E. Kazdin (Eds.), *Advances in clinical child psychology* (Vol. 4, pp. 91–114). New York: Plenum.

Matsueda, R. (1988). The current state of differential association theory. *Crime and delinquency, 34,* 277–306.

Matsueda, R. L. (1989). The dynamics of moral beliefs and minor deviance. *Social Forces, 68,* 428–457.

Matsueda, R. L., & Heimer, K. (1987). Race, family structure, and delinquency: A test of differential association and social control theories. *American Sociological Review, 52,* 826–840.

Matt, C. (1992). *Violence and delinquency in abused and neglected emotionally disturbed children.* Unpublished master's thesis, University at Albany, State University of New York.

May, R. (1953). *Man's search for himself.* New York: Norton.

May, R. (1972). *Power and innocence: A search for the sources of violence.* New York: Norton.

Mazur, A., & Lamb, T. (1980). Testosterone, status, and mood in human males. *Hormones and Behavior, 14,* 236–246.

McCord, J. (1983). A forty year perspective on effects of child abuse and neglect. *Child Abuse and Neglect, 7,* 265–270.

McCord, J. (1986). Instigation and insulation: How familes affect antisocial aggression. In D. Olweus, J. Block, & M. Radke-Yarrow (Eds.), *Development of antisocial and prosocial behavior: Research, theories and issues* (pp. 343–357). San Diego, CA: Academic Press.

McCord, J. (1991). Questioning the value of punishment. *Social Problems, 38,* 167–177.

McDaniel, J. W., O'Neal, E., & Fox, E. S. (1971). Magnitude of retaliation as a function of the similarity of available responses to those employed by attacker. *Psychonomic Science, 22,* 215–217.

McDermott, J. J. (1979). *Rape victimization in 26 American cities: Applications of the National Crime Survey victimization and attitude data* (Analytic Rep. SD-VAD-6). Washington, DC: U.S. Department of Justice.

McDougall, W. (1908). *Introduction to social psychology.* London: Methuen.

McNeely, R. L., & Mann, C. R. (1990). Domestic violence is a human issue. *Journal of Interpersonal Violence, 5,* 128–135.

Mead, M. (1935). *Sex and temperament in primitive societies.* New York: Morrow.

Mednick, S. A., Gabrielli, W. F., & Hutchings, B. (1984). Genetic influences in criminal convictions: Evidence from an adoption cohort. *Science, 224,* 891–894.

Megargee, E. I. (1970). Undercontrolled and overcontrolled personality types in extreme antisocial aggression. In E. I. Megargee & J. E. Hokanson (Eds.), *The dynamics of aggression* (pp. 108–120). New York: Harper & Row.

Mehrabian, A. (1972). *Nonverbal communication.* Chicago: Aldine.

Meichenbaum, D., & Gilmore, J. B. (1984). The nature of unconscious processes: A cognitive–behavioral perspective. In K. Bowers & D. Meichenbaum (Eds.), *The unconscious reconsidered* (pp. 273–298). New York: Wiley.

Meier, R. F., & Johnson, W. T. (1977). Deterrence as social control: the legal and extralegal production of conformity. *American Sociological Review, 42,* 292–304.

Melburg, V., & Tedeschi, J. T. (1981). Risk-taking, justifiability, recklessness, and responsibility. *Personality and Social Psychology Bulletin, 7,* 509–515.

Melburg, V., & Tedeschi, J. T. (1989). Displaced aggression: Frustration or impression management? *European Journal of Social Psychology, 19,* 139–145.

Merton, R. (1957). *Social theory and social structure.* New York: Free Press of Glencoe.

Messick, D. M., Bloom, S., Boldizar, J. P., & Samuelson, C. D. (1985). Why we are fairer than others. *Journal of Experimental Social Psychology, 21,* 480–500.

Messner, S. F. (1986). Television violence and violent crime: An aggregate analysis. *Social Problems, 33,* 218–235.

Messner, S. F. (1991, April). *Socio-cultural determinants of female homicide victimization and offending: A state-level analysis of gender inequality, pornography, and cultural support for violence.* Paper presented at the 61st annual meeting of the Eastern Sociological Society, Providence, RI.

Messner, S. F., & Blau, J. R. (1987). Routine leisure activities and rates of crime: A macro-level analysis. *Social Forces, 65,* 1035–1052.

Metts, S., & Cupach, W. R. (1989). Situational influence on the use of remedial strategies in embarrassing predicaments. *Communication Monographs, 56,* 151–162.

Meyer, T. P. (1972a). The effects of sexually arousing and violent films on aggressive behavior. *Journal of Sex Research, 8,* 324–331.

Meyer, T. P. (1972b). Effects of viewing justified and unjustified real film violence on aggressive behavior. *Journal of Personality and Social Psychology, 23,* 21–29.

Meyers, R. M. (1988). *The likelihood of knowledge.* Norwell, MA: Kluwer Academic.

Michener, H. A., & Cohen, E. D. (1973). Effects of punishment magnitude in the bilateral threat situation: Evidence for the deterrence hypothesis. *Journal of Personality and Social Psychology, 28,* 427–438.

Michener, H. A., Vaske, J. J., Schleifer, S., Plazewski, J. G., & Chapman, L. (1975). Factors affecting concession rate and threat usage in bilateral conflict. *Sociometry, 38,* 62–80.

Miethe, T. D., Stafford, M. C., & Long, J. S. (1987). Social differentiation in criminal victimization: A test of routine activities/lifestyle theories. *American Sociological Review, 52,* 184–194.

Mikula, G. (1984). Personal relationships: Remarks on the current state of research. *European Journal of Social Psychology, 14,* 339–352.

Mikula, G. (1993). On the experience of injustice. *European Review of Social Psychology, 4,* 223–244.

Mikula, G., & Heimgartner, A. (1992). *Experiences of injustice in intimate relationships.* Unpublished manuscript, University of Graz, Graz, Austria.

Mikula, G., Petri, B., & Tanzer, N. (1989). What people regard as unjust: Types and structures of everyday experiences of injustice. *European Journal of Social Psychology, 20,* 133–149.

Milavsky, J. R., Stipp, H. H., Kessler, R. C., & Rubens, W. S. (1982). *Television and aggression: A panel study.* San Diego, CA: Academic Press.

Milgram, S. (1974). *Obedience to authority: An experimental view.* New York: Harper & Row.

Miller, G. A., Galanter, E., & Pribram, K. H. (1960). *Plans and the structure of behavior.* New York: Holt.

Miller, M. E., Adesso, V. J., Fleming, J. P., Gino, A., & Lauerman, R. (1978). Effects of alcohol on the storage and retrieval processes of heavy social drinkers. *Journal of Experimental Psychology: Human Learning and Memory, 4,* 246–255.

Miller, N. E. (1941). The frustration–aggression hypothesis. *Psychological Review, 48,* 337–342.

Miller, N. E. (1948). Theory and experiment relating psychoanalytic displacement to stimulus–response generalization. *Journal of Abnormal and Social Psychology, 43,* 155–178.

Miller, N. E., & Bugelski, R. (1948). Minor studies in aggression: The influence of frustration imposed by the in-group on attitudes expressed toward the out-groups. *Journal of Psychology, 25,* 437–442.

Miller, P., Danaher, D., & Forbes, D. (1986). Sex-related strategies for coping with interpersonal conflict in children aged five and seven. *Developmental Psychology, 22,* 543–548.

Miller, W. B. (1958). Lower class culture as a generating milieu of gang delinquency, *Journal of Social Issues, 14*(3), 5–19.

Milowe, I., & Lourie, R. (1964). The child's role in the battered child syndrome. *Society for Pediatric Research, 65,* 1079–1081.

Mitchell, R., & Byrne, D. (1973). The defendant's dilemma: Effects on juror's attitudes and authoritarianism on judicial decisions. *Journal of Personality and Social Psychology, 25,* 123–129.

Mitchell, R. E. (1971). Some social implications of high density housing. *American Sociological Review, 36,* 18–29.

Molm, L. D. (1988). The structure and use of power: A comparison of reward and punishment power. *Social Psychology Quarterly, 51,* 108–122.

Money, J. (1980). *Love and love sickness.* Baltimore: Johns Hopkins University Press.

Mongrain, S., & Standing, L. (1989). Impairment of cognition, risk-taking, and self-perception by alcohol. *Perceptual and Motor Skills, 69,* 199–210.

Morse, C., Sahler, O., & Friedman, S. (1970). A three-year follow-up study of abused and neglected children. *American Journal of Diseases of Children, 12,* 439–446.

Motowidlo, S., Packard, J. S., & Manning, M. R. (1986). Occupational stress: Its causes and consequences for job performance. *Journal of Applied Psychology, 71,* 618–629.

Moyer, K. E. (1971). The physiology of aggression and the implications for aggression control. In J. L. Singer (Ed.), *The control of aggression and violence* (pp. 61–93). San Diego, CA: Academic Press.

Moyer, K. (1987). *Violence and aggression: A physiological perspective.* New York: Paragon House.

Muehlenhard, C. L. (1988). Misinterpreted dating behaviors and the risk of date rape. *Journal of Social and Clinical Psychology, 6,* 20–37.

Muehlenhard, C. L., & Cook, S. W. (1987). Men's self-reports of unwanted sexual activity. *Journal of Sex Research, 24,* 58–73.

Muehlenhard, C. L., & Hollabaugh, L. C. (1988). Do women sometimes say no when they mean yes? The prevalence and correlates of women's token resistance to sex. *Journal of Personality and Social Psychology, 54,* 872–879.

Mueller, C. W. (1983). Environmental stressors and aggressive behavior. In

R. G. Geen & E. I. Donnerstein (Eds.), *Aggression: Theoretical and empirical reviews* (Vol. 2, pp. 51–76). San Diego, CA: Academic Press.

Muir, D., & Weinstein, E. (1962). The social debt: An investigation of lower-class and middle-class norms of social obligation. *American Sociological Review, 27*, 532–539.

Mummendey, A., Linneweber, V., & Löschper, G. (1984). Actor or victim of aggression: Divergent perspectives—divergent evaluations. *European Journal of Social Psychology, 14*, 291–311.

Murnen, S. K., Perot, A., & Byrne, D. (1989). Coping with unwanted sexual activity: Normative responses, situational determinants, and individual differences. *Journal of Sex Research, 26*, 85–106.

Murphy, W. D., Coleman, E. M., & Haynes, M. R. (1986). Factors related to coercive sexual behavior in a nonclinical sample of males. *Violence and Victims, 1*, 255–278.

Myer, J. S., & Baenninger, R. (1966). Some effects of stress and punishment on mouse-killing by rats. *Journal of Comparative and Physiological Psychology, 62*, 292–297.

Nacci, P. L., & Tedeschi, J. T. (1977). Displaced aggression: Drive reduction or equity restoration. *Human Relations, 30*, 1157–1167.

Napier, J. (1970). *The roots of mankind.* Washington, DC: Smithsonian Institution.

Nasby, W., Hayden, B., & DePaulo, B. M. (1979). Attributional bias among aggressive boys to interpret unambiguous social stimuli as displays of hostility. *Journal of Abnormal Psychology, 89*, 459–468.

National Institute of Mental Health. (1982). *Television and behavior: Ten years of scientific progress and implications for the eighties.* Washington, DC: U.S. Government Printing Office.

Neiss, R. (1988). Reconceptualizing arousal: Psychobiological states in motor performance. *Psychological Bulletin, 103*, 345–366.

Nemeth, C. (1970). Bargaining and reciprocity. *Psychological Bulletin, 74*, 297–308.

Nesdale, A. R., Rule, B. G., & Hill, K. A. (1978). The effect of attraction on causal attributions and retaliation. *Personality and Social Psychology Bulletin, 4*, 231–234.

Nichols, R. C., & Bilbro, W. C. (1966). The diagnosis of twin zygosity. *Acta Genetica, 16*, 265–275.

Nickel, T. W. (1974). The attribution of intention as a critical factor in the relation between frustration and aggression. *Journal of Personality, 42*, 482–492.

Niem, T. C., & Collard, R. (1971, September). *Parental discipline of aggressive behaviors in four-year-old Chinese and American children.* Paper presented at the 79th Annual Convention of the American Psychological Association, Washington, DC.

Nisbett, R. E. (1993). Violence and U.S. regional culture. *American Psychologist, 48*, 441–449.

Nisbett, R. E., & Schachter, S. (1966). Cognitive manipulation of pain. *Journal of Experimental Social Psychology, 2*, 227–236.

Novaco, R. W. (1976). The functions and regulation of the arousal of anger. *American Journal of Psychiatry, 133*, 1124–1128.

Nucci, L. P., & Turiel, E. (1978). Social interactions and the development of social concepts in preschool children. *Child Development, 49*, 400–407.

O'Brien, R. M. (1987). The interracial nature of violent crimes: A reexamination. *American Journal of Sociology, 92*, 817–835.

O'Carroll, P. W., & Mercy, J. A. (1989). Regional variation in homicide rates: Why is the West so violent? *Violence and Victims, 4*, 17–25.

Ogles, R. M. (1987). Cultivation analysis: Theory, methodology and current research on television-influenced constructions of social reality. *Mass Communication Review, 14*, 43–53.

Ohbuchi, K. (1991). *Interpersonal conflicts among Japanese and Americans.* Unpublished manuscript, Tohoku University, Sendai, Japan.

Ohbuchi, K., & Izutsu, T. (1984). Retaliation by male victims: Effects of physical attractiveness and intensity of attack of female attacker. *Personality and Social Psychology Bulletin, 10*, 216–224.

Ohbuchi, K., & Kambara, T. (1985). Attacker's intent and awareness of outcome, impression management, and retaliation. *Journal of Experimental Social Psychology, 21*, 321–330.

Ohbuchi, K., Kameda, M., & Agarie, N. (1989). Apology as aggression control: Its role in mediating appraisal of and response to harm. *Journal of Personality and Social Psychology, 56*, 219–227.

Ohbuchi, K., Ohno, T., & Mukai, H. (1993). Empathy and aggression: Effects of self-disclosure and fearful appeal. *Journal of Social Psychology, 133*, 243–253.

Oldershaw, L., Walters, G. C., & Hall, D. K. (1986). Control strategies and noncompliance in abusive mother–child dyads: An observational study. *Child Development, 57*, 722–732.

Olds, J. (1953). The influence of practice on the strength of approach drives. *Journal of Experimental Psychology, 46*, 232–236.

Olweus, D. (1977). Aggression and peer acceptance in adolescent boys: Two short-term longitudinal studies of ratings. *Child Development, 48*, 1301–1313.

Olweus, D. (1978). *Aggression in the schools: Bullies and whipping boys.* Washington, DC: Hemisphere.

Olweus, D. (1979). Stability of aggressive reaction patterns in males: A review. *Psychological Bulletin, 86*, 852–875.

Olweus, D. (1984). Aggressors and their victims: Bullying at school. In N. Frude & H. Gault (Eds.), *Disruptive behaviors in schools* (pp. 57–76). New York: Wiley.

Orne, M. T. (1962). On the social psychology of the psychological experiment: With particular reference to demand characteristics and their implications. *American Psychologist, 17*, 776–783.

Orvis, B. R., Kelley, H. H., & Butler, D. (1976). Attributional conflict in young couples. In J. H. Harvey, W. J. Ickes, & R. F. Kidd (Eds.), *New directions in attribution research* (Vol. 1., pp. 353–386). Hillsdale, NJ: Erlbaum.

Osgood, C. E., May, W. H., & Miron, M. S. (1975). *Cross-cultural universals of affective meaning.* Urbana: University of Illinois Press.

Osgood, D. W., Johnston, L. D., O'Malley, P. M., & Bachman, J. G. (1988). The generality of deviance in late adolescence and early adulthood. *American Sociological Review, 53,* 81–93.

Owens, D. J., & Straus, M. A. (1975). The social structure of violence in childhood and approval of violence as an adult. *Aggressive Behavior, 1,* 193–211.

Page, M. M., & Scheidt, R. J. (1971). The elusive weapons effect: Demand awareness, evaluation apprehension, and slightly sophisticated subjects. *Journal of Personality and Social Psychology, 20,* 304–318.

Pagelow, M. D. (1984). *Family violence.* New York: Praeger.

Palmer, C. T. (1988). Twelve reasons why rape is not sexually motivated: A skeptical examination. *Journal of Sex Research, 25,* 512–530.

Palmer, C. T. (1991). Human rape: Adaptation or by-product? *Journal of Sex Research, 28,* 365–386.

Panksepp, J. (1971). Aggression elicited by electrical stimulation of the hypothalamus in albino rats. *Physiological Behavior, 6,* 321–329.

Parke, R. D., Berkowitz, L., Leyens, J. P., West, S., & Sebastian, R. J. (1977). Some effects of violent and nonviolent movies on the behavior of juvenile delinquents. In L. Berkowitz (Ed.), *Advances in experimental social psychology* (Vol. 10, pp. 135–172). San Diego, CA: Academic Press.

Parke, R. D., & Collmer, C. W. (1975). Child abuse: An interdisciplinary analysis. In E. M. Hetherington (Ed.), *Review of Child Development Research* (Vol. 5, pp. 509–590). Chicago: University of Chicago Press.

Parke, R. D., Sawin, D. B., & Kreling, B. (1974). *The effect of child feedback on adult disciplinary choices.* Unpublished manuscript, Fels Research Institute, Philadelphia, PA.

Pastore, N. (1952). The role of arbitrariness in the frustration–aggression hypothesis. *Journal of Abnormal and Social Psychology, 47,* 728–731.

Patchen, M. (1993). Reciprocity of coercion and cooperation between individuals and nations. In R. B. Felson & J. T. Tedeschi (Eds.), *Aggression and violence: Social interactionist perspectives* (pp. 119–144). Washington, DC: American Psychological Association.

Paternoster, R. (1989). Absolute and restrictive deterrence in a panel of youth. *Social Problems, 36,* 289–309.

Patterson, G. R. (1976). The aggressive child: Victim and architect of a coercive system. In L. A. Hamerlynck, E. J. Mash, & L. C. Handy (Eds.), *Behavior modification and families: I. Theory and research: II. Applications and developments* (pp. 267–316). New York: Brunner/Mazel.

Patterson, G. R. (1982). *Coercive family processes.* Eugene, OR: Castalia.

Patterson, G. R. (1984). Siblings: Fellow travelers in coercive family processes. In R. J. Blanchard & D. C. Blancard (Eds.), *Advances in the study of aggression.* (Vol. 1, pp. 173–215). San Diego, CA: Academic Press.

Patterson, G. R., & Cobb, J. A. (1971). A dyadic analysis of "aggressive" behavior. In J. P. Hill (Ed.), *Minnesota symposia on child psychology* (Vol. 5, pp. 72–129). Minneapolis: University of Minnesota Press.

Patterson, G. R., & Forgatch, M. (1982). *Parents and adolescents: Living together.* Eugene, OR: Castalia.

Patterson, G. R., Littman, R. A., & Bricker, W. (1967). Assertive behavior in children: A step toward a theory of aggression. *Monographs of the Society for Research in Child Development, 32*(5, Serial No. 113).

Paul, L., Foss, M. A., & Galloway, J. (1993). Sexual jealousy in young women and men: Aggressive responsiveness to partner and rival. *Aggressive Behavior, 19,* 401–420.

Pavlov, I. P. (1927). *Conditioned reflexes.* Oxford, England: Oxford University Press.

Peirce, R. S., Pruitt, D. G., & Czaja, S. J. (1991). *Complainant–respondent differences in procedural choice.* Unpublished manuscript, State University of New York, Buffalo.

Pellegrini, R. J., Hicks, R. A., & Meyers-Winton, S. (1978). Effects of simulated approval-seeking and avoiding on self-disclosure, self-presentation, and interpersonal attraction. *Journal of Psychology, 98,* 231–240.

Pennebaker, J. W., Burnam, M., Schaeffer, M. A., & Harper, D. C. (1977). Lack of control as a determinant of perceived symptoms. *Journal of Personality and Social Psychology, 35,* 167–174.

Pepitone, A. (1974). Aggression—a matter of stimulus and reinforcement control. *Contemporary Psychology, 19,* 769–770.

Pepitone, A. (1984). Violent aggression from the multiple perspectives of psychology. *Journal of Social and Economic Studies, 1,* 321–355.

Perry, D. G., Kusel, S. J., & Perry, L. C. (1988). Victims of peer aggression. *Developmental Psychology, 24,* 807–814.

Perry, D. G., Perry, L. C., & Rasmussen, P. (1986). Cognitive social learning mediators of aggression. *Child Development, 57,* 700–711.

Peters, R. S. (1958). *The concept of motivation.* New York: Humanities Press.

Petersilia, J., Greenwood, P., & Lavin, M. (1977). *Criminal careers of habitual felons.* Santa Monica, CA: Rand.

Pettiway, L. E. (1987). Arson for revenge: The role of environmental situation, age, sex, and race. *Journal of Quantitative Criminology, 3,* 169–184.

Phillips, D. P. (1983). The impact of mass media violence on U.S. homicides. *American Sociological Review, 48,* 560–568.

Phillips, D. P. (1986). The found experiment: A new technique for assessing the impact of mass media violence on real-world aggressive behavior. In G. Comstock (Ed.), *Public communication and behavior* (Vol. 1, pp. 259–307). San Diego, CA: Academic Press.

Phillips, D. P., & Bollen, K. A. (1985). Same time last year: Selective data dredging for unreliable findings. *American Sociological Review, 50,* 364–371.

Pietromonaco, P. R., & Rook, K. S. (1987). Decision style in depression: The contribution of perceived risks versus benefits. *Journal of Personality and Social Psychology, 52,* 399–408.

Pihl, R., Zeichner, A., Niaura, R., Nagy, K., & Zacchia, C. (1981). Attribution and alcohol-mediated aggression. *Journal of Abnormal Psychology, 90,* 468–475.

Pisano, R., & Taylor, S. P. (1971). Reduction in physical aggression: The effects of four different strategies. *Journal of Personality and Social Psychology, 19,* 237–242.

Plomin, R. (1981). Heredity and temperament: A comparison of twin data for self-report questionnaires, parental ratings, and objectively assessed behavior. In L. Gedda, P. Parisi, & W. E. Nance (Eds.), *Twin research 3: Intelligence, personality and development* (pp. 269–278). New York: Alan R. Liss.

Plomin, R., DeFries, J. C., & McClearn, G. E. (1990). *Behavioral genetics* (2nd ed.). New York: Freeman.

Plomin, R., & Rowe, D. C. (1979). Genetic and environmental etiology of social behavior in infancy. *Developmental Psychology, 15,* 62–72.

Plomin, R., Willerman, L., & Loehlin, J. C. (1976). Resemblance in appearance and the equal environments assumption in twin studies of personality traits. *Behavior Genetics, 6,* 43–52.

Ploog, D., & Melnechuk, T. O. (1970). Primate communication. In F. O. Schmitt, T. O. Melnechuk, G. C. Quarton, & G. Adelman (Eds.), *Neurosciences research symposium summaries* (Vol. 4, pp. 103–190). Cambridge, MA: MIT Press.

Ploughman, P., & Stensrud, J. (1986). The ecology of rape victimization: A case study of Buffalo, New York. *Genetic, Social, and General Psychology Monographs, 112*(3), 303–342.

Poulton, E. C. (1978). A new look at the effects of noise upon performance. *British Journal of Psychology, 69,* 435–437.

Powers, P. C., & Geen, R. G. (1972). Effects of the behavior and the perceived arousal of a model on instrumental aggression. *Journal of Personality and Social Psychology, 23,* 175–183.

Preston, K., & Stanley, K. (1987). "What's the worst thing . . . ?" Gender-directed insults. *Sex Roles, 17,* 209–219.

Pruitt, D. G., & Johnson, D. F. (1970). Mediation as an aid to face saving in negotiation. *Journal of Personality and Social Psychology, 14,* 239–246.

Pruitt, D. G., Mikolic, J. M., Peirce, R. S., & Keating, M. (1993). Aggression as a struggle tactic in social conflict. In R. B. Felson & J. T. Tedeschi (Eds.), *Aggression and violence: Social interactionist perspectives* (pp. 99–118). Washington, DC: American Psychological Association.

Pruitt, D. G., & Rubin, J. Z. (1986). *Social conflict: Escalation, stalemate, and settlement.* New York: Random House.

Queen's Bench Foundation. (1976). *Rape prevention and resistance* (pp. 59–76, 79–87, 92–94). San Francisco: Author.

Quigley, B. M., Croom, K., & Tedeschi, J. T. (1993, April). *Value and likelihood of the outcome predict attributions of intent for aggressive behavior.* Paper presented at the annual meeting of the Eastern Psychological Association, Arlington, VA.

Quinsey, V. L., Chaplin, T. C., & Varney, G. A. (1981). A comparison of rapists' and non-sex offenders' sexual preferences for mutually consenting sex, rape, and physical abuse of women. *Behavioral Assessment, 3,* 127–135.

Rada, R. T., Laws, D. R., & Kellner, R. (1976). Plasma testosterone levels in the rapist. *Psychosomatic Medicine, 38,* 257–268.

Ransford, H. E. (1968). Isolation, powerlessness, and violence: A study of attitudes and participation in the Watts riot. *American Journal of Sociology, 73,* 581–591.

Rapaport, K., & Burkhart, B. R. (1984). Personality and attitudinal characteristics of sexually coercive college males. *Journal of Abnormal Psychology, 93,* 216–221.

Rausch, H. L. (1965). Interaction sequences. *Journal of Personality and Social Psychology, 2,* 487–499.

Reckless, W. C. (1961). A new theory of delinquency and crime. *Federal Probation, 25,* 42–46.

Reed, J. S. (1971). To live-and die-in Dixie: A contribution to the study of southern violence. *Political Science Quarterly, 86,* 429–443.

Reid, J. B., Kavanagh, K., & Baldwin, D. V. (1987). Abusive parents' perceptions of child problem behaviors: An example of parental bias. *Journal of Abnormal Child Psychology, 15,* 457–466.

Reid, J. B., Taplin, P., & Loeber, R. (1981). A social interactional approach to the treatment of abusive families. In R. B. Stuart (Ed.), *Violent behavior: Social learning approaches to prediction, management, and treatment.* New York: Brunner/Mazel.

Reisenzein, R. (1983). The Schachter theory of emotion: Two decades later. *Psychological Bulletin, 94,* 239–264.

Reiss, I. L. (1986). *Journey into sexuality: An exploratory voyage.* Englewood Cliffs, NJ: Prentice Hall.

Reynolds, V. (1965). Some behavioral comparisons between the chimpanzee and the mountain gorilla in the wild. *American Anthropologist, 67,* 691–706.

Richardson, D., Leonard, K., Taylor, S., & Hammock, G. (1985). Male violence toward females: Victim and aggressor variables. *Journal of Psychology, 119,* 129–135.

Riordan, C. A., Marlin, N. A., & Kellogg, R. T. (1983). The effectiveness of accounts following transgression. *Social Psychology Quarterly, 46*, 213–219.

Roberts, W. W., & Kiess, A. O. (1964). Motivational properties of hypothalamic stimulation in cats raised in social isolation. *Journal of Comparative and Physiological Psychology, 58*, 187–193

Robertson, L. S. (1977). Car crashes: Perceived vulnerability and willingness to pay for crash protection. *Journal of Community Health, 3*, 136–141.

Robinson, B. W., Alexander, M., & Bowne, G. (1969). Dominance reversal resulting from aggressive responses evoked by brain telestimulation. *Physiology and Behavior, 4*, 749–752.

Roediger, H. L., III, & Stevens, M. C. (1970). The effects of delayed presentation of the object of aggression in pain induced fighting. *Psychonomic Science, 21*, 55–56.

Rogers, M. L., & Harding, S. S. (1981). Retrospective and daily menstrual distress measures in men and women using Moos's instruments (Forms A & T), and modified versions of Moos's instruments. In P. Komnenich, M. McSweeney, J. A. Noack, & N. Elder (Eds.), *The menstrual cycle: Vol. 2. Research and implications for women's health* (pp. 71–81). New York: Springer-Verlag.

Rokeach, M. (1979). (Ed.). *Understanding human values: Individual and societal.* New York: Free Press.

Rose, R., Bernstein, I., & Gordon, T. (1975). Consequences of social conflict on plasma testosterone levels in rhesus monkeys. *Psychosomatic Medicine, 37*, 50–61.

Rosen, B., & Jerdee, T. H. (1974). Factors influencing disciplinary judgments. *Journal of Applied Psychology, 59*, 327–331.

Rosenberg, M. J. (1969). The conditions and consequences of evaluation apprehension. In R. Rosenthal & R. Rosnow (Eds.), *Artifacts in behavioral research* (pp. 280–349). San Diego, CA: Academic Press.

Rosenkrantz, P., Vogel, S. R., Bee, H., Broverman, I. K., & Broverman, D. M. (1968). Sex-role stereotypes and self-concepts in college students. *Journal of Counseling and Clinical Psychology, 32*, 289–295.

Rosenzweig, S. (1944). An outline of frustration theory. In J. McV. Hunt (Ed.), *Personality and the behavior disorders* (pp. 379–388). New York: Ronald.

Ross, L. (1977). The intuitive psychologist and his shortcomings: Distortions in the attribution process. In L. Berkowitz (Ed.), *Advances in experimental social psychology* (Vol. 10, pp. 174–221). San Diego, CA: Academic Press.

Rossi, P. H., Waite, E., Bose, C., & Berk, R. E. (1974). Seriousness of crimes: Normative structure and individual differences. *American Sociological Review, 39*, 224–237.

Rowe, A. R., & Tittle, C. R. (1977). Life cycle changes and criminal propensity. *Sociological Quarterly, 18*, 223–236.

Rubin, K. H. (1982). *Social and social-cognitive developmental characteristics of young isolate, normal and sociable children.* New York: Springer-Verlag.

Ruble, T. L. (1983). Sex stereotypes: Issues of change in the 1970s. *Sex Roles, 9,* 397–402.

Rule, B. G., Bisanz, G. L., & Kohn, M. (1985). Anatomy of a persuasion schema: Targets, goals, and strategies. *Journal of Personality and Social Psychology, 48,* 1127–1140.

Rule, B. G., Dyck, R., & Nesdale, A. R. (1978). Arbitrariness of frustration: Inhibition or instigation effects on aggression. *European Journal of Social Psychology, 8,* 237–244.

Rule, B. G., & Ferguson, T. J. (1986). The effects of media violence on attitudes, emotions, and cognitions. *Journal of Social Issues, 42,* 29–50.

Rule, B. G., & Leger, G. L. (1976). Pain cues and differing functions of aggression. *Canadian Journal of Behavioural Science, 8,* 213–223.

Rule, B. G., & Nesdale, A. R. (1976a). Emotional arousal and aggressive behavior. *Psychological Bulletin, 83,* 851–863.

Rule, B. G., & Nesdale, A. R. (1976b). Environmental stressors, emotional arousal and aggression. In I. G. Sarason & C. D. Spielberger (Eds.), *Stress and anxiety* (Vol. 3, pp. 87–103). Washington, DC: Hemisphere.

Rule, B. G., & Nesdale, A. R. (1976c). Moral judgments of aggressive behavior. In R. G. Geen & E. C. O'Neal (Eds.), *Perspectives on aggression* (pp. 37–60). San Diego, CA: Academic Press.

Rumsey, M. G. (1976). Effects of defendant background and remorse on sentencing judgements. *Journal of Applied Social Psychology, 6,* 64–68.

Runciman, W. G. (1966). *Relative deprivation and social justice.* London: Routledge & Kegan Paul.

Rushton, J. P., Fulker, D. W., Neale, M. C., Nias, D. K. B., & Eysenck, H. J. (1986). Altruism and aggression: The heritability of individual differences. *Journal of Personality and Social Psychology, 50,* 1192–1198.

Russell, D. E. H. (1984). *Sexual exploitation: Rape, child sexual abuse and workplace harassment.* Beverly Hills, CA: Sage.

Ryan, W. (1971). *Blaming the victim.* New York: Random House.

Sampson, R. J., & Laub, J. H. (1990). Crime and deviance over the life course. *American Sociological Review, 55,* 609–627.

Sampson, R. J., & Laub, J. H. (1993). *Crime in the making: Pathways and turning points through life.* Cambridge, MA: Harvard University Press.

Sanday, P. R. (1981). The socio-cultural context of rape: A cross-cultural study. *Journal of Social Issues, 37,* 5–27.

Sanjo, K. (1975). Posterior hypothalamic lesions in the treatment of violent behavior. In W. S. Fields & W. H. Sweet (Eds.), *Neural bases of violence and aggression* (pp. 401–428). St. Louis, MO: Warren H. Green.

Sapolsky, B. S. (1984). Arousal, affect, and the aggression-moderating effect of erotica. In N. M. Malamuth & E. Donnerstein (Eds.), *Pornography and sexual aggression* (pp. 83–115). San Diego, CA: Academic Press.

Sarrel, P. M., & Masters, W. H. (1982). Sexual molestation of men by women. *Archives of Sexual Behavior, 11,* 117–131.

Savitsky, V. C., Czyzewski, D., Dubord, D., & Kaminsky, S. (1976). Age and emotion of an offender as determinants of adult punitive reactions. *Journal of Personality, 44,* 311–320.

Scarr, S. (1966). Genetic factors in activity and motivation. *Child Development, 37,* 663–673.

Scarr, S. (1968). Environmental bias in twin studies. *Eugenics Quarterly, 15,* 34–40.

Scarr, S., & Carter-Saltzman, L. (1979). Twin method: Defense of a critical assumption. *Behavior Genetics, 9,* 527–542.

Schachter, S. (1964). The interaction of cognitive and physiological determinants of emotional state. In L. Berkowitz (Ed.), *Advances in experimental social psychology* (Vol. 1, pp. 49–80). San Diego, CA: Academic Press.

Schachter, S., & Singer, J. (1962). Cognitive, social and physiological determinants of emotional state. *Psychological Review, 69,* 379–399.

Schafer, S. (1977). Sociosexual behavior in male and female homosexuals: A study of sex differences. *Archives of Sexual Behavior, 6,* 355–364.

Schank, R., & Abelson, R. (1977). *Scripts, plans, goals and understanding.* Hillsdale, NJ: Erlbaum.

Schecter, D., & Gandelman, R. (1981). Intermale aggression in mice: Influence of gonadectomy and prior fighting experience. *Aggressive Behavior, 7,* 187–193.

Scheff, T. J. (1988). Shame and conformity: The difference-emotion system. *American Sociological Review, 53,* 395–406.

Scheier, M. F., Fenigstein, A., & Buss, A. H. (1974). Self-awareness and physical aggression. *Journal of Experimental Social Psychology, 10,* 264–273.

Schlenker, B. R. (1980). *Impression management: The self-concept, social identity and interpersonal relations.* Monterey, CA: Brooks/Cole.

Schlenker, B. R., & Darby, B. W. (1981). The use of apologies in social predicaments. *Social Psychology Quarterly, 44,* 271–278.

Schmutte, G. T., Leonard, K. E., & Taylor, S. P. (1979). Alcohol and expectations of attack. *Psychological Reports, 45,* 163–167.

Schneider, S. L., & Lopes, L. L. (1986). Reflection in preferences under risk: Who and when may suggest why. *Journal of Experimental Psychology: Human Perception and Performance, 12,* 535–548.

Schönbach, P. (1990). *Account episodes: The management or escalation of conflict.* New York: Cambridge University Press.

Schönbach, P., & Kleibaumhüter, P. (1990). Severity of reproach and defensiveness of accounts. In M. J. Cody & M. L. McLaughlin (Eds.), *The psychology of tactical communication* (pp. 229–243). Philadelphia: Multilingual Matters.

Schruijer, S. G. L. (1990). *Norm violation, attribution and attitudes in intergroup relations.* Tilburg, The Netherlands: Tilburg University Press.

Schruijer, S., Blanz, M., Mummendey, A., Tedeschi, J. T., Banfai, B., Dittmar, H., Kleibaumhüter, P., Mahjoub, A., Mandrosz-Wroblewska, J., Molinari, L., & Petillon, X. (1994). The group-serving bias in evaluating and explaining harm-doing behavior. *Journal of Social Psychology, 134,* 47–54.

Schutz, A. (1967). *Phenomenology of the social world.* Evanston, IL: Northwestern University Press.

Schwartz, G. S., Kane, T. R., Joseph, J. M., & Tedeschi, J. T. (1978). The effects of post-transgression remorse on perceived aggression, attribution of intent, and level of punishment. *British Journal of Social and Clinical Psychology, 17,* 293–297.

Scott, J. P. (1958). *Aggression.* Chicago: University of Chicago Press.

Scott, J. P. (1970). Biology and human aggression. *American Journal of Ortho-psychiatry, 40,* 568–576.

Scott, J. P. (1971). Theoretical issues concerning the origin and causes of fighting. In B. E. Eleftherious & J. P. Scott (Eds.), *The physiology of aggression and defeat* (pp. 11–42). New York: Plenum.

Scott, M. R., & Lyman, S. M. (1968). Accounts. *American Sociological Review, 33,* 46–62.

Scully, D., & Marolla, J. (1985). Riding the bull at Gilley's: Convicted rapists describe the rewards of rape. *Social Problems, 32,* 251–263.

Sebastian, R. J. (1978). Immediate and delayed effects of victim suffering on the attacker's aggression. *Journal of Research in Personality, 12,* 312–328.

Semin, G. R., & Rubini, M. (1990). Unfolding the concept of person by verbal abuse. *European Journal of Social Psychology, 20,* 463–474.

Sermat, V. (1967). The possibility of influencing the other's behavior and cooperation: Chicken vs. prisoner's dilemma. *Canadian Journal of Psychology, 21,* 204–219.

Shaver, K. G. (1970). Defensive attribution: Effects of severity and relevance on the responsibility assigned for an accident. *Journal of Personality and Social Psychology, 14,* 101–113.

Sheehan, P. W. (1986). Television viewing and its relation to aggression among children in Australia. In L. R. Huesmann & L. D. Eron (Eds.), *Television and the aggressive child: A cross-national comparison* (pp. 161–200). Hillsdale, NJ: Erlbaum.

Sherman, L. W., & Berk, R. A. (1984). The specific deterrent effects of arrest for domestic assault. *American Sociological Review, 49,* 261–272.

Sherman, L. W., & Smith, D. A. (1992). Crime, punishment and stake in conformity: Milwaukee and Omaha experiments. *American Sociological Review, 57,* 680–690.

Shields, N. M. (1979). Accounts and other interpersonal strategies in a credibility detracting context. *Pacific Sociological Review, 22,* 255–272.

Shields, W. M., & Shields, L. M. (1983). Forcible rape: An evolutionary perspective. *Ethology and Sociobiology, 4,* 115–136.

Short, J. F., & Strodtbeck, F. L. (1965). *Group process and gang delinquency.* Chicago: University of Chicago Press.

Shortell, J., Epstein, S., & Taylor, S. P. (1970). Instigation to aggression as a function of degree of defeat and the capacity for massive retaliation. *Journal of Personality, 38,* 313–328.

Shortell, J. R., & Miller, H. B. (1970). Aggression in children as a function of sex of subject and of opponent. *Developmental Psychology, 3,* 143–144.

Shotland, L., & Craig, J. M. (1988). Can men and women differentiate between friendly and sexually interested behavior? *Social Psychology Quarterly, 51,* 66–73.

Shotland, R. L., & Goodstein, L. I. (1984). The role of bystanders in crime control. *Journal of Social Issues, 40,* 9–26.

Shuck, J., & Pisor, K. (1974). Evaluating an aggression experiment by the use of simulating subjects. *Journal of Personality and Social Psychology, 29,* 181–186.

Shupe, L. M. (1954). Alcohol and crime: A study of the urine-alcohol concentration found in 882 persons arrested during or immediately after the commission of a felony. *Journal of Criminal Law and Criminology, 44,* 661–664.

Siegel, A. E., & Kohn, L. G. (1959). Permissiveness, permission and aggression: The effect of adult presence or absence on aggression in children's play. *Child Development, 30,* 131–141.

Silver, R. L., Boon, C., & Stones, M. H. (1983). Searching for meaning in misfortune: Making sense of incest. *Journal of Social Issues, 39,* 81–101.

Silverman, I., & Kleinman, D. (1967). A response deviance interpretation of the effects of experimentally induced frustration on prejudice. *Journal of Experimental Research in Personality, 2,* 150–153.

Simon, H. A. (1979). Information processing models of cognition. *Annual Review of Psychology, 30,* 311–396.

Simons, L. S., & Turner, C. W. (1976). Evaluation apprehension, hypothesis awareness, and the weapons effect. *Aggressive Behavior, 2,* 77–87.

Simpson, J. A., & Gangestad, S. W. (1991). Individual differences in sociosexuality: Evidence of convergent and discriminant validity. *Journal of Personality and Social Psychology, 60,* 870–883.

Singer, B. (1985). A comparison of evolutionary and environmental theories of erotic response: Part II. Empirical arenas. *Journal of Sex Research, 21,* 345–374.

Slaby, R. G., & Guerra, N. G. (1988). Cognitive mediators of aggression in adolescent offenders: 1. Assessment. *Developmental Psychology, 24,* 580–588.

Smith, D., & Visher, C. A. (1981). Street level justice: Situational determinants of police arrest decisions. *Social Problems, 29,* 169–177.

Smith, M. D. (1979). Hockey violence: A test of the violent subculture hypothesis. *Social Problems, 27,* 235–247.

Smith, R. T. (1965). A comparison of socio-environmental factors in monozygotic and dizygotic twins, testing an assumption. In S. G. Vandenberg (Ed.), *Meth-*

ods and goals in human behavior genetics (pp. 45–62). San Diego, CA: Academic Press.

Smith, W. P., & Leginski, W. A. (1970). Magnitude and precision of punitive power in bargaining strategy. *Journal of Experimental Social Psychology, 6,* 57–76.

Sobell, M. B., & Sobell, L. C. (1973). Individualized behavior therapy for alcoholics. *Behavior Therapy, 4,* 49–72.

Sorenson, S. B., Stein, J. A., Siegel, J. M., Golding, J. M., & Burnam, M. A. (1987). The prevalence of adult sexual assault: The Los Angeles Epidemiologic Catchment Area Project. *American Journal of Epidemiology, 126,* 1154–1164.

South, S. J., & Felson, R. B. (1990). The racial patterning of rape. *Social Forces, 69,* 71–93.

Southwick, C. H. (1967). An experimental study of intragroup agonistic behavior in rhesus monkeys (*Macaca mulatta*). *Behavior, 28,* 182–209.

Stafford, M. C., & Gibbs, J. P. (1993). A theory about disputes and the efficacy of control. In R. B. Felson & J. T. Tedeschi (Eds.), *Aggression and violence: Social interactionist perspectives* (pp. 69–98). Washington, DC: American Psychological Association.

Stapleton, R. E., Joseph, J. M., & Tedeschi, J. T. (1978). Perceived aggression and competitive behavior. *Journal of Social Psychology, 105,* 277–289.

Stapleton, R. E., Nelson, B. L., Franconere, V. T., & Tedeschi, J. T. (1975). The effects of harm-doing on interpersonal attraction. *Journal of Social Psychology, 96,* 109–120.

Stark, R., & McEvoy, J. (1970, November). Middle-class violence. *Psychology Today, 4,* pp. 52–54, 111–112.

Starr, R. H. (1982). A research-based approach to the prediction of child abuse. In R. H. Starr (Ed.), *Child abuse prediction: Policy implications* (pp. 105–134). Cambridge, MA: Ballinger.

Starr, R. H. (1988). Physical abuse of children. In V. B. Van Hasselt, R. L. Morrison, A. S. Bellack, & M. Hersen (Eds.), *Handbook of family violence* (pp. 119–155). New York: Plenum.

Steadman, H. J., & Felson, R. B. (1984). Self-reports of violence: Ex-mental patients, ex-offenders, and the general population. *Criminology, 22,* 321–342.

Steele, B. F., & Pollock, C. B. (1968). A psychiatric study of parents who abuse infants and small children. In R. Helfer & C. Kempe (Eds.), *The battered child* (pp. 103–148). Chicago: University of Chicago Press.

Steele, C. M., & Southwick, L. (1985). Alcohol and social behavior: 1. The psychology of drunken excess. *Journal of Personality and Social Psychology, 48,* 18–34.

Stockman, C. L., & Glusman, M. (1969). Suppression of hypothalamically produced flight responses by punishment. *Physiology and Behavior, 4,* 523–525.

Stotland, E. (1976). Self-esteem and violence by guards and state troopers at Attica. *Criminal Justice and Behavior, 3,* 85–96.

Stouffer, S. A., Suchman, E. A., DeVinney, L. C., Star, S. A., & Williams, R. M., Jr. (1949). *The American soldier: Adjustment during army life* (Vol. 1, pp. 97–125). Hillsdale, NJ: Erlbaum.

Strack, S., & Coyne, J. C. (1983). Social confirmation of dysphoria: Shared and private reactions to depression. *Journal of Personality and Social Psychology, 44,* 798–806.

Straus, M. A. (1971). Some social antecedents of physical punishment: A linkage theory of interpretation. *Journal of Marriage and the Family, 33,* 658–663.

Straus, M. A. (1980). Stress and child abuse. In C. H. Kempe & R. F. Helfer (Eds.), *The battered child* (3rd ed., pp. 86–103). Chicago: University of Chicago Press.

Straus, M. A. (1991). Discipline and deviance: Physical punishment of children and violence and other crime in adulthood. *Social Problems, 38,* 133–153.

Straus, M. A., Gelles, R. J., & Steinmetz, S. K. (1980). *Behind closed doors: Violence in the American family.* Garden City, NY: Anchor Books.

Stryker, S. (1968). Identity salience and role performance: The relevance of symbolic interaction theory for family research. *Journal of Marriage and the Family, 30,* 558–564.

Sturup, G. K. (1960). Sex offenses: The Scandinavian experience. *Law and Contemporary Problems, 25,* 361–375.

Sturup, G. K. (1968). Treatment of sexual offenders in Herstedvester, Denmark: The rapist. *Acta Psychiatrica Scandinavica, 44*(Suppl. 204).

Sundberg, S. L., Barbaree, H. E., & Marshall, W. L. (1991). Victim blame and the disinhibition of sexual arousal to rape vignettes. *Violence and Victims, 6,* 103–120.

Surgeon General's Scientific Advisory Committee on Television and Social Behavior. (1972). *Television and growing up: The impact of televised violence* (Report to the Surgeon General, U.S. Public Health Service, HEW Publication No. HSM 72–9090). Rockville, MD: National Institute of Mental Health, U.S. Government Printing Office.

Svare, B., & Gandelman, R. (1975). Postpartum aggression in mice: Inhibitory effect of estrogen. *Physiology and Behavior, 14,* 455–461.

Svare, B., & Kinsley, C. H. (1987). Hormones and sex-related behavior. In K. Kelley (Ed.), *Females, males and sexuality: Theories and research* (pp. 13–58). Albany: State University of New York Press.

Swart, C., & Berkowitz, L. (1976). Effects of a stimulus associated with a victim's pain on later aggression. *Journal of Personality and Social Psychology, 33,* 623–631.

Sykes, G., & Matza, D. (1957). Techniques of neutralization: A theory of delinquency, *American Sociological Review, 22,* 664–670.

Sykes, G., & Matza, D. (1961). Juvenile delinquency and subterranean values. *American Sociological Review, 26,* 712–719.

Sykes, R. E., & Clark, J. P. (1975). A theory of deference exchange in police–civilian encounters. *American Journal of Sociology, 81,* 584–600.

Symons, D. (1979). *The evolution of human sexuality.* New York: Oxford University Press.

Tajfel, H. (1978). *Differentiation between social groups: Studies in the social psychology of intergroup relations.* San Diego, CA: Academic Press.

Tavris, C. (1982). *Anger: The misunderstood emotion.* New York: Simon & Schuster.

Taylor, D. M., & Jaggi, V. (1974). Ethnocentrism and causal attribution in a South Indian context. *Journal of Cross-Cultural Psychology, 5,* 162–171.

Taylor, S. P. (1970). Aggressive behavior as a function of approval motivation and physical attack. *Psychonomic Science, 18,* 195–196.

Taylor, S. P., & Epstein, S. (1967). Aggression as a function of the interaction of the sex of the aggressor and the sex of the victim. *Journal of Personality, 35,* 474–485.

Taylor, S. P., & Gammon, C. B. (1975). Effects of type and dose of alcohol on human physical aggression. *Journal of Personality and Social Psychology, 32,* 169–175.

Taylor, S. P., Gammon, C. B., & Capasso, D. R. (1976). Aggression as a function of alcohol and threat. *Journal of Personality and Social Psychology, 34,* 938–941.

Tedeschi, J. T. (1970). Threats and promises. In P. Swingle (Ed.), *The structure of conflict* (pp. 155–192). San Diego, CA: Academic Press.

Tedeschi, J. T. (1979). Frustration, fantasy aggression, and the exercise of coercive power. *Perceptual and Motor Skills, 48,* 215–219.

Tedeschi, J. T. (Ed.). (1981). *Impression management theory and social psychological research.* San Diego, CA: Academic Press.

Tedeschi, J. T. (1989). Self-presentation and social influence: An interactionist perspective. In M. J. Cody & M. L. McLaughlin (Eds.), *Psychology of tactical communication* (pp. 301–323). Clevedon, United Kingdom: Multilingual Matters.

Tedeschi, J. T., Bonoma, T. V., & Novinson, N. (1970). The behavior of a threatener: Retaliation vs. fixed opportunity costs. *Journal of Conflict Resolution, 14,* 69–76.

Tedeschi, J. T., Horai, J., Lindskold, S., & Faley, T. E. (1970). The effects of opportunity costs and target compliance on the behavior of a threatening source. *Journal of Experimental Social Psychology, 6,* 205–213.

Tedeschi, J. T., & Lindskold, S. (1976). *Social psychology: Interdependence, interaction, and influence.* New York: Wiley.

Tedeschi, J. T., Lindskold, S., & Rosenfeld, P. (1985). *An introduction to social psychology.* St. Paul, MN: West.

Tedeschi, J. T., & Melburg, V. (1984). Impression management and influence in the organization. In S. B. Bacharach & E. J. Lawler (Eds.), *Perspectives in organizational psychology: Theory and research* (pp. 31–58). Greenwich, CT: JAI Press.

Tedeschi, J. T., Melburg, V., & Rosenfeld, P. (1981). Is the concept of aggression useful? In P. Brain & D. Benton (Eds.), *A multi-disciplinary approach to aggression research* (pp. 23–38). Amsterdam: Elsevier and North-Holland.

Tedeschi, J. T., & Norman, N. (1985a). Self, self-presentation, and social power. In B. Schlenker (Ed.), *Self and identity: Presentation of self in social life* (pp. 293–322). New York: McGraw-Hill.

Tedeschi, J. T., & Norman, N. (1985b). Social mechanisms of displaced aggression. In E. J. Lawler (Ed.), *Advances in group processes: Theory and research* (Vol. 2, pp. 29–56). Greenwich, CT: JAI Press.

Tedeschi, J. T., & Riess, M. (1981). Predicaments and verbal tactics of impression management. In C. Antaki (Ed.), *Ordinary language explanations of social behavior* (pp. 271–309). San Diego, CA: Academic Press.

Tedeschi, J. T., Schlenker, B. R., & Bonoma, T. V. (1971). Cognitive dissonance: Private ratiocination or public spectacle? *American Psychologist, 26,* 685–695.

Tedeschi, J. T., Schlenker, B. R., & Bonoma, T. V. (1973). *Conflict, power, and games.* Chicago: Aldine.

Tedeschi, J. T., Schlenker, B. R., & Bonoma, T. V. (1975). Attraction and esteem of the source and compliance to threats. *Sociometry, 38,* 81–98.

Tedeschi, J. T., Schlenker, B. R., & Lindskold, S. (1972). The source of influence: The exercise of power. In J. T. Tedeschi (Ed.), *The social influence processes* (pp. 287–345). Chicago: Aldine.

Tedeschi, J. T., Smith, R. B., III, & Brown, R. C., Jr. (1974). A reinterpretation of research on aggression. *Psychological Bulletin, 89,* 540–563.

Teger, A. I. (1980). *Too much invested to quit.* Elmsford, NY: Pergamon Press.

Tellegen, A., Bouchard, T. J., Wilcox, K. J., Segal, N. L., Lykken, D. T., & Rich, S. (1988). Personality similarity in twins reared apart and together. *Journal of Personality and Social Psychology, 54,* 1031–1039.

Tennen, H., & Affleck, G. (1991). Blaming others for threatening events. *Psychological Bulletin, 108,* 209–232.

Tetlock, P., & Manstead, T. (1985). Impression management versus intrapsychic explanations in social psychology. *Psychological Review, 92,* 59–77.

Thibaut, J. W., & Coules, J. (1952). The role of communication in the reduction of interpersonal hostility. *Journal of Abnormal and Social Psychology, 47,* 770–777.

Thibaut, J. W., & Kelley, H. H. (1959). *The social psychology of groups.* New York: Wiley.

Thibaut, J. W., & Riecken, H. W. (1955). Some determinants and consequences of the perception of social causality. *Journal of Personality, 24,* 113–133.

Thomas, M. H., Horton, R. W., Lippincott, E. C., & Drabman, R. S. (1977). Desensitization to portrayals of real-life aggression as a function of exposure to television violence. *Journal of Personality and Social Psychology, 35,* 450–458.

Thorndike, E. L. (1913). *Education psychology: The psychology of learning* (Vol. 2). New York: Teachers College.

Thornhill, R., & Thornhill, N. W. (1983). Human rape: An evolutionary analysis. *Ethology and Sociobiology, 4,* 137–173.

Tinbergen, N. (1953). The curious behavior of the stickleback. In *Scientific American Reader* (pp. 433–440). New York: Simon & Schuster.

Tittle, C. R., & Logan, C. H. (1973). Sanctions and deviance: Evidence and remaining questions. *Law and Society Review, 7,* 371–392.

Tjosvold, D. (1983). Social face in conflict: A critique. *International Journal of Group Tensions, 13,* 49–64.

Toby, J. (1957). Social disorganization and stake in conformity: Complementary factors in the predatory behavior of young hoodlums. *Journal of Criminal Law, Criminology and Political Science, 48,* 12–17.

Toch, H. H. (1969). *Violent men: An inquiry into the psychology of violence.* Chicago: Aldine-Atherton.

Toch, H. (1980). *Violent men: An inquiry into the psychology of violence.* Washington, DC: American Psychological Association.

Toch, H. H. (1993). Good violence and bad violence: Self-presentations of aggressors through accounts and war stories. In R. B. Felson & J. T. Tedeschi (Eds.), *Aggression and violence: Social interactionist perspectives* (pp. 193–208). Washington, DC: American Psychological Association.

Tollman, J., & King, J. A. (1956). The effects of testosterone propionate on aggression in male and female C57BL/10 mice. *British Journal of Animal Behaviour, 4,* 147–149.

Tolman, E. C. (1966). *Behavior and psychological man: Essays in motivation and learning.* Berkeley: University of California Press.

Triandis, H. C. (1972). *The analysis of subjective culture.* New York: Wiley.

Trickett, P. K., & Kuczynski, L. (1986). Children's misbehaviors and parental discipline strategies in abusive and nonabusive families. *Developmental Psychology, 22,* 115–123.

Trickett, P. K., & Susman, E. J. (1988). Parental perceptions of child-rearing practices in physically abusive and nonabusive families. *Developmental Psychology, 24,* 270–276.

Turkat, D., & Dawson, J. (1976). Attributions of responsibility for a chance event as a function of sex and physical attractiveness of target individual. *Psychological Reports, 39,* 275–279.

Turnbull, C. (1965). *Wayward servants: The two worlds of the African pygmies.* Garden City, NY: Natural History.

Turner, C. W., & Simons, L. S. (1974). Effects of subject sophistication and evaluation apprehension on aggressive responses to weapons. *Journal of Personality and Social Psychology, 30,* 341–348.

Turner, C. W., Simons, L. S., Berkowitz, L., & Frodi, A. (1977). The stimulating and inhibiting effects of weapons on aggressive behavior. *Aggressive Behavior, 3,* 355–378.

Tyler, T. R. (1988). What is procedural justice? Criteria used by citizens to assess the fairness of legal procedures. *Law and Society Review, 22,* 103–135.

Valenstein, E. S. (1973). *Brain control: A critical examination of brain stimulation and psychosurgery.* New York: Wiley.

Vandenberg, S. G. (1968). The contribution of twin research to psychology. *Psychological Bulletin, 66,* 327–352.

Veitch, R., & Piccione, A. (1978). The role of attitude similarity in the attribution process. *Social Psychology Quarterly, 41,* 165–169.

Venables, P. H. (1984). Arousal: An examination of its status as a concept. In M. G. H. Coles, J. R. Jennings, & J. A. Stern (Eds.), *Psychophysiological perspectives* (pp. 134–142). New York: Van Nostrand Reinhold.

Vernon, W., & Ulrich, R. (1966). Classical conditioning of pain-elicited aggression. *Science, 152,* 668–669.

Vidmar, N., & Crinklaw, L. D. (1974). Attributing responsibility for an accident: A methodological and conceptual critique. *Canadian Journal of Behavioural Science, 6,* 112–130.

Virkunen, M. (1974). Alcohol as a factor precipitating aggression and conflict behavior leading to homicide. *British Journal of Addictions, 69,* 149–154.

Vogel, W., & Lazare, A. (1990). The unforgivable humiliation: A dilemma in couples' treatment. *Contemporary Family Therapy, 12,* 139–151.

vom Saal, F. S. (1979). Prenatal exposure to androgen influence morphology and aggressive behavior of male and female mice. *Hormones and Behavior, 12,* 1–12.

Vuchinich, R. E., & Sobell, M. B. (1978). Empirical separation of physiological and expected effects of alcohol on complex perceptual motor performance. *Psychopharmacology, 60,* 81–85.

Wachtel, P. L. (1973). Psychodynamics, behavior therapy, and the implacable experimenter: An inquiry into the consistency of personality. *Journal of Abnormal Psychology, 83,* 324–334.

Wagner, A. R. (1966). Frustration and punishment. In R. N. Haber (Ed.), *Current research in motivation* (pp. 229–238). New York: Holt, Rinehart & Winston.

Wallgreen, H., & Barry, H. B., III. (1970). *Actions of alcohol: Biochemical, physiological, and psychological aspects* (Vol. 1). Amsterdam: Elsevier.

Walster, E. (1966). Assignment of responsibility for an accident. *Journal of Personality and Social Psychology, 3,* 73–79.

Walster, E., Berscheid, E., & Walster, G. W. (1973). New directions in equity research. *Journal of Personality and Social Psychology, 25,* 151–176.

Walters, G. C., & Grusec, J. E. (1977). *Punishment.* New York: Freeman.

Walters, G. D. (1992). A meta-analysis of the gene–crime relationship. *Criminology, 30,* 595–613.

Walters, R. H., & Brown, M. (1963). Studies of reinforcement of aggression: III. Transfer of responses to an interpersonal situation. *Child Development, 34,* 536–571.

Walton, R. E., & McKersie, R. B. (1965). *A behavioral theory of labor negotiations.* New York: McGraw-Hill.

Warner, C. T. (1986). Anger and similar delusions. In R. Harré (Ed.), *Social construction of emotions* (pp. 135–165). Cambridge, MA: Basil Blackwell.

Washburn, S. L., & DeVore, I. (1961). The social life of baboons. *Scientific American, 204,* 62–71.

Wasman, M., & Flynn, J. P. (1962). Direct attack elicited from the hypothalamus. *Archives of Neurology, 6,* 60–67.

Weigold, M. F., & Schlenker, B. R. (1991). Accountability and risk taking. *Personality and Social Psychology Bulletin, 17,* 25–29.

Weiner, B. (1985). "Spontaneous" causal thinking. *Psychological Bulletin, 97,* 74–84.

Weiner, B., Amirkhan, J., Folkes, V. S., & Verette, J. A. (1987). An attributional analysis of excuse giving: Studies of a naive theory of emotion. *Journal of Personality and Social Psychology, 52,* 316–324.

Weinstein, N. D. (1984). Why it won't happen to me: Perceptions of risk factors and susceptibility. *Health Psychology, 3,* 431–457.

Weis, K., & Borges, S. S. (1973). Victimology and rape: The case of the legitimate victim. *Issues in Criminology, 8,* 71–115.

Weiss, B., Dodge, K. A., Bates, J. E., & Pettit, G. S. (1992). Some consequences of early harsh discipline: Child aggression and a maladaptive social information processing style. *Child Development, 63,* 1321–1335.

Weiss, R. L., & Heyman, R. E. (1990). Observation of marital interaction. In F. D. Fincham & T. N. Bradbury (Eds.), *The psychology of marriage: Basic issues and applications* (pp. 87–117). New York: Guilford Press.

Weiss, W. (1969). Effects of the mass media of communication. In G. Lindzey & E. Aronson (Eds.), *Handbook of social psychology* (Vol. 5, 2nd ed., pp. 77–195). Reading, MA: Addison-Wesley.

West, D. J. (1982). *Delinquency: Its roots, careers, and prospects.* Cambridge, MA: Harvard University Press.

West, D. J., & Farrington, D. P. (1977). *The delinquent way of life.* London: Heinemann.

Westley, W. A. (1970). *Violence and the police: A sociological study of law, custom, and morality.* Cambridge, MA: MIT Press.

Weston, J. (1968). The pathology of child abuse. In R. Helfer & C. Kempe (Eds.), *The battered child* (pp. 61–88). Chicago: University of Chicago Press.

White, J. W., & Roufail, M. (1989). Gender and influence strategies of first choice and last resort. *Psychology of Women Quarterly, 13,* 175–189.

White, L. A. (1979). Erotica and aggression: The influence of sexual arousal, positive affect, and negative affect on aggressive behavior. *Journal of Personality and Social Psychology, 37,* 591–601.

White, R. K. (1968). *Nobody wanted war: Misperception in Vietnam and other wars.* Garden City, NY: Doubleday.

Wiatrowski, M. D., Griswold, D. B., & Roberts, M. K. (1981). Social control theory and delinquency. *American Sociological Review, 46,* 525–541.

Wicklund, R. A. (1975). Objective self-awareness. In L. Berkowitz (Ed.), *Advances in experimental social psychology* (Vol. 8, pp. 233–275). San Diego, CA: Academic Press.

Widom, C. S. (1989a). The cycle of violence. *Science, 244,* 160–166.

Widom, C. S. (1989b). Does violence beget violence? A critical examination of the literature. *Psychological Bulletin, 106,* 3–28.

Wiley, M. G., & Hudik, T. L. (1974). Police–citizen encounters: A field test of exchange theory. *Social Problems, 22,* 119–129.

Williams, C. A. (1966). Attitudes toward speculative risks as an indicator of attitudes toward pure risks. *Journal of Risk and Insurance, 33,* 577–586.

Williams, R. M., Goldman, M. S., & Williams, D. L. (1981). Expectancy and pharmacological effects of alcohol on human cognitive and motor performance: The compensation for alcohol effect. *Journal of Abnormal Psychology, 90,* 267–270.

Wills, T. A. (1981). Downward comparison principles in social psychology. *Psychological Bulletin, 90,* 245–271.

Wilson, J. Q., & Herrnstein, R. J. (1985). *Crime and human nature.* New York: Simon & Schuster.

Wilson, L., & Rogers, R. W. (1975). The fire this time: Effects of race of target, insult, and potential retaliation on Black aggression. *Journal of Personality and Social Psychology, 32,* 857–864.

Wilson, M. I., & Daly, M. (1992). Who kills whom in spouse killings?: On the exceptional sex ratio of spousal homicides in the United States. *Criminology, 30,* 189–215.

Witkin, H. A., Mednick, S. A., Schulsinger, F., Bakkestrom, E., Christiansen, K. O, Goodenough, D. R., Hirschhorn, K., Lunsteen, C., Owen, D. R., Philip, J., Rubin, D. B., & Stocking, M. (1976). Criminality in XYY and XXY men. *Science, 196,* 547–555.

Wolfe, D. A. (1985). Child-abusive parents: An empirical review and analysis. *Psychological Bulletin, 97,* 483–496.

Wolfe, D. A. (1987). *Child abuse: Implications for child development and psychopathology.* Newbury Park, CA: Sage.

Wolfe, D. A., Fairbank, J. A., Kelly, J. A., & Bradlyn, A. S. (1983). Child abusive parents' physiological responses to stressful and non-stressful behavior in children. *Behavioral Assessment, 5,* 363–371.

Wolfgang, M. E. (1958). *Patterns in criminal homicide.* Philadelphia: University of Pennsylania Press.

Wolfgang, M., & Ferracuti, F. (1967). *The subculture of violence: Toward an integrated theory of criminality.* London: Tavistock.

Wolfgang, M. E., & Strohm, R. B. (1956). The relationship between alcohol and criminal homicide. *Quarterly Journal of Studies on Alcohol, 17,* 108–123.

Wong, W. P. T., & Weiner, B. (1981). When people ask "why" questions, and the heuristics of attributional search. *Journal of Personality and Social Psychology, 40,* 650–663.

Wood, W., Wong, F. Y., & Chachere, J. G. (1991). Effects of media violence on viewers' aggression in unconstrained social interaction. *Psychological Bulletin, 109*, 371–383.

Worchel, S. (1974). The effect of three types of arbitrary thwarting on the instigation to aggression. *Journal of Personality, 42*, 301–318.

Worchel, S., Arnold, S. E., & Harrison, W. (1978). Aggression and power restoration: The effects of identifiability and timing on aggressive behavior. *Journal of Experimental Social Psychology, 14*, 43–52.

Wright, J. D., & Rossi, P. H. (1986). *Under the gun: Weapons, crime, and violence in America.* New York: Aldine de Gruyter.

Wright, J., Rossi, P., & Daly, K. (1983). *Under the gun: Weapons, crime, and violence in America.* New York: Aldine de Gruyter.

Yarrow, L. (1948). The effects of antecedent frustration on projective play. *Psychological Monographs, 62*(6, Whole No. 293).

Yates, W. R., Perry, P., & Murray, S. (1992). Aggression and hostility in anabolic steroid users. *Biological Psychiatry, 31*, 1232–1234.

Yegidis, B. L. (1986). Date rape and other forced sexual encounters among college students. *Journal of Sex Education and Therapy, 12*, 51–54.

Young, L. (1964). *A study of child neglect and abuse.* New York: McGraw-Hill.

Zahn-Waxler, C., & Chapman, M. (1982). Immediate antecedents of caretakers' methods of discipline. *Child Psychiatry and Human Development, 12*, 179–192.

Zeichner, A., & Pihl, R. O. (1979). Effects of alcohol and behavior contingencies on human aggression. *Journal of Abnormal Psychology, 88*, 153–160.

Zillmann, D. (1971). Excitation transfer in communication-mediated aggressive behavior. *Journal of Experimental Social Psychology, 7*, 419–434.

Zillmann, D. (1979). *Hostility and aggression.* Hillsdale, NJ: Erlbaum.

Zillmann, D. (1983). Arousal and aggression. In R. G. Geen & E. I. Donnerstein (Eds.), *Aggression: Theoretical and empirical reviews* (Vol. 1, pp. 75–101). San Diego, CA: Academic Press.

Zillmann, D. (1988). Cognition–excitation interdependencies in aggressive behavior. *Aggressive Behavior, 14*, 51–64.

Zillmann, D., & Bryant, J. (1974). Effects of residual excitation on the emotional response to provocation and delayed aggressive behavior. *Journal of Personality and Social Psychology, 30*, 782–791.

Zillmann, D., Bryant, J., Cantor, J. R., & Day, K. D. (1975). Irrelevance of mitigating circumstances in retaliatory behavior at high levels of excitation. *Journal of Research in Personality, 9*, 282–293.

Zillmann, D., Bryant, J., Comisky, P. W., & Medoff, N. J. (1981). Excitation and henonic valence in the effect of erotica on motivated intermale aggression. *European Journal of Social Psychology, 11*, 233–252.

Zillmann, D., & Cantor, J. R. (1976). Effect of timing of information about mitigating circumstances on emotional responses to provocation and retaliatory behavior. *Journal of Experimental Social Psychology, 12*, 38–55.

Zillmann, D., Hoyt, J. L., & Day, K. D. (1974). Strength and duration of the effect of aggressive, violent, and erotic communications on subsequent aggressive behavior. *Communications Research, 1,* 286–306.

Zillmann, D., & Johnson, R. C. (1973). Motivated aggressiveness perpetuated by exposure to aggressive films and reduced by exposure to nonaggressive films. *Journal of Research in Personality, 7,* 261–276.

Zillmann, D., Johnson, R. C., & Day, K. D. (1974). Attribution of apparent arousal and proficiency of recovery from sympathetic activation affecting excitation transfer to aggressive behavior. *Journal of Experimental Social Psychology, 10,* 503–515.

Zillmann, D., Katcher, A. H., & Milavsky, B. (1972). Excitation transfer from physical exercise to subsequent aggressive behavior. *Journal of Experimental Social Psychology, 8,* 247–259.

Zillmann, D., & Sapolsky, B. S. (1977). What mediates the effect of mild erotica on annoyance and hostile behavior in males? *Journal of Personality and Social Psychology, 35,* 587–596.

Zimbardo, P. G. (1970). The human choice: Individuation, reason, and order versus deindividuation, impulse, and chaos. In W. J. Arnold & D. Levine (Eds.), *Nebraska Symposium on Motivation* (Vol. 17, pp. 237–307). Lincoln: University of Nebraska Press.

AUTHOR INDEX

89, 90, 94, 98, 106, 103, 111, 113, 114, 117, 119, 155, 156, 159, 167, 182, 198, 224, 246n. 14, 278, 349n. 1, 364, 364n. 5, 366, 368, 369

Berndt, T. J., 113

Berne, E., 83

Bernstein, I. S., 12, 25, 27

Berscheid, E., 214

Best, A., 216

Bierhoff, H., 233

Bies, R. J., 219

Bilbro, W. C., 18

Birnbaum, H. J., 313, 332

Bisanz, G. L., 181–182

Bitter, E., 65

Bjorkqvist, K., 186

Black, D. J., 139, 141, 169, 193, 214, 245, 266, 354

Blackburn, R., 360

Blanchard, E. B., 318

Blanz, M., 231

Blau, J. R., 116

Blegen, M. A., 204, 206

Block, J., 197

Bloom, S., 219

Blum, B., 242

Blumberg, S. R., 272

Blumenthal, M., 227, 288

Blumstein, A., 150, 193

Blumstein, P. W., 241

Bober, J., 216, 225n. 7

Boelkins, C. R., 14

Boezio, S. L., 339, 341

Boldizar, J. P., 190, 219

Bollen, K. A., 118

Bolles, R. C., 16, 67

Bond, C. F., 200

Bond, M. H., 262

Bonoma, T. V., 177–178, 191, 202, 245, 251, 265, 367n. 9

Booker, A., 62

Boon, C., 238

Borden, R. J., 275

Borgess, S. S., 325

Boriskin, J. A., 295, 296

Bornerwasser, M., 81, 226

Bose, C., 133, 245

Bouchard, T. J., 19–20

Boulding, K. A., 35, 183

Bower, G. H., 96, 102

Bowne, G., 31

Braaten, D. O., 242

Bradlyn, A. S., 303

Brain, P. F., 27

Brain, P. H., 30, 34, 34n. 2

Braine, L. G., 294

Bramel, D., 46, 242

Brand, P. A., 203

Brantingham, P. J., 146

Braten, D. O., 239

Brehm, J. W., 265

Brehm. S. S., 265

Brennan, P., 150n. 20

Brenner, A. R., 253

Brent, E. E., 267

Bricker, W., 107, 206

Briere, J., 339, 342

Briggs, J. L., 186, 234

Brittain, R. P., 22

Brockner, J., 185

Bronfenbrenner, U., 304

Bronson, F. H., 25

Broude, G. J., 320

Broverman, D. M., 255

Broverman, I. K., 255

Brown, B. R., 276

Brown, B., 258

Brown, J. S., 44, 97, 334

Brown, P. A., 43

Brown, P., 95, 255, 263, 264, 266, 271

Brown, R. C., Jr., 44, 108, 166, 225, 226

Brown, R., 196

Brown, S. A., 199

Brownmiller, S., 331, 331n. 21, 334

Brunn, K., 17

Brunnquell, D., 295

Brunton, M., 22

Bryant, J., 79, 80, 81, 85, 86

Buck, R., 92

Buehler, R. E., 96

Bugelski, R., 47, 48, 366n. 8

Bunker, B. B., 210

Bunting, K., 101

Burgess, A. W., 310, 318, 327n. 17, 329, 332

Burgess, M., 76

Burgess, R. L., 169, 298, 304

Burkhart, B. R., 339, 341

Burman, M., 57

Burnam, M. A., 324, 324n. 14

Burt, M. R., 342, 339

Buss, A. H., 27, 44, 54, 55, 62, 87, 93, 97, 98–99, 100, 101, 102, 125,

154–156, 198, 200, 257, 273, 279, 312, 330
Buss, D. M., 310
Buss, E., 62
Butler, D., 229
Bybee, R., 295
Byrne, D., 55, 230, 279, 324, 336

Cahalan, D., 197
Cahn, E., 225
Cairns, B. D., 209
Cairns, R. B., 209
Calder, B. J., 118
Calhoun, K. S., 30
Camino, L., 117, 119
Camp, D. S., 97
Canter, S., 17
Cantoni, L., 207
Cantor, J. R., 81, 225
Capasso, D. R., 199
Caprara, G, V., 102
Carey, G., 17
Carlsmith, J. M., 253
Carlson, B., 203
Carlson, M., 62, 63
Carnevale, P. J., 206
Carpenter, C. R., 13
Carroll, D., 34
Carroll, J. S., 180
Carssow, K. G., 241
Carter-Saltzman, L., 19
Carver, C. S., 279
Cattell, R. B., 92
Caulfield, C., 303
Cederlof, R., 18
Ceniti, J., 90, 332
Chachere, J. G., 117n. 5, 119
Chagnon, N. A., 184, 234, 252
Chandler, T. A., 208
Chaplin, T. C., 318
Chapman, L., 206
Chapman, M., 291, 293
Chappell, D., 319, 329, 332, 333
Chasdi, E. H., 97
Check, J. V. P., 119n. 7, 336, 342, 339
Chiricos, T. G., 232
Christenson, C. V., 316
Christiansen, K. O., 18, 22
Church, R. M., 97
Cialdini, R. B., 269
Cicchetti, D., 303
Claerhout, S., 207

Clark, J. P., 266, 267
Clark, R. D., III, 310
Clark, W. B., 197
Clarke, R., 152, 180, 371
Clarkson, F. E., 255
Clary, B., 57
Claster, D. S., 190
Cleaver, E., 330
Cline, V. B., 106
Cloninger, C. R., 17
Cloward. R. A., 137n. 14
Cobb, J. A., 298
Coccaro, E. F., 20
Cochran, S. T., 56
Cody, M. J., 239, 242
Cohen, A. R., 44, 130, 225
Cohen, A., 130n. 4, 221
Cohen, D. J., 18
Cohen, E. D., 206
Cohen, J., 150, 193
Cohen, L. E., 145, 146, 169, 192, 319, 336
Cohen, S., 57
Coie, J. D., 209, 233, 369
Coleman, E. M., 325
Coleman, K. H., 208
Collard, R., 291
Collins, W. A., 113
Collmer, C. W., 146, 289, 296, 297, 300
Comisky, P. W., 85, 86
Conger, R. D., 304
Conklin, J. E., 205
Connor, R. L., 26
Connor-Linton, J., 255
Cook, P. J., 205
Cook, T. D., 117, 118, 121n. 12, 122
Cornish, D., 152, 180, 371
Corwin, R., 60
Cottesman, I. I., 17
Cotton, J. L., 92
Coules, J., 46
Courrier, S., 106
Cowan, P. A., 96
Coyne, J. C., 272
Craig, J. M., 325
Craig, M. E., 330, 339
Crick, N. R., 182
Crinklaw, L. D., 227
Crockenberg, S., 293
Croft, R. G., 106
Croom, K., 158
Crotty, W. J., 254

Crowe, L. C., 200
Crum, R., 195
Cupach, W. R., 269, 270
Cusson, M., 194
Czaja, S. J., 186
Czyzewski, D., 242

Dahl, R. A., 188, 201
Dahlback, O., 196
Dalton, K., 28, 29
Daly, K., 189
Daly, M., 191, 203, 219, 355n. 1
Danaher, D., 256
Darby, B. W., 241, 242
Darwin, C., 7
D'Augello, D., 102
Davis, K. E., 223
Davitz, J. R., 103
Dawson, J., 230
Day, K. D., 79, 79, 83
Dedrick, D. K., 241
DeFries, J. C., 20
Del Rosario, M. L., 118
Deming, M. B., 255, 332
Dengerink, H. A., 87, 202, 245
DePaulo, B. M., 232
DeRidder, R., 215, 218n. 4, 225, 227
Desheilds, T. L., 237
Desjardins, C., 25
Deur, J. L., 300
Deutsch, M., 184, 190, 262
DeVinney, L. C., 217
DeVore, I., 14
Dibble, E., 18
DiLalla, L. F., 124
D'Imperio, G., 102
Dinero, T. E., 322, 325, 328, 330, 339
Dion, K. K., 230
Disbrow, M. A., 303
Ditrichs, R., 101, 189
Dittmar, H., 231
Dix, T., 293, 302
Dobash, R. E., 191, 203
Dobash, R. P., 191, 203
Dobbs, A. R., 225
Dodge, K. A., 182, 209, 232, 233, 288, 369
Doerr, H., 303
Dollard, J., 37, 39, 40, 42, 43, 68, 71, 140, 156, 238, 246n. 14, 260
Donnerstein, E., 57, 77, 84, 87, 88, 89, 90, 101, 117, 169, 244n. 13, 246

Donnerstein, M., 84, 101, 189
Donovan, W., 297
Doob, A. N., 48
Doob, N., 37, 39, 40, 42, 43, 68, 71, 156, 238, 246n. 14
Dorros, K., 197
Doyle, D. P., 136, 187
Drabman, R. S., 115
Dreiser, T., 156
Dressler, W. W., 217
Dretske, F. I., 160n. 5
Drost, B., 190
DuBois, C., 214
Dubord, D., 242
Duncan, B. L., 231
Durkee, A., 27, 330
Dyck, R. J., 52, 225

Eagly, A. H., 66, 186
Edney, J., 14
Edwards, S., 31
Egeland, B., 295, 297n. 5, 303
Egger, M. D., 31
Egolf, B. P., 289, 295
Elder, J., 207
Elias, M., 27
Eliasz, H., 66
Eliot, R., 91
Elliot, D., 138, 146
Elliott, R., 95
Ellis, B. J., 310
Ellis, D. P., 29, 62
Ellis, L., 311, 341
Ellison, C. G., 288, 303
Ellison, G. D., 32
Ellsworth, P. C., 253
Elmer, E., 300
Embree, M. C., 56
Emler, N. P., 214
Ennis, P. H., 319
Eppy, A., 255, 332
Epstein, S., 43–44, 87, 101, 189, 201, 215, 223–224, 257, 367
Erlanger, H. S., 132, 133, 133n. 10
Eron, L. D., 120, 120n. 9, 121
Ervin, F. R., 34n. 2
Estes, W. K., 98
Evans, G. W., 57
Evans, R., 84
Exline, R. V., 253
Eysenck, H. J., 17
Eysenck, H., 310, 312

Fagot, B. I., 303
Fairbank, J. A., 303
Faley, T. E., 187, 263
Farber, I. E., 44, 97
Farnsworth, M., 138n. 15
Farrington, D. P., 147, 150
Feeney, F., 179, 188
Feild, H. S., 333
Feingold, J., 84, 87
Felleman, E. S., 234
Felon, D. K., 298
Felson, M., 145, 146, 169, 188, 192, 319, 336
Felson, R. B., 134, 146, 169, 184, 191, 203, 209, 217, 218, 221, 222, 237, 237n. 10, 243, 255, 257, 258, 259, 261, 264, 265, 271, 274, 277, 310, 316, 319, 320, 328, 328n. 19, 329, 330, 367
Felstiner, W. L. F., 215
Fenigstein, A., 279
Fenton, M., 265
Ferguson, T. J., 169
Fernandez, L. E., 109
Ferracuti, F., 130, 131, 136, 187, 249
Feshbach, S., 44, 65, 86, 113, 119
Feshbach, S., 84, 87
Fifield, J., 227
Fincham, F. D., 222, 227, 239
Fine, J., 185
Fine, M., 215n. 2
Fingerhut, L. A., 128
Finklehor, D., 328
Fischer, C. S., 184, 202
Fischer, D. G., 62
Fisher, R., 164
Flanagan, T. J., 193
Fleming, J. P., 198
Flynn, J. P., 31, 32
Foa, U. G., 183
Folger, R., 218
Folkes, V. S., 241
Follingstad, D. R., 330, 339
Foote, W., 31
Forbes, D., 256
Ford, C. S., 311, 317
Ford, R., 204, 206
Forde, D. R., 146
Forehand, R., 291
Forgas, J. P., 223
Forgatch, M., 291
Foss, M. A., 355, 355n. 2

Fox, E. S., 245
Fox, R., 277
Fox, V., 258
Fraczek, A., 121
Franconere, V. T., 291, 231
Freedman, J. L., 117, 118, 120, 121
French, J. R. P., Jr., 209, 251
Freud, S., 15, 16, 37, 38–39, 41, 67–68, 71, 83, 147–148
Friberg, L., 18
Frick, R. W., 263
Friedman, S., 296
Friedrich, L. K., 119
Friedrich, W. N., 295, 296
Friedrich-Cofer, L., 117–118, 119n. 8, 121n. 12, 122
Frodi, A. M., 62, 63, 87, 87n. 3, 232, 295, 297, 303
Froming, W. J., 279
Fulker, D. W., 17
Furer-Haimendorf, C. von, 214
Furniss, J. M., 96

Gabrielli, W. F., 20
Gaes, G. G., 223
Gagnon, J. H., 311, 316, 320
Galanter, E., 157
Galef, B. G., Jr., 24
Galloway, J., 355, 355n. 2
Gammon, C. B., 198, 199
Gamson, W. A., 202
Gandelman, R., 26
Gangestad, S. W., 311
Garbarino, J., 305
Gariepy, J., 209
Garner, K. A., 263, 265
Gastil, R. D., 131
Gecas, V., 210
Geen, R. G., 44, 46, 50, 59, 65, 76, 77, 99, 107, 113, 115, 118, 167, 215
Geis, G., 331n. 21
Gelles, R. J., 203, 208, 288, 291, 293, 303, 305
Genthner, R., 101
Gentry, R. A., 251
Gentry, W. D., 44, 87n. 3, 215
George, W. H., 200
Gerbner, G., 115
Gerstel, E. K., 197
Gest, S. D., 209
Gibbs, J. P., 143, 19, 215
Gibson, R. H., 255

Heimer, K., 144, 145
Heimgartner, A., 215, 228, 229
Heironimus, M., 60
Heiser, J. F., 14
Helm, B., 245
Helmreich, R. L., 255
Hendrick, C., 231
Hennigan, K. M., 118
Henson, A., 253
Herbert, V., 29
Herrenkohl, E. C., 289, 295
Herrenkohl, R. C., 289, 295
Herrnstein, R. J., 138, 152, 208, 360
Hess, V. L., 113
Hewitt, J. P., 241, 244
Heyman, R. E., 239
Hicks, D. J., 104
Hicks, R. A., 251
Hilderbrandt, K., 227
Hilgrad. E. R., 96, 102
Hill, K. A., 230
Hindelang, M. J., 205
Hinkle, S., 265
Hinton, J. W., 33
Hirschhorn, K., 22
Hirschi, T., 21, 128, 138, 139, 143, 144,
       148, 149, 150, 151, 169, 181, 192,
       328, 341
Hitchcock, J., 57
Hobbes, T., 7, 9
Hoebel, E. A., 261
Hoffman, L. W., 21
Hoffman, M. L., 105, 292
Hoffman, R., 241
Hogan, R., 214
Hokanson, J. E., 45, 76, 272
Hollabaugh, L. C., 321
Holmes, D. S., 246, 268
Holmes, J. G., 214
Holmes, T. H., 221
Holmstrom, L. L., 318, 327n. 17, 329, 332
Holtgraves, T., 185
Homans, G. C., 178, 189, 216
Hooton, E. A., 258
Hope, D., 242
Horai, J., 187, 229, 245, 263
Horn, J. M., 17
Hornstein, H. A., 201
Horowitz, R., 251, 260
Horton, R. W., 115
Hosoda, M., 182
Houlihan, D., 293

Howard, J. A., 339, 341
Howells, K., 339
Hoyt, J. L., 83, 113
Hu, H. C., 250
Hudik, T. L., 267
Hudson, J. R., 267
Huesmann, L. R., 120, 120n. 9, 121, 182,
       369
Huizinga, D., 138
Hull, C., 39, 67, 93
Hull, J. G., 198, 200
Huston, A. C., 117–118, 119n. 8,
       121n. 12, 122
Hutchings, B., 20
Hutchinson, R. R., 24, 54
Hutton, D. G., 362n. 4
Hyde, J. S., 25
Hynan, D. J., 361

Infante, D. A., 208
Inn, A., 199
Instone, D., 210
Isenberg, D. J., 196
Ishem, E., 241
Izutsu, T., 231

Jacobs, P. A., 22
Jaffe, Y., 84, 87
Jaggi, V., 231
James, J., 319, 329, 332, 333
James, W., 210
Janes, C., 207
Jansen, M. A., 208
Jaspars, J. M., 222
Jay, T. B., 261
Jegard, S., 44
Jellison, J. M., 251
Jemmott, J. B., 30
Jenkins, J. O., 237
Jerdee, T. H., 227
John, J. R., 150n. 20
Johnson, D. F., 277
Johnson, G. D., 321, 322
Johnson, R. C., 78, 79
Johnson, R. N., 24, 28, 65, 367
Johnson, W. T., 193
Johnston, C., 301
Johnston, L. D., 150
Jones, E. E., 18, 200, 223, 230, 232, 252,
       253
Jones, R. N., 293
Jonsson, E., 18

Lagerspetz, K., 120n. 9, 121
Lallemand, S., 260
Lamb, M. E., 232, 297, 303
Lamb, T., 27
Land, K., 146
Landy, D., 245
Lang, A. R., 200
Larrance, D. T., 232, 303
Laschet, U., 28
Laub, J. H., 144
Lauer, E., 291
Lauerman, R., 198
Laughhunn, D. J., 195
Lavin, M., 188
Lawler, E. J., 205, 206
Lawrence, M. S., 97
Laws, D. R., 330
Lawson, R., 44–45
Lazare, A., 242, 259
Lazarus, R. S., 57
Leary, M. R., 256
Leavitt, L., 297
Lefever, H. G., 260
Lefkowitz, M. M., 120, 121
Leger, G. L., 65
Leginski, W. A., 201
Leiber, M. J., 138n. 15
Leland, J., 197
Le Maire, L., 316
Leonard, K. E., 199, 262, 338, 339, 342
LePage, A., 61, 62, 86, 94
Lerner, M. J., 213
Leshner, A. I., 97
Letkemann, P., 180, 188, 191, 202
Levendusky, O. G., 202
Levenson, R. W., 197
Leventhal, H., 92
Levine, E. N., 198
Levine, J. M., 198
Levine, R. A., 315, 321, 334, 337, 337n. 30
Levine, S., 26
Levinson, D., 219, 291
Levinson, S. C., 263, 264, 266, 271
Levy, R. I., 291
Levy, S., 254
Lewontin, R. C., 22
Leyens, J. P., 117, 119
Libbey, P., 295
Liebert, R. M., 109
Light, R. J., 305

Lindskold, S., 178, 186, 187, 209, 210, 249, 263, 280
Linneweber, V., 226, 228
Linz, D., 90
Lippincott, E. C., 115
Lipton, D. M., 325
Liska, A. E., 132, 133, 134, 138, 144, 145, 255
Litman, C., 293
Littman, R. A., 107, 206
Lizotte, A. J., 308
Lockwood, D., 309, 317–318, 319
Loeber, R., 124, 289, 290, 298
Loehlin, J. C., 17, 18
Loew, C. A., 99
Logan, C. H., 143
Long, J. S., 146
Lopes, L. L., 195
LoPiccolo, L., 313
Lopyan, K. J., 279
Lorber, D., 294
Loren, L. E. A., 336
Lorenz, K., 8, 10–13, 15, 71
Loschper, G., 226, 228
Lourie, R., 296
Luckenbill, D. F., 136, 169, 179, 180, 187, 188, 190, 191, 205, 257, 258, 261, 264, 28n.2 0
Luengo, M. A., 20
Lunsteen, C., 22
Lykken, D. T., 19–20
Lyman, S. M., 169, 240, 273
Lysak, H., 225
Lytton, H., 291, 294, 296

Macaulay, J., 87
MacDonald, J. M., 328, 329
MacLean, G., 186
Magenau, J., 206
Mahjoub, A., 231
Major, B. R., 210, 227
Malamuth, N. M., 84, 86, 87, 90, 119n. 7, 332, 335, 338, 339, 340, 342
Malin, H., 197
Mallick, S. K., 46
Mandell, A., 29
Mandell, M., 29
Mandler, G., 72
Mandrosz-Wroblewska, J., 231
Mann, C. R., 203
Manning, M. R., 221

Manstead, T., 251
Marcus-Newhall, A., 62, 63
Marion, M., 292
Mark, V. H., 34n. 2
Markkanen, T., 17
Marlatt, G. A., 200
Marlin, N. A., 241
Marolla, J., 325n. 16, 329, 330, 333
Marshall, C., 291
Marshall, D., 312
Marshall, G., 92
Marshall, W. L., 318
Martin, C., 218
Martin, H. P., 297
Martin, J. A., 289, 295, 304
Maruniak, J. A., 25
Mash, E. J., 301
Maslach, C., 92
Mason, W. A., 12
Massey, J. L., 140
Masson, S. F. 231
Masters, J. C., 234
Masters, W. H., 310
Masuda, M., 221
Matsueda, R. L., 129, 133n. 10, 144, 145
Matt, C., 124
Matza, D., 130, 137n. 13, 148, 149, 241,
    273, 339
Maurer, C. P., 241
May, M. A., 148
May, R., 257
May, W. H., 250
Mazur, A., 27
McCandless, B. R., 46
McClearn, G. E., 20
McCord, J., 123, 124, 300n. 8
McDaniel, J. W., 245
McDermott, J. J., 308, 334, 336
McDonel, E. C., 325
McDougall, W., 8
McElrath, K., 205
McEnvoy, J., 273, 288, 291, 292, 303
McFall, R. M., 325
McGillis, D., 230, 232
McGrade, B. J., 227
McKersie, R. B., 239
McKinnon, C., 191
McLaughlin, M. L., 239
McNeely, R. L., 203
McNulty, T., 133, 134
Mead, M., 291

Mednick, S. A., 20
Medoff, N. J., 85, 86
Megargee, E. I., 238
Meichenbaum, D., 219, 234
Meier, R. F., 193
Melburg, V., 155, 228, 269, 252, 356, 365
Melnechuk, T. O., 9–10
Melville, M, M., 22
Mendick, S. A., 22, 150n. 20
Mercy, J. A., 131n. 6
Merton, R., 137–138, 210
Messick, D. M., 219
Messner, S. F., 116, 341
Metts, S., 259, 270
Meyer, T. P., 60, 83
Meyers, R. M., 154n. 2
Meyers-Abel, J., 208
Meyers-Winton, S., 251
Michener, H. A., 206
Midanik, L., 197
Miethe, T. D., 146
Mikolic, J. M., 240
Mikula, G., 169, 183, 215, 218, 219, 227,
    228, 229
Milavsky, B., 78
Milavsky, J. R., 120, 121
Milgram, S., 106, 272, 276
Miller, D. T., 214, 217
Miller, G. A., 157
Miller, L., 62, 37, 39, 40, 42, 43, 68, 71,
    156, 198, 238
Miller, N. E., 37, 39, 40, 40n. 1, 42, 43,
    47, 48, 62, 63, 68, 71, 95, 156,
    198, 238, 246n. 14, 366, 366n. 8
Miller, P., 256
Miller, S. M., 197
Miller, W. B., 129, 130n, 249
Milm, L. D., 207
Milowe, I., 296
Miron, M. S., 250
Mischel, W., 104–105
Misner, R. P., 266
Mitchell, R., 230, 292
Mitchell, T. R., 182
Moag, J. S., 219
Molinari, L., 231
Money, J., 28
Mongrain, S., 200
Morris, L. W., 109
Morris, S. L., 223
Morse, C., 296

Motowidlo, S., 221
Mowrer, O. H., 37, 39, 40, 42, 43, 68, 71, 93, 156, 238, 246n. 14
Moyer, K., 15, 29, 32, 33, 34, 34n. 2
Muehlenhard, C. L., 321, 325, 326
Mueller, C. W., 57, 58, 220
Mueller, P., 227
Muir, D., 244
Mukai, H., 66, 368
Mummendey, A., 81, 226, 228, 231, 368
Murnen, S. K., 324
Murphy, W. D., 325
Murray. S., 27
Myer, J. S., 24
Myers, M. A., 140

Nacci, P. L., 109, 246
Nagin, D., 205
Nagy, K., 200
Napier, J., 9
Nasby, W., 232
Neale, M. C., 17
Neckderman, H. J., 209
Neiss, R., 74, 82, 91, 91n. 5
Nelson, B. L., 192, 231
Nemeth, C., 109
Nesdale, A. R., 57, 222, 223n. 6, 225, 227, 230
Nesler, M. S., 182
Newlin, D. B., 197
Newman, J. P., 197, 232
Nias, D. K. B., 17
Niaura, R., 200
Nichols, R. C., 17, 18
Nickel, T. W., 215, 224
Niem, T. C., 291
Nisbett, R. E., 74, 128, 131, 131n. 5, 134
Norman, N., 60, 246, 365, 365n. 6
Novaco, R. W., 229, 235
Novinson, N., 367n. 9
Nucci, L. P., 293

O'Brien, R. M., 330
O'Callaghan, M. A. J., 34
O'Carroll, P. W., 131n. 5
O'Connor, K. V., 223
Ogles, R. M., 115
Ohbuchi, K., 66, 224, 231, 238, 242, 368
Ohlin, L. E., 137n. 14
Ohno, T., 66, 368
Oldershaw, L., 297, 300
Olds, J., 43

Olweus, D., 123, 147, 206, 209, 245, 273
O'Malley, P. M., 150
O'Neal, E. C., 76, 77, 245
Orne, M. T., 99
Oros, C. J., 339
Orvis, B. R., 229
Osgood, C. E., 250
Osgood, D. W., 150
Owen, D. R., 22
Owens, D. J., 123

Packard, J. S., 221
Page, M. M., 61, 62
Pagelow, M. D., 305
Palileo, G. J., 321, 322
Palmer, C. T., 312, 313, 317
Panksepp, J., 31
Parke, R. D., 117, 119, 146, 289, 296, 297, 300
Partanen, J., 17
Pastore, N., 44, 224
Patchen, M., 244n. 12
Paternoster, R., 193
Patten, C., 293
Patterson, G. R., 95, 96, 107, 193, 206, 207, 289, 290, 291, 292n. 4, 298, 300
Paul, L., 355, 355n. 2
Pavlov, I. P., 93, 94
Payne, J. W., 195
Peirce, R. S., 186
Pellegrini, R. J., 251
Pennebaker, J. W., 57
Pepitone, A., 110, 214
Perice, R. S., 240
Perot, A., 324
Perry, D. G., 107, 180, 190, 206
Perry, L. C., 107, 180, 190, 206
Perry, P., 27
Peters, R. S., 161
Peters, S. D., 272
Petersilia, J., 188
Petillon, X., 231
Petri, B., 218, 219
Pettit, G. S., 288
Pettiway, L. E., 245
Pfeiffer, C., 373
Philip, J., 22
Phillips, D. P., 118, 122
Piccione, A., 230
Pietromonaco, D. P., 367
Pigg, R., 99

Sarat, A., 215
Sarrel, P. M., 310
Savitsky, V. C., 242
Sawin, D. B., 296
Scarr, S., 17, 18, 19
Schachter, S., 72–75, 83, 91, 92
Schaeffer, M. A., 57
Schafer, S., 311
Schank, R., 181
Schecter, D., 26
Scheff, T. J., 259
Scheidt, R. J., 61, 62
Scheier, M. F., 279
Schleifer, S., 206
Schlenker, B. R., 177–178, 191, 196, 202,
    241, 242, 249, 251, 256, 265
Schmidt, S. M., 201
Schmutte, G. T., 199
Schneider, S. L., 195
Schoenfeld, W. N., 96
Schonbach, P., 243, 273
Schruijer, S. G. L., 215, 217, 218n. 4,
    231
Schulsinger, F., 22
Schutz, A., 159
Schwartz, G., 242, 251, 260
Scott, J. P., 9, 15, 16, 35, 65, 95
Scott, M. R., 169, 240, 273
Scully, D., 325n. 16, 329, 330, 333
Sears, R. R., 37, 39, 40, 42, 43, 68, 71,
    156, 238, 246n. 14
Sebastian, R. J., 119
Secord, P. F., 160
Segal, N. L., 19–20
Semin, G. R., 262
Sermat, V., 367n. 9
Shaver, K. G., 227
Sheehan, P. W., 121
Sher, K. J., 197
Sherkat, D. E., 288, 303
Sherman, D., 305
Sherman, L. W., 194
Shetler, S., 76
Shields, L. M., 311, 313
Shields, N. M., 242
Shields, W. M., 311, 313
Shope, G. L., 46
Short, J. F., 134–135, 258
Shortell, J., 189
Shotland, L., 325
Shotland, R. L., 193
Shuck, J., 357

Shultz, T. R., 227
Shuntich, R., 101
Shupe, L. M., 197
Siegel, A. E., 109
Siegel, J. M., 324, 324n. 14
Siegel, M., 277
Silver, R. L., 238
Silverman, I., 366n. 8
Simon, H. A., 157, 179
Simon, S., 101, 189
Simon, W., 311
Simons, L. S., 63, 64, 64n
Simpson, J. A., 311
Singer, B., 313
Singer, J., 57, 73, 74, 92
Singer, R., 119
Skinner, B. F., 93
Slaby, R. G., 182–183, 207–208
Sloane, H. N., 293
Smith, D. A., 193, 194, 266, 275
Smith, K., 265
Smith, M. D., 275
Smith, R. B., III, 44, 108, 166, 225
Smith, R. T., 18
Smith, W. P., 201
Sobell, L. C., 200
Sobell, M. B., 198, 200
Sorenson, S. B., 324, 324n. 14
South, S., 133, 134, 330
Southwick, C. H., 11
Southwick, L., 198, 201
Spence, J. T., 255
Spens, D., 241
Sprafkin, J., 119
Srofe, L. A., 303
Stafford, M. C., 146, 215
Standing, L., 200
Stanley, K., 261
Stapleton, R. E., 192, 226, 231
Stark, R., 273, 288, 291, 292, 303
Starr, R. H., 296, 298, 301, 302, 305
Steadman, H. J., 191, 183, 209, 221, 243,
    258
Steele, B. F., 304
Steele, C. M., 198, 201
Steffen, V. J., 66, 186
Stein, A. H., 119
Stein, J. A., 324, 324n. 14
Steinmetz, S. K., 203, 288, 291, 293, 303
Stevens, J., 34n. 2
Stevens, M. C., 24
Stiles, W. B., 65

Stillwell, A., 229, 236
Stipp, H. H., 120, 121
Stocking, M., 22
Stockman, C. L., 97
Stokes, R., 241, 244
Stokols, D., 57
Stones, M. H., 238
Stonner, D., 46, 99
Stotland, E., 265
Stouffer, S. A., 217
Stouthamer-Loeber, M., 124
Strack, S., 272
Straus, M. A., 113, 114, 123, 203, 220,
    288, 291, 293, 303, 305, 340, 341
Strodtbeck, F. L., 134–135, 258
Strohm, R. B., 197
Stryker, S., 261
Sturup, G. K., 28, 317
Suchman, E. A., 217
Suggs, R., 312
Sundberg, S. L., 318
Susman, E. J., 299, 300
Svare, B., 25–26, 29–30
Swart, C., 65
Sykes, G., 130, 137n. 13, 148, 149, 241,
    273, 339
Sykes, R. E., 266, 267
Symons, D., 310, 311, 313, 315
Syroit, J., 225

Tait, R. C., 237
Tajfel, H., 231
Tanzer, N., 218, 219
Taplin, P., 289, 290
Taub, B., 242
Tavris, C., 235, 236
Taylor, D. M., 231
Taylor, J., 241
Taylor, S. P., 44, 87, 101, 189, 198, 199,
    201, 215, 223–224, 231, 342,
    257, 262, 275, 367
Tedeschi, J. T., 44, 60, 108, 109, 155,
    158, 163, 165, 166, 169, 177–178,
    182, 186, 187, 191, 192, 202, 209,
    210, 223, 225, 226, 228, 231, 240,
    242, 245, 246, 249, 251, 252, 263,
    265, 268, 269, 273, 356, 365,
    365n. 6, 367n. 9
Teger, A. I., 185
Tellegen, A., 19–20
Tennen, H., 227, 238
Tennent, G., 29

Tetlock, P., 251
Thibaut, J. W., 46, 189, 216, 232, 238
Thomas, B., 185
Thomas, M. H., 115
Thomas, S. V., 117, 121n. 12, 122
Thome, P. R., 56, 87
Thorndike, E. L., 93, 94, 97, 164
Thornhill, N. W., 311, 312, 313, 319
Thornhill, R., 311, 312, 313, 319
Tice, D. M., 362n. 4
Tinbergen, N., 8, 9, 13
Tittle, C. R., 143, 144, 194
Tjosvold, D., 257
Toby, J., 143
Toch, H. H., 196, 208, 232, 249, 254,
    266, 274
Tollman, J., 26
Tolman, E. C., 93, 157, 160
Travaglia, G., 102
Triandis, H. C., 250
Trickett, P. K., 291, 292n. 4, 294, 297,
    298, 300, 303
Tripathi, R. C., 215, 218n. 4
Turetsky, B., 185
Turiel, E., 293
Turkat, D., 230
Turnbull, C., 184
Turner, C. W., 63, 64, 64n
Tversky, 195
Twentyman, C. T., 232, 302
Tyler, T. R., 219, 220

Ulrich, R., 24
Ury, W., 164

Valenstein, E. S., 33
Van Alstyne, D. J., 193
Vanegas, H., 31
Varney, G. A., 318
Vaske, J. J., 206
Vaughn, B., 297n. 5
Veitch, R., 230
Venables, P. H., 91
Venus, C. K., 262
Verette, J. A., 241
Vernon, W., 24
Vidmar, N., 227
Viemero, V., 121
Virkunen, M., 197
Visher, C. A., 193, 266, 275
Vogel, S. R., 255
Vogel, W., 242, 259

vom Saal, F. S., 26
Voss, H., 146
Vuchinich, R. E., 198

Wachtel, P. L., 254
Wagner, A. R., 44
Waite, E., 133, 245
Walder, L. O., 120, 121
Waldo, G. P., 232
Walker, G. R., 279
Wallgreen, H., 197
Walster, E., 214, 227
Walster, G. W., 214
Walters, G. C., 18, 44, 97, 164, 297, 300
Walters, R. E., 239
Walters, R. H., 44, 48, 96, 105
Warner, C. T., 229
Washburn, S. L., 14
Wasman, M., 31
Waterhouse, A., 57
Weeks, G., 336
Weigold, M. F., 196
Weinberg, M. S., 319n. 11
Weiner, B., 227, 241
Weiner, P., 62
Weinstein, E., 244
Weinstein, N. D., 195
Weis, K., 325
Weiss, B., 288
Weiss, R. L., 239
Weiss, W., 46
Werner, C, M., 231
West, D. J., 145, 150
West, S., 119
Westley, W. A., 266, 267
Weston, J., 295
Wharton, J. D., 118
White, J. W., 182
White, L. A., 85
White, R. K., 234
Wiatrowsji, M. D., 144
Wicklund, R. A., 278
Widom, C. S., 123, 124
Wilcox, K. J., 19–20
Wiley, M. G., 267
Willerman, L., 18
Williams, C. A., 195

Williams, D. L., 198
Williams, R. M., 198
Williams, R. M., Jr., 217
Wills, T. A., 268, 269
Wilson, D. W., 57, 77
Wilson, G., 197
Wilson, J. Q., 138, 152, 208, 360
Wilson, L., 101, 189
Wilson, M., 191, 203, 219, 355n. 2
Winsborough, H. H., 133, 133n. 10
Winters, L. C., 253
Wisniewski, N., 320, 322
Witkin, H. A., 22
Wolfe, D. A., 289, 295, 299, 301, 303, 304
Wolfgang, M., 130, 131, 136, 142, 179, 187, 197, 220, 249
Wong, F. Y., 117n. 5, 119
Wong, W. P. T., 197
Wood, L., 48
Wood, W., 117n. 5, 119
Worchel, S., 225, 357
Wotman, S. R., 229, 236
Wright, E., 339
Wright, J., 189
Wrightsman, L. S., 309, 331–332

Yarrow, L., 43–44
Yates, W. R., 27
Yegidis, B. L., 333
Yllo, K., 328
Young, L., 300, 303
Youngblade, L., 303

Zacchia, C., 200
Zahn-Waxler, C., 291, 293
Zambarano, R. J., 293, 302
Zeichner, A., 198, 200
Zeisel, H., 230
Zellman, G. L., 326
Zillmann, D., 66, 72, 75–76, 76n. 1, 77, 78, 79, 80, 81, 82, 83, 85, 86, 91, 92, 106, 115, 198, 225, 366
Zimbardo, P. G., 92, 280
Zimmerman, D. L., 241
Zukerman, M., 339
Zwirner, W., 291, 294

SUBJECT INDEX

453

Berkowitz, L. (*continued*)
    goal of aggression, 165
    pain cues, 106
    reactive aggression, 37, 50–53, 366–
        367, 368
    research generated by, 53–67
    on violent films, 114
    on weapons effect, 61, 63
Bias crimes, 330
Biological factors. *See* Genetics; Socio-
        biology
Birth control, 29
Blacks, 140, 217, 231–232, 330
Blame, 225–228
    attribution of, 222–223, 352
    aversiveness and, 367n
    children and, 302
    expectations and, 230
    forgiveness and, 242
    grievances and, 213–248
    perceived aggression and, 225–227
    self-justification and, 229
    See also Guilt; Responsibility
Blocked opportunity theory
    crime and, 137–142, 145–146, 151
    education and, 130n
    goals and, 129
    violence and, 139–142, 210
Blood pressure, 45, 57
Bobo experiments, 108–109, 110
Bodily force, 168
Boulding, K., 183
Brain centers, 30–35
Break the camel's back effect, 238
Brownmiller, S., 331
Bullies, 254, 273
Buss, A. H.
    aggression defined by, 160–161
    aggression machine, 198
    instrumental theory of, 98–102, 125
Buss–Durkee Hostility Inventory, 27

California Personality Inventory, 18
Canadian Urban Victim Survey, 146
Capital punishment, 114
Castration, 25, 28, 317
Catharsis, 364–366
    Berkowitz on, 51–52
    displacement and, 47–48, 364–366
    energy and, 45–46
    Freud on, 39, 41, 67–68
    frustration on, 51–52

Cavitt, D., 208
Central nervous system, 15, 31, 32, 34
Character contest, 257
Child abuse, 287–306
Class differences, 128, 133
Classical conditioning, 8, 94, 161, 292n
Coalition formation, 202
Coercion, 162–168, 216
    aggression and, 159–176, 225, 347–
        371
    alcohol and, 197–201
    anger and, 233–235, 247, 259
    authority and, 267, 281
    aversive stimuli and, 367
    children and, 289–291 compliance
        and, 351–352
    conflict and, 184
    costs of, 187–197, 211, 334
    decision making and, 177–212, 350
    disinhibition and, 279–280
    downward comparisons and, 268–270
    facilitators of, 270
    failure and, 267–268
    frequency of, 292
    gender and, 255, 290–298
    goals of, 351–355
    identity and, 249–270, 280, 290–298
    individual differences in, 308, 358–
        361
    inhibition and, 270
    language of, 348
    legitimation of, 272–273
    miscommunication and, 325
    parental, 289–290
    persuasion and, 293
    power and, 201–203
    protective, 256–270
    punishments and, 168, 170, 171
    reputation and, 254
    secondary gains for, 357–358
    self-awareness and, 278–279
    self-presentation and, 249–250, 256–
        270
    social interaction theory of, 155–157,
        174–176, 348–355
    stress and, 367
    threats, 262–263
    types of, 348
    values, 183–187
    See also Punishment; Sexual coercion
Cognitive processes, 247
    anger and, 234

Empathy, and pain, 368
Endangerment, defined, 75
Energy concepts, 15, 39, 45. *See also* Catharsis
Environmental cues, 9, 57, 182
Equal-environment assumption, 18–19, 23
Equity-restoring actions, 214
Eros, in Freud, 38
Erotic films, 78, 83–84, 88, 280
Escalation
    crime and, 354
    cycles in, 280–281
    de-escalation, 240
    parental coercion and, 297–300
    process of, 295, 297–298
Estrogens, 29
Ethnicity, 53, 266, 304
Ethnocentric bias, 231
Ethological theory, 10, 71
Evaluation apprehension, 62–64
Evolution, 7, 11, 13
Excitation transfer, 72, 75, 79, 91, 198
Excuses, 240–241
Exercise, 78, 80, 82

Face saving, 263–264, 269
Facilitators, 69, 270, 333
Failure-based predicaments, 256, 267–268
Fairness, 217–218
Family, 207
    child abuse in, 287–306
    conflicts in, 184
    delinquency and, 145–146
    domestic violence, 146, 193, 203, 208, 219, 252
    power in, 207
    sibling fights, 222
    See also Parents
Fear, 115–116, 366
Females, 26, 28–30, 311, 312
Feminists, 331, 339
Fight–flight reactions, 50–52
Films. *See* Media
Foreseeability, 227–228
Forgiveness, 241–243
Freud, S., 15–16, 37–39, 71, 83
Frustration and Aggression (Dollard et al.), 37, 39
Frustration–aggression theory, 37–49, 269n
    aggression and, 37–69
    arbitrary, 51, 224

    Berkowitz on, 49–67, 364
    catharsis and, 46
    defined, 39, 44–45
    displacement in, 42–43, 246
    factors in, 40
    kinds of, 44
    Miller, N. E., on, 40n
    no-reward and, 97
    provocation and, 76, 269n
    reactive aggression, 348
    reinforcement in, 39–40
    research generated by, 43–49
    substitution and, 53

Gang violence, 260
Gaze, 253
Gender differences
    alcohol and, 197
    biological, 26–30, 311, 312
    double standard, 338
    genetic, 26
    hormonal, 26
    injustices, 219
    insults and, 262
    measures of, 340
    parental, 304–305
    testosterone, 26–27
    third parties and, 193
    sexual coercion and, 324–326, 330
    sexual identity, 255, 268, 310, 333
    sexual scripts, 321, 339
    violence and, 87, 101, 203, 330
    See also Women
Generalized reinforcement, 96
Genetics, behavior, 16–23, 26, 123
Grievance
    accounts and, 273
    cultural context, 238
    definition of, 215
    expression of, 213–217, 235–247, 353–354
    formation of, 247
    inhibition of, 237–238
    justice and, 352–354
    procedures for, 214
    punishment and, 248
    rape and, 330
    social control and, 326
Guilt
    apology and, 241–242
    aversion and, 367

catharsis and, 51–52
cognitive bias and, 229
shame and, 149
target substitution and, 366
See also Blame
Guns, 60–63

Habits, and instincts, 9
Harassment, sexual, 307
Hate crimes, 273
Heat, effects of, 55–56
Hedonic tone hypothesis, 84–85
Hippocampus, 33
Hobbes, T., 7, 9
Holmes, D. S., 246–247
Homicide rate, 118, 128, 222, 341
Homosexuality, 28, 88, 203, 310–331
Honor, 260
Hormonal factors, 13, 15, 25–30, 72
Hostility biases, 232–233, 362, 369
Hull, C., 39
Human Relations Area Files, 219
Humiliation
    coercive responses, 270
    defined, 259, 270n
    forgiveness and, 242
    grievence and, 357
    rape and, 329
Hyperactivity, 20, 24
Hypothalamus, 31, 32

Identity attacks, 258–259, 275, 280
Imitative aggression, 104, 111–112
Impression management, 249–250, 331–333, 354
Impulsive behavior, 20, 75, 361
In-group bias, 231
Incarceration, 143
Incentive conditions, 44
Incompetence, 256
Individual differences, 63, 359
Influence theory, 181, 355–356
Informal control, 192
Infrahuman research, 30–32
Inhibition, 38
    coercion and, 270, 333
    costs and, 351
    defined, 69
    generalized, 47
    learned, 41–42
    sexual coercion and, 333

Innate drives, 15–16
Instigation, defined, 68
Instincts, 8–10, 14
Instrumental aggression, 65, 99–100, 349
Instrumental learning theory, 94
Instrumental values, 183
Insult
    arousal and, 45, 74–76, 85
    authority and, 281
    dozens game, 260
    frustration and, 44
    heat effects and, 55
    imitation and, 104–105
    purpose of, 174, 259
    response to, 357
    ritualistic, 261
    sexual, 208
    Zillmann, D., on, 79–80, 85
Intelligence, 20, 22, 138, 268
Intention
    attribution of, 172, 223–224
    concept of, 163–165, 347
Interaction norms, 219–221
Intergenerational transmission, 123–125
Internal controls, 147
Interpersonal power, 201
Intimate contact, 219
Intimidation, 252, 354
Irritability, 102

Justifiability, 228, 240
Justice
    behavior, 214
    blocked opportunity and, 371
    coercive actions, 213–248
    defined, 213
    grievances and, 352–354
    restoration process, 214–215, 246
    retributive, 27, 213, 244–247
    self-presentation and, 356–357
    See also Grievances; Punishments
Juvenile delinquency, 124

Kanin, E. J., 316–317
Kaplan paradox, 160

Labeling process, 74
Lamarckian theory, 23
LaMotta, J., 208

Language, of coercion, 348–350
Law of effect, 97, 170
Learning theory
    aggression and, 93–126
    drive theory and, 67, 71
    inhibitions and, 41–42
    instrumental aggression and, 94–95
    major classes of, 94
    See also Social learning theory; *specific concepts*
Legal system, 143, 214
Legitimate Violence Index, 114
Legitimation, 112, 272–273
Lesbians, 203, 331
Limbic system, 31
Longitudinal analyses, 119–122
Lorenz, K., 8, 10–11, 15, 71

Machismo, 255, 261
Males
    biology of, 26–30, 311, 312
    intermale fighting, 24
    testosterone, 25–28, 83
    See also Gender differences
Masochism, 83
Mating rituals, 13
McDougall, W., 8
Media, violence in, 59–60, 76–78, 86, 111–123
Mediators, 248, 250. *See also* Third parties
Medroxyprogesterone acetate, 28
Men
    sexual coercion, 308–313
    sexual identity, 255, 268, 310, 321, 333
    testosterone, 25–28, 83
Menstrual cycle, 28–29
Merton's theory, 137–142
Meta-analysis, 62–64, 117, 119, 198–199
Miller, N. E., 39, 42
Minimax criterion, 180
Minorities, 266, 371
Misattribution, 71, 82, 92
Miscommunication, and coercion, 325
Modeling, 104, 111–112
Morality, 250–251, 270n, 360
Motivational bias, 228
Motive, defined, 165
Movies. *See* Media

National Crime Survey, 146, 308, 309
Negative affect, 52, 65, 95

Negative face, 263, 281
Negative identity, 258
Negative judgment, 216–218
Negative reinforcement, 95
Negative relationships, 144
Negativity bias, 229, 230
Negligence, 227–228
Negotiation, 238–240. *See also* Third parties
Neurosystems, 30–35
Neutralization techniques, 148–149
Noise, 57, 80, 366
Nominalistic error, 8
Noncoercion, 190, 206–211
Noncontingent threat, 169–170, 174
Norm violations, 214, 215–222, 224–225
Nurturant models, 105

Obedience, 276
Observation, and learning, 103–104, 159
Opportunities, blocked. *See* Blocked opportunity theory
Opportunity costs, 187–189
Overpopulation, 13

Pacifism, 360
Pain, 23–24, 36, 65–68, 364–366
Parents
    abusive, 123–125, 299–300, 303
    commands by, 293
    cross-cultural comparisons, 291, 301–305
    expectations of, 301
    punishment and, 105, 185, 193, 298–305
    stress and, 301
    See also Domestic violence
Partial reinforcement effect, 96
Patriarchy, 331
Pavlov, I., 94
Peer groups, 96, 209
Performance, and stress, 221
Personality theory, 93, 101–102
Persuasion, 181, 184, 292, 293, 356
Phenotypes, 23
Physiological effects, 45, 71–92, 197–199
PMTS. *See* Premenstrual tension syndrome
Police, 143, 194, 216, 266–267
Politeness norms, 263, 271, 281
Political values, 227
Pornography, 72, 84, 87–92, 117, 280, 315, 339

individual differences, 359
intent in, 165
symbolic interactionism and, 159n
Social learning theory, 126, 369–370
  aggression and, 103–116
  arousal and, 83
  drive theory and, 103
  influence of, 93
  media and, 111–116
  pain cues and, 106
Social stereotypes, 101
Socialization, 21–22, 134–136, 251
Sociobiology, 311–312, 363. *See also* Animal behavior; Genetics
Southerners, 128, 130
Speech acts, 264
Sponsor effect, 117n
Spousal violence, 146, 193, 203, 208, 219, 252
Staring, 253
Status hierarchies, 12, 333, 356
Steroids, 27
Stimulus generalization, 42
Strategy, 242
Stress, 57, 221–222, 271, 301, 367
Subcultural theories, 128–129, 130–132, 147–148, 151, 187
Suicide rates, 118, 122
Sunk costs, 185
Symbolic interactionism, 159n
Symbolic models, 103

Taboo behavior, 86
Target selection, 206, 365
Task interference, 43
Teacher–learner paradigm, 55, 62, 65, 78, 279
Television. *See* Media
Temperament, 20, 101–102
Terminal values, 183, 308, 359
Territoriality, 10, 13–14
Testosterone, 25–28, 83
Thanatos, 38
Theory construction, 156
Third parties, 274–275, 354
  costs and, 192
  intervention by, 202
  as mediators, 248–250

parental coercion and, 305
social identity and, 274–275
Threats
  coercion and, 204, 262–263, 348
  commands and, 294
  contingent, 174
  defined, 168
  identity and, 356
  implied, 205
  punishment and, 263
  two types of, 169–170
Time-out, 44
Tinbergen, N., 8, 13
Trustworthiness, 356
Twin studies, 17–23
Two-factor theory of emotions, 72, 73, 88

Unemployment, 138
Unprovoked aggression, 76–77

Values, 132–133, 178, 183–187, 196
Vandalism, 139, 245
Vicarious reinforcement, 112

Weakness, appearance of, 256
Weapons effects, 60–65, 68, 368
Whipping boys, 206
White, L. A., 85
Women
  alcohol and, 197
  attitudes toward, 255, 261, 338–342
  domestic violence, 146, 193, 203, 208, 219, 252
  feminism, 331, 339
  media violence and, 59–60, 76–78, 86, 111–123
  PMTS and, 28–29
  pornography, 72, 84–92, 117, 280, 315, 339
  See also Gender differences; Parents; Sexual Coercion

Y chromosome, 22

Zillmann's theory, 75–83, 91, 92

ABOUT THE AUTHORS

James T. Tedeschi is a professor of psychology at the University of Albany, State University of New York. He is a Fellow of the American Psychological Association and has served as a Consulting Editor for both the *Journal of Personality and Social Psychology* and *Social Psychology Quarterly*. Tedeschi has won an Outstanding Teacher Award at the University of Miami, Florida, and an Outstanding Educator Award from the American Education Association. He has edited *The Social Influence Processes: Perspectives on Social Power*, *Impression Management Theory*, and *Social Psychological Research*, and, with Richard B. Felson, edited *Aggression and Violence: Social Interactionist Perspectives*. He was the senior author of *Conflict, Power, and Games*, *Social Psychology*, and *Introduction to Social Psychology*. In addition, he has written numerous journal articles and chapters for edited books on social power, self-presentation, and aggression.

After obtaining his PhD in sociology at Indiana University in 1977, **Richard B. Felson** joined the faculty at the University of Albany, State University of New York. He is currently a professor of sociology and adjunct professor of psychology there. Felson has received funding for his research from the National Science Foundation and the National Institute of Mental Health. He has written numerous journal articles and edited, with James T. Tedeschi, *Aggression and Violence: Social Interactionist Perspectives*. His articles on interpersonal violence and on the self-concept have appeared in such journals as the *Journal of Personality and Social Psychology*, *Social Forces*, *Criminology*, and *Social Psychology Quarterly* (for which he served on the editorial board). Felson has researched situational factors in homicide and assault, sibling aggression, and rape. He has also written about the impact of ideology on social science, partly in response to the controversy over his research on rape.